# ENVIRONMENTAL LAW HANDBOOK

## Fourteenth Edition

*Thomas F. P. Sullivan*
*Editor*

*Authors*

Thomas L. Adams
R. Craig Anderson
F. William Brownell
David R. Case
Lynn M. Gallagher
Wayne T. Halbleib
Stanley W. Landfair
Robert T. Lee

Marshall Lee Miller
Karen J. Nardi
Austin P. Olney
John M. Scagnelli
James W. Spensley
Thomas F. P. Sullivan
Stephen E. Williams

Government Institutes, Inc.
Rockville, MD
1997

Government Institutes, Inc., 4 Research Place, Rockville, Maryland 20850
Phone: (301) 921-2355
Fax: (301) 921-0373
Email: giinfo@govinst.com
Internet Address: http://www.govinst.com

00    99    98    97         5    4    3    2    1

ISSN: 0147-7714
ISBN: 0-86587-560-X

Library of Congress Catalog Card Number: 92-75400

Printed in the United States of America

# SUMMARY TABLE OF CONTENTS

# TABLE OF CONTENTS

## CHAPTER 1: FUNDAMENTALS OF ENVIRONMENTAL LAW

# CHAPTER 2: ENFORCEMENT AND LIABILITY

# CHAPTER 3: CLEAN AIR ACT

# CHAPTER 4: CLEAN WATER ACT

# CHAPTER 5: OIL POLLUTION ACT

# CHAPTER 6: SAFE DRINKING WATER ACT

# CHAPTER 7: TOXIC SUBSTANCES CONTROL ACT

# CHAPTER 8: PESTICIDES

# CHAPTER 9: RESOURCE CONSERVATION AND RECOVERY ACT

# CHAPTER 10: UNDERGROUND STORAGE TANKS

# CHAPTER 11: FEDERAL FACILITY COMPLIANCE ACT

# CHAPTER 12: NATIONAL ENVIRONMENTAL POLICY ACT

# CHAPTER 13: COMPREHENSIVE ENVIRONMENTAL, RESPONSE, COMPENSATION, AND LIABILITY ACT

# CHAPTER 14: EMERGENCY PLANNING AND COMMUNITY RIGHT-TO-KNOW ACT

# CHAPTER 15: POLLUTION PREVENTION ACT

# CHAPTER 16: OCCUPATIONAL SAFETY AND HEALTH ACT

# PREFACE

This Fourteenth Edition of the *Environmental Law Handbook* marks the 24th anniversary of this preeminent authoritative resource in the environmental field. As the reader will learn, the term "environmental" has evolved to encompass health and safety concerns.

For this new revision we have invited no fewer than fifteen nationally recognized experts—representing major law firms and institutions in the forefront of this field—to completely update the *Environmental Law Handbook.*

The goal of the *Environmental Law Handbook*, however, has remained constant through all of its editions: to give its users reliable, accurate and practical compliance information from some of the most respected people in the field in each subject area—all presented in a clear, concise manner, with a minimum of legal jargon.

This new edition begins with a chapter on the "Fundamentals of Environmental Law" to provide a foundation for understanding and applying the information in the chapters that follow.

Over the years, the government has seen the value of bringing personal criminal charges for violation of many of the laws. Thus, the second chapter, " Enforcement and Liability," has become critically important for many of our readers because their personal freedom has been placed at risk by working in this challenging field. This chapter explains the negative consequences of failure to comply with the requirements of the laws and regulations, which can range from administrative fines to criminal prosecution for a growing number of unfortunate individuals. This chapter also provides many good reasons to comply with the law and to read the remaining chapters carefully to learn your obligations.

Each of the major environmental, health, and safety laws and issues are then covered in individual chapters: Clean Air Act; Clean Water Act; Oil Pollution Act; Safe Drinking Water Act; Toxic Substances Control Act; Pesticides; Resource Conservation and Recovery Act; Underground Storage Tanks; Federal Facilities Compliance Act; National Environmental Policy Act; Comprehensive Environmental Response, Compensation, and Liability Act; Emergency Planning and Community Right-to-Know Act; Pollution Prevention Act; and the Occupational Safety and Health Act.

We sincerely hope that readers will find this to be a useful reference. I encourage all those who want additional information in a given area to see the many references listed in the back of this handbook.

As always, we welcome the opportunity to hear from our readers as to how well this "flagship" publication, as well as all of our products, continues to help meet our mutual goals of compliance with the "spirit" as well as the "letter" of the environmental, health and safety laws.

Thomas F.P. Sullivan, *Editor*
President, Government Institutes

# ABOUT THE AUTHORS

## Thomas L. Adams

Thomas L. Adams is of counsel to the law firm of Perkins Coie, in Washington, DC, where he specializes in international, federal, and state environmental counseling. Prior to joining Perkins Coie, Mr. Adams represented International Paper Corporation as environmental director and independent consultant, and has also served as the assistant administrator for enforcement and compliance monitoring for the U.S. Environmental Protection Agency. He has also served as the assistant director of governmental relations for Republic Steel Corporation, as assistant general counsel for legislation to the U.S. Federal Trade Commission, and has served on the minority counsel subcommittee on environment and consumer affairs for the U.S. Senate. He holds a B.A. in history from the University of Virginia and a law degree from Vanderbilt University.

## R. Craig Anderson

Craig Anderson is with Duvall, Harrigan, Hale & Hassan in Fairfax, Virginia, focusing his work in all areas of environmental law. Before retiring from the U.S. Air Force in 1994, he served most recently as the senior environmental law attorney for the Air Combat Command at Langley Air Force Base, Hampton, Virginia. As the chief of environmental law, he advised the command leadership and environmental engineers on all aspects of environmental law requirements. He also supported the individual base legal offices at more than 30 subordinate installations worldwide on matters related to environmental law questions and issues. He is a frequent speaker on environmental law issues and has written several law review articles on personal civil and criminal responsibility under environmental law statutes and regulations.

## F. William Brownell

William Brownell is a member of the Hunton & Williams law firm's Energy and Environmental Team in Washington, D.C. His practice covers a broad range of environmental law issues in proceedings before federal agencies, state and federal courts, and Congress. He has represented clients in many of the major rulemakings and judicial review proceedings under the Clean Air Act, as well as in citizen suits and enforcement actions. Mr. Brownell's practice also extends to issues arising under many other environmental statutes. He is a member of the American Bar Association's sections on Administrative Law and Natural Resources Law. He speaks and writes frequently on environmental and administrative law issues, and is an author of the *Clean Air Handbook*.

## David R. Case

David Case is general counsel for the Environmental Technology Council, a trade association for the hazardous waste treatment, recycling and disposal industry in Washington, D.C. He represents member firms before the EPA, Congress, and the courts on a broad range of environmental issues related to RCRA, Superfund, TSCA, the Clean Air Act and Clean Water Act. He was the lead attorney on many RCRA rule-review cases setting legal precedents on hazardous waste identification, recycling, treatment standards, and land disposal restrictions. He is a former chairman of the Environmental Pollution Committee of the Federal Bar Association, a member of the American Bar Association's section on Natural Resources Law, and has written and lectured extensively on environmental law.

## Lynn M. Gallagher

Lynn Gallagher is a counsel with Swidler & Berlin of Washington, D.C. and a member of the bars of Maryland and the District of Columbia. She has a wide range of environmental experience, concentrating on compliance counseling and permit work in the water and hazardous waste areas. Her experience includes NPDES and RCRA permit proceedings for a wide variety of facilities; citizen suits under the Clean Water Act and EPCRA; variance requests under RCRA and the Clean Water Act; transactional counseling; comments on environmental rulemakings; and environmental enforcement actions. She also has broad litigation experience, including environmental loss recovery and toxic tort litigation. In addition, Ms. Gallagher coauthored the *NPDES Permit Handbook* and has lectured extensively on clean water and other environmental issues. She holds a B.A. degree from the University of Florida and a J.D. degree from Georgetown University.

## Wayne T. Halbleib

Wayne Halbleib is counsel to the Energy and Environmental Practice Group of the law firm of Mays & Valentine in Richmond, Virginia. He provides environmental compliance and enforcement counseling, as well as litigation services for banks, corporations, trade associations and local governments throughout Virginia. Mr. Halbleib was an assistant attorney general for the Commonwealth of Virginia and also served as the first state director of the SARA Title III Office in Virginia's Department of Waste Management. He regularly lectures and writes on a wide variety of environmental issues.

## Stanley W. Landfair

Stanley Landfair is a partner with the law firm of McKenna & Cuneo, L.L.P. in its Los Angeles office and specializes in environmental law, administrative law, and state and federal litigation. He provides TSCA counseling to many companies in the chemical, aerospace and electronics industries and has litigated numerous actions arising under TSCA, FIFRA, NEPA, the Freedom of Information Act and the Federal Food, Drug and Cosmetic Act, as well as many civil and criminal actions in state and federal courts. Previously, Mr. Landfair was a judicial law clerk in the U.S. Court of Appeals, for the Fourth Circuit. He also served as a Judge Advocate in the U.S. Navy, and was chief trial counsel at the Naval Legal Service Office in Japan. Mr. Landfair's coauthor, **Elizabeth Coppage Brown**, is an associate in the Los Angeles office of McKenna & Cuneo.

## Robert T. Lee

Robert Lee is an attorney in the Washington, D.C. office of Ogletree, Deakins, Nash, Smoak & Stewart, L.L.P., where he specializes in environmental compliance and litigation, including all facets of hazardous waste management and remediation and major Superfund litigation. Previously, he served in the Environmental Enforcement Section of the Land and Natural Resources Division of the U.S. Department of Justice. He has also been a government contract attorney, trial judge and trial attorney with the Office of the Judge Advocate General of the U.S. Air Force. During 1994, he served as chairman of the Natural Resources Committee on Governor George Allen's (VA) Commission on Government Reform. In 1995, Governor Allen appointed him Northern Virginia's Representative on the Commonwealth Transportation Board, which sets transportation policy for Virginia. He frequently lectures and writes on a variety of environmental issues.

## Marshall Lee Miller

Marshall Miller is a partner in the Washington, D.C. office of the law firm of Baise & Miller, where he specializes in the areas of environmental law, occupational health and safety, and international transactions. Mr. Miller was previously special assistant to the first administrator of the U.S. Environmental Protection Agency, chief EPA judicial officer, associate deputy attorney general in the U.S. Department of Justice, and deputy administrator and acting head of the Occupational Safety and Health Administration. He was educated at Harvard, Oxford, Heidelberg and Yale.

## Karen J. Nardi

Karen Nardi is a partner in the San Francisco office of McCutchen, Doyle, Brown & Enersen L.L.P., where she specializes in compliance issues and administrative law proceedings. She has assisted clients involved in underground tank cleanups, the closure of property contaminated with hazardous wastes, and the cleanup of complex groundwater problems in the Silicon Valley. She was also a legislative analyst for the California state legislature on resources, land use, and energy.

## Austin P. Olney

Austin P. Olney is a partner in the Washington, D.C. office of LeBoeuf, Lamb, Greene & MacRae, L.L.P. For the last 15 years he has specialized in representing domestic and foreign clients on marine safety and pollution matters. He has testified before the U.S. Congress on oil pollution matters, represented shipowners in oil spills, advised clients on corporate issues arising under the Oil Pollution Act of 1990, and lectured extensively on oil pollution issues in both the United States and Europe. Previously, Mr. Olney served as secretary of natural resources and environmental control for the State of Delaware. He also served as counsel to the U.S. House of Representatives Committee on Merchant Marine and Fisheries.

## John M. Scagnelli

John Scagnelli heads the environmental department of Whitman Breed Abbott & Morgan, where he has had extensive involvement with environmental issues in a business and public advisory context. Previously, he served as legal counsel with Cheesebrough-Pond's, Inc., and as vice president and general counsel of Allied Maintenance Corporation, a subsidiary of Ogden Corporation. A member of the National Institute for Environmental Auditing, Mr. Scagnelli has also published widely in the environmental law field and has written articles on natural resource damages, underground storage tanks, international environmental legal issues, regulation of sanitary landfills and other topics. **Kathleen A. Pierce** is an environmental associate at the firm of Whitman Breed Abbott & Morgan.

## James W. Spensley

James Spensley heads the Rocky Mountain office of Jellinek, Schwartz, and Connelly, "JSC/Spensley" in Denver, Colorado. He worked for the President's Council on Environmental Quality after NEPA was first enacted and assisted in the development of the first federal guidelines on preparing an environmental impact statement. As counsel to several committees of the U.S. House of Representatives, he managed the first and only amendment to NEPA and was involved in developing other major environmental legislation concerning atmospheric science, ocean dumping, and environmental research and development issues. In addition, Mr. Spensley serves as an adjunct professor of law and environmental management at the University of Denver, and lectures at the University of Colorado. He holds a science degree in Industrial Engineering and a law degree from George Washington University National Law Center.

## Thomas F. P. Sullivan

Academically, Thomas Sullivan has a B.A. in philosophy, a B.S. in physics and math, and a J.D. in law. He has been in the forefront of the environmental field since the 1960s. He gained experience in industry before practicing law and representing clients in the environmental field. In 1973 he founded Government Institutes, and has authored and edited more than 100 books including *The Greening of American Business*, *Environmental Health and Safety Manager's Handbook*, and *Directory of Environmental Information Sources*. He is a regular lecturer internationally on environmental topics and serves as president of Government Institutes.

## Stephen E. Williams

Stephen Williams is counsel to the law firm, Bayh & Connaughton, P.C. and a principal in the firm's affiliated environmental consulting firm of RegNet Environmental Services. He has provided legal and technical consulting assistance to major trade associations and Fortune 500 companies in litigation, legislation, and regulatory proceedings under all of the environmental statutes. His experience extends from working on problems associated with air, water, groundwater, and waste pollution to handling complex land use issues involving the National Environmental Policy Act and natural resource damage regulations. He has represented major trade associations and Fortune 500 companies before Congress, federal and state agencies, including EPA and many of its regional offices, and the courts.

# ENVIRONMENTAL LAW HANDBOOK

**Fourteenth Edition**

# CHAPTER 1

# FUNDAMENTALS OF ENVIRONMENTAL LAW

Thomas F. P. Sullivan, Esquire[1]
Government Institutes
Rockville, Maryland

This chapter covers the fundamentals of the environmental law field, so that the reader has a foundation to comprehend and use the information provided in the chapters that follow.

## 1.0 ENVIRONMENTAL LAW AS A SYSTEM

Environmental law is more than simply a collection of statutes on environmental subjects. The field is one which cannot be mastered simply by learning the specific requirements of some individual laws impacting the environment. Over the past few decades, "Environmental Law" has evolved into a *system* of statutes, regulations, guidelines, factual conclusions and case-specific interpretations which relate one to another. The system is complex in itself and is made even more challenging by the difficulty of the interdisciplinary subject matter to be regulated (health, safety and environment) and the problems which the law often has in dealing with the scientific issues and uncertainties nearly always faced in environmental cases.

Understanding this environmental law system, its unifying principles and the ways in which the individual elements work together to achieve the system's objectives is a challenge for those who try to comply with environmental laws. This book is intended to provide assistance in meeting the challenge of understanding this system.

## 2.0 DEFINING OUR SUBJECT MATTER—WHAT IS ENVIRONMENTAL LAW?

The key to understanding a system as complex as environmental law is the definition of the subject. The best definition, I believe, is:

> The environmental law system is an organized way of using all of the laws in our legal system to minimize, prevent, punish or remedy the consequences of actions which damage or threaten the environment, public health and safety.

---

[1]Author's Note: The author thanks James Aloysius Hogan, Esquire, for his research and assistance in the preparation of these materials. The author also thanks J. Gordon Arbuckle, Esquire, who provided contributions to this chapter.

This definition reflects the great expansion over the years of the term "environment" to encompass the protection of public health and workers' safety in addition to the environment.

By this definition, what makes a law or regulation a part of the environmental law system is not its label or original function but the purpose for which it is used. For example, a compilation of the federal environmental statutes does not include the entire body of environmental law. The criminal code and the Administrative Procedure Act also play important roles in the environmental law system.

When we talk about the "environmental law system," then, we are referring to all aspects of our legal system—the Constitution, statutes, regulations, rules of evidence, rules of procedure, judicial interpretations, the common law and, indeed, the criminal law—to the extent that these elements are being applied towards environmental ends. "Environmental law" is best defined—not as a book or compilation of certain laws, but, instead, as a *system* for using *all* of the laws for environmental, public health and safety purposes.[2]

In summary, environmental law encompasses all the protections for our environment that emanate from the following sources:

1. Laws: federal and state statutes and local ordinances,
2. Regulations promulgated by federal, state and local agencies,
3. Court decisions interpreting these laws and regulations,
4. The common law,
5. United States Constitution and state constitutions, and even
6. Treaties.

## 2.1 How a Federal or State Environmental Law Is Made[3]

Federal and state legislative processes are similar; the federal procedure is used here for illustration. First a bill is introduced in either the House of Representatives or the Senate. Bills are referred to committee for consideration. The committee(s), in considering a bill, may hold hearings, study, investigate, and issue a report and a recommendation on whether or not the bill should pass. When a bill is reported out of committee, it is placed on a calendar in the respective house, considered, debated, and, if passed, becomes an act.

In the environmental field, the House and Senate generally pass different bills, and a conference of House and Senate representatives is needed to resolve the differences. After passage in both the House of Representatives and the Senate, the act is sent to the President of the United States. The act will become law if it is signed by the President of the United States or if the act is not vetoed within ten days.

---

[2]An article by Robert G. Schwartz entitled "Criminalizing Occupational Safety Violations: The Use of Knowing Endangerment Statutes to Punish Employers Who Maintain Toxic Working Conditions" excellently illustrates both the expansion of the term "environmental law"and the utilization of seemingly non-environmental statutes toward environmental ends. 14 *Harvard Environmental Law Review* 487 (1990).

[3]For a more comprehensive treatment of how laws and regulations are made the reader is referred to Al Coco's, *Finding the Law* (Government Institutes, 1982).

This often is a long and arduous process resulting in confusing language to embody the compromises necessary to obtain agreement among all the differing factions and thus a majority vote and the approval of the President.

## 2.2 How Environmental Regulations Are Made[4]

Environmental statutes generally empower an administrative agency, like the U.S. Environmental Protection Agency (EPA), to develop and promulgate regulations. The President may also empower an executive agency to promulgate regulations through an executive order.

Rule-making is a process of publishing proposed regulations in the *Federal Register;* providing opportunity for the public to comment either through submission of written comments or through public hearings that concern the regulations; and publishing final regulations in the *Federal Register,* which have the force and effect of law when they become effective. Annually the regulations are combined into the *Code of Federal Regulations (C.F.R.).*

## 3.0 LAWS THAT ESTABLISH COMPLIANCE OBLIGATIONS

The natural resource laws such as the Endangered Species Act and those related to fish, wildlife, oil and gas exploration, forests and mining are covered in the *Natural Resources Law Handbook* published by Government Institutes. Although they are important for protection of our ecology, we have elected to approach them from the natural resource perspective. In this *Environmental Law Handbook,* we focus herein on environmental laws, specifically those intended to protect the human environment, health and safety.

## 3.1 Major Environmental Laws

Subsequent chapters of this book describe the regulatory programs in place under the major federal environmental statutes. These environmental laws define most of the substantive compliance obligations of the environmental law system. The major federal environmental statutes do not, however, operate alone. There are other components of "environmental laws" that supplement or complement the programs which the federal environmental statutes establish.

## 3.2 State Statutes and Regulations Implementing the Federal Statutes

Many of the federal statutes, like the Clean Air Act or Clean Water Act, establish federal-state regulatory programs in which the states are given the opportunity to enact and enforce laws, meeting federal minimum criteria, to achieve the regulatory objectives which the Congress has established. In most instances where the states have had the opportunity to take over regulatory programs in their jurisdictions, they have done so. States are generally the primary permitting and enforcement authorities subject to federal intervention only if they do not enforce effectively or rigorously enough.

---

[4]The reader is encouraged to read *How the Environmental Regulatory System Works: A Business Primer* by Aaron Gershonowitz (Government Institutes, 1993).

Generally, the states are not precluded from enforcing criteria more stringent than those required by the federal laws, and are given considerable leeway to follow enforcement interpretations which may not be fully consistent with those applied at the federal level. Thus the laws and interpretations used to apply and enforce the federal laws may vary considerably from state to state and these variations may not be readily apparent. Government Institutes has published a comprehensive environmental law handbook on each state. Reference should be made to these to fully understand all the environmental obligations in a specific state.

### 3.3 State Laws Independent of the Federal Requirements

The trend is for states—particularly certain states like California and New Jersey—to take initiatives to provide their citizens and their environment with protection beyond that generally available under the federal statutes. Examples of laws generated by this trend include:

- Toxic Waste Minimization Laws like one in Massachusetts[5] which imposes mandatory waste reduction objectives on companies which use or generate toxic or hazardous wastes.
- Environmental Full Disclosure Laws like California Proposition 65,[6] which requires extraordinary efforts to make the public aware of health risks associated with products or environments to which they are exposed.
- Property Transfer Environmental Laws like the New Jersey law,[7] which requires extensive investigation and cleanup of contaminated sites before they are sold or transferred.
- State Groundwater Protection Laws. Although the federal government has not yet adopted comprehensive groundwater protection legislation, many, if not most of the states, have detailed permit programs.[8]

The list could go on, including state citizens' action laws, laws compelling response at hazardous substance sites not on the federal superfund list, facility siting laws, laws governing the operation of publicly owned treatment works and landfills, asbestos abatement and so on. State laws in many states may be a more important factor in dictating the focus of compliance programs than the laws which exist at the federal level. Commensurate attention is clearly warranted.

---

[5]Massachusetts Toxics Use Reduction Act added by St. 1989, c. 265, §3, approved July 24, 1989.

[6]California Safe Drinking Water and Toxic Enforcement Act, adopted as Prop. 65 in 1986, Cal. Health and Safety Code §§25249.5-25249.13 (West Supp. 1987).

[7]NJ Stat. Anno. 13:1K-6 et seq., Environmental Cleanup Responsibility Act L. 1983, c. 330, §1.

[8]Ground Water Permit Act (Cities, Villages, and Municipal Corporations), Neb. Rev. Stat. 1943, 46-638 *et seq.,* Ground Water Exploration and Protection Act, Kan. Stat. Anno. 82a-1201 *et seq.;* Ground Water Basin Protection Act (Porter-Dolwig), Cal. Water Code §12920 *et seq.*

### 3.4 Tax Laws

There is a trend at both the state and federal levels towards using the tax laws to create incentives towards environmentally benign products and activities and disincentives against products and activities considered to be environmentally detrimental. Gas-guzzler taxes, recycling tax credits, taxes on use of virgin materials, taxes on hazardous waste generation and excise taxes on various products are among the approaches which have been adopted or seriously discussed. These approaches and other economic incentive-oriented strategies are expected to be vigorously promoted in the future.

### 3.5 Business Regulatory Laws

The Federal Trade Commission and a number of state attorneys general have initiatives to use their ordinary business regulatory authorities to police environmental claims made for products. The Securities and Exchange Commission has for some time required full disclosure of environmental liabilities in statements and reports falling under its jurisdiction.

The innovative abilities of both state and federal officials will continue to be applied to effective utilization of all the laws in their arsenal in an effort to enforce increasingly stringent standards of protection for health, safety and the environment. The limits on this kind of creativity are yet to be seen and are unlikely to be reached in the immediate future because environmental protection is a political asset.

### 3.6 Local and Municipal Laws

Localities do have great powers to control the location and operation of facilities within their jurisdictions and are often able to effectively utilize this authority. Active community involvement and participation in consideration of local ordinances is, for a number of businesses, essential to continued ability to operate profitably. While it is difficult to generalize, issues which warrant particularly careful attention include the operation of the local waterworks and waste treatment plants, local recycling initiatives and associated product initiatives, zoning and noise control ordinances, nuisance laws, air emission requirements, landfill restrictions or closures, local emergency planning and initiatives relating to waste site cleanup. In every instance, the impact of this kind of local action can be as immediate and severe as that of any taken at the state or federal level. From the perspective of an environmental law compliance program, local does not mean trivial. It means immediate, important, largely unreviewable, and deserving of considerable attention. Effective environmental compliance requires acceptance of these facts of life.

### 3.7 Environmental Law and Judicial Decisions

As the courts interpret the environmental laws and regulations and apply them to specific factual situations, they are continually determining what the law actually means in factual situations. In order to gain the proper understanding of court decisions, a basic knowledge of the United States court system is needed. The courts and their role are described later in this chapter (see 6.2).

### 3.8 Common Law

Underlying the development of legal theory in the United States is a body of rules and principles relating to the government and security of persons and property which had its origin, development and formulation in England. Brought to the American colonies by peoples of Anglo-Saxon stock, these basic rules were formally adopted in the states in which they were in force after the American Revolution. Known as the "common law," these principles are derived from the application of natural reason, an innate sense of justice and the dictates of conscience. The common law is not the result of legislative enactment. Rather, its authority is derived solely from usages and customs which have been recognized, affirmed and enforced by the courts through judicial decisions.

It is important to realize that "common law" is not a fixed or absolute set of written rules in the same sense as statutory or legislatively enacted law. The unwritten principles of common law are flexible and adaptable to the changes which occur in a growing society. New institutions and public policies; modifications of usage and practice; changes in values, trade, and commerce; inventions; and increasing knowledge—all generate new factual situations which require application and reinterpretation of the fundamental principles of common law by the courts.

As the courts examine each new set of facts in the light of past precedent, an orderly development of common laws occurs through a slow and natural process. Thus, the basic principles underlying American jurisprudence remain fundamentally constant, evolving slowly and progressively.

The common law, so far as it has not been expressly abrogated, is recognized as an organic part of the jurisprudence of most of the states. The major exception is Louisiana jurisprudence, which is based on Roman law—a relic of French rule prior to the Louisiana Purchase. However, since the state court systems have functioned independently of each other, subject only to federal review in cases of national importance, the common law varies slightly from state to state.

The common law actions that we will discuss in subsequent sections are civil suits in which the plaintiff (the party bringing the lawsuit) seeks to remedy a violation of a right. Civil actions are distinguished from criminal proceedings. Criminal actions are those in which the state seeks to redress a breach of public or collective rights which are established in codified penal law. Subsequent sections of this chapter review the three most frequently used types of common law actions that can be the basis of a lawsuit in the pollution control field.

### 4.0 COMMON LAW ENVIRONMENTAL REQUIREMENTS: TORTS

"Tort" is the word used to denote a common law civil wrong for which a court will provide a remedy.

A tort arises from the existence of a generalized legal duty to avoid causing harm to others, through acts of omission, as well as of commission. Every adult person is obliged to fulfill a duty of care for the personal and property rights of others while engaged in daily life. Carelessness in exercising this responsibility may give rise to a cause of action (a lawsuit) by means of which the injured party may seek restitution. This duty is noncontractual; that is, it does not arise from an explicit promissory agreement between the parties to the action. So a tort is also distinguished from a contract right which is dependent upon the contract itself.

Tens of thousands of tort lawsuits have been filed involving asbestos cases and other toxic chemical litigation. These cases have prompted some writers to allege that this is the era of "toxic torts." It is clear that tort law is of major interest in the environmental field as more and more tort lawsuits are filed.

The three types of torts most commonly encountered in the environmental field are: (1) nuisance, (2) trespass and (3) negligence, which are each described in the following sections.

## 4.1 Nuisance

Nuisance is defined as "that activity which arises from the unreasonable, unwarrantable or unlawful use by a person of his own property, working an obstruction or injury to the right of another or to the public, and producing such material annoyance, inconvenience, and discomfort that the law will presume resulting damage."[9]

The general rule is that a person may use his land or personal property in any manner he sees fit. However, this rule is subject to limitation: The owner must use his property in a reasonable manner. A nuisance arises whenever a person uses his property to cause material injury or annoyance to a reasonable neighbor.

In determining whether a given act constitutes a nuisance, the court considers the nature of the act itself. The discomfort must amount to a material injury or annoyance. It must tangibly affect the physical or mental health of ordinary people under normal circumstances or conditions.

### 4.1.1 Noise Nuisance

Noise produced by human activities is a common environmental problem. In order to constitute a nuisance in the legal sense, generally, noise must be of such magnitude and intensity as to cause actual or psychological discomfort to persons of ordinary sensibilities. Noise from the operation of an industrial plant constitutes an actionable nuisance if it injures the health or comfort of *ordinary* people in the plant's vicinity to an *unreasonable* extent. The courts and legislatures have had difficulty in setting an absolute standard, so this determination rests on the facts.

*O'Neill v. Carolina Freight Carriers Corp.*[10] is an example of a "noise nuisance" case in which a homeowner was awarded both an injunction and damages against the operators of a nearby business. In this case, the plaintiffs showed that they were ordinary people and that the noise from trucks and loading operations at a terminal located immediately adjacent to their home was unreasonable. It caused them loss of sleep and prevented general enjoyment of their home. The court ruled that the truck terminal noises between 11:00 p.m. and 6:00 a.m. were unreasonable and that every property owner must make reasonable use of his land so as not to cause unnecessary annoyance to his neighbors.

---

[9]*Black's Law Dictionary* 1065 (6th ed. 1990).
[10]156 Conn. 613, 244 A.2d 372 (1968).

In the *O'Neill* case, the facts lead readily to a conclusion of injury to health because the noise during the night could logically cause loss of sleep and resulting injury to health.

The case of *Rose v. Chaikin*[11] presents another interesting situation in which noise constituted a nuisance. On the New Jersey Shore just north of Atlantic City, the energy conservation-minded and environmentally conscious Joseph Chaikin erected a windmill on his residence. When it began to produce offensive noise exceeding levels permissible under the controlling city ordinance, Joel Rose and other neighbors initiated suit to enjoin the operation of the windmill.

The court announced the following standard: "The essence of a private nuisance is an unreasonable interference with the use and enjoyment of land. The elements are myriad. . . . The utility of the defendant's conduct must be weighed against the quantum of harm to the plaintiff. The question is not simply whether a person is annoyed or disturbed, but whether the annoyance or disturbance arises from an unreasonable use of the neighbor's land. . . . Unreasonableness is judged not according to exceptionally refined, uncommon or luxurious habits of living, but according to the simple tastes and unaffected notions generally prevailing among plain people."[12] Due to the unreasonable character, volume, frequency, duration, time, and locality of the noise, the court issued an injunction against any further operation of the windmill.

There is no fixed standard as to what degree or kind of noise constitutes a nuisance. The circumstances of each case must be considered independently. Generally, the key determination is whether or not the noise is unreasonable and causes some physical or psychological harm. This determination varies from one community to another and from one period of time to another depending on local attitudes and customs.

### 4.1.2 Other Nuisances

Odors, dust, smoke, other airborne pollutants, water pollutants and hazardous substances have also been held to be nuisances as the following cases illustrate.

The case of *Washington Suburban Sanitary Commission v. CAE-Link Corp. et al*[13] provides an example of an odor being classified as a nuisance. In this 1993 case, the Washington, D.C., area faced a health and safety emergency because sewage was increasingly being discharged into the Potomac River in violation of the Clean Water Act. As a result, the United States District Court for the District of Columbia ordered the Washington Suburban Sanitary Commission to build a sewage sludge composting facility next to the Montgomery Industrial Park. However, when the facility began operating, it emitted noxious odors. Companies in the Montgomery Industrial Park such as the Washington Post Company, AT&T Resource Management Corporation, and CAE-Link Corporation claimed these odors were a nuisance, and the parties went to court.

---

[11]187 N.J. Super. 210 (1982).
[12]*Ibid.* at 216.
[13]37 ERC 1863 (1993).

The Maryland Court of Appeals established that, "To prove the existence of a nuisance, therefore, the complained of interference must cause actual physical discomfort and annoyance to those of ordinary sensibilities, tastes and habits; it must interfere seriously with the ordinary comfort and enjoyment of the property." "[I]n Maryland, nuisance is a matter of strict liability and . . . 'liability for nuisance may arise even where there is compliance with applicable laws and regulations or where the offending instrumentality is authorized or permitted . . . by state statute.'" Following these established principles, the court reasoned that, like the purchase of the property for the sewage treatment facility, the elimination of odors or the compensation of those affected was a cost of the new facility. Thus the court ruled the Washington Suburban Sanitary Commission strictly liable for the odors as a nuisance. This ruling demonstrates Maryland's adherence to the traditional formulation of the law of nuisance.

In 1984 Vernon Lever sued Wilder Mobile Homes, Inc.[14] because Wilder's improperly maintained sewage treatment lagoon emitted offensive odors that interfered with gardening, family picnics, and church groups at Lever's residence. The court found that, "In South Carolina `anything' causing inconvenience or damage, or interfering with the enjoyment of life or property is a nuisance. More to the point, it is a nuisance to use property in such a way that annoying or injurious odors are emitted."[15] Accordingly, the appellate court affirmed that Wilder Mobile Homes, Inc. was liable for maintaining a nuisance.

Likewise, too, in 1993 a federal court in Kentucky ruled for the plaintiff on a nuisance claim in *Fletcher v. Tenneco, Inc.*[16] The three-generation Fletcher family lived on two farms in Powell County, Kentucky, next to a natural gas pipeline station owned by Tenneco, Inc. PCBs, toxic chemicals which were in a lubricant used at the pipeline station, leaked into the ground beneath the station and migrated in the soil and drainage water to the Fletchers' parcels of land. The PCBs found their way into the Fletchers' beef cattle as well as the blood of at least two of the Fletchers themselves.

The court ruled, notwithstanding Tenneco's scientific affidavit to the contrary, that PCBs were indeed hazardous as Congress concluded when it passed the Toxic Substances Control Act (TSCA), the Clean Water Act, and the Comprehensive Environmental Response, Compensation and Liability Act (CERCLA). Thus "the lack of any genuine issue of material fact as to Tenneco's 1) unreasonable use of its land, and 2) the resultant grave harm to the plaintiffs required that Tenneco be deemed liable as a matter of law for the creation of a nuisance."[17]Note that the two criteria for nuisance liability in Kentucky — 1) the reasonableness of the defendant's use of his property, and 2) the gravity of harm to the plaintiff"[18]—put Kentucky in the group of states that follows the traditional formulation of the law of private nuisance.

It should be noted that air pollutants only constitute a nuisance under certain circumstances. Normal air is usually considered as that common to a locality and so

---

[14]*Lever v. Wilder Mobile Homes, Inc.* 322S.E.2d692 (S.C.App. 1984).
[15]*Ibid.* at 693-4.
[16]37 ERC 1237 (E.D. KY 1993).
[17]*Ibid.* at 1241.
[18]*Ibid.* at 1239.

varies from one area to another. To be a nuisance, the air pollution must cause harm and discomfort to ordinary people to an unreasonable extent.

In the case of *Chicago v. Commonwealth Edison*[19] the court refused to rule against the electric company for alleged air pollution. The court found that although the public had a right to clean air, the notion of pure air has come to mean clean air consistent with the character of the locality and the attending circumstances. The court ruled that the city had failed to answer the threshold question of whether Commonwealth Edison's Indiana facility caused substantial harm so as to constitute an actionable invasion of a public right. In order to be entitled to injunctive relief a substantial harm or injury must be clearly demonstrated. This case is a strict interpretation of the law of nuisance because it was a request for an injunction to cease operation which would have had a broad impact on employment and local economies. If the action had been for damages, the court may have decided it differently by not using a strict interpretation of the law.

In *Harrison v. Indiana Auto Shredders,*[20] the Seventh Circuit Court of Appeals also refused to permanently enjoin operation of an automobile shredding and recycling plant based on a nuisance action. The court held that under the evidence presented and in the absence of an imminent hazard to health or welfare—none of which was established—the defendant could not be prevented from continuing to engage in its operation. In addition, the court believed that the operation should be allowed a reasonable time to correct any defects not posing threats of imminent or substantial harm.

In essence, the courts were not convinced by the evidence presented in these last two cases that harm caused by the alleged nuisance was so great as to justify forcing the defendant to cease operation. If these facilities were shut down, many families would be injured by the forced unemployment. So the weighing of equities by the court resulted in a determination based on all the evidence presented in favor of allowing continued operations. This is generally called "balancing the equities."

The Earthline Corporation, a subsidiary of SCA Services, Inc., attempted to operate an industrial waste recovery, treatment, storage and disposal site on a 130-acre site in Illinois. Ninety acres are located within the Village of Wilsonville and the remaining acres are adjacent to the village. The operation accepted hazardous wastes and toxic substances. The Village sued Earthline to stop the operation and also to require the removal of those hazardous wastes and toxic substances that had been deposited on the site.[21] The court ruled that the site was a public/private nuisance, issued an injunction against Earthline's further operation of the site and required them to remove all wastes and contaminated soil.

It is most important to note that this case was decided against SCA even though there was no showing that SCA had violated any government regulation. Compliance with government regulations is not a defense against a common law nuisance action.

Also, the lower court decision emphasized that a nuisance does not require a showing of any negligence on the part of the defendant. Nuisance and negligence are

---

[19]24 Ill. App. 624, 321 N.E. 2d 412, 7 ERC 1974.

[20]528 F.2d 1107, 8 Env't Rep. Cas. ERC 1569 (7th Cir. 1975).

[21]*Village of Wilsonville v. SCA Services, Inc.,* 77 Ill. App. 3d 618, 396 N.E. 2d 522 (1979), aff'd 86 Ill. 2d 1, 426 N.E. 2d 824 (1981).

distinct torts, and except in the cases of nuisances created by negligence, liability for nuisance does not depend upon the existence of negligence. Negligence is not an essential or material element of a cause of action for nuisance and need not be proved especially where the thing complained of is a nuisance per se or a public nuisance or results from ultra-hazardous conduct on the part of the defendant. A nuisance is a condition and not an act or a failure to act on the part of the person responsible for the condition.

In a more recent case, a different result—but the case was decided in a different jurisdiction, namely, Ohio versus Illinois. In 1993 Greenpeace pursued a nuisance claim[22] to block operation of a hazardous waste incinerator in East Liverpool, Ohio. In Ohio, however, if one has obtained from the state the required authority to operate, one cannot be a nuisance. Thus, though the hazardous waste incinerator may omit offensive odors and toxic dioxins, it will not be held liable in a cause of action for nuisance. Remember that the application of the law can vary from one jurisdiction to another and that often the factual situations are distinguishable even though at first glance they may appear the same.

### 4.1.3 Some Defenses to Nuisance Actions

Nuisance actions have often been decided by balancing the equities (weighing the impact of the injuries to respective parties involved in litigation). In any balancing of the equities, the good faith efforts of the polluter, while not absolving him, would be a factor.[23]

The availability of pollution control devices is, of course, a significant factor that can be considered by the court. For example, in *Renkin v. Harvey Aluminum,*[24] the court noted Harvey Aluminum's failure to keep pace with technological advances in pollution controls. In that case the court ordered adoption of such controls.

In general, courts are moving to strict liability for environmental nuisances so that practically speaking, there are few good defenses. The solution is: do not create nuisances. If you have an existing nuisance, you are best advised to abate it.

### 4.1.4 Coming to a Nuisance

"Coming to a nuisance" is the phrase used to describe a defense that the complainant or plaintiff affected by the nuisance moved into the area where the "complained about activity" had already been in existence.

An example of "coming to a nuisance" occurs when someone moves onto property near an airport or industrial complex and then complains of the nuisance that existed prior to his moving there. Generally, the fact that an individual purchases property with the knowledge of the existence of a nuisance or that he came to the nuisance will not

---

[22]*Greenpeace, Inc. v. Waste Technologies Industries,* 37 ERC (BNA) 1736 (N.D. Ohio 1993).

[23]*McElwain v. Georgia Pacific,* 245 Or. 247, 421 P.2d 957 (1986).

[24]226 F. Supp. 169 (D. Or. 1963).

defeat his right to the abatement of the nuisance or recovery of damages[25] nor will his right to recovery be affected if the property is sold to another while the lawsuit is pending.[26]

However, some cases have held that if the complainant came to a nuisance, this constitutes a defense to a nuisance lawsuit. This minority view is probably a result of an old axiom of law that one who voluntarily places himself in a situation whereby he suffers an injury will not prevail. The test of liability in these cases is often the knowledge of the plaintiff regarding the consequences of his conduct.

The majority rule, however, is that the fact alone that a person moved into the vicinity of a nuisance by purchasing or leasing property in the area does not bar him from complaining in an action against the continued operation or maintenance of the nuisance.[27] The majority rule is based on the theory that the right to pure air and the comfortable enjoyment of property belong to property as much as the right of possession and occupancy. If population where there was none before approaches a nuisance, it is the duty of those liable to put an end to it.

## 4.2 Trespass

Trespass is distinguished from nuisance in that trespass is interference with the possession of property whereas nuisance is interference with the use and enjoyment of property. Trespass is commonly divided into two types:

1. Trespass to chattels is an injury to or interference with the possession of personal property, with or without the exercise of personal force. This trespass involves destruction of personal property, taking from the possession of another, or a refusal to surrender possession.

.2. Trespass to land is an unlawful, forcible entry on another's realty. An injury to the realty of another or an interference with possession, above or below ground, is a trespass, regardless of the condition of the land and regardless of negligence.

Both types of trespass are categorized as intentional interferences with property. However, the concept of intent in trespass is subtle and tricky. In order to support a lawsuit under the theory of trespass to land, the Second Restatement of Torts, §163, Comment b, indicates that the intent necessary is simply an intent to be at the place on the land where the trespass allegedly occurred. As long as the defendant voluntarily interfered with the personal property, trespass to chattels will be appropriate. For both types of trespass, the "intent" requires no wrongful motive. For example, it is no defense that the defendant thought the land or chattels were his own. The property right is protected at the expense of an innocent mistake.[28]

---

[25]*Fertilizing Co. v. Hyde Park,* 97 U.S. 659 (1987); *Rentz v. Roach,* 154 Ga. 491, 115 S.E. 94 (1922); *Vann v. Bowie Sewerage Co.,* 127 Tex. 97, 90 S.W. 2d 561 (1936) are a few cases.

[26]*Abbott v. City of Princeton, Texas,* 721 S.W. 2d 872 (Tex.App. -Dallas 1986).

[27]A comprehensive article on this subject is found in 42 A.L.R. 3rd 344 (1972). This article includes a listing of cases by jurisdictions that recognize the majority rule.

[28]Prosser and Keeton on Torts 87 (5th ed. 1984).

Trespass to land is the type of trespass action that is generally used in pollution control cases. In an action for trespass to land, entry upon another's land need not be in person. It may be made by causing or permitting a thing to cross the boundary of the premises. The trespass may be committed by casting material upon another's land, by discharging water, soot or carbon, by allowing gas or oil to flow underground into someone else's land, but not by mere vibrations or light which are generally classed as nuisances.

In the case of *Martin v. Reynolds Metal Co.,*[29] the deposit on Martin's property of microscopic fluoride compounds, which were emitted in vapor form from the Reynolds' plant, was held to be an invasion of this property—and so a trespass.

The line between trespass and nuisance is sometimes difficult to determine. "The distinction which is now accepted is that trespass is an invasion of the plaintiff's interest in the exclusive possession of his land, while nuisance is an interference with his use and enjoyment of it."[30]

Negligence and trespass have also been used interchangeably as seen in the case of *Stacy v. VEPCO.*[31] In this case, the court ruled that there was "negligence and/or trespass on the part of VEPCO" because of damage caused to Stacy's trees by emissions from VEPCO's Mount Storm power plant. It is interesting to note that the court in this case was convinced by the expert meteorologist's testimony that the emissions could travel the 22-mile distance from the plant to damage the trees. The important point to remember is that courts can and do minimize the importance of the form of the action—namely, whether it is a nuisance, trespass or negligence—but endeavor to make a relatively just decision based on all the evidence presented.

## 4.3 Negligence

"Negligence" is "the omission to do something which a reasonable man, guided by those ordinary considerations which ordinarily regulate human affairs, would do, or the doing of something which a reasonable and prudent man would not do."[32] Negligence is that part of the law of torts which deals with acts not intended to inflict injury.

The standard of care required by law is that degree which would be exercised by a person of ordinary prudence under the same circumstances. This is often defined as the "reasonable man" rule, what a reasonable person would do under all the circumstances.

In order to render the defendant liable, his act must be the proximate cause of injury. Proximate cause is that which in the natural and continuous sequence, if unbroken by an efficient intervening act, produces injury and without which the result would not have happened.

*Nissan Motor Corp. v. Maryland Shipbuilding and Drydock Company*[33] exemplifies a negligence action in an environmental case. The shipbuilding company's employees failed to follow company regulations when painting ships, allowing spray

---

[29]221 Or. 86, 342 O. 2d 790 (1959), *cert. denied,* 362 U.S. 912 (1960).
[30]Prosser and Keeton on Torts 622 (5th ed. 1984).
[31]7 Env't. Rep. Cas. 1443 (1975).
[32]*Black's Law Dictionary* 1032 (6th ed. 1990).
[33]544 F.Supp. 1104 (1982).

paint to be carried by the wind onto Nissan's cars. The shipbuilders had knowledge of the likely danger of spraypainting, yet failed to exercise due care in conducting the painting operations in question. This failure to exercise due care amounted to negligence.

Persons harmed as a result of careless and improper disposal or handling of hazardous waste can recover for their losses under a negligence cause of action. Indeed, state and federal courts have long recognized this common law theory of recovery against defendants who engage in the negligent disposal of pollutants such as hazardous waste.[34] Where negligence can be established, it is no defense that the negligent action was in full compliance with all government regulations[35] and permit conditions.[36] On the other hand, noncompliance with regulations or a permit may be *prima facie* evidence (proof without any more evidence) of liability in some states.[37]

Generations of creative lawyers have eased the burden of proving negligence or fault in some circumstances by developing the negligence theories described in the following two sections.

### 4.3.1 Violation of a Statute or Ordinance Can Be Negligence

Generally, the violation of a statute or ordinance which was passed to promote safety is negligence, but the violation of such law does not of itself give rise to civil liability. The plaintiff must show that the violation of the law was the proximate cause of the injury. The violation of a statute or ordinance which is not designed to prevent the sort of harm about which the plaintiff is complaining is not negligence.

An example of the application of this doctrine in an environmental lawsuit is the case of *Springer v. Schlitz Brewing Company.*[38] Mr. and Mrs. Springer owned a large farm downriver from a newly constructed Winston Salem, N.C., brewery of Schlitz. They sued Schlitz for overloading the city's sewage treatment, causing it to pollute the Yadkin River, resulting in fish kills and so interfering with their fishing rights. In North Carolina, as in many other states, a landowner has a right to the fishing, agricultural, recreational and scenic use and enjoyment of the stream bordering his land. A city sewage ordinance prohibited the discharge of pollutants that interfere with the city's waste treatment process.

In this case the plaintiff did not, according to the court's opinion, prove that Schlitz was negligent in the conventional sense. Instead, the court looked to the theory that violation of a city sewage ordinance is negligence "per se." The appeals court directed that the jury should decide if Schlitz violated the city's ordinance. If the jury decided that the ordinance was violated, then the violation was negligence per se; and if the negligence proximately caused injury, then the industry was liable irrespective of any good faith efforts of Schlitz. The case was settled out of court.

---

[34]See, e.g., *Knabe v. National Supply Div. of Armco Steel Corp.,* 592 F.2d 841 (5th Cir. 1979).

[35]*Greater Westchester Homeowners Assoc. v. City of Los Angeles,* 26 Cal. 3d 86, 603 P.2d 1329 (1979), 160 Cal. Rptr. 733, *cert. denied,* 499 U.S. 820 (1980).

[36]*Brown v. Petroland, Inc.,* 102 Cal. App. 3d 720, 162 Cal. Rptr. 551 (1980).

[37]See *Martin v. Hersog,* 288 N.Y. 164, 126 N.E. 814, 439 N.Y.S. 2d 922 (1920).

[38]510 F.2d 468, 7 ERC 1516 (4th Cir. 1975).

So, violations of environmental or pollution control statutes or ordinances which are generally designed to protect the public health or safety could result in a successful negligence lawsuit by the injured party even though there is no factual showing of negligence.

### 4.3.2 Strict Liability and Dangerous Substances

The assessment of liability for damages without requiring a showing of negligence is called "strict liability." A landowner keeping a potentially dangerous substance on his land which, if permitted to escape, is certain to injure others, must make good the damage caused by the escape of the substance, regardless of negligence on his part.

This strict liability theory is very old. It was used in a 1907 case in which oil escaped into the Potomac River in Washington, D.C. and resulted in injury to boats in a downstream boathouse.[39] In this case, it was determined that a potentially dangerous substance is anything which, if permitted to escape, is certain to injure others. This description of a potentially dangerous substance is so broad as to include oil in the case under discussion as well as thousands of other substances in subsequent litigation.

The reasoning for this strict liability standard is that, when persons suffer loss, no good reason can be found to charge the loss against anyone who did not contribute to it. But if someone is engaged in an ultra-hazardous or dangerous activity for profit, he should bear the burden of compensating others who are harmed by his activities.

Not surprisingly, courts have applied strict liability theories in cases involving the disposal of hazardous waste and hazardous materials management.

In *Crawford v. National Lead Company,*[40] Ohio residents who lived near a federally owned uranium metals production plant alleged that the defendants failed to prevent the emission of uranium and other harmful materials from the plant and that this failure caused emotional distress and diminished property values. The court determined that the provision of uranium in various forms to nuclear facilities throughout the country is an abnormally dangerous activity.

The court then looked to the elements of strict liability for harm caused by an abnormally dangerous activity:

1.    One who carries on an abnormally dangerous activity is subject to liability for harm to the person, land or chattels of another resulting from the activity, although he has exercised the utmost care to prevent the harm.
2.    This strict liability is limited to the kind of harm the possibility of which makes the activity abnormally dangerous.[41]

Ruling that emotional distress and property damage will support a claim of strict liability in Ohio, the court ruled in favor of the residents.

Strict liability takes on a huge role in the burgeoning environmental law field. In fact, the Environmental Protection Agency itself states, "Most of the statutes which the EPA administers are strict liability,"illustrating its widespread use.[42]

---

[39]*Brennan Constr. Co. v. Cumberland,* 29 App. D.C. 554 (1907).
[40]784 F.Supp. 439 (S.D. Ohio 1989).
[41]Restatement (Second) of Torts §519 (1977).
[42]*Environmental Protection Agency Civil Penalty Policy* (February 16, 1984) at 24.

Take, for instance, the courts' application, developed over the past decade and a half, of strict liability to the Federal Water Pollution Control Act. The federal courts have recognized the application of strict liability to the Federal Water Pollution Control Act[43], referring back to the grandfather of this line of cases, *United States v. Earth Sciences, Inc.*[44]

In *United States v. Earth Sciences, Inc.,* a gold leaching operation owned by defendant Earth Science discharged cyanide into the Rito Seco Creek in Costilla County, Colorado during the process of separating gold from ore. Earth Sciences argued that the pertinent statute made only intentional discharges unlawful. The court stated, "The regulatory provisions of the FWPCA were written without regard to intentionality, however, making the person responsible for the discharge of any pollutant strictly liable."[45]

In 1993 the case titled *In Re: Sundance Corp.*[46] decided, in a matter of first impression, "whether receivers or trustees personally are strictly liable for acts done in the course of their official duties."[47] The case involved some of Washington state's renowned apples, specifically a bankrupt apple orchard in receivership, the trees of which needed to be staked to prevent wind damage. Hazardous substances used to treat the wooden stakes to prevent their deterioration when stuck in the soil as well as other hazardous materials used as pesticides and stored in various spots around the orchard dripped into the ground. The court's policy-based decision stated that "if a receiver was personally liable for any damage that results from an abnormally dangerous activity despite the lack of showing of a negligent or knowingly wrongful act, courts would be unable to obtain the services of a receiver for any site where abnormally dangerous acts are a routine part of business."[48] Strict liability was thus not applied to this situation of an abnormally dangerous activity.

The lesson here is that, especially in cases with no precedent right on point, one should remember to appeal to policy considerations to win the day in court.

## 5.0 LAWS THAT ENFORCE PERMITS, PROHIBITIONS AND PENALTIES

Although the environmental law's mechanisms for enforcing its mandates are essentially the same as those available in other legal disciplines, there are distinctive aspects to the overall enforcement program—the ways in which the available mechanisms are used together to effectively compel fulfillment of the environmental compliance obligations.

### 5.1 Permits

Perhaps the most distinctive aspect of environmental enforcement is its extensive and effective use of permitting mechanisms. Particularly with laws as complex and

---

[43] *United States v. Winchester Municipal Utilities,* 944 F.2d 301 (6th Cir. 1991).

[44] 599 F.2d 368 (10th Cir. 1979)

[45] *Ibid.* at 374.

[46] 36 ERC 1470 (U.S. Bankruptcy Ct. E.D. Wash. 1993).

[47] *Ibid.* at 1476.

[48] *Ibid.* at 1477.

technical as most of the environmental statutes, it is critical that there be an effective mechanism for bridging from generalities like "Effluents shall be treated in compliance with best available technology" to specifics like:

> Permittee is authorized to discharge from outfall number 001 "x" pounds per day of pollutant "y," subject to the condition that the discharge be monitored in accordance with specified protocols and that periodic reports be provided.

The permit fulfills this need by, in effect, establishing the "law" for a particular discharge or activity. The requirement to obtain a permit and operate in compliance with it is an individualized and highly effective way of insuring that regulators are notified of releases or activities of which they need to be aware. It is also an effective way of assuring and demonstrating that the person required to comply is on notice of his obligations. The role of permits in bridging the substantive requirements of the environmental laws—notification, discharge controls and so forth—and the other enforcement mechanisms is discussed below.

Permitting requirements, however, are by no means the only weapon in environmental law's enforcement arsenal.

## 5.2 Enforcement Provisions of the Federal and State Environmental Statutes

Each of the major federal environmental statutes provides an array of enforcement tools to compel compliance with its mandates. Generally, these include:

- Civil penalties ranging from $10,000 to $50,000 per violation or day of violation
- Administrative orders to respond or abate, enforceable by civil and criminal sanctions
- Civil action for relief including prohibition or mandatory injunction enforced by judicial decree
- Citizens' civil actions to compel compliance with or collect damages for violation of the statute
- Criminal sanctions against organizations and responsible individuals for misrepresentation or knowing or negligent violation of the statutes

There is no doubt that the federal environmental statutes and the regulations under them present a formidable set of reasons for a business or other organization to institute programs for aggressive compliance with the environmental laws. They are supported and complemented by similar enforcement provisions in the state environmental statutes as well as in local laws and ordinances.

## 5.3 General Purpose Criminal Laws

The last major category of "environmental laws that enforce" are laws from the criminal code, originally enacted to punish more traditional crimes, which have been adopted and adapted to the prosecution of crimes which are essentially environmental. The criminal code provisions which have proven particularly useful in this connection include:

- Prohibition Against False Statements to the Federal Government—18 U.S.C. 1001
- Mail Fraud Statutes—18 U.S.C. 1341, 1343
- Conspiracy Laws—18 U.S.C. 371

Even more traditional criminal laws, such as the murder statutes, have been used, at least at the state level, to successfully prosecute environmental offenses. These non-environmental laws have become almost as important as the environmental statutes in defining the liability of violators.

The environmental law enforcement package, then, is a carefully structured combination of methods—environmental and general purpose, traditional and newly conceived—which work together to bring bad consequences to those who fail to fulfill their environmental compliance obligations. This interaction has been extremely effective and will become even more formidable as the environmental law system matures.

## 6.0 LAWS THAT DEFINE THE ENVIRONMENTAL LAW FRAMEWORK

Having discussed the substantive mandates of the environmental laws and the enforcement methods which make compliance mandatory, we now need to examine the laws that establish the framework within which the system operates. The fact is that many of the questions which are most critical to successful compliance efforts and most difficult to answer fall within this category:

- What level of government has authority to regulate?
- What protections are available to the regulated?
- How do questions of scientific fact get answered?
- Who can go to court and who pays for it?

Answers to these and similar questions—critical to the resolution of environmental cases—are found not in the "environmental" statutes or regulations, but in organic laws such as constitutions—federal and state—and city charters, and procedural laws such as Administrative Procedure Acts, judicial codes and rules of evidence. These determine how our overall legal system works in environmental contexts as well as in others. It is, of course, impossible in one chapter of one volume to do more than highlight some of these important requirements which are particularly germane to the subject at hand.

### 6.1 The Organic Laws—Constitutions and Charters

In our system, the powers of government and the rights of individuals are defined primarily in the "organic acts" by which governments are created—constitutions in the case of federal and state governments and, generally, charters in the case of local governmental units like cities and counties. These laws provide the foundation for the environmental law system just as they do for the legal system in general. We look to this foundation to give us answers to the most basic and often most important questions encountered.

#### 6.1.1 Federal, State and Local Roles

A question which arises in the development of environmental regulatory programs revolves around which level of government—state, federal or local—is to play the primary role in regulating particular activities affecting the environment. The federal government is a government of limited authority which may act only through the exercise of the enumerated powers granted to it under the Constitution. In practice, however, the enumerated powers—particularly the power to regulate interstate and foreign commerce—have been broadly construed and there are few, if any, recent instances where federal laws enacted to protect public health and welfare have been held to be in excess of constitutional authority.

Once federal authority has been exercised, and a federal system of regulation has been established, important questions arise about the continuing ability of state and local governments to operate in that same area. While state and local governments have broad "police powers" to do what is necessary to protect the health and safety of their citizens, that authority may be displaced where a scheme of federal regulation, pursuant to enumerated authority, preempts the field of regulation and precludes the further exercise of state and local authority. The judicial trend in these "preemption cases" is towards upholding continued state authority except where the U.S. Congress has explicitly expressed a clear intention to fully occupy the field and displace state authority to regulate. The trend in the Congress is to explicitly preserve the states' continuing authority to regulate.

### 6.1.2 Commerce Clause

One line of constitutional cases dealing with this question of "who can regulate?" involves the issue of whether, even in the absence of preemptive federal action, a state or local law may be unconstitutional because it improperly restrains interstate or foreign commerce.

Article I, Section 8, of the U.S. Constitution is called the "Commerce Clause." It grants to Congress the authority ". . . to regulate Commerce with foreign Nations, and among the several States, and with the Indian Tribes." If the courts find that state statutes or regulations impermissibly burden interstate commerce, then they are unconstitutional and unenforceable.

It is well settled that a state regulation validly based on police power does not impermissibly burden interstate commerce if the regulations neither discriminate against interstate commerce nor operate to disrupt its required uniformity. Where there is a reasonable basis to protect the social, as distinguished from the economic welfare of a community, the courts will not deny this exercise of sovereign power and hold it to violate the Commerce Clause.

The U.S. Supreme Court examined a Commerce Clause case involving Alabama's Emelle facility, the nation's largest commercial hazardous waste landfill and one of our oldest. For disposal of hazardous waste at the Emelle facility, Alabama charged $72 more per ton for waste generated *outside* Alabama than it did for waste generated *inside* Alabama. The Supreme Court ruled that the additional fee discriminated against hazardous waste generated in states other than Alabama and that such burdensome taxes on interstate commerce were forbidden.[49]

Another Commerce Clause case involved the Chicago ordinance banning the sale of detergents containing phosphates.[50] The Seventh Circuit Court of Appeals held that the ordinance did not violate the Commerce Clause because, although it had some minor effect on interstate commerce, the benefits far outweighed these effects, and the ordinance was a reasonable method of achieving a legitimate goal of improving Lake Michigan.

Another result favorable to legislators was reached in Missouri when the constitutionality of the City of Columbia's five-cent refund on beverage containers was challenged.[51] "The declared purpose of the ordinance is to reduce littering and to promote recycling and reuse of empty beverage containers."[52] The Court held, "The Columbia ordinance does not discriminate between intrastate and interstate commerce."[53]

The trend is definitely to try to uphold environmental legislation, the rationale based on a balancing of environmental benefits against detrimental effects.

We can expect the debate along these lines to intensify and revitalize as international laws and treaties establish product standards and regulate activities, like marine transportation, potentially affecting the environment. While questions of "unreasonable burden" may be philosophically the same in the global context as within the national borders, the political dynamics and level of complexity will increase radically and new solutions may indeed be required.

### 6.1.3 Equal Protection

Another category of cases of interest to the environmental field are those limiting the ability of federal and state governments to regulate conduct under the Constitutional mandate of "equal protection."

Section One of the Fourteenth Amendment to the Constitution prohibits governments from denying to any person the equal protection of the laws. This provision has been applied, essentially, to prevent inappropriate discrimination.

In Hawaii several environmental groups sought to stop an interstate highway project known as the "H-3" project.[54] Congress thwarted their efforts in 1986 when they passed Public Law No. 99-591. Section 114 of this law provided for specific exemption of the H-3 project from federal "4(f) statutes" requiring that no public parks,

---

[49]*Chemical Waste Management, Inc. v. Hunt*, ---U.S.---, 112 S.Ct. 2009, 119 L.Ed.2d.2d121, 60 U.S.L.W. 4433, 34 ERC 1721, 22 Envtl. L. Rep. 20909 (1992); See also *Fort Gratiot Sanitary Landfill, Inc. v. Michigan Dept. of Natural Resources*, ---U.S.---, 112 S.Ct. 2019, (1992).

[50]*Procter and Gamble Co. vs. Chicago*, 509 F.2d69, 7 ERC 1328 (7th Cir 1975), *cert. denied*, 421 U.S. 978 (1975).

[51]*Mid-State Distributing Company v. City of Columbia*, 617 S.W.2d 419 (Mo.App. 1981).

[52]*Ibid*, at 421.

[53]*Ibid*, at 430.

[54]*Stop H-3 Association v. Transportation Department*, 870 F.2d 1419, 29 ERC 1390 (CA 9th Cir. 1989).

wildlife refuges, or historical sites be used for any project unless "no feasible and prudent alternative" exists and unless harm to the area is minimized.

The environmental groups asked the court to hold that section 114 violated the equal protection component of the U.S. Constitution. They argued that the right to a healthy environment is an "important" individual right and that Congress violated constitutional principles of federalism in enacting a provision which discriminates against the citizens of Hawaii. They claimed that section 114 "creates an arbitrary classification [based on state citizenship] by denying residents of Hawaii the environmental protections provided by the 4(f) statutes."

The U.S. Court of Appeals for the 9th Circuit ruled against the Hawaiian environmental groups, remarking that no court had yet found a constitutional right to a healthy environment to exist. The court held that Congress had the power to exempt specific projects from certain federal laws, and that exempting this particular project did not amount to arbitrarily or categorically discriminating against Hawaii.

Courts generally hold that for a classification to violate the constitutional guarantee of equal protection, there must be a showing that there is no reasonable basis for the distinction. A law is presumptively valid. Unless clear and convincing proof demonstrates that a law is arbitrary and unreasonable, the law must be upheld. The result is that few laws are ever held to violate the equal protection clause.

So, effective arguments have been made that there is a need to limit the number of regulators by either giving all power to the states and keeping the federal government out or vice versa. The end result of all these arguments has been continued reaffirmation that, in environmental contexts, federal, state and local governments will continue to exercise concurrent, but not always coordinated, jurisdiction. This fact of life is one of the things that makes this field a challenge.

## 6.2 The Courts' Role

The organic laws define the authorities of the legislative and executive branches of the government as well as the judiciary. To understand the law as applied, one must understand the courts' role.

### 6.2.1 State and United States Court Systems

There are two primary judicial systems in the United States: (1) the state and local courts, established in each state under the authority of the state government, and (2) federal courts, set up under the authority of the Constitution by the Congress of the United States.

The state courts have general, unlimited power to decide almost every type of case, subject only to the limitation of state law. State and local courts are located in every town and county and are the tribunals with which citizens most often have contact. The great bulk of legal business, such as divorce, probate of estates, traffic accidents and all other matters except those assigned to the U.S. courts is handled by these state and local courts.

The U.S. courts, on the other hand, have the authority to hear and decide only selected types of cases, which are specifically enumerated in the Constitution. The U.S. courts are located principally in the larger cities while state and local courts are found throughout the country.

### 6.2.2 United States Court System

The structure of the U.S. court system has evolved throughout the historical development of our country. The Constitution merely provides: "The Judicial Power of the United States, shall be vested in one Supreme Court, and in such inferior Courts as the Congress may from time to time ordain and establish." Thus, the only court which is constitutionally indispensable is the Supreme Court. The authority to establish and abolish other U.S. courts is vested in and has been exercised by the Congress.

The United States court system is pyramidal in structure with three levels. At the apex of the pyramid stands the Supreme Court of the United States, the highest court in the land. On the second level are the 12 United States courts of appeals. On the third level are the 94 United States district courts.

A person involved in a suit in a U.S. court may proceed through the three levels of decision. Generally, the case will first be heard and decided by one of the courts on the district court level. If either party is dissatisfied with the decision, it will usually have a right of review in one of the courts of appeals. Then, if still dissatisfied, it may petition for review in the Supreme Court of the United States. However, review is granted by the Supreme Court only in cases involving matters of national importance.

This pyramidal organization of the courts serves two purposes. First, the Supreme Court and the courts of appeals can correct errors which have been made in the decisions of the trial courts. Secondly, the higher courts can assure uniformity of decision by reviewing cases in which two or more lower courts have reached different decisions.

State courts have a similar pyramid structure, with a basic court of original jurisdiction, an appellate court and then a supreme court. Often states do not use the same terminology in naming their courts. So, at the state level the nomenclature can be confusing, but the system of a lower court deciding a case in the beginning with opportunity for review of the decision by appellate courts is similar to the federal system.

### 6.2.3 Courts in Practical Perspective

From a practical viewpoint, when you learn about a judicial decision of interest to you, ask which court decided the case. If the Supreme Court of the U.S. decided the case, it is a very important decision for the entire country. If a local court decided the case, it is generally of limited interest nationally but of major interest to that local jurisdiction. However, any decision on a point of law is better than none at all.

Also, be aware that courts do differ in their opinions. There are many examples of two lower courts reaching conflicting opinions on a point of law. This is an extremely difficult concept for many to accept. If you are originally trained in engineering or the sciences, you are probably accustomed to dealing in data and facts. To move into the realm of "ifs" and "yes, but" seems like going from the world of black and white into a world of gray. For those who find this troubling, remember that in almost everything, we are talking about degrees of certitude. The field of environmental law may involve a higher degree of incertitude than most other areas because of its newness and changeability. As a result, you do your best to understand what is the meaning of the laws, regulations and court opinions, and you then take into your consideration the degree of certitude involved in a particular legal issue before proceeding to a decision.

Also, keep in mind that your court system, although hailed as one of the fairest systems ever developed by mankind, is subject to human frailties. Human interactions like those of dealing with judges, lawyers, plaintiffs, defendants and jurors are another source of uncertainties.

### 6.2.4 Court Jurisdiction and Forum Shopping

The question of which court has jurisdiction can be a complex issue. Also, the question of the specific court in which a case is initiated is generally a key move in the overall strategy for winning a lawsuit. This is called "forum shopping." When initiating a lawsuit a good lawyer will evaluate which court is more inclined toward his client's position. For example, the judges of the U.S. Courts in the District of Columbia are known for their pro-environmental record. So organizations such as the Environmental Defense Fund (EDF) and the Sierra Club are inclined to initiate their lawsuits in the U.S. District Courts for the District of Columbia. Industrial firms are generally more inclined to file a lawsuit in a district court in Louisiana or other such geographic area with a more conservative judicial record.

### 6.2.5 When Can Courts Act?

According to Article III, Section 2, clause 1, of the United States Constitution, federal courts can only act on actual "cases" or "controversies," meaning:

1. "Moot" questions cannot be decided,
2. "Advisory opinions" cannot be issued,
3. Cases must be "ripe" for decision—concrete and focused, having reached "finality" on the part of the executive and legislative branches, and not premature and abstract,
4. "Collusive" and "feigned" cases will be dismissed, and
5. Parties must have standing to sue.

The following examples illustrate these principles.

In *Woodland Private Study Group v. New Jersey Department of Environmental Protection*[55] the U.S. Court of Appeals for the Third Circuit ordered a complaint dismissed as moot when 3M (the Minnesota Mining and Manufacturing Company) and R&H (the Rohm and Haas Company) challenged the New Jersey Spill Compensation and Control Act as unconstitutional. Before their case was decided, however, the New Jersey Supreme Court in two different cases performed what the court called "judicial surgery" on the act, bringing it into conformity with the federal constitution. Both 3M and R&H agreed in letters to the court that this action rendered their case moot, and it was dismissed.

In *TJ Baker, Inc. v. Aetna Casualty and Surety Co.*,[56] plaintiff Baker was named as a potentially responsible party (PRP) for environmental pollution at several sites. Aetna Casualty and Surety Co. had issued comprehensive general liability [CGL] insurance policies to Baker, and Baker sought "partial summary judgment on the legal

---

[55]846 F.2d 921, 27 ERC 1911 (3rd Cir. 1988).
[56]28 ERC 1237 (DC NJ 1988).

interpretation, under New Jersey law, of a provision contained in the CGL policies which defined an 'occurrence'—the event which triggers coverage under each policy."

"What the plaintiff seeks, in essence, is an advisory opinion on the state of New Jersey law regarding the widely-used `occurrence' definition in CGL policies. This requested ruling would not require an examination of any of the facts, disputed or otherwise, involved in this matter, nor would this determination dispose of any claim or any part of any claim asserted by plaintiff."[57] Accordingly, the federal district court dismissed the case, illustrating the rule against issuing advisory opinions.

Ripeness was the issue of *In re Combustion Equipment Associates, Inc.*[58] There the EPA sent the appellant a letter naming it a *potentially* responsible party (PRP) for groundwater contamination at two landfill sites. The appellant sought judgment that any CERCLA liability it may have had was discharged by its subsequent Chapter 11 bankruptcy reorganization. The court ruled that there was no finality to the EPA's action of naming the appellant a PRP, and since there was not yet any determination that the appellant was actually responsible, there might never be a need to assess the effect of the bankruptcy reorganization on such responsibility. The court dismissed the action as not ready or "ripe" for determination.

In 1993 the Third Circuit Court of Appeals faced the issue of ripeness in *New Hanover Township v. Army Department.*[59] New Hanover Corporation (NHC) sought to use land located within New Hanover Township as a municipal waste landfill. Under the Clean Water Act, the Secretary of the Army through the Army Corps of Engineers has the authority to issue permits to persons who want to discharge dredged or fill material into navigable waters. New Hanover Township objected to the Corps' issuance of a permit to NHC for the municipal waste landfill. The court set out the standard for ripeness:

> In determining whether this case involves an abstract disagreement or a dispute which requires judicial intervention, the court should examine 1) whether the issues are fit for judicial resolution and 2) whether withholding judicial resolution will result in hardship to the parties.[60]

The court pointed out that though the Corps had made a decision, NHC still needed to obtain a water quality permit from the Pennsylvania Department of Environmental Resources (PADER). The court also noted, "not all decisions that represent an agency's last word on an issue are final for purposes of review. . . Rather, finality is to be interpreted in a pragmatic way."[61] Effectively PADER has a veto over the Corps. Because, then, no one was hurt by the court refraining from hearing the case at that time, "a pragmatic view of the facts mandates a decision that this case is not ripe for review."[62]

---

[57]*Ibid.,* at 1239.
[58]838 F.2d 35, 27 ERC 1227 (2nd Cir. 1988).
[59]37 ERC 1189 (3d Cir. 1993).
[60]*Ibid.* at 1191.
[61]*Ibid.*
[62]*Ibid.*

### 6.2.6 Who May Sue?

To sue, a party must have "standing" or an appropriate individuated interest in the outcome of the case. In the 1989 case of *McCormick v. Anshutz Mining Corp.,*[63] the plaintiff, Walter McCormick, alleged that Anshutz Mining had violated CERCLA. However, McCormick testified in deposition that he had not been injured in any way by alleged discharges of pollution from a mine owned by Anshutz Mining. While McCormick was worried that he might be exposed to *future* liability because he had been in charge of the refinery at the mine until it was closed, "The mere possibility of future injury is not enough." Hence, the court dismissed McCormick's case for lack of standing.

In the context of actions to compel or obtain review of agency actions, the required interest is described in the Administrative Procedure Act (APA). Under APA, standing exists only when a plaintiff can satisfactorily demonstrate that (a) the agency action complained of will result in an injury in fact and that (b) the injury is to an interest "arguably within the zone of interests to be protected" by the statute in question.

The leading cases addressing the "injury in fact" question are cases involving the National Environmental Policy Act and environmental impact statements. The key case is the Supreme Court decision in *Sierra Club v. Morton.*[64] This case involved the recreational development of the Mineral King Valley. The question in *Sierra v. Morton* was: What must be alleged by persons who claim injury of a non-economic nature to widely shared interests to give them standing? The court recognized that environmental well-being, like economic well-being, is an important ingredient of our society. The fact that environmental interests are shared by many rather than few does not make them less deserving of legal protection. But the "injury in fact" test, according to the Court, requires that the party seeking review be himself among the injured. The Sierra Club did not allege and show that it or its members would be affected in any of their activities or pastimes by the development. So the Court ruled against them. However, this has since proven to be an easy matter to remedy by the plaintiffs alleging that an aesthetic or other non-economic interest was injured. So the Sierra Club established in this decision that environmental interests could be the basis for standing.

In a subsequent Supreme Court case, *SCRAP v. U.S.*[65] the Supreme Court gave some law students standing to sue the Interstate Commerce Commission (ICC) in a rate increase case involving recyclables. The Supreme Court ruled that standing to sue was demonstrated by the students, showing that they used forests and streams in the Washington, D.C. area for camping and hiking and that this was disturbed by the adverse environmental impact caused by the nonuse of recyclable goods brought on by the ICC rate increase on recyclable commodities.

In one of its most recent visits to the case or controversy and standing issue the Supreme Court has indicated that environmental organizations do not get a free ride to judgment but must allege and prove individuated injury in fact. In *Lujan v. National Wildlife Federation,*[66] the Supreme Court reversed a decision which held that two

---

[63]29 ERC 1707 (1989).
[64]405 U.S. 727 3 ERC 2039 (1972).
[65]412 U.S. 669 (1973)
[66]110 S.Ct. 3177 (1990).

affidavits filed on behalf of the National Wildlife Federation had satisfactorily alleged injury in fact, even though they were not specific as to the actual injury. The affidavits were filed in support of a challenge to a program of the Bureau of Land Management. The Court stated that "whether one of respondent's members has been, or is threatened to be, 'adversely affected or aggrieved' by Government action—Rule 56(e) is assuredly not satisfied by pleadings which state only that one of respondent's members uses unspecified portions of an immense tract of territory, on some portions of which mining activity has occurred or probably will occur by virtue of the governmental action."[67]

The U.S. Supreme Court's current trend is definitely to make it harder for a plaintiff to establish standing to sue. The 1992 case of *Lujan v. Defenders of Wildlife*[68] continues this trend. This lawsuit challenged the view that U.S. agencies' funding of development projects overseas does not have to comply with the Endangered Species Act. The court did not rule on the question of whether the law's provisions extend to overseas projects, but rather dismissed the case on the legal ground that the plaintiffs lacked standing to sue. One of the plaintiffs in this lawsuit, Joyce Kelly, had asserted that she would suffer harm because the Bureau of Reclamation's project to rebuild the Aswan Dam in Egypt threatened the endangered Nile crocodile. Amy Silbred said she would be harmed by the Mahaweli water resource project in Sri Lanka, funded by the U.S. AID, which threatened the endangered Asian elephant and leopard.

Justice Scalia, writing for the court majority, said that although both women had visited the area of the projects and alleged their intention to return, that was not enough to demonstrate that they were in immediate danger of suffering harm. He said plaintiffs must prove they suffer individual, concrete harm as a result of the government's procedural violation to have standing to sue.

## 6.3 Defining The Rights of the Regulated and Limits of Governmental Authority

While we normally think about "Constitutional Rights" in contexts other than environmental law, there is little doubt that the scope and availability of rights which some regard as "fundamental freedoms" will continue to be matters of vigorous contention in this field. Some of these areas of debate are summarized below.

### 6.3.1 Search Warrants and the Fourth Amendment

The Fourth Amendment of the Constitution provides that:

> The right of the people to be secure in their persons, houses, papers, and effects, against unreasonable searches and seizures shall not be violated, and no Warrants shall issue, but upon probable cause, supported by oath or affirmation and particularly describing the place to be searched and the persons or things to be seized.

The warrant issue arises most frequently in connection with the collection or obtaining of evidence. Evidence is necessary for any civil or criminal enforcement

---

[67]*Id.* at 3189.
[68]110S.Ct. 3177 (1990).

program. However, federal and state evidence collection is limited by Fourth Amendment prohibitions. Generally warrants are only sought after entry is refused, because there is no need for a search warrant when the owner or operator has given his consent.

The courts have held that the Fourth Amendment applies to the corporate entity as well as to the private citizen. The Supreme Court has held that the requirement for a search warrant even applies to routine inspections.[69] In the *Camara* case, the Court held that the warrant requirement applied to a municipal health inspector's search of a private residence. A similar conclusion was reached with respect to a fire inspector's attempted search of a commercial warehouse.[70] In these cases, the Court indicated that a lesser degree of "probable cause" would be required for an administrative search warrant than for the typical criminal search warrant. So there can be routine periodic searches of all structures in a given area based on an appraisal of conditions in the area as a whole rather than on a knowledge of conditions in a particular building. The reasonableness of such inspections is to be weighed against the invasion of rights that the search entails.

In November of 1989, the Supreme Court of Pennsylvania upheld warrantless, unannounced inspection provisions of Pennsylvania's Solid Waste Management Act.[71] The act allowed a Department of Environmental Resources (DER) employee to go into a "transfer station" where trash was compacted, since the employee entered the transfer station "to ascertain the compliance or noncompliance by any person or municipality with the provisions of this act." The DER employee had seen one of the appellant's loaded trash trucks enter the transfer station, which the appellant had not been issued a permit to operate. The court reasoned that the "Colonade-Biswell exception"[72] to the warrant requirement of the Fourth Amendment allows greater latitude to conduct warrantless inspections of commercial property because "the expectation of privacy that the owner of commercial property enjoys in such property differs significantly from the sanctity accorded an individual's home. . ."[73]

To avoid this need for search warrants, Congress has authorized warrantless searches in some statutes. In the famous *Barlow* case[74] the constitutionality of these legislative waivers was reviewed by the Supreme Court. The Court held that Section 8 of the Occupational Safety and Health Act (OSHA), which authorized warrantless inspections, violated the Fourth Amendment prohibition against warrantless searches and was unconstitutional. Despite this Constitutional protection, the wisdom of demanding a warrant for a normal inspection is dubious at best, and few businesses challenge inspections without warrants because to do so indicates that a problem probably exists. The warrant requirement does put some minimal restraint on the federal government's ability to conduct repetitive or needless inspections.

---

[69]*Camara v. Municipal Court of San Francisco,* 387 U.S. 523 (1967).

[70]*See v. City of Seattle,* 387 U.S. 541 (1967).

[71]*Com., DER v. Blosenski Disposal Serv,* 523 Pa 274, 566 A2d 845, 30 ERC 1835 (1989).

[72]*Colonade Catering Corp. v. United States,* 397 U.S. 72, 90 S.Ct. 774, 25 L.Ed.2d 60 (1970), *United States v. Biswell,* 406 U.S. 311, 92 S.Ct. 1593, 32 L.Ed.2d 87 (1972).

[73]*Com., DER v. Blosenski Disposal Serv.,* 566 A2d 845, 848 (1989).

[74]*Marshall v. Barlow's Inc.,* 436 U.S. 307 (1978).

The Environmental Protection Agency (EPA) has avoided any test of the constitutionality of the warrantless search authorizations given to them by Congress in the Noise Control Act and the Resource Conservation and Recovery Act by not challenging the issue. If an EPA inspector is refused admission, EPA, as standard procedure, will then obtain a search warrant and not even try to use the statutory authority. This avoids the constitutional confrontation.

It is common, in the field of environmental law, to find exceptions to the general rules. An example of an exception to the search warrant requirement is the so-called "open fields" exception described in the Supreme Court case, *Air Pollution Variance Board v. Western Alfalfa*.[75] In this case, an inspector of a Division of the Colorado Department of Health entered the premises of Western Alfalfa Corporation without its knowledge or consent to make a Ringelmann reading of plumes of smoke being emitted from the company's chimneys. Western Alfalfa Corporation claimed that the inspection violated the Fourth Amendment by entering its property to collect evidence without a search warrant. The U.S. Supreme Court ruled that the inspector was within an exception to the Fourth Amendment and had not violated the rights of Western Alfalfa Corporation. The Court held the general rule to be that the act of conducting tests on a defendant's premises without either a warrant or the consent of defendant constitutes an unreasonable search within the Fourth Amendment. However, in this case the inspector did not enter the plant or offices. Basically he sighted what anyone in the area near the plant could see in the sky. He was on the defendant's property, but there was no showing that he was on premises from which the public was excluded. The Court held that there is an "open fields" exception to the constitutional requirement for a search warrant which was applicable in this case.

Another case describing the "open fields" exception is in the interesting case of *Forsythe v. Commonwealth of Pennsylvania*.[76]

After various discussions with appellant Barb Forsythe about the condition of her property, Larry Smith, Franklin Township's code enforcement officer, periodically inspected her premises. Smith observed "numerous junked cars, piles of trash, washers, mailboxes, wheel rims, water heaters, concrete blocks, and miscellaneous car parts on her property."[77] Barb Forsythe claimed she was operating a "recycling center" and admitted she had a business sign with the designation "Jay's Auto Parts" erected at the entrance to her yard. Forsythe was convicted of operating a junkyard without a license.

On appeal Forsythe argued that because enforcement officer Smith had entered her property without a warrant, her conviction should be overturned. The appellate court disagreed, however, noting that "[t]he condition of [appellant's] land was easily ascertainable from a public road. She could have no expectation of privacy in an open field."[78] Since the only evidence used in her conviction was easily ascertainable from a public road, the open fields exception applied and Forsythe's conviction was upheld.

In the vast majority of practical situations, consent is given for collection of evidence. The consent may be oral or written, and is commonly given by employees

---

[75] 416 U.S. 861, 6 ERC 1571 (1974).
[76] 601 A2d 864 (Pa Cmwealth 1992).
[77] *Ibid*, at 865.
[78] *Ibid*, at 866.

simply admitting the inspectors to the company premises or giving answers to oral or written questions by government employees.

One method of avoiding the necessity of obtaining a search warrant is to require the owner or operator of the pollution source to get a permit or license to operate which includes a condition allowing inspections without warrants. The U.S. Supreme Court has not yet ruled on the constitutionality of this method. Since permit systems are now being used more and more by federal, state and local agencies to control pollution, this method of obtaining desired evidence will be the trend of the future and provides the government with the consent needed.

### 6.3.2 Prohibition Against Self-Incrimination: The Fifth Amendment

The Fifth Amendment to the Constitution prohibits compulsory self-incrimination. The protection applies in criminal cases. If the government agency collecting the evidence will use it only for civil actions, such as fines or injunctions, the Fifth Amendment is not applicable. In addition, the Fifth Amendment applies only to persons and not to corporations or partnerships.

In *Braswell v. United States*[79] the Supreme Court reiterated many of the protections against self-incrimination. The petitioner Randy Braswell purchased and sold timber, land, equipment, and oil and gas interests through his two corporations. When a federal grand jury subpoenaed Braswell as president of both corporations to produce the corporations' books and records, Braswell claimed that according to the Fifth Amendment he should not be compelled in any criminal case to be a witness against himself.[80]

In the decision Chief Justice Rehnquist explained that the Fifth Amendment neither applies to "collective entities" such as corporations, unions or partnerships, nor to people acting as agents of collective entities. Rather, the Fifth Amendment applies to people in personal capacities and protects individuals' private papers. Notably, a sole proprietorship is considered personal and is protected by the Fifth Amendment.

The Supreme Court ruled against Braswell. Because the subpoena identified Braswell as an agent of "collective entities,"—specifically, president of the corporations—the Fifth Amendment's protections did not apply. If, on the other hand, Braswell had been operating sole proprietorships as he had in the past, he would have been protected by the Fifth Amendment.

Most environmental statutes provide penalties for both individuals and corporations. Therefore, in a case where the evidence or samples taken might be used in a criminal action, the person in authority at the place where evidence is to be taken should be advised of his rights to remain silent, to an attorney, and that any evidence taken may be used against him in a subsequent criminal action. If these rights are not formally observed, the evidence so collected may not be admissible in a criminal action. See section 6.5.6 of this chapter on Your Own Reports as Evidence Against You.

### 6.3.3 Due Process, the Fifth and Fourteenth Amendments

The requirement that government entities provide due process of law is found in the Fifth and Fourteenth Amendments.

---

[79]487 U.S. 11 (1988).
[80]Fifth Amendment.

The Fifth Amendment to the U.S. Constitution says: "No person shall . . . be deprived of life, liberty, or property, without due process of law; nor shall private property be taken for public use, without just compensation."

The Fourteenth Amendment to the U.S. Constitution states: "Section 1 . . . No State shall make or enforce any law which shall abridge the privileges or immunities of citizens of the United States; nor shall any State deprive any person of life, liberty, or property without due process of law; nor deny to any person within its jurisdiction the equal protection of the law."

The Fifth Amendment prohibition applies to the federal government and the Fourteenth applies to the states.

An example of the application of the legal concept of due process is found in the case, *Construction Industry Ass'n. v. Petaluma.*[81] In this case the Court held that a city ordinance that limits issuance of new building permits to achieve a goal of preserving "small town" character, open spaces and low density population does not violate the due process clause of the Fourteenth Amendment.

The Court's opinion explained that, to satisfy the due process mandate, zoning regulations must find their justification in some aspect of the police power asserted for the public welfare. The Court found that the concept of the public welfare is sufficiently broad to uphold Petaluma's desire to preserve its small town character, open spaces and low density population.

The due process argument was used against the beverage container ordinance of the City of Bowie, Maryland.[82] The Court ruled that there was not a violation of due process since there was not a showing that the police power was exercised arbitrarily, oppressively or unreasonably. The opinion also held that a law should not be held void if there are any considerations of public welfare which can support it.

*Massachusetts v. Blackstone Valley Electric Co.*[83] applied the due process protections to the Comprehensive Environmental Response, Compensation, and Liability Act (CERCLA, a.k.a. Superfund). According to CERCLA, a Remedial Investigation/Feasibility Study (RI/FS) must be conducted once a hazardous waste site has been identified. CERCLA further requires that the alleged generators of a site's hazardous waste be notified of cleanup efforts, be allowed access to the RI/FS, and have a chance to comment on the work plan and data. This input becomes important because it establishes the administrative record from which the cleanup costs owed by the individual hazardous waste generators can eventually be calculated.

In this case, the Massachusetts Department of Environmental Protection did not notify Blackstone Valley Electric Company of the cleanup until approximately one year after it had begun. Blackstone Valley Electric Company argued that its due process rights would be violated if it were forced to pay for cleanup efforts about which it knew nothing and over which it had no input or control. The court agreed with Blackstone Valley Electric Company. The court ordered the Massachusetts Department of Environmental Protection to supplement the administrative record with comments

---

[81]522 F.2d 897, 8 ERC 1001 (9th cir. 1975), *cert. denied,* 424 U.S. 924 (1976).
[82]*Bowie Inn v. City of Bowie,* 274 Md. 230, 335 A.2d 679, 7 ERC 2083 (1975).
[83]37 ERC 1383 (1992).

submitted by Blackstone, to hold meetings for Blackstone to comment on the selected cleanup actions, to accept written submissions by Blackstone for 30 days following the date of the last of these meetings, and to certify to the court a supplemented administrative record including any decreases in the cleanup costs it sought from the defendants. Thereby, defendant Blackstone Valley Electric Company had its important Fourteenth Amendment due process rights protected.

### 6.3.4 Police Power and Due Process

Police power is the inherent right of a government to pass laws for the protection of the health, welfare, morals, and property of the people within its jurisdiction. Police power may not be bartered away by contract. It extends to all public needs. It may be put forth in aid of what is sanctioned by usage or what is held by prevailing opinion to be greatly or immediately necessary for public welfare. By exercise of reasonable police power, government may regulate the conduct of individuals and of the use of their property and, in some instances, take property without compensation.

Although the police power of a state is very broad, it is not without limitation. It is always within the power of the court to declare a law void which, although enacted as a police regulation, is not justified as such. In other words, a law enacted as a police regulation must be reasonable. If the law is unreasonable or exercised in an arbitrary manner, it is taking life, liberty or property without due process of law.

The case of *Browning-Ferris Industries (BFI) of Alabama, Inc. v. Alabama Department of Environmental Management (ADEM)*[84]illustrates the interplay of police power and due process rights. BFI was trying to open a hazardous waste facility when the Alabama legislature passed the Minus Act prohibiting hazardous waste facilities to open without prior legislative approval. BFI challenged the statute as violative of the Fourteenth Amendment's Due Process Clause.

The court announced that the storage of hazardous waste is an appropriate area for control by the Alabama legislature under its police power. "The Court emphasizes that the Constitution does not foreclose legislative restrictions on hazardous waste facilities. Such restrictions appear to this Court to be essential for the protection of the health and safety of Alabama residents."[85]

However, the federal court found that the statute provided absolutely no standards by which to decide for approval of hazardous waste facilities. The court stated that, "the guarantee of due process . . . demands only that the law shall not be unreasonable, arbitrary and capricious and that the means selected shall have some real and substantial relationship to the object sought to be obtained . . . "[86] Thus, while in an area appropriate for police power protection, the pertinent provision of the Minus Act was held an unconstitutional violation of due process.

Another example of the valid exercise of police power which did not violate the due process principle was in the Supreme Court case, *Village of Belle Terre v. Borass.*[87] In this case a New York village ordinance restricted land use to one-family houses and

---

[84]710 F.Supp. 313, 30 ERC 1166 (M.D. Ala. 1987).

[85]*Ibid,* at 30 ERC 1169.

[86]*Ibid,* at 30 ERC 1168.

[87]416 U.S. 1 (1974).

precluded occupancy by more than two unrelated persons. The Court held this ordinance to be a valid exercise of the city's police power, stating:

A quiet place where yards are wide, people few, and motor vehicles restricted are legitimate guidelines in a land use project addressed to family needs. The police power is not confined to elimination of filth, stench, and unhealthy places. It is ample to lay out zones where family values, youth values, and the blessings of quiet seclusion and clean air make the area a sanctuary for people.

### 6.3.5 Prohibition Against Taking Property Without Compensation

The Fifth Amendment to the Constitution states that ". . . private property [shall not] be taken for public use, without just compensation."

Despite numerous court opinions on this issue, the line between "takings" which require compensation and valid exercises of "police power" which do not require compensation has never been clearly drawn. It is difficult to predict the outcome when the principles in this area are applied to factual situations.

It may be said that the state takes property by eminent domain because it is useful to the public. This taking requires compensation. When the state takes property because it is harmful, it is done under the police power and does not require compensation. What is useful to one person may be harmful to another. So, the perspective of all the conditions and circumstances is often the determining factor in choosing between useful and harmful.

The problem often comes down to one of degree. In both circumstances damages result. If the damage is suffered by many similarly situated and is in the nature of a restriction and ought to be borne by the individual as a member of society for the good of the public, it is a reasonable exercise of police power not requiring compensation. However, if the damage is so great to the individual that he ought not to bear it under generally accepted standards, then courts are inclined to treat it as a "taking," or unreasonable exercise of police power requiring compensation. .

A developer, Southview Associates Ltd. had purchased 88 acres with the intent to build a residential subdivision. When it became known that this land was a winter habitat for white-tailed deer, the Vermont Department of Fish and Wildlife opposed the development project. Southview's land use permit application was then turned down by the District III Environmental Commission as was its appeal to the Vermont Environmental Board.

In *Southview Associates Ltd. v. Vermont Environmental Board,*[88] the court ruled that Southview had not lost the right to possess the allegedly occupied land that forms part of the deeryard and exclude people and even deer therefrom; that Southview retained substantial control over the property including the right to build on up to 10 acres for any purpose and to camp, walk, ski, or even hunt deer—irrespective of whether these activities caused the deer to abandon the deeryard; and that Southview's right to sell the land was by no means worthless. The court ruled that no absolute, exclusive physical occupation existed. The property was not "emptied. . .of any value"[89] by the permit denial. "Indeed, the deer activity displaces only a few sticks in the bundle of

---

[88] *36 ERC 1024 (1992)*
[89] *Ibid.* at 1032.

rights that constitute ownership."[90] The court dismissed Southview's physical taking claim saying, "Denial of the. . .permit—foreclosing one configuration of a development plan—represents a regulation of the use of Southview's property, rather than a *per se* physical taking."[91]

Another case involved the denial of operational drilling permits in the Santa Barbara Channel, *Union Oil v. Morton.*[92] In this case the court reviewed the question of the degree to which government may interfere with enjoyment of private property by exercise of police power without compensation, and concluded that there was not a simple answer to this question. The courts under a variety of tests have recognized that regulation of private property can become so onerous that it amounts to a taking of that property. The court in this case held that a permanent unconditional suspension of permits to install drilling platforms is a taking that requires compensation or violation of the Fifth Amendment.

Two cases decided by the U.S. Court of Claims confirm that failure to issue permits can constitute a taking. The cases, *Florida Rock Industries, Inc. v. United States,* No. 266-82L (Cl. Ct. July 23, 1990), and *Loveladies Harbor, Inc. v. United States,* No. 243-83L (Cl. Ct. July 23, 1990), both were the result of lengthy administrative proceedings which led to the denial of permits under Section 404 of the Clean Water Act. The major import of the court's decisions is twofold: (1) under certain circumstances, the Government's denial of a permit to fill wetlands under Section 404 of the Clean Water Act is an interference with a property owner's legitimate entitlement to the proposed use of its property, and is thus compensable under the Takings Clause; and (2) in determining the market value of such property following the taking, recreational and/or conservation uses carry minimal value.[93]

A series of cases have held that airport noise can constitute a taking of property rights. In the landmark case of *United States v. Causby,*[94] the Supreme Court held that frequent low flights over the Causby's land by military aircraft landing at a nearby airport operated by the United States constituted a taking of the Causby's property without compensation in violation of the Fifth Amendment of the Constitution. The noise from the aircraft rendered it impossible to continue the property use as a commercial chicken farm. Although the flights did not completely destroy the enjoyment and use of the land, they were held to be so low and frequent as to constitute a direct and immediate interference with the full enjoyment of the land, limiting the utility of the land and causing a diminution in its value, and therefore constituted a taking under the Fifth Amendment.

In another major Supreme Court decision on this issue, *Griggs v. Allegheny County,*[95] the Court held that Allegheny County, which owned and operated the Greater

---

[90]*Ibid.* at 1032.

[91]*Ibid.* at 1033.

[92]12 F.2d 743, 7 ERC 1 587 (9th Cir. 1975).

[93]In *Loveladies,* the court placed such value at $1,000 per acre, while in *Florida Rock* it was set at a "nominal" $500 per acre for "future recreational/water management purposes. . . to a government agency".

[94]328 U.S. 256 (1946).

[95]369 U.S. 84 (1962).

Pittsburgh Airport, was liable for a taking of property under the Fifth Amendment where the noise from taking off and landing at the airport on flight paths over the Griggs' property rendered the property undesirable and unbearable for residential use. The Court saw no difference between the county's responsibility to pay for land on which runways were built and its responsibility for air easements necessary for airport operation. The glide path for the northwest runway is as necessary for the operation of the airport as is a surface right-of-way, wrote the Court. Several states have interpreted their own constitutions to require compensation under less strict circumstances when noise from aircraft has diminished the market value of the homeowner's property. Interference must be substantial and sufficiently direct in the majority of jurisdictions.

Trade secrets also may be the subject of takings. In *Ruckelshaus v. Monsanto Company*,[96] Monsanto objected to data-disclosure and data-consideration provisions of the Federal Insecticide, Fungicide, and Rodenticide Act (FIFRA), alleging that these provisions amounted to a taking without just compensation in violation of the Fifth Amendment. The Supreme Court held that to the extent that Monsanto, as an applicant for the registration of pesticides, had an interest in its health, safety and environmental data recognizable as a trade-secret property right under Missouri law, that property right was protected by the taking clause of the Fifth Amendment.

While the constitutional rights of individuals and organizations may be more difficult to uphold in contexts where these private rights arguably contend with public rights to a safe and healthy environment, it has often been suggested that constitutional rights are most important in the most unpopular cases and it is here we need to work the hardest to uphold them. The Constitution is, and will continue to be, a major aspect of environmental law.

### 6.4 Administrative Law and Procedure

As with most areas of law, the business of environmental law is to find the facts and decide what to do about them. While the substantive and organic laws outlined above will greatly affect the way this business is conducted, the required procedures will be influential in determining the outcomes of cases.

In cases where there is significant scientific opinion on both sides of an issue, the critical issue is not what the facts are, but who has the burden of proof and what must be done to carry it. In a case where an administrative agency has made a decision, the issue is not whether the rule or decision is good or bad, but whether it is within the agency's authority, consistent with required procedures, and otherwise in accordance with law. For example, a federal court in Iowa examined the EPA's interpretation of the Superfund Amendment and Reauthorization Act of 1986 (SARA) in the case *Dico v. EPA*.[97] When SARA became effective on October 17, 1986, it created a new right of a non-liable party who "receives and complies with the terms of any administrative order. . ."[98] to be reimbursed for cleanup costs. However, "EPA's interpretation of the statute denies reimbursement 'to anyone who was unfortunate enough to have received

---

[96]467 U.S. 986, 104 S.Ct. 2862, 81 L.Ed 2d 815 (1984).
[97]37 ERC 1246 (1993).
[98]CERCLA § 106 (b)(2), 42 U.S.C. § 9606(b)(2).

a clean-up order before Congress made provision for reimbursement.'"[99] Dico, Inc. felt not only unfortunate to have received a cleanup order less than 3 months before Congress made provision for reimbursement, but positively wronged and so filed suit.

In considering EPA's interpretation of the statute, the court observed, "The EPA is charged with administering CERCLA. Interpretation of [CERCLA] is the [EPA's] responsibility in the first instance (citations omitted)."[100] The U.S. Supreme Court pointed out in *Chevron U.S.A., Inc. v. Natural Resources Defense Council, Inc.*[101] that the questions for the court are: 1) whether Congress has directly addressed the precise issue at question, and 2) if not, whether the agency's answer is based on a permissible construction of the statute. "The Court has long recognized that considerable weight should be accorded to an executive department's construction of a statutory scheme it is entrusted to administer. If the agency's action is a reasonable accommodation of conflicting policies that were committed to the agency's care by the statute, the agency's action should be upheld unless it appears from the statute or its legislative history that the accommodation is not one that Congress would have sanctioned."[102] The court thus upheld EPA's interpretation and dismissed the Dico, Inc. suit.

The critical questions of environmental law—the cutting edge issues of science, risk assessment, application of technology and analytical methods—are often resolved not through the scientific and engineering disciplines, but through argument and procedural determinations. Any detailed discussion of the rules for those determinations is well beyond the scope of this text. However, a few brief comments may be helpful.

Administrative law may not be a favorite course in law school, and it is probably not an area in which the average lawyer has much experience. Few non-lawyers feel comfortable dealing with these rules. It is probable, however, that administrative law issues are at or close to the heart of somewhere between eighty and ninety percent of all disputes concerning the federal environmental laws and regulations. And there is no doubt that a basic familiarity with the administrative process will substantially improve the effectiveness and understanding of those who deal with environmental law.

Following is a thumbnail sketch of the most important things we need to know about administrative law.

- Administrative agencies have no inherent or residual authority but can act only pursuant to authority "delegated" to them in the statutes enacted by Congress. If an agency acts beyond the scope of its delegated authority, its action is illegal and void.
- Agencies' opinions in interpreting their own regulations and the statutes they administer will, particularly if consistently held over a substantial period of time, be granted deference by the courts.
- Agencies must act in accordance with the procedures specified in their enabling legislation, or, if no other procedures are specified, in accordance with the Administrative Procedure Act. The required procedures normally

---

[99]op. cit. at 37 ERC 1251 (1993); Also see *Wagner Seed Co. v. Bush* , 946 F.2d 918, 920, 33 ERC 1897 (D.C. Cir. 1991), cert. denied, 112 S. Ct. 1584 [37 ERC 1784] (1992).

[100]*Ibid.* at 37 ERC 1250 (1993).

[101]467 U.S. 837, 21 ERC 1049 (1984).

[102]op. cit. at 37 ERC 1251 (1993).

entail publication in the *Federal Register,* opportunity for public comment, sometimes a public hearing, response to public comment and final publication.

- Agencies must act in accordance with their own rules and regulations. Failure to follow those rules results in invalid actions.

- Agencies must maintain a docket or record in support of their action and there must be evidence in that record to support the agency action. The record must be open for public examination throughout the period when public comments are being received.

- Agency actions may not be "arbitrary and capricious" . . . which means that there must be at least some evidence in the record to support the agency decision. When a statute specifically requires so, agencies must support their decisions with "substantial evidence." Although the difference between "some evidence" and "substantial evidence" is somewhat obscure, agencies hate substantial evidence requirements.

- Agency decisions may be appealed to the courts under either specific judicial review provisions in the enabling statutes or the general provision in the Administrative Procedure Act. You can't go to court, however, unless you have standing, the issue is "ripe," you have exhausted administrative remedies and a final agency decision has been issued.

- On appeal, administrative agency actions are generally upheld in the absence of some glaring procedural defect or a clearly inadequate record. However, these circumstances occur frequently and successful appeals, while not the rule, are far from a rarity.

## 6.5 Rules of Evidence

Most environmental issues don't get to court, but of those that do, the majority of them probably involve the questions of who did it and what does it take to prove it. Some of these questions turn on evidentiary determinations, others on questions of responsibility, liability sharing and contribution. Here is a summary of some of the major concepts.

### 6.5.1 Burden of Proof and Presumptions

Where, as is very often the case, the scientific facts of a controversy are being hotly debated in the scientific community or the facts are otherwise unclear, the outcome of the case may turn on the question of who has the "burden of proof" and the obligation of going forward with the evidence.

Fortunately, in our legal system, plaintiffs in civil cases normally have the burden of proving their cases. They must do so by a "preponderance of the evidence." However, attorneys and courts have developed special liability concepts, like strict liability, to shift the burden to defendants in some circumstances. Since the party with the burden will often lose the case, the question of who bears the burden of proof is one of the most contentious issues in civil litigation in the environmental context.

In criminal cases, the prosecutor has the burden of proving guilt "beyond a reasonable doubt" and defendants are presumed innocent until proven guilty, though that presumption is not always reflected in public opinion.

Finally, where the issue involves an effort to set aside an agency regulation or other action, there is a presumption of validity and the contesting party has the obligation of proving conclusively that the action is arbitrary and capricious, unsupported by the evidence or otherwise not in accordance with law.

### 6.5.2 Hearsay

Hearsay is evidence which depends for its truth or falsity solely upon statements of a person other than the witness. Hearsay, in itself, has no evidentiary value. The witness cannot be cross-examined regarding hearsay, because the statements are those of another. Generally, hearsay is inadmissible, but there are numerous exceptions.

In the case of documents, a statute usually provides for an official custodian or witness who will certify to their authenticity or validity to overcome the hearsay objection.

### 6.5.3 Opinion Evidence and Expert Witnesses

Generally, the testimony of a witness is confined to a statement of concrete facts based upon his own observation or knowledge. However, expert opinion evidence, though often based largely on hearsay, opinions, or conclusions not normally admissible into evidence, is admissible when it concerns scientific or technical matters and is presented by an appropriately qualified expert.

The *Daubert* decision (*Daubert v. Merrell Dow Pharmaceutical, Inc.*)[103] was an important Supreme Court opinion that defined the scientific testimony that can be used in court. It stated, first, that the trial judge should act as gatekeeper and make a decision about whether the methodology of the expert testimony is scientifically valid. If not, the judge can strike the evidence *even before the case goes to trial*, so that it is never presented to a jury. The *Daubert* opinion also specified a series of criteria, from the Federal Rules of Evidence, that should be used as the standard for determining whether the scientific evidence can be used.

Three guides to evaluate expert evidence that can be derived from the *Daubert* decision are:

1) Has the expert's theory or technique been adequately tested and can the results be replicated?
2) Has the theory or technique been subjected to peer review and publication?
3) Have scientifically accepted protocols or standards been followed in the research that the expert is using as a basis for his/her opinion?

Non-expert witnesses may be asked to express an opinion to help understand what was observed, but conjecture is not admissible.

### 6.5.4 Witnesses

Generally, all persons are competent to testify, but their credibility can be attacked. Leading questions (ones which suggest an answer), may generally only be asked of

---

[103]*Daubert v. Merrel Dow Pharmaceuticals Inc.*, 113 B Sup. Ct. Rep. 2786 (1993).

unwilling witnesses or adverse parties. A witness must answer all questions asked which will provide information on the issue under investigation—unless this testimony may subject the witness to criminal prosecution. The opposing party has a right to cross-examine the witness. If the witness refuses to answer on cross-examination, his entire testimony may be expunged from the record. Generally, cross-examinations are limited to facts on which a witness testified during direct examination.

### 6.5.5 Privileged Communication and Environmental Audits

Privilege is an exception to the rule that the public has the right to know every man's evidence. The reason for the exception is public policy.

In environmental lawsuits, the concern is with the attorney-client relationship. It is the duty of a lawyer to preserve his client's confidences. This duty outlasts the lawyer's employment.

The concept of privileged communications can be used not only in lawsuits but also when providing legal advice in connection with environmental audits and assessments. Thus, though there is no absolute assurance that the privilege can be maintained, it may be useful to have a lawyer supervise the information-gathering process during an audit and establish procedures for controlling access to all documents generated during the audit.

### 6.5.6 Your Own Reports as Evidence Against You

Many of the environmental laws and regulations require reports or data to be filed with the government. Even the reports to the Securities and Exchange Commission require disclosure of information on pollution. Most of these reports are available to the public and to competitors.

The extent to which the results of an investigation or inspection are available in private liability litigation remains uncertain. A corporation is not protected by the self-incrimination provisions of the Fifth Amendment to the U.S. Constitution. So, it may not object to the use of its records as evidence against it.[104]

### 6.5.7 Samples or Physical Evidence

One of the common evidentiary problems raised in court cases involves physical evidence. In environmental cases, the evidence is often a sample or some data. Some of the key issues normally involved with physical evidence are: (1) has the evidence or data been altered or contaminated, (2) was the equipment used in evidence collection properly calibrated, (3) were scientifically acceptable and standard methods of analysis used in evaluation and (4) who has handled the evidence (chain of custody)?

In order to lay a proper foundation for the admission of evidence, an attorney should be able to present the principals in the "chain of custody" to testify as to their involvement and their appropriate expertise in the proper handling of the evidence. The courts will frequently require the parties to stipulate authenticity of evidence to avoid this tedious form of proof. In legal terminology, "to stipulate" is to agree initially on conduct or evidence for the purpose of shortening the legal proceedings.

---

[104]*Essgee Co. v. U.S.*, 262 U.S. 151 (1923). Also see Section 6.3.2 of this chapter.

### 6.5.8 Evidence Collection and Constitutional Rights

A problem that may arise in the collection of evidence concerns the Fourth Amendment or Constitutional rights of corporate entities and private persons.

The Fourth Amendment to the U.S. Constitution prohibits all unreasonable searches and requires a search warrant for most investigations. However, no search warrant is needed in three situations: (1) when there is an emergency, (2) when the owner or operator gives his consent, or (3) when the samples could be taken from outside of the property (open fields exception). See the previous section on search warrants.

In most states, search warrants are used for searches for the implements or fruits of a crime and not for mere investigation of conditions which may lead to either civil or criminal penalties. A few states authorize a special kind of search warrant, sometimes called an inspection warrant, which may be used to investigate conditions.

The Fifth Amendment prohibition against criminal self-incrimination was described earlier. In evidence collection involving criminal charges against private parties, this Fifth Amendment right must be properly observed or the courts will not allow evidence to be introduced in the case. The Fifth Amendment protections apply only to private persons and not to corporations or partnerships.

## 7.0 JOINT AND SEVERAL LIABILITY, INDEMNITY, AND CONTRIBUTION

In toxic tort cases, the concepts of joint and several liability, indemnity, and contribution arise when deciding how much money potentially responsible parties will have to pay for the environmental cleanup (of a hazardous landfill, for example).

Contribution is an equitable concept which dictates that parties share the loss incurred. The loss is apportioned according to the relative responsibility of the parties. The right of contribution assumes joint fault and partial reimbursement. An instance of contribution occurred in the 1994 case of *Akzo Coatings Inc. v. Aigner Corp.*[105] In that case, after Akzo Coatings Inc. was ordered to perform an initial emergency cleanup at a Superfund site (over $1.2 million), it later sought pro rata payment from Aigner Corp. for Aigner's share of the responsibility. The court ruled that Akzo had a right to contribution from Aigner for the emergency cleanup of the polluted site, though not for voluntary costs incurred in attempting to anticipate future claims.

Indemnity, in contrast, is a principle which dictates that the entire loss incurred by a party be shifted to another. The parties do not share the loss. The right of indemnity assumes derivative fault or a special pre-tort relationship and total reimbursement. For example, an instance of indemnity arises when a potentially responsible party has previously contracted with an insurance company for complete coverage of an environmental accident. The insurance company thus indemnifies the party and bears the entire loss.

Joint and several liability is a concept which dictates that parties who tortiously contribute to a site's pollution are each liable as though they alone polluted that site. Under this concept any one party can be held liable (by the United States Environmental

---

[105]CA 7, No. 92-3820, 7/11/94

Protection Agency, for example) for *all* the costs of a remedial action. In such a case, this one party may be responsible for identifying others to share the liability, i.e. to contribute to the cost of the cleanup.

This tough policy of joint and several liability for toxic tort and cleanup cases springs from the extreme difficulty of apportioning liability among what may be numerous polluters of a site. The theory is that the public or the injured party should not bear the risk and cost of sorting out these complex situations, but, instead, should rest the burden on those who caused the problems.

## 8.0 ENVIRONMENTAL COMPLIANCE PRINCIPLES

Once a basic understanding of the environmental law system and its requirements is achieved, the next step is to apply that knowledge to achieve or maintain an acceptable compliance posture in the organization you work for or advise. The last approach to the development of an effective compliance program rests on the basic premise that aggressive compliance is the most effective protection.

Government Institutes has published many books discussing and detailing the elements of an appropriate compliance program.[106] The following principles derived from these works may be instructive:

- Everyone is responsible for environmental law compliance and, to protect against individual liability, everyone should continually demonstrate due concern and diligent efforts to comply.
- Providing appropriate education and training as well as sufficient informational resources is a good demonstration of concern for compliance and key to a successful environmental management program.
- The best answer to the question of what can be done to prevent violations and minimize liability is an appropriate corporate "culture" or management structure formulated with a view to environmental objectives and aggressively implemented.
- Outside consultants and counsel can help, but can't comply for you any better than they could run your company. The objective of an effective program is to provide the organization's officers and employees with the knowledge, resources and motivation required to meet and exceed requirements.
- After your compliance system is in place, periodic "audits" to verify compliance and identify areas where compliance can be improved will be helpful. "We had a good program but got sloppy" is not a mitigating factor, but an aggravating admission of failure. Don't start what you don't intend to finish and don't do anything half-way.

## 9.0 ENVIRONMENTAL LAW KNOWLEDGE IS CRUCIAL

The need for a working understanding of the environmental law system is probably more crucial now than it ever has been. Our actions and inactions, what we know and—perhaps most importantly—what we ought to know, can have dramatic effects on the financial well-being of organizations as well as the financial and personal futures of

---

[106]For additional information, the reader is referred to the publications described at the end of this handbook.

the individuals who work for them. Failure to know is no excuse. Under the legal theory of constructive knowledge, for those involved in the environmental field, knowledge may be presumed.

Knowledge of and strict adherence to the mandates of the environmental laws is not a luxury for companies and organizations. Financial viability and profitability—the bottom line for businesses—and personal freedom—the bottom line for individuals—may rest on this knowledge and how we use it. I hope this handbook will be helpful in that connection and that you aggressively seek more information and learning in the future.

# CHAPTER 2

# ENFORCEMENT AND LIABILITY

Thomas L. Adams, Esquire[1]
Perkins Coie
Washington, D.C.

## 1.0 INTRODUCTION

The process of enforcement of the environmental laws has been in continual transition since the inception of the United States Environmental Protection Agency (EPA), when the Department of Justice (DOJ), Land and Natural Resources Division and EPA endeavored to prosecute environmental violators under archaic laws. Through the years, with the passage of the air, water, and waste laws, the EPA and the DOJ have become increasingly systematic, sophisticated, and skilled at finding and punishing corporations and individuals for environmental violations.[2] Traditionally, the EPA's enforcement philosophy has been driven by civil and criminal command and control requirements to maintain accountability for noncompliance and to punish wrongdoers. With the reorganization of the EPA in 1994, new compliance approaches and attitudes were developed regarding the best means to attain the goal of environmental protection.[3] According to Steve Herman, the Assistant Administrator of the EPA's Office of Enforcement and Compliance Assurance (OECA), "only a combination of approaches will be effective. These approaches feed off each other. A strong traditional civil and criminal enforcement program is necessary to give credibility to the compliance incentives approach."[4]

The EPA's post-reorganization goal has been to increase the level of compliance for regulated entities, rather than emphasizing deterrence through penalties alone. This new national approach follows earlier state activity and supplements the old school civil and criminal prosecution for penalties with initiatives targeting compliance assurance and noncompliance prevention. The EPA's goal is to use enforcement resources more efficiently without sacrificing environmental protection. But to date, the agency has had

---

[1]Wishes to acknowledge the support of colleagues at Perkins Coie and in particular, Michelle Dauphinais Echols, who assisted in updating this chapter and Jeffrey G. Miller of Pace Law School, for his editorial and substantive input.

[2]Interview of August 13, 1996 with Deputy Assistant Administrator for Enforcement and Compliance Assurance; Ms. Sylvia K. Lowarance. Ms. Lowarance explained that, "The EPA enforcement world had gone high tech in that with compliance records, geographic studies, required submission, Dunn and Bradstreet. . . 17 major information systems in all — EPA knows more than many companies do about their own compliance — especially those without computers."

[3]*See* U.S. EPA, *Executive Summary of the EPA Enforcement Reorganization Task Force*, Envtl. L. Inst., Number AD-124 (Sept. 1, 1993).

[4]Steven A. Herman, *Past Accomplishments and Future Challenges in Enforcement and Compliance Assurance*, Assistant Administrator's Address at the National Enforcement Conference, Apr. 9, 1996.

difficulty in loosening its litigation oriented grip on regulated entities and states to allow compliance-oriented programs to develop.

The EPA has struggled to balance its old penalty-based ideology with new initiatives. However, when its level of civil enforcement actions dropped in 1995, the EPA came under fire from environmentalists and their political allies. As a result, penalties for violations are growing increasingly larger and non-litigation programs intended to encourage compliance are not meeting expectations.[5] The resulting swing of the schizophrenic enforcement pendulum leaves the regulated public confused as to what is coming next and hesitant to participate in new enforcement compliance initiatives.

## 2.0 FORMAL ENFORCEMENT MECHANISMS

### 2.1 Administrative and Civil Actions

#### 2.1.1 Administrative Orders

Administrative orders may be used by EPA to order monitoring and information gathering, e.g., Resource Conservation Recovery Act (RCRA) § 3013; compliance with regulation requirements, e.g., Clean Water Act (CWA) § 309(a); or remedial action, e.g., Comprehensive Environmental Response, Compensation and Liability Act (CERCLA) 42 USCA § 106(a). Such orders normally are not subject to pre-enforcement review, or judicial review unless and until the EPA attempts to enforce them.[6] Failure to comply with such an order, however, may lead to the imposition of a penalty in addition to a penalty for the underlying violation the order was issued to correct, e.g., RCRA § 3008(a), CWA § 309(d), CERCLA § 106(b)(1). Finally, administrative orders may be used to assess penalties. Under some statutes administrative orders are the only way in which penalties can be assessed against violators, e.g., Federal Insecticide, Fungicide, Rodenticide Act (FIFRA) § 14. Some statutes provide for assessment of penalties of the same magnitude by either the EPA or the courts, e.g., RCRA § 3008(a), (g). Under other statutes, the EPA may also assess relatively small penalties with the courts imposing more significant ones, e.g., CWA § 309(d) and (g). The EPA's assessment of administrative penalties is guided by an elaborate penalty policy, as discussed below.

For several reasons, the vast majority of enforcement actions taken by the EPA are in the form of administrative orders rather than judicial action: 1) administrative action is usually faster and requires less resources, and 2) it also allows the EPA to control both the conduct and outcome of the action rather than sharing it with the DOJ, which it must do when cases go to court. The EPA may, and often does, issue an order without the agreement of the party to whom it is directed.

---

[5]Enforcement personnel at both EPA and DOJ have continued to increase since the inception of the programs.

[6]*United States v. City of Baton Rouge*, 620 F.2d 478 (5th Cir. 1980).

### 2.1.2 Suspension, Debarment and Listing

Suspension and debarment are governmental mechanisms which allow the EPA to prohibit federal governmental entities from contracting or subcontracting with particular companies upon a finding that the company lacks integrity or business ethics, including findings of environmental violations.[7] Suspension refers to the interim prohibition from contracting with the Federal government, pending further investigation. Debarment is the prohibition from contracting for a set period of time. Prior to any conviction, the EPA can suspend a company indicted of a crime, since suspension and debarment were developed as protection for the government, not as punishment.[8] Listing is the mandatory debarment of an entity. Under the Clean Water Act and the Clean Air Act, the EPA "lists" a company to prohibit them from obtaining new government contracts until they achieve compliance.[9]

### 2.1.3 Judicial Civil Actions

Under most statutes, the EPA may request that the DOJ initiate a civil action for a federal court to order: 1) compliance with regulatory requirements; 2) penalties for violations of regulatory requirements; and/or 3) abatement of imminent and substantial endangerments to public health or the safety from environmental contamination, regardless of whether regulatory requirements are violated, e.g., CWA §§ 308(a) and 504. Penalties can and are often authorized up to $25,000 or even $50,000 per day, per violation, e.g., CWA § 309, RCRA § 3008. While courts are not bound by the EPA's penalty policy, they often find it a useful framework for determining the amount of the penalty to assess.[10] Because the DOJ normally does not file cases it is not confident of winning, defendants usually find it advantageous to settle civil cases prior to trial and as a consequence, few civil actions are tried. Indeed, the government often negotiates settlements even before filing complaints, and it is not unusual to see a complaint filed simultaneously with the lodging of a consent decree for the court's approval. The DOJ customarily requires that consent decrees be subject to public notice and opportunity to consent prior to moving the court to approve a consent decree.[11]

---

[7]*See* U.S. EPA, *Suspension, Debarment and Ineligibility for Contracts, Assistance, Loans and Benefits*, 60 Fed. Reg. 47,135 (Sept. 11, 1995); *See generally*, Judson W. Starr & Valerie K. Mann, *The Collateral Consequences of an Environmental Violation*, 31 Chem. Waste Litig. Rep. 423 (Feb. 1996).

[8]*E.g.*, CWA, 33 U.S.C.A. § 1368 (1986 & Supp. 1996) (debarment); CAA, 42 U.S.C.A. § 7606 (1995 & Supp. 1996) (debarment).

[9]Previously a separate function, in October 1994, the administration of "listing" was consolidated with the administration of suspension and debarment functions in the EPA's Office of Assistant Administrator for Administration of Resources Management. *See Suspension, Debarment and Ineligibility for Contracts, Assistance, Loans and Benefits*, 60 Fed. Reg. 47,135 (Sept. 11, 1995).

[10]*Chesapeake Bay Found. v. Gwaltney of Smithfield Ltd.*, 611 F. Supp. 1542 (E.D. Va. 1985), *cert. granted*, 479 U.S. 1029 (1987).

[11]28 C.F.R. § 50.7.

### 2.1.4 Monetary Liabilities

The EPA has developed two policies which are used when it negotiates the settlement of civil penalties, whether assessed in an administrative or a judicial order. The oldest and most basic is its civil penalty policy, under which it calculates the size of the penalty for which it will settle. The other is its Supplemental Environmental Project (SEP) policy, under which it may mitigate a portion of the penalty in consideration for the defendants undertaking some environmental improvement which it is not otherwise legally bound to undertake. Finally, under some statutes, the EPA may recover its costs for remedying environmental contamination and for damages to natural resources.

#### *2.1.4.1 Civil Administrative and Judicial Fines, and Penalties*

The EPA has published a general policy establishing its goals for penalty assessments in administrative and judicial environmental actions reflecting both the gravity of the violation and the economic benefit derived from the violation.[12] It has further published policies specifying the process by which penalties are to be calculated under each of the major statutes which it enforces. The gravity component factors are the seriousness of the violation and the extent to which the violation deviates from statutory or regulatory requirements.[13] The economic benefit component determines an amount that equals or exceeds the gains realized by the company's noncompliance or delayed compliance.[14]

Once a base penalty is calculated using the two components, the EPA may adjust the penalty based on a variety of factors, including: 1) degree of willfulness and/or negligence of the violation; 2) degree of cooperation/noncooperation of the violator; 3) the violator's history of noncompliance; and 4) any other factors unique to the violation.[15] The defendant has the burden of demonstrating any mitigating factors to the

---

[12]U.S. EPA, *A Framework for Statute-Specific Approaches to Penalty Assessments: Implementing EPA's Policy on Civil Penalties* (Feb. 16, 1984), *reprinted in* 17 ELR 35,073 (Oct. 1987).

[13]The EPA will rank specific violations using several factors to determine seriousness: a) actual or possible harm; b) importance of requirement to the regulatory scheme; c) availability of data from other sources for reporting or recordkeeping violations; and d) size of the violator. *Id.* at 35,077.

[14] The EPA uses a computer model, BEN, to calculate the benefits realized by the entity. However, BEN does not factor benefits related to competitive advantage through noncompliance, such as reducing product prices through failure to purchase pollution inhibiting equipment as compliance requires. The EPA may revise its calculations to include the competitive advantage economic benefit in the near future. Cheryl Hogue, *EPA Evaluating, May Revise, Method For Calculating Economic Benefit Penalties*, Daily Env't Rep. (BNA), d6 (Oct. 9, 1996).

[15] In October 1996, the EPA reduced a $4.75 million fine assessed under TSCA by 90 percent because the offending company agreed to invest several million dollars in an internal audit. *$4.75 Million Fine For PMN Violations Cut 90 Percent As Company Agrees To Audit*, Daily Env't Rep. (BNA) A-11 (Oct. 25, 1996).

EPA. Further, the entity may propose participating in supplemental environmental projects which can reduce the amount of the agreed upon penalty.[16]

### 2.1.4.2 Supplemental Environmental Projects

As stated, violators of environmental laws may mitigate penalties by voluntarily performing projects benefiting the environment that are distinctly related to the violations they have committed. The offending regulated entity must pay for the Supplemental Environmental Project (SEP). In some cases, the actual amount paid by the entity for the SEP and a reduced penalty may be greater than the original penalty without the mitigation for the SEP. Typically, SEPs will arise in the settlement of enforcement actions and are negotiated between the parties.[17] An entity's penalty will be mitigated to reflect how well the SEP achieves several factors, such as: 1) benefits to the public or environment at large; 2) innovativeness; 3) existence of damage mitigation or risk reduction to minority or low income communities; 4) multimedia impacts; and 5) pollution prevention.[18] The EPA negotiated some 350 SEPs in Fiscal Year 1995, which it valued at $103 million.[19]

In addition, the EPA will consider a violator's ability to pay any penalties imposed. However, the defendant carries the burden to demonstrate an inability to pay, usually by providing a significant amount of specific financial information to be reviewed by the EPA. Once it is determined that the violator cannot pay the penalty, the EPA may consider several payment options, such as a delayed payment schedule, non-monetary alternatives, joinder of the violator's individual owners, or, as a last resort, a straight penalty reduction. The EPA uses another computer model, referred to as ABEL, to compute the ability of the entity to pay the penalties.

### 2.1.4.3 Remedial and Natural Resource Damages

When the EPA takes civil action against a violator seeking injunctive relief, the equitable remedies of the court include the power to remediate environmental damages resulting from the pollution. Such remedial orders are most common in cases addressing the unpermitted filling of wetlands in violation of CWA § 404, but they can be used to address virtually any kind of environmental damage.

The statutes also addresses pollution which damages or endangers public health or the environment regardless of whether the damage or endangerment results from a violation of the statute. Most of the statutes authorize the government to bring an action against persons causing imminent and substantial endangerment to health or the environment to abate the endangerment, e.g., CWA § 504, RCRA § 2003, CERCLA

---

[16] *See generally* Steven A. Herman, *EPA's Revised Supplemental Environmental Projects Policy Will Produce More Environmentally Beneficial Enforcement Settlements*, 10 Ntl. Envtl. Enf. J. 9 (July 1995).

[17] There are seven categories of allowable projects, including those addressing public health, pollution reduction, environmental restoration and protection, assessment and audit environmental compliance promotion, emergency planning and preparedness. *Id.* at 10.

[18] *Id.* at 11.

[19] U.S. EPA, Office of Enforcement, *Enforcement and Compliance Assurance Accomplishments Report FY 1995*, EPA 300-R-96-006, 3-13 (July 1996) (hereinafter "FY 1995 EPA Report").

§ 106. Some statutes authorize the government to abate the endangerment itself and recover its costs from those causing the endangerment, e.g., CERCLA § 107, CWA § 311, OPA § 1321, while other statutes allow governmental entities, as trustees of natural resources, to recover for damages to the environment from those responsible, e.g., CERCLA § 107, CWA § 113, OPA § 1321.

These costs can be significant. Average remedial costs under CERCLA §§ 106, 107 are in the $30-40 million range, but can exceed $1 billion, e.g. Rocky Flats Arsenal, Colorado. Even oil spill cleanup and damage liability under CWA § 311 can exceed $1 billion, e.g., the Exxon Valdez.

## 2.2 Criminal Penalties and Consequences

For over a decade the EPA and the DOJ have sought and obtained increasing numbers of environmental criminal indictments against corporate and individual defendants. This trend continued in 1995 when 256 criminal cases were referred to the DOJ.[20] The rate of criminal referrals has steadily increased from 107 in 1992, to 140 in 1993 and to 220 in 1994.[21]

### 2.2.1 Theories of Liability

Every federal environmental statute establishes some form of criminal liability for violators, with the exception of the National Environmental Protection Act (NEPA).[22] Under this statute, violators are subject to charges that vary from simple negligence to endangerment of injury or death. Because the environmental statutes are considered public welfare statutes, Congress can make violations of these statutes a crime without a requirement of knowledge or other evidence of criminal intent by the violator.[23] For the most part, however, Congress has not done so, but has required knowledge for criminal convictions. Because they are public welfare statutes, however, the courts have interpreted the knowledge requirements leniently.[24]

#### 2.2.1.1 Criminal Negligent Violations

Simple negligence, a failure to exercise due care, combined with an entity's non-compliance can lead to criminal charges under the Clean Water Act.[25] Intent or knowledge on the part of the violator need not be proven for conviction of such an offense.

#### 2.2.1.2 "Knowing" Violations

Most of the statutes require a knowing state of mind be proven for some or all of the elements of the offense. Under traditional principles of criminal law, "knowing" violations require some level of conscious wrongdoing or blameworthiness.[26] This does

---

[20]FY 1995 EPA Report at 3-11.

[21]FY 1995 EPA Report at 3-12.

[22]*E.g.,* CWA, 33 U.S.C.A. § 1319(c) (1986 & Supp. 1996); RCRA, 42 U.S.C.A. § 6928(d) (1995); CAA, 42 U.S.C.A. § 7413(c) (1995); CERCLA, 42 U.S.C.A. § 9603(b) (1995).

[23]*United States v. Morrisette*, 342 U.S. 246 (1952).

[24]*United States v. T. Owens*, 860 F.2d 1076 (3rd Cir. 1988)

[25]*E.g.,* CWA, 33 U.S.C.A. § 1319(c) (1986 & Supp. 1996).

[26]*E.g., United States v. Park*, 421 U.S. 658 (1975).

not mean that the defendant knows the applicable law, but rather that he knows the relevant facts.[27] However, even here, the courts have lessened the degree of knowledge required.[28] For instance, the courts have ruled under RCRA that the government is not required to prove that the defendant actually knew that the hazardous material it handled was regulated, but only that it knew the material was dangerous.[29] In *United States v. Laughlin*, the court stated, "(w)here, as here...dangerous or deleterious devices or products or obnoxious waste materials are involved, the probability of regulation is so great that anyone who is aware that he is in possession of them or dealing with them must be presumed to be aware of the regulation."[30] The jury must find that "the defendant knew that the stored material had the potential to be harmful to others or to the environment, in other words, that it was not an innocuous substance like water."[31] In *United States v. Hopkins*, the court stated that the knowledge requirement in the Clean Water Act does not require the government to prove the defendant intended to violate the law or even that it had specific knowledge of the regulations at issue.[32]

Circumstantial evidence, as well as direct evidence, may be used to establish proof of knowledge.[33] As with the responsible corporate officer doctrine, the position and responsibility of a defendant can be used as circumstantial evidence.[34] Likewise, knowledge of prior illegal activity may also be circumstantial evidence to infer knowledge of a subsequent violation.[35] Ignorance of the law is not an acceptable defense to an environmental charge.[36] Willful or intentional avoidance of knowledge regarding environmental violations is not a defense.[37] However, a defendant's good faith belief in a material fact, which was actually in error, can be used as a defense against a criminal charge of "knowing" violation.[38]

---

[27] *United States v. International Minerals & Chem. Corp.*, 402 U.S. 588 (1971)

[28] *See* Ruth Ann Weidel, et al., *The Erosion of Mens Rea in Environmental Criminal Prosecution*, 21 Seton Hall L. Rev. 1100 (1991).

[29] 42 U.S.C.A. § 6928(d) (1995) and *United States v. Hopkins*, 53 F. 3d 533, 538 (2d Cir. 1995), *cert. denied*, 116 S.Ct. 773 (1996) (citing *United States v. Laughlin*, 10 F. 3d 961, 966 (2d Cir. 1993), *cert. denied*, 114 S.Ct. 1649 (1994) and *United States v. Wagner*, 29 F. 3d 264, 265-66 (7th Cir. 1994)).

[30] *Laughlin*, 10 F.3d at 965; *United States v. Weitzenhoff*, 1 F.3d 1523, 1530 (9th Cir. 1993) *modified*, 35 F.3d 1275 (9th Cir. 1994) *cert. denied*, 115 S.Ct. 939 (1995) (quoting *United States v. International Minerals & Chem. Corp.*, 402 U.S. 558, 565 (1971)).

[31] *United States v. Goldsmith*, 978 F.2d 643, 645 (11th Cir. 1992) and *United States v. Hoflin*, 880 F.2d 1033, 1039 (9th Cir. 1989) *cert. denied*, 493 U.S. 1083 (1990).

[32] *United States v. Hopkins*, 53 F.3d 533, 536, 540 (2d Cir. 1995) *cert denied.*, 116 S.Ct. 773 (U.S. 1996) (citing *International Minerals & Chem. Corp.*, 402 U.S. at 564 and *Weitzenhoff*, 1 F.3d at 1529-30).

[33] *Hopkins*, 53 F.3d at 536.

[34] *United States v. Self*, 2 F.3d 1971, 1088 (10th Cir. 1993).

[35] *Id.*

[36] *Hopkins*, 53 F.3d at 538 (citing *International Minerals & Chem. Corp.* 402 U.S. at 563).

[37] *Id.*, 53 F.3d at 537.

[38] *Self*, 2 F.3d at 1091; *See also International Minerals and Chemicals*, 402 U.S. at 563-64.

### 2.2.1.3 Knowing Endangerment

A regulated entity that "places another person in imminent danger of death or serious bodily injury" can be charged with knowing endangerment.[39] For example, in *United States v. Protex*, inadequate safety provisions failed to protect employees from exposure to toxic chemicals and increased their risk of solvent poisoning, thus leading to a charge of knowing endangerment.[40] For successful production, the government must demonstrate that the entity actually knew that its violation created imminent danger of death or serious bodily injury. For knowing endangerment determinations, "the defendant is responsible only for actual awareness or actual belief possessed and knowledge possessed by a person other than the defendant. . . may not be attributed to the defendant."[41] Circumstantial evidence may be used to prove knowledge. Ignoring or avoiding information regarding a violation can constitute circumstantial evidence to demonstrate actual knowledge.[42]

### 2.2.1.4 Miscellaneous Laws

The government may charge a violator with additional criminal counts, sometimes not specifically associated with environmental laws, to increase the severity of their criminal liability. Enforcement of environmental laws often relies upon self-monitoring and self-reporting, invoking the traditional criminal remedies in the United States Code, Title 18, Section 1001, for submitting false information to the government. Willful falsification of a statement or concealment of any false writing by a private party to the federal government can lead to fines up to $10,000 or imprisonment of up to five years, or both.[43] The use of the postal system, airwaves, or interstate wires to defraud or to obtain money or property with false representation constitutes mail fraud (under 18 U.S.C. Sections 1341 and 1343) and violators can also be prosecuted on these counts.[44] Conspiracy (18 U.S.C. Section 371) between two or more employees of a corporation to violate environmental laws can result in fines up to $10,000 and/or imprisonment of up to five years.[45] Prosecution for murder and manslaughter charges for chemical

---

[39]*See United States v. Protex Indust., Inc.*, 874 F.2d 740, 743 (10th Cir. 1989); *See also United States v. Borowski*, 977 F. 2d 27 (1st Cir. 1992); *See also* CWA, 33 U.S.C.A. § 1319(c)(3)(A) (1986 & Supp. 1996).

[40]*Protex*, 874 F.2d at 742. It has been held, however, that the knowing endangerment provision does not apply in the workplace environment. *Borowski*, 977 F.2d 27 (1st Cir. 1992).

[41]CWA, 33 U.S.C.A. § 1319(c)(3)(B) (1986 & Supp. 1996); CAA, 42 U.S.C.A. § 7413(c)(5)(B) (1995); RCRA, 42 U.S.C.A. § 6928(e) (1995).

[42]CWA, 33 U.S.C.A. § 1319(c)(3)(B) (1986 & Supp. 1996); CAA, 42 U.S.C.A. § 7413(c)(5)(B) (1995); RCRA, 42 U.S.C.A. § 6928(f)(2) (1995).

[43]18 U.S.C.A. § 1001 (1976 & Supp. 1996); RCRA, 42 U.S.C.A. § 6928(d)(3) (1995); CWA 33 U.S.C.A. § 1319(c)(4) (1986 & Supp. 1996); *See also Self*, 2 F.3d at 1083.

[44]18 U.S.C.A. § § 1341, 1343 (1984 & Supp. 1996); *See also Self*, 2 F.3d at 1084*; See also United States v. Paccione*, 949 F.2d 1183 (2d Cir. 1991) *cert. denied sub nom.*, 505 U.S. 1220 (1992).

[45]18 U.S.C.A. § 371 (1966 & Supp. 1996).

exposure resulting in death have also accompanied prosecution for the violation of environmental laws.[46]

### 2.2.2 Responsible Corporate Officer Doctrine

Upper-level company officials are increasingly becoming the targets of the EPA environmental criminal actions, in addition to, and sometimes in lieu of, corporations as a whole. In 1991, 80 percent of the environmental criminal defendants were companies, and by 1995, 80 percent were individuals.[47] In 1995, 245 corporate officers and individuals were indicted.[48] Thirty-one corporate defendants and 116 individual defendants were found guilty.[49] As noted, even if the official did not have direct knowledge of the violation, a presumption of knowledge may be imputed if they had "a responsible share in the furtherance of the transaction which the statute outlaws."[50] The official can also be held responsible for a subordinate's illegal actions if the official knew of or had responsibility over the actions in question.[51] As discussed above, the courts have justified the application of a strict liability standard on corporate officials through their findings that environmental laws are public welfare statutes. "The requirements of foresight and vigilance imposed on responsible corporate agents are beyond question demanding, and perhaps onerous, but they are no more stringent than the public has a right to expect of those who voluntarily assume positions of authority in business enterprises whose services and products effect the health and well-being of the public."[52] Thus, company officials risk criminal liability merely from their position within the company, greatly increasing their incentive to ensure compliance with environmental laws.

### 2.2.3 Department of Justice Prosecutorial Policy

The DOJ will consider several factors before prosecuting a case criminally: 1) whether the regulated entity voluntarily discloses its violation or cooperates with the authorities; 2) whether the entity has a pervasive level of noncompliance; 3) whether the regulated entity establishes preventive measures and compliance programs; and 4) whether an entity promulgates its own internal disciplinary actions and produces subsequent compliance.[53]

---

[46]*See Owners of Electroplating Co. Charged in Employee's Death*, 1 Mealey's Litig. Rep. 7 (Aug. 1994).

[47]3 Envtl. Compl. Bull. (BNA) 21 (Sept. 23, 1996) at 1.

[48]FY 1995 EPA Report at 3-11.

[49]FY 1995 EPA Report at 3-11.

[50]*United States v. Cordoba-Hincapie*, 825 F. Supp. 485, 508 (E.D.N.Y. 1993) (quoting *United States v. Dotterweich*, 320 U.S. 277, 284 (1943)).

[51]*Cordoba-Hincapie* at 508 (discussing *United States v. Park*, 421 U.S. 658 (1975)).

[52]*United States v. Latex Surgeons' Gloves*, 799 F. Supp. 1275 (D.P.R. 1992) (citing *United States v. Park* at 421 U.S. 672).

[53]U.S. DOJ, *Factors in Decisions on Criminal Prosecutions For Environmental Violations in the Context of Significant Voluntary Compliance or Disclosure Efforts by the Violator* (July 1, 1991).

### 2.2.4 EPA Factors for Referral to DOJ for Criminal Prosecution

The EPA will examine the degree of actual or threatened harm to the environment or human health and the level of culpable conduct by the regulated entity when determining whether a case should be prosecuted criminally.[54] When considering the level of harm created, the EPA will also take into account whether the violation was voluntarily reported and whether a regulated entity's illegal conduct, which in itself will not cause significant harm, represents a trend or common attitude within the regulated community, which can result in significant harm. In addition, as previously mentioned in *Protex*, the EPA will examine the adequacy of established safety provisions within a facility when determining whether to bring a criminal enforcement action. The "woefully inadequate" safety provisions at the Protex facility put their employees at an increased risk of serious injury and lead to charges of "knowing" endangerment.[55]

Culpable conduct is indicated by: a) a history of repeat violations; b) direct or circumstantial evidence of deliberate misconduct resulting in violation; c) concealment of misconduct or falsification of required records; d) tampering with monitoring or control equipment; and e) operation without a required permit, license, manifest, or other required documentation.[56]

### 2.2.5 Consequences of Criminal Prosecution

More than one consequence may apply to an offending regulated entity or individual. Both criminal and civil charges may be brought against a company by the federal government for the same illegal conduct. Further, the Double Jeopardy clause of the Constitution does not apply to suits brought by different sovereigns. Thus, state, tribal, and federal governments may prosecute a company for the same conduct if the company violated each jurisdiction's environmental laws. For example, in May 1996, the Iroquois Pipeline Operating Company and four of its officials pled guilty to violating the Clean Water Air Act.[57] As part of their plea agreement, the company must clean up 30 wetlands and streams damaged during their construction of a pipeline and pay $22 million in criminal and civil penalties. Further, four company officials are now subject to one year in jail and a $100,000 fine.

### 2.2.5.1 Fines

Just as administrative or civil judicial actions can impose monetary penalties, fines may also be pursued against offenders in a criminal action. In FY 1995, $23 million in criminal fines was paid to the EPA.[58] In September 1996, a federal judge assessed a $75

---

[54]Internal memorandum from Earl Devaney, Director Office of Criminal Enforcement at EPA, *The Exercise of Investigative Discretion* (Jan. 12, 1994).

[55]*Protex*, 874 F.2d at 742.

[56]Internal memorandum from Earl Devaney (Jan. 12, 1994).

[57]Steven A. Herman, *Iroquois, PSC Settlements Demonstrate Benefits of Strong Innovative Enforcement of Environmental Laws*, 11 Natl. Envtl. Enf. J. 11 (July 1996).

[58]FY 1995 EPA Report at 3-11.

million criminal fine against three related companies for their role in the spill of more than 750,000 gallons of oil in waters off Puerto Rico in January of 1994.[59]

Federal criminal statutes enumerate penalty amounts for specific criminal violations. The Clean Water Act, for instance, specifies that negligent violations can result in a fine up to $25,000 per day, per violation.[60] "Knowing" violations can lead to a fine as great as $50,000 per day, per violation and knowing endangerment can accrue up to $250,000 for individuals or up to $1,000,000 for companies. Repeat violations of any conviction, cause the fine maximum to double. Further, judges have an option to assess fines in the amount established by the specific statute or to assess fines up to twice the profits gained and/or twice the loss or harm caused by noncompliance.[61]

### 2.2.5.2 Imprisonment

Punishment for criminal conviction includes not only the possibility of large fines, but also the threat of incarceration for individuals, including company officials.[62] For example, in August 1996, a businessman was sentenced to serve 41 months in prison without parole for violating RCRA.[63] The man told two employees to bring six 55-gallon drums containing chemicals to a salvage yard that did not have a permit to treat, store or dispose of hazardous waste. In another case, a part-owner of a sludge disposal contractor pled guilty to a Clean Water Act violation and was sentenced to six months in a halfway house, five years probation, and a $50,000 fine for the illegal disposal of sewage sludge.[64] In the increasingly tougher stance against individual violators, pending legislation would further increase the maximum sentences for violations of federal environmental crimes causing serious injury or death.[65]

The United States Sentencing Commission Guidelines include a section establishing a range of appropriate prison terms specifically for environmental violations committed by individuals, including corporate officers. A prison sentence can vary from

---

[59]*Record $75 Million Criminal Penalty Levied for 1994 Incident in Waters Off Puerto Rico*, 27 Env't Rep. 1235 (Oct. 4, 1995).

[60]CWA, 33 U.S.C.A. § 1319(c)(1) (1986 & Supp. 1996).

[61]Alternative Fines Act, 18 U.S.C.A. § 3571(d) (Supp. 1996).

[62]The United States Sentencing Commission also provides guidance in determining appropriate fines, as well as criminal jail sentences. *U.S. Sentencing Commission Guidelines Manual*, Ch. 2Q (guidelines for individuals committing environmental violations); Ch. 8 (guidelines for sentencing organizations). Reprinted in *Practice Under the Federal Sentencing Guidelines*, 3rd Ed., Vol. 2, Appendix A; (1996 Supplement) (hereinafter "U.S.S.G. Manual").

[63]*Wisconsin Man Sentenced to 41 Months For Illegally Dumping Hazardous Waste*, 27 Env't Rep. 916 (Aug. 23, 1996).

[64]*Co-Owner of Sludge Disposal Contractor Sentenced For Criminal CWA Violation,* Daily Env't Rep. (BNA) A1 (Sept. 25, 1996).

[65]Cheryl Hogue, *Reno Unveils Bill to Give Prosecutors New Powers to Fight Environmental Crimes*, Daily Env't Rep. (BNA) d6 (Sept. 20, 1996).

zero to 63 months depending on the charge, but it cannot exceed the statutory maximum.[66]

The Organizational Sentencing Guidelines, established in 1991, may also be used by the federal courts to impose restitution and probation on organizations convicted of environmental crimes, although they do not apply exclusively to environmental violations.[67] In 1993, draft organizational sentencing guidelines were developed by the U.S. Sentencing Commission Advisory Working Group, specifically for environmental crimes.[68] Recommendations for a level of penalty assessment and procedures necessary for sentence reduction are also detailed in the draft provisions. In December 1993, two members of the advisory group filed their opposition to the draft guidelines with the U.S. Sentencing Commission.[69] Public comment on the guidelines lasted until late 1995 and has been followed with a lengthy review process.[70]

As a corollary to punishment, violation of an environmental law by a regulated entity may also indirectly impact the entity's own financial standing and reputation. Fines and requirements to pay for cleanup or compensation are typically not covered by insurance and are not tax deductible. Noncompliance, in some instances, can financially ruin a corporation. Financial standing may also be directly affected since certain violations, legal proceedings, and other environmental obligations must be reported to the Securities and Exchange Commission (SEC), pursuant to regulation S-K.[71] Further, the negative publicity from a suit claiming personal injury of private individuals can also severely impact an entity's business.

## 3.0 ALTERNATIVE DISPUTE RESOLUTION

Environmental litigation has become increasingly expensive over the years with cases involving multiple parties and enormous remedial and punitive costs. Regulators,

---

[66]Five categories of environmental crimes exist for individuals: Knowing Endangerment from Mishandling, Hazardous or Toxic Substances can result in a prison term of 51 to 63 months. Mishandling hazardous or toxic substances, pesticides, recordkeeping, tampering and falsification can lead up to six months in prison. A violator who mishandles other environmental pollutants, recordkeeping, tampering and falsification can also get sentenced up to six months. Tampering or attempted tampering with the public water system is more serious resulting in 27 to 33 months in jail, while threatened tampering will lead to six to twelve months of imprisonment. *U.S.S.G. Manual, Ch. 2Q1.1 - Q1.5, 5G.*

[67]*U.S.S.G. Manual Ch. 8A1.1.*

[68]The draft was released by the Advisory Group in: *Draft Sentencing Guideline Issued For Corporate Environmental Crimes*, 8 Tox. L. Rep. (BNA) 736 (Nov. 24, 1993). The draft guidelines are reprinted at page 739.

[69]*Advisory Group Members File Dissent, Urge Sentencing Commission To Reject Draft*, 8 Tox. L. Rep. (BNA) 921 (Jan. 12, 1994).

[70]*Comments Sought on Sentencing Guidelines; Review Process Could Last Until Late 1995*, 8 Tox. L. Rep. (BNA) 897 (Jan. 5, 1994).

[71]Securities and Exchange Commission Act of 1934 § 10(b)(5); 15 U.S.C.A. § 78o(d) (1981); 17 C.F.R. § 240.15d (1996); *See generally,* Judson W. Starr & Valerie K. Mann, *The Collateral Consequences of an Environmental Violation*, 31 Chem. Waste Litig. Rep. 425 (Feb. 1996). See also George Van Cleve, The Changing Intersection of Environmental Auditing, Environmental Law, and Enforcement Policy, Cardoza Law Review, Vol. 12, #5, April 1991, p. 1236.

courts, and private party litigants have increasingly sought private and governmental sponsored Alternative Dispute Resolution (ADR) as an alternative to court proceedings. In at least 250 environmental actions the DOJ has used or considered using ADR.[72] By way of example, of which there are many, the DOJ used ADR to achieve a settlement agreement with 56 parties to clean up a Superfund site.[73] In April, 1995, the U.S. Attorney General, Janet Reno, issued an order to further promote the greater use of ADR.[74]

Since 1987, the EPA has encouraged the use of ADR in its guidance statements and by 1995, ADR was used in more than 50 enforcement actions.[75] Also in 1995, the EPA established eight pilot projects to resolve Superfund site issues using a third-party neutral to allocate costs.[76] The EPA provides ADR training to all its regional offices and headquarters.[77] Several statutes, including the Administrative Dispute Resolution Act of 1990[78] and the aforementioned Civil Justice Reform Act,[79] encourage the use of ADR to settle federal disputes. Recently, the President issued an order encouraging the use of ADR.[80] As enforcers are discovering more efficient means to achieve compliance, ADR offers an effective and efficient alternative to standard environmental litigation.

## 4.0 TRANSBOUNDARY ENVIRONMENTAL ENFORCEMENT

Government regulators also enforce environmental laws which prohibit the importation and/or exportation of specific items or substances.[81] *In the Matter of: Wego Chemical & Mineral Corporation*[82] is an example of EPA's efforts to enforce Section 8 of the Toxic Substances Control Act (TSCA).[83] Wego imported urea-formaldehyde polymer and oxalic and citric acid without submitting the requisite reports with the EPA in a timely manner. EPA brought charges under TSCA and, through an administrative hearing, Wego was fined $42,000.

The EPA may work in conjunction with other government entities and citizens' groups to enforce these types of environmental statutes. In *USS Cabot v. United States*

---

[72]Michael P. Vandenberg and Peter L. Winik, *Environmentally Sound*, Legal Times, Sept. 16, 1996 at S43.

[73] *Parties Agree to Clean Up West Virginia Site; Cleanup Geared Toward Future Industrial Use*, 27 Env't Rep. (BNA) 25 (May 3, 1996).

[74]U.S. DOJ, *Policy on the Use of Alternative Dispute Resolution, and Case Identification Criteria for Alternative Dispute Resolution*, 61 Fed. Reg. 36,895 (July 15, 1996).

[75]Vandenberg, at S40, S43.

[76]*Id.*

[77]FY 1995 EPA Report at 7-5.

[78]Administrative Dispute Resolution Act of 1990, Pub. L. No. 101-552 104 Stat. 2736 (1990).

[79]Currently implemented through Exec. Order No. 12988, 61 Fed. Reg. 4729 (Feb. 7, 1996).

[80]*Id.*

[81]TSCA, 15 U.S.C.A. § 2612 (1982 & Supp. 1996); FIFRA, 7 U.S.C.A. § 136o (1980 & Supp. 1996).

[82]*In the Matter of: Wego Chem. & Mineral Corp.*, 4 E.A.D. 513 (1993); *See also 3M Co. v. Browner,* 17 F.3d 1453 (D.C. Cir. 1994).

[83]TSCA, 15 U.S.C.A. § 2607 (1982 & Supp. 1996).

*Customs Service,*[84] the EPA, U.S. Customs Service, and the DOJ sought to prevent the exportation of a former aircraft carrier to India because of its illegal levels of PCBs (polychlorinated biphenyls), which violated TSCA.[85] In *Earth Island Institute v. Secretary of Commerce,*[86] citizens' groups filed suit against the government to compel its enforcement of the Marine Mammal Protection Act. The Act bans the importation of commercial fish or fish products caught with fishing technology that incidentally kills or injures ocean mammals in excess of the United States' standards.[87] Thus, the enforcement capacity of the EPA, and other governmental entities, extends beyond the borders of the United States and, in some instances can have global impact.

## 5.0 ENFORCERS OF ENVIRONMENTAL LAW

### 5.1 Federal

#### 5.1.1 Environmental Protection Agency
The EPA is the primary enforcer of all federal environmental statutes. The 1994 reorganization of EPA allied the expertise of its lawyers with its technical experts to create a new Office of Enforcement and Compliance Assurance.[88] Through its headquarters in Washington, DC, and 10 regional offices, the EPA is responsible for issuing administrative orders and penalties, negotiating settlements with entities or individuals in noncompliance, and initiating civil proceedings. The EPA refers cases to the DOJ and assists them with civil and criminal environmental investigations[89] and proceedings.

#### 5.1.2 Department of Justice
The Department of Justice Environmental and Natural Resources Division consists of, among others, an Environmental Enforcement Section and an Environmental Crimes Section, which represents the EPA in civil and criminal proceedings.[90]

### 5.2 States

#### 5.2.1 Federal Delegation of Authority
Under specific federal environmental statutes, the EPA delegates implementation and enforcement authority to states demonstrating the establishment of adequate

---

[84]*USS Cabot Dedalo Museum Found. v. United States Customs Service*, 1995 U.S. Dist LEXIS 4068, 41 ERC (BNA) 1020 (E.D. La. 1995).

[85]15 U.S.C.A. §§ 2605(e), 2611(a)(2) (1982), § 2614 (1982 & Supp. 1996).

[86]*Earth Island Institute, Marine Mammal Fund v. Brown,* 28 F.3d 76 (9th Cir. 1994), *cert. denied,* 115 S.Ct. 509 (1994). *See also Earth Island Institute v. Mosbacher,* 785 F. Supp. 826 (N.D. Cal. 1992) (district court decision).

[87]Marine Mammal Protection Act, 16 U.S.C.A. § 1371(a)(2)(C) (1996).

[88]See OECA organizational chart.

[89]A part of the OECA organization is the NEIC National Enforcement Investigation Center which provides technical support, trains officials in enforcement at all levels of government, and conducts criminal investigations.

[90]See DOJ organizational chart.

environmental programs and the capability to enforce those programs.[91] The EPA may establish "cooperative agreements" with a state to develop state involvement where a statute does not allow delegation of authority to the states.[92] The EPA maintains authority to issue enforcement actions concurrently with, or in lieu of, state agencies maintaining oversight and responsibility for ensuring that federal laws are enforced. For the most part, the EPA will become directly involved when: a) a state requests the U.S. EPA's involvement; b) a state acts untimely or inappropriately; c) a national legal or program precedent could result from a specific case; or d) a U.S. EPA or federal court order is violated.[93] Additionally, the EPA may permit state inspectors to act in the place of federal inspectors and can allow states to perform the work on an issue, while the EPA retains oversight authority.[94] For example, Mississippi assessed its largest fine in State history for two Clean Water Act violations, under its federal delegation authority.[95] The offending company paid $2.5 million in criminal fines and $1.5 million in restitution to the State for tampering with waste water discharge monitoring and for illegally storing hazardous waste.

### 5.2.2 Enforcement of State Laws

States, cities, and counties may enforce their own environmental laws independent of federal authority. In some instances, states may have requirements which are more stringent than federal laws, and are therefore allowed to enforce the laws as such.[96] For example, over ten states have enacted "bad actor" statutes to revoke, suspend, or deny waste-handling permits for repeat environmental offenders.[97] Additionally, several states have enacted statutes that provide privileges for performing self-audits or for voluntarily disclosing violations, despite the EPA's opposition to the statutes.

### 5.3 Local Governments

Local governments also may assist in enforcing federal and state regulations. For example, in *City of New York v. Exxon*, the City of New York brought suit, under CERCLA, to obtain damages for the clean up of five landfills in the city.[98] In recognition of the increased assistance of local officials with enforcement actions, the EPA has bolstered and expanded training programs for them.[99]

---

[91]*See*, for example, CAA, 42 U.S.C.A. § 7410 (1995 & Supp. 1996); CWA, 33 U.S.C.A. § 1342 (1986 & Supp. 1996); RCRA, 42 U.S.C.A. § 6926 (1995 & Supp. 1996); TSCA, 15 U.S.C.A. § 2684 (1982 & Supp. 1996).

[92]*E.g.*, FIFRA, 7 U.S.C.A. § 136u (1980 & Supp. 1996).

[93]U.S. EPA, Office of Enforcement, *Principles of Environmental Enforcement*, EPA/300-F-93-001 (July 1992).

[94]See, for example, U.S. EPA Office of Solid Waste and Emergency Response, *RCRA Inspection Manual*, EPA/520-R-94-007 (1993).

[95]*Firm Pays $2.5 Million Fine, Restitution For Waste Water, Hazardous Waste Crimes*, Daily Env't Rep. (BNA) A-5 (Sept. 30, 1996).

[96]*E.g.*, RCRA, 42 U.S.C.A. § 6991(g) (1995).

[97]*See*, for example, Cal. Health & Safety Code § 25099.1 (1996).

[98]*New York v. Exxon Corp.*, 697 F. Supp. 677 (S.D.N.Y. 1988).

[99]*More Agents, New Enforcement Programs Will Increase Prosecutions, Agency Says*, 24 Env't. Rep. (BNA) 1956 (Mar. 18, 1994).

## 5.4 American Indian Tribes

In most cases, tribes enforce federal environmental laws and standards within their territory as state programs created by the EPA. tribes receive authority from the EPA to be treated as a state for specific federal statutory and regulatory programs, and become the primary enforcers of federal environmental law established under these programs. tribes are also enforcers of their own tribal environmental laws and standards.

### 5.4.1 Delegated Tribal Environmental Enforcement Established Through the EPA "Treatment as State" (TAS) Programs

In several major federal statutes, Congress granted EPA the authority to treat Indian tribes as states to delegate the principal enforcement responsibility of the statute to the tribe, and to authorize the establishment of tribal environmental standards for some regulations.[100] The tribes must satisfy criteria specified in the statute before treatment as a state will be authorized. These criteria include verifying federal recognition, demonstrating tribal jurisdiction over the functions of the program, and establishing capacity to carry out the program.[101]

Once the EPA grants a tribe TAS status for a particular statute, the tribes are authorized to regulate and enforce the standards as their own tribal law.[102] A tribe, in some instances, can also establish its own tribal environmental standards within the framework of the federal law. However, just as with state delegated authority, EPA retains its authority as the ultimate enforcer.[103] It should be noted that the procedures for administrative and judicial review for delegated and authorized programs are primarily hypothetical at this point, since they have not yet been challenged.

---

[100]*See* for example, Clean Water Act, 33 U.S.C.A. § 1377 (Supp. 1996); Safe Drinking Water Act (SDWA) 42 U.S.C.A. § 300j-11(a)(1)(1991); Clean Air Act, 42 U.S.C.A. § 7601(d) (1995); CERCLA/Superfund 42 U.S.C.A. § 9626 (1995); *See generally* David F. Coursen, *Tribes as States: Indian Tribal Authority to Regulate and Enforce Federal Environmental Law and Regulations*, 23 Envtl. L. Rep. 10579 (Oct. 1993).

[101]*See*, for example, SDWA, 42 U.S.C.A. § 300j-11(b)(1) (1991).

[102]Since TAS is a relatively new idea, only a handful of tribes have been granted TAS authority. For an example of delegated authority, see the National Pollution Discharge Elimination System (NPDES) program of the CWA, under which two tribes have pending approval. 33 U.S.C.A. § 1377(e) (Supp. 1996). Likewise, 17 tribes have been granted TAS authority to establish water quality standards under the CWA, and approval is pending for 9 other Tribes. *Id. See also* U.S. EPA, American Indian Environmental Office, *U.S. EPA Treatment of Tribes in the Same Manner as States Matrix*, Apr. 1996. See also authorized authority under subtitle D of RCRA and CWA.

[103]Just as with a state, if a tribe is not enforcing the environmental standards, persons may request that the EPA withdraw the tribe's TAS status. To date, EPA has never withdrawn a tribe's TAS status, although this is partly due to the recent development of TAS grants of authority to tribes.

In addition, tribes do not have criminal jurisdiction over non-Indians for some crimes.[104] Accordingly, under some environmental statutes, Congress could not have intended that tribes have authority over criminal enforcement. Thus, tribes must establish an agreement for referral of potential criminal violations to EPA for enforcement.[105]

### 5.4.2 Tribal Environmental Laws and Standards

Tribes hold a unique position in their trust relationship with the United States government. The inherent sovereignty of tribes entitles them to self-governance, allows them to create their own laws, and immunizes them from suit by individuals and states.[106] Enforcement of their environmental laws within Tribal territory belongs to the tribes themselves. Thus, individuals or organizations seeking to enforce tribal environmental laws must seek recourse through the tribes.[107] "The rule requiring exhaustion of tribal remedies in matters related to the reservation affairs is an important aspect of the federal government's long-standing policy of supporting tribal self-government."[108] Further, the EPA has released its policy recognizing tribal governments "as the primary parties for setting standards, making environmental policy decisions and managing programs for reservations."[109]

### 5.4.3 Federal Environmental Laws

In some instances, tribal sovereignty may be preempted with respect to activities by the federal government. "The tribes have been described as 'domestic dependent nations,' exercising many of the sovereign powers of an independent nation, yet existing in a ward-guardian relationship with the federal government and thus subject to its superior and plenary powers."[110] Enforcement of federal environmental standards is primarily held with the EPA, even on tribal lands. "EPA remains responsible for ensuring that the federal standards are met on the reservations."[111] The DOJ can represent a tribe if violation of the federal standard occurs on Indian territory. However, if the tribe is violating a federal standard, individuals or organizations may request that the EPA enforce the standards against the tribe. The EPA will try to assist the tribe into

---

[104]*See* Indian Major Crimes Act, 18 U.S.C.A. § 1153 (1984 & Supp. 1996); *See also Duro v. Reina*, 495 U.S. 676, 682 (1990) (citing *Oliphant v. Suquamish Indian Tribe*, 435 U.S. 191 (1978)).

[105]*See*, for example, 40 C.F.R. § 123.34 (1995).

[106]*See Blatchford v. Native Village of Noatak*, 501 U.S. 775 (1991).

[107]*National Farmers Union Ins. Cos. v. Crow Tribe of Indians*, 471 U.S. 845, 857 (1985).

[108]*Reservation Tel. Coop. v. Three Affiliated Tribes of Fort Berthold Reservation*, 76 F.3d. 181, 184 (8th Cir.). *reh'g, en banc denied*, 1996 U.S. App. LEXIS 8829 (1996).

[109]U.S. EPA, *EPA Policy for the Administration of Environmental Programs on Indian Reservations* (Nov. 8, 1984) at 2.

[110]*United States v. Red Lake Band of Chippewa Indians*, 827 F.2d 380, 383 (8th Cir. 1987), *cert. denied*, 485 U.S. 935 (1988).

[111]*Washington Dep't of Ecology v. United States EPA*, 752 F.2d 1465, 1472 (9th Cir. 1985). *See also Blue Legs v. United States Bureau of Indian Affairs*, 867 F.2d, 1094, 1096-97 (8th Cir. 1989).

compliance. And, if they do not comply, the tribe's sovereign immunity may be waived, and they may be sued for noncompliance with federal environmental law.

At times, federal statutes conflict with tribal ordinance. Some federal statutes may preempt Tribal laws and limit the tribes' regulatory control on their lands.[112] Further, the sovereign immunity of a tribe may be waived to allow a suit to be brought against them for violation of a federal statute.[113] "Indian tribes have long been recognized as possessing common-law immunity from suit traditionally enjoyed by sovereign powers. This aspect of tribal sovereignty, like all others, is subject to the superior and plenary control of Congress. But without congressional authorization, the Indian Nations are exempt from suit. It is settled that a waiver of sovereign immunity cannot be implied but must be unequivocally expressed."[114]

## 5.5 Citizen Enforcement

### 5.5.1 Enforcement Actions
All of the major federal environmental statutes include provisions permitting suits to be brought by citizens, with the exception of the Federal Insecticide, Fungicide, and Rodenticide Act (FIFRA).[115] Private individuals can enforce statutory, regulatory, and permit requirements through suits seeking compliance orders and/or penalties. [116] Citizens may also seek to require compliance of a regulator's duty to enforce environmental provisions. However, under the CAA, CWA, and RCRA, a citizen cannot pursue a citizen suit where the government is "diligently prosecuting" an action for the same violations. In order to initiate a suit, the citizen typically must give notice to: 1) the EPA-DOJ; 2) the state where the purported violation occurred; and 3) the alleged violator. Notice provides the federal government with the opportunity to initiate their own suit, precluding the citizen's suit, or to allow the violator to comply and correct its violation. EPA plans to initiate a program to boost public participation in

---

[112]*Northern States Power Co. v. Prairie Island Mdewakanton Sioux Indian Community*, 991 F.2d 458, 462 (8th Cir. 1993) (held that tribal ordinance is preempted by the Hazardous Materials Transportation Act since the regulatory scheme of the ordinance interfered with the purpose of the Act). See also *South Dakota v. Bourland, 508 U.S. 679*, 697 (1993). (held that the Flood Control and Cheyenne River Acts abrogated the Tribe's treaty rights to regulate non-Indian hunting and fishing on lands and in waters within their reservation that were acquired by the federal government for the operation of a reservoir and dam).

[113]*Northern States Power Co.*, 991 F.2d at 462; *See also United States v. Yakima Tribal Court*, 806 F.2d 853,861 (9th Cir. 1986), *cert. denied*, 481 U.S. 1069 (1987).

[114]*Santa Clara Pueblo v. Martinez*, 436 U.S. 49, 58-59 (1978). *See also Northern States Power Co.* 991 F.2d at 462.

[115]*See*, for example, CAA, 42 U.S.C.A. § 7604 (1995 & Supp. 1996); CWA, 33 U.S.C.A. § 1365 (1986 & Supp. 1996); TSCA, 15 U.S.C.A. § 2619 (1982 & Supp. 1996).

[116]In *Natural Resources Defense Council v. Texaco Refining & Mktg.*, 2 F. 3d 493 (3d Cir. 1993) (over $1.5 million in penalties was paid resulting from a citizen suit).

enforcement, including training citizens to monitor local facilities, permitting them to target entities for enforcement actions, and allowing them to assist in negotiations.[117]

### 5.5.2 Individual Injury Claims

Citizens may also initiate private damages actions against environmental violators. These "toxic tort" suits include damages for injury to a person or property and often these suits are in the form of class action litigation. Individual(s) claims of emotional distress, personal injury, property damage, and financial damage are included in these suits. For example, toxic torts include suits ranging from someone suing a restaurant for food poisoning to landowners claiming that their drinking water has become contaminated from a nearby chemical storage facility. Toxic tort lawsuits may be pursued even if the violating company is being prosecuted or has enforcement actions pending against it by another government entity or individual. Suits will typically be brought on the theory that the company was negligent or that they are strictly liable.[118]

Moreover, common law nuisance and trespass charges may be initiated by citizens to compensate for losses due to the violation of environmental regulations. In addition, courts allow recovery for medical monitoring, when a plaintiff must be medically monitored for exposure to hazardous substances, even if there is currently no detectable injury.

## 5.6 Other Federal Agencies

The EPA joins forces with other agencies and departments of the government to coordinate and facilitate environmental enforcement. Formal agreements are often established if the violation of particular environmental laws impact the jurisdictions of both agencies. For example, on March 4, 1996, the EPA and U.S. Customs Service signed a Memorandum of Understanding (MOU) to address the importation and exportation of illegal toxic substances, chemicals, hazardous waste, and pesticides.[119] Coordination between these agencies increases their enforcement and investigative strength and provides enhanced training for Customs officials' detection of unlawful substances at the United States borders. The alliance also integrates Customs' databases with those at the EPA to better identify potentially illegal shipments. The Federal Bureau of Investigation (FBI) and the EPA have also signed a MOU to increase the FBI's involvement in environmental crime investigations.[120] The EPA and the U.S. Coast Guard entered into a MOU to coordinate their enforcement efforts regarding the assessment of civil penalties for the discharge of oil and hazardous substances, pursuant

---

[117]U. S. EPA, *Notice of Availability of Permits Improvement Team Concept Paper on Environmental Permitting and Task Force Recommendations; Correction,* 61 Fed. Reg. 41,252 (Aug. 7, 1996).

[118]*See,* for example, *Atkins v. Harcross Chem. Co,* La. Dist. Ct. Orleans Parish, No. 89-2396 (Oct. 17, 1996) ($51.6 million settlement was reached between 3,800 people and a pesticide manufacturer); *See also Louisiana Judge Approves $51.6 Million Accord for Neighbors of New Orleans Pesticide Plant,* 11 Tox. L. Rep. 635 (Oct. 30, 1996).

[119]Steven A. Herman, *EPA, Customs Service Join Forces to Fight Pollution at the Border,* 11 Natl. Envtl Enf. J. 9 (Apr. 1996.)

[120]*See* U.S. DOJ, *Internal Review of the Department of Justice Environmental Crimes Program, Part 1* (Mar. 10, 1994).

to the Clean Water Act §311.[121]   A Memorandum of Agreement (MOA) also exists between the White House Council of Environmental Quality (CEQ) and EPA to coordinate their responsibilities for the implementation of the National Environmental Policy Act (NEPA).[122]   In addition, on November 26, 1990, the Occupational Safety and Health Administration (OSHA) signed an MOU with the EPA to promote their exchange of information.[123]   The EPA has signed numerous Memoranda of Understanding and Agreement with other governmental entities including:   the Department of the Army; U.S. Fish and Wildlife Service; U.S. Bureau of Land Management; National Oceanic and Atmospheric Administration; Nuclear Regulatory Commission; and the Federal Drug Administration.

Additionally, some environmental statutes are or may be delegated to other federal agencies as enforcers.  For example, President Clinton granted CERCLA enforcement authority to several government entities including the Departments of Interior, Commerce, Agriculture, Defense, and Energy.[124]

## 6.0 REORGANIZATION:  "CLEANER, CHEAPER, SMARTER"
The reorganization of EPA's enforcement program has brought forth new experimental approaches to enforcement in the form of compliance assurance projects.

### 6.1 Common Sense Initiative
The Common Sense Initiative (CSI) was designed during the early days of the reorganization to address and develop strategies for environmental management based on and tailored for specific industries.[125]   A panel of representatives from companies, trade associations, environmental groups, and state and local officials was created to suggest policy changes and to ensure that the EPA programs were "cleaner, cheaper, and smarter" in the specific industry areas.  A CSI Council was formed to guide the program and resolve any issues that could arise in the program's implementation.[126]  The program addresses several areas in each industry: a) regulation;  b) pollution prevention;  c)

---

[121]U.S. EPA, *Memorandum of Understanding Between the U.S. Environmental Protection Agency and the U.S. Coast Guard concerning the Enforcement of § 311 of the Clean Water Act*, 58 Fed. Reg. 19,420 (April 14, 1993) (codified at 40 C.F.R. Pt. 112, Appendix B).

[122]*See* U.S. EPA, Office of Enforcement, Envtl L. Inst. Number AD-658.

[123]*See* U.S., EPA, Office of Enforcement, *Enforcement Accomplishments Report FY 1990* EPA (Feb. 1991).

[124]*See* U.S. President, *Amendment to Executive Order No. 12580*, U.S. President, *Superfund Implementation*, Exec. Order 13016, 61 Fed. Reg. 45,871 (Aug. 30, 1996); *See also* Exec. Order 12580, 52 Fed. Reg. 2923 (Jan. 29, 1987).

[125]Metal finishing and plating, electronics and computers, iron and steel, auto assembly, petroleum refining, and printing were the industry areas/sectors EPA selected at the program's inception.  U.S. EPA, *Administrator's Update No. 12, Common Sense Initiative 1* (1994).  *See also Instrument Panel Suppliers For Autos Sought by EPA for Common Sense Initiative*, 27 Env't Rep. (BNA) 10 (May 3, 1996).

[126]U.S. EPA, *Common Sense Initiative Council Federal Advisory Committee Establishment*, 59 Fed. Reg. 55,117 (Nov. 3, 1994).

reporting; d) compliance; e) permitting; and f) environmental technology. The structure and concept of the CSI program has been appraised to have great potential.[127]

## 6.2 Environmental Leadership Program[128]

The Environmental Leadership Program (ELP) was established to allow particular companies with exemplary environmental performance to experiment in using innovative management and compliance techniques.[129] The net effect of this program is to produce the same end-product environmental result, utilizing more economical processes. In exchange for their experimentation, the EPA will recognize the companies publicly, allow them fewer facility inspections, and provide them with a limited time to correct any violations which occur. Twelve pilot facilities, made up of private firms and federal facilities, were selected by the EPA in April 1995 to participate in the program.[130] Each facility is to explore innovations in one or more areas including: a) determining the best methods to incorporate environmental management systems comparable to ISO 14000; b) examining the benefits of using third-party auditors to verify compliance; c) establishing evaluation techniques the public can employ to analyze a company's compliance; and d) developing procedures for multimedia (non industry-specific) compliance, community involvement, and mentoring for small business compliance.[131] In December 1996, EPA will launch full-scale ELP and solicit applications for facilities wanting to participate for six years at a time.[132]

## 6.3 Project XL (Excellence and Leadership)

Project XL allows regulated entities flexibility in achieving compliance, as long as their alternative techniques achieve greater results than the current federal standards

---

[127]*See* Daniel J. Fiorino, *Toward a New System of Environmental Regulation: The Case for an Industry Sector Approach*, 26 Envtl. L. 457 (Summer 1996).

[128]There is a web page on the World Wide Web for more information regarding ELP at (http://es.inel.gov.elp).

[129]U.S. EPA, *Environmental Leadership Program Overview 1* (1995). *See* Steven A. Herman, *EPA Launches Environmental Leadership Program*, 10 Ntl. Envtl. Enf. J. 14 (May 1995) at 14; *See also* Fiorino, at 475-76.

[130]FY 1995 EPA Report at 4-2.

[131]Ciba-Geigy, a chemical manufacturer, will test innovations in environmental management systems, multimedia compliance, and community involvement. Gillette, a producer of toiletries and appliances, is experimenting with third-party auditors and is also in the Star Track program, see below. Salt River Project, a public power utility and water supplier, is examining self-certification standards for an environmental management system and methods for customer compliance and pollution prevention training. Duke Power's Riverbend Stream Station, the John Roberts Company, McClellan Air Force Base, Motorola, Inc., Ocean State Power, Puget Sound Naval Shipyard, Arizona Public Service, Simpson Tacoma Kraft Company, and WMX Technologies, Inc. are also participating in the pilot ELP. *See EPA Launches Environmental Leadership Program*, at 14; *See also* Fiorino at 475-76.

[132]*See* Cheryl Hogue, *EPA Preparing for 1997 Launch of Environmental Leadership Program*, Daily Env't Rep. d6 (Oct. 16, 1996).

require.[133] Once selected, participating facilities join with state or local environmental agencies to develop a Final Project Agreement (FPA) which details the facility's plans to achieve outstanding compliance and the exemptions the regulators will provide the facility in exchange.[134] If federal and state enforcers and other stakeholders, including community organizations and environmental groups, do not oppose the FPA, it becomes a binding contract. Some debate exists over whether the EPA has the authority to provide such flexibility in enforcement, and whether the entities are still vulnerable to citizen enforcement.[135] Further, Project XL and other compliance incentive initiatives, such as CSI, are not meeting the expectations of many in the regulated community.[136] Many companies that have considered taking part in the incentive-based voluntary initiatives are rethinking their participation in the programs.

### 6.4 Star Track

Region I, of the EPA, has established a program to allow private third parties to assess a regulated entity's management and compliance.[137] Regulated entities, with a history of exemplary compliance records and environmental performance beyond the requirements of law, are selected to participate in the program. Several of the companies that piloted the program were also earlier involved with the ELP. In exchange for their participation in the program, the EPA allows limited penalty amnesty for violations which are voluntarily corrected and reduces reporting requirements. Also the EPA conducts no routine inspections and expedites the permitting process for participants.

### 6.5 "Cluster Rule"

The EPA is in the process of formalizing a rule, often referred to as the "Cluster Rule," which creates incentives to reduce the discharge of water pollutants and emissions of hazardous air pollutants, for certain segments of the pulp, paper, and paperboard industries.[138] In the development of the "Cluster Rule," the EPA has released the new National Emissions Standard for Hazardous Air Pollutants (NESHAP) to establish the Maximum Available Control Technology (MACT) in order to regulate

---

[133]U.S. EPA, *Regulatory Reinvention (XL) Pilot Projects*, 60 Fed. Reg. 27,282 (May 23, 1995).

[134]*See* Fiorino, at 472 -73.

[135]*See* William H. Freedman and Karen A. Caffee, *EPA's Project XL: Regulatory Flexibility*, Nat. Res. & Env't, (Spring 1996) at 59.

[136]*See Inflexibility?: EPA Clings to Command and Control; 3M Shelves Project XL Proposal*, 19 Envtl. Remed. Tech. 4 (Sept. 18, 1996); *See also Frustrated by Pace of Project XL, States Draft Federal Legislation*, Daily Env't Rep. AA-1 (Sept. 9, 1996).

[137]U.S. EPA, New England Press Office, *EPA Moves To Privatize Corporate Environmental Oversight; Twenty Hailed As Environmental Leaders*, Environmental News Press Release, Release No. 96-5-4 (May 6, 1996).

[138]U.S. EPA, *Effluent Limitations Guidelines, Pretreatment Standards, and New Source Performance Standards: Pulp, Paper, and Paperboard Category; National Emission Standards for Hazardous Air Pollutants for Source Category: Pulp and Paper Production*, 58 Fed. Reg. 66,078 (Dec. 17, 1993).

hazardous air emissions.[139] In July 1996, the EPA issued the framework for the "Cluster Rule" and announced the Advanced Technology Incentives Program which provides benefits for facilities going beyond the Best Available Technology (BAT) requirements in order to control wastewater discharges.[140] The incentives for providing greater-than-compliance performance include, providing fast-track permitting and reduced monitoring, allowing water quality permits to last longer than the standard permit term, and providing mitigation credit for enforcement actions.

## 7.0 INCENTIVES: PREVENTING NONCOMPLIANCE

Post-reorganization, the EPA also expanded and created several programs to supplement their traditional deterrence-oriented enforcement programs with initiatives which focus on preventing noncompliance.

### 7.1 Auditing and Voluntary Disclosure

In 1986, the EPA issued their policy statement encouraging effective auditing practices, as part of their initiative to improve compliance and environmental management. They defined auditing as "a systematic, documented and objective review by regulated entities of facility operations and practices relating to meeting environmental requirements."[141] The EPA stated that the policy "was developed to help (a) encourage regulated entities to institutionalize effective audit practices as one means of improving compliance and sound environmental management, and (b) to guide internal EPA actions directly related to regulated entities' environmental auditing programs."[142] They provided several characteristics of an effective environmental program, however, the policy statement is not binding as an environmental standard. Additionally, the EPA has stated that it would not "routinely" request audit reports from regulated entities as part of its initiative to encourage audits.

In December 1995, the EPA revised its policy statement regarding self-auditing. The policy reduces civil penalties, by diminishing or eliminating the gravity component of a penalty, for violations voluntarily and promptly disclosed and corrected by the regulated entity. However, the statement continues to be guidance and is not binding

---

[139]U.S. EPA, *National Emission Standards for Hazardous Air Pollutants for Source Category: Pulp and Paper Production*, 61 Fed. Reg. 9383 (Mar. 8, 1996).

[140]U.S EPA, *Effluent Limitations Guidelines, Pretreatment Standards, and New Source Performance Standards: Pulp, Paper, and Paperboard Category; National Emission Standards for Hazardous Air Pollutants for Source Category: Pulp and Paper Production; Availability*, 61 Fed. Reg. 36,835 (July 15, 1996).

[141]U.S EPA, *Environmental Auditing Policy Statement* (1986 EPA Audit Statement"), 51 Fed. Reg. 25,004, 25,006 (July 9, 1986).

[142]*Id.*

as a regulation, maintaining the EPA's discretion to use information discovered in an audit against a regulated entity.[143]

The DOJ internal guidelines allow voluntary disclosure of environmental violations to be calculated as a mitigating factor in criminal environmental enforcement actions as encouragement for self-audits and voluntary disclosure of violations.

### 7.1.1 Benefits

Audits are positively utilized by regulated entities to detect and correct a facility's compliance risks and/or to review the entity's management procedures for identifying and remedying environmental violations or potential violations. Theoretically, audits allow regulated entities to achieve compliance before governmental agencies or citizen groups initiate action against them for their violations.

### 7.1.2 Disadvantages - Disincentives

The principle disadvantage of completing a self-audit is the increased, or perceived increased, risk of liability for an entity, since an audit report can be a significant resource for prosecutors, citizens, and government entities. As discussed above, there is no guarantee that the EPA or DOJ will not use an audit report to hold an entity or its officials liable for violations discovered through the audit.[144] Neither governmental entity has offered protection of audit results from disclosure to other parties.[145] Consequently, much debate surrounds the government's policies regarding auditing[146]

---

[143]U.S. EPA, *Incentives for Self-Policing: Discovery, Disclosure, Correction and Prevention of Violations*, 60 Fed. Reg. 66,706 (Dec. 22, 1995). *See also* James T. Banks, *EPA's New Enforcement Policy: At Last, a Reliable Roadmap to Civil Penalty Mitigation for Self-Disclosed Violations*, 26 Envtl. L. Rep. 10227, (May 1996) (discusses the evolution of the EPA's auditing policy and details the revised policy and its impact).

[144]*See Chemical Makers Pay Maximum Penalty as CAP Garners $22 Million in Fines*, Daily Env't Rep. (BNA) d12 (Oct. 3, 1996) (123 companies in a voluntary audit program were fined combined penalties of more than $22 million for filing late reports that divulged the health and ecological effects of their products. E.I. duPont de Nemours & Co. filed 1,386 late reports during a five year audit. Dow Chemical Co. filed 967 late and Union Carbide filed 933 late reports.)

[145] In some situations the attorney-client privilege, the work-product privilege, or the self-evaluation privilege may be used to prevent disclosure of audit reports to the regulating authorities. The use of these privileges are limited to the situations where specific elements are present in order to trigger their protection. *See United States Postal Serv. v. Phelps Dodge Refining Corp.*, 852 F. Supp. 156 (E.D.N.Y. 1994) (discussing attorney-client privilege); *See also Logan v. Commercial Union Ins. Co.*, 96 F.3d 971 (7th Cir. 1996) (discussing work product privilege). *See also In Re: Grand Jury Proceedings*, 861 F. Supp. 386 (D. Md. 1994) (discussing self-evaluative privilege).

[146]*See* James R. Moore, David Dabroski, John Daniel Ballbach - Perkins Coie, *Why Risk Criminal Charges By Performing Environmental Audits?* 6 Tox. L. Rep. (BNA) 503 (Sept. 18, 1991); *But see* David Ronald, *The Case Against an Environmental Audit Privilege*, 9 Ntl. Envtl. Enf, J. 8 (Sept. 1994).

and critics of the government's approach suggest the enactment of a federal self-audit privilege and voluntary disclosure legislation that would eliminate the disincentive.[147]

### 7.1.3 States: Self-Audit Privileges and Voluntary Disclosure Legislation

Eighteen states have enacted their own self-audit privilege and/or voluntary disclosure legislation to encourage self-auditing by regulated entities.[148] While the statutes vary somewhat among the states, audit protection typically only extends to those audits not required by law, to those conducted without fraudulent intent, and to companies that promptly remedy any violations found as a result of the audit. Further, in criminal proceedings, the privilege may not protect audit information from reaching the hands of the prosecutor.[149] Additionally, only those violations discovered as a result of a voluntary audit, promptly disclosed, and corrected may receive penalty mitigation.

Several citizens groups have advocated that EPA consider withdrawing federally delegated programs from the states that have enacted privilege and voluntary disclosure legislation, arguing that it impedes their ability to enforce federal environmental laws and standards.[150] The EPA may increase its enforcement efforts in a state with an audit

---

[147]"Despite the new Policy, there remains a real need for federal legislation to provide i) balanced incentives that encourage regulated entities to disclose voluntarily instances of noncompliance discovered either through an audit or as a consequence of a compliance management system; and ii) limited privilege protection for members of the regulated community that move beyond required compliance monitoring and undertake voluntary audits to promote better environmental protection. By itself, the EPA Policy cannot eliminate the impediments to improved environmental compliance currently created by our legal system." James R. Moore and Nancy W. Newkirk - Perkins Coie, *Continuing Need for Federal Audit Disclosure and Use Immunity and Privilege Legislation*, Comments of the Compliance Management & Policy Group, submitted for the record to the Subcommittee on Administrative Oversight and the Courts of the Senate Committee on the Judiciary for the Hearing on "S. 582 and Voluntary Environmental Audits," May 21, 1996.

In 1991, the EPA developed the Compliance Audit Program (CAP) under TSCA § 8(e). U.S. EPA, *Registration and Agreement for TSCA Section 8(e) Compliance Audit Program*, 56 Fed. Reg. 4128 (Feb. 1, 1991); 15 USC § 2607(e) (1982), which requires TSCA regulated entities to perform audits, to disclose the results to the EPA, and to remedy any violations. In exchange, EPA will not prosecute the entity criminally and will cap the amount of civil penalties the government can assess. Thus, the EPA has demonstrated some amenability to an audit privilege in certain statutory situations.

[148]*See*, for example: Or. Rev. Stat. § 468.96 (1993) Colo. Rev. Stat. §§ 13.25-126.5 (1994); Ind. Code § 13-10 (1994); Ky. Rev. Stat. Ann §§ 224.01-040 (1996); 1996 Mich. Pub. Acts 132, 1996 N.H. Laws 4.

[149]*See* David Sorenson, *The U.S. Environmental Protection Agency's Recent Environmental Auditing Policy and Potential Conflict With State-Created Environmental Audit Privilege Laws*, 9 Tul. Envtl. L. J. 483 (Summer 1996) (discussing the disadvantages of the state audit privilege statutes).

[150]For example, Northwest Environmental Advocates petitioned the EPA to withdraw Idaho's authority to administer federal programs, arguing that the State's audit privilege and voluntary disclosure statute reduce the State's enforcement authority. In June 1996, the EPA questioned its approval of Idaho's application to administer a Clean Air Act program because of its audit statute. *Group Asks EPA to Withdraw Delegation for RCRA, Underground Injection,*

(continued...)

privilege statute.[151] Moreover, in its opposition to the establishment of a statutory privilege, the EPA stated that, as of July 1996, its revised policy has lead 76 companies to voluntarily disclose violations. Most of the companies were not required to pay penalties.[152] Consequently, the debate continues over the best way to encourage efficient self-monitoring practices without simultaneously creating disincentives.

## 7.2 International (Non-EPA) Program to Encourage Effective Environmental Management

### 7.2.1 ISO 14000/14001

The International Organization for Standardization (ISO) has developed voluntary environmental management standards to guide regulated entities in developing their own management systems.[153] There are over 100 countries which are members of the International Organization for Standardization.[154] Each has its own Technical Advisory Group made up of accredited standards institutes, government and industry representatives, and other interested parties which convey the nation's official opinion

---

(...continued)
*SDWA*, Daily Env't Rep. d16 (Oct. 15, 1996); *See also State Privilege-Immunity Laws for Audits Could Hurt Program Delegation, Official Says, 26 Env't Rep. (BNA) 2253 (March 29, 1996); See also Audits, Takings, Public Participation Thwart Delegation of NPDES Program*, Daily Env't Rep. d15 (Sept. 30, 1996) (Texas' application for authority over the NPDES program is incomplete because it does not discuss the impact of the State's audit privilege statute on the State's capacity to carry out the program).

[151]For example, during debate over Virginia's adoption of its audit privilege statute, EPA threatened to increase federal enforcement in Virginia. *State Lawmakers Ask for Relief From EPA Enforcement Scrutiny*, Daily Env't Rep. (BNA) A206 (Oct. 25, 1995).

[152]*New Federal Audit Leads 76 Companies to Disclose Environmental Violations, EPA Says*, 27 Env't Rep. (BNA) 784 (Aug. 2, 1996).

[153]*See* American National Standards Institute (ANSI)/International Organization of Standardization (ISO) publication of the 14000 series including: ISO 14001 "Environmental Management Systems-Specification With Guidance For Use" contains the requirements to establish and implement an EMS for certification under ISO 14000 standards or for self-declaration purposes. ISO 14004 "Environmental Management Systems - General Guidelines on Principles, Systems, and Supporting Techniques" contains guidelines and options to implement or enhance and EMS. ISO 14010 "Guidelines for Environmental Auditing - General Principles," guides regulated entities, auditors, and their clients through the general principles of environmental auditing. ISO 14011 "Guidelines for Environmental Auditing - Audit Procedures - Auditing of Environmental Management Systems," provides procedures for conducting EMS audits. ISO 14012 "Guidelines for Environmental Auditing - Qualification Criteria for Environmental Auditors" includes qualification criteria for internal and external environmental auditors. ISO 14020-14024.2 addresses the general principles of environmental labeling. ISO 14040 and 14041.2 provide the principles and goals of environmental management life cycle assessments. ISO 14050 addresses the vocabulary of environmental management. For more information, ANSI has a web page on the World Wide Web at (http://www.ansi.org).

[154]*See generally* Carey A. Mathews, *The ISO 14001 Environmental Management System Standard: An Innovative Approach to Environmental Protection*, 2 Envtl. Law. 817, 818 (June 1996); *See also* Warren A. Bird, *ISO 14000: How to Decide What is Right for Your Company?*, 102 Chem. Eng'g 9 (Sept. 1995) at 94.

regarding the standards.[155] ISO 14001 guides the development of an Environmental Management System (EMS) which will shape, develop, implement, and review an entity's environmental policy, and attempts to improve the environmental performance of an entity. The requirements of an effective EMS are detailed in 14001, including: a) the development of a policy statement;  b) establishing planning methods for implementation;  c) providing resources and procedures for management and employees to manage and maintain the EMS;  d) creating procedures to monitor, remedy, and prevent operations which can negatively impact the environment; and e) continually evaluating the EMS and providing documentation of its reviews.

A participating entity may receive ISO 14001 certification once it has achieved and demonstrated the core requirements of an EMS. While the requirements were not developed as a basis for a regulation, certification may provide several benefits to participating entities. Certification may provide a company with an advantage in the global market.[156] In the future, many major corporations might well require that suppliers be certified in order to do business with them. As discussed, the EPA's Environmental Leadership Program uses standards similar to ISO 14000 and demonstrates that the ISO EMS requirements are somewhat compatible with current practices and programs.[157] Consequently, ISO 14000 has the potential to become a required operating standard among all regulated entities in the near future.

## 8.0 RECENT CASE LAW AND LEGISLATION IMPACTING ENVIRONMENTAL ENFORCEMENT

### 8.1 "Fair Warning" Defense Doctrine

Recent case law has developed and solidified a constitutional defense to environmental civil or criminal penalty enforcement actions.[158] The courts have reasoned that due process in the environmental arena requires fair notice be given to an entity before depriving them of their property. Thus, due process protection is triggered when a regulation does not provide fair warning by clearly establishing the conduct constituting a violation and results in the assessment of a fine.[159] In *General Electric v. EPA,* the court stated that "where, as here, the regulations and other policy statements are unclear, where the petitioner's interpretation is reasonable, and where the agency itself struggles to provide a definitive reading of the regulatory requirements, a regulated

---

[155]Mathews, at 818.

[156]Mathews, at 827,833.

[157]Mathews, at 828, 832.

[158]*General Elec. Co. v. United States EPA,* 53 F.3d 1324, 1328-29 (D.C. Cir. 1995); *See also In re CWM Chem. Servs. Inc.,* TSCA Appeal No. 93-1 TSCA LEXIS 10,41 (EAB May 15, 1995) (notice must derive from regulatory language or approval document); *See also Rollins Envt'l. Servs. v. United States EPA,* 937 F.2d 649 (D.C. Cir. 1991); *See also United States v. Trident Seafoods Corp.,* 60 F.3d 556, 559 (9th Cir. 1995) *petition for cert. filed* Nov. 5, 1996 (when violation of a regulation subjects private parties to criminal or civil sanctions, a regulation cannot be construed to mean what an agency had intended but did not adequately express).

[159]*General Electric v. EPA,* 53 F.3d at 1324, 1328 (D.C. Cir 1995). *See also* Roy S. Belden, *Reinvigorating the Due Process Defense: EPA Required to Give Fair Warning of Rule Interpretations,* 26 Envt' Rep. (BNA) 2449 (Apr. 26, 1996).

party is not 'on notice' of the agency's ultimate interpretation of the regulations, and may not be punished."[160] The effect of this decision requires that regulations be written using clear and understandable language, and that drafters of regulations are now on notice that not to do so will produce confusion in enforcement, as well as a potential loophole for non compliance. Consequently, ambiguous regulations or unclear interpretations may provide enforcement problems for the EPA, with the development of the "fair warning" doctrine in the environmental context.

## 8.2 Small Business Regulatory Enforcement Fairness Act

Legislation which passed this past session of Congress may also have a major impact on environmental regulations and enforcement. On March 29, 1996, President Clinton signed into law the Small Business Regulatory Enforcement Fairness Act of 1996 (SBREFA).[161] See 201, *et seq.*, 110 Stat. 857. The legislation establishes a government-wide congressional review mechanism for most rules, in effect, allowing Congress the opportunity to review a rule before it takes effect. Likewise, the legislation directs attention to the problems of small businesses and in some instances, of large corporations that have to operate with overly burdensome rules or extraordinary enforcement actions, policy and guidance. The working parts of this new law have not yet been tested, however, the potential for change in environmental enforcement is great.[162]

## 9.0 CONCLUSION

The new reorganization of the EPA's enforcement office will not be the last. More changes and newer approaches will be tried with the end result that compliance will increasingly become the no option norm for the regulated community. With required reporting to the government on various emissions and an almost inclusive inventory of ingredients utilized in producing a product, the government will, and to some extent now has, the ability to determine any number of violations of environmental laws simply by looking at submitted reports. For an enforcement back up, if the submissions are false, the violator can be prosecuted criminally. In effect, environmental enforcement has become increasingly sophisticated and risk taking on noncompliance has become increasingly unwise when 1) the chances of being caught are greater, and 2) the downside of not adhering to the laws can lead to an economic detriment in terms of penalties paid and negative investor reaction.

---

[160]*General Elec.*, 53 F.3d. at 1333-34.

[161]Pub L. No. 104-121, 110 Stat. 857 (1996).

[162]In addition, see *U.S. EPA Policy on Compliance Incentives for Small Businesses.* 60 Fed. Reg. 2,0621 (April 26, 1995).

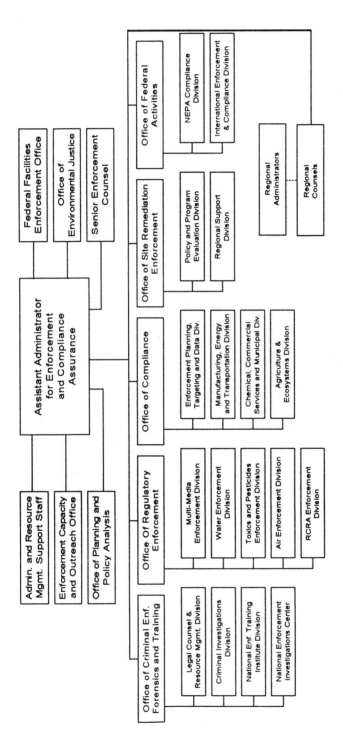

**Figure 2.1. Office of Enforcement and Compliance Assurance**

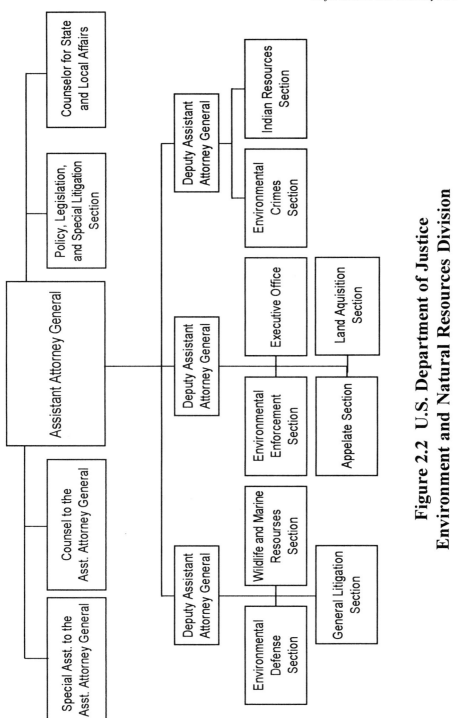

**Figure 2.2  U.S. Department of Justice Environment and Natural Resources Division**

# CHAPTER 3

# CLEAN AIR ACT

F. William Brownell[1]
Hunton & Williams
Washington, D.C.

## 1.0 OVERVIEW

Over the past three decades, the Clean Air Act (Act or CAA) has evolved from a set of principles designed to guide states in controlling sources of air pollution (the 1967 Air Quality Act), to a series of detailed control requirements (the 1970, 1977, and 1990 Amendments to the Act) that the federal government implements and the states administer. The Clean Air Act regulatory programs have traditionally fallen into three categories.

First, all new and existing sources of air pollution are prohibited from emitting pollution that exceeds ambient air quality levels designed to protect public health and welfare. This ambient air quality program is implemented through source-specific emission limits contained in state implementation plans (SIPs). Second, new sources are subject to more stringent control technology and permitting requirements. Third, the Act addresses specific pollution problems, including hazardous air pollution and visibility impairment.

In 1990, Congress amended this three part system of regulation in significant respects (e.g., by revamping the system of hazardous air pollution regulation, and by addressing new air pollution problems such as acid deposition), and added a fourth program–a comprehensive operating permit program to focus in one place all of the Clean Air Act requirements that apply to a given source of air pollution. This chapter reviews briefly each of these Clean Air Act regulatory programs, with a particular focus on changes made by the 1990 Amendments to the Act.

## 2.0 THE CLEAN AIR ACT REGULATORY PROGRAMS

### 2.1 Air Quality Regulation

The centerpiece of the Clean Air Act has traditionally been the national ambient air quality standard (NAAQS) program. The NAAQS addresses pervasive pollution that endangers public health and welfare, and have been established for six pollutants: sulfur dioxide ($SO_2$), nitrogen oxides ($NO_x$), particulate matter, carbon monoxide (CO), ozone, and lead. *See* 40 C.F.R. Part 50. For each of these pollutants, NAAQS are set at a level designed to protect public health with an adequate margin of safety (referred to as the "primary" NAAQS), and to promote public welfare (the "secondary" NAAQS).[2]

---

[1]The author wishes to acknowledge the support of colleagues at Hunton & Williams who assisted in updating this chapter.

[2]CAA §109.

NAAQS are to be reviewed and revised as appropriate every five years.[3] As a practical matter, EPA has had difficulty meeting this schedule. Nevertheless, EPA has more recently–largely as a result of pressure from the courts–made a number of decisions regarding the NAAQS program that could have important implications for future regulation under the CAA.

On May 22, 1996, EPA promulgated a decision *not* to tighten the NAAQS for $SO_2$.[4] This decision followed an earlier EPA proposal in November 1994 to revise the $SO_2$ ambient standard, to include a 0.6 ppm, 5-minute average standard (1 exceedance per year). Instead of tightening the $SO_2$ NAAQS, EPA proposed on January 2, 1997 a program for monitoring and regulation of 5-minute average peak $SO_2$ concentrations under § 303 of the Act.

On October 8, 1996, EPA issued its decision *not* to set a short-term NAAQS for $NO_2$.[5] More significantly, EPA in December 1996 proposed to tighten substantially the NAAQS for particulate matter and ozone.

EPA's proposed particulate matter NAAQS would address fine particles of 2.5 microns or less (i.e.,PM-2.5). EPA has proposed to adopt an annual standard of about 50 $\mu g/m^3$ (98th percentile), and a 24-hour standard of 15 $\mu g/m^3$ (spatially averaged). These standards are much more stringent than the current PM-10 standards (which would remain in place under the current proposal, except that the daily PM-10 standard would be based on the 98th percentile reading). As a result, the proposed PM-2.5 standards, if adopted, will create many new nonattainment areas. Because gaseous emissions react in the atmosphere to form PM-2.5, this new standard will result in significant new $SO_2$, $NO_X$, and VOC controls for many industrial sources. Moreover, because PM-2.5 is considered a regional pollutant such controls might well be sought on sources significantly outside the boundaries of the nonattainment areas. EPA is currently under court order to promulgate this new standard by July 19, 1997.

At the same time it proposed the PM-2.5 standard, EPA also proposed to replace the current hourly ozone NAAQS with a new, more stringent NAAQS for ozone of 0.08 ppm, eight-hour average, with compliance determined on the basis of the third highest reading. In addition, EPA has asked for comment on an even-more-stringent 3-month standard to protect crops. These new ozone standards would also result in many new nonattainment areas, greatly complicating the ozone attainment problem in many areas of the country. As a result, one can anticipate substantial litigation and perhaps new legislation in this area.

### 2.1.1 State Implementation Plans

Sections 107 and 110 of the Clean Air Act give each state primary responsibility for assuring that air quality within its borders is maintained at a level consistent with the NAAQS. This is achieved through the establishment of source-specific requirements in state implementation plans (SIPs) addressing the primary and secondary air quality standards. The Act contains substantive and procedural requirements governing the

---

[3]*See* CAA §109(d).
[4]62 Fed. Reg. 210 (1997).
[5]61 Fed. Reg. at 52852.

development and approval of these SIP requirements.[6] The stringency of the substantive requirements depends upon whether an area attains or does not attain the level of air quality specified in the NAAQS.

### 2.1.1.1 Requirements Regarding SIP Content

Section 110(a)(2) requires that all SIPs must be adopted after reasonable notice and public hearing, and must include the following information:

**Enforceable emission limitations.** A SIP must include enforceable emission limitations and other control measures, including economic incentives and timetables, as necessary to comply with the Act.[7] These emission limitations are typically established by modeling the air quality impact of individual sources to determine an emission level adequate to ensure attainment of the NAAQS.

**Air quality data.** A SIP must include provisions for developing data on ambient air quality to be made available to EPA, which data are used to classify areas as attainment or nonattainment.

**Enforcement.** A SIP must establish a program for enforcement of the emission limitations and control measures established by the state for individual sources.[8] Stationary sources are also subject to enforcement under the operating permit program established by Title V of the 1990 Amendments.

**Interstate air pollution.** A SIP must prohibit emissions activities that interfere with attainment and maintenance of the NAAQS, new source requirements, or visibility protection in another state.[9] CAA §110(a)(2)(D). A SIP must also include provisions insuring compliance with sections of the Act relating to interstate and international air pollution abatement.[10]

**Adequate personnel, funding, and authority.** A SIP must provide assurances that the designated control authority has adequate resources and power to carry out the SIP under state or local laws. See CAA §128. The state must also retain ultimate responsibility for implementation and enforcement despite any delegation of authority to local agencies.[11]

**Monitoring and emission data.** A SIP must require monitoring and periodic reporting of emissions by stationary sources, in order to enable state enforcement and EPA oversight. The state must correlate emission reports with relevant emission limitations and make the reports available to EPA and for public inspection.[12]

**Contingency plans.** A SIP must provide authority for certain emergency powers similar to the provisions contained in §303 of the Act, and for adequate contingency plans to restrict emissions of pollutants that present an imminent and substantial danger

---

[6]*See* CAA §§110 and 172.
[7]CAA §110(a)(2)(A).
[8]CAA §110(a)(2)(C).
[9]CAA § 110(a)(2)(D)
[10]*See* CAA §§115 and 126.
[11]CAA §110(a)(2)(E).
[12]CAA §110(a)(2)(F).

to the public.[13] EPA plans to require states to develop specific programs for prevention of peak $SO_2$ concentrations under the authority of this provision.

**Revision of the SIP.** A SIP must provide for revision as necessary to take into account any changes in the NAAQS, any improved methods of attainment, or any finding by EPA of substantial inadequacy of the current plan. CAA §110(a)(2)(H).

**Part D requirements.** A SIP must meet the additional requirements of Part D of the Act (discussed below), relating to construction of new sources and operation of existing sources in areas that do not attain the NAAQS.[14]

**Preconstruction review and notification requirements.** A SIP must meet the requirements of Part C, relating to the prevention of significant deterioration (PSD) program for approval of construction of "major" new sources of air pollution in attainment areas.[15] A SIP must also contain requirements for preconstruction review of "minor" sources of air pollution in both attainment and nonattainment areas.[16]

**Air quality modeling.** A SIP must provide for air quality modeling and submission of related data as prescribed by the Administrator. This modeling is used to predict the effect of the emissions of regulated pollutants on ambient air quality, in order to evaluate the adequacy of individual source emission limitations and the adequacy of an area's classification as attainment or nonattainment.[17]

**Permit fees.** A SIP must include provisions requiring the owner or operator of each major stationary source to pay, as a condition of any permit, fees to cover the reasonable costs of reviewing, acting on, and enforcing the permit, until superseded by a fee program under Title V of the 1990 Amendments.[18]

**Local consultation.** A SIP must provide for consultation with and participation by local political subdivisions affected by the plan.[19]

Traditionally, determining the contents of a SIP has been difficult because, as states have developed their air quality programs, not every provision has been submitted to EPA for approval as part of the SIP. Of those submitted to EPA, some have been approved as part of the SIP and some have not. And when a state revises a SIP provision, that revised regulation may or may not be submitted for EPA approval (if it is not, the old provision that is no longer in the state rules may remain part of the SIP). SIP identification has been a problem under the new Title V operating permit program (discussed below), which requires a source to identify all "federally" applicable requirements. To address this problem, state environmental agencies and EPA regional offices have developed SIP compilations for use in preparing Title V permit applications.

---

[13]CAA §110(a)(2)(G).
[14]CAA §110(a)(2)(I).
[15]CAA §110(a)(2)(J).
[16]CAA § 110(a)(2)(C).
[17]CAA §110(a)(2)(K).
[18]CAA §110(a)(2)(L).
[19]CAA §110(a)(2)(M).

### 2.1.1.2 Procedural Requirements Regarding SIP Development

The SIP is a constantly evolving regulatory document, that must be updated as federal requirements and local conditions change. States are responsible for developing SIPs and keeping them up-to-date. SIPs must be submitted to EPA, however, for review and approval. Until a SIP is approved by EPA, it is enforceable only as a matter of state, not federal, law.

States must ensure that their SIPs are adequate to attain and maintain the NAAQS, and must revise the SIP within three years of issuance of any new or revised NAAQS (or such shorter time as is prescribed by EPA). Moreover, whenever the Administrator finds that a SIP is "substantially inadequate" (I) to attain or to maintain a NAAQS; (ii) to mitigate adequately interstate air pollution;[20] or (iii) to comply with any other requirement of the Act, the Administrator must publicly notify the state and establish reasonable deadlines for SIP revisions.[21]

SIP revisions required in response to a finding by EPA of plan inadequacy (i.e., a "SIP call") must correct the deficiency and meet all other applicable requirements of CAA §110 and Part D (addressing additional requirements for areas that do not attain the NAAQS). In order to facilitate submittal of adequate and approvable plans, EPA issues written guidelines, interpretations, and information to the states and the public.[22]

Clean Air Act section 110(k) outlines the requirements for EPA action on new and revised SIP submittals. Generally, within sixty days of receiving a plan or plan revision, the Administrator will determine whether the submission is "complete."[23] Completeness criteria were published in the *Federal Register* in August 1991. 56 Fed. Reg. 42216 (1991). If, after six months, the Administrator has failed to determine whether these criteria have been met, the SIP submittal is automatically deemed complete.[24] If, however, the Administrator determines that the plan or any portion of the plan does not meet the completeness criteria, the state is treated as not having made the submission.[25]

Once a plan submission is deemed complete, the Administrator is required to approve or to disapprove the plan within 12 months.[26] A plan that meets all of the applicable requirements of the Act will be approved in whole. However, the Administrator may also approve a plan in part, or approve a plan revision on condition that the state will adopt specific enforceable measures within one year.[27] This is referred to as a "conditional" SIP approval or a "committal" SIP.

If a state fails to make a required submission, or if the Administrator disapproves a SIP submission in whole or in part, EPA must promulgate a Federal Implementation Plan (FIP) for the state within two years of the date on which the SIP submission was

---

[20] *See* CAA §§176A, 184.
[21] CAA §110(k)(5).
[22] *See* CAA §172(d).
[23] CAA §110(k)(1)(A).
[24] CAA §110(k)(l)(B).
[25] CAA §110(k)(l)(C).
[26] CAA §110(k)(2).
[27] CAA §110(k)(3) & (4).

required. A federal plan is not required, however, if the state corrects the deficiency before the expiration of this two-year period.[28]

### 2.1.1.3 Sanctions for Failure to Develop a SIP

If a SIP deficiency has not been corrected within 18 months of notice from EPA, the Administrator must choose either to cut off federal highway funds, or to require additional emissions offsets of at least two-to-one for new or modified sources seeking new source permits, until the state has corrected the deficiency.[29] The Administrator may also withhold support grants for air pollution planning and control programs. Further, if the Administrator finds "lack of good faith," or if the deficiency has not been corrected within six months after imposition of one of the above sanctions, both of the above sanctions are to apply until the state has come into compliance.[30]

The Administrator has authority under § 110(m) of the Act to apply the § 179(b) sanctions discussed above at the time of a SIP deficiency finding, or at any time thereafter prior to the expiration of the 18-month period for state correction of the deficiency. The Administrator has issued regulations on how EPA will exercise this discretionary authority to apply § 179(b) sanctions prior to the date for mandatory application of sanctions.[31] The Administrator has also issued regulations specifying the sequence in which the § 179(b) sanctions will be applied at the end of the 18-month period.[32]

Sanctions are not politically popular, and the development of a FIP is burdensome for EPA. As a result, EPA often seeks alternatives to sanctions or FIP development. The most significant of the recent efforts to find alternatives to sanctions and FIPs–the Ozone Transport Assessment Group (OTAG)–is discussed below regarding ozone nonattainment area issues.

### 2.1.2 Additional SIP Requirements in Nonattainment Areas

The Clean Air Act contains general requirements governing development of SIPs in areas that do not attain the NAAQS. Title I of the 1990 Amendments includes additional, specific requirements addressing nonattainment areas for CO, fine particles (or PM-10), and the two precursors of ozone–volatile organic compounds (VOCs) and $NO_X$. The 1990 Amendments emphasize an incremental approach to achieving attainment of the NAAQS for each of these pollutants. That is, attainment deadlines have been relaxed as compared to the 1977 Clean Air Act, but more stringent control requirements apply as an area's nonattainment problems become more severe. Specific nonattainment provisions are highlighted below.

### 2.1.2.1 Substantive Requirements for Nonattainment SIPs

In addition to complying with the general requirements for SIPs discussed above, nonattainment area SIPs must include the following additional provisions:

---

[28]CAA §110(c)(1).
[29]*See* CAA §179(b)(1).
[30]CAA §179(a) & (b).
[31]59 Fed. Reg. 1481 (1994).
[32]59 Fed. Reg. 39859 (1994).

**Reasonably available control technology.** Plans must provide for application of all reasonably available control measures for stationary sources as expeditiously as practicable with adoption, at a minimum, of reasonably available control technology (RACT) for existing sources.[33]

**Reasonable further progress.** Plans must provide for such "annual incremental reductions" in emissions of nonattainment pollutants as required by Title I of the 1990 Amendments, or that are reasonably required in order to assure reasonable further progress in attaining the NAAQS by the applicable date.[34]

**Inventory of current emissions.** Plans must include a provision for obtaining a current inventory of actual emissions from all sources of the nonattainment pollutant(s), including periodic revisions as may be required by EPA.[35]

**Permits for new and modified major stationary sources.** Plans must require permits for the construction and operation of new or modified "major" or "minor" stationary sources anywhere in the nonattainment areas. Plans must contain the more restrictive requirements of the nonattainment new source review program for "major" sources.

**Quantify new emissions to be allowed.** Plans must expressly identify and quantify emissions that will be allowed in accordance with all new source permits and demonstrate that such emissions will be consistent with the achievement of reasonable further progress and eventual attainment of the NAAQS.[36] In essence, an "emissions budget" will be developed for each nonattainment area that will govern future environmental control strategies and economic growth in the area.

**Contingency measures.** Plans must provide specific measures that will automatically be implemented if the area fails to make reasonable further progress or to attain the NAAQS by the applicable date.[37]

**Equivalent techniques.** The Administrator may allow, upon application from the state, the use of modeling, emission inventory, and planning techniques equivalent to those prescribed by EPA, provided that they are not, in the aggregate, less effective than the EPA methods.[38]

### 2.1.2.2 Specific Nonattainment Pollutants

In order to address persistent nonattainment problems, Congress in 1990 wrote into the Clean Air Act detailed substantive requirements applicable to specific nonattainment pollutants. These requirements increase in stringency as the severity of an area's nonattainment problem increases. The 1990 Amendments also set new deadlines for attainment, again depending upon the severity of the nonattainment problem. Since these provisions were all keyed to the existing NAAQS, EPA and perhaps Congress will have to revisit these pollutant-specific attainment strategies if the ozone and particulate NAAQS are tightened, as EPA has proposed.

---

[33]CAA §172(c)(1).
[34]CAA §§171(1), 172(c)(2).
[35]CAA §172(c)(3).
[36]CAA §172(c)(4),(5).
[37]CAA §172(c)(9).
[38]CAA §172(c)(8).

**Ozone.**[39] Under the 1990 Amendments, ozone nonattainment areas are designated as marginal, moderate, serious, severe, or extreme, depending on the severity of the nonattainment problem. Marginal areas were required to attain the ozone NAAQS within three years of enactment of the 1990 Amendments (i.e., by November 15, 1993), moderate areas within six years, serious areas within 9 years, severe areas within 15 years, and extreme areas (Southern California) within 20 years.

New provisions address the obligation of existing sources to install reasonably available control technology (RACT). EPA was required by the 1990 Amendments to list source categories for which control technique guidelines for RACT have not been published, and then to publish the guidelines pursuant to a rolling schedule contained in the legislation. Stationary sources that are not otherwise covered by control technique guidelines and that emit certain levels of VOCs would also be required to install RACT. States with ozone nonattainment areas have to revise their SIPs to address various new requirements, including annual, incremental reductions in emissions of VOCs. States are also given authority to require $NO_x$ emission reductions in ozone nonattainment areas that are ranked as having "moderate" or more serious nonattainment problems, and EPA is required to develop guidance with respect to control techniques for $NO_x$ reductions.

Along with its December 1996 proposal to tighten the ozone NAAQS, EPA issued an implementation paper addressing how the transition from the current ozone NAAQS to the new more stringent NAAQS would be handled. The intent of this transition policy is to ensure that the progress required under the existing CAA provisions continues as states implement any revised ozone NAAQS through SIP revisions.

**Carbon Monoxide.**[40] CO nonattainment areas are designated as either moderate or serious. Moderate areas must attain the CO NAAQS by December 31, 1995, and serious areas by December 31, 2000.

The 1990 Amendments require that states with CO nonattainment areas include in their plans specific emission reduction requirements (e.g., RACT for major sources and mobile source fleet requirements) that must be met by specific deadlines in order that the overall deadline for attainment be met. If a state fails to meet these interim "milestones," EPA must impose sanctions and require revisions to the SIP to ensure compliance.

**PM-10.**[41] Under the 1990 Amendments, all PM-10 nonattainment areas are initially classified as moderate, and were to be reclassified later as serious if the area cannot practically attain the PM-10 NAAQS by December 31, 1994. Serious PM-10 nonattainment areas are given until December 31, 2001 to attain the NAAQS.

The 1990 Amendments contain requirements for PM-10 similar to those for ozone and CO nonattainment areas. For example, states must implement reasonably available control measures for sources contributing to nonattainment of the PM-10 standard, and designate periodic emission reduction milestones until attainment is achieved. EPA is

---

[39] *See* CAA §§181-185B.
[40] *See* CAA §§186-87.
[41] *See* CAA §§188-90.

directed to promulgate control technique guidelines for reasonably available control measures and best available control measures for PM-10 emissions from stationary sources contributing to nonattainment of the NAAQS.

As with ozone and CO, PM-10 SIP revisions are to provide for automatic implementation of contingency measures if the area fails to attain the PM-10 NAAQS by the mandated deadline. States are to adopt these contingency measures as regulations prior to the deadline for attainment, to ensure that these back-up measures go into effect without delay if the target date is missed.

If EPA promulgates the proposed PM-2.5 NAAQS (discussed above), states will be required to revise their SIPs to ensure attainment and maintenance of this more stringent standard. If the PM-10 NAAQS is left in place so that there are NAAQS for both PM-10 and PM-2.5 (as EPA has proposed to do), ongoing PM-10 efforts will continue as the PM-2.5 standard is implemented.

### 2.1.2.3 The Conformity Program

The Clean Air Act's federal "conformity" provisions in § 176© provide that no federal department may engage in, support in any way or provide financial assistance for, or license or approve any activity that does not conform to a SIP. The 1990 Clean Air Act Amendments put teeth in this provision by expanding the "conformity" program from a simple check on the implementation of transportation control measures, to ensuring that all relevant state actions (1) conform to the purpose of the SIP (i.e., to eliminate or reduce the severity and number of ambient standard exceedances), and (2) do not cause or contribute to new violations of an ambient standard, increase the severity or frequency of existing violations, or otherwise delay attainment.

The federal conformity provisions have been implemented through two lengthy rules. As to transportation plans, programs and projects requiring funding or approval from the U.S. Department of Transportation, the Federal Highway Administration or the Federal Transit Administration, the conformity provision is implemented by the "Transportation Conformity" rule issued on November 24, 1993. [42]This rule establishes the process by which federal and state transportation agencies and metropolitan planning organizations determine that highway and transportation projects conform to the emission budget established by the SIP. For all other federal actions (including EPA and Corps of Engineers licensing and permit actions), the conformity program is implemented by the "General Conformity" rule issued by EPA on November 30, 1993.[43]

The Transportation Conformity rules are particularly complex, and failure to comply with these rules can result in a cut-off of federal highway funds. In this sense, the conformity program operates as a strong *de facto* sanction for failure to meet SIP deadlines, or to account adequately for transportation growth in SIP planning. And while the conformity program does not apply in attainment areas, the tightening of the ozone and PM NAAQS will expand the reach of the conformity program by creating more nonattainment areas.

---

[42]40 C.F.R. § 51.390 *et seq.*, 58 Fed. Reg. 62188.
[43]40 C.F.R. § 51.850 *et seq.*, 58 Fed. Reg. 63214.

### 2.1.3 Enhanced Monitoring and Periodic Monitoring

In recognition that many SIPs do not clearly specify the methods to be used to determine compliance with emission limitations, EPA proposed a rulemaking under § 114 of the 1990 Amendments to the Act to establish requirements for "enhanced monitoring" of industrial emissions. This rulemaking was later split into two separate proceedings–the so-called "credible evidence" and "compliance assurance monitoring" (CAM) rules. The credible evidence rule, scheduled for promulgation in late 1996, will provide that any measurement technique that generates emissions data comparable to (and of the same duration as) EPA's reference methods (typically found in Appendix A to 40 C.F.R. Part 60), can be used to determine compliance with an emission limitation. As a practical matter, this rule could make many existing emission standards that were based on periodic stack tests more stringent, by making short-term average continuous emission monitor data the new compliance method.

The compliance assurance monitoring rule is scheduled for promulgation in mid-1997. It will require the development of monitoring plans in which industrial facilities will identify emission "trigger" levels below the level of applicable emission limitations, and specify "quality improvement programs" that apply when the trigger level is exceeded. As currently written, the second exceedance of a trigger level would itself constitute a violation of the Act. CAM plans will be implemented through the Title V operating permit program, which is discussed below.

## 2.2 New Source Control Programs

In enacting the 1970 and 1977 Amendments to the Act, Congress expressed concern that the costs of retrofitting existing sources with state-of-the-art control technologies could be prohibitively expensive. Congress concluded that it would be more cost-effective to require high levels of technological performance at new sources, because they have more flexibility as to location and design of control equipment than do existing sources.[44] As a result, new sources are subject to more stringent levels of control under the Act than existing sources.

### 2.2.1 New Source Performance Standards (NSPS)

Under §111 of the Act, Congress required the EPA Administrator to identify categories of new and modified sources that contribute significantly to air pollution that endangers public health or welfare. To date, EPA has identified over 60 such source categories, including most major industrial processes.[45]

For these source categories, EPA must set emission standards that reflect the "degree of emission reduction achievable" through the best technology that the Agency determines has been "adequately demonstrated," taking into consideration "non-air quality health and environmental impacts and energy requirements."[46] NSPS may be promulgated as design, equipment, work practice, or operational standards where numerical emission limitations are not feasible.[47]

---

[44]S. Rep. No. 91-1196, 91st Cong., 2d. Sess. 15-16 (1970).
[45]*See* 40 C.F.R. Part 60.
[46]CAA §111.
[47]CAA §111(h)(1).

Each NSPS in 40 C.F.R. Part 60 identifies the types of facilities (e.g., in terms of size and type of process) to which the standards apply. NSPS apply to any facility so identified on which construction is begun after the date of *proposal* of the NSPS. In addition, the NSPS apply to facilities that are "reconstructed" or "modified" after the date of proposal of the NSPS.

Once set, NSPS serve as the *minimum* level of control that must be achieved by new or modified sources, through the new source preconstruction permitting program (discussed below). In theory, NSPS must be reviewed at least every eight years and, if appropriate, revised through notice and comment rulemaking.[48] In practice, further review of NSPS takes place only infrequently.

In part as a result of the infrequent revision of NSPS, Congress in 1990 mandated several revisions to specific NSPS. For example, the 1990 Amendments repealed §111(a)(1) of the Act, which includes the percentage reduction requirement for large fossil fuel-fired boilers (1990 Amendments §403(a)), and required the Administrator to promulgate revised NSPS for $SO_2$ for this source category. The Administrator currently is under court order to propose revised NSPS for $NO_x$ emissions from fossil-fuel fired steam generating units.[49]

The Amendments also set a new regulatory schedule for source categories that were listed under §111, but not regulated, prior to enactment of the Amendments.[50] NSPS that EPA has undertaken to develop or revise in response to the 1990 Amendments include the NSPS for municipal waste combustion (MWC) units, municipal solid waste landfills and medical waste incinerators.[51]

### 2.2.2 New Source Review

Large new sources of air pollution (and, under certain conditions, major modifications to large existing sources) are subject to preconstruction review and permitting under the Clean Air Act. The nature of the preconstruction permitting requirements depends upon whether the source is to be located in an area that attains, or has failed to attain, the NAAQS for the pollutant in question.

Sources located in attainment areas are subject to the prevention of significant deterioration (PSD) permit program; sources in nonattainment areas are subject to the nonattainment permit program.[52] The PSD program applies to sources that have the potential to emit at least 250 tons per year (tpy) of a regulated pollutant, or at least 100 tpy of a regulated pollutant if the source falls within one of 28 listed source categories.[53] The nonattainment program applies to sources that have the potential to emit at least 10

---

[48]CAA §111(b)(1)(B).

[49]CAA §407(c).

[50]CAA §111(f)(1); 40 C.F.R. § 60.16 (source category priority list).

[51]The NSPS for MWC units was vacated by the D.C. Circuit on December 6, 1996. *Davis County SWM District v. EPA*, Nos. 95-1611, *et al.* (D.C. Cir., decided December 6, 1996).

[52]The PSD Program is contained in Title I, Part C, of the Clean Air Act, and the nonattainment program is contained in Title I, Part D of the Act.

[53]*See* 40 C.F.R. §52.21(b)(1).

to 100 tpy of the nonattainment pollutant, depending upon the pollutant in question and the seriousness of the nonattainment problem in the area in which the source is located.[54]

Whether a source has the "potential to emit" at these levels has traditionally been determined based on the maximum capacity of the source to emit under its physical and operational design, taking into account any regulatory limits on source operations that are "federal enforceable" (e.g., operating limits included in a SIP or new source permit).[55] In *National Mining Association v. EPA*, however, the D.C. Circuit set aside the requirement of the air toxics program that operational limits could be considered in defining a source's potential to emit only where the limit was "federally enforceable."[56] The D.C. Circuit subsequently applied this decision to vacate the federally enforceable requirement in the new source review and Title V potential to emit rules.[57] The court suggested that any limit that was "effective as a practical matter" should be considered in defining a source's potential to emit. EPA has issued several guidance documents addressing how potential to emit will be calculated pending issuance of revised rules.[58]

### 2.2.2.1 The PSD Program

Under the Clean Air Act, before one can construct a "major" (i.e., 100/250 tpy) new source, or undertake a "major modification" of an existing major source (as discussed below), in an area that attains the NAAQS, one must obtain a permit under the PSD program.[59] In order to receive a PSD permit, the owner or operator of the proposed new source or major modification must show that the source (1) will comply with ambient air quality levels designed to prevent deterioration of air quality (the "PSD increments"), (2) will employ "best available control technology" (BACT) for each pollutant regulated under the Act that it will emit in "significant" amounts, and (3) will avoid adverse impacts on federal "Class I" areas (including national wilderness areas and parks in existence on August 7, 1977 and greater than 5,000 or 6,000 ares in size, respectively).[60] BACT is defined as the "maximum degree of [emission] reduction . . . achievable," taking into account economic, energy, and environmental factors. BACT must be at least as stringent as any NSPS applicable to the source category.

Traditionally, both the amount of PSD increment a new source is allowed to consume and the BACT determination have been matters of state discretion. The BACT

---

[54]*See*, e.g., CAA §182(b)-(e).

[55]*See* 40 C.F.R. § 52.21(b)(4).

[56]59 F.3d 1351 (D.C. Cir. 1995).

[57]*Clean Air Implementation Project v. EPA*, No. 96-1224 (D.C. Cir. June 28, 1996); *Chemical Manufacturers Ass'n v. EPA*, No. 89-1514 (September 15, 1995).

[58]J. Seitz, Director EPA OAQPS, "Extension of January 25, 1995 PTE Transition Policy" (August 27, 1996); J. Seitz, Director EPA OAQPS, "Release of Interim Policy on Federal Enforceability of Limitations on Potential to Emit" (January 22, 1996); M. Nichols and S. Herman, EPA Assistant Administrator for Air Programs and Enforcement, "'Effective' Limits on Potential to Emit: Issues and Options" (January 31, 1996).

[59]*See generally* 40 C.F.R. §52.21.

[60]"Significance" levels are provided at 40 C.F.R. §52.21(b)(23).

determination, for example, has traditionally been based on the state's balancing of the economic, energy, and environmental impacts of alternative control technologies.[61]

With respect to the BACT determination, EPA in December 1987 issued guidance (referred to as the "top-down" BACT guidance) that, as applied, substantially restricted state discretion in making BACT determinations. In response to a judicial challenge, EPA agreed in 1991 to issue a *Federal Register* notice clarifying its position on BACT review. In July 1996, EPA finally proposed a rule addressing a variety of new source reform issues–including BACT, special requirements applicable to sources locating near national parks and other "Class I" areas (discussed below), and the definition of "major modification" (discussed below).

With respect to BACT determinations, the proposed rule would confirm that states that have developed PSD permitting programs as part of their SIPs would be able to continue to exercise broad discretion in determining BACT. Those few states that have been delegated authority to implement EPA's PSD program would have to continue to apply to top-down BACT policy.[62]

Since BACT review applies to any regulated pollutant that a source has the potential to emit in a "significant" amount (as defined by the PSD rules),[63] BACT review has traditionally focused on *both* criteria pollutants (i.e., pollutants subject to NAAQS) and air toxics. The 1990 Amendments to the Act, however, state that substances listed under the new air toxics program are *not* subject to the PSD program.[64] Since the air toxics list is extensive (i.e., 189 substances and compounds are currently listed), this provision should obviate the need for BACT review for regulated hazardous air pollutants once states revise their PSD programs in response to the 1990 Amendments. However, states may also choose to continue to require such analyses under state law. Moreover, state permitting authorities may require the applicant to consider the implications of any proposed BACT decision for the control of air toxics.

While the BACT determination is perhaps the most important and controversial aspect of PSD permitting, a variety of other issues must also be resolved in order to receive a permit to construct a major new source, or to modify a major existing source. As noted above, the applicant must show that the proposed source will not cause or contribute to exceedances of either NAAQS or PSD increments.[65] For sources proposed to be located near national parks or other "Class I" areas (as defined in CAA § 162), the applicant might also have to address allegations of the Federal Land Manager (FLM) of that area that the proposed source adversely impacts air quality-related values (AQRVs) of that area, such as visibility.

Special requirements applicable to sources located near Class I areas are addressed in more detail in a new source reform rule proposed in July 1996. This proposal would give the Federal Land Managers for Class I areas authority to identify the AQRVs of their Class I areas and to define what constitutes an "adverse impact" on those values. Under this proposal, pre-application notice must be given to FLMs for any source

---

[61]*See, e.g.*, 1980 PSD Workshop Manual I-B-2.

[62]*Compare* 61 Fed. Reg. 38332 (proposed § 51.166(j)(5) *with* 61 Fed. Reg. 38340 (proposed § 52.21(j)(5)).

[63]*See* 40 C.F.R. § 52.21(b)(23).

[64]CAA §112(b)(6).

[65]*See* CAA §§163, 166.

proposed to be located within 100 Kms of a Class I area. A computer data base would be created for sources to be located further away, and permit applicants would have to register on this data base in order to give FLMs an opportunity to object to the permitting of these sources as well.[66] A permit application could not be found "complete" and processed by a state permitting authority until the applicant had performed the analyses dictated by the FLM, and a state could not reject the findings of the FLM without detailed justification. In order to avoid permitting delays, the proposed rule encourages permit applicants to obtain emission offsets to mitigate potential Class I area impacts, and to undertake post-construction AQRV monitoring in Class I areas.

### 2.2.2.2. The Nonattainment Program

In areas that have not attained the NAAQS for a given pollutant (i.e., "nonattainment" areas), new major stationary sources, or major modifications of existing major sources, must receive a nonattainment permit before construction can begin. A "major" source for purposes of the nonattainment program is generally one that has the potential to emit in excess of 100 tpy of a nonattainment pollutant. The 1990 Amendments lower this threshold for areas with more serious nonattainment problems (e.g., to 50 tpy for VOC and $NO_x$ in serious ozone nonattainment areas, to 25 tpy for severe areas, and to 10 tpy for extreme areas). Moreover, in areas that are attainment for some regulated pollutants and nonattainment for others, both PSD and nonattainment permits may be required.

States are responsible for implementing the nonattainment permit program. State permit programs must include, among other things, a requirement that major new or modified existing sources commit to achieve the "Lowest Achievable Emission Rate" (LAER). LAER is to be based on "the most stringent emission limitation" contained in any SIP, or that is "achieved in practice" by the same or a similar source category, whichever is more stringent. If the owner or operator of the proposed source can demonstrate that the most stringent technology is not feasible for the proposed facility, the next most stringent level of control can be established as LAER.

In order to ensure progress towards attainment of the NAAQS, the state permit program must also require that the proposed new or modified source offset its potential to emit nonattainment pollutants by securing emission reductions from nearby facilities at a greater than one-to-one ratio. The Administrator is given authority to set rules for determining the "baseline" against which emission offsets are to be credited,[67] and EPA has issued extensive guidance on this issue.[68] Moreover, the Clean Air Act Amendments of 1990 define the offset ratios that apply in ozone, CO, and PM-10 nonattainment areas, and these ratios increase as the nonattainment problem becomes more severe. For example, the offset ratio in ozone nonattainment areas varies between 1.1 and 1.5 to 1, according to the seriousness of the area's nonattainment problem.

Finally, the source owner or operator must certify that its other sources are in compliance (or on a schedule to comply) with all applicable air quality requirements,

---

[66]61 Fed. Reg. 38285-86 (1996).

[67]CAA §173(a)(1)(A)

[68]*See*, e.g., 51 Fed. Reg. 43814 (1986) (Emissions Trading Policy Statement); 40 C.F.R. Part 51, Appendix S.

and that the benefits of the proposed source outweigh its environmental and social costs.[69]

### 2.2.3 The Reconstruction and Modification Rules

As noted above, new source requirements apply not only to new sources, but to existing sources that are "reconstructed" (for the NSPS program) or "modified" (for any of the new source programs).

**Reconstruction.** EPA promulgated the "reconstruction" rule in 1975 to address projects designed to extend the useful life of existing industrial facilities.[70] The rule defines when a project to rebuild an existing facility becomes so extensive that it is substantially equivalent to replacing the facility "at the end of its useful life."[71] The reconstruction rule triggers application of only the NSPS program, and *not* the PSD or nonattainment permit programs. A reconstruction rule has also been adopted in the context of the new air toxics program (discussed below).

In general, work to rebuild or to replace parts of an existing facility triggers the reconstruction rule when the project involves expenditures that are fifty percent or more of the capital cost of a comparable new facility.[72] Triggering the reconstruction rule does not, however, automatically result in application of NSPS. Rather, recognizing that control technology standards developed for new facilities may not be appropriate for reconstructed, existing facilities, EPA has provided that NSPS will not be applied to reconstructed facilities where the NSPS is shown to be technologically or economically infeasible, or where consideration of costs, remaining useful life, and potential emission reductions make it inappropriate to apply NSPS.[73]

When EPA promulgated the reconstruction rule, it stated that it did not anticipate that many facilities would trigger reconstruction review, and that it would address more specific concerns with "life extension" of existing sources in rulemakings establishing NSPS for specific source categories.[74] It is important, therefore, to examine the NSPS rules applicable to individual source categories for further guidance on when capital expenditures trigger application of NSPS.

**Modification.** Unlike the reconstruction rule, the modification rule can trigger application of the PSD and nonattainment permit programs as well as NSPS. The modification rule has the same basic elements for all of these programs. First, there must be a "physical or operational change" at the source. Second, this change must "result in" an "increase in emissions" of the regulated pollutant. Third, the modification rules list specific activities (e.g., routine repair, replacement, and maintenance) that do not constitute a modification, even if there is otherwise a physical or operational change that results in an emissions increase.

---

[69]*See* CAA §173(a).
[70]40 Fed. Reg. 58417 (1975); 40 C.F.R. §60.15.
[71]40 Fed. Reg. 58417 (1975).
[72]40 C.F.R. §60.15(b)(1).
[73]40 C.F.R. §60.15(b)(2), (f).
[74]39 Fed. Reg. 36948 (1974).

Application of the modification rule has been the subject of much controversy over the past decade. Starting with the so-called *WEPCo* guidance issued by EPA in 1987, EPA adopted what it called an "activist" approach to interpretation of the modification rules under which virtually *any* activity designed to restore lost capacity at an existing industrial facility (e.g., as a result of equipment breakdown), and that does not constitute "routine repair, replacement, or maintenance," would trigger NSPS and the new source permit programs. Under this activist interpretation of the modification rules, virtually any construction activity at an industrial facility, save the most routine maintenance or repair activity, would have to be preceded by preconstruction permit review. While the U.S. Court of Appeals for the Seventh Circuit largely accepted EPA's position regarding NSPS, it rejected key elements of its position regarding the PSD permit program.[75]

In 1990, Congress made several attempts to address and to clarify the *WEPCo* decision in the Clean Air Act Amendments. The final legislation contained no generic "fix", however, because EPA committed to undertake administrative action to clarify the modification rule along the lines of the Administration's legislative proposal.[76] The first set of clarifying rules (the so-called "*WEPCo* rule") was promulgated in July 1992.[77]

The *WEPCo* rule governing modification of major existing sources has two parts. First, the preamble to the rule contains the Agency's interpretations of the existing modification rules, which apply to all industry. This interpretive rule confirms that the Agency will in most respects return to its pre-*WEPCo* interpretations of the modification rules. For example, where an existing source has begun operation, the Agency will not calculate an "emissions increase" in the case of a proposed modification based on a comparison of past actual emissions and future potential to emit, but rather will apply a past-to-future-actual comparison. Moreover, the Agency will continue to exclude pollution control projects from the new source permitting rules. These interpretive rulings are important since they apply to *all* industry, whereas the formal legislative rule discussed below applies only to large utility boilers.

Second, in the legislative rule, the Agency clarified certain aspects of the modification rule as applied to large utility boilers subject to the acid deposition program (Title IV) of the 1990 Amendments. This rule has several general characteristics. First, the rule confirms that new source permitting requirements are not triggered when a facility has experienced equipment failure and has merely undertaken a project to return the facility to its former, representative production capacity. Second, while the rule confirms that pollution control projects do not trigger new source review, it tightens the traditional pollution control exclusion as applied to large utility boilers by extending the exclusion only to pollution control projects that result in a net environmental benefit. At the same time, the Agency confirms that virtually all pollution control projects do result in such a benefit. Third, the rule confirms that the test for new source review is whether a specific project "results in" (i.e., causes) an increase in emissions. As a result, where an emissions increase results from an increase in demand or in general economic activity, new source review is not required.

---

[75]*Wisconsin Electric Power Company [WEPCo] v. Reilly*, 893 F.2d 901 (7th Cir. 1990).

[76]Letter from William K. Reilly, EPA, to Michael Boskin, Council of Economic Advisors (Oct. 26, 1990).

[77]57 Fed. Reg. 32314 (1992).

In 1992, EPA formed a New Source Review Workshop to discuss further changes in the modification rule. As a result of the discussions of that group, EPA, in July 1994, issued a guidance memorandum discussing when pollution control projects at nonelectric utility sources should be excluded from NSR. This memorandum provides "interim guidance" pending promulgation of a "formal regulatory exclusion" for such projects in a future rulemaking.

In contrast to the *WEPCo* rule and EPA's description of the existing modification rule in the preamble of the *WEPCo* rule, this pollution control guidance would require that (1) existing sources obtain applicability determinations *before* installing pollution control equipment, (2) air quality modeling be performed whenever there is a significant increase in emissions in any pollutant from the pollution control project, and (3) any collateral emissions be "minimized," with offsets in nonattainment areas and risk assessments in the case of air toxics.

In July 1996, EPA published in the *Federal Register* a proposed rule revising the modification rules.[78] The draft proposal would codify the 1994 guidance on the pollution control exclusion in some respects, and further restrict the use of this exclusion by requiring analysis of impacts on "air quality related values" associated with significant emissions increases. The proposal solicits comment on whether this new approach should be extended to electric utility boilers, in place of the exclusion contained in the *WEPCo* rule.

This proposal also asks for comment on whether the NSR "emissions increase" determination should be based on a comparison of past actual versus future potential emissions, thereby reversing the 7th Circuit's *WEPCo* decision (although allowing a ten-year look back to establish past actual emissions). EPA also requests comment on whether it should eliminate the "demand growth" exclusion, under which emissions increases that result from changes in demand or economic conditions, as opposed to physical or operational changes, are not counted for purposes of calculating an "emissions increase." EPA also proposes to create a new exclusion from the modification rule for sources meeting BACT or LAER levels of emission reductions.

In many respects, this proposal represents a return to EPA's activist approach to the modification rule that preceded the 7th Circuit's *WEPCo* decision. As a result, this proposed rule is likely to be controversial since it could create significant obstacles to industry efforts to maintain reliable and efficient operations in an increasingly competitive international marketplace.

### 2.2.4 Minor New Source Review

Under § 110(a)(2) of the Act, states are to include in their SIPs programs for pre-construction review of minor new or modified sources to the extent necessary to attain and to maintain compliance with the NAAQS. States have substantial authority as to the coverage, the substantive content, and the procedural format of minor new source review programs.

The minor new source review requirement received increased attention in the wake of the 1990 Amendments to the Clean Air Act, as a way of imposing federally enforceable operating limits on industrial facilities to avoid triggering applicability of

---

[78]61 Fed. Reg. 38260-63 (1996).

major new source review or Title V operating permit programs. In the proposed new source review reform rule, EPA envisions the minor new source review program as playing a more important role–e.g., as the vehicle for implementing the new restrictions it would impose on the pollution control project exclusion (discussed above).[79] Given the potentially broad coverage of minor new source review program and the requirement for annual compliance certifications under the new Title V operating permit program (discussed below), it is important that all source owner/operators familiarize themselves with their state's minor new source review program.

## 2.3 Specific Pollution Problems

Besides establishing generally applicable air quality and control technology requirements, the Clean Air Act addresses a number of specific pollution problems. The most important of these programs involve air toxics emissions, acid rain, visibility degradation, and stratospheric ozone-depleting substances. The Act also addresses the special concerns presented by mobile source emissions.

### 2.3.1 Air Toxics

Congress, in the 1990 Amendments, altered the principal focus of the air toxics program under §112 of the Clean Air Act from health-based to technology-based regulation. The following discussion summarizes the key elements of this new air toxics regulatory program.

#### 2.3.1.1 Pollutants and Source Categories Subject to Regulation

Under the 1990 Amendments, 189 substances will be regulated including both hazardous organics and metals.[80] Substances can be added to or deleted from this list after rulemaking.

The Act provides that any stationary source having the "potential to emit" (a concept discussed under the new source review program) more than 10 tons per year of any of the listed substances, or 25 tons per year of any combination of the substances, is considered a major source and is subject to regulation under the major source program. Whether a source is "major" for purposes of the air toxics program is defined by adding together the potential to emit of all emission units located at a common site and subject to common ownership, regardless of whether those emission units belong to the same industrial category or are otherwise functionally related.[81] EPA must examine all other sources for regulation (i.e., any isolated minor emission units) under an "area source" program. This program was to be developed within five years of enactment of the 1990 Amendments (i.e., by November 15, 1995), but area source standards have been issued for only a handful of source categories.

In July 1992, EPA published an initial list of 174 major source categories of hazardous air pollutants, such as oil refineries, chemical plants and the like, which are to be regulated under §112.[82] In September 1992, EPA followed this list of source categories with a draft schedule for promulgation of emission standards, which specifies

---

[79]61 Fed. Reg. 38263 (1996).
[80]*See* CAA §112(b). Prior to 1990, EPA had addressed 33 substances under §112.
[81]*NMA v. EPA*, 59 F.3d 1351 (D.C. Cir. 1995).
[82]57 Fed. Reg. 31576 (1992); *see* CAA §112(c).

when each of the listed source categories will be regulated.[83]  EPA updates this list periodically and, according to EPA's latest § 112 list, air toxics standards have been issued or are in various stages of development for well over 50 source categories of emissions.[84]

### 2.3.1.2 Maximum Achievable Emission Limitations

For each listed category of major sources, EPA must promulgate standards requiring the installation of technology that will result in the "maximum degree of reductions" that is "achievable," in light of economic, energy and environmental considerations.  (This requirement has been referred to as the "maximum achievable control technology," or "MACT," standard.)  EPA is to base the standard on the best technology currently available for the source category in question, and these standards must be at least as stringent as the level achieved in practice by the best controlled source in the source category (for new source MACT standards) or for the best performing group of sources (for existing source MACT standards).[85]  For existing source MACT standards, EPA defines the "MACT floor" (i.e., the minimum stringency level for existing source MACT) in terms of the central tendency (i.e., arithmetic mean or median) of the best performing 12 percent of sources in the source category (where there are 30 or more sources in the category) or the best performing 5 sources (where there are fewer than 30 sources in the category).

These MACT standards are to be issued according to the schedule originally issued by EPA in September 1992.  The first proposed MACT standards, referred to as the hazardous organic NESHAP or "HON," were finalized in March 1994.  The HON addresses emissions of 112 air toxics from approximately 370 synthetic and nonsynthetic organic chemical manufacturers, and over 940 chemical manufacturing processes.  The proposed standards require control of emissions from distillation, reactor and air oxidation process vents, waste water operations, storage vessels, transfer operations, and equipment leaks.

Other source categories regulated by MACT standards include coke ovens, industrial cooling towers, halogenated solvent cleaning, magnetic tape manufacturing operations, gasoline terminals and pipeline breakout stations, petroleum refinery sources, aerospace manufacturing, wood furniture manufacturing, printing and publishing, and various aspects of polymer and resin production.[86]  An updated schedule for future MACT development was published by EPA on June 4, 1996.[87]  Over a dozen additional MACT standards are due to be issued by November 15, 1997, including standards for primary and secondary aluminum production, ferroalloys production, steel foundries, oil and natural gas production, agricultural chemicals production, pharmaceutical production, and certain types of resin, polymer, and inorganic chemical

---

[83]57 Fed. Reg. 44147 (1992).
[84]*See* 61 Fed. Reg. 28197 (1996).
[85]*See* CAA §112(d).
[86]*See generally* 40 C.F.R. Part 63.
[87]61 Fed. Reg. 28197 (1996).

production. A complete list of MACT rules under development is contained in the Agency's semi-annual regulatory agenda.[88]

EPA has also issued regulations allowing exemptions from the MACT standards for existing sources where the source demonstrates that it has achieved a voluntary reduction of 90 percent or more in emissions of a hazardous air pollutant before proposal of the MACT standard (95 percent for hazardous air pollutants that are particulates). In this case, the source may be eligible for an extension of the MACT compliance deadline.[89] Final rules implementing this early reduction program were signed by the EPA Administrator in November 1992, and were amended in November 1993.[90] A final rule defining "high risk" pollutants for purposes of this "early reduction" program (i.e., pollutants for which the use of offsets to establish program eligibility is limited) was issued in June 1994,[91] and a final rule providing a temporary permit mechanism to make early reductions enforceable was published in November 1994.[92]

### 2.3.1.3 Case-specific MACT

Where EPA has missed the deadline for establishing a federal MACT standard for a source category, § 112(j) of the CAA requires that the Title V permit program be used to establish case-specific MACT standards. In June 1994, EPA promulgated rules providing guidance for establishment of case-specific MACT standards when EPA fails to promulgate a federal standard.[93] In general, states with approved Title V programs must establish source-specific MACT standards through a Title V permit proceeding, within 18 months of the missed regulatory deadline. In May 1996, EPA extended the effective date of the § 112(j) program to November 15, 1996, to avoid forcing states to establish case-specific MACT standards for source categories subject to the November 1994 MACT deadline.[94]

Under § 112(g) of the Act, permitting authorities must also establish case-by-case MACT standards for new, modified or reconstructed sources, where no federal MACT standard has been set.[95] Such standards would be set through a pre-construction review procedure. As of this writing, EPA plans to revise and to reissue its original § 112(g) proposed rules, in order to require case-specific MACT standards for only new and reconstructed sources, *not* modified sources. A new unit would trigger review if it had the potential to emit 10 tons or more of an individual air toxic, or 25 tons or more of a combination of air toxics. It is unclear, however, whether the reconstruction test (discussed above under the new source heading) would apply to individual emission units theoretically requiring MACT determination for individual valves or vents) or to some aggregation of emission units.

---

[88]61 Fed. Reg. 63183 (1996).
[89]*See* CAA §112(i)(5).
[90]58 Fed. Reg. 62539 (1993).
[91]59 Fed. Reg. 32165 (1994).
[92]59 Fed. Reg. 59921 (1994).
[93]59 Fed. Reg. 26429 (1994).
[94]61 Fed. Reg. 21370 (1996).
[95]59 Fed. Reg. 15504 (1994).

Finally, EPA has issued rules under § 112(l) of the Act providing guidance on the development of federally approvable state air toxics programs.[96] Under these rules (which were upheld by the D.C. Circuit in response to industry and environmental group challenges[97]), state air toxics programs could be substituted for the federal air toxics program where the state could demonstrate that its program was at least as stringent as the federal program.

### 2.3.1.4 Residual Risks

Because the MACT standards are technology rather than health-based, the 1990 Amendments provide for a second phase of regulatory controls aimed at protecting public health with an "ample margin of safety." This health-based inquiry would generally take place no later than eight years after a MACT standard has been established for a source category. As a result, the first residual risk standards are theoretically due by the year 2001. For known or suspected carcinogens, this subsection would require consideration of further control if the MACT standard does not reduce life time risk to the most exposed individual to a level of less than one-in-one million.[98]

In January 1997, EPA announced a "Risk Identification Program" to be used to set priorities for regulating hazardous air pollutants, source categories, and geographic areas pursuant to the § 112(f) residual risk program. EPA intends to file a report with Congress during 1997 describing its plans for implementation of § 112(f).

### 2.3.1.5 Control of Accidental Releases

The 1990 Amendments require EPA to promulgate regulations to control and to prevent accidental releases of regulated hazardous pollutants or any other extremely hazardous substances defined by the Act.[99] Owners and operators of facilities at which such substances are present in more than a threshold quantity must prepare risk management plans for each substance used at the facility. EPA may also require annual audits and safety inspections to prevent leaks and other episodic releases. EPA promulgated its List of Regulated Substances under §112(r) on January 31, 1994,[100] and issued regulations implementing the Accidental Release Prevention Program on June 20, 1996.[101]

### 2.3.2 Acid Rain

One of the major new regulatory programs of the 1990 Amendments concerns the control of sulfur dioxide ($SO_2$) and nitrogen oxides ($NO_x$), precursors of acid deposition. The centerpiece of Title IV of the 1990 Amendments is the establishment of an emissions allowance and trading program for $SO_2$.

---

[96]58 Fed. Reg. 62262 (1993); 61 Fed. Reg. 36295 (1996).
[97]*Louisiana Environmental Action Network v. EPA*, 87 F.3d 1379 (D.C. Cir. 1996).
[98]*See* CAA §112(f).
[99]*See* CAA §112(r).
[100]59 Fed. Reg. 4478.
[101]61 Fed. Reg. 31668 (1996).

On January 11, 1993, EPA published final rules addressing acid rain permits,[102] $SO_2$ emission allowance tracking and trading,[103] emissions monitoring, [104]excess emissions penalties and offset plans,[105] and the administrative appeals process.[106] EPA also issued the standard forms needed for permit applications and compliance plans. Final $SO_2$ allowance allocations were published in March 1993.[107] Proposed adjustments of allowance allocations for a limited number of electric utility units are scheduled for publication in December 1996.

Sources subject to emission limitations under Title IV were assigned $SO_2$ allowances under formulas prescribed in the statute.[108] An allowance is defined as an authorization to emit one ton of $SO_2$. A unit's annual $SO_2$ emissions will not be allowed to exceed the allowances allocated to or purchased or otherwise acquired by the unit for a given calendar year, or the unit's owner/operator will be subject to penalties that are designed to be more costly than compliance. The 1990 Amendments specify that allowances are not a property right and can be limited, revoked or modified by the federal government.

The Act makes specific $SO_2$ allowance allocations to Phase I utility boilers (i.e., utility boilers that must meet reduction targets by January 1, 1995), and specifies formulas for other boilers. A unit's allowance allocation is made part of its Title IV permit. In addition, source owners and operators may submit compliance plans to pursue certain optional control strategies.[109] In November 1994, EPA revised the rules governing compliance plans in a way that would greatly reduce the number of allowances that a utility would receive for voluntarily bringing Phase II units into Phase I compliance, although EPA agreed as part of a litigation settlement to provide some additional allowances in the case of plans that utilities had already submitted.

EPA's Title IV regulations set up an allowance auction to be held annually.[110] Anyone eligible to hold allowances may purchase at the auction. In addition, holders of allowances can also contribute to the auction and receive a pro rata share of the monies collected. EPA has held auctions every March beginning in 1993. All of the Phase I and Phase II allowances offered by EPA were purchased each year. The average price in the first auction was approximately $150/allowance, and the average price decreased to a low of about $70 in the 1996 auction.

In April 1995, the Agency promulgated regulations addressing criteria and procedures for allowing owners and operators of industrial boilers, small utility boilers, and other combustion sources not subject to the mandatory requirements of Title IV voluntarily to opt into the Title IV program.[111] The purpose of the opt-in program is to increase the amount of allowances available, while expanding the scope of sources

---

[102]40 C.F.R. Part 72
[103]40 C.F.R. Part 73
[104]40 C.F.R. Part 75
[105]40 C.F.R. Part 77
[106]40 C.F.R. Part 78
[107]58 Fed. Reg. 15634 (1993).
[108]*See* CAA §403.
[109]CAA §408.
[110]*See* CAA §416.
[111]CAA §410.

subject to the Title IV control requirements. Sources that opt into the program, of course, are subject to all of the permitting and monitoring requirements of this program. Some aspects of these rules were challenged in court; on one issue, the court upheld the Agency's interpretation of the statute in October 1996, and other issues are subject to settlement negotiations. Units at only two plants in the country have "opted in" as of the date of this publication.

Title IV of the Act also addresses emissions of nitrogen oxides ($NO_x$). Under §407 of the Act, EPA was to establish allowable emission rates for $NO_x$ emissions from certain categories of coal-fired electric utility boilers subject to Phase I of the acid deposition program by May 1992. These rules were proposed in November 1992 and, after litigation before the U.S. Court of Appeals for the District of Columbia Circuit, were finally promulgated in April 1995.[112] A second set of $NO_x$ emission standards applicable to the remaining categories of Phase I and Phase II boilers–and more stringent standards for the boilers subject to the 1995 rule–are scheduled to be promulgated in December 1996.[113]

### 2.3.3 Visibility Protection and Air Quality Related Values

#### 2.3.3.1 Best Available Retrofit Technology

In the 1977 Clean Air Act Amendments, Congress established a national goal of eliminating "any" manmade visibility impairment in "mandatory Class I areas,"[114] and required that states make "reasonable progress" towards attaining that goal. To achieve that goal, states are to develop requirements for best available retrofit technology (BART) and long-term strategies that address sources contributing to visibility impairment in Class I areas as part of the SIP process.

In 1980, EPA adopted regulations addressing the criteria for SIPs for visibility impairment, and directed states to focus regulatory attention on sources that cause "plume blight" (i.e., visible plumes in a Class I area). Another more controversial issue—the regulation of sources contributing to "regional haze"—was specifically deferred.

During the 1980s, EPA found that, for all but one state and one Class I area, there were no sources to which plume blight could be "reasonably attributed." Accordingly, in reviewing the adequacy of SIPs, EPA concluded that the 1980 visibility rules were satisfied by current SIP requirements except to the extent that the states needed to incorporate in their SIPs procedural requirements to ensure that visibility impairment would be addressed (e.g., through establishment of BART limits) if it were to occur. In the early 1990s, however, EPA concluded that visibility impairment in the Grand Canyon in Arizona could be "reasonably attributed" to the Navajo Generating Station (an electric utility plant), and therefore initiated a regulatory program to address this issue. This finding was based on a Park Service study in 1987 and a study by the owners of the Navajo Generating Station in 1990, both of which involved the release of an

---

[112]60 Fed. Reg. 18751 (1995).

[113]61 Fed. Reg. 1443 (1996) (proposed rule).

[114]Mandatory class I areas include international parks, national wilderness areas and national memorial parks which exceed 5,000 acres in size, and national parks which exceed 6,000 acres in size, if the areas were in existence on August 7, 1977. CAA §162(a).

artificial tracer from the stacks of the Navajo Generating Station. Based on these studies and extensive public comment, EPA published a formal BART rule on October 3, 1991 that calls for 90-percent scrubbing on a plant-wide, annual average basis.[115] This proceeding establishes important precedent for future efforts to regulate existing sources that contribute to visibility impairment.

### 2.3.3.2 Visibility Impairment, AQRVs, and the New Source Review Program

Under the prevention of significant deterioration (PSD) permit program, before a permitting authority can issue a permit authorizing construction of a new or modified source, it must consider whether emissions from the proposed source "will have an adverse impact on air quality-related values (*including visibility*)."[116] Based on this provision, Federal Land Managers (FLMs) have raised the issue of visibility impairment in a number of new source permit proceedings over the past several years. The Forest Service, for example, has developed a workbook to guide local FLMs in deciding whether proposed new sources would have an adverse impact on the air quality-related values (AQRVs) of Class I areas. This workbook indicates that the Forest Service is dissatisfied with the current air quality in many Class I areas and advises FLMs to challenge the licensing of any new source. The National Park Service has taken a similar approach (e.g., with respect to facilities proposed to be located in the vicinity of the Shenandoah National Park), urging that proposed new facilities obtain offsetting emission reductions to ensure that there is no contribution to atmospheric loadings of emissions that the FLMs regard as unacceptable.

As part of the NSR reform rulemaking proposed in July 1996, EPA has proposed to give the FLM a more important role in permit proceedings for new and modified sources. Under this proposed rule, the FLM would be responsible for defining the AQRVs for the parks they manage, as well as what constitutes an adverse impact on those values. Permit applicants would have to provide notice of new source permit applications to the FLM and, if the FLM filed a notice alleging that emissions from the proposed facility might cause an adverse impact on an AQRV, the permit applicant would have to complete AQRV analyses dictated by the FLM before the state could find the application "complete" (a finding that triggers a statutory one-year deadline for action on the permit application). Ultimately, a state could not issue a permit until the concerns of the FLM were resolved. According to the proposed rule, one way of resolving the FLM's concerns would be to mitigate any adverse impact by purchasing emission offsets and installing additional control technology.[117]

Because this proposed rule shifts significant permitting authority from states to FLMs, it is controversial and the outcome of this rulemaking is uncertain. Nevertheless, a number of FLM are attempting to exercise the type of authority contemplated by the proposed rule in individual permit proceedings.[118]

---

[115]56 Fed. Reg. 50172 (1991).

[116]*See* CAA §165(d) (emphasis added).

[117]61 Fed. Reg. 38283-95 (1996).

[118]*See, e.g.,* Letter from J. Daniel, Director Air Division, Virginia Dep't of Envt'l Quality, to , Wegman, EPA OAQPS (September 19, 1996).

### 2.3.3.3 Visibility Impairment and the 1990 Amendments

The 1990 Amendments to the Act also addressed visibility in several respects. First, Congress authorized a $40 million, 5-year research program to evaluate Class I area visibility impairment.

Second, Congress established a procedure for creating Visibility Transport Commissions made up of Governors from states with sources that contribute to interstate air pollution in Class I areas. These commissions are to produce recommendations for EPA within four years after their creation about whether compliance with other programs of the 1990 Amendments (e.g., the acid rain program) would solve air quality problems in the Class I areas.

Finally, EPA plans to undertake rulemaking addressing development of a regulatory program requiring regional (multi-state) planning to address regional visibility in groupings of Class I areas. Controls on industrial sources would be required based on a balancing of costs versus visibility and environmental benefits.

### 2.3.4 Stratospheric Ozone Protection

Title VI of the Clean Air Act Amendments of 1990 addresses stratospheric ozone depletion and global warming, establishing a program for the phaseout of ozone depleting substances generally along the lines called for by the *Montreal Protocol.*

In Title VI, Congress has established initial lists of so-called Class I substances (*i.e.*, chlorofluorocarbons (CFCs), halons, carbon tetrachloride, and methyl chloroform) and Class II substances (*i.e.*, hydrochlorofluorocarbons (HCFCs)). EPA is directed to list additional substances, as warranted, and to assign ozone-depletion and global warming "potential values" to each listed substance.

Beginning in 1991, it is unlawful for any person to produce any Class I substance in an annual quantity greater than certain percentages specified in a table set forth in the statute. Exceptions are made for "essential uses" of methyl chloroform, for medical devices that employ Class I substances, and where aviation safety (*e.g.*, nondestructive testing for metal fatigue and engine corrosion) demands the use of such substances. Beginning in 2000 (or, 2002 for methyl chloroform), all production of Class I substances is prohibited. Title VI also calls for the complete phaseout of the use and production of Class II substances (again, with an exception for medical devices) by 2030. In February 1992, the Bush Administration initiated efforts to accelerate this schedule, and a final rule implementing the accelerated phaseout was promulgated on November 30, 1993. Pursuant to this rule, the production of all CFCs, methyl chloroform, and carbon tetrachloride was eliminated by January 1, 1996. The production of halons was phased out by January 1, 1994. As for HCFCs, the final rule provides for a phaseout schedule on a compound-specific basis depending on the ozone depleting potential of these Class II substances. The earliest phaseout date is January 1, 2003; the latest is January 1, 2030.

EPA is further directed to establish transferable "allowances" for the production and use of Class I and Class II substances, and to issue regulations concerning (1) the safe use, recycling, disposal, and release of Class I and Class II substances from appliances and industrial process refrigeration, (2) the servicing of motor vehicle air conditioners, (3) the eventual prohibition of nonessential products using Class I and Class II substances, and (4) the labeling of products made with or containing Class I and Class II substances. Title VI also orders EPA to develop a "safe alternatives" policy.

Rules establishing the allowance trading system were promulgated in July 1992. In addition, the Agency has now issued the refrigerant recycling rule (May 1993), regulations on motor vehicle air conditioner servicing (July 1992), the nonessential products ban (January 1993 for Class I substances; December 1993 for Class II substances), the labeling rule (February 1993 and October 1994), and the safe alternatives policy (March 1994).[119]

### 2.3.5 Mobile Sources, Fuels, and Fuel Additives

Besides addressing stationary source issues, the 1990 Amendments substantially tighten mobile source emission standards. The Amendments require automobile manufacturers to reduce tailpipe emissions of hydrocarbons (HC) and $NO_x$ by 35 percent and 60 percent, respectively, beginning with 40 percent of the vehicles sold in 1994 and increasing to 100 percent of vehicles sold in 1996.[120] The Amendments also require a further 50-percent reduction in mobile source emissions of these pollutants beginning in 2003, unless EPA finds that these more stringent standards are not necessary, technologically feasible, or cost effective.

In addition to establishing new mobile source emission standards, the Amendments establish two new fuel-related programs designed to achieve emission reductions.[121] The first of these fuel programs—the reformulated fuel program—requires the use of reformulated gasoline in certain CO and severe ozone nonattainment areas beginning in 1992 and 1995, respectively. Among other things, reformulated gasoline must be blended to achieve reductions in volatile organic compounds and toxic tailpipe emissions. Regulations implementing this provision were published in February 1994.[122]

The second fuel program is the clean fuel vehicle program. Under this program, automobiles operating on "clean alternative fuels" (e.g., methanol, ethanol, natural gas, and reformulated gasoline) must meet even more stringent emission standards. The clean fuel vehicle program will be implemented in two ways: (1) by establishing a California pilot test program which requires the production and sale of 300,000 clean fuel vehicles annually by 1999; and (2) by requiring operators of centrally fueled fleets of ten or more vehicles in certain CO and ozone nonattainment areas to purchase and use clean fuel vehicles beginning in 1998.

Finally, the Agency issued its long-awaited rules on registration of fuels and fuel additives in June 1994.[123] Under these rules, a new fuel or fuel additive cannot be introduced into commerce until the manufacturer completes potentially extensive testing addressing the public health risks associated with use of the product. Existing fuels and fuel additives are given six years to comply with these testing requirements.

While Congress clearly envisioned the continued use of traditional emission control technology to achieve the emission reductions required by the Amendments, the success or failure of the new program for clean fuels will have a dramatic impact on attainment of the ozone NAAQS in many areas of the country.

---

[119] 40 C.F.R. Part 82.
[120] *See* CAA §202.
[121] *See* CAA §§211(k) and 241-50.
[122] 59 Fed. Reg. 7716 (1994).
[123] 59 Fed. Reg. 33042 (1994).

## 2.4 The Operating Permit Program

Prior to 1990, the only permit program contained in the Clean Air Act was the preconstruction permitting program for new and modified sources. While EPA issued guidance in the late 1980s addressing how a state, through its SIP, could create a federally enforceable operating permit program,[124] few states took advantage of this guidance. As a result, from the standpoint of federal law, existing sources were regulated almost exclusively through provisions established in state implementation plans (SIPs) and preconstruction permits, rather than through source-specific operating permits.

Title V of the 1990 Clean Air Act Amendments changed the basic approach to source-specific regulation under the Act, by requiring each state to develop and implement a comprehensive operating permit program for most sources of air pollution. The purpose of this new permit program is to consolidate in a single document all of the federal regulations applicable to a source, in order to facilitate source compliance and enforcement. With few exceptions, Title V does not authorize the creation of new substantive federal requirements. Permit programs will be administered by the states, but EPA will retain authority to review and to approve not only the overall permit program, but also each individual permit issued by the state.

In July 1992, EPA issued final regulations addressing the minimum requirements for state operating permit programs.[125] Based on these minimum requirements, most states have developed Title V operating permit programs and have submitted these programs to EPA for approval. (EPA's "Clean Air Act Operating Permits Program Fact Sheet" provides a continuously updated source of information on the status of each state and local Title V permit program.) Once the state permit programs have received EPA approval, sources subject to the program generally have one year to submit permit applications. In some cases, states may require the submittal of permit applications even before final EPA approval of state programs.

Immediately after promulgation of the July 1992 regulations, several industry groups, environmental organizations, and states challenged the Title V rules in the D.C. Circuit.[126] The parties jointly requested a stay in briefing for most issues, in order to encourage settlement. A number of the issues raised in the litigation are the focus of rulemaking proposals issued by EPA on August 29, 1994,[127] and August 31, 1995.[128] These proposals would amend several elements of the existing Part 70 regulations, including those pertaining to when sources must seek revisions to their operating permits and the procedures applicable to each type of revision.

The following discussion summarizes the general features of the current program and, where possible, notes areas where change is likely.

### 2.4.1 Applicability

Section 70.3(a) of the Title V regulations requires a state program to provide for the permitting of at least the following sources:

---

[124]54 Fed. Reg. 27274 (1989).

[125]57 Fed. Reg. 32250 (1992), codified at 40 C.F.R. Part 70.

[126]Docket No. 92-1303, and consolidated cases.

[127]59 Fed. Reg. 44460 (1994).

[128]60 Fed. Reg. 45530 (1995).

1.  Any major source, defined in §70.2 of the rules as any stationary source belonging to a single major industrial grouping and that is:
    (i)   a major source under §112 of the Act;
    (ii)  a major source of air pollutants that directly emits or has the potential to emit 100 tons per year or more of any air pollutant (including any major source of fugitive emissions of any such pollutant); and
    (iii) a major source as defined in Part D of Title I of the Act;
2.  Any source subject to a standard, limitation, or other requirement under §111 of the Act;
3.  Any source subject to a standard or other requirement under §112 of the Act (although a source is not required to obtain a permit solely because it is subject to regulation under §112(r) dealing with accidental release prevention);
4.  Any affected source under Title IV of the Act; and
5.  Any source in a source category designated by EPA.

A state may defer for five years regulation of nonmajor sources, and EPA has provided for additional deferrals for certain non major sources of air toxics in specific § 112 standards.[129] Section 70.5(c) also allows the states to develop exemptions for insignificant activities because of size, emission levels, or production rate. The rules preclude establishment of exemptions, however, if they would interfere with the determination or imposition of any applicable requirement or the calculation of fees.[130]

### 2.4.2 Permit Applications

A source subject to the Title V program must submit a complete permit application, including a compliance plan describing how the source plans to comply with all applicable requirements where there is noncompliance, to the state permitting authority within one year after the permit program becomes effective.[131] A permit program becomes effective upon approval by EPA, whether that approval is interim, partial, or full.

If a state fails to implement an adequate Title V program of their own, a federal operating permit program will be applied, either by EPA or by the state under a delegation of authority from EPA. EPA issued rules governing this federal operating permit program on July 1, 1996, which rules appear at 40 C.F.R. Part 71.[132]

The permitting authority must determine whether the application is complete within sixty days after receipt of an application. Unless the permitting authority requests additional information or otherwise notifies the applicant of incompleteness within this time period, the application is deemed complete.[133]

---

[129]J. Seitz, Director EPA OAQPS, "Title V Permitting for Nonmajor Sources in Recent § 112 MACT Standards" (May 16, 1995).

[130]57 Fed. Reg. 32273.

[131]40 C.F.R. §70.5(a)(1), §503(a) of the Act. However, §70.5(a)(1)(i) stipulates that the permitting authority may establish an earlier date for submission of a permit application.

[132]61 Fed. Reg. 34202 (1996).

[133]40 C.F.R. §70. 7(a)(4).

In general, if a source submits a timely and complete permit application, failure to have a permit is not considered a violation of the statutory requirement to operate with a permit, at least until the permitting authority takes final action on the application.[134] This protection is called the "application shield."

A permit application must contain all information listed in §70.5(c), including: (i) all emissions of pollutants for which the source is major and all emissions of "regulated air pollutants;" (ii) identification of all points of emissions; (iii) emission rates in tons per year and in other terms necessary to establish compliance; (iv) description of air pollution control equipment; (v) identification of all federal air pollution control requirements; (vi) monitoring and measurement techniques used to demonstrate compliance with federal applicable requirements; and (vii) a statement of current compliance status with respect to all federally applicable requirements, and a schedule for compliance in the event of noncompliance. A responsible corporate official must certify the truth, accuracy and completeness of the application. States have developed standard application forms for use in satisfying the Title V permit application requirement.

### 2.4.3 Permit Issuance

The permitting authority must take final action within 18 months after receiving a complete application.[135] However, anticipating the administrative burden of establishing the new permitting program, Congress, in §503(c) of the Act, provided for a phased schedule over three years for acting on initial Title V permit applications. The permitting authority must act on one third of the permit applications received in the first year of the program in each year over a three year period following program approval by EPA. EPA makes clear in the preamble to the Title V rules that "act on" means final action rather than initial review.[136]

The permitting authority must issue permits for a fixed term of no more than five years. Each permit must include: (i) applicable emission limitations and standards; (ii) monitoring and related recordkeeping and reporting requirements; (iii) a permit condition prohibiting emissions of sulfur dioxide exceeding any allowances held under Title IV of the Act (for affected sources); (iv) a severability clause to ensure continued validity of remaining permit requirements if any provisions are challenged; (v) a statement that the permit may be modified, revoked, reopened, and reissued or terminated for cause; and (vi) a provision to ensure that a source pays fees consistent with an approved state permitting fee schedule. Insignificant emission units must be covered by the permit to the extent they are subject to applicable requirements.[137]

The permit also must contain the compliance requirements listed in §70.6(c), including (i) compliance certification, testing, monitoring, reporting, and recordkeeping requirements to assure compliance with the permit (including any terms needed to "fill gaps" in applicable compliance requirements); (ii) inspection and entry requirements for permitting authority officials; and (iii) a schedule of compliance and provisions for regular progress reports. When EPA issues the "compliance assurance monitoring"

---

[134]40 C.F.R. §70.7(b).
[135]40 C.F.R. §70.7(a)(2).
[136]57 Fed. Reg. 32266.
[137]61 Fed. Reg. 39335 (1996).

(CAM) rule in mid-1997 (discussed above), CAM plans will have to be included in Title V permits. If promulgated in its current form, exceedances of the emission level in the CAM plan that triggers implementation of a quality improvement program will have to be reported as an exception to the Title V compliance certification.

Finally, pursuant to §70.6(b)(2), the permit must "specifically designate as not being federally enforceable . . . any terms and conditions included in the permit that are not required under the Act or any of its applicable requirements" (e.g., state-only requirements). Such terms and conditions are not subject to Title V requirements regarding permit issuance, permit modification, and EPA and affected state review. Any terms not otherwise designated, however, *are federally enforceable* by either EPA or citizens under the citizen suit provisions of the Act.

Prior to permit issuance, the permitting authority must provide procedures for public notice, a comment period of at least 30 days, and the opportunity to request a public hearing on the draft permit.[138]

### 2.4.4 EPA and Affected State Review of Permit Applications

Section 70.8(a) requires the permitting authority to provide to EPA a copy of each permit application, draft permit, and final permit issued under Part 70. EPA may comment on a permit application or draft permit.

The permitting authority must also give notice of each draft permit to any affected state on or before the time public notice is provided.[139] An affected state is one whose air quality may be affected *and* that is contiguous to the state in which the source is located, or within 50 miles of the source.

If EPA objects to a proposed final permit within 45 days of receipt, the permitting authority may not issue the permit. Under §70.8(c), EPA must object to issuance of any proposed permit deemed not to be in compliance with the requirements of Part 70. If the permitting authority fails to revise and resubmit the proposed permit to EPA within 90 days of receipt of the objection notice, EPA must issue or deny the permit.[140]

If EPA does not object to the proposed permit, any person (including an affected state) may petition the Agency to object within sixty days after expiration of the 45-day EPA review period.[141] The petition must be based on objections to the permit that were raised with reasonable specificity during the public comment period, unless the petitioner demonstrates that it was impracticable to raise such objections within that period, or unless the grounds for the objection arose after that period. A petition for review does not stay the effectiveness of a permit if it was issued after EPA's original 45-day review period.[142]

### 2.4.5 The Permit Shield

Section 504(f) of the Act provides that compliance with the permit shall be deemed compliance with applicable provisions of the Act. This permit shield is optional with the states, however. Section 70.6(f) provides that the permitting authority may include

---

[138]40 C.F.R. §70.7(h).
[139]40 C.F.R. §70.8(b)(1).
[140]40 C.F.R. §70.8(c).
[141]40 C.F.R. §70.8(d).
[142]40 C.F.R. §70.8(d).

in a permit an express statement that compliance with the conditions of the permit shall be deemed compliance with any applicable requirements *as of the date of issuance* if (i) the applicable requirements are specifically identified in the permit, or (ii) the permitting authority determines in writing that other requirements specifically identified do not apply to the source and the permit includes that determination. If the permit does not expressly state that a permit shield applies, then no shield will be presumed.

### 2.4.6 Permit Revision and Operational Flexibility

The present Title V rules establish several categories of permit revisions. These requirements were the subject of intense debate throughout the rulemaking and the ensuing litigation, with industry and state agencies generally arguing for limited review of permit revisions during the five-year permit term and environmental groups in favor of more extensive interim review. At the heart of this debate is the issue of how much flexibility a source should have to change its operations without having to undertake a full-blown permit proceeding.

As a result of the judicial challenges to the final rule, EPA proposed revisions to the flexibility provisions of 40 C.F.R. Part 70 in 1994[143] and then again in August 1995.[144] EPA's 1994 proposal would have provided for four revision tracks, rather than the three that exist under the current rules. The complexity of this proposal, however, raised questions as to whether the proposed rule would in fact increase source flexibility to change operations in response to competition and other market conditions. Numerous parties, including states and regulated industries, criticized the proposal as too complex for both sources and permitting authorities.

In response to such criticism, EPA in August 1995 proposed a fundamental restructuring of the permit revision portions of the Title V rule. Under this proposed approach, during the five-year permit term, a source could undertake many changes in operations that require a permit revision simply by notifying the permitting authority at the time of the change and submitting a statement describing the revised permit term or new applicable requirements. This statement would be attached to the permit itself. For "environmentally significant" changes (a term to be defined by the rule), this procedure would be available for those changes for which a review process was afforded in conjunction with development or implementation of the applicable requirement if that review process was essentially equivalent to the Title V permit procedures. States would have more flexibility as to the procedures afforded for less environmentally significant changes. Formal review under the Title V program would occur subsequently, during the next permit renewal. The Agency is scheduled to promulgate this rule during 1997. States would have between 12 and 24 months to conform their programs to any amendments to the Title V rule.

Below is a summary of the permit revision system as set forth in the current Title V rule. The simplification proposal issued in August 1995 would principally affect the "significant" and "minor" permit revision categories, allowing these types of revisions to take place without new permit proceedings as described above.

---

[143]59 Fed. Reg. 44460 (1994).
[144]60 Fed. Reg. 45530 (1995).

### *2.4.6.1 Scope*

Under the current Title V rule, a source must seek a permit revision *only* if the contemplated change could not be operated without violating a term of the existing permit, or if the change would trigger an applicable requirement to which the source had not previously been subject.

### *2.4.6.2 Administrative Permit Amendments*

An administrative permit amendment is generally a simple revision that corrects typographical errors, identifies a change in name or similar information, requires more frequent monitoring, or incorporates requirements into the operating permit from a preconstruction review permit (if the state review also satisfies the procedural participation requirements of Title V). No public notice is required for administrative amendments. Administrative amendments may typically be implemented upon the filing of an application. No permit shield is available.

### *2.4.6.3 Minor Permit Revisions*

Minor permit revisions are subject to limited review requirements and streamlined procedures. The existing Title V rules do not require public review of such revisions, but do require that EPA and affected states be notified of the application. To qualify for the minor permit revision procedure, the source may not be in violation of the permit term it seeks to change; further, the revision may not violate any requirement applicable to the source. The source may make the proposed change immediately but, once it makes the change, the source may be liable for violating its permit if the revision is ultimately denied (e.g., in response to EPA or affected state comments, or a citizen suit challenging the state's failure to object to the proposed change).

### *2.4.6.4 Significant Permit Revisions*

Significant permit revisions are those that would not qualify as administrative or minor revisions. They are subject to the procedural requirements applicable to permit issuance and renewal, including the requirements for public participation and review by affected states and EPA.

### *2.4.6.5 Operational Flexibility/Trading*

Pursuant to § 502(b)(10) of the Act, states must allow sources to engage in trading under a federally enforceable cap established in the permit.

### *2.4.6.6 Alternative Operating Scenarios*

By far the best way to ensure operational flexibility is to write a permit that specifies operation under all of the reasonably anticipated operating scenarios of the facility. A source owner or operator would merely have to give notice of a change in operating scenarios, and no permit revision would be required. In the preamble to the final Title V rules, EPA also recognizes that an appropriate way to avoid the need for permit revisions is to base permit terms and conditions on reasonably conservative assumptions regarding source emissions and operations.

### 2.4.7 Permit Fees

Section 70.9(b) requires states to establish a fee schedule that results in collection of revenue sufficient to cover permit program costs. The costs to be covered by the fee schedule are listed in §70.9(b)(1). A state fee schedule may include emissions fees, application fees, service-based fees or other types of fees.[145] EPA will assume that the fees are adequate to cover the costs of the state program if the fees are equal to $25 per year multiplied by the total tons of the *actual* emissions of each regulated pollutant emitted.[146] The fee schedule ultimately adopted by the state must be increased annually by the percentage increase in the Consumer Price Index, in order to ensure adequate funding of the state program.[147]

### 3.0 ENFORCEMENT OF THE CLEAN AIR ACT

The Title V operating permit program will make it easier to identify a source's applicable Clean Air Act requirements as well as the compliance status of the source. Moreover, the 1990 Amendments to the Clean Air Act give EPA and the courts much broader enforcement authority and significantly increase the civil and criminal penalties for violations. As a result, Clean Air Act enforcement cases are likely to increase over the coming years as the Title V program is implemented. The following sections summarize the enforcement provisions of the Act.

### 3.1 Civil Enforcement

One of the most significant changes in civil enforcement under the 1990 Amendments to the Act is the ability of the Administrator to bring administrative enforcement actions against violators directly without going through the Department of Justice (DOJ) and the courts. The administrative enforcement provisions, modeled after similar provisions in the Clean Water Act, authorize the Administrator to impose administrative penalties up to $200,000 or more if the Administrator and the Attorney General agree that a stiffer penalty is appropriate. The Administrator must give written notice to the alleged violator. The violator then has 30 days within which to request an adjudicatory hearing. Administrative enforcement is attractive to EPA because it not only allows EPA to avoid having to coordinate first with DOJ, but also enables EPA to reach agreements with violators more quickly than in litigation.[148]

The Amendments also authorize the Agency to establish a "field citation" program for minor violations. This program would allow Agency officials inspecting a facility to issue environmental "traffic tickets" with fines of up to $5000 per day per violation. Violators may request a hearing or simply pay the fine.[149] A final rule governing the field citation program is scheduled to be issued in early 1997.[150]

In addition to expanding the Agency's authority to enforce the Act, the Amendments also authorize private citizens to seek civil penalties for violations of the Act. Under the pre-1990 Act, when citizens brought suits against EPA for failure to

---

[145]40 C.F.R. §70.9(b)(3).
[146]40 C.F.R. §70.9(b)(2).
[147]40 C.F.R. §70.9(b)(2).
[148]CAA §113(d).
[149]CAA §113(d)(3).
[150]*See* 59 Fed. Reg. 22776 (1994) (proposed rule).

perform a nondiscretionary act or against a particular source for violations of the statute, the court only had authority to order EPA to take action or to order the source to comply. As under the original citizen suit provision, plaintiffs must provide at least 60 days notice of the action to the Administrator, the state, and the alleged violator.[151]

To underscore how serious Congress is about enforcement of the Clean Air Act, it has authorized EPA to pay a "bounty" of up to $10,000 to anyone who provides information that leads to a criminal conviction or civil penalty.[152]

### 3.2 Criminal Penalties

The Clean Air Act imposes criminal liability in §113(c) on "any person" who knowingly violates the statute, and makes a knowing violation of the Act a felony offense. Significantly, the definition of "person" includes individuals as well as corporations and partnerships, and while some enforcement provisions can only be enforced against "senior management personnel" or "corporate officers," the knowing violation provisions of the Act can be enforced against *anyone* involved in the violation. The 1990 Amendments have increased fines to $250,000 per day per violation and up to 5 years in jail. Corporations are subject to even larger fines, up to $500,000 per violation.

The Amendments have also expanded the crimes related to record keeping. Individuals are subject to fines up to $250,000 and two years in jail not only for making false statements to the Agency, but also for failing to file or maintain records or reports required under the Act. Corporations face fines of up to $500,000 for the same violation. This provision is particularly important for Title V permittees, because the Clean Air Act requires each permittee to certify at least once a year that the permitted facility "is in compliance with any applicable permit, and to promptly report any deviations from permit requirements . . . ."[153]

Knowing failure to pay any fee owed to the government under the Act, such as permit fees, is also a criminal act and is punishable by fines up to $100,000 and one year in jail for individuals and fines up to $500,000 for corporations. Penalties are doubled for repeat offenders.

Two new sections of the Clean Air Act impose criminal penalties for *knowing or negligent* release of air toxics which place another person in "imminent danger of death or serious bodily injury." An individual who *knowingly* releases any hazardous air pollutant or any "extremely hazardous substance" which places another person in "imminent danger of death or serious bodily injury" is subject to fines up to $250,000 per day and up to a 15-year imprisonment. Corporations may be fined up to $1 million per day. This provision requires actual knowledge that the release placed others in imminent danger of death or serious bodily injury.[154]

Lack of actual knowledge, however, does not let a violator off the hook altogether. An individual who *negligently* releases any air toxic which places another person in "imminent danger of death or serious bodily injury" is subject to fines up to $100,000 and up to one year in jail. Corporations may be fined up to $200,000. Because it

---

[151]CAA §304.
[152]CAA §113(f).
[153]CAA §503(b)(2).
[154]CAA §113(c)(5).

criminalizes negligent behavior, this provision has serious implications for anyone with responsibility for environmental compliance and creates a particular need for effective compliance procedures and a clear delineation of responsibilities for ensuring compliance.[155]

In addition to stiffer criminal penalties for violations of the Clean Air Act, Congress has required EPA to substantially increase the number of criminal investigators to enforce all environmental laws. The Pollution Prosecution Act of 1990 required EPA to have at least 200 trained criminal investigators by October 1995.

### 3.3 Compliance Audits

In light of the expansion of criminal liability under the Act, any company whose activities are subject to environmental regulation is well-advised to implement an internal compliance program. Regular comprehensive audits will reduce the chance of criminal actions against the company by enabling the company to detect and correct problems early and will be considered a mitigating factor by a court imposing penalties.

A common concern in connection with environmental audits is how to deal with violations once they are discovered and whether the company must report them to the Agency. Title V specifically requires permittees to report any deviation from a permit requirement to the Agency, and failure to do so carries civil and criminal penalties of its own. A comprehensive internal compliance program, however, can reduce a permittee's potential liability for violations.

In 1991, the Department of Justice released guidelines on the factors prosecutors should consider in making criminal enforcement decisions under federal environmental statutes. The guidelines state that it is the policy of the Agency to *encourage* self-auditing and voluntary disclosure of environmental violations by the regulated community. To that end, the guidelines list several factors that will weigh against criminal enforcement action including: regular, comprehensive environmental audits; timely voluntary disclosure of violations; good faith efforts to remedy noncompliance; an effective internal disciplinary system; and prompt, good faith efforts to reach compliance agreements with federal and state authorities. Thus, although the company will have an affirmative duty to report violations of the Act when it discovers them, voluntary disclosure and cooperation with enforcement authorities should mitigate against enforcement action based on those violations. These same themes are repeated in a guidance memorandum issued in January 1994 by EPA's Director of Criminal Enforcement, entitled "The Exercise of Investigative Discretion."

More recently, the Agency undertook a formal review of the environmental auditing guidelines it adopted in 1986.[156] The 1986 guidelines encouraged the use of routine audits in order to avoid or to mitigate the results of environmental enforcement proceedings. Key elements of the audit are explicit top management support, an environmental auditing function independent of audited activities, adequate staffing and training, prompt reporting of compliance problems to management, and prompt corrective action. In December 1995, EPA issued a notice concluding its review of the

---

[155]CAA §113(c)(4).
[156]59 Fed. Reg. 38455 (1994).

1986 audit policy.[157]  In this notice, EPA provided that it would generally seek lower civil penalties (by eliminating the gravity component) and not pursue criminal enforcement where a company discovered, voluntarily reported, and promptly corrected violations pursuant to a properly designed and implemented environmental audit program.

Finally, numerous states have adopted or are considering adopting audit privilege or immunity legislation. EPA has generally opposed such legislation, and has issued guidance describing circumstances in which such legislation will render a state's Title V program inadequate (based on the concern that such legislation could interfere with state enforcement of Title V permits).[158]  In particular, EPA has expressed concern that the Idaho and Michigan Title V programs might be inadequate based on audit legislation in those states.

### 3.4  Enforcement Priorities

EPA typically targets specific industries and substantive issues for enforcement attention. For fiscal year 1998-99, "national priority sectors" for enforcement attention are petroleum refining, dry cleaners, and primary nonferrous metals.  "Significant sectors" include pulp mills, mining, iron and steel production, plastics and synthetics production, and coal-fired power plants. "Priority air program issues" identified for enforcement purposes include NSPS and MACT applicability determinations, excursions reported in Title V compliance certification, and MACT standards with fiscal year 1998 compliance data.[159]

### 4.0  CONCLUSION

The Clean Air Act as amended in 1990 contains numerous complex regulatory requirements.  Over the coming years EPA will continue to face implementation responsibilities that far surpass those that have been assigned to virtually any other administrative agency.

Establishing the numerous new programs called for by the 1990 Amendments has fostered the development of new approaches to rulemaking and alternatives to formal rules.  Interpretive rulings, policy guidance, direct final rulemaking, negotiated rules, and advisory committees have all been used extensively over the past six years to implement general statutory requirements as statutory deadlines make it increasingly difficult for the Agency to conduct traditional rulemaking.

As a practical matter, these developments call on those affected by the Clean Air Act to become involved earlier than ever before in the implementation process.  This requires more careful monitoring of Agency priorities and schedules, in order to identify issues that may be of interest early in the rule or guidance development stage, and perhaps even before regulatory proceedings are announced.

---

[157]60 Fed. Reg. 66706 (1995).

[158]M. Nichols and S. Herman, EPA Assistant Administrator for Air Programs and Enforcement, "Effect of Audit Immunity/Privilege Laws on States' Ability to Enforce Title V Requirements" (April 5, 1995).

[159]Memorandum from E. Stanley, Director EP Office of Compliance, "Draft FY 98/99 National Enforcement and Compliance Assurance Priorities" (October 1996).

Enforcement of CAA rules will receive more attention as proceedings to implement the 1990 Amendments are completed, and as source owners and operators begin to confront the compliance monitoring and certification requirements of the Title V operating permit program. Owners and operators of industrial facilities will need to define their compliance obligations with thoroughness and care, and to develop appropriate compliance/audit strategies.

As the 1990 Amendments are implemented, clean air regulation will have a greater impact on day-to-day business decisions than perhaps any other piece of environmental legislation. Given the breadth of the Act and of EPA's new enforcement powers, comprehensive environmental planning has become crucial to sound business decisions.

# CHAPTER 4

# CLEAN WATER ACT

Lynn M. Gallagher, Esquire
Swidler & Berlin, Chartered
Washington, D.C.

## 1.0 OVERVIEW

Federal water pollution control law, as embodied in the Clean Water Act (CWA), 33 U.S.C. §§ 1251-1387, contains a comprehensive program for protecting our nation's waters. The federal Environmental Protection Agency (EPA), along with other federal, state, and local agencies, administers the numerous programs established under the Act, including the National Pollutant Discharge Elimination System (NPDES) permit program, the dredge and fill permit program, and municipal wastewater treatment programs. This chapter will focus primarily on those CWA programs that are most likely to affect industrial and municipal dischargers of pollutants into surface waters.

## 2.0 A BRIEF HISTORY

The earliest federal law affecting water pollution in the United States was the Refuse Act, passed in 1899.[1] This act focused primarily on the protection of navigation rather than on the quality of the nation's waters. During the late 1960s, however, federal regulators began to use the broad language of the Refuse Act to establish an environmentally oriented program to control water pollution. Although it is no longer a major element of the federal water pollution control program, the Refuse Act is still in effect and is used in some enforcement cases to reach activities that fall outside other more recent environmental laws.[2]

The modern Clean Water Act traces its roots to the Federal Water Pollution Control Act, passed by Congress over President Nixon's veto in 1972.[3] This statute required the EPA to set nationwide effluent standards on an industry-by-industry basis based on the capabilities of pollution control technologies and their costs to the regulated industries. The Act provided that more stringent pollution controls could be imposed where technology-based limitations were insufficient to assure that the quality of receiving waters did not deteriorate to, or remain at, unacceptable levels. The 1972 Act established the NPDES permit program, which could be administered by states after federal authorization. This basic framework—effluent limitations guidelines, water quality requirements, the permit program, and other provisions— remains in place today.

---

[1]33 U.S.C. § 407 (1899).
[2]*See, e.g., United States v. Hercules, Inc.*, 961 F.2d 796 (8th Cir. 1992); *United States v. Ashland Oil Inc.*, 705 F. Supp. 270 (W.D. Pa. 1989).
[3]Pub. L. No. 92-500, 86 Stat. 816 (1972).

EPA, in carrying out the mandates of the 1972 Act, focused primarily on the control of conventional pollutants, such as biological oxygen demand and suspended solids, rather than toxic pollutants. Unhappy with EPA's progress toward reducing toxic water pollution, environmental groups sued the Agency for its failure to meet statutory deadlines. This lawsuit resulted in a consent decree, known as the Flannery Decree, in 1976.[4] This decree refocused the federal water pollution program on toxics control and spelled out a detailed toxics strategy. The decree required EPA to promulgate effluent guidelines, new source performance standards, and pretreatment standards covering 65 toxic pollutants (the "priority pollutants") for each of 21 major industrial categories by December 31, 1979.[5] Congress endorsed the Flannery Decree's approach to toxics regulation in 1977 amendments to the Act, writing several portions of the decree into law.[6]

In 1987, the Act was amended again to focus the Act's programs for toxics control by, among other things, establishing a "Toxic Hot Spots" program to identify and improve waterways that are expected to remain polluted with toxic pollutants even after the strictest technology-based requirements have been met. In addition, the 1987 amendments established a timetable for regulation of storm water, strengthened water quality-related requirements, tightened requirements for the fundamentally different factors variance, established a revolving loan fund for construction of sewage treatment plants, and expanded EPA's enforcement tools.[7]

In 1990, in response to the *Exxon Valdez* oil spill, Congress overhauled the oil spill provisions of the Act in the Oil Pollution Act of 1990, sometimes referred to as OPA 90.[8] In addition to its amendments to the existing oil spill provisions in Section 311 of the CWA, the Oil Pollution Act also created a new statutory section on oil spill liability and compensation.[9]

## 3.0 CLEAN WATER ACT GOALS AND POLICIES

Like many of the federal environmental statutes, the Clean Water Act contains a statement of "goals, objectives, and policies." The Act's stated objective is to "restore and maintain the chemical, physical and biological integrity of the nation's waters."[10] To achieve this objective, the Act establishes the following "goals":

- elimination of the discharge of pollutants into surface waters; and

---

[4]*NRDC v. Train*, 8 E.R.C. 2120 (D.D.C. 1976), *modified*, 12 E.R.C. 1833 (D.D.C. 1979); *aff'd, Environmental Defense Fund, Inc. v. Costle*, 636 F.2d 1229 (D.C. Cir. 1980).

[5]EPA completed issuance of the effluent guidelines required by the decree in 1987.

[6]Pub. L. No. 95-217, 91 Stat. 1567 (1977).

[7]Water Quality Act, Pub. L. No. 100-4 (1987).

[8]Pub. L. 101-380 (1990).

[9]33 U.S.C. § 2701-2761.

[10]Section 101(a), 33 U.S.C. § 1251(a).

- achievement of a level of water quality which "provides for the protection and propagation of fish, shellfish and wildlife" and "for recreation in and on the water."[11]

The Act also establishes a "national policy" that the "discharge of toxic pollutants in toxic amounts" shall be prohibited.[12]

While these objectives, goals, and policies are not legal mandates, EPA and the courts rely on them as a means of interpreting the intent of Congress on Clean Water Act issues. For example, the term "toxic pollutants in toxic amounts" was the principal support for the Flannery Decree, and has been a primary focus of the Act's implementation since 1977.

## 4.0 ELEMENTS OF THE CLEAN WATER ACT

The Clean Water Act contains a broad range of regulatory tools and mechanisms designed to attain the statutory objectives and goals. These tools include the following major elements:

- a prohibition of discharges, except as in compliance with the Act (Section 301);
- a permit program to authorize and regulate certain discharges (Section 402);
- a system for determining the limitations to be imposed on regulated discharges (Sections 301, 306, 307);
- a process for cooperative federal/state implementation (Sections 401, 402);
- a system for preventing, reporting, and responding to spills (Section 311);
- a permit program governing the discharge or placement of dredged or fill material into the nation's waters (Section 404); and
- strong enforcement mechanisms (Sections 309, 505).

These elements and other aspects of the federal Clean Water Act program will be discussed in some detail in the rest of this chapter.

## 5.0 THE DISCHARGE PROHIBITION

Section 301 of the Clean Water Act establishes a broad prohibition against "the discharge of any pollutant by any person" except as in compliance with the Act's permit requirements, effluent limitations and other enumerated provisions.[13] EPA and the courts have interpreted this language broadly.[14]

---

[11]Section 101(a)(1) & (2), 33 U.S.C. § 1251(a)(1) & (2).

[12]Section 101(a)(3), 33 U.S.C. § 1251(a)(3).

[13]Section 301(a), 33 U.S.C. § 1311(a).

[14]The effect of the "except as in compliance" language is to shift the burden of proof in an enforcement action. This language requires the discharger to prove that the discharge *was in compliance* with the Act, rather than requiring the government to prove that a discharge *was out of compliance*.

Because the Section 301 prohibition establishes the Act's scope, it is useful to examine closely the language of the statute. First, the "discharge of a pollutant" is defined to mean, in relevant part, "any addition of any pollutant to navigable waters from any point source."[15] Thus, the terms "addition," "pollutant," "navigable waters," and "point source" are of critical importance.

## 5.1 "Addition"

EPA and the courts have interpreted the term "addition" broadly. Generally, any introduction of a pollutant into a body of water is an addition. EPA's regulations make an exception to this principle for pollutants that are present in a discharge only by reason of their presence in the discharger's intake water, if the intake water is drawn from the same body of water as the one into which the discharge is made and if the pollutants are not removed by the discharger as part of its normal operations.[16] In addition, discharges of water from dams, even if a dam's operations adversely affect the temperature or dissolved oxygen content of the water, have been determined not to be "additions" of pollutants.[17] An EPA administrative law judge recently held that a company could be liable for exceedances of metals in its outfall that result from metals in rainfall and from leaching of building materials caused by acid rain.[18] This ruling has been appealed to the EPA Environmental Appeals Board.

## 5.2 "Pollutant"

"Pollutant" is defined in the Act to include dredged spoil, solid waste, incinerator residue, sewage, garbage, sewage sludge, munitions, chemical wastes, biological materials, radioactive materials, heat, wrecked or discarded equipment, rock, sand, cellar dirt, and industrial, municipal, and agricultural waste discharged into water.[19] Despite this specific definition, however, the term has been broadly interpreted by the courts to include virtually any material, as well as characteristics such as toxicity or acidity.[20]

## 5.3 "Point Source"

"Point source" is defined in the Act to include "any discernable, confined and discrete conveyance . . . from which pollutants are or may be discharged."[21] This definition has been interpreted to cover almost any conveyance from which a pollutant

---

[15]Section 502(12), 33 U.S.C. § 1362(12).

[16]40 C.F.R. § 122.45(h). This credit for pollutants in uptake water, referred to as a "net/gross credit," is available only for technology-based limitations.

[17]*National Wildlife Federation v. Consumers Power* Co., 862 F.2d 580 (6th Cir. 1988); *National Wildlife Federation v. Gorsuch*, 693 F.2d 156 (D.C. Cir. 1982). *But see Committee to Save the Mokelumne River v. East Bay Mun. Utility Dist.*, 13 F.3d 305 (9th Cir. 1993), *cert. denied*, 115 S. Ct. 198 (1994) (discharges from dam used to collect acid mine drainage from abandoned mine subject to CWA permit requirement).

[18]*In the Matter of General Motors Corp., CPC-Pontiac Fiero Plant*, No. CWA-A-O-011-93 (June 28, 1996).

[19]Section 502(6), 33 U.S.C. § 1362(6).

[20]*E.g., Natural Resources Defense Council v. EPA*, 859 F.2d 156 (D.C. Cir. 1988); *U.S. v. Hamel*, 551 F.2d 107, 110-12 (6th Cir. 1977).

[21]Section 502(14), 33 U.S.C. § 1362(14).

may be discharged, including pipes, ditches, erosion channels, and gullies. The conveyance need not be manmade. Vehicles, such as bulldozers or tank trucks, have also been held to be point sources.[22] Human beings have been held not to be point sources, at least for purposes of criminal enforcement of the Act.[23]

Point sources include sources from which pollutants "may be" discharged. Thus, the term includes not only sources from which pollutants are routinely discharged, but also conveyances from which a pollutant may be discharged only in extreme conditions, such as during an unusual storm event.

### 5.4 "Navigable Waters" (Waters of the United States)

"Navigable waters" is defined by the Act to include all "waters of the United States."[24] EPA's regulations define the term "waters of the United States" to include (1) waters used in interstate commerce, including all waters subject to the tides; (2) interstate waters; (3) intrastate lakes, rivers, streams, wetlands, etc. (a) which are used by interstate travelers for recreation and other purposes, or (b) which are sources of fish or shellfish sold in interstate commerce, or (c) which are utilized for industrial purposes by industries engaged in interstate commerce; (4) impoundments and tributaries of waters within these first three categories; and (5) wetlands adjacent to waters within these categories.[25] Excluded from the definition of "waters of the United States" are manmade waste treatment systems, such as treatment ponds or lagoons, designed to meet Clean Water Act requirements.[26]

Deciding whether an intrastate water falls within this definition is often controversial. For the most part, EPA and the courts have supported the broadest possible interpretation of the scope of the Act's coverage that would be allowed under the Commerce Clause of the U.S. Constitution. For example, in 1986, EPA issued a policy that intrastate waters may be waters of the United States if they are used by migratory birds.[27] EPA has also ruled that springs and seeps that support unusual flora or fauna which attract many out-of-state scientists for study are subject to Clean Water Act jurisdiction.[28] Seasonal ponding in pits formerly used for salt production has also been held to be within the scope of waters of the United States.[29]

---

[22]*E.g., Concerned Area Residents for Environment v. Southview Farm*, 34 F.3d 114 (2d Cir. 1994), *cert. denied*, 115 S. Ct. 1793 (1995).

[23]In other words, a person dumping pollutants into a water body, other than through a hose or pipe, for example, would not be in violation of the Act's prohibition of discharges from point sources without a permit. The person may, however, be in violation of other laws and regulations. *U.S. v. Plaza Health Laboratories, Inc.*, 3 F.3d 643, 649 (2d Cir. 1993), *cert. denied*, 114 S. Ct. 2764 (1994) (dumping of vials of medical waste into Hudson River).

[24]Section 502(7), 33 U.S.C. § 1362(7).

[25]40 C.F.R. § 122.2.

[26]*Id.* Cooling ponds meeting the definition of 40 C.F.R. § 423.11(m) are not within this exclusion, and so may be considered waters of the United States.

[27]51 Fed. Reg. 41206, 41217 (Nov. 13, 1986).

[28]EPA Office of General Counsel, "Clean Water Act Jurisdiction over Springs in Ash Meadows, Nevada" (July 5, 1983).

[29]*Leslie Salt Co. v. U.S.*, 896 F.2d 354 (9th Cir. 1990), *cert. denied*, 498 U.S. 1126 (1991).

Although the federal jurisdiction is interpreted broadly, courts have limited this jurisdiction in some cases. For example, in one case, the court held that a one-acre wetland located 750 feet from a small creek was not within the scope of "waters of the United States."[30]

Groundwaters are not within the scope of "waters of the United States." EPA has taken the position that it has jurisdiction over discharges to groundwater where there is a hydrological connection between the groundwater and surface water. The courts, however, are divided on whether EPA's jurisdiction extends to discharges to such groundwaters.[31] Groundwater is included in many states' definitions of "waters of the state" and, in these states, point source discharges into groundwater are covered by the state water permit program.[32]

## 6.0 THE NPDES PERMIT PROGRAM

### 6.1 What Is an NPDES Permit?

The National Pollutant Discharge Elimination System (NPDES) permit program implements the Clean Water Act's prohibition on unauthorized discharges by requiring a permit for every discharge of pollutants from a point source to waters of the United States. Permits, which are issued by EPA or authorized states pursuant to Section 402 of the Act, give the permittee the right to discharge specified pollutants from specified outfalls, normally for five years. The permit normally sets numerical limitations on the authorized discharges and imposes other conditions on the permittee.[33]

---

[30]*Hoffman Homes, Inc. v. EPA*, 999 F.2d 256, 260-61 (7th Cir. 1993). In this case, there was no evidence that the wetland was used by migratory birds or had characteristics commonly of value to migratory birds. 999 F.2d at 262.

[31]*Compare Village of Oconomowoc Lake v. Dayton Hudson Corp.*, 24 F.3d 962 (7th Cir.), *cert. denied*, 115 S. Ct. 322 (1994) (EPA has no jurisdiction over discharges to groundwater regardless of hydrological connection to surface water); *and Kelley v. U.S.*, 618 F. Supp. 1103 (W.D. Mich. 1985) (discharges to groundwater not within Act's prohibition even though contaminants eventually were discharged into bay); *with Sierra Club v. Colorado Refining Co.*, 838 F. Supp. 1428 (D. Colo. 1993) (Act's prohibition on discharges to navigable waters extends to discharges reaching navigable water as result of discharge to connected groundwater); *McClellan Ecological Seepage Situation (MESS) v. Weinberger*, 707 F. Supp. 1182, 1193-96 (E.D. Cal. 1988), *vacated on other grounds*, 47 F.3d 325 (9th Cir.), *cert. denied*, 116 S. Ct. 51 (1995) (discharge to groundwater that has effect on surface water may violate Act); *United States v. GAF Corp.*, 389 F. Supp. 1379, 1383 (S.D. Tex. 1975) (permit not required for disposal of wastes into groundwater which does not flow into or otherwise affect surface waters).

[32]In 1991, EPA and states began developing Comprehensive State Groundwater Protection Programs (CSGWPP), a non-regulatory approach that seeks better coordination between federal and state groundwater activities and prioritization of protection efforts based on groundwater uses and values. EPA has approved only four CSGWPPs--for New Hampshire, Connecticut, Alabama, and Wisconsin. Other states are expected to submit CSGWPPs.

[33]For a full discussion of the NPDES permit program, see the *NPDES Permit Handbook* (2d ed. Gov't. Inst. 1992).

## 6.2 What Discharges Require an NPDES Permit?

As stated previously, an NPDES permit is required for any discharge of a "pollutant" from a "point source" to "waters of the United States." Discharges that require an NPDES permit include such waste streams as industrial process water, non-contact cooling water, and collected or channeled storm water runoff. In other words, a permit is required for all discharges except sheet runoff (which is not a point source discharge), discharges into wholly intrastate waters (i.e. waters not falling within the definition of "waters of the United States") or wastewater treatment systems, and certain exempted activities.[34]

## 6.3 State and Federal Roles

An NPDES permit is issued either by EPA or by a state if the state has received permitting authority from EPA pursuant to Section 402(b) of the Act.[35] Currently, 41 states and territories have received permitting authority.[36] Upon EPA approval of a state program, EPA and a state enter into a Memorandum of Understanding (MOU) concerning the specific elements of the authorized state program.[37] In states that are not authorized to administer the NPDES program, permits are issued by the 10 EPA Regional Offices.

Permitting procedures for state-issued permits normally follow the EPA procedures described below. EPA's regulations mandate that state permit programs include certain elements, such as signatory requirements, certain boilerplate provisions, limitations calculation methods, and issuance procedures.[38] It is not unusual, however, for aspects of state programs that are not mandated by the EPA regulations, such as appeal procedures, to differ from federal procedures.

Substantively, state programs must be at least as stringent as the federal program. States are free to implement requirements that are more stringent than the federal program.[39]

---

[34]Certain discharges of pollutants are exempted from the NPDES permit requirement. These include discharges of sewage from vessels, discharges from some agricultural and silvicultural activities, discharges into publicly owned treatment works, and discharges in compliance with instructions from an On-Scene Coordinator responding to a spill incident. 40 C.F.R. § 122.3.

[35]State-issued permits are sometimes referred to as State Pollutant Discharge Elimination System (SPDES) permits. See 40 C.F.R. Part 123 for EPA's regulations regarding the process for approval of state programs.

[36]Currently, only the following "states" do *not* have permitting authority: Alaska, Arizona, District of Columbia, Florida, Idaho, Maine, Massachusetts, New Hampshire, New Mexico, Oklahoma, Texas, and five U.S. territories. EPA Region VI has announced that intends to approve Oklahoma's request to assume NPDES responsibility. 61 Fed. Reg. 45420 (Aug. 29, 1996). Indian tribes are also considered to be states for CWA purposes. A federal court recently affirmed EPA's position that tribal governments have authority under the Act to apply their own water quality standards to the activities of nonmembers operating on tribal lands. *State of Montana v. U.S. EPA,* 42 E.R.C. 1922 (D. Mont. 1996).

[37]40 C.F.R. § 123.24.

[38]40 C.F.R. § 123.25.

[39]40 C.F.R. § 123.1(i).

Permits issued by authorized states are subject to review by EPA.[40] If EPA objects to a state permit and the state does not change the permit to address EPA's concerns, EPA may issue its own permit for the facility.[41] EPA has the power to withdraw its approval of a state permit program and to take over the program if it finds that the state is not administering the program in accordance with the Act's requirements.[42]

Where EPA is the permitting authority, the state in which the discharger is located must certify that the discharge authorized in the permit will comply with state water quality standards and other requirements.[43] If the state does not either certify the permit or deny certification within a reasonable time, it is deemed to have waived the certification requirement.[44] States often use the certification requirement as a means of persuading EPA to adopt more stringent conditions in a permit.

## 6.4 The Permit Process

### 6.4.1 The Permit Application

The NPDES permit application, whether for a new discharge or for an existing discharge, requires extensive information about the facility and the nature of the discharges from the facility. EPA application forms include Form 1 (general information), Form 2C (detailed information for existing sources), Form 2D (detailed information for new sources and new discharges), Form 2E (for facilities that discharge only nonprocess wastewater), and Form 2F (for storm water discharges).[45] State application forms must at a minimum require the information required by EPA's forms.[46]

The permit application must be signed by a "responsible corporate officer" as defined in EPA's regulations.[47] The person signing the application must certify as follows: "*I certify under penalty of law that this document and all attachments were prepared under my direction or supervision in accordance with a system designed to assure that qualified personnel properly gather and evaluate the information submitted. Based on my inquiry of the person or persons who manage the system, or those persons directly responsible for gathering the information, the information submitted is, to the best of my knowledge and belief, true, accurate and complete. I am aware that there are significant penalties for submitting false information, including the possibility of*

---

[40]Section 402(d), 33 U.S.C. § 1342(d). EPA has 90 days in which to make its comments, objections, or recommendations to the state permitting agency. 40 C.F.R. § 123.44(a)(1).

[41]Section 402(d)(4), 33 U.S.C. § 1342(d)(4).

[42]Section 402(c)(2), 33 U.S.C. § 1342(c)(2).

[43]Section 401(a), 33 U.S.C. § 1341(a); 40 C.F.R. Part 121. *See also PUD No. 1 of Jefferson County v. Washington Dept. of Ecology*, 114 S. Ct. 1900 (1994) (state certification may include requirement to maintain certain level of flow from hydropower facility).

[44]Section 401(a)(1), 33 U.S.C. § 1341(a)(1).

[45]See 40 C.F.R. § 122.21 for a full discussion of the information required in NPDES permit application forms. EPA has proposed to revise and consolidate the existing permit application forms. See U.S. EPA, "Summary Overview of Office of Water Preliminary Report: Review of the Code of Federal Regulations" (March 24, 1995).

[46]40 C.F.R. § 122.1(d).

[47]40 C.F.R. § 122.22(a).

*fine and imprisonment for knowing violations.*"[48] Because the person signing the application may have little direct knowledge of the application's contents, some companies have adopted the practice of having the application signed in a "signing ceremony" during which the responsible corporate officer may question those directly responsible for the application in order to ensure the correctness of its contents. This ceremony is then memorialized in a memorandum or other writing so that a record of this inquiry will exist if the accuracy of the application becomes an issue in the future.

If the discharger is located in an authorized state, it must submit its permit application to the state permitting agency. If the discharger's state is not authorized, the application must be submitted to the EPA Regional Office for the discharger's state. The application must be submitted at least 180 days prior to the date a proposed discharge is to commence or 180 days prior to the expiration of an existing permit.[49]

If a complete application is filed at least 180 days prior to the expiration of an existing permit, the existing permit will be "continued" (i.e. will remain in effect) until a new permit is issued by the permitting authority. Because it often takes up to a year for a state or EPA Regional Office to issue a renewed permit, it is essential that a permittee ensure that its renewal application is both timely and complete.[50]

### 6.4.2 The Draft Permit and Comment Period

Normally, when a permit involves complicated or unusual features, EPA or the state will initiate early informal discussions with the discharger about the permit terms. Often the permitting agency will issue a "pre-draft" permit, sometimes accompanied by what is called a "14-day letter," upon which the discharger can submit comments, so that the draft permit, when it is issued for public comment, reflects the input of the discharger.

The draft permit, when it is issued, must be accompanied by a "Fact Sheet" or "Statement of Basis" explaining how the permit terms and conditions were calculated and developed.[51] The permitting agency must publish a notice of the issuance of the draft permit in a local newspaper and must accept comments from the public during a comment period of at least 30 days.[52] If there is significant public interest in the draft permit, EPA or the state agency will hold a public hearing.[53]

The permittee must raise all reasonably ascertainable issues and submit all reasonably available arguments supporting its positions during the comment period on

---

[48]40 C.F.R. § 122.22(d).

[49]40 C.F.R. § 122.21(c) and (d).

[50]This permit continuance policy is in effect for EPA-issued permits and in at least 31 authorized states. *See Natural Resources Defense Council v. EPA*, 859 F.2d 156, 213-14 (D.C. Cir. 1988) (upholding EPA policy to continue expired permits, reasoning that policy is necessary to prevent undue hardships on permittees).

[51]40 C.F.R. §§ 124.7, 124.8, 124.56. In some states, this document is referred to as a "Rationale."

[52]40 C.F.R. §§ 124.10(c), 124.11.

[53]40 C.F.R. § 124.12. There must be at least 30 days' notice of a hearing on a draft permit. Thus, the grant of a hearing extends the comment period at least until the end of the hearing.

the draft permit.[54] If an issue is not raised during the comment period, the permittee may never raise that issue during subsequent administrative or judicial challenges to the permit.[55]

### 6.4.3 Appealing the Final Permit

After accepting comments, the permitting agency will issue a final NPDES permit, which normally is effective for five years.[56] This permit normally becomes final in 30 days unless the permittee requests an administrative hearing on the permit.[57]

Any person may appeal a final NPDES permit by filing a written request for an evidentiary hearing within 30 days of the permit's issuance.[58] The request for hearing must identify all legal and factual issues to be raised in the appeal.[59]

Under EPA's regulations, if a request for a hearing is filed, the entire permit is stayed until review is granted or denied.[60] In practice, however, it is not unusual for an EPA Region or a state to take the position that only the contested provisions are stayed by a request for a hearing.

The request for a hearing must be granted or denied by the permitting authority within 30 days. The grant of an evidentiary hearing stays all contested provisions in the permit.[61] The hearing is an on-the-record trial-like proceeding presided over by an administrative law judge.[62]

EPA has recently announced that it plans to eliminate the existing evidentiary hearing and appeals procedures for NPDES permits. Under the expected proposal, an NPDES permit could be appealed directly to the EPA Environmental Appeals Board

---

[54]40 C.F.R. § 124.13.

[55]*See, e.g., Mueller V. EPA*, 993 F.2d 1354, 1357 (8th Cir. 1993).

[56]See 40 C.F.R. § 122.46.

[57]40 C.F.R. § 124.15(b). If no comments requesting a change in the permit are received during the public comment period, the final permit will become effective immediately upon issuance. 40 C.F.R. § 124.15(b)(3).

[58]40 C.F.R. § 124.74. This discussion describes the federal appeal process. State procedures may vary. For example, states are not required to provide evidentiary hearings for permit appeals. 40 C.F.R. § 123.25(a).

[59]A hearing will be granted only if a factual issue is raised. While a request that raises purely legal issues will be denied, those issues would be reviewable on appeal of the denial to the Administrator. 40 C.F.R. § 124.74(b). It is important to note that a request for an evidentiary hearing is a prerequisite to an appeal to the Administrator, even if it is clear that the only issue raised is a purely legal question on which an evidentiary hearing will be denied. Moreover, an appeal to the Administrator is a prerequisite to judicial review. 40 C.F.R. § 124.91(e).

[60]40 C.F.R. § 124.15(b).

[61]40 C.F.R. § 124.16(a). For a permit for a new source, the grant of the request for a hearing results in the facility being without a permit until final Agency action on the appeal. 40 C.F.R. § 124.60(a)(1). For a permit renewal, the uncontested portions of the new permit and the provisions of the existing permit that correspond to the contested portions of the new permit will be in effect and enforceable pending resolution of the appeal. 40 C.F.R. § 124.60(e).

[62]See 40 C.F.R. §§ 124.71-124.91. Some states do not provide for evidentiary hearings to review permit decisions.

(EAB) without going through an evidentiary hearing first. This change is expected to reduce the average appeal process from about 21 months to about 9 months.[63]

The administrative law judge's decision (or the denial of a request for a hearing) may be appealed to the EPA EAB.[64] The permittee must file a notice of appeal and petition for review with the EAB within 30 days of the initial decision or denial. The petition for review must demonstrate that there is a finding of fact or conclusion of law that is clearly erroneous, or that there are policy issues warranting review.[65] Where appeal is granted, there will normally be a hearing before the EPA EAB or the state equivalent.[66] This hearing will result in "final agency action" that may be appealed in the courts.

Where EPA is the permitting authority, the final agency action is subject to judicial review in the federal Courts of Appeals.[67] Where the state issues the permit, judicial review is in accordance with state procedures.[68] Normally, judicial appeal is a review of the agency's decision based solely on the administrative record. The court will review the record to determine whether the agency's decision was arbitrary and capricious, an abuse of discretion, contrary to a constitutional right, or otherwise not in accordance with law.[69]

### 6.5 NPDES Permit Conditions

Normally, the primary purpose of an NPDES permit is to establish enforceable effluent limitations. In addition to effluent limitations, which are discussed in Part 6.7 below, the NPDES permit establishes a number of other enforceable conditions, such as monitoring and reporting requirements (which are discussed in more detail in Part 6.6 below), a duty to properly operate and maintain systems, upset and bypass provisions,[70] record keeping, and inspection and entry requirements.[71] Although these other conditions are often "boilerplate," some may be subject to some degree of negotiation with the permit writer and should not be accepted if they would impose an unreasonable

---

[63]See BNA, Daily Envt Rptr p. A-5 (Aug. 29, 1996).

[64]40 C.F.R. § 124.91. In most authorized states, the initial decision may be appealed to the head of the state permitting agency.

[65]40 C.F.R. § 124.91(a)(1).

[66]*See* 40 C.F.R. § 22.04(a). The hearing before the EAB or state equivalent is not a trial-like proceeding. Rather, it consists of an opportunity to submit briefs and an oral argument before the appellate board.

[67]Section 509(b)(1)(F), 33 U.S.C. § 1369(b)(1)(F).

[68]EPA recently issued a rule requiring authorized states to allow citizens as well as permittees to challenge final permit decisions in court. 61 Fed. Reg. 20972 (May 8, 1996).

[69]5 U.S.C. § 706.

[70]See Part 11.3 below.

[71]40 C.F.R. § 122.41.

burden upon a facility.[72] State boilerplate may be more stringent than EPA; for example, omitting the upset defense provision or establishing more stringent standards for the use of the defense.[73]

In addition, NPDES permits may require the permittee to perform best management practices (BMPs).[74] BMPs are procedures designed to prevent or minimize the release of toxic or hazardous pollutants. BMPs are often simple "housekeeping" measures such as requirements to store drums in specific locations or to clean up spills promptly. BMPs are especially appropriate for nontraditional NPDES permits, such as storm water permits or permits for mining operations.

Where it is impossible for a permittee immediately to come into compliance with a permit, the permit may contain a schedule of compliance. Such a schedule may contain interim limitations, and dates for the submittal of compliance plans designed to achieve full compliance by a date certain.

### 6.6 Monitoring Requirements

The implementation and enforcement of the NPDES program depend to a large extent on self-monitoring. Permits require dischargers to monitor their compliance with permit limitations on a regular basis and to report the results of this monitoring to the permitting authority on standardized discharge monitoring reports (DMRs).[75]

Monitoring must take place at the point of discharge into the receiving waters unless monitoring at that location is infeasible. For example, the permit may require the monitoring of internal waste streams where the final discharge point is inaccessible, where wastes at the point of discharge are so diluted as to make compliance monitoring impracticable, or where interference among pollutants at the point of discharge would prevent accurate detection or analysis.[76]

Permits normally contain requirements for the maintenance and proper installation of monitoring equipment, and specify the monitoring and analytical methods that must

---

[72]The NPDES regulations were substantially revised in September 1984. The Federal Register preamble to that revision, found at 49 Fed. Reg. 37998 (Sept. 26, 1984), contains useful discussions of EPA policies concerning the NPDES program, including some boilerplate requirements. The D.C. Circuit Court of Appeals' discussion of these regulations also provides useful information about the permit program. *Natural Resources Defense Council, Inc. v. EPA*, 859 F.2d 156 (D.C. Cir. 1988).

[73]40 C.F.R. § 123.25(a). *See Atlantic States Legal Foundation, Inc. v. Eastman Kodak Co.*, 12 F.3d 353, 358-59 (2d Cir.), *cert. denied*, 115 S. Ct. 62 (1994) (state requirement more stringent than federal requirement may be enforced by state or EPA but not through citizen suit provisions of Act).

[74]See Section 304(e), 33 U.S.C. § 1314(e).

[75]EPA's regulations require that permits contain monitoring requirements that are sufficient to yield representative data. 40 C.F.R. § 122.48. The regulations, however, establish only minimal specific requirements for monitoring method and frequency, leaving most such decisions to the discretion of the permit writer. Regardless of monitoring frequency, monitoring results must be reported to the permitting agency at least once per year. 40 C.F.R. § 122.44(i)(2).

[76]40 C.F.R. § 122.45(h).

be used.[77] Tampering with monitoring equipment or submitting false monitoring data to the permitting authority are criminal violations of the Act.[78] The Act gives the permitting authority the right to enter the premises of any permittee to inspect the facility's monitoring and other records, inspect monitoring equipment, and take samples to verify monitoring results.[79]

## 6.7 Effluent Limitations

The Clean Water Act mandates a two-part approach to establishing effluent limitations. First, all dischargers are required to meet treatment levels based on EPA's assessment of the capabilities of treatment technologies that are technologically and economically achievable in the discharger's particular industry. This technology-based treatment level is considered to be the baseline for dischargers. Second, more stringent treatment requirements must be met where they are found to be necessary to achieve water quality goals for the particular body of water into which a facility discharges. Water quality-based controls may be a combination of chemical-specific limitations, whole effluent toxicity control, and a biological criteria/bioassay and biosurvey approach.[80]

### 6.7.1 Forms of Permit Limitations

Permit limitations may be expressed in several ways. Most technology-based or water quality-based limitations are expressed either as a mass limitation (e.g., 2 pounds per day or 2 pounds per X units of production) or a concentration limitation e.g., 50 parts per million). Other types of permit limitations include visual observations (e.g., no visible sheen, foam, or floating solids), monitor-only requirements, requirements to perform specified tests, limitations on "indicator" parameters (e.g., biological oxygen demand, total organic carbon), flow limitations, pH range limitations, and temperature limitations.

Most permits impose both maximum limitations (i.e. the discharge may not exceed the limit during any monitoring event during the permit term, known as a "daily maximum" limitation) and "monthly average" limitations (i.e. the average of discharge levels as revealed in daily, weekly or monthly monitoring throughout the month may not exceed the limitation). For some parameters, particularly pH, a permit may require continuous monitoring and virtually continuous compliance.[81]

---

[77]EPA-approved analytical methods are contained in 40 C.F.R. Part 136.

[78]Section 309(c)(4), 33 U.S.C. § 1319(c)(4).

[79]Section 308(a), 33 U.S.C. § 1318(a).

[80]40 C.F.R. § 122.44(d)(1)(iv). See U.S. EPA, *Technical Support Document for Water Quality-Based Control* at 1 (March 1991) (hereinafter *"TSD"*).

[81]Permittees measuring compliance with a pH limitation through the use of a continuous pH monitor are allowed to exceed the pH limitations on a limited basis. No individual pH excursion may exceed 60 minutes in length and the total time of noncompliance during any calendar month may not exceed seven hours and 26 minutes. 40 C.F.R. § 401.17(a).

### 6.7.2 Technology-Based Limitations

EPA establishes national "effluent guidelines" (or "effluent limitations guidelines") for industrial categories through notice and comment rulemakings.[82] These guidelines establish limitations for all types of dischargers within the industrial category (i.e. direct and indirect dischargers, existing and new sources), and for specific types of discharges (e.g., process water, cooling water, sanitary wastewater). The effluent guidelines are enforceable only through their incorporation into an NPDES permit.

EPA has issued effluent guidelines for more than 50 industrial categories.[83] In a 1992 consent decree EPA agreed to meet a schedule for issuing 19 effluent guidelines over an 11-year period.[84]

For dischargers in industrial categories for which EPA has not yet issued effluent guidelines, and for types of discharges not covered by an applicable effluent guideline, permit writers will apply "best professional judgment" (BPJ) to establish permit limitations.[85] Normally, in applying BPJ, the permit writer will assess potentially applicable technologies applied to similar discharges in other industrial categories and may evaluate effluent treatability and analytical methods to develop limitations roughly equivalent to what an applicable effluent guideline would prescribe.[86]

Permit limitations established based on BPJ are subject to EPA's "anti-backsliding policy." This policy, which was codified in the 1987 amendments to the Act,[87] prohibits, with a few exceptions, the relaxation of BPJ limitations in subsequent permits, even if subsequently promulgated effluent guidelines would allow less stringent limitations.

The 1972 amendments to the Clean Water Act established a two-step program for the reduction of water pollution through the imposition of technology-based controls. In the first phase, industrial dischargers were required to meet a level of pollutant control based on the application of the "best practicable control technology currently available" (BPT) by July 1, 1977.[88] The second level of pollution control, to be

---

[82]Despite the "guideline" nomenclature, the effluent guidelines are not merely guidance to permit writers in setting limitations in NPDES permits. The guidelines establish substantive requirements that must be met by facilities within the regulated industrial categories. *E.I. DuPont de Nemours & Co. v. Train*, 430 U.S. 112 (1977).

[83]40 C.F.R. Parts 405-471.

[84]*See* U.S. EPA, Effluent Guidelines Plan, 61 Fed. Reg. 52582 (Oct. 7, 1996).

[85]See 40 C.F.R. § 125.3(c).

[86]A major difference between BPJ requirements and requirements based on effluent guidelines is that a permittee can challenge the propriety of a BPJ limitation when the permit is issued. Where a permit limitation is based on an effluent guideline, the validity of the guideline itself cannot be challenged in a permit appeal; rather, the permittee may challenge only the application of the guideline to the specific discharge and the permit writer's translation of the guideline into limitations.

[87]Section 402(o), 33 U.S.C. § 1342(o). *See also Natural Resources Defense Council v. EPA*, 859 F.2d 156, 197-203 (D.C. Cir. 1988) (upholding EPA's pre-1987 nonstatutory anti-backsliding policy).

[88]Section 301(b)(1)(A), 33 U.S.C. § 1311(b)(1)(A).

achieved by July 1, 1983, was based on the "best available technology economically achievable" (BAT).[89]

The BAT standards do not apply to conventional pollutants (biological oxygen demand, total suspended solids, fecal coliform, pH, and oil and grease). In 1977, Congress enacted Section 301(b)(2)(E) of the Act, which allows the application of a more lenient "best conventional pollutant control technology" (BCT) rather than BAT for conventional pollutants.

The BPT/BAT/BCT system of standards does not apply to "new sources."[90] Direct discharges that are new sources must meet "new source performance standards" (NSPS), which are based on "best available demonstrated control technology."[91]

Industrial dischargers that discharge into publicly owned treatment works (POTWs) (known as "indirect dischargers") are not regulated by the standards applicable to direct dischargers. Instead, they are regulated under the Section 307(b) pretreatment program, which is discussed in Part 7 below.

### 6.7.2.1 BPT

EPA sets BPT standards by surveying the particular industry, determining the types of treatment facilities typical of the industry, and determining the levels of pollution control achieved by the better run facilities using the typical technologies. The Agency then considers the category-wide or subcategory-wide cost of applying the technology in relation to the effluent reduction benefits.[92] This results in a control level reflecting the "average of the best" achieved by the industry.[93]

Although the 1977 deadline for meeting BPT limitations is long past, EPA has continued to promulgate BPT standards for conventional pollutants.[94] It is EPA's position that Congress did not intend BCT standards to displace BPT standards for conventional pollutants. Instead, EPA believes that BCT, which places cost-effectiveness constraints on incremental technology requirements that exceed BPT, was intended only to supplement BPT.[95]

### 6.7.2.2 BAT

BAT controls are intended to represent the maximum feasible pollution reduction for an industry. In making this determination, EPA often looks beyond the technologies

---

[89]Section 301(b)(2)(A), 33 U.S.C. § 1311(b)(2)(A). The Water Quality Act of 1987 extended this deadline to March 31, 1989.

[90]See discussion of "new source" in Part 6.7.2.4. below.

[91]Section 306, 33 U.S.C. § 1316.

[92]See, e.g., 52 Fed. Reg. 42522, 42525, 42533-38 (Nov. 5, 1987) (discussion of development of BPT limitations for OCPSF industrial category).

[93]EPA develops extensive supporting documentation for its categorical effluent guidelines. These "Development Documents" provide EPA's technical basis for the promulgated limitations and for its decision to regulate particular pollutants and waste streams under the guidelines. These Development Documents are often essential sources when challenging permit limitations.

[94]See, e.g., 40 C.F.R. Part 414; 52 Fed. Reg. 42522 (Nov. 5, 1987) (BPT limitations established for OCPSF industrial category).

[95]See Chemical Manufacturers Ass'n v. EPA, 870 F.2d 177, 207 (5th Cir. 1989), cert. denied, PPG Industries Inc. v. EPA, 495 U.S. 910 (1990).

usually employed by an industry, basing its standards on technologies used in other industries or on pilot plant data. Although no cost-benefit analysis is required, the standards must be "economically achievable." EPA considers BAT standards to be economically achievable if they would not force the closure of a large portion of the plants in an industrial category or subcategory.[96]

### 6.7.2.3 BCT

Congress created the BCT category of controls because it was concerned that the costs of moving beyond BPT to BAT for conventional pollutants were likely to be unreasonable considering the nature of conventional pollutants. It therefore required BCT standards to meet a "cost-reasonableness" test.[97] In most industrial categories, the BCT limitations are no more stringent than those established for BPT.

### 6.7.2.4 NSPS

"New sources" are subject to "new source performance standards" (NSPS). The question of whether a discharge is a "new source" is often disputed. "New source" is defined in the Act as "any source, the construction of which is commenced after the publication of proposed regulations prescribing a standard of performance . . . which will be applicable to such source, if such standard is thereafter promulgated . . . ."[98] EPA regulations modify this definition somewhat, defining a new source as a facility for which construction begins after the promulgation of an applicable final NSPS, or after proposal of such NSPS if the proposed NSPS is finally promulgated within 120 days of its proposal.[99]

The determination of whether a facility is a "new source" can be far more complicated than suggested by the regulatory definition. For one thing, the circuits of the U.S. Courts of Appeal are in conflict regarding the validity of the 120-day provision.[100] Further, it is not always clear when "construction" has begun. EPA's regulations define commencement of construction to include the placement, assembly, or installation of facilities or equipment, or significant site preparation work, or the entering into of a binding contract for the purchase of facilities or equipment.[101] Controversy may also arise as to whether construction at an existing facility should be considered a new source or simply a facility modification. To answer this question, EPA uses a "substantial independence" test, which looks at the degree to which the new unit functions independently of the existing facility, the degree of integration, and the

---

[96]*See, e.g.*, 52 Fed. Reg. 42522, 42538-45 (Nov. 5, 1987) (discussion of development of BAT for OCPSF category).

[97]This "cost reasonableness" test is discussed in detail at 51 Fed. Reg. 24973 (July 9, 1986).

[98]Section 306(a)(2), 33 U.S.C. § 1316(a)(2).

[99]40 C.F.R. § 122.2. It is virtually impossible for EPA to issue a final NSPS within 120 days of its proposal. Thus, for practical purposes, new sources are sources for which construction begins after promulgation of the final NSPS.

[100]*See National Ass'n of Metal Finishers v. EPA*, 719 F.2d 624 (3d Cir. 1983), *rev'd on other grounds sub nom. CMA v. NRDC*, 470 U.S. 116 (1985) (120-day provision not valid interpretation of congressional intent); *Natural Resources Defense Council, Inc. v. EPA*, 822 F.2d 104, 114 (D.C. Cir. 1987) (120-day provision valid).

[101]40 C.F.R. § 122.29(b)(4).

extent to which the new unit is engaged in the same general type of activity as the existing source.[102]

NSPS are intended to reflect "the greatest degree of effluent reduction . . . achievable through application of the best available demonstrated control technology, processes, operating methods, and other alternatives, including, where practicable, standards permitting no discharge of pollutants."[103] Although NSPS often are very similar to BAT standards, they can be more stringent than BAT, based on EPA's position that it can require the installation of state-of-the-art treatment technology in new facilities where requiring existing facilities to retrofit their processes and systems to include such technology would be economically unreasonable. In addition, because EPA must consider alternative production processes and operating methods, NSPS can also effectively dictate the choice of production processes used by a new source. For example, the NSPS for the steam electric category prohibit the discharge of fly ash transport water, effectively requiring "new source" plants in this category to use a dry ash handling system.[104]

One benefit of being a new source is that any new source facility constructed to meet all applicable NSPS may not be subjected to any more stringent standards for ten years after the date construction is completed or for the period of depreciation under the Internal Revenue Code, whichever is shorter.[105] This ten-year protection, however, applies only to technology-based limitations; it does not prevent more stringent water quality-based limitations from being imposed on a new source. In addition, at the end of the ten-year period, immediate compliance with the standards in effect at that time will be required. No implementation period for compliance is allowed.[106]

### 6.7.3 Water Quality-Based Limitations

#### *6.7.3.1 Water Quality Standards*

Water quality standards are established by the states and consist of two elements: (1) use classifications, and (2) criteria that, if not exceeded, will protect those uses. The Clean Water Act requires all states to classify the waters within the state according to intended use, e.g., public drinking water supplies, propagation of fish and wildlife, recreational purposes, and industrial, agricultural and other uses.[107] The state standards must attain the Act's goal of fishable, swimmable waters wherever possible, and, under EPA's "anti-degradation policy," must maintain both the uses designated in the standards and the current uses, unless the state can demonstrate that the designated use is unattainable or infeasible for reasons specified in EPA's regulations.[108]

---

[102]40 C.F.R. § 122.29(b)(1)(iii); 49 Fed. Reg. 37998, 38043-45 (Sept. 26, 1984); 45 Fed. Reg. 59343 (Sept. 9, 1980).

[103]Section 306(a)(1), 33 U.S.C. § 1316(a)(1).

[104]See 40 C.F.R. § 423.15(g).

[105]Section 306, 33 U.S.C. § 1316.

[106]Section 306(d), 33 U.S.C. § 1316(d).

[107]Section 303(c)(2), 33 U.S.C. § 1313(c)(2); 40 C.F.R. § 131.10(a).

[108]40 C.F.R. §§ 131.10(g), 131.12.

Water quality criteria quantitatively describe the physical, chemical, and biological characteristics of waters necessary to support the designated uses. State criteria are normally based on federal water quality criteria, which have been published for more than 50 pollutants.[109] The federal criteria are not enforceable standards, but are guidance that can be used by states in determining appropriate numerical criteria for water bodies within the state. A state may, however, choose to set site-specific criteria based on the characteristics of the local water body. For example, site-specific criteria may be appropriate in water bodies with species different from those used in the development of the Section 304(a) federal criteria or where adaptive processes have enabled a viable, balanced aquatic community to exist with levels of pollutants that exceed the national criteria.[110] The Water Quality Act of 1987 required states to establish numerical water quality standards rather than narrative standards for toxic pollutants.[111]

Normally, a state water quality standard consists of a numeric level of a pollutant that cannot be exceeded in the ambient water in order to protect the designated use. For example, the standard may state that the level of arsenic in a stream designated for trout propagation may not exceed 0.2 milligrams per liter.

### 6.7.3.2 Translating Standards Into Chemical-Specific Permit Limitations

EPA's regulations require permits to include water quality-based limitations for all pollutants that "are or may be" discharged at levels that cause, have a "reasonable potential to cause, or contribute to an excursion above any State water quality standard."[112] In setting a permit limitation to meet a water quality standard, the permit writer will calculate how much of the pollutant the permittee may discharge without causing the ambient standard to be exceeded. Normally, limitations based on chronic health effects are defined as four-day averages, and limitations based on acute health effects are defined as 1-hour or 24-hour limitations.

To calculate an appropriate permit limitation based on a numerical state standard, the permit writer will take into account the dilution provided by the receiving water. Where mixing with the receiving water occurs rapidly, the permit writer will normally consider the flow of the receiving stream (usually the 7Q10 low flow[113]) as compared

---

[109]Section 304(a)(1), 33 U.S.C. § 1314(a)(1).

[110]U.S. EPA, *Water Quality Standards Handbook* at iii (1983, updated Aug. 1994).

[111]Section 303(c)(2)(B), 33 U.S.C. § 1313(c)(2)(B). In December 1992, EPA issued what is referred to as the National Toxics Rule (NTR) which established numerical water quality standards for the 14 states that failed to meet the statutory deadline for developing their own numerical standards. 57 Fed. Reg. 60848 (Dec. 22, 1992). The NTR was modified somewhat as the result of litigation challenging the rule. 60 Fed. Reg. 22229 (May 4, 1995) (rule modified to base criteria for metals on measurement of total dissolved metals rather than total recoverable metals).

[112]40 C.F.R. § 122.44(d)(1)(i).

[113]The 7Q10 flow is the historical low flow for a period of seven days during a ten-year period, normally expressed as million gallons per day (MGD) or cubic feet per second (cfs). The 7Q10 flow may occur on nonconsecutive days during any one year.

to the flow of the outfall, and will develop a "dilution factor."[114] For example, an outfall that discharges 50,000 (0.05 million) gallons per day into a receiving stream with a low flow of 1.0 million gallons per day would be assigned a dilution factor of 20. The ambient water standards would then be multiplied by this dilution factor to determine the permit limitations.[115]

In most states, where mixing occurs less rapidly, a permit writer will set permit limitations based on a "mixing zone." A mixing zone is that portion of the receiving water that immediately receives an effluent discharge and in which the initial dilution of the discharge takes place. Normally, permit writers will allow water quality standards to be exceeded within the mixing zone so long as acutely toxic conditions do not exist.[116] Some states will take mixing into account through the use of dynamic modeling which models the fate of a discharge in the receiving waters.

In addition, where there are other dischargers into the receiving water, the permit limitation may be based on a total maximum daily load (TMDL) calculation.[117] A TMDL is an estimate of the total load of pollutants (from point, nonpoint, and natural background sources) that a segment of water can receive without exceeding applicable water quality criteria. Once the TMDL is determined, the permitting authority will allocate this total amount among the individual dischargers into the water body. Most states allocate the allowable discharge levels based on the proportion of the total discharges a facility has discharged into the water body in the recent past.

### 6.7.3.3 The Section 304(l) "Toxic Hot Spots" Program

The Water Quality Act of 1987 required states to develop lists of "impaired" water bodies within their boundaries, i.e. those waters that will not meet water quality standards even after the imposition of all technology-based requirements. For water bodies on those lists, states were required to identify specific point sources of toxic pollutants preventing or impairing the achievement of water quality standards, and to develop "individual control strategies" (ICSs) designed to attain such standards within three years. To comply with the ICS requirement, most states chose to issue new permits or permit modifications to point sources identified in the Section 304(l) process. In other words, because of the Section 304(l) program, many facilities' permits have been modified mid-term to include more stringent water quality-based limitations.

---

[114]See U.S. EPA Region VIII, "Mixing Zones and Dilution Policy" (Dec. 1994).

[115]This calculation is significantly more complicated for parameters such as pH, temperature, and biological oxygen demand. In these cases, permit limitations are often based on modeling of the effects of a discharge on the receiving waters.

[116]See *TSD* at 33-34.

[117]Section 303(d) of the Act requires states to identify water bodies for which technology-based effluent limitations are not stringent enough to meet water quality standards, and to develop TMDLs for those water bodies. These TMDLs must be submitted to EPA for approval. 33 U.S.C. § 1313(d). See also 40 C.F.R. § 130.7. A federal district court recently ordered EPA to take over Georgia's TMDL program, because the state had failed to develop TMDLs for its impaired waters. EPA took the position in the lawsuit that water quality-based effluent limits are an adequate substitute for TMDLs. There are other lawsuits pending against 14 other states' TMDL programs.

EPA made the Section 304(l) program a high priority within the Agency and all of the actions required by the Act have now been completed.[118] Revised NPDES permits have been issued to more than 800 point sources identified in the Section 304(l) process.

### 6.7.3.4 Pollutant Trading

In June 1996, EPA issued a guidance document describing its proposed approach to watershed-based "trading" of pollutants in effluents.[119] Under the proposed effluent trading approach, facilities that can reduce pollution to meet water quality standards at lower costs could accumulate credits by going beyond their permit requirements. Once these reductions are achieved, a trading program would allow companies to sell or barter credits to other facilities within the same watershed. Small dischargers are expected to be able to purchase these credits at a lower price than they would pay to install the technology needed to reduce pollution to meet water quality standards. The total pollutant reduction under trading would be the same as or greater than the reduction that would be achieved if no trading occurred. Trading participants must meet all applicable technology-based requirements. EPA's framework document provides information on various types of pollutant trading within a watershed, including point-point source trading, intra-plant trading, pretreatment trading, point-nonpoint source trading, and nonpoint-nonpoint source trading.

### 6.7.4 Toxicity-Based Limitations

Because of the enormous difficulties associated with setting individual water quality-based permit limitations, EPA and the states have begun to rely more extensively on limitations based on whole effluent toxicity (WET).[120] WET limitations are imposed in the form of a requirement to perform toxicity testing on the permittee's effluent. Effluent toxicity tests involve exposing selected species of aquatic life to one or more concentrations of an effluent in a laboratory setting to determine the short-term and/or long-term effects of exposure to the effluent.

Most permits now require dischargers to conduct toxicity tests with their effluent on a regular basis (e.g., monthly or quarterly). For example, a permit may require the permittee to conduct a 24-hour acute toxicity test on a species of water flea known as *Daphnia Magna,* using 100-percent effluent. In some cases, the permit may require

---

[118]The Ninth Circuit in 1990 remanded portions of the § 304(l) regulations and instructed EPA to require states to develop more comprehensive lists of point sources and develop ICSs for all listed point sources. *NRDC v. EPA*, 915 F.2d 1314 (9th Cir. 1990). EPA amended its regulations to require states to submit expanded point source lists "as soon as possible." The Agency, however, retained its original requirement to submit ICSs only for point sources on the "short list" pending a reconsideration of the scope of the ICS requirement. 57 Fed. Reg. 33040, 33042 (June 24, 1992).

[119]61 Fed. Reg. 29563 (June 11, 1996).

[120]Toxicity-based permit limitations may also be imposed on a chemical-specific basis. This approach imposes concentration limitations on specific toxic pollutants based on established concentrations known to prevent toxic effects of the particular pollutants. In recent years, EPA and most states have concentrated their toxicity-based permitting on WET rather than chemical-specific limitations.

longer-term chronic toxicity testing on a species of fish, such as the Fathead Minnow.[121] This toxicity testing can be very expensive, in some cases more expensive than all of the other monitoring and testing required by a permit.

In addition, a permit may establish a limitation on the results of the testing, such as providing that the mortality rate in an acute toxicity test may be no more than 10 percent. With this type of permit, the failure of a toxicity test will be considered a violation of the permit and could subject the permittee to penalties. In other permits, the failure of a toxicity test is not a permit violation, but triggers a requirement to perform a toxicity identification evaluation (TIE) or toxicity reduction evaluation (TRE) to identify and eliminate the source of the effluent toxicity.[122]

In early 1990, EPA began to focus on a third approach for controlling water pollution. In addition to chemical-specific and WET requirements, EPA turned its attention to biological assessments (i.e. evaluating the integrity of receiving waters directly by comparing various in-stream characteristics, such as species diversity and number, to the characteristics representative of "unaffected" waters).[123] It is now EPA's policy that states must fully integrate chemical-specific limitations, toxicity testing, and biological criteria (or "biocriteria") into their water quality programs.[124]

### 6.7.5 Variances

The statutory mechanisms for obtaining a variance from a technology-based standard are very limited. One such variance is the fundamentally different factors (FDF) variance.[125] The FDF variance mechanism allows a discharger to obtain a variance from technology-based limitations (including pretreatment limitations) other than NSPS. The variance is not available for water quality-based limitations.

To obtain an FDF variance, a discharger must demonstrate that the factors applicable to its facility are fundamentally different from those considered in the development of the effluent limitations guidelines applicable to the facility. Factors that may be fundamentally different include (1) the nature or quality of the pollutants contained in the discharge; (2) the volume of the discharge; (3) non-water quality environmental impacts of control and treatment of the discharge; (4) energy requirements of the treatment technology; and (5) age, size, land availability and configuration as they relate to the discharger's equipment, facilities, and processes. The

---

[121]EPA has proposed guidance for biomonitoring using five species, three for fresh water and two for salt water. 54 Fed. Reg. 50216 (Dec. 4, 1989).

[122]*See* 55 Fed. Reg. 30082, 30110 (July 24, 1990). EPA has published guidance for conducting TREs, including "Generalized Methodology for Conducting Industrial Toxicity Reduction Evaluations" (EPA/600/2-88/070).

[123]See U.S. EPA, "Policy on the Use of Biological Assessments and Criteria in the Water Quality Program" (June 19, 1991); U.S. EPA, "Notice of Availability: Biological Criteria: Technical Guidance for Streams and Small Rivers," 61 Fed. Reg. 42610 (Aug. 16, 1996).

[124]*TSD* at 41.

[125]Section 301(n), 33 U.S.C. § 1311(n); 40 C.F.R. § 125.30-125.32. Only EPA may grant an FDF variance, even where the state is the permit-issuing authority.

variance is not available, simply because the cost of compliance with the limitations would force plant closure.[126]

Under the 1987 amendments to the Act, a permittee must file a request for an FDF variance within 180 days after the publication of the applicable effluent guideline or standard.[127] In addition, an applicant for an FDF variance must show that it raised the fundamentally different factors during the development of the effluent guideline or show why it did not have a reasonable opportunity to raise such issues. This requirement makes it imperative that affected industries monitor and participate in the development and revision of effluent guidelines.

Several other variances are available under the Act, although they are rarely, if ever, granted. Under Section 301(c), EPA may modify BAT requirements or pretreatment requirements affecting nonconventional, nontoxic pollutants if it can be shown that the economic capability of the discharger requires less stringent limitations. The modified limitation must be shown to result in further progress toward elimination of the discharge of pollutants. Under Section 301(g), EPA may grant a variance from BAT for several nonconventional nontoxic pollutants (ammonia, chlorine, color, iron, and total phenols) where the applicable BAT limits are unnecessarily stringent.

## 6.8 Storm Water Discharges

### 6.8.1 Requirements Applicable to Storm Water Discharges

The problem of how to regulate storm water discharges has plagued EPA for more than two decades. Although the CWA has prohibited since 1972 the discharge of any pollutant to navigable waters from a point source, unless authorized by an NPDES permit, EPA and the courts struggled long and hard to develop a feasible program to reconcile the statutory requirement with the practical problems of regulating possibly millions of diverse point source discharges of storm water. Yet, EPA continued to identify storm water runoff as a significant source of water quality impairment. Ultimately, the storm water program required Congressional action.

In the Water Quality Act of 1987, Congress established a schedule under which EPA was required to establish regulations and issue permits for storm water discharges. That Act required EPA first (by October 1, 1992) to regulate storm water discharges "associated with industrial activity" and discharges from municipal separate storm sewer systems serving more than 100,000 people.[128]

---

[126]40 C.F.R. § 125.31.

[127]Section 301(n)(2), 33 U.S.C. § 1311(n)(2); 40 C.F.R. § 122.21(m)(1). For effluent guidelines promulgated before February 4, 1987, the request was required to be submitted by July 3, 1989. The statutory provisions regarding FDF variances apply only to variances from BAT limitations and pretreatment standards. FDF variances from BPT or BCT would presumably be handled under the regulatory provisions in 40 C.F.R. Part 125 Subpart D.

[128]Section 402(p), 33 U.S.C. § 1342(p). Storm water discharges included in an NPDES permit as of February 4, 1987, and discharges determined by EPA to contribute to a violation of a water quality standard or to be a significant contributor of pollutants to waters of the United States, were also required to have a permit by October 1992.

"Storm water" is defined as "storm water runoff, snow melt runoff and surface runoff and drainage."[129] The definition does not include infiltration (water that enters a sewer system from below the surface of the ground through defective pipes, pipe joints, connections, or manholes) or street wash waters.

The definition of "storm water discharge associated with industrial activity" is long and complex and requires careful reading.[130] In general, the term means the discharge from any point source used for collecting and conveying storm water which is directly related to manufacturing, processing, or materials storage areas at an industrial plant. This definition includes two subparts. First, the regulations define what types of facilities are considered to have "industrial activity" based on the facilities' SIC codes. Second, the regulations define what portions of these facilities are considered to include "industrial activity." These portions include industrial plant yards, material handling sites, refuse sites, shipping and receiving areas, manufacturing buildings, raw material storage areas, and other areas.[131]

For a limited number of industries, identified in § 122.26(b)(14)(xi), discharges are considered to be "associated with industrial activity" only where material handling equipment or activities, raw materials, intermediate products, final products, waste materials, by-products, or industrial machinery are exposed to storm water. For all other facilities subject to the storm water regulations, the permit requirement applies even if all activities at the facility are conducted indoors.[132]

The definition of "storm water associated with industrial activity" excludes discharges from facilities engaged in wholesale, retail, service, or commercial activities.[133] This definition also excludes storm water discharged from areas that are separate from industrial activities, such as office buildings and parking lots, unless the drainage is combined with storm water drained from areas used for industrial activities.[134] EPA or the state retains the authority to require a permit for discharges falling outside this definition that contribute to water quality violations or are significant contributors of pollutants to water bodies.[135]

---

[129]40 C.F.R. § 122.26(b)(13).

[130]The scope of "associated with industrial activity" is discussed at length at 55 Fed. Reg. 48007-15 (Nov. 16, 1990).

[131]40 C.F.R. § 122.26(b).

[132]EPA is in the process of developing guidance to encourage facilities to ensure that their industrial materials and processes do not come into contact with storm water. An earlier draft of this guidance, which was prepared by a federal advisory panel rather than EPA, would have exempted from the Section 402(p) permit requirement facilities that certify that all industrial activities and materials are within a permanent enclosed structure so that they are not exposed to storm water. It is not known at this time whether EPA's guidance will allow a similar exemption.

[133]55 Fed. Reg. 48007 (Nov. 16, 1990). See discussion of Phase II of the storm water program, below.

[134]*Id.* at 48010.

[135]Section 402(p)(2)(E), 33 U.S.C. § 1342(p)(2)(E).

The EPA recently issued an interim policy statement which provides that numeric water quality-based effluent limitations will not apply to storm water discharges.[136] The interim approach will rely on best management practices to meet water quality standards. This interim policy will not affect technology-based limitations on storm water discharges based on effluent guidelines or BPJ.

Discharges into municipal separate storm sewers are considered discharges to waters of the United States and require a storm water permit to the same extent as direct discharges. A municipal separate storm sewer is defined as a conveyance or system of gutters, ditches, manmade channels or storm drains, which is owned by a state, county, municipality, or other public entity, is designed or used for conveying storm water, and is not a combined sewer or part of a publicly owned treatment works.[137] This permit requirement applies regardless of the size of the municipality, whether or not the discharge from the storm sewer itself is subject to the permit requirement.

The EPA may issue permits for municipal storm sewer systems either for a particular system or on a jurisdiction-wide basis. Permits for municipal storm sewer systems must control pollutants "to the maximum extent practicable."[138] Such permits must include a requirement to effectively prohibit nonstorm water discharges into the system's storm sewers.

During the second phase of storm water regulation, EPA was required to identify storm water sources other than municipal and industrial sources, to determine the nature and extent of pollutants in such discharges, and, where appropriate, to issue permits for such additional discharges by October 1, 1992. This second phase of EPA's storm water program covers such sources as small municipal storm systems, commercial facilities, institutional facilities, some light industrial facilities, and construction activities disturbing less than five acres of land (potentially 19,000 small municipal systems and more than 7.5 million other small dischargers).

On August 7, 1995, EPA issued a final rule regulating the Phase II discharges.[139] Under the rule, sources that are determined to be significant contributors to water quality problems will be required to apply for a discharge permit within 180 days of receiving notice of such a determination.[140] The remaining dischargers will be required to apply for permits within six years of the effective date of the regulation, but only if the Phase II regulatory program in place at that time requires permits.

The preamble to the Phase II rule states that EPA is open to, and committed to, exploring a number of nonpermit control strategies for the Phase II program that will allow efficient and effective targeting of real environmental problems. EPA has established the Storm Water Phase II Federal Advisory Subcommittee to include stakeholders in the development of a supplemental Phase II rule. This supplemental rule

---

[136]U.S. EPA, "Interim Permitting Approach for Water Quality-Based Effluent Limitations in Storm Water Permits," 61 Fed. Reg. 43761 (Aug. 26, 1996).

[137]40 C.F.R. § 122.26(b)(8).

[138]Section 402(p)(3)(B)(iii), 33 U.S.C. § 1342(p)(3)(B)(iii).

[139]60 Fed. Reg. 40230 (Aug. 7, 1995). The rule superseded a direct final rule issued by EPA on April 7, 1995. 60 Fed. Reg. 17950 (April 7, 1995).

[140]EPA expects that most of these types of dischargers have already been included under Phase I of the storm water program. See 60 Fed. Reg. at 40230.

is scheduled to be finalized by March 1, 1999 and will determine the nature and extent of the requirements, if any, that will apply to the various types of Phase II facilities prior to the end of the six-year period.[141]

### 6.8.2 The Storm Water Permit Process

EPA published its final regulations addressing permit application requirements for storm water discharges in November 1990.[142] Under those regulations, dischargers had three options for obtaining coverage under a storm water permit: (1) coverage under a general permit; (2) application for a permit through a group application; or (3) obtaining an individual storm water permit. With the passage of time, only the general permit and individual permit options remain.

#### 6.8.2.1 General Permits

A storm water discharger may apply for an NPDES permit by filing a notice of intent to be covered by a general permit issued by EPA or an authorized state. EPA issued general permits for storm water discharges associated with industrial activity and discharges associated with construction activity in September 1992.[143] Although EPA's general permits would apply only in the 10 states, the District of Columbia, and five territories where EPA is the permitting authority, a number of authorized states have adopted EPA's general permits or have developed general permits of their own.

In September 1995, EPA issued a multi-sector general storm water permit which would apply to 11,000 facilities in 29 industrial segments in the unauthorized states and territories.[144] Under the multi-sector program, any facility that falls into one of the 29 industrial sectors would be allowed to apply for coverage under the five-year permit, including facilities already covered by one of the baseline general permits. Under the permit, storm water dischargers would have to develop site-specific pollution prevention plans based on industry-specific best management practices specified in the permit. For most facilities, the requirements under the more tailored multi-sector permit are less stringent than those under the baseline general permit. EPA is encouraging authorized states to use the multi-sector permit as a model for state-issued general permits.

#### 6.8.2.2 Individual Storm Water Permits

If a facility cannot qualify for coverage under a general permit, it must submit an individual storm water permit application. The preparation of the individual application is very burdensome, requiring not only detailed information about the facility but also

---

[141]An EPA official has stated that the Agency envisions a flexible permitting approach for small municipal dischargers within Phase II, including: education, outreach and public involvement; a clamp-down on illicit connections; provisions that address runoff from development and redevelopment and from construction activities; and good housekeeping practices at federal, state and local government facilities. *See* BNA, Daily Envt Rptr, "Work on Storm Water Rule To Continue Despite Concerns About Key Elements," (Aug. 14, 1996).

[142]55 Fed. Reg. 47990 (Nov. 16, 1990).

[143]57 Fed. Reg. 41178, 41236 (Sept. 9, 1992). The deadline for filing a notice of intent to be covered by these general permits was October 1, 1992.

[144]60 Fed. Reg. 50804 (Sept. 29, 1995).

quantitative data based on sampling of storm water discharges collected during storm events.[145]

### 6.8.2.3 Storm Water Management Plans and Pollution Prevention Plans

EPA believes that a pollution prevention approach is the most environmentally sound and cost-effective way to control the discharge of pollutants in storm water runoff from industrial facilities.[146] Thus, a primary component of all state and federal general permits is the requirement to develop and implement a storm water pollution prevention plan, also referred to as a storm water management plan, to control the pollutants carried by storm water discharges into surface waters. These plans generally contain various best management practices (BMPs), which may be general, industry-specific, or site-specific.

The major objectives of such plans are: (1) to identify sources of pollution potentially affecting the quality of storm water discharges associated with industrial activity from the facility; and (2) to describe and ensure implementation of practices to minimize and control pollutants in storm water discharges associated with industrial activity from the facility and to ensure compliance with the terms and conditions of the general permit.[147]

The general permits prescribe a four-step process for meeting these objectives: (1) formation of a team of qualified plant personnel who will be responsible for preparing the plan and assisting the plant manager in its implementation; (2) assessment of potential storm water pollution sources; (3) selection and implementation of appropriate management practices and control methods; and (4) periodic evaluation of the ability of the plan to prevent storm water pollution and comply with the terms and conditions of the permit.[148]

### 6.9 Thermal Discharges

Section 316 of the Act establishes special criteria for the discharge of heat, which is defined as a pollutant under the Act and is therefore subject to technology-based limitations. Under Section 316(a), if a discharger can demonstrate that the applicable technology-based limitation is more stringent than necessary to assure protection and propagation of a balanced, indigenous population of shellfish, fish, and wildlife in and on the receiving water, EPA or the state may adjust the limitation to a less stringent level. Section 316 is of particular importance to electric generating facilities because heat is a significant part of their discharge.

---

[145]EPA estimates that the individual storm water permit application takes approximately 60 hours to complete. *See* EPA, Guidance Manual for the Preparation of NPDES Permit Applications for Storm Water Discharges Associated with Industrial Activity (April 1991). EPA has proposed to simplify these permit application requirements. EPA recently issued interpretive policy guidance that allows permit writers considerable discretion to customize appropriate and streamlined reapplication requirements on a case-by-case basis for large municipal dischargers. This streamlining could include the use of the fourth-year annual report as the principal reapplication document. 61 Fed. Reg. 41698 (Aug. 9, 1996).

[146]57 Fed. Reg. at 41243 (Sept. 9, 1992).

[147]*Id.* at 41242.

[148]*Id.*

The Section 316 process is quite complex and requires the discharger to develop substantial amounts of scientific data. Today, most Section 316 applications are supported by extensive computer modeling of the effects of a thermal discharge on the receiving waters.

### 6.10 Ocean Discharges

No NPDES permit may be issued for a discharge into the territorial seas, the contiguous zone, or the oceans, unless the permittee complies with special criteria.[149] The permitting authority may issue a permit for such a discharge only if it determines that the discharge is in the public interest and will not result in the "unreasonable degradation of the marine environment." "Unreasonable degradation of the marine environment" is defined as either (1) a significant adverse change in ecosystem diversity, productivity, and stability of the biological community within the discharge area and surrounding biological communities; (2) a threat to human health through direct exposure to pollutants or through consumption of exposed aquatic organisms; or (3) a loss of aesthetic, recreational, scientific, or economic values which is unreasonable in relation to the benefit to be derived from the discharge.[150] Permit conditions may be imposed to ensure that such degradation does not occur.

The dumping of materials into the oceans (i.e. discharges that are not through outfalls) is regulated under the Marine Protection Research and Sanctuaries Act (MPRSA).[151] Under the MPRSA, the transportation of material from the United States for the purpose of dumping it into ocean waters is prohibited except as authorized by a permit issued under the Act.[152] The only ocean dumping activity of any significance that is currently permitted is the disposal of dredged spoil.[153] Under the MPRSA, the U.S. Army Corps of Engineers is authorized to issue permits for the transportation of dredged materials for ocean disposal.[154] EPA may designate ocean sites for dumping and may designate other sites as protected from ocean dumping. More than 140 dredged material disposal sites have been designated.[155]

---

[149]Section 403, 33 U.S.C. § 1343. "Territorial seas," "contiguous zone," and "ocean" are defined in CWA Section 502, 33 U.S.C. § 1362.

[150]40 C.F.R. § 125.121(e). The permitting authority may not issue a permit if it is uncertain whether the discharge will result in an unreasonable degradation, unless the permittee (1) agrees to provide additional data, such as a chemical analysis of the discharge, bioassays, or a dilution analysis, at a later date; and (2) can demonstrate that there are no reasonable alternatives to the disposal and that the discharge will not result in irreparable harm to the marine environment while the data are being obtained. 40 C.F.R. § 125.123(c).

[151]33 U.S.C. § 1401-14.

[152]33 U.S.C. § 1411(a).

[153]33 U.S.C. § 1413. The dumping of fish wastes is also allowed under the ocean dumping program, except for dumping in harbors or other areas where such wastes could endanger health, the environment, or ecological systems. 33 U.S.C. § 1412(d).

[154]33 U.S.C. § 1413; 33 C.F.R. Part 324.

[155]40 C.F.R. § 228.12.

The Ocean Dumping Ban Act of 1988, which amended the MPRSA, imposed strict prohibitions on the types of materials that can be dumped in the oceans. Under that Act, it is unlawful to dump into ocean waters sewage sludge or industrial waste.[156]

Ocean dumping is also regulated by the Coast Guard under Annex V of the International Convention for the Prevention of Pollution from Ships, known as MARPOL V. This treaty restricts the discharge of garbage and plastics in the ocean from ships of the signatory countries. Provisions of MARPOL V were codified as part of the Marine Plastic Pollution Research and Control Act of 1987.[157] In addition, the discharge of sewage from vessels is controlled under the Marine Sanitation Device Program.[158]

## 7.0 THE PRETREATMENT PROGRAM

Industrial discharges that do not discharge directly into "waters of the United States" but instead discharge into a public sanitary sewer system are regulated under the Clean Water Act pretreatment program.[159] Under the pretreatment program, limitations are imposed on industrial users (IUs) of a POTW through a permit, order or contract issued by the POTW or municipality rather than the state or EPA.

The pretreatment program involves a three-part system for controlling the pollution caused by IUs of POTWs. This system includes: (1) national general and specific discharge prohibitions, (2) national categorical standards, and (3) local limits developed by POTWs.

### 7.1 General Prohibitions

Discharges of pollutants that may interfere with a POTW's operations are regulated through the general pretreatment regulations found at 40 C.F.R. Part 403.[160] The regulations contain both general discharge prohibitions and specific prohibitions. The general prohibitions prohibit an IU from introducing into a POTW any pollutant that causes "pass through" or "interference."[161] Pass through is defined as a discharge that exits the POTW into waters of the United States in quantities or concentrations which, alone or in conjunction with a discharge or discharges from other sources, cause a violation of any requirement of the POTW's NPDES permit (including an increase in the magnitude or duration of a violation).[162] Interference is defined as a discharge which, alone or in conjunction with a discharge or discharges from other sources, both (1) inhibits or disrupts the POTW, its treatment processes or operations, or its sludge processes, use or disposal; and (2) therefore is a cause of a violation of any requirement

---

[156]33 U.S.C. § 1414b.

[157]33 U.S.C. § 1901 *et seq.*

[158]40 C.F.R. Part 140.

[159]Section 307(b), 33 U.S.C. § 1317(b). Discharges *from* publicly owned treatment works must comply with NPDES permits for direct dischargers, including "secondary treatment standards" for biological oxygen demand ($BOD_5$), suspended solids, and pH. 40 C.F.R. Part 133.

[160]EPA substantially revised its general pretreatment regulations in 1988. The preamble to that regulatory revision, found at 53 Fed. Reg. 40562 (Oct. 17, 1988), provides extensive discussions of several important aspects of the pretreatment program.

[161]40 C.F.R. § 403.5(a)(1).

[162]40 C.F.R. § 403.3(n).

of the POTW's NPDES permit (including an increase in the magnitude or duration of a violation) or of the prevention of sewage sludge use or disposal in compliance with applicable statutory provisions and regulations.[163]

## 7.2 Specific Prohibitions

The regulations establish eight specific prohibitions that are generally intended to prevent interference with the POTW's operations. These prohibitions include prohibitions on pollutants that may be fire or explosion hazards, pollutants that will cause corrosive structural damage to the POTW, solid or viscous pollutants that would cause an obstruction in flow, heat that would inhibit the biological activity at the POTW, and pollutants that could cause acute worker health and safety problems.

## 7.3 National Categorical Standards

The prohibition on discharges that "pass through" POTWs is implemented through categorical effluent guidelines. Effluent guidelines for an industrial category will normally include pretreatment standards for existing sources (PSES) and pretreatment standards for new sources (PSNS). The standards establish specific numerical limitations on pollutants considered "incompatible" pollutants — that is, pollutants other than biological oxygen demand, suspended solids, pH, and fecal coliform bacteria.

## 7.4 Removal Credits

The categorical standards are intended to result in the same level of treatment prior to discharge from the POTW as would have been required if the industrial facility had discharged those pollutants directly to the receiving waters. Thus, the user must meet the equivalent of BAT control unless the stringency of the standard is reduced through the mechanism of "removal credits," which gives an industrial discharger "credit" for the actual level of removal of a pollutant consistently achieved by the POTW.[164] In other words, the industrial discharger may meet a less stringent limitation if treatment of the pollutant occurs at the POTW. "Removal" does not include dilution or volatilization that occurs at or on the way to the POTW.[165]

In 1986, the U.S. Court of Appeals for the Third Circuit interpreted the Act to require EPA to promulgate comprehensive sewage sludge regulations before any removal credits could be authorized.[166] Congress codified this interpretation in the Water Quality Act of 1987.[167] Removal credits were thus not available for several years because EPA had failed to promulgate final regulations governing the disposal and use of POTW sludge.

---

[163] 40 C.F.R. § 403.3(i).

[164] 40 C.F.R. § 403.7.

[165] 40 C.F.R. § 403.7(a)(i) (dilution); 52 Fed. Reg. 42522, 42547 (Nov. 5, 1987) (volatilization).

[166] *Natural Resources Defense Council v. EPA*, 790 F.2d 289 (3d Cir. 1986), *cert. denied*, 479 U.S. 1084 (1987).

[167] Water Quality Act of 1987 § 406(e).

Regulations governing sludge that is co-disposed in municipal solid waste landfills were promulgated in October 1991[168] and were upheld by the D.C. Circuit Court of Appeals in December 1993.[169] EPA promulgated Phase I of its comprehensive sludge use and disposal regulations in February 1993.[170] Phase I established numerical pollutant limits for ten metals when sewage sludge is applied to the land, for three metals when it is disposed of at surface disposal sites, and for seven metals and total hydrocarbons when it is incinerated.[171]

Removal credits are thus now available for (1) pollutants sent to POTWs that co-dispose of their sludge in municipal landfills, and (2) the pollutants listed in 40 C.F.R. § 403 Appendix G that are discharged to other POTWs that comply with the sludge regulations.[172]

### 7.5 Local Limits

Both the Act and the federal pretreatment regulations specifically endorse more extensive requirements based on state and/or local law.[173] Two factors that often require local limits are the prevention of fume toxicity to workers and reducing POTW air emissions.

POTWs may establish local limits that are more stringent than the federal categorical standards. For example, the local limits may impose more stringent limitations on pollutants regulated under the federal standards, or may establish limits on pollutants that are not limited in the federal standards. Where the local limit is more stringent than the federal standard, the local limit supersedes the federal standard. A local limit that is less stringent than a federal standard, however, does not relieve the IU of its obligation to meet the federal standard.

### 7.6 Pretreatment Program Enforcement

Although the pretreatment program is primarily implemented by the municipality operating the POTW, EPA and the states retain enforcement authority.[174] If EPA becomes aware of a pass through or interference at a POTW and sends notice of the incident to the POTW and the POTW does not take appropriate enforcement action within 30 days, EPA may bring an enforcement action for the violation.[175] Similarly, an authorized state has the power to bring an action for penalties even though a POTW has

---

[168]56 Fed. Reg. 50978 (Oct. 9, 1991).

[169]*Sierra Club v. EPA*, 992 F.2d 337 (D.C. Cir. 1993).

[170]40 C.F.R. Part 503; 58 Fed. Reg. 9248 (Feb. 19, 1993). Under the terms of a consent decree, *Gearhart v. Reilly*, Civil No. 89-6266-JO (D. Ore.), EPA must promulgate Phase II of the sludge regulations by December 15, 2001.

[171]EPA withdrew the limits for chromium in October 1995. 60 Fed. Reg. 54764 (Oct. 25, 1995).

[172]See 40 C.F.R. Part 403 App. G.

[173]See Section 307(b)(4), 33 U.S.C. § 1317(b)(4); 40 C.F.R. § 403.4.

[174]Section 309, 33 U.S.C. § 1319; 40 C.F.R. § 403.10(f)(1). *See also*, EPA, Effluent Guidelines Plan, 59 Fed. Reg. 25859, 25861 (May 18, 1994).

[175]Section 309(f), 33 U.S.C. § 1319(f); 40 C.F.R. § 403.5(e).

sought penalties for the same noncompliance, if the state determines that the penalty sought by the POTW is insufficient.[176]

POTWs with approved pretreatment programs may enforce against violations of pretreatment permits, including violations of the national pretreatment standards.[177] POTWs, to be approved under the federal pretreatment program, must have the authority to seek injunctive relief for noncompliance and to seek or assess civil or criminal penalties of at least $1,000 per day for each violation of a pretreatment requirement.

## 8.0 NONPOINT SOURCE DISCHARGES

Nonpoint sources of pollution, i.e. discharges other than those defined as "point source" discharges, are a major source of pollution of our nation's waters. The largest nonpoint source contributor of pollutants is agricultural runoff. Siltation, salinity, pesticides, and nutrient discharges are the primary impacts on surface waters caused by nonpoint sources.

### 8.1 The Section 319 Program

Section 319 of the 1987 amendments to the Act created a system for the control of nonpoint sources of water pollution that depends primarily on state implementation. Under the Section 319 program, states were required to submit to EPA for approval an assessment of waters within the state that, without additional action to control nonpoint sources of pollution, cannot reasonably be expected to attain or maintain applicable water quality standards.[178] The states also were required to submit to EPA for approval state management programs that identify the measures to be undertaken by the state to reduce the pollutant loadings resulting from nonpoint source discharges, the state programs to achieve these measures, and a schedule for implementing the measures.[179] State programs must be developed in cooperation with local, sub-state regional and interstate entities involved in the nonpoint source issue. Congress authorized up to $400 million over four years to fund the state management programs.[180] This statutory provision has been greatly weakened, however, by Congress' failure to appropriate the money. Additionally, the statute provides no sanction against states for failing to submit an adequate plan.[181]

---

[176]40 C.F.R. § 403.10(f)(iv).

[177]*See* U.S. EPA, *Pretreatment Program Guidance to POTWs for Enforcement of Industrial Categorical Standards* (Nov. 1, 1984).

[178]Section 319(a)(1), 33 U.S.C. § 1329(a)(1).

[179]Section 319(b), 33 U.S.C. § 1329(b).

[180]Section 319(j), 33 U.S.C. § 1329(j).

[181]In May 1996, EPA and the states issued an agreement titled "Nonpoint Source Program & Grants Guidance for Fiscal Year 1997 & Future Years." This agreement gives states more flexibility in administering their nonpoint source control programs and streamlines the grants program.

## 8.2 Coastal Zone Management Program

The protection of coastal areas from nonpoint sources of pollution is managed under Section 319 of the Act and the Coastal Zone Management Program.[182] EPA and the National Oceanic and Atmospheric Administration (NOAA) jointly administer the Coastal Zone Management Program. Under the Program, the 29 coastal states were required to submit coastal nonpoint pollution control plans to EPA and NOAA by July 1995. States that fail to submit such plans risk losing a percentage of nonpoint source pollution control grants provided by EPA and NOAA under the Coastal Zone Management Act (CZMA), and may face penalties. The states must fully implement the management measures by January 1999.[183]

EPA and NOAA issued guidance on the development of state coastal nonpoint source management plans in January 1993.[184] These guidance documents establish specific management measures to control nonpoint pollution from various sources, including agriculture, silviculture, urban runoff, hydromodification, and marinas.

## 8.3 National Estuary Program

The 1987 amendments to the CWA also created the National Estuary Program (NEP) in order to promote long-term planning and management for nationally significant estuaries threatened by pollution, development, or overuse.[185] This program is a major vehicle for the implementation of nonpoint source controls. The NEP requires the preparation of Comprehensive Conservation and Management Plans (CCMP) which recommend approaches for correcting and preventing problems for estuaries nominated by state governors or the EPA Administrator. A CCMP is prepared through a Management Conference, to which federal, state, and local governments and representatives of industry and the general public may be invited. There are currently 28 estuaries included in the NEP.

## 9.0 DREDGE AND FILL PERMITS

The NPDES permit program does not apply to the disposal or placement of dredged or fill material into waters of the United States. Generally, any discharge or placement of dredged or fill material from a point source (e.g., a bulldozer) into any surface water is prohibited by Section 301 of the Act unless carried out under a permit issued by the U.S. Army Corps of Engineers under Section 404. As part of the permit process, the Corps of Engineers may designate areas for the placement or disposal of dredged or fill materials.

---

[182]Coastal Zone Management Act, 33 U.S.C. § 1451-1464, as amended by the Coastal Zone Act Reauthorization Amendments of 1990 (Pub. L. 101-508); *see* 58 Fed. Reg. 5182 (Jan. 19, 1993); 56 Fed. Reg. 57892 (Nov. 14, 1991).

[183]In February 1995, EPA and NOAA proposed to amend these requirements to give the agencies the option of granting conditional program approval for up to five years, and to provide flexibility in the implementation of the plans.

[184]U.S. EPA, *Guidance Specifying Management Measures for Sources of Nonpoint Pollution in Coastal Waters* (Jan. 1993); NOAA, *Coastal Nonpoint Pollution Control Program: Program Development and Approval Guidance* (Jan 1993).

[185]Section 320, 33 U.S.C. § 1330. See also 54 Fed. Reg. 40798 (Oct. 3, 1989).

## 9.1 Waters Within the Scope of the Program

As discussed above, "waters of the United States" includes wetlands that are adjacent to or tributary to other waters of the United States.[186] In addition, nonadjacent wetlands are usually found to be waters of the United States on the grounds that their potential use by migratory waterfowl or interstate travelers constitutes a nexus to interstate commerce sufficient to establish federal jurisdiction.[187] Section 404 thus substantially affects development in areas that could be considered to be wetlands.

Generally, "wetlands" are defined as areas that are inundated or saturated by surface or groundwater at a frequency and duration sufficient to support, and that under normal circumstances do support, a prevalence of vegetation typically adapted for life in saturated soil conditions, including swamps, marshes, bogs, and similar areas.[188] In 1987, the EPA, Corps of Engineers, Fish and Wildlife Service, and Soil Conservation Service issued a guidance manual for identifying wetlands subject to the Section 404 program.[189] This document describes technical criteria, field indicators and other methods for identifying and delineating jurisdictional wetlands. A 1989 revision of this manual led to an outcry from industry groups who complained that it would block development in many areas. A 1991 version of the manual proved to be extremely controversial, with environmentalists charging that it would open millions of acres of wetlands to development, and wetlands scientists labeling it as scientifically flawed. Because of this controversy, EPA and the Corps continue to rely on the 1987 manual, along with a 1992 technical supplement.

## 9.2 Covered Activities

The Section 404 permit program covers only the actual discharge or placement of dredged and fill material into waters of the United States. The Act does not cover pure dredging activities.[190] The Corps has clarified that incidental fallback of dredged soil from a normal dredging operation is not subject to the permit requirement. The test for "incidental fallback" is whether the "intent of the dredging operator is to remove material from the water and the results support this intent."[191]

"Redeposit" of dredged materials into a wetland has been held to be subject to the Section 404 program. For example, in one case, the court held that the rearrangement of indigenous materials in a riverbed, undertaken to cut off high water channels to protect riverbanks from erosion, required a permit under Section 404.[192] In another case, the court held that Section 404 applied to the owners of a tugboat that had propellers

---

[186]*See also United States v. Riverside Bayview Homes, Inc.*, 474 U.S. 121 (1985) (upholding Corps definition as including wetlands adjacent to navigable waters even if not inundated or frequently flooded by the navigable water).

[187]*See* 40 C.F.R. § 122.2. *See also Leslie Salt Co. v. U.S.*, 55 F.3d 1388 (9th Cir.), *cert. denied*, 116 S. Ct. 407 (1995) (seasonally dry wetlands used by migratory birds).

[188]*Id.*

[189]*Federal Manual for Identifying and Delineating Jurisdictional Wetlands* (1987).

[190]*But see Salt Pond Assoc. v. Army Corps of Engineers*, 815 F. Supp. 766 (D. Del. 1993).

[191]51 Fed. Reg. 41210 (Nov. 13, 1986).

[192]*U.S. v. Sinclair Oil Co.*, 767 F. Supp. 200 (D. Mont. 1990).

which cut into the river bottom, uprooting and destroying sea grass, and depositing bottom sediment on adjacent sea grass beds.[193]

Some fill activities are exempted from Section 404 if specified effects on navigable waters are avoided. These exempted activities include maintenance of dams, dikes, and similar structures, the construction of temporary sedimentation basins and temporary farm, forest, and mining roads, and several types of agricultural activities.[194]

## 9.3 Individual Permits

The Corps regulations governing the issuance of Section 404 permits are found at 33 C.F.R. § 325.1. In addition to these national regulations, there are local procedures and policies developed and implemented by the Corps district engineers. These local procedures must allow potential applicants to contact the local office for pre-application consultation for major projects.[195]

In reviewing an application for an individual Section 404 permit, the Corps will conduct what is referred to as a "Public Interest Review." This review involves an evaluation of the probable impacts of the proposed activity and its intended use on the public interest; and consideration and balancing of conservation, economics, aesthetics, general environmental concerns, historic values, fish and wildlife values, flood damage prevention, water supply, water quality, energy, and other factors.[196] The Corps cannot deny a permit solely on the basis of economics unrelated to environmental impacts.[197]

In reviewing a permit application, the Corps must apply EPA's Section 404 guidelines.[198] Under EPA's guidelines, no discharge of dredged or fill material shall be permitted if there is a practicable alternative to the proposed discharge which would have less adverse impact on the aquatic ecosystem.[199] An alternative is practicable if it is "capable of being done" taking into account "cost, technology and logistics in light of overall project purposes."[200] There is a presumption that a permit will not be granted for work in a wetland or "special aquatic area" for a nonwater-dependent project unless there are no practicable alternatives which are less environmentally damaging. A heavy burden is placed on the applicant to overcome thispresumption.[201] EPA's guidelines also contain a policy statement that a discharge may not cause or contribute to "significant degradation" of the aquatic ecosystem.[202]

---

[193]*U.S. v. M.C.C. of Florida, Inc.*, 772 F.2d 1501 (11th Cir. 1985), *vacated and remanded on other grounds*, 107 S. Ct. 1968 (1987). *See also Avoyelles Sportsman's League v. Marsh*, 715 F.2d 897 (5th Cir. 1983).

[194]See Section 404(f), 33 U.S.C. § 1344(f).

[195]33 C.F.R. § 325.1(b).

[196]33 C.F.R. § 320.4(a).

[197]*Mall Properties v. Marsh*, 672 F. Supp. 561 (D. Mass. 1987).

[198]33 C.F.R. §§ 320.4(a)(4); 325.2(a)(6).

[199]40 C.F.R. § 230.10(a).

[200]40 C.F.R. § 230(a).

[201]40 C.F.R. § 230.10(a)(3).

[202]40 C.F.R. §§ 230.1(c) and (d); 230.10(c).

No Section 404 permit may be granted by the Corps unless a certification from the affected state or states is obtained.[203] The Corps must also consult with EPA and the federal Fish and Wildlife Service prior to issuing a permit.[204] In addition, permits issued under Section 404 are subject to the requirements of the National Environmental Policy Act (NEPA).[205] This means that if a project authorized by a Section 404 permit would result in significant effects on the human environment, the Corps of Engineers is required to prepare an environmental impact statement before the permit can be issued. This requirement can significantly delay development and construction projects.

The Corps' regulations require that permit applications must be concurrently processed at federal, state and local levels. Some states and Corps districts are working to streamline the permit application process. For example, the Pennsylvania Department of Natural Resources (DNR) and the Corps have created a new general wetlands permit, called the Pennsylvania State Programmatic General Permit, for activities that have a limited environmental impact on wetlands less than one acre in size or on less than 250 linear feet of streams. This general permit will allow developers to submit only one application for authorization, and will allow the DNR to approve an activity without it undergoing extensive federal review.

### 9.4 The Mitigation Policy

The Section 404(b)(1) guidelines require applicants to take all practicable steps to minimize the adverse effects of proposed filling activities. Once the amount of wetland damage has been reduced to its barest minimum, the remaining damage must be mitigated.

Under a February 1990 memorandum of understanding between EPA and the Corps of Engineers, the Corps committed to strive to minimize the loss of wetlands resulting from its permit decisions.[206] This "no net loss" policy requires the Corps first to determine that potential impacts have been avoided to the maximum extent practicable, and then determine whether any remaining impacts have been mitigated "to the extent appropriate and practicable by requiring steps to minimize impacts, and then

---

[203]Section 401, 33 U.S.C. § 1341; 33 C.F.R. § 325.2(b). The certifying agency may be deemed to have waived its certification if it does not act within 60 days. 33 C.F.R. § 325.2(b)(1)(ii). *See also U.S. v. Marathon Dev. Co.*, 867 F.2d 96 (1st Cir. 1989).

[204]Section 404(q), 33 U.S.C. § 1344(q). EPA may veto a Section 404 permit if it determines that the discharge would have an unacceptable adverse effect on municipal water supplies, shellfish beds, fishing areas, wildlife, or recreation areas. Section 404(c), 33 U.S.C. § 1344(c). *Alameda Water & Sanitation Dist. v. Reilly*, 930 F. Supp. 486 (D. Colo. 1996).

[205]42 U.S.C. §§ 4321-4370d.

[206]Memorandum of Agreement Between the Environmental Protection Agency and the Department of the Army Concerning the Determination of Mitigation Under Clean Water Act Section 404(b)(1) Guidelines (Feb. 6, 1990).

to compensate for aquatic values." Unavoidable wetlands impacts often may be offset by wetlands restoration or creation.[207]

In most cases, a minimum of 1:1 acreage replacement of wetlands will be required to achieve no net loss of values. Compensatory mitigation (e.g., restoration of existing degraded wetlands or creation of manmade wetlands) should be undertaken, when practicable, on-site. If this is not practicable, it should be undertaken in the same geographical area (e.g., the same watershed).[208]

## 9.5 Nationwide Permits

The Corps is authorized to issue nationwide and general (state, regional or nationwide) Section 404 permits for specific categories of activities involving the discharge of dredged or fill materials determined to have minimal adverse environmental effects. An activity covered by a nationwide or general permit may be performed without obtaining an individual Section 404 permit, so long as the requirements of the nationwide or general permit are complied with.[209] The general and nationwide permits are intended to allow certain minor-impact activities to take place without delay or paperwork.

Currently, nationwide permits have been issued for 36 activities, including such things as some survey activities, backfilling of utility lines, minor road crossings, construction of outfall structures, bank stabilization, oil and gas structures, hydropower projects, and maintenance activities.[210] Only 13 of the nationwide permits require that special notice be given to the Corps prior to proceeding with an activity. The other 23 nationwide permits are technically self-executing, although it is normally prudent to contact the Corps when planning an activity within a possible wetland area.

---

[207]The February 1990 MOA contains a controversial provision limiting mitigation requirements where a high proportion of the land is wetlands. In addition, the MOA states that the sequencing set forth in the MOA (avoidance, minimization, compensation) may not be required where wetland alterations constitute "insignificant environmental losses."

[208]The Interagency Working Group on Federal Wetlands Policy – a workgroup established by President Clinton's August 1993 wetlands initiative, *Protecting America's Wetlands: A Fair, Flexible, and Effective Approach* – has proposed national guidance for wetlands mitigation banking. Mitigation banking is defined as "wetlands restoration, creation, enhancement, and in exceptional circumstances, preservation undertaken expressly for the purpose of mitigating unavoidable adverse wetland losses in advance of development actions, when compensatory mitigation cannot be achieved at the development site or is not environmentally beneficial." Mitigation banking works by allowing developers to use mitigation bank wetlands acreage and functions – known as "credits" – to replace the anticipated loss of wetlands acreage and functions at the development site. See also *Federal Guidance for the Establishment, Use, and Operation of Mitigation Banks* (proposed), 60 Fed. Reg. 12286 (March 6, 1995).

[209]See 33 C.F.R. Parts 320-330; 56 Fed. Reg. 59110 (Nov. 22, 1991).

[210]33 C.F.R. Part 330, App. A.

## 9.6 Potential Liabilities Under the Section 404 Program

Like violations of other parts of the Act, violations of the Section 404 permit requirement may result in penalties of up to $25,000 per day.[211] In addition, the Corps may bring an action to compel the restoration of areas that have been filled without obtaining the required permit, or dredged in violation of permit conditions. Extensive restoration, including replication of natural topography and hydrology, has been ordered in some cases.[212]

Discharging dredged or fill material without a Section 404 permit can also lead to criminal penalties. Criminal penalties will normally be imposed only for cases of extreme conduct, such as refusing to obey a cease and desist order, or causing severe damage to a wetland.[213]

## 10.0 PREVENTING, REPORTING AND RESPONDING TO SPILLS

### 10.1 Spill Prevention

Section 301 of the Clean Water Act establishes a national policy "that there should be no discharges of oil or hazardous substances into or upon the navigable waters of the United States, adjoining shorelines, or into or upon the waters of the contiguous zone"[214] Section 311 of the Act creates a comprehensive scheme of prohibitions, reporting requirements, penalties, and cleanup obligations to implement this policy.

The Act requires many facilities to develop and maintain plans for preventing and responding to spills of oil and hazardous substances, called Spill Prevention Control and Countermeasure (SPCC) Plans. As amended by the Oil Pollution Act of 1990 (OPA), the Act now also requires owners and operators of some facilities to prepare and submit a more extensive plan for responding to a worst case spill of oil, called a "Facility Response Plan."

#### 10.1.1 SPCC Plans

A facility must prepare an SPCC plan if it engages in drilling, producing, gathering, storing, processing, refining, transferring, distributing, or consuming oil and if, due to its location, it could reasonably be expected to discharge oil in "harmful quantities," as defined in Part 110 of the regulations,[215] into or upon surface waters or

---

[211]Section 309(d), 33 U.S.C. § 1319(d). See the discussion of Clean Water Act enforcement in Part 11 below.

[212]*See, e.g., U.S. v. Cumberland* Farms, No. 91-10051-MLW (D. Mass. July 25, 1996), 61 Fed. Reg. 40248 (Aug. 1, 1996) (settlement under which company will establish 30-acre wildlife and wetlands corridor on site it allegedly damaged and will turn over additional 225 acres to state for permanent conservation); *U.S. v. Larkins,* 657 F. Supp. 76 (W.D. Ky. 1987), *aff'd,* 852 F.2d 189 (6th Cir. 1988); *U.S. v. Board of Trustees, Florida Keys Comm. College,* 531 F. Supp. 267 (S.D. Fla. 1981).

[213]*See U.S. v. Ellen,* 961 F.2d 462 (4th Cir. 1992), *cert. denied,* 113 S. Ct. 217 (1992); *U.S. v. Pozsgai,* 897 F.2d 524 (3d Cir.), *cert. denied,* 498 U.S. 812 (1990).

[214]Section 301(b)(1); 33 U.S.C. § 1321(b)(1).

[215]See discussion in Part 10.2 below.

adjoining shorelines.[216] Exempted from this requirement are facilities where (1) the total underground storage capacity is 42,000 gallons or less of oil, and (2) the aboveground storage capacity is 1,320 gallons or less of oil, provided no single container has a capacity in excess of 660 gallons.[217]

The SPCC plan is a plan describing steps the facility will take to prevent spills and to minimize the risk of harm to surface waters in the event of a release of oil. The SPCC plan need not be submitted to the regulatory agency, but must be maintained at the facility at all times and may be reviewed during state or federal inspections.[218] Owners or operators of new facilities must prepare an SPCC plan within six months after the date the facility begins operations and must implement the plan as soon as possible but not later than one year after the facility begins operations.[219]

The SPCC plan must be amended whenever there is a change in facility design, operation or maintenance that materially affects the facility's potential for the discharge of oil. Notwithstanding this requirement, the plan must be reviewed and evaluated for adequacy at least once every three years.[220] Plans must be reviewed and certified by a Registered Professional Engineer.[221] The failure to maintain and implement an SPCC plan in accordance with the regulations may result in a civil penalty of not more than $5,000 for each day the violation continues.[222]

If a facility discharges more than 1,000 gallons of oil into the waters of the United States or upon adjoining shorelines, or discharges a harmful quantity of oil to waters of the United States or adjoining shorelines twice within a 12-month period, the owner or operator of the facility must submit additional information to the EPA Regional Administrator within 60 days.[223] After reviewing this information, the Regional Administrator may require the facility to amend the SPCC plan if he or she finds that the existing plan does not meet the requirements of the regulations or that amendment of the plan is necessary to prevent or contain discharges from the facility.[224]

---

[216] 40 C.F.R. § 112.1(b). Although the Act requires EPA to issue regulations requiring SPCC plans for discharges of oil or hazardous substances, 33 U.S.C. § 1321(j)(5)(A), EPA has issued such regulations only for discharges of oil (40 C.F.R. Part 112). Regulations requiring SPCC plans for discharges of hazardous substances that apply to the Department of the Army have been issued by the Department of Defense. See 32 C.F.R. § 650.208 et seq. In addition, states may require SPCC plans for hazardous substances under state programs.

[217] 40 C.F.R. § 112.1(d)(2).

[218] 40 C.F.R. § 112.3(e). SPCC plans must be maintained at a facility if the facility is normally attended at least eight hours a day. If the facility is normally attended less than eight hours, the plan may be maintained at a nearby field office. 40 C.F.R. § 112.3(e).

[219] 40 C.F.R. § 112.3(b).

[220] 40 C.F.R. § 112.5.

[221] 40 C.F.R. § 112.3(d). The engineer must certify that the plan has been prepared in accordance with good engineering practices.

[222] 40 C.F.R. § 112.6. The procedures for imposing such penalties are set forth in 40 C.F.R. § 114.

[223] 40 C.F.R. § 112.4(a).

[224] 40 C.F.R. § 112.4(d). Section 112.4(e) and (f) set forth the procedures for appealing a decision by the Regional Administrator requiring amendment of an SPCC plan.

EPA's regulations set forth detailed guidelines for the preparation of SPCC plans.[225] The plan must contain a description of recent spill events, and, in some circumstances, a prediction of the direction, rate of flow, and total quantity of oil that could be discharged from the facility as a result of a failure in containment.[226] The regulations specify the types of containment structures and other spill control mechanisms that may, or in some cases must, be included in the plan. For example, where a facility has above-ground bulk petroleum storage tanks, it must provide a containment structure large enough to contain the entire contents of the largest single tank plus sufficient freeboard to allow for precipitation.[227]

The plan must also identify a designated person who is accountable for oil spill prevention and who reports to line management.[228] Owners and operators are responsible for properly instructing their personnel in the operation and maintenance of equipment to prevent oil discharges, and in applicable pollution control laws and regulations.[229]

### 10.1.2 Facility Response Plans

Under the OPA, a nontransportation-related onshore facility is required to prepare a Facility Response Plan if it handles, transports, or stores oil, and if it, "because of its location, could reasonably be expected to cause substantial harm to the environment by discharging into or on the navigable waters, adjoining shorelines, or the exclusive economic zone."[230] Facilities that do not meet EPA's "substantial harm criteria" must complete and maintain a certification stating that the criteria do not apply.[231]

EPA has established criteria for determining which facilities may cause "substantial harm" in the event of a discharge of oil. Facility Response Plans must be prepared for: (1) facilities that transfer oil over water to or from vessels that have a total oil storage capacity greater than or equal to 42,000 gallons; (2) facilities with total oil storage capacity of at least one million gallons, where one or more of the following is true: (a) the facility does not have secondary containment for each aboveground storage area sufficiently large to contain the capacity of the largest tank plus sufficient freeboard for precipitation; (b) the facility is located at a distance from fish and wildlife or sensitive environments such that a discharge could cause injury to them; (c) the facility is located such that a discharge would shut down operations at a public drinking water intake; or (d) the facility has had a reportable spill greater than or equal to 10,000 gallons within the past five years.[232]

The Regional Administrator may require facilities other than "substantial harm facilities" to prepare and submit a facility response plan after a consideration of: (1) the

---

[225]40 C.F.R. § 112.7.

[226]40 C.F.R. § 112.7(a) and (b). This information is required if experience indicates that there is a reasonable potential for equipment failure (such as tank overflow, rupture, or leakage).

[227]40 C.F.R. § 112.7(e)(2). Some states require this allowance for precipitation to be equal to 10 percent of the contents of the largest tank.

[228]40 C.F.R. § 112.7(e)(10)(ii).

[229]*Id.*

[230]Section 311(j)(5)(B)(iii), 33 U.S.C. § 1321(j)(5)(B)(iii).

[231]40 C.F.R. § 112.20(e).

[232]40 C.F.R. § 112.20(f); 59 Fed. Reg. 34070 (July 1, 1994).

type of transfer operation; (2) the oil storage capacity; (3) a lack of secondary containment; (4) proximity to fish and wildlife and sensitive environments and other areas determined to possess ecological value; (5) proximity to drinking water intakes; (6) spill history; and (7) other site-specific characteristics and environmental factors that the Regional Administrator determines are relevant to protecting the environment from harm.[233]

The OPA required "substantial harm facilities" to submit Facility Response Plans to EPA for approval by February 1993. Facilities that have not submitted such plans are not permitted to operate.[234] Facilities may operate for up to two years pending federal approval of submitted plans if the owner of the facility certifies that he or she has ensured by contract or other means the availability of private personnel and equipment necessary to respond to a worst case discharge. If that period expires, or if approval is denied, the facility must discontinue its storage, transportation and handling of oil.[235]

The Facility Response Plan is intended to be a plan for responding to a worst case release of oil.[236] EPA's regulations include a worksheet that is to be used to calculate what this worst case event would be.[237] The regulations also set forth a model plan that is to be followed in developing facility plans.[238] The plan must, among other things, identify the person with authority to implement the plan; require immediate communication to appropriate federal officials; ensure that adequate private personnel and equipment will be available to respond to the discharge; describe the immediate measures that will be taken in the event of a spill to secure the source of the discharge and provide containment; contain plans for evacuation; and require training, drills and equipment testing.[239] The Plan must be consistent with the National Oil and Hazardous Substance Pollution Contingency Plan (NCP).[240]

## 10.2 Spill Notification

Section 311(b)(5) of the Act requires persons in charge of facilities to immediately report to the National Response Center discharges[241] of harmful quantities of oil or a

---

[233]40 C.F.R. § 112.20(b), (f)(2).

[234]Section 311(j)(5)(E), 33 U.S.C. § 1321(j)(5)(E). EPA's regulations amending its OPA requirements allowed owners or operators that failed to meet the February 1993 deadline to submit their SPCC plans by August 30, 1994. 59 Fed. Reg. 34070 (July 1, 1994).

[235]Section 311(j)(5)(F), 33 U.S.C. § 1321(j)(5)(F).

[236]The plan must include discussions of planning for a worst case spill and for other possible spill scenarios, including (i) a discharge of 2,100 gallons or less, and (ii) a discharge of between 2,100 and 36,000 gallons or 10 percent of the capacity of the largest tank at the facility, whichever is less. 40 C.F.R. § 112.20(h)(5).

[237]40 C.F.R. Part 112, App. D.

[238]40 C.F.R. Part 112, App. F.

[239]Section 311(j)(5)(C), 33 U.S.C. § 1321(j)(5)(C).

[240]40 C.F.R. Part 300.

[241]For purposes of the Section 311 program, "discharge" is defined as including, but not limited to, "any spilling, leaking, pumping, pouring, emitting, emptying or dumping." Section 311(a)(2), 33 U.S.C. § 1321(a)(2).

hazardous substance to navigable waters or adjoining shorelines. It is a criminal offense to fail to make such a report, punishable by up to five years in prison.[242]

For spills of oil,[243] EPA has determined that a "harmful quantity" is any quantity causing a film or sheen on the receiving waters, any quantity causing a sludge or emulsion to be deposited beneath the surface of the water or upon adjoining shorelines, or any quantity that violates an applicable water quality standard.[244]

EPA has designated approximately 300 substances as hazardous substances subject to the Section 311 reporting requirement,[245] and has identified the "reportable quantity" for each of these substances.[246] Any release of more than the reportable quantity of a hazardous substance within a 24-hour period must be reported to the National Response Center.[247] This reporting requirement is in addition to reporting requirements under the Comprehensive Environmental Response, Compensation, and Liability Act (CERCLA), the Emergency Planning and Community Right-to-Know Act (EPCRA), and other federal or state requirements.

Under certain conditions, an NPDES permit may insulate a permittee from the statutory notification requirement. For purposes of Section 311, "discharge" is defined to exclude (1) discharges in compliance with an NPDES permit; (2) discharges resulting from circumstances identified, reviewed and made a part of the public record with respect to an NPDES permit, and subject to a condition in such permit; and (3) continuous or anticipated intermittent discharges from a point source, identified in an NPDES permit or permit application, that are caused by events occurring within the scope of the relevant operating or treatment systems.[248]

## 10.3 Spill Response and Liability

The discharge of harmful quantities of oil or a hazardous substance into waters of the United States or onto adjoining shorelines or the contiguous zone is prohibited.[249] Owners and operators of facilities from which oil or a hazardous substance is discharged to navigable waters, shorelines, or into the contiguous zone in quantities greater than the reportable quantity are strictly liable for: (1) penalties, (2) the costs of cleaning up the

---

[242]Section 311(b)(5), 33 U.S.C. § 1321(b)(5).

[243]"Oil" is defined as "oil of any kind or in any form, including, but not limited to, petroleum, fuel oil, sludge, oil refuse, and oil mixed with other than dredged spoil." Section 311(a)(1), 33 U.S.C. § 1321(a)(1).

[244]40 C.F.R. § 110.3. *See Orgulf Transport Co. v. U.S.*, 711 F. Supp. 344 (W.D. Ky. 1989) (EPA determination that any discharge of oil causing a sheen may be harmful is authorized by the Act, even though all spills of oil create a sheen). The use of a dispersant or emulsifier to prevent a sheen in order to circumvent the notice requirement is prohibited. 40 C.F.R. § 110.8.

[245]40 C.F.R. Part 116.

[246]40 C.F.R. Part 117.

[247]40 C.F.R. § 117.21.

[248]Section 311(a)(2), 33 U.S.C. § 1321(a)(2); 52 Fed. Reg. 10712 (April 2, 1987). For a complete discussion of the exclusions from Section 311 notification requirements, see the *NPDES Permit Handbook*, Appendix 2 (2d ed. Gov't. Inst. 1992).

[249]Section 311(b)(3), 33 U.S.C. § 1321(b)(3).

spill, and (3) natural resource damages caused by the spill.[250] Defenses to liability are very limited.[251]

The OPA increased the penalties to which a discharger may be subject. Any owner, operator, or person in charge may be fined up to $25,000 per day for a discharge, or up to $1,000 per barrel of oil discharged.[252] Where a discharge results from gross negligence or willful misconduct, the minimum penalty is $100,000 and the maximum penalty is $3,000 per barrel of oil or unit of reportable quantity of hazardous substance discharged.

As stated above, liability under Section 311 is strict, i.e. it may be imposed without regard to fault or negligence.[253] For response costs, however, unless the government proves that the discharge resulted from "willful negligence or willful misconduct within the privity and knowledge" of the responsible person, liability is capped at $50 million for a facility, and for a vessel at $150 per gross ton or (for a vessel carrying oil or a hazardous substance as a cargo) $250,000, whichever is greater.[254] The liability of an owner or operator of a vessel or facility from which a prohibited discharge of oil or a hazardous substance occurs includes costs incurred by the federal or state government in the restoration and replacement of natural resources damaged or destroyed as the result of the discharge.[255] Sums recovered from such owners and operators are to be used to restore, rehabilitate, or acquire the equivalent of such natural resources.[256]

---

[250]For example, in December 1994, in a settlement of a complaint under the Clean Water Act and Oil Pollution Act, six Chinese and Japanese ship operators agreed to pay $9 million in civil penalties, cleanup costs, and natural resource damages for a 1991 spill of 450,000 gallons of oil off the Olympic Peninsula in Washington. (*U.S. v. Marutha Corp.*, D. Wash., No. 94-1537 WD, Oct. 14, 1994).

[251]Section 311(f), 33 U.S.C. § 1321(f). Defenses include: (1) an act of God; (2) an act of war; (3) negligence on the part of the U.S. government; and (4) an act or omission of a third party. *Id.*

[252]For discharges of hazardous substances, the quantity-based penalty is $1,000 per reportable quantity unit. In other words, if the reportable quantity for a substance is 10 pounds and 10,000 pounds are discharged, the penalty would be $1,000,000 (10,000 ÷ 10 X $1,000). Section 311(b)(7)(A), 33 U.S.C. § 1321(b)(7)(A).

[253]For example, in November 1994, a Port Arthur, Texas, refinery was ordered to pay a $400,000 criminal fine and was placed on probation for three years for two relatively small oil spills into the Neches River. The case was based on a spill of three barrels of No. 6 fuel oil and a spill of one barrel of light mixed product. The spills were reported by the company and were promptly cleaned up by company employees. The company cooperated fully with all governmental agencies and there was no evidence of fish kills or other environmental damage. (*U.S.A. Fina Oil and Chemical Co.*, D. E. Tex., No. 194CR65, Oct. 31, 1994). In a 1994 Tennessee case, Alamco Inc. was fined $124,000 in administrative penalties for a release of about 174 barrels of oil that occurred after vandals cut off the lock securing the valve on an oil storage tank. In assessing the fine, EPA recognized that vandalism was the cause of the discharge and that the surrounding wildlife and vegetation were not significantly affected by the spill.

[254]Section 311(f)(1)-(3), 33 U.S.C. § 1321(f)(1)-(3). For an inland oil barge, the response cost cap is $125 per gross ton or $125,000, whichever is greater.

[255]Section 311(f)(4), 33 U.S.C. § 1321(f)(4).

[256]Section 311(f)(5), 33 U.S.C. § 1321(f)(5).

A discharge in violation of Section 311(b) may also subject the discharger to criminal penalties under Section 309(c) of the Act. In addition, a person in charge of a vessel or facility who fails to report a reportable discharge to the NRC may be guilty of a criminal violation, punishable by a fine and/or imprisonment for up to five years.[257]

## 11.0 ENFORCEMENT

### 11.1 Federal and State Roles

The Clean Water Act's enforcement mechanisms are structured to allow states (and local governments in the case of the pretreatment program) to assume an active role in the Act's enforcement. The federal government, however, has traditionally been more active in the enforcement of the Clean Water Act than state and local governments. Part of the reason for this is surely financial; the federal government has had more resources allocated to the Act's enforcement than have state and local governments. Many states have only recently made environmental enforcement in general, and water pollution enforcement in particular, a priority budget item.

To obtain approval of its NPDES permit program, a state must demonstrate that its environmental control agency has adequate powers of enforcement, roughly equivalent to those exercised by EPA under the Act.[258] At a minimum, authorized states must have civil and criminal enforcement authority, and virtually all have some form of administrative enforcement authority.

State enforcement programs are not required to be identical to the federal program. For example, states may impose maximum civil penalties as low as $5,000 per day per violation (compared to the daily maximum of $25,000 under the federal program) and may impose maximum criminal penalties as low as $10,000 per day per violation (compared to $50,000 per day under the federal program).[259] In addition, EPA currently does not require authorized states to provide a mechanism for citizen suits under the state program. States are required only to allow intervention of citizens in enforcement actions, to investigate and respond in writing to citizen complaints, and to provide notice and opportunity for comment on proposed settlements of state enforcement actions.[260]

In states with authorized permit programs, EPA retains the right to initiate an enforcement action despite a state's determination that no action is warranted.[261] EPA must first notify the alleged violator and the state of its intent to bring an enforcement action and must allow the state 30 days to commence a state enforcement action.

Moreover, EPA may bring a federal enforcement action even though an authorized state has brought a parallel action that is pending in state court. Where a final judgment

---

[257]Section 311(b)(5); 33 U.S.C. § 1321(b)(5). The first criminal action to enforce the OPA included a charge for failure to report the discharge of a waste oil and water mixture into the ocean off the coast of Florida. The company was fined $500,000 for the failure to report and for the discharge itself. *U.S. v. Palm Beach Cruises S.A.*, D.C. S. Fla., No. 94-08049, May 19, 1994.

[258]Section 402(b)(7), 33 U.S.C. § 1342(b)(7); 40 C.F.R. § 123.27(a).

[259]40 C.F.R. § 123.27(a)(3). *See also Natural Resources Defense Council v. EPA*, 859 F.2d 156, 180 (D.C. Cir. 1988).

[260]40 C.F.R. § 123.27(d).

[261]Section 309(a), 33 U.S.C. § 1319(a).

has been issued in the state action, however, EPA is generally foreclosed from relitigating the factual issues decided in the state proceeding.[262]

In addition, if EPA finds that permit violations within a state are widespread and appear to result from the state's failure to enforce its permits, EPA must so notify the state. If the state's failure to enforce extends more than 30 days beyond the notice, EPA must assume responsibility for enforcing permits within the state. This period of federally assumed enforcement ends only after EPA determines that the state will adequately enforce its permit program.[263]

In states where EPA retains permitting authority, EPA (usually through the Regional Offices) is the primary enforcement authority. Nonauthorized states may enforce in state courts any state statutes and regulations that are not inconsistent with or duplicative of the federal scheme.

## 11.2 Enforcement Theories

The Clean Water Act is viewed by many as the easiest of the federal environmental statutes to enforce. This is because the persons regulated under the Act, primarily holders of NPDES permits, must report their own compliance and noncompliance to the regulating agency on a regular basis on their discharge monitoring reports (or DMRs). On the DMRs, a permittee must report the results of all monitoring of its discharges, and must indicate where those discharges exceeded permit limitations.[264] In addition, permittees must report any noncompliance that may endanger health or the environment within 24 hours from the time the permittee becomes aware of the circumstances.[265] Permittees are also required to report any anticipated noncompliance,[266] any noncompliance not required to be reported under any other specific provision,[267] and any noncompliance that the permittee failed to report as required elsewhere by the regulations or the permit.[268]

The most common substantive basis for a federal enforcement action is Section 301(a) of the Act, the discharge prohibition discussed earlier in this chapter.[269] Because this provision effectively prohibits the discharge of any pollutant except as in compliance with the Act, it imparts broad enforcement authority. For example, any discharge in excess of a permit limitation is not only a potential violation of Section 402 (which sets out the permit program), but also a violation of Section 301(a). Likewise, any discharge without a permit would potentially violate Section 301(a).

For civil enforcement purposes, and arguably for some criminal violations, the Clean Water Act is a strict liability statute. This means that the intent of the violator is irrelevant; once the violation is established, liability attaches. A person need not have

---

[262]*U.S. v. ITT Rayonier, Inc.*, 627 F.2d 996, 1001 (9th Cir. 1980).

[263]Section 309(a)(2), 33 U.S.C. § 1319(a)(2). We are not aware of any occasions on which EPA has exercised this right to assume enforcement responsibility.

[264]40 C.F.R. § 122.41(l)(4) and (7).

[265]40 C.F.R. § 122.41(l)(6).

[266]40 C.F.R. § 122.41(l)(2).

[267]40 C.F.R. § 122.41(l)(7).

[268]40 C.F.R. § 122.41(l)(8).

[269]33 U.S.C. § 1311(a).

acted negligently or with any intent to violate the statute to be found liable.[270] Moreover, impossibility and data errors have been held not to be defenses to Clean Water Act enforcement actions.[271] Thus, enforcement actions may be brought based on little, if anything, more than the DMRs and other reports submitted by the permittee itself. In addition, EPA or the state may generate additional evidence of violations through inspections of the permitted facility.

EPA often enforces in cycles, focusing its enforcement efforts on a particular issue or industrial group in a coordinated manner. For example, at various times, EPA has targeted such issues as unpermitted discharges, pretreatment violations, Oil Pollution Act violations, municipal permit violations, and discharges of toxic chemicals.[272] That is not to say that when EPA is focusing on a particular type of activity it will ignore all other types of violations. It is probably safe to say, however, that when the Agency is targeting a certain type of activity, all entities participating in that activity should be aware that they are likely to be scrutinized.

## 11.3 Defenses

Because liability under the Act is strict, there are few defenses available to the permittee accused of violating its permit. For example, assertions of the good faith of the defendant, the pendency of a permit modification request, and the need for federal funding for a public system have all been rejected as defenses to enforcement actions under the Act.[273] Two defenses that exist under EPA's regulations are theories of "upset" and "bypass." A third defense, known as "permit-as-a-shield," may also be available in some situations.

### 11.3.1 Upset

Several courts have ruled that, since the equipment underlying the technology-based permit limitations is inherently subject to failure for reasons beyond the control

---

[270]*E.g.*, *U.S. v. Texas Pipeline Co.*, 611 F.2d 345 (10th Cir. 1979); *U.S. v. Amoco Oil Co.*, 580 F. Supp. 1042 (W.D. Mo. 1984).

[271]*California Public Interest Research Group v. Shell Oil Co.*, 840 F. Supp. 712 (N.D. Cal. 1993). *But see Public Interest Research Group of New Jersey, Inc. v. Elf Atochem North America, Inc.*, 817 F. Supp. 1164 (D.N.J. 1993) (laboratory error is partial defense to enforcement action; permittee will not be held liable for discharge violation, but will be liable for each measurement proved to be erroneous).

[272]In 1996, the EPA water enforcement program announced that it will focus its enforcement efforts on discharges into streams and basins in about a dozen high-risk watersheds, and on wet weather flows and wetlands. *See* BNA, Daily Envt Rptr, "Water Program to Focus on Wetlands, Watersheds, Wet Weather Flow Violations," (Sept. 6, 1996).

[273]*United States v. Amoco Oil. Co.*, 580 F. Supp. 1042 (W.D. Mo. 1984) (good faith); *Public Interest Research Group of New Jersey v. Monsanto*, 600 F. Supp. 1479 (D.N.J. 1985) (permit modification pendency); *Pacific Legal Foundation v. Quarles*, 440 F. Supp. 316 (C.D. Cal. 1977), *aff'd*, 614 F.2d 225 (9th Cir.), *cert. denied*, 449 U.S. 825 (1980) (lack of federal funding).

of the operator, EPA must allow for upsets in applying those standards.[274] EPA's regulations define an "upset" as "an exceptional incident in which there is unintentional and temporary noncompliance with technology-based permit effluent limitations because of factors beyond the reasonable control of the permittee."[275] The term does not include noncompliance "caused by operational error, improperly designed treatment facilities, inadequate treatment facilities, lack of preventive maintenance, or careless or improper operation."[276] An upset constitutes an affirmative defense in an enforcement action for violations of technology-based permit limitations.[277]

To claim upset as a defense, the permittee must submit notice of the upset within 24 hours of the event.[278] The permittee must be able to show, through properly signed contemporaneous operating logs or other relevant evidence, the cause of the upset,[279] that the facility was being operated properly at the time of the upset, and that appropriate remedial measures were taken.[280] The permittee seeking to establish the upset defense has the burden of proving that the defense applies.[281]

The upset defense is available to a permittee only if it is incorporated into the permit expressly or by reference to the relevant regulatory provisions.[282] It is also important to note that, since state permit programs can be more stringent than the federal program, a state can choose not to allow the upset defense.[283]

### 11.3.2 Bypass

A more limited defense may be offered through EPA's regulations governing "bypasses." A "bypass" is defined as the intentional diversion of waste streams from

---

[274]*See Marathon Oil Co. v. EPA*, 564 F.2d 1253 (9th Cir. 1977); *FMC Corp. v. Train*, 539 F.2d 973 (4th Cir. 1976).

[275]40 C.F.R. § 122.41(n)(1). *See also* 40 C.F.R. § 403.16(a). *See also Chesapeake Bay Foundation, Inc. v. Bethlehem Steel Corp.*, 652 F. Supp. 620 (D. Md. 1987) (violations of permit nearly every day during two-month period were not upsets).

[276]40 C.F.R. § 122.41(n)(1).

[277]40 C.F.R. § 122.41(n)(2). In 1988, the U.S. Court of Appeals for the D.C. Circuit ruled that EPA's refusal to extend the upset defense to water quality-based permit limits was arbitrary and capricious. *Natural Resources Defense Council v. EPA*, 859 F.2d 156, 209-10 (D.C. Cir. 1988). Upon remanding the regulation to the Agency, the court specifically stated that it did not mean to imply that EPA must allow the defense for water quality-based limitations, only that if the Agency decides not to extend the defense, it must provide a reasoned basis for its decision. EPA appears to have taken no action in response to the court's holding, but appears to consider the issue on a case-by-case basis.

[278]40 C.F.R. § 122.41(n)(3)(iii); *Public Interest Research Group of New Jersey v. U.S. Metals Refining Co.*, 681 F. Supp. 237 (D. N.J. 1987).

[279]The "cause" may be shown through circumstantial evidence, although the permittee must at least perform a thorough investigation of the causes of an incident. 49 Fed. Reg. 38039 (Sept. 26, 1984).

[280]40 C.F.R. § 122.41(n)(3).

[281]40 C.F.R. § 122.41(n)(4).

[282]*Sierra Club v. Union Oil Co. of California*, 813 F.2d 1480, 1487 (9th Cir. 1987), *vacated on other grounds*, 485 U.S. 931 (1988), *reinstated on remand*, 853 F.2d 667 (9th Cir. 1988).

[283]40 C.F.R. § 123.25(a)[Note].

any portion of a treatment facility.[284] Bypasses are allowed only in very limited circumstances. Even a bypass that does not cause effluent limitations to be exceeded is allowed only for essential maintenance to ensure efficient operation.[285] Essential maintenance is not routine maintenance that can be performed during periods of non-process operations, but includes only repairs and maintenance that cannot wait until the production process is not in operation to be performed.[286] For example, if a seal on a valve malfunctions or a pipe bursts during production hours, the facility operator may bypass that particular unit process in order to perform corrective maintenance.[287]

Bypasses that cause effluent limitations to be exceeded are prohibited except in circumstances where they are necessary to avoid severe property damage, personal injury, or loss of life.[288] Under these circumstances, bypass is permitted only if there are no feasible alternatives, such as the use of auxiliary treatment facilities, retention of untreated waste waters, or maintenance during normal periods of down time.[289] In addition, if the permittee knows in advance of the need for a bypass, it must submit prior notice, if possible, at least ten days before the date of the anticipated bypass.[290] The regulatory agency must be notified within 24 hours of any unanticipated bypass.[291] Where all of these conditions are met, a bypass will not be considered a violation of a permit. Bypass may be used as an affirmative defense in an enforcement action.[292]

### 11.3.3 Permit-as-a-Shield

Under Section 402(k) of the Act, compliance with an NPDES permit acts as a "shield" against enforcement. In other words, so long as a permittee is in compliance with the limitations and conditions in its NPDES permit, neither the state nor EPA can bring an enforcement action against it for violation of the Act, such as for discharging pollutants not limited in the permit.[293] The Supreme Court has noted that the purpose of Section 402(k) "seems to be . . . to relieve [permit holders] of having to litigate in an

---

[284]40 C.F.R. § 122.41(m)(1)(i). *See also* 40 C.F.R. § 403.17(a).

[285]40 C.F.R. § 122.41(m)(2). *See also Natural Resources Defense Council, Inc. v. EPA*, 822 F.2d 104 (D.C. Cir. 1987) (upholding bypass prohibition even where limitations not exceeded).

[286]49 Fed. Reg. 38037 (Sept. 26, 1984).

[287]*Id.*

[288]40 C.F.R. § 122.41(m)(4).

[289]40 C.F.R. § 122.41(m)(4)(B). This condition is not satisfied if adequate backup equipment should have been installed in the exercise of reasonable engineering judgment to prevent a bypass that occurred during normal periods of equipment down time or preventive maintenance. *Id.*

[290]40 C.F.R. § 122.41(m)(3)(i).

[291]40 C.F.R. § 122.41(m)(3)(ii).

[292]*See, e.g., U.S. v. CPS Chemical Co.*, 779 F. Supp. 437, 454 (E.D. Ark. 1991); *Student Public Interest Research Group of New Jersey v. AT&T Bell Laboratories*, 617 F. Supp. 1190, 1204 (D. N.J. 1985).

[293]U.S. EPA, "Policy Statement on Scope of Discharge Authorization and Shield Associated with NPDES Permits," Memorandum from Robert Perciasepe, Assistant Administrator for Water, *et al.*, to Regional Administrators and Regional Counsels (July 1, 1994). This policy statement clarifies the applicability and scope of the permit shield under various scenarios.

enforcement action the question whether their permits are sufficiently strict."[294] The shield does not apply to violations of the Act outside the scope of the NPDES program (e.g., spill reporting, Section 404 violations).

In *Atlantic States Legal Foundation, Inc. v. Eastman Kodak Co.*, 12 F.3d 353 (2d Cir.), *cert. denied*, 115 S. Ct. 62 (1994), a citizens group sued an NPDES discharger for discharging, over a four-year period, more than a million pounds of pollutants which were not limited in the discharger's permit. The court held that Section 402(k) prohibited an enforcement action against the discharger for discharging the pollutants since the discharger was in compliance with its permit at all relevant times. The court stated,

> Viewing the regulatory scheme as a whole, . . . it is clear that the permit is intended to identify and limit the most harmful pollutants while leaving the control of the vast number of other pollutants to disclosure requirements. Once within the NPDES or SPDES scheme, therefore, polluters may discharge pollutants not specifically listed in their permits so long as they comply with the appropriate reporting requirements and abide by any new limitations when imposed on such pollutants.[295]

## 11.4 Enforcement Options

Federal enforcement may take the form of (1) an administrative order requiring compliance and/or assessing an administrative penalty, (2) an action for civil penalties and/or an injunction, or (3) an action for criminal penalties. State enforcement schemes generally follow the federal system.

EPA will normally choose the least resource-consuming enforcement option, which in most cases will be an administrative order.[296] A civil judicial action may be appropriate when there is a need for a court order directing immediate or long-term compliance measures (i.e. a temporary restraining order or injunction), such as where the noncompliance is serious and continuing and the violator is uncooperative. In addition, civil judicial action is needed to assess a penalty of more than $125,000. Criminal enforcement actions will be brought for serious violations that are knowing or negligent.[297]

## 11.5 Administrative Orders

The Water Quality Act of 1987 authorized EPA to issue administrative orders assessing penalties for Clean Water Act violations, including permit violations. Class I penalties may not exceed $10,000 per violation, up to a maximum of $25,000. Before assessing a Class I penalty, EPA must give the alleged violator written notice of the

---

[294]*E.I. du Pont de Nemours & Co. v. Train*, 430 U.S. 112, 138 n.28 (1977).

[295]12 F.3d at 357.

[296]U.S. EPA, "Guidance on Choosing Among Clean Water Act Administrative, Civil and Criminal Enforcement Remedies" (Aug. 28, 1987).

[297]*Id.*

proposed assessment and an opportunity to request an informal hearing.[298] A Class II penalty may not exceed $10,000 per day for each violation, up to a maximum of $125,000. Class II penalties may be imposed only after notice and an opportunity for a full adjudicatory hearing.[299]

EPA may also issue an administrative order requiring compliance with the Act.[300] Administrative orders for permit violations often include a compliance schedule and may also include interim limitations that must be met while the scheduled activities are being performed. Administrative compliance orders are administrative commands; they are not adjudications of rights or liabilities and do not impose any sanctions for the underlying violations or for a violation of the compliance order itself. Because they lack such determinative effect, such orders lack finality and are not reviewable by a court until EPA brings an action in federal district court to enforce an administrative order.[301] Although an order is not enforceable until EPA brings such an action, failure to comply with an administrative order could form the basis of a criminal prosecution for a "knowing" violation or of a civil action where a claim of bad faith is made.

### 11.6 Civil Judicial Enforcement

EPA, through its U.S. Department of Justice attorneys, may bring an action in federal district court seeking civil penalties for violations of the Act.[302] Civil penalties may be imposed without a showing of negligence or fault on the part of the defendant, and may be assessed at up to $25,000 per day for each violation.[303] An alleged violator is entitled to a jury trial to determine liability for civil penalties. Once liability is established, however, the court retains the power to determine the amount of penalty to be imposed.[304]

EPA's Clean Water Act Penalty Policy[305] establishes a method for calculating an appropriate penalty as part of a settlement of a Clean Water Act enforcement action. The penalty is to consist of an "economic benefit component" plus a "gravity component," plus or minus adjustments. It is EPA's policy that penalties should recover the full economic benefit of noncompliance, calculated from the beginning of the noncompliance until the point when the facility was or will be in compliance. Under the Penalty Policy, EPA normally calculates this benefit using the BEN computer program. The gravity component is based on (1) the significance of the violation, (2) the actual or potential harm to human health or the environment, (3) the number of violations, and (4) the duration of noncompliance. Adjustments may be made for (1) a history of recalcitrance, (2) ability to pay, (3) litigation considerations (e.g., the potential for

---

[298]For guidance on Class I penalty procedures, see 52 Fed. Reg. 30730 (Aug. 17, 1987).
[299]Section 309(g), 33 U.S.C. § 1319(g).
[300]Section 309(a), 33 U.S.C. § 1319(a).
[301]Section 309(b), 33 U.S.C. § 1319(b).
[302]*Id.*
[303]Section 309(d), 33 U.S.C. § 1319(d).
[304]*U.S. v. Tull*, 481 U.S. 412 (1987).
[305]EPA, Clean Water Act Penalty Policy for Civil Settlement Negotiations (Feb. 11, 1986), revised effective March 1, 1995.

protracted litigation and the maximum penalty likely to be awarded by a court), and (4) other equitable considerations.

EPA may also initiate a civil action to obtain an injunction. The district court has the power to enter preliminary and permanent injunctions to restrain and abate violations of the Act, regulations, and permits, including state permits. If an injunction is violated, the violator is subject to the criminal and civil penalty provisions of the Act, as well as the criminal and civil contempt powers of the court.

## 11.7 Criminal Enforcement

EPA may refer a matter to the Department of Justice for the institution of a criminal action against any discharger who knowingly or negligently violates the Act.[306] The penalties for an initial conviction for a negligent violation include a fine of from $2,500 to $25,000 per day, imprisonment for not more than one year, or both. The penalties for a knowing violation are a fine of from $5,000 to $50,000 per day, imprisonment for not more than three years, or both. In both cases, the maximum penalties for subsequent convictions are doubled.[307]

In a recent case, the Ninth Circuit Court of Appeals held that the manager and assistant manager of a sewage treatment plant were criminally liable under the Act for "knowing" violations even though the two men did not know that the discharges of sludge violated the facility's permit. The Court held that criminal sanctions may be imposed on an individual who knowingly engages in conduct that results in a permit violation, regardless of whether he is cognizant of the requirements or even the existence of the permit.[308]

A person who knowingly violates a permit or other requirement of the Act and knows at the time that he thereby places another person in imminent danger of death or serious bodily injury is subject to a fine of up to $250,000 ($1,000,000 for an organization) and imprisonment for up to 15 years. Penalties are doubled for second offenses.[309] An action for such "knowing endangerment" may, for example, be brought if a person knowingly contaminates a water supply or deliberately dumps hazardous materials into sewers or waterways.[310]

Criminal penalties may also be imposed against any person who makes a false statement, representation, or certification to the government, or any person who falsifies,

---

[306]Section 309(c), 33 U.S.C. § 1319(c).

[307]*Id.*

[308]*U.S. v. Weitzenhoff*, 1 F.3d 1523 (9th Cir. 1993), *amended and superseded on denial of reh'g en banc*, 35 F.3d 1275 (9th Cir. 1993), *cert. denied*, 115 S. Ct. 939 (1995). *Accord U.S. v. Hopkins*, 53 F.3d 533 (2d Cir. 1995) (defendant only had to know of the commission of the illegal act, not that the act violated the company's discharge permit).

[309]Section 309(c)(3), 33 U.S.C. § 1319(c)(3).

[310]*See U.S. v. Borowski*, 977 F.2d 27 (1st Cir. 1992) (prosecution for knowing endangerment cannot be premised on danger that occurs before pollutant reaches water); *U.S. v. Villegas*, 784 F. Supp. 6 (E.D. N.Y. 1991), *rev'd and remanded*, *U.S. v. Plaza Health Laboratories, Inc.*, 3 F.3d 643 (2d Cir. 1993), *cert. denied*, 114 S. Ct. 2764 (1994) (defendant who placed vials of blood into river bulkhead could not be convicted of knowing endangerment because there was insufficient evidence that he knew there was a high probability that by placing the vials in the river he was placing another person in imminent danger).

tampers with, or knowingly renders inaccurate any monitoring device required under the Act.[311] These violations may subject a violator to a fine of not more than $10,000, imprisonment for not more than two years, or both, with penalties doubled for a subsequent violation.

Criminal penalties may be imposed against corporations, persons directly involved in a violation, and "responsible corporate officers."[312] Corporate officers that deliberately shield themselves from knowledge of violations are likely to be considered "responsible" under the Act.

## 11.8 Citizen Suits

Section 505 of the Act allows any person "having an interest which is or may be adversely affected"[313] to commence a civil action against any person for violation of any effluent standard, limitation or order, or against EPA for failure to perform a nondiscretionary duty.[314] This citizen suit provision has been frequently used by citizen groups, particularly in actions against dischargers for violations of NPDES permits. These suits are rather straightforward, since NPDES permittees must report all exceedances of permit limitations to the permitting agency on a monthly or quarterly basis. A citizen group may therefore bring an action for a permit violation using the permittee's own reports as evidence.

A citizen suit may be brought only if neither EPA nor a state is "diligently prosecuting" the violation.[315] An EPA or state enforcement action that results in a compliance order and not a penalty assessment, however, has been held not to constitute a diligent prosecution that would foreclose a citizen suit.[316]

The plaintiff must give the alleged violator, EPA and the state 60 days' notice prior to initiation of the lawsuit, unless the action involves a violation of Sections 306 or 307(a) of the Act. The notice must include a parameter-by-parameter description of the

---

[311]Section 309(c)(4), 33 U.S.C. § 1319(c)(4). See *U.S. v. Sinskey and Kumm*, Nos. 96-400/0-01 & 02 (D. S.D. July 26, 1996) (jury verdict finding men guilty of deliberately falsifying DMRs and of rigging a water sampling test to render it inaccurate).

[312]Section 309(c)(6), 33 U.S.C. § 1319(c)(6).

[313]This standing requirement of this section has been broadly construed. Normally, a citizen group can demonstrate standing by showing that one or more of its members makes use of the water body that is affected by the discharge at issue. See *Natural Resources Defense Council, Inc. v. Texaco Refining and Marketing, Inc.*, 2 F.3d 493 (3d Cir. 1993); *Public Interest Research Group of New Jersey, Inc. v. Powell-Duffryn Terminals, Inc.*, 913 F.2d 64 (3d Cir. 1990), cert. denied, 498 U.S. 1109 (1991). But see *Friends of the Earth Inc. v. Crown Central Petroleum Corp.*, 95 F.3d 358 (5th Cir. 1996) (citizen group does not have standing where members used waters three tributaries and 18 miles downstream from facility and no evidence that pollutants had migrated from facility to those waters).

[314]Section 505(a), 33 U.S.C. § 1365(a).

[315]Section 505(b), 33 U.S.C. § 1365(b).

[316]*Natural Resources Defense Council, Inc. v. Fina Oil & Chem. Co.*, 806 F. Supp. 145 (E.D. Tex. 1992). See also *Citizens for a Better Environment v. Union Oil Co. of California*, 83 F.3d 1111 (9th Cir. 1996) (citizen suit not barred by company's settlement with state under which it paid $780,000 to push back a compliance date); *Knee Deep Cattle Co. v. Bindana Investment Co.*, 94 F.3d 514 (9th Cir. 1996) (state prosecution for solely past violations did not constitute diligent prosecution for ongoing violations).

alleged violations[317] and must specify a time period in which the alleged violations occurred.[318]

Most citizen suits settle under a consent agreement providing for some combination of (1) payment of a civil penalty,[319] (2) payment of attorney's fees and costs to the plaintiffs, (3) a compliance schedule to bring the permittee into compliance, along with (4) stipulated penalties for failure to meet the compliance schedule, and (5) payment of money to support an environmental activity selected by the plaintiff. EPA has the right to review and object to any consent agreement entered in a citizen suit.[320] The plaintiff may not recover personal remedies, such as damages.

Citizen suits may be brought only for continuing or intermittent violations.[321] To meet this requirement, however, a plaintiff need only make a good faith allegation of a continuous or intermittent violation at the time the statutory 60-day notice of intent to sue is given. A violation will be considered to be continuing for jurisdictional purposes unless it is "absolutely clear that the allegedly wrongful behavior could not reasonably be expected to occur."[322] A court has jurisdiction only over violations included in the plaintiff's 60-day notice letter and post-complaint continuing violations of the same type.[323]

---

[317]*Natural Resources Defense Council, Inc. v. Texaco Refining and Marketing, Inc.*, 2 F.3d 493, 499 (3d Cir. 1993).

[318]*Hudson Riverkeeper Fund Inc. v. Putnam Hosp. Ctr. Inc.*, 891 F. Supp. 152 (S.D. N.Y. 1995).

[319]Any civil penalty recovered goes to the U.S. Treasury. *New Jersey Public Interest Research Group v. Powell-Duffryn Terminals, Inc.*, 913 F.2d 64 (3d Cir. 1990). If a suit is settled without a finding or admission of a violation of the Act, the money recovered is not required to be paid to the Treasury, although it often will be. *Sierra Club v. Electronic Controls Design, Inc.*, 909 F.2d 1350 (9th Cir. 1990).

[320]Section 505(c)(3), 33 U.S.C. § 1365(c)(3). Often, EPA or the U.S. Department of Justice will require that any environmental activity receiving settlement funds be related to the alleged violation (*e.g.*, money paid in settlement of an alleged water permit violation would not be allowed to be designated for an air monitoring project).

[321]*Gwaltney of Smithfield Ltd. v. Chesapeake Bay Foundation, Inc.*, 484 U.S. 49 (1987).

[322]484 U.S. at 66. The Fourth Circuit, on remand in the *Gwaltney* case, stated, "Intermittent or sporadic violations do not cease to be ongoing until the date when there is no real likelihood of repetition." *Gwaltney of Smithfield Ltd. v. Chesapeake Bay Foundation, Inc.*, 844 F.2d 170, 172 (4th Cir. 1988). *But see Allen County Citizens for the Environment v. BP Oil Co.*, 762 F. Supp. 733 (N.D. Ohio 1991), *aff'd*, 966 F.2d 1451 (6th Cir. 1992) (violation not "continuing" where no exceedances had occurred during the 42 months preceding the date the complaint was filed, even though two exceedances occurred after complaint was filed).

[323]*Public Interest Research Group v. Hercules, Inc.*, 830 F. Supp. 1549, 1556 (D. N.J. 1993).

# CHAPTER 5

# OIL POLLUTION ACT

Austin P. Olney[1]
LeBoeuf, Lamb, Greene & MacRae, L.L.P.
Washington, D.C.

## 1.0 OVERVIEW

The Oil Pollution Act of 1990 (OPA)[2] brought about massive changes in the oil production, transportation, and distribution industry. Its stringent legal regime and its extensive operational requirements caused significant restructuring in the industry, created overnight demand for oil spill prevention and response technology and equipment, and set in motion the issuance of sweeping new requirements at the federal, state, and local levels.

In the six years since its enactment, most of the OPA regulations have been issued, leaving an extensive regulatory legacy, the impact of which is still being absorbed. Although OPA has been tested in several major incidents, comparatively few cases have been brought to court, and the precise contours of the statute have yet to be drawn by the courts. Consequently, the primary guidance for the interpretation of OPA is still found in the statute itself, its legislative history, and the implementing regulations. The following provides a summary of the statute, its regulatory regime, and the application of OPA's provisions in the limited number of civil and criminal cases reported to date.

OPA is far more comprehensive and stringent than any previous United States or international oil pollution liability and prevention law. OPA is divided into nine titles. Title I of OPA creates a new section on oil pollution liability and compensation in Title 33 of the U.S. Code.[3] In Title I, OPA imposes strict liability for a comprehensive and expansive list of damages from an oil spill into the water from vessels and facilities. The law contains limits on this liability, but the limits are far higher than under prior U.S. law or international law. These limits are subject to important exceptions. OPA creates a $1 billion supplemental compensation fund for oil spills and details procedures for obtaining access to it.

Title IV of OPA amends provisions of the Federal Water Pollution Control Act[4] concerning oil spills. Title IV expands the authority and capability of the federal government to direct and manage oil spill clean up operations. It requires vessel and facilities operators to file detailed oil spill response plans evidencing the availability of private-sector clean up and removal resources. Also in OPA Title IV are amendments

---

[1]The author is indebted to his LeBoeuf colleague, Robert J. Kinney, for his invaluable assistance in preparing this chapter.

[2]Pub. L. 101-380, August 18, 1990.

[3]33 U.S.C. §§ 2701-2761.

[4]33 U.S.C. §§ 1251-1376, renamed the Clean Water Act of 1977. OPA Subtitles B and C in Title IV make extensive amendments to section 311 of the Clean Water Act, 33 U.S.C. § 1321.

to the title of the U.S. Code on shipping and navigation safety.[5] OPA mandates numerous operational requirements for vessels to prevent oil spills, including the replacement of single hull oil tankers and barges with double hull vessels. Title IV of OPA also substantially increases the civil and criminal penalties for causing spills and for violating many marine safety and environmental protection laws.

Of the seven other OPA titles, Title III concerns the implementation of international conventions. Title III does not require the United States to adopt any international conventions on oil spills. Titles II, VI and IX contain technical and conforming amendments to other laws. The remainder of the act addresses subjects primarily concerned with Alaska and is beyond the scope of this chapter. Title V contains provisions on oil spill prevention and removal in Prince William Sound[6], Title VII sets up an oil pollution research and development program[7], and Title VIII amends the Trans-Alaska Pipeline System Act.[8]

## 2.0 BACKGROUND

While the grounding of the *Exxon Valdez* on March 24, 1989 and several subsequent accidents in 1989 and 1990 are generally viewed as the inspiration for the enactment of OPA, the law is actually the product of nearly 20 years of Congressional debate on oil pollution liability and tanker safety. This debate frequently centered on whether federal law should preempt state law and whether federal law should be circumscribed by international treaties.

In the 1970s Congress responded to concern over water pollution by enacting the Federal Water Pollution Control Act. Section 311 addressed oil spills from vessels and facilities by imposing strict liability to the federal government for clean up and removal costs.

In addition, three specialized statutes addressed oil spills in specific circumstances: the Trans-Alaska Pipeline Authorization Act,[9] the Deepwater Port Act of 1974,[10] and the Outer Continental Shelf Lands Act Amendments of 1978.[11] These statutes set up strict liability schemes and supplemental compensation funds for spills occurring in their respective areas. Congress also enacted laws to promote safer port operations and safer vessels: the Ports and Waterways Safety Act of 1972[12] and the Port and Tanker Safety Act of 1978.[13]

Individual U.S. state governments also adopted their own oil pollution laws. Although a few states, notably California, Florida and Maine, adopted oil pollution laws in the late 1970s, a majority of the 24 coastal states enacted special oil spill laws or amendments after 1986.

---

[5]Title 46 U.S. Code.
[6]46 U.S.C. § 2731-37.
[7]46 U.S.C. § 2761.
[8]43 U.S.C. § 1653.
[9]43 U.S.C. § 1651.
[10]33 U.S.C. § 1517.
[11]43 U.S.C. § 1801.
[12]86 Stat. 424.
[13]33 U.S.C. § 1221.

Roughly contemporaneous with U.S. efforts, the International Convention on Civil Liability for Oil Pollution Damage was signed in 1969 and came into force in 1975.[14] The CLC established a strict liability regime subject to limits on liability for tankers carrying persistent oil. The International Convention on the Establishment of an International Fund for the Compensation for Oil Pollution Damage[15] created a supplemental compensation fund, financed by the cargo interests. The Fund Convention was signed in 1971 and came into force in 1978.

Although the United States participated in the diplomatic conferences for these two conventions, neither the CLC nor the Fund Convention was ratified by the United States for two reasons. Their limits of liability were perceived to be too low, and the CLC and Fund Convention would have preempted federal and state law. Nevertheless, partly at the behest of the United States, two protocols to the CLC and the Fund Convention were adopted at a diplomatic conference held in 1984.[16] The 1984 Protocols increased the limits of liability, expanded the scope of compensable damages, and increased the size of the supplemental compensation fund. Neither of the Protocols is in force internationally.[17]

Many of the structural and operational requirements of the 1978 Port and Tanker Safety Act were enacted internationally by the Protocol of 1978 Relating to the International Convention for the Prevention of Pollution from Ships, 1973.[18]

### 3.0 TITLE I: OIL POLLUTION LIABILITY AND COMPENSATION

Title I[19] establishes the federal liability scheme for vessels and facilities that spill oil on waters subject to United States jurisdiction. It sets out the scope of the Act: the waters, vessels and facilities to which OPA applies. It defines the standard of liability and enumerates compensable damages. The provisions of Title I also set up the claims procedures, financial responsibility requirements, and the uses of the $1 billion Oil Spill Liability Trust Fund.

---

[14]International Convention on Civil Liability for Oil Pollution Damage, 1969, I.L.M. 45 (1970) (CLC).

[15]The International Convention on the Establishment of an International Fund for Oil Pollution Damage, 1971, 11 I.L.M. 284 (1972) (Fund Convention).

[16]Protocol of 1984 to the International Convention on Civil Liability for Oil Pollution Damage and the Protocol of 1984 to the International Convention on the Establishment of an International Fund for Compensation for Oil Pollution Damage (1984 Protocols).

[17]The 1984 Protocols have been superseded by two protocols adopted in 1992, both of which were done in London on November 27, 1992: The Protocol of 1992 to Amend the International Convention on Civil Liability for Oil Pollution Damage, 1969; and the Protocol of 1992 to Amend the International Convention on the Establishment of an International Fund for Compensation for Oil Pollution Damage, 1971 (1992 Protocols). The 1992 Protocols entered into force on May 30, 1996.

[18]20 I.L.M. 561 (1981).

[19]33 U.S.C. §§ 2701-2719.

## 3.1 Definitions

Section 1001 of OPA contains 37 definitions which are used throughout the Act.[20] OPA restates verbatim many of the definitions of the Clean Water Act.

**Vessels.** Except where otherwise limited, OPA applies to all vessels, not just tankers. Consequently, a spill involving fuel from a pleasure craft or bunkers from a general cargo vessel is subject to OPA liability. On the other hand, these vessels are not subjected to the operational and construction requirements applicable to tankers. Vessels are defined to include "every description of watercraft or other artificial contrivance used, or capable of being used, as a means of transportation on water, other than a public vessel." Public vessels are non-commercial government vessels.

**Tank Vessels.** These are vessels constructed, adapted to carry, or that carry oil or hazardous materials in bulk as cargo or cargo residue and that are United States documented vessels, operate in United States waters, or transfer oil or hazardous material in a place subject to the jurisdiction of the United States. This definition of tank vessels is not limited to oil tankers and barges, but also includes tankers and barges carrying hazardous materials such as explosives, liquefied petroleum gas and liquefied natural gas.[21]

OPA provisions vary in scope. For example, OPA liability is imposed only on vessels which discharge oil (section 1002). Financial responsibility requirements apply to all tank vessels carrying oil and hazardous materials (section 1016). Double hull requirements apply only to tank vessels which carry oil (section 4115).

**Mobile Offshore Drilling Units** (MODUs) are drilling units capable of use as an offshore facility; self-elevating lift vessels are not included in this definition.

**Facility** is any structure, group of structures, equipment, or device (other than a vessel) which is used for any of the following purposes: exploring for, drilling for, producing, storing, handling, transferring, processing, or transporting oil. The term also includes any motor vehicle, rolling stock, or pipeline used for these purposes.[22] Facilities are further subdivided into onshore and offshore facilities.

**Oil** covers oil of any kind, including petroleum, fuel oil, sludge, oil refuse, and oil mixed with wastes, other than dredge spoils. The definition goes on to exclude any part of oil which is defined as a "hazardous substance" by the Comprehensive Environmental Response, Compensation and Liability Act (CERCLA).[23] Thus, there is intended to be no overlap between the liability provisions of OPA and those of CERCLA. Agencies charged with implementing OPA regulations have interpreted this definition to include non-petroleum oils, such as animal fat and vegetable oils. In response to industry concerns about over-regulation of such edible oils, Congress enacted the Edible Oil

---

[20]33 U.S.C. § 2701.

[21]These materials are listed at 49 C.F.R. § 172.101 (1995).

[22] Facility does not include locomotive fuel tanks. *See United States v. Southern Pac. Transp. Co.,* Civ. No. 94-6176-HO, 1995 U.S. Dist. LEXIS 5247, 40 ERC (BNA) 1158 (D. Or. Jan. 20, 1995).

[23]42 U.S.C. § 9601.

Regulatory Reform Act which requires agencies regulating oil under laws such as the OPA to differentiate between edible oils and petroleum oils.[24]

**Person** is defined broadly to include both natural persons and commercial and government entities, including states, municipalities, commissions, political subdivisions and interstate bodies.

**Owner or Operator** is the person(s) who bears the burden for the substantive obligations of OPA. In the case of a vessel this means a person who owns, operates or demise (bareboat) charters a vessel. With respect to facilities, it is those persons owning or operating the facility. For an abandoned vessel or facility, it is the person who would have been the owner or operator immediately prior to abandonment.

**Responsible Party** is the person(s) liable for removal costs and damages under section 1002. Generally, the term means the owner or operator whose vessel or facility is the source of an oil discharge or which poses the substantial threat of a discharge. For deepwater ports, the responsible party is the licensee and for offshore facilities the responsible party is the lessee or the permittee of the area in which the facility is located. Public entities are not considered responsible parties in connection with onshore facilities.

**Discharge** is any sort of emission in the navigable waters, the adjoining shoreline, or the exclusive economic zone. A discharge of oil triggers OPA liability. A discharge of CERCLA hazardous substances[25] triggers OPA containment and removal provisions.

**Incident.** One or more discharges from the same source constitutes an "incident."

**Navigable waters** means all waters of the United States beginning with marshes and extending seaward 12 miles to the limits of the territorial sea. A discharge in these waters or on the adjoining shoreline is covered by OPA.

**Guarantor** means any person who provides financial responsibility for a responsible party under OPA; it does not include the responsible party, however.

**Exclusive Economic Zone** includes those waters which extend seaward 200 miles. Discharges in these waters are also covered by OPA.

**Remove or Removal,** means that under Title IV of OPA, public and private entities are to carry out the effective and immediate removal of a discharge and mitigate or prevent the substantial threat of a discharge. Remove or removal is defined as containment and removal of the oil or hazardous substance from the water and shorelines and taking other actions to minimize or mitigate damage.

## 4.0 ELEMENTS OF LIABILITY

OPA makes responsible parties for vessels and facilities liable for the results of oil spills without regard to fault, subject only to certain narrow defenses. While this is essentially the same liability that vessel and facility owners and operators had under the Clean Water Act, the damages that can be recovered from them after an oil spill under OPA are potentially much greater.

---

[24]Pub. L. No. 104-55, 109 Stat. 546 (1995) (codified at 33 U.S.C. § 2701 et. seq.). It is not clear whether in fact this will result in substantially different regulatory treatment of edible oils.
[25]40 C.F.R. Part 116 (1996).

## 4.1 Standard of Liability

Section 1002 states that liability under OPA exists "[n]otwithstanding any other provision or rule of law. . ." This removes any prerequisite to liability and means no other law will affect the ability of a claimant to recover under OPA such as the requirement that a claimant show physical damage to his property. This also means that a vessel owner is unable to limit his liability to the value of this vessel and its freight under the Limitation of Liability Act.[26]

OPA further states that each responsible party for a vessel or facility is liable for removal costs and damages. This envisions that in some circumstances multiple responsible parties could be liable for the entire amount of removal costs and damages. This is called joint and several liability.

## 4.2 Removal Costs

A responsible party is liable for all removal costs incurred by the federal government, state governments, or Indian tribes. The only restriction on these removal costs is that they be incurred under the authority of either the Clean Water Act as amended by OPA, or the Intervention on the High Seas Act,[27] which governs discharges in international waters which threaten the United States. OPA provides that removal costs can include expenses of actions taken by virtually any agency or department of federal, state, and local governments to avert the threat of a discharge, and to ensure the immediate and effective containment, dispersal and removal of the oil or hazardous substance. [28] These costs and expenses could also include those resulting from whatever action is necessary to protect fish, shellfish, wildlife, public and private property, shorelines, beaches, and living and nonliving natural resources.

A responsible party is liable for any removal costs incurred under authority of state law. Finally, a responsible party is also liable for any removal costs incurred by any person, that is private individuals and organizations, for actions taken which are consistent with the National Contingency Plan. In one recent case, attorneys' fees incurred in compelling the operators of an oil field to conduct a study of oil spill threats at the field and the feasibility of remedial action were held to be recoverable removal costs under OPA.[29]

---

[26]46 U.S.C. § 183; *See also, In re Complaint of Plaintiffs Jahre Spray II K/S,* Civ. Nos. 95-3495 (JEI) and 95-6500 (JEI) (consolidated cases), 1996 U.S. Dist. LEXIS 11594 (D.C. N.J. Aug. 5, 1996) ("Not only does the specific language of the OPA indicate that it supersedes the Limitation of Liability Act, but also the existence of provisions in the OPA such as § 2703 creating specific defenses to OPA claims and §2704 establishing liability limitations suggests that the OPA governs oil spill claims because these provisions would otherwise be redundant.").

[27]33 U.S.C. § 1471.

[27]Costs of monitoring removal activities incurred by the Coast Guard are recoverable. *United States v. Murphy Exploration and Production Co.,* Civ. No. 95-2372C(3), 1996 U.S. Dist. LEXIS 14133 (E.D. La. Sept. 21, 1996); *United States v. Conoco, Inc.,* 916 F. Supp. 581 (E.D. La. 1996).

[29]*Avitts v. Amoco Production Co.,* 840 F. Supp. 1116 (S.D. Tex. 1994).

### 4.3 Compensatory Damages

In addition to removal costs, OPA makes a responsible party liable for six categories of compensatory damages:[30]

**Natural Resources.** The United States, states, Indian tribes, and foreign governments are entitled to recover from a responsible party for damages, injury to, destruction, loss of, and loss of use of natural resources. Natural resource damages also include the reasonable cost of assessing those damages.

**Real or Personal Property.** If an oil spill injures real or personal property or diminishes the earnings from that property due to its destruction, the owner, or anyone who leases that property, may claim damages.

**Subsistence Use.** Any person who relies on natural resources for subsistence (as opposed to commercial reliance which is covered under loss of profits and earnings) may recover damages for injury to natural resources regardless of who owns or manages those resources. One court interpreting this term has held that it relates to use of a natural resource, such as water, to obtain the minimum necessities for life.[31]

**Revenues.** Federal, state, and local governments are entitled to recover damages equal to the net loss of taxes, royalties, rents, fees, or net profit shares resulting from the destruction or loss of real or personal property, or natural resources.

**Profits and Earning Capacity.** Any claimant is entitled to loss of profits or impairment of earning capacity from injury, destruction, or loss of real or personal property or natural resources.[32]

**Public Services.** State and local governments are entitled to recover damages for the net costs of providing increased or additional public services resulting from removal activities, including fire, safety, and health protection.

### 4.4 Interest

A responsible party, or his insurer, may be liable to a claimant for interest on the amount to be paid in satisfaction of a claim.[33] The interest period begins 30 days after the claim is presented to the responsible party, and continues until the claim is paid. An offer of the amount claimed can suspend the interest period, as will reasons beyond the control of the responsible party. Interest payments are not included in liability limit calculations.

### 5.0 NATURAL RESOURCE DAMAGES

OPA establishes a standard for measuring natural resource damages applicable to all actions for such damages. Government bodies are identified as the trustees of natural resources to whom a responsible party is liable in the event of damage to their respective natural resources. Each of these government entities is to develop a plan for repairing

---

[30]Section 1002; 33 U.S.C. § 2702.

[31]*Petition of Cleveland Tankers*, 791 F. Supp. 669 (E.D. Mich. 1992).

[32]In one case where a claim under this section was made, the court ruled that to succeed, the claimants must assert that their "injury, destruction or loss" was to property owned by them and that, without such an allegation, the claimants cannot recover. *See Petition of Cleveland Tankers*, 791 F. Supp. 669, 678-79 (E.D. Mich. 1992).

[33]Section 1005; 33 U.S.C. § 2705.

damage to its natural resources, and the cost of carrying out these plans constitutes the major component of natural resource damages. The federal government is charged with issuing timely regulations for the assessment of natural resource damages.

A responsible party is liable to the federal government, state, and foreign governments, as well as Indian tribes for injury to, destruction of, or loss of natural resources. Authorized representatives of these government entities are to be designated as trustees of their respective natural resources, to present claims for, and recover for damages to, natural resources. The different entities have jurisdiction over natural resources belonging to, managed by, controlled by, or appertaining to them. Where there is joint jurisdiction, the trustees are to exercise joint management or control over the shared resources; no group of trustees can preempt another group.

The designated federal, state, foreign, and Indian trustees are also charged with assessing damages to their natural resources, and determining the assessment costs. They are to develop and implement plans for the restoration, rehabilitation, and replacement of the natural resources of which they are trustees. The plans are also to include provisions for the acquisition of equivalent resources — that is, resources comparable to the injured resources — to restore the damaged ecosystem. This alternative is to be utilized only if the trustees determine that restoration, rehabilitation or replacement is not feasible. The trustees are to determine the cost of implementing these plans. The trustees are also to calculate the diminution in value of the damaged resources pending restoration. These trustee plans are to provide the basis for the calculation of natural resource damages for which a responsible party is liable.

Also prescribed is the standard measure of damages to natural resources that is to apply to all actions brought under the Act. This consists of (1) the cost of restoring, rehabilitating, replacing, or acquiring the equivalent of the damaged natural resources; (2) the diminution in value of those natural resources pending restoration; and (3) the reasonable cost of assessing the damage. Since double recovery for natural resource damages is prohibited, government entities and tribes are directed to consolidate their efforts to assess and recover natural resource damages.

Amounts recovered by the respective trustees for natural resource damages are to be retained by the trustees in their own trust accounts to be used, without further appropriation, exclusively for the costs of carrying out their restoration plans. Excess amounts are to be deposited in the Oil Spill Liability Trust Fund. Any person can obtain judicial review of trustees' actions in federal court.

The Undersecretary of Commerce for Oceans and the Atmosphere, in consultation with the Environmental Protection Agency, the Fish and Wildlife Service, and other affected federal agencies, is to promulgate regulations for the assessment of natural resource damages. Trustees' natural resource damage assessments made according to these regulations are treated legally as rebuttable presumptions. This means that they are presumed to be correct; although the presumption can be overcome, the opponent has the burden of proof to do so.

### 5.1 NRDA Regulations

The National Oceanic and Atmospheric Administration (NOAA) published final regulations on natural resource damage assessments (NRDA) under OPA, effective

February 5, 1996.[34] The regulations describe measures that may be taken by designated federal, state, foreign and Indian tribe trustees in assessing natural resource damages resulting from an oil spill.

The regulations set forth three major components of a damage assessment:
1. Preassessment Phase;
2. Restoration Planning; and
3. Restoration Implementation.

Under the regulations, trustees determine in the preassessment phase threshold criteria that establish their authority to begin a natural resource damage assessment. They then make a preliminary determination whether natural resources or natural resource services have been injured. Following this determination, the trustees then determine, in coordination with response agencies, whether response actions will eliminate the threat of ongoing injury.

The restoration planning phase has two basic components: (1) injury assessment; and (2) restoration selection. Under the regulation, injury is defined as an observable or measurable adverse change in a natural resource or impairment of a natural resource service. Once trustees have determined that an injury has occurred, they must also quantify the degree, and spatial and temporal extent of the injury. Upon completion of the injury assessment, the trustees must develop both a Draft and Final Restoration Plan which take into account a reasonable range of restoration alternatives. The Draft Restoration Plan must consider public comments.

Restoration alternatives selected by the trustees may be primary restoration, in which injured natural resources are returned to baseline on an accelerated time-frame, compensatory restoration, which encompasses actions to compensate for interim losses of natural resources pending recovery, or a combination of the two. The regulation requires that the identified restoration alternatives be evaluated based upon several factors, including:

1. the cost to carry out the alternative;
2. the extent to which each alternative is expected to meet the goals and objectives of the trustees in returning the injured resources or services to baseline and/or compensate for interim losses;
3. the likelihood of success of each alternative;
4. the extent to which each alternative will prevent future injury and avoid collateral injury as a result of implementing the alternative;
5. the extent to which each alternative benefits more than one natural resource and/or service; and
6. the affect of each alternative on public health and safety.

---

[34]61 Fed. Reg. 440; January 5, 1996 (to be codified at 15 C.F.R. Part 990). Author's Note: References to regulations in this chapter include both the Code of Federal Regulations (C.F.R.) citation as well as the Federal Register citation for the final or interim final rule in order to aid the reader in locating useful preamble and explanatory language which is not codified in the C.F.R.

The regulation further provides that the trustees select the most cost-effective of two or more equally preferable alternatives.

The proposed regulations provided for a contingent valuation (CV) methodology in determining equivalent values for lost services. The final regulations allow for the use of CV or other valuation methodologies, but only where a resource-to-resource or service-to-service approach to scaling the restoration action is inappropriate

Finally, following public comment and, where appropriate, compliance with National Environmental Policy Act[35] (NEPA) requirements, the Final Restoration Plan is presented to the responsible parties to implement or to fund the trustees' costs of implementing the plan.

## 6.0 DEFENSES TO LIABILITY

Strict liability is a legal doctrine which imposes on a person who engages in a particular activity the responsibility for compensating others for the harm he causes, regardless of fault. OPA makes a responsible party strictly liable for oil spill damages. There are only four defenses which exonerate a responsible party from liability: three complete defenses to liability and one defense to particular claimants.[36]

The complete defenses require showing the intervention of outside forces: an act of God, an act of war, and an act or omission of a third party. If one or more of these events, or a combination of them, is the sole cause of the discharge or threat of a discharge of oil and the resulting damages or removal costs, then the responsible party is exculpated. However, the responsible party is only able to avail himself of these defenses if he fulfills his other obligations under the Act. He must report the spill, he must cooperate and assist with removal efforts, and he must comply with official removal orders.

A responsible party also has a defense to the claim of a particular claimant to the extent that the incident giving rise to the claim is caused by the gross negligence or willful misconduct of the claimant himself.

## 6.1 Third Party Liability

When a responsible party is able to establish that the threat or spill, and resulting removal costs and damages, were caused solely by the act or omission of one or more third parties, then the third parties are treated as the responsible parties instead of the original responsible party.[37]

However, a third party will be treated as a responsible party only in limited circumstances. The third party cannot be an employee or agent of the responsible party. Nor will the third party be treated as the responsible party if the third party's act or omission, causing the threat or spill, occurred in connection with a contract between the

---

[35]42 U.S.C. § 4321 et seq.
[36]Section 1003; 33 U.S.C. § 2703.
[37]Section 1002(d); 33 U.S.C. § 2702(d).

responsible party and the third party,[38] unless the contract only involves carriage of oil by a common carrier by rail. The responsible party must prove that he exercised due care in handling the oil and took precautions against foreseeable acts of the third party and any foreseeable consequences of those actions.

Furthermore, the responsible party must first pay removal costs and damages to any claimant. Only at that point is the responsible party entitled to be subrogated to the claimants' rights and recover the amount for any claims paid from the third party or from the Fund.

## 7.0 LIMITS ON LIABILITY

The Act limits the liability of a responsible party for removal costs and damages to specified dollar amounts depending on the type of vessel or facility involved in the spill.[39] However, egregious or aberrant behavior by a responsible party, or his failure to fulfill his reporting and assistance obligations under OPA, create circumstances in which these limits do not apply.

### 7.1 The Standard for Limiting OPA Liability

The right of a vessel or facility owner to limit its liability is a conditional right. The right to limit is lost if the incident was proximately caused by the gross negligence, willful misconduct or violation of an applicable federal safety, construction or operating regulation by the responsible party. Similarly, the failure of a responsible party to fulfill his reporting, cooperation and compliance obligations under OPA will render the liability limits inapplicable. The actions of an agent, employee, or contracted party (not including rail common carriers) are considered to be the acts of the responsible party. These exceptions to the limits on liability are far broader and more numerous than the ones under prior law. Previously, under the Clean Water Act, only if the government could show that the discharge was the result of willful negligence or willful misconduct within the privity and knowledge of the owner or operator, would the limits on liability not apply.[40]

### 7.2 Specific Liability Limits

OPA increases the liability limits for vessel and facility owners or operators from the limits under the Clean Water Act. For vessel owners, the limits have been increased by a factor of almost ten. Furthermore, the OPA limits are now the only limits available for vessels owners, since other statutory limits have been abrogated.

For tank vessels, the limit is the greater of $1,200 per gross ton or either $2 million for vessels 3,000 gross tons or smaller, or $10 million for vessels larger than 3,000 gross

---

[38]*See National Shipping Co. of Saudi Arabia v. Moran Mid-Atlantic Corp.*, 924 F. Supp. 1436, 1446, n.4 (E.D. Va. 1996) ("[defendant] Moran is not a responsible party, and, because it was operating under a contractual relationship with NSCSA, it may not be treated as a responsible party").

[39]Section 1004; 33 U.S.C. § 2704.

[40]33 U.S.C. § 1321(f)(1).

tons. For other vessels, the limit is the greater of $600 per gross ton or $500,000.[41] For vessels which carry oil as cargo from outer continental shelf facilities, these limits only apply to liability for damages. The owner or operator of such vessels is liable for all removal costs, without limit, resulting from a discharge.

For onshore facilities and deepwater ports, the limit is $350 million, and for offshore facilities (except deepwater ports) the limit is $75 million plus the total of all removal costs. For outer continental shelf facilities, these limits only apply to liability for damages. The owner or operator of such facilities is liable for all removal costs, without limit, resulting from a discharge. Liability limits for mobile offshore drilling units which operate as offshore facilities and are involved in a discharge or the threat of a discharge are the same as for vessels. However, if the removal costs and damages exceed the vessel liability limits, then the facility liability limits apply.

These liability limits also apply to third parties. If the act or omission of a third party that causes an incident occurs in connection with a vessel or facility owned or operated by the third party, then his liability is subject to the limits under OPA. In other cases, the liability of a third party is restricted in amount to the limit of the responsible party for the vessel or facility from which the discharge occurred, as if the responsible party were liable.

### 7.3 Adjustment of Liability Limits

The president is directed to report periodically to the Congress on the desirability of adjusting the statutory limits of liability. No authority is conferred in this section to actually adjust the limits on the liability for vessels in general. The president does have the authority to adjust the limits on liability for onshore facilities and deepwater ports without an amendment to the statute.[42]

With respect to onshore facilities, the president may set by regulation specific limits of liability between $8 million and $350 million for any class or category of onshore facility. The secretary of transportation is also required to report on the relative risks associated with the use of deepwater ports as compared with the risks associated with other ports and is authorized to lower the limits of liability by regulation for deepwater ports from $350 million to $50 million.

The president may also amend triennially the limits of liability by regulation to reflect significant increases in the Consumer Price Index.

### 8.0 RECOVERY BY A FOREIGN CLAIMANT

Section 1007 permits a foreign claimant (a person residing in a foreign country or a foreign government) to bring an OPA claim in the United States for a discharge in the territorial sea, internal waters, or adjacent shoreline of a foreign country. Section 1007

---

[41]Vessels carrying non-petroleum, edible oils are considered "other vessels," subject to the lesser limits of liability and corresponding lesser requirements for demonstrating evidence of financial responsibility. *See* Edible Oil Regulatory Reform Act, Pub. L. No. 104-55, 109 Stat. 546 (1995) (codified at 33 U.S.C. § 2701 et. seq.).

[42]Section 1004(d); 33 U.S.C. § 2704(d). The Final Rule has been issued; *see* 60 Fed. Reg. 39849; Aug. 4, 1995 (codified at 33 C.F.R. Part 137 (1996)).

is the only specific statutory authority for a foreign claimant to bring an OPA action in U.S. courts.

There are a number of conditions that must be fulfilled for a foreign claimant to bring an OPA action in a U.S. court. These conditions essentially ascertain that the origin of the spill had a strong connection with the United States. The foreign claimant must demonstrate that it has not received compensation for removal costs and damages and, except for Trans-Alaska Pipeline Oil spilled in Canada, that recovery under OPA is provided for in a treaty or executive agreement or by reciprocal right. At present, there are no such agreements or rights.

## 9.0 RECOVERY BY THE RESPONSIBLE PARTY

A responsible party entitled to a defense to liability under section 1003 or entitled to limit its liability under section 1004 can assert a claim under section 1013 for amounts paid.[43] The responsible party with a complete defense to liability can recover all payments of removal costs and damages. The responsible party entitled to limit its liability under section 1004 can recover amounts paid exceeding the limit.

## 10.0 CONTRIBUTION AND INDEMNIFICATION

Where multiple parties are involved in an oil spill, any person can bring a contribution action against any other person who is liable or potentially liable under OPA or another law.[44]

No responsible party may divest itself of OPA liability by contract. However, any person potentially liable under OPA may agree to have others contractually assume the responsibility to pay for some or all of those liabilities through insurance contracts or indemnity agreements and hold harmless agreements.[45]

## 11.0 OIL SPILL LIABILITY TRUST FUND

Some of the principal sections applicable to the creation and operation of the Fund are: section 1012, Use of Fund; section 1013, Claims Procedure; section 1014, Designation of Source & Advertisement; section 1015, Subrogation; and section 6002, Annual Appropriations. Also relevant are section 1007, Recovery by Foreign Claimants; section 1008, Recovery by Responsible Party, and section 9509 of the Internal Revenue Code.[46]

### 11.1 Abolition of Existing Funds

#### 11.1.1 Deepwater Port Liability Fund[47]

This fund was established in 1974 to pay for cleanup costs and damages associated with deepwater ports. It was funded by a two cent tax on the owners of deepwater port oil. It was never utilized, and its balance of $6.6 million was transferred to the Fund.

---

[43]Section 1008; 33 U.S.C. § 2708.
[44]Section 1009; 33 U.S.C. § 2709.
[45]Section 1010; 33 U.S.C. § 2710.
[46]26 U.S.C. § 9509.
[47]33 U.S.C. § 1517(f).

### 11.1.2 Offshore Oil Pollution Compensation Fund[48]

This fund was established in 1978 to cover uncompensated economic losses including removal costs from OCS activities. It was financed by a three cent tax on OCS producers. It, too, was never utilized and its balance of $171 million was transferred to the Fund.

### 11.1.3 Trans-Alaska Pipeline Fund[49]

This fund was established in 1973 to cover damages and removal costs in excess of $14 million and less than $100 million from vessels carrying oil loaded at the pipeline terminal in Valdez, Alaska. It was financed by a five cent tax on the owners of TAPS oil. Claims against the fund filed from the *Glacier Bay* and *Exxon Valdez* spills have been resolved. Several claims against the fund regarding the *American Trader* spill are still outstanding. The fund is retained under OPA until certification that these claims have been resolved.

### 11.1.4 Federal Water Pollution Control Act Fund[50]

This was called the "311 or 311(k)" Fund. It was set up in 1973 to be a $35 million revolving fund for federal responses to oil and hazardous substance spills. However, its balance never exceeded $25 million. It was financed through initial appropriations and recoveries from responsible parties. Availability of its funds was subject to appropriation. Its $20 million balance was transferred to the Oil Pollution Liability Trust Fund.

## 11.2 Preservation of State Funds

OPA preserves the right of the states to establish or continue any state oil pollution compensation fund, or the right of the states to tax for the purpose of oil pollution compensation funds.

## 11.3 Funding of the Fund

At the end of August 1994 the Fund had a balance of $780 million. This sum resulted from the five cents per barrel tax on oil received at United States refineries, or petroleum products entering the United States for consumption, use, or warehousing and the integration of existing funds into the Fund. Future penalties from Clean Water Act section 311 violations, Deepwater Port Act violations, and Trans-Alaska Pipeline Authorization Act violations will be paid into the Fund as will be excess natural resource damages.

The Attorney General is authorized to recover any compensation paid by the Fund and all administrative costs of the claim. The Fund is also authorized to borrow up to $1 billion from the Treasury.

---

[48]43 U.S.C. § 1812.
[49]43 U.S.C. § 1653(c).
[50]33 U.S.C. § 1321(k).

### 11.4 Uses of the Fund

The Internal Revenue Code sets a $1 billion per incident limit on government and private uses of the Fund.

#### 11.4.1 Government Uses:

1. Up to $50 million per fiscal year, including $250,000 at the request of a state, is made immediately available without further appropriation, for federal and state removal and monitoring costs to provide a quick response to an incident.[51]
2. Up to $500 million per incident is provided for natural resource damages.
3. Payment of removal costs and damages resulting from a discharge from a foreign offshore unit must be consistent with the National Contingency Plan.
4. OPA also provides for payment of administrative, operational, and personnel costs and expenses for implementation, administration, and enforcement. Certain of these expenditures are specifically authorized.

#### 11.4.2 Private Uses:

The Fund can be used for payment of uncompensated removal costs and damages consistent with the National Contingency Plan for claims submitted according to the claims procedure. These amounts are available for payment without further appropriation by Congress. Uncompensated claims could result from defenses to liability and liability limits or the financial inability to pay claims.

### 12.0 CLAIMS

OPA sets up a notification and claims procedure to facilitate the prompt filing and payment of claims for damages from oil spills.[52] Procedures are also detailed for the processing of claims by the Fund. The Fund is available to satisfy claims which are not promptly or fully compensated by the responsible party. The Coast Guard issued interim final regulations which address the presentation, processing, settlement and adjudication of claims against the Fund in 1992.[53]

### 12.1 Designation of the Source and Advertisement

OPA requires the person in charge of a vessel or a facility to report a spill to federal authorities. Failure to notify the authorities is grounds for imposing penalties and abolishing defenses to or limits on liability. Under OPA, upon receiving information about a spill, federal authorities will designate the source and notify the responsible party and insurer. If the spill does not involve damages or removal costs, no designation need be made.

---

[51]Section 1012 (d) and (e); 33 U.S.C. § 2712(d) and (e). Interim Final Rules regarding access to the Fund by State officials were issued on Nov. 13, 1992. *See* 57 Fed. Reg. 53, 968 (codified at 33 C.F.R. Part 133 (1996)).

[52]Section 1013; 33 U.S.C. § 2713.

[53]57 Fed. Reg. 36, 314; Aug. 12, 1992 (codified at 33 C.F.R. Part 136 (1996)).

Depending on whether the responsible party accepts liability or not, either the responsible party or the federal authorities will advertise the source of the spill and the claims procedure.[54]

**Responsible Party Advertises.** If the responsible party or its guarantor does not deny designation within five days, thus accepting liability for the spill, they must advertise the designation and the claims procedure within 15 days of the designation and continue to do so for 30 days.

**Government Advertises.** If the federal authorities are unable to designate the source, if the source is a government vessel, or if the responsible party accepts the designation but fails to advertise, the government will advertise at the responsible party's expense. The implementing regulations were issued in interim final form on August 12, 1992.[55]

### 12.2 Procedure

Claims for removal costs and damages must be presented first to the designated responsible party or its guarantor. If the responsible party or guarantor denies liability for the claim, or the claim is not settled 90 days after submission or the date of advertisement, whichever is later, the claimant has the option of bringing a lawsuit against the responsible party or its guarantor or presenting the claim to the Fund.

Two courts have upheld the presentation requirement of section 1013, holding that a failure to first present all claims for removal costs and damages to the responsible party or guarantor precludes a claimant from bringing a court action under OPA.[56] OPA claims in both cases were dismissed since the claimants had not first presented their claims under section 1013.

Claims can be presented first to the Fund if the responsible party denies the designation, if the authorities are unable to designate the source, or if the source is a government vessel. Insufficiently compensated claims submitted according to the claims procedure can be presented directly to the Fund.[57]

Claims are also subject to a statute of limitations. The time limit for presentation of claims for recovery of removal costs from the Fund is six years after completion of the removal action. Claims for recovery of removal costs from the responsible party must be presented within three years after completion of the removal action. Claims for damages must be submitted within three years of discovery of loss. Claims for damages to natural resources must be submitted within three years of discovery of loss or completion of the natural resource damage assessment.

---

[54]Section 1014; 33 U.S.C. § 2714.

[55]57 Fed. Reg. 36, 314; Aug. 12, 1992 (codified at 33 C.F.R. Part 136 (1996)).

[56]*Boca Ciega Hotel, Inc. v. Bouchard Transp. Co., Inc.*, 844 F. Supp. 1512 (M.D. Fla. 1994), *aff'd*, 51 F.3d 235 (11th Cir. 1995); *Johnson v. Colonial Pipeline Co.*, 830 F. Supp. 309 (E.D. Va. 1993); *but see Marathon Pipe Line Co., v. Laroche Indus., Inc.*, Civ. No. 96-2187N, 1996 U.S. Dist. LEXIS 17002 (E.D. La. Nov. 7, 1996) (presentation requirement of § 2713 does not apply to claims by a responsible party against allegedly sole-cause third party).

[57]57 Fed. Reg. 36, 314; August 12, 1992 (codified at 33 C.F.R. Part 136 (1996)).

## 13.0 FINANCIAL RESPONSIBILITY

OPA continues the Clean Water Act requirement that owners and operators of vessels and facilities demonstrate the financial capacity to pay claims up to their limits of liability.[58] However, because the amounts of the liability limits have been increased dramatically, the amounts of financial responsibility which must be demonstrated are also much larger.

### 13.1 Vessels

The financial responsibility requirements apply to any vessel over 300 gross tons, except a barge (non-self-propelled vessel) which is not carrying oil on board, either as fuel or cargo. Thus not only tankers, but also other classes of vessels, such as passenger vessels and dry bulk cargo vessels, must comply with the financial responsibility requirements.

The requirements also apply to any vessel, regardless of tonnage, which is either transshipping or lightering oil within the exclusive economic zone. The financial responsibility requirements do not apply to vessels in innocent passage or vessels transferring oil not destined for the United States.

### 13.2 Facilities

The financial responsibility requirements apply to offshore facilities and deepwater ports, but not to onshore facilities. The Minerals Management Service (MMS) of the U.S. Department of Interior is charged with issuing financial responsibility regulations for offshore facilities. As of the end of 1996, the agency had only issued an advance notice of proposed rulemaking.[59]

### 13.3 Calculation of Financial Responsibility Amounts

For vessels, the owner or operator must show financial responsibility sufficient to meet its limit of liability. For tank vessels carrying oil or hazardous materials, the amount is $1,200 per gross ton. For other vessels, it is $600 per gross ton. The owners or operators of multiple vessels must only cover the limit of liability of the largest vessel in their fleet.

For offshore facilities, the general requirement is for $150 million of financial responsibility. For deepwater ports, the amount is $350 million. The Secretary of Transportation may lower these limits. Owners or operators of multiple facilities must cover only the limit of liability of the largest facility.

### 13.4 Methods of Demonstrating Financial Responsibility

Financial responsibility may be evidenced by one or more of the following methods: insurance, surety bond, guarantee, letter of credit, self-insurance, or "other evidence of financial responsibility." The President (in the case of facilities) and the Secretary of Transportation (in the case of vessels) may issue regulations which set standards for policy or contract defenses, conditions, and terms.[60] An entity other than the responsible party which provides evidence of financial responsibility is a "guarantor."

---

[58]Section 1016; 33 U.S.C. § 2716.
[59]58 Fed. Reg. 44,797; August 25, 1993.
[60]Section 1016(e); 33 U.S.C. § 2716(e).

## 13.5 The Role of Guarantor

The stated purpose of having a guarantor of the owner's liability is to "provide claimants with a full range of options for pursuing their claims."[61] Consequently, OPA requires guarantors to be directly liable to claimants for removal costs and damages, subject to very limited defenses. Claimants are intended to have direct access to recovery, regardless of whether the responsible party is insolvent or otherwise unavailable to pay claims.

## 13.6 Financial Responsibility Regulations

The Coast Guard issued interim final regulations relating to financial responsibility on July 1, 1994.[62] These regulations specify what types of evidence vessel owners and operators must submit to the Coast Guard to demonstrate ability to pay for damages and removal costs arising from an oil or hazardous substance spill. The regulations mirror the requirements of the act in allowing only insurance, surety bond, guarantee, and self-insurance to serve as evidence of financial responsibility. The interim final regulations contained another category of "other evidence of financial responsibility," but this category was left undefined.

The interim final regulations superseded the financial responsibility regulations issued prior to the enactment of OPA and consolidated financial responsibility requirements for both OPA and CERCLA in one rulemaking. The interim final regulations contained a phased-in schedule for implementation. Self-propelled tankers had to submit new evidence of financial responsibility by December 28, 1994, although new Certificates of Financial Responsibility (COFRs) issued by the Coast Guard do not have to be carried on board a tanker until December 28, 1995.

Non-self-propelled tank vessels had to submit new evidence of financial responsibility and apply for a new COFR by July 1, 1995. After this date, these vessels had to carry a new COFR on board.

For a non-tank vessel, the date for compliance with the OPA/CERCLA regulations depended on the vessel's date of expiration of its current pre-OPA COFR. If the old COFR expired prior to December 28, 1994, the vessel had to renew its old COFR for three more years. If the old COFR expired after December 28, 1994, the vessel had to obtain a new OPA/CERCLA COFR prior to the expiration of the old COFR. All vessels must be in compliance with the new regulations by December 28, 1997.

The interim final regulations required guarantors providing evidence of financial responsibility to agree to be sued directly for any damages or removal costs that could be obtained from the vessel owner or operator. The new regulations repeat the statutory defenses that will be allowed guarantors in these direct actions: willful misconduct of the vessel owner or operator; and any defense available to the person for whom the COFR is issued. The Coast Guard added three "defenses": (1) the claims exceed the amount of the guaranty provided by the guarantor; (2) the claim is not one made under OPA or CERCLA; or (3) the COFR does not serve as a guaranty under any state law without the guarantor's permission. The effect of the latter "defense" is uncertain since OPA specifically preserves state statutes.

---

[61]H.R. Conf. Rep. No. 653, 101st Cong., 2d Sess. (OPA Conf. Rep.) 119 (1990).
[62]59 Fed. Reg. 34,210; July 1, 1994 (codified at 33 C.F.R. Part 138 (1996)).

In addition, the Coast Guard regulations provide that, in instances where multiple guarantors issue a guarantee, such co-subscribing guarantors may limit liability to the extent of their participation in the guaranty. This alters somewhat the guarantors' joint and several liability in pre-existing financial responsibility undertakings.

For vessel owners providing evidence of self-insurance, the Coast Guard is requiring demonstration of net worth[63] and working capital[64] each in amounts equal to or greater than the amount needed to satisfy the COFR regulations.

The Coast Guard subsequently issued final rules on March 7, 1996 which made some minor technical adjustments to the interim final rule. The most significant amendment was to surety bond provisions; up to ten co-guarantors may now participate in a single surety bond.[65]

## 14.0 SUBROGATION

Any person who compensates a claimant for removal costs or damages is subrogated to all the rights that the claimant may have under OPA and any other law.[66] The Fund is subrogated in respect to any claims it pays and can assume the claimant's rights under any law, including state law.

## 15.0 LITIGATION AND JURISDICTION

Although OPA channels the resolution of claims first to the responsible party and its guarantor and then to the Trust Fund, courts will consider claims for damages and can be petitioned to review OPA rules. Section 1017 sets out the rules for this litigation and defines the role of state courts.[67]

### 15.1 Jurisdiction

United States federal district courts have exclusive original jurisdiction over all OPA cases. However, petitions to review OPA regulations are filed with the United States Circuit Court of Appeals for the District of Columbia.[68] A state trial court with jurisdiction over removal costs and damages may consider OPA claims and state claims.

### 15.2 Limitations

Claims for removal costs must be brought within three years after the removal actions have been completed. Claims for damages must be brought within three years of the date of the discovery of the loss, and in the case of natural resources damages, within three years after the completion of the natural resource damage assessment performed

---

[62]"Net worth" means the amount of all assets located in the United States minus all liabilities anywhere in the world.

[64]"Working capital" means the amount of current assets located in the United States less all current liabilities anywhere in the world.

[65]61 Fed. Reg. 9264; March 7, 1996 (codified at 33 C.F.R. Parts 4, 130, 131, 132, 137 and 138 (1996)).

[66]Section 1015; 33 U.S.C. § 2715.

[67]Section 1017; 33 U.S.C. § 2717.

[68]Section 1017(a); 33 U.S.C. § 2717(a).

by the trustees. Contribution actions must be brought within three years after judgment on costs and damages or approval of settlement. Subrogation actions must be commenced within three years after the payment of a claim for removal costs or damages.

## 16.0 RELATIONSHIP TO OTHER LAWS

Congress declined to enact an exclusive federal oil pollution law and instead chose a system which preserved state law.

### 16.1 Preservation of State Law

OPA does not preempt state law. State and local governments may impose additional liability or requirements related to oil spills by statute or ruling as well as imposing additional civil or criminal penalties.[69] States may establish oil pollution funds to pay for removal costs and damages. States may also enforce federal financial responsibility requirements in state waters.[70]

### 16.2 Preservation of Federal Laws

OPA does not affect the Solid Waste Disposal Act.[71] Nothing in the OPA creates a cause of action against federal officials or employees.[72] In addition, OPA does not preclude federal officials from pursuing claims for cleanup costs or damages under any other applicable federal statutes or general maritime law.[73]

### 16.3 Tanker Design and Construction Standards

The Conference Report states that OPA does not affect the ruling of the United States Supreme Court in the *Ray v. Atlantic Richfield Co.,*[74] a case striking down state tanker construction regulations which conflicted with federal regulations. This suggests that federal authority to regulate vessel design and construction is preserved and that OPA does not grant states any additional authority in this area.[75]

---

[69]Section 1018; 33 U.S.C. § 2718; *See also, e.g., International Ass'n. of Indep. Tanker Owners v. Lowry,* No. C95-1096C, slip op. at 10 (W.D. Wa. Nov. 18, 1996) ("[N]one of the provisions of OPA 90 preempt the ability of the states to add to federal requirements in the areas addressed by the Act."); *National Shipping Co. of Saudi Arabia v. Moran Mid-Atlantic Corp.,* 924 F. Supp. 1436, 1448 (E.D. Va. 1996) ("The savings clause * * * was meant to allow the states to go beyond the basic protection of federal law.").

[70]Section 1019; 33 U.S.C. § 2719.

[71]42 U.S.C. § 6901.

[72]Section 1018(d); 33 U.S.C. § 2718(d).

[73]*See In re Cropwell Leasing Co.,* 5 F.3d 899 (5th Cir. 1993) (addressing federal remedies beyond the Clean Water Act or CERCLA).

[74]OPA Conf. Rep. at 122. *Ray v. Atlantic Richfield Co.,* 435 U.S. 151 (1978).

[75]*Cf. International Ass'n.. of Indep. Tanker Owners v. Lowry,* Civ. No. C95-1096C (W.D. Wa. Nov. 18, 1996) (while states may be preempted from establishing vessel design and construction standards, states may impose additional requirements with regard to all aspects of oil pollution liability, compensation, prevention and removal, so long as these requirements do not directly conflict with federal regulation).

## 17.0 TITLE II: CONFORMING AMENDMENTS

Title II contains conforming amendments transferring the balance of funds under the Clean Water Act[76], the Deepwater Port Act[77], and the Outer Continental Shelf Lands Act[78] to the Oil Spill Liability Trust Fund. The Secretary of Transportation is also authorized to utilize the Fund for removal activities under the Intervention on the High Seas Act.[79]

## 18.0 TITLE III: INTERNATIONAL OIL POLLUTION PREVENTION AND REMOVAL

A contentious issue in the OPA debate was United States participation in international oil pollution liability and compensation conventions. Generally, the House of Representatives advocated participation in the international conventions for reasons of comity and international uniformity. On the other hand, members of the Senate found that the international compensation levels were too low and that the preemption of federal and state laws by the conventions was unacceptable.

The compromise proposed in Title III of OPA[80] stated the opinion of Congress that the best interests of the United States would be served by participation in an international prevention and compensation regime that was at least as effective as domestic law.

Title III also contains provisions regarding cooperation between the United States and Canada on oil pollution matters.[81]

## 19.0 TITLE IV: PREVENTION AND REMOVAL

Title IV is divided into three subtitles. Subtitle A changes many of the laws governing the manning and operation of tank vessels to prevent oil spills. Subtitle B establishes a national planning and response system to insure the prompt and effective removal of oil spills that do occur. Subtitle C substantially increases the severity of criminal and civil penalties that can be imposed on vessel and facility owners and operators for discharges of oil under OPA, the Clean Water Act, and marine safety laws.

## 20.0 SUBTITLE A: PREVENTION

The OPA contains new or more stringent licensing and operating requirements designed to ensure the safe transportation and transfer of oil and hazardous substance.

### 20.1 Licensing Requirements and Drug and Alcohol Testing

The Secretary of Transportation is given the authority to require additional information on driving records, criminal records, and results from mandatory drug and alcohol tests of applicants for new merchant mariners' papers, for renewal applicants,

---

[76]Section 2002.
[77]Section 2003.
[78]Section 2004.
[79]Section 2001.
[80]Section 3001.
[81]Sections 3002-3005.

and for current holders of licenses, certificates, and merchant mariners' documents.[82] Current holders will be tested for drug and alcohol use on a random, periodic, reasonable cause and post-accident basis.[83]

OPA also adds additional grounds for suspension and revocation of current papers. Holders of licenses, certificates, and merchant mariners' documents who perform safety sensitive functions may have their papers suspended for drug and alcohol violations. Holders also may have their papers suspended or revoked for a violation of safety or pollution laws and regulations and incompetence, misconduct or negligence.

To ensure that all holders of current papers will be subjected to background checks, the terms of all licenses, certificates and merchant mariners' documents are changed to five years with five year renewal periods.[84] Existing papers without renewal dates will now be renewed on the date after the enactment of the OPA which is the five-year multiple of the date of issuance. Regulations establishing a five-year term of validity and providing a schedule for the expiration of existing certificates and merchant mariners' documents were issued in September 1994.[85]

The master or individual in charge of a vessel may be relieved of command if he is under the influence of alcohol or drugs and is incapable of commanding the vessel.[86]

### 20.2 Foreign Tank Vessel Manning Standards

The Coast Guard is required to evaluate the manning, training, qualification and watchkeeping standards of a foreign country that issues vessel documentation to determine whether that country's standards are equivalent to United States or international standards and whether those standards are being enforced adequately. A rulemaking on this subject was withdrawn in 1995. The Coast Guard also is required to conduct periodic review for each country as well as a post-casualty review.[87]

### 20.3 Tank Vessel Manning

The Coast Guard is to consider additional factors in formulating manning standards for tank vessels. These factors now include the navigation, cargo handling, and maintenance functions of a tank vessel for protection of life, property and the environment.[88] The Secretary of Transportation is to initiate a rulemaking on the operation of tank vessels in navigable waters under automatic-pilot or an unattended engine room. Regulations on use of automatic-pilot were issued in May 1993.[89]

On self-propelled tank vessels, officers and crew members are restricted to working no more than 15 hours in any 24-hour period, or no more than 36 hours in any 72-

---

[82]Section 4101. Final Rules were issued at 60 Fed. Reg. 65,478; Dec. 19, 1995 (codified at 46 C.F.R. Parts 10 and 12 (1996)).

[83]Section 4103. Final Rules were issued at 60 Fed. Reg. 4522; Jan. 23, 1995 (codified at 46 C.F.R. Parts 10, 12, and 16 (1996)).

[84]Section 4102.

[85]59 Fed. Reg. 49,294; September 27, 1994 (codified at 46 C.F.R. Parts 10 and 12 (1996)).

[86]Section 4104.

[87]Section 4106.

[88]Section 4114.

[89]58 Fed. Reg. 27,628; May 10, 1993 (codified at 33 C.F.R. Part 164 (1996) and 46 C.F.R. Part 35 (1996)).

hour period. For these purposes, "work" includes administrative functions associated with the vessel, whether these functions are conducted on board the vessel or ashore.[90]

## 20.4 Marine Casualty Reporting

OPA expands existing marine casualty reporting requirements to include marine casualties involving "significant harm to the environment." Casualty reporting requirements for foreign tank vessels are expanded to include casualties occurring in the exclusive economic zone.[91]

## 20.5 Pilotage Requirements

The Secretary of Transportation will designate on which United States waters tankers over 1,600 gross tons will be required to have a licensed master or mate on the bridge in addition to the pilot. Also, the Secretary will designate waters in the Northwest in which single hull tankers will be required to be escorted by two tugs.[92] Final regulations have been issued which designate Prince William Sound, Alaska, Rosario Strait and Puget Sound, Washington, as waters where single hull tankers over 5000 gross tons must be escorted by at least two towing vessels.[93]

OPA requires non-United States flag and Canadian flag vessels to retain a Canadian or United States pilot on the Great Lakes. This requirement applies to any vessel, not just to tank vessels.[94]

More stringent requirements are also imposed for Prince William Sound, Alaska.

## 20.6 Studies and Regulations [Sections 4107-4113]

These sections call for a number of studies and regulations on safety-related issues. The Secretary of Transportation is required to conduct a study of vessel traffic systems and report the results to Congress.[95] Coast Guard regulations establish requirements and procedures for Vessel Traffic Services (VTS) and make participation in all VTS mandatory.[96] The Secretary was required to issue regulations on minimum standards for plating thickness and periodic gauging of plating thickness, as well as minimum standards for and use of overfill devices and tank level or pressure monitoring devices.[97] The regulations establishing minimum plating thickness standards for tank vessels and requiring periodic gauging of vessels over 30 years old were published on October 8, 1993.[98] Regulations setting minimum standards for tank level and pressure monitoring devices were issued on August 21, 1995.[99] Additional regulations have been published to reduce the likelihood of oil spills caused by overfilling of cargo tanks on oil tankers

---

[90]Section 4114(b), amending 46 U.S.C. § 8104.

[91]Section 4106(b).

[92]Section 4116.

[93]59 Fed. Reg. 42,962; August 19, 1994 (codified at 33 C.F.R. Part 168 (1996)).

[94]Section 4108.

[95]Section 4107.

[96]59 Fed. Reg. 36,321; July 15, 1994 (codified at 33 C.F.R. Parts 1, 26, 160, 161, 162, 164 and 165 (1996)).

[97]Section 4109 and section 4110.

[98]58 Fed. Reg. 52,599; October 8, 1993 (codified at 46 C.F.R. Parts 30, 31 and 32 (1996)).

[99]60 Fed. Reg. 43,427; August 21, 1995 (codified at 46 C.F.R. Part 16 (1996))

and barges.[100] These regulations apply to both United States and foreign tank vessels and went into effect on January 19, 1995. The Secretary also is required to issue regulations on radio equipment for vessels subject to the Vessel Bridge-to-Bridge Radiotelephone Act.[101]

The Secretary has completed a comprehensive study to evaluate the adequacy of existing navigation laws and regulations for safe operation of tankers.[102] The Secretary evaluated crew size and qualifications, electronic navigation and position-reporting equipment, navigation procedures, inspection standards, and whether to impose tanker-free zones. The Secretary also analyzed whether there is a correlation between tanker size, cargo capacity, national origin, and oil spills. The Secretary further considered the use of computer simulators and remote alcohol testing.

Other requirements include a report by the Secretary of the Army on the feasibility of modifying dredges to be used in cleaning up oil spills,[103] a report by the President on whether liners or other containment devices should be required at shoreside facilities,[104] and a study of the feasibility of a maritime oil pollution prevention training program.[105]

## 20.7 Double Hull Requirements for Tank Vessels

The requirement that a tank vessel have a double hull went into effect upon enactment for a new vessel and according to a phase-out schedule for an existing vessel.[106] The phase-out schedule began in 1995 and runs until 2015. Older and larger vessels are retired first. An existing vessel is one for which a contract for construction or for a major conversion had been placed prior to June 30, 1990 and the vessel was delivered under that contract prior to January 1, 1994. Consequently, a future major conversion on an existing vessel could result in that vessel being treated as a new vessel for double hull purposes. Major conversion means a substantial change in the type, carrying capacity, or dimensions of the vessel, or a conversion that substantially prolongs the life of the vessel or makes it a new vessel. A major reconstruction of the hull structure that enhances environmental compatibility also constitutes a major conversion.

OPA does not define what constitutes a "double hull," but the Coast Guard has published regulations on March 10, 1995 setting forth standards for double hulls.[107] The Coast Guard specifically rejected design alternatives to double hull construction. The regulations require tank vessels contracted for after September 12, 1992, to have a double-hull construction with dimensions consistent with International Maritime

---

[100]59 Fed. Reg. 53,286; October 21, 1994 (codified at 33 C.F.R. Parts 155 and 156 (1996)).

[101]Section 4118.

[102]Section 4111.

[103]Section 4112.

[104]Section 4113.

[105]Section 4117.

[106]Section 4115. A domestic operator has sued the United States in the United States Court of Federal Claims, alleging that the premature retirement of its single-hull tank vessels constitutes an unconstitutional taking of property without compensation. *Maritrans Inc. v. United States*, No. 96-483C (Cl. Ct. filed Aug. 8, 1996).

[107]60 Fed. Reg. 13,318; March 10, 1995 (codified at 33 C.F.R. Parts 155 and 157 (1996); 46 C.F.R. Parts 30, 32, 70, 90 and 172 (1996)).

Organization (IMO) standards adopted in March 1992. The technical standards include the required clearances between the minor hull and the outer hull on the sides and on the bottom. Vessels for which construction was begun according to a contract awarded prior to September 11, 1992 and after June 30, 1990 must have a double hull construction consistent with Coast Guard standards adopted in Navigation and Vessel Inspection Circular (NVIC) No. 2-90. The interim final regulation contains some additional mandates beyond NVIC No. 2-90: piping requirements must be consistent with IMO Rules 13F and 13G; the vessel must have protected ballast tanks; and there must be clearance between framing on inland vessels.

NVIC No. 2-90 provides policy guidance on double hull dimensions to assist in planning and designing tank vessels that must be fitted with double hulls under OPA. Vessels built under plans that are approved in accordance with NVIC No. 2-90 prior to the effective date of final regulations will be deemed to be in compliance with the double hull requirement in section 4115 of OPA.

### 20.7.1 Exceptions to the Requirements

New tank vessels are required to be built with a double hull. The only exceptions are vessels used only to respond to oil spills and newly constructed vessels less than 5,000 gross tons. The latter category must be equipped with a double containment system which has been determined to be as effective as a double hull.

The double hull requirement does not go into effect until the year 2015 in three cases: (1) for vessels unloading at deepwater ports; (2) for vessels delivering to lightering vessels in established lightering zones at least 60 miles offshore;[108] and (3) for existing vessels less than 5,000 gross tons.

### 20.7.2 Additional or Alternative Requirements

Additionally, the Secretary of Transportation was directed to complete a rulemaking proceeding to determine whether any structural or operational requirements should be imposed on existing vessels subject to the double hull requirements during the period before the requirement goes into effect.[109] In partial fulfillment of this mandate the Coast Guard issued a final rule consisting of requirements for lightering equipment and the reporting of a vessel's international IMO number prior to port entry was published in August 1994.[110] The Coast Guard also issued a final rule for single hull tank vessels requiring written bridge procedures; vessel specific training measures; enhanced surveys; cargo and mooring system surveys; autopilot alarm systems; maneuvering tests; and calculation and notification of keel clearance prior to entering ports.[111] The Secretary is also required to conduct a study and issue a report based on

---

[108]The Coast Guard established four such lightering zones in the Gulf of Mexico in a Final Rule published August 29, 1995 (60 Fed. Reg. 45,006) (codified at 33 C.F.R. Part 156 (1996)).

[109]Section 4115(b).

[110]59 Fed. Reg. 40, 186; Aug. 5, 1994 (codified at 33 C.F.R. Parts 157 and 160 (1996)).

[111]61 Fed. Reg. 39,770; July 30, 1996 (codified at 46 C.F.R. Parts 31 and 35, and at 33 C.F.R. Part 157 (1996)). On November 27, 1996, the Coast Guard announced the suspension of the portion of this rule which required owner notification of a vessel's under-keel clearance. *See* 61 Fed. Reg. 60,189.

recommendations from the National Academy of Sciences, on whether other structural and operational requirements would provide equal or better protection than double hulls.[112] This report was submitted to Congress in January, 1993. The Secretary, also in conjunction with the National Academy of Sciences, is to review periodically the impact of double hulls on environmental safety and is to consider other methods of increasing tank vessel safety.

### 20.7.3 Title XI Loan Guarantees

The Secretary of Transportation can provide loan guarantees under the current provisions of Title XI of the Merchant Marine Act, 1936, for the construction of replacement vessels or reconstruction of vessels rendered inoperable by changes in the law.[113] The borrower must be already operating this type of vessel and must agree to use the newly constructed or reconstructed vessels as replacements. The new vessels must not be larger than the vessels they replace. These provisions essentially restate existing authority.

### 21.0 SUBTITLE B: REMOVAL

Under OPA, federal authorities have the responsibility for averting threats of oil spills and cleaning up ones that happen. These activities are conducted according to the National Response System and the National Contingency Plan. Although the OPA oil spill response system utilizes governmental planning and direction, it relies primarily on private resources to mitigate or remove spills. To ensure the availability of private response personnel and equipment, OPA requires approved individual vessel and facility response plans for vessel and facility owners and operators. Private response efforts are encouraged by conferring immunity from liability for removal costs and damages on those rendering care, assistance or advice in response to a spill.

### 21.1 Federal Removal Authority

OPA emphasizes federal direction of public and private efforts both of the response to avert the threat of an oil spill and of removal of oil that has been spilled. Under the Clean Water Act, federal authorities were authorized to act at any time to remove oil in the event of a spill or the threat of a spill, but removal could be entrusted to the vessel or facility owner or operator. However, OPA states that federal authorities are to insure the immediate removal of a discharge and mitigate and prevent the substantial threat of a discharge.[114] This authority applies to spills or threats in navigable waters, shorelines, and the waters of the exclusive economic zone. It also applies to situations where federal natural resources are affected.

OPA is more explicit than the Clean Water Act about federal responsibility for responding to the threat of a spill and removing a spill, and it also provides the government with a wider range of alternative actions to accomplish immediate removal. The federal authorities may merely direct or monitor federal, state, and private removal and mitigation actions. More actively, the federal authorities may assume the

---

[112]Section 4115(e).
[113]Section 4115(f).
[114]Section 4201.

responsibility and costs of the actions subject to reimbursement from the responsible party. This is referred to as "federalizing" the effort. They may go so far as to remove and destroy a discharging vessel using any means available.

### 21.1.1 Discharges That Constitute a Substantial Threat to Public Welfare

The federal government has extensive authority over containment and removal of a particular class of spills: those which are deemed to pose a substantial threat to the public health or welfare of the United States. The public health or welfare of the United States includes fish, shellfish, wildlife, other natural resources, or public and private shorelines and beaches. Criteria for identification of these spills, as well as procedures for responding to them, are to be addressed in the National Contingency Plan.

In the case of spills such as the *Exxon Valdez* in Alaska, the *American Trader* in California, and the *Mega Borg* in the Gulf of Mexico, the act states unequivocally that the federal government shall direct all federal, state, and private actions to remove the discharge or to prevent a substantial threat of a discharge. This delineation of authority is intended to eliminate confusion which allegedly impeded response efforts to such spills.

OPA requires federal direction of federal, state, local, and private response and removal efforts for spills which constitute a substantial threat to public health and welfare. Like lesser spills, they can be federalized by the government who undertakes response and removal and seeks reimbursement from the responsible parties. The federal government also has the authority to remove and, if necessary, destroy a vessel. At least in regard to emergency response measures, the federal government is exempted from contract and employment laws. However, this exemption is not intended to apply to long-term removal actions.

### 21.2 State and Local Removal Authority

The act specifies federal preeminence in undertaking and directing response actions, but preserves state authority over significant aspects of removal activities. State and local governments may impose additional requirements with respect to removal activities.[115] Further, in regard to the conclusion of removal activities, the federal government is required to consult with the governors of affected states before making a determination that removal with respect to any discharge is considered complete.[116]

### 21.3 Responder Immunity

To induce vessel operators, cleanup contractors, and cleanup cooperatives to undertake prompt and effective measures in response to spills and threats of spills, OPA exempts them from liability.[117] When a person is rendering care, assistance, or advice, he is not liable for removal costs or damages which result from his acts or omissions. However, his acts or omissions must be consistent with the National Contingency Plan or as directed by the federal government. It was also recognized that the National Contingency Plan and federal orders may not cover every detail or eventuality of a spill

---

[115]Section 1018; 33 U.S.C. § 2718.
[116]Section 1011; 33 U.S.C. § 2711.
[117]Section 4201(a), amending 33 U.S.C. § 1321(c).

response. Consequently, responder immunity is extended to actions that are in keeping with the overall objectives of the National Contingency Plan or federal directives.

However, this immunity does not apply to a responsible party, that is, the owner or operator of the vessel or facility from which the discharge originates. It only applies to other individuals or entities whom they retain. Furthermore, although the responder may be relieved of liability for removal costs and damages, that liability is borne by the responsible party.

The immunity does not apply in cases of personal injury or wrongful death, or if the person is grossly negligent or engages in willful misconduct. It does not apply to CERCLA cleanups, nor does OPA immunity prevent states from imposing their own requirements for the liability of persons involved in the removal of oil.[118]

### 21.4 National Planning and Response System

OPA keeps the National Contingency Plan under the Clean Water Act, which establishes the overall methodology for the containment, dispersal, and removal of oil and hazardous substances.[119] The plan is required to address the assignment of duties and responsibilities among federal departments and agencies, state and local agencies, and port authorities, and sets up Coast Guard strike teams, manned by trained personnel and specially equipped to deal with oil spills. These teams can be called in by the federal on-scene coordinator to provide assistance and training.

The plan also creates a national surveillance and notice system intended to give immediate warning of threatened spills or actual spills to state and federal officials and a national center to coordinate and direct the implementation of the plan.

The plan provides that federal and state officials work jointly to formulate a schedule for the use of dispersants and other chemicals to mitigate or remove a spill, and that the schedule detail both the waters in which it is deemed appropriate to use such chemicals and the amounts of the chemicals that can be used. The plan must now include provisions for the protection of fish and wildlife resources.

OPA also creates a new National Planning and Response System under the Clean Water Act.[120] This system creates a federal, state, and local hierarchy for spill response. The elements of this system are the National Response Unit, Coast Guard Strike Teams, Coast Guard District Response Groups, Area Committees, Area Contingency Plans, and vessel and facility response plans. One of the primary purposes of this system is to prevent duplication of federal and private response efforts. While much of the planning and organization is conducted by public agencies and officials, the objective of this system is to have response equipment and personnel primarily provided by private entities.

---

[118]Section 1018; 33 U.S.C. § 2718.

[119]Section 4201(b), amending 33 U.S.C. § 1321(d).

[120]Section 4202(a), amending 33 U.S.C. § 1321(j). This section also requires tank vessels to carry oil spill response equipment that is the best technology economically feasible and compatible with safe operation of the vessel. Interim Final Rules were published on December 22, 1993 (58 Fed. Reg. 67,988) and amended January 26, 1994 (59 Fed. Reg. 3749). The rules are codified at 33 C.F.R. Part 155 (1996).

Local Area Committees composed of federal, state and local agencies are to be established to prepare, and update periodically, detailed local area contingency plans to respond to a worst case oil discharge, or the threat of such a discharge, from a vessel, offshore facility, or onshore facility in or near the area. These plans must be federally reviewed and approved. The plans must describe the area that they cover and identify any sub-areas of special economic and environmental importance. They are to integrate with the operating procedures of the National Response Unit, other area plans, and individual vessel and facility response plans. The area plans are to list all available federal, state, local, and private response equipment and personnel, as well as fire-fighting equipment, and are to delegate respective responsibilities between federal, state, and local agencies and owners and operators. The plans are also to contain procedures for obtaining expedited decisions on the use of dispersants.

The President is required to revise and republish the National Contingency Plan (NCP) to ensure coordination among the various response organizations under the act. These revisions were published by the Environmental Protection Agency in September 1994.[121] Among other things, the regulations established the National Strike Force Coordination Center to coordinate spill responses, revised the list of acceptable dispersants and bioremediation agents, and added a new appendix to the NCP with spill response procedures and assignment of responsibility among various federal and state agencies.

### 21.5 Vessel and Facility Response Plans

Owners and operators of tank vessels, offshore facilities and certain onshore facilities are required to prepare response plans to remove discharges of oil. These plans must be consistent with the National Contingency Plans and Area Contingency Plans. Vessel and facility response plans must identify the qualified individual having full authority to implement removal actions and must require immediate communications between federal officials and private removal contractors. The response plans must identify and ensure by contract or other approved means the availability of private personnel and equipment necessary to remove to the maximum extent practicable a worst-case discharge (including a discharge resulting from fire or explosion) and to mitigate or prevent a substantial threat of such a discharge. A "worst case discharge" for a vessel is a discharge of its entire cargo in adverse weather conditions. For a facility it is the largest foreseeable discharge in adverse weather conditions.

The plans must also describe training, equipment testing, periodic unannounced drills, and response actions of vessel and facility personnel to mitigate or prevent the discharge. The plans must be updated periodically and be resubmitted for approval of each significant change. Removal equipment will be inspected periodically. Interim Regulations requiring vessel and facility owners and operators to have an approved response plan for a worst case discharge of oil have been issued. Plans had to be

---

[121]59 Fed. Reg. 47,384; September 15, 1994 (codified at 40 C.F.R. Part 300 (1996)).

submitted for approval by February 18, 1993.[122] Final regulations requiring vessels carrying oil as cargo to carry discharge removal equipment were issued on January 12, 1996.[123] It is not a defense to liability that an owner or operator was acting in accordance with an approved response plan.

The Coast Guard took the initial steps in implementing regulations for vessels and facilities handling hazardous substances by issuing an Advanced Notice of Proposed Rulemaking on May 3, 1996.[124]

### 21.5.1 Vessel Response Plan Regulations

The requirements for vessel response plans became fully effective on August 18, 1993. All owners and operators of vessels handling, storing or transporting oil in bulk as cargo in waters under United States jurisdiction must submit a vessel response plan. The submitted plan must be approved by the Coast Guard or the owner or operator must be granted written authorization to continue operations pending approval of the plan. The required sections of the submitted plan and the letter approving the plan or providing authorization to continue operations must be maintained aboard the vessel. Items which must be in the plan are:

1. Identification of the Qualified Individual and alternate;
2. Accurate representation of the quantity involved in a worst case discharge;
3. Training and drills adequately described;
4. Private resources identified and ensured by contract or other approved means to respond to a worst case discharge; and
5. Adequate notification procedures about a discharge.

The certification of adequate response resources may be provided separately from the submitted plan.

If a plan contains this information, and upon certification of the adequacy of the response resources, the Coast Guard will tentatively approve the plan pending a more detailed review of the plan.

The regulations establish two different planning standards: one for vessels carrying oil as primary cargo and one for vessels carrying oil as a secondary cargo. The plan must address not only response to worst case spill scenarios, but also responses to the "average most probable discharge" and "maximum most probable discharge."

Plans must provide for mobilizing response resources within two hours of a spill's discovery and for resources to be in place within 12 hours in high volume port areas; within 24 hours in river, inland, nearshore and offshore areas; and within 24 hours "plus travel time" for spills occurring in the open ocean more than 50 miles from shore.

The regulations provide for "tiering" of resources in responding to a worst case spill. Tier 1 resources must arrive at the scene within 12 hours in high volume port areas

---

[122]58 Fed. Reg. 7376, February 5, 1993 (codified at 33 Part 155 (1996) (vessels)). 58 Fed. Reg. 7330; February 5, 1993 (codified at 33 C.F.R. Part 154 (1996) (marine transportation-related facilities)). Regulations for non-transportation-related onshore facilities were issued by EPA on July 1, 1994 (59 Fed. Reg. 34,070 (codified at 40 C.F.R. Part 112 (1996)).

[123]61 Fed. Reg. 1052. (codified at 33 C.F.R. Part 155 (1996)).

[124]61 Fed. Reg. 20,084.

or 24 hours in other areas. Tier 2 and tier 3 resources "must be capable of arriving in 24-hour increments thereafter." Responsible parties must notify Tier 1 resources within 30 minutes of the spills discovery.

The Coast Guard has also issued an interim final regulation requiring vessels carrying oil in bulk as cargo to carry discharge removal equipment, install spill prevention coamings, and install emergency towing arrangements.[125] The regulation details specific requirements for vessels measuring 400 feet or more in length as well as smaller vessels. There are also requirements for inland oil barges, and vessels that carry oil as secondary cargo. Vessels measuring 400 feet or more in length must have equipment and supplies capable of containing and removing on-deck cargo spills of at least 12 barrels. Vessels under 400 feet must carry equipment and supplies capable of handling an on-deck spill of at least seven barrels. Inland oil barges must have equipment capable of handling an on-deck spill of at least one barrel and vessels carrying oil as secondary cargo must be able to handle a spill of one-half barrel.

### 21.5.2 Facility Response Plan Regulations

The Coast Guard has published final regulations requiring the development and submission of oil response plans by coastal marine transportation-related facilities which took effect May 29, 1996.[126] Any facility transferring more than 250 barrels of oil to or from a vessel over water must develop a response plan. The regulation covers trucks and trains loading or unloading cargo at facilities as "mobile facilities" subject to OPA plan requirements.

Facilities that are determined to have either "substantial harm" or a "significant and substantial harm" in the event of a discharge must submit response plans. The criteria used to determine which facilities must submit plans include: (1) the type of facility; (2) storage capacity and material stored; (3) the number of tanks, their age and the presence of secondary containment; (4) proximity to navigable waters and public supply intakes or wells; (5) proximity to sensitive environmental areas; (6) spill history; and (7) the likelihood of natural disasters, such as floods, hurricanes and earthquakes. The Coast Guard will also consider operational items such as (1) the number of annual tank barge or tank vessel transfers; (2) the type or quantity of petroleum project transferred each year; (3) the ability of the facility to perform multiple transfers; and (4) other unidentified "risk factors."

Each facility must address a worst case discharge, as well as the substantial threat of a worst case discharge, such as loss of the entire facility or loss of the single largest tank or battery of tanks within the same secondary containment system. The plan must also address an "average most probable discharge" and a "maximum most probable discharge."

For non-transportation-related facilities, EPA issued a final rule that requires these facilities to prepare and submit oil spill response plans.[127] The rule took effect on August 30, 1994 and requires facility owners or operators to plan for worst case discharges, as well as small and medium discharges of oil. Like marine transportation

---

[125] 58 Fed. Reg. 67,988; December 22, 1993 (codified at 33 C.F.R. Part 155 (1996)).

[126] 58 Fed. Reg. 7330; February 5, 1993 (codified at 33 C.F.R. Part 154 (1996)).

[127] 59 Fed. Reg. 34,070; July 1, 1994 (codified at 40 C.F.R. Part 112 (1996)).

facilities, only those non-transportation related facilities that meet EPA's criteria for "substantial harm" will be required to prepare response plans.

For onshore pipelines, the Research and Special Programs Administration (RSPA) of the Department of Transportation requires pipeline operators to compute "worst case discharges" for response zones that take into account pipeline proximity to navigable waters and to environmentally sensitive areas, and prepare response plans.[128]

## 22.0 SUBTITLE C: PENALTIES

OPA significantly increases the severity of criminal and civil penalties resulting from discharges of oil into navigable waters and other offenses contributing to a discharge of oil.

### 22.1 Criminal Penalties

Under the OPA amendments, a violation of section 311(b)(3) of the Clean Water Act can constitute a criminal offense under section 309, rather than a civil matter.[129] Previously, there was no criminal penalty for a simple negligent discharge of oil. Other existing criminal penalties for deficient operation of a tank vessel have been increased, about five times for individuals and about ten times for organizations. An organization under federal criminal statutes includes any form of entity other than a natural person.

#### 22.1.1 Clean Water Act Criminal Penalties

Section 309(c)(1) of the Clean Water Act provides that any person who negligently violates section 301 of the Act is subject to criminal penalties.[130]

Section 309(c)(2) provides that any person who knowingly violates section 301 of the act is subject to criminal prosecution.[131]

Section 309(c)(3) penalizes violations involving knowing endangerment.[132] This section is triggered when a person, at the time of committing a knowing violation, has actual knowledge that his actions pose a serious threat to human health and life.

OPA amended section 309(c) to include within its coverage violations of section 311(b)(3). Thus, an oil discharge in violation of section 311(b)(3) now can be treated as a criminal offense.[133]

Under section 309(c)(1) a conviction of negligently discharging oil carries a criminal fine of $2,500--$25,000 per day of violation, up to one year imprisonment, or both.

---

[128]58 Fed. Reg. 244; Jan. 5, 1993 (codified at 49 C.F.R. Part 194 (1996)).

[129]Section 4301(c), amending 33 U.S.C. § 1319(c).

[130]33 U.S.C. § 1319(c)(1).

[131]33 U.S.C. § 1319(c)(2).

[132]33 U.S.C. § 1319(c)(3).

[133]In one of the early examples of enforcement of these provisions, the captain of the *Emily S* was charged with criminal violations of the Oil Pollution Act and Clean Water Act for negligently causing a barge under tow, the *Morris S. Berman*, to break loose and run aground, spilling 750,000 gallons of oil off the coast of San Juan, Puerto Rico in January, 1994. The captain pleaded guilty and was sentenced. In the related criminal case against the corporate defendants, three corporations and several corporate officers were convicted after a jury trial and fined and sentenced. Fines against the corporate defendants totaled $75 million. *See United States v. Bunker Group, et al*, No. 95-84 (HL) (D. P.R. Sept. 25, 1996).

A prior conviction doubles the fines and term of imprisonment. Under section 309(c)(2) the crime of a knowing discharge of oil carries a criminal fine of $5,000-$50,000 per day of violation and up to three years' imprisonment. A prior conviction also doubles the penalties.

If a knowing discharge of oil is committed with the knowledge that another person is placed in imminent danger of death or serious bodily harm, section 309(c)(3) provides a maximum criminal fine of $250,000 and up to 15 years' imprisonment. For an organization, knowing endangerment carries a maximum fine of $1,000,000.

### 22.1.2 Criminal Penalties for Failure to Notify

OPA also increases the criminal penalty for failure to notify the appropriate federal official of a discharge of which a person is aware under section 311(b)(5) of the Clean Water Act. The previous penalty was $10,000 and up to one year imprisonment. The new penalty is a maximum $250,000 fine and up to five years imprisonment for individuals and a maximum fine of $500,000 for organizations.

### 22.1.3 Criminal Penalties for Violations of Vessel Inspection, Manning and Operation Requirements

Criminal penalties are also increased for violations of the vessel inspection, manning and operation provisions of Title 46, U.S. Code.[134] Operation of a vessel in a grossly negligent manner, previously a Class A misdemeanor with a penalty of a $5,000 fine and up to one year imprisonment, now carries a fine of up to $100,000 for an individual or $200,000 for an organization. Should the gross negligence result in death, the maximum penalty for an individual is $250,000 and up to one year imprisonment and the maximum penalty for an organization is $500,000. The criminal penalty for operating a vessel while intoxicated is identical.

The maximum penalty for a willful and knowing violation of the bulk dangerous cargoes rules in 46 U.S.C. Chapter 37 has been increased from $50,000 and up to five years' imprisonment to a $250,000 fine and up to six years' imprisonment for an individual, and a $500,000 fine for an organization. The bulk dangerous cargoes rules govern the design, construction, operation, and manning of tank vessels.

Section 4301(a) eliminates all use immunity for organizations arising from spill notification and eliminates personal derivative use immunity.

Section 4302 strengthens penalties under a number of other marine transportation safety laws.

The maximum penalty for a willful violation of a regulation, order or direction under the Intervention on the High Seas Act,[135] Deepwater Port Act of 1974,[136] and the Ports and Waterways Safety Act[137] has been increased to a fine of $100,000 for individuals and a fine of $200,000 for organizations. If death occurs as a result of a violation, the penalty is a $250,000 fine and up to one year in prison for an individual and a $500,000 fine for an organization.

---

[134]Section 4302.
[135]33 U.S.C. § 1471.
[136]33 U.S.C. § 1501.
[137]33 U.S.C. § 1221.

## 22.2 Civil Penalties

In addition to the imposition of criminal penalties, OPA establishes new Class I and Class II penalties for discharges of oil in violation of section 311(b)(3) of the Clean Water Act or for failure to comply with regulations under section 311(j) of the Clean Water Act governing the National Contingency Plan, Area Contingency Plans and vessel and facility response plans. The maximum Class I penalty for a prohibited discharge or for a failure to comply with the contingency or response plan regulations is $10,000 per violation, not to exceed $25,000. This penalty may be assessed only after the liable party is given notice and a reasonable opportunity to be heard and present evidence concerning the imposition of the penalty.

The maximum Class II penalty for a prohibited discharge or for a violation of a contingency or response plan regulation is $10,000 per day of violation not to exceed $125,000.[138] Procedural prerequisites for the imposition of a Class II penalty are notice and an opportunity for a hearing on the record comporting with the Administrative Procedure Act at which interested persons are afforded the opportunity to testify. Judicial review of the assessment is available, otherwise the penalty becomes final 30 days after issuance.

OPA provides an alternative civil penalty scheme for owners, operators, and persons in charge of vessels or facilities. The penalty for discharges violating the Clean Water Act is up to $25,000 per day of violation or up to $1,000 per barrel of oil discharged. If the discharge results from gross negligence or willful misconduct, the minimum penalty is $100,000 and up to $3,000 per barrel of oil discharged. The alternative civil penalties for failure to comply with presidential orders relating to discharges is up to $25,000 per day of violation or an amount up to three times the costs incurred by the Oil Spill Liability Trust Fund resulting from the failure to comply. Failure to comply with contingency plan regulations carries a penalty of $25,000 per day of violation. This penalty can be assessed against any person who fails to comply with the contingency plan requirements and is not limited in applicability to the owner, operator, or person in charge of the vessel or facility. This penalty is imposed by the United States District Court. In order to expedite the processing of civil penalties for spills of 100 gallons or less, or for violations of pollution prevention regulations involving penalties not more than $2,500, the Coast Guard issued regulations for so-called "fast track resolution."[139]

OPA also sets out a number of criteria to be used in determining the level of civil penalties. The official imposing the penalty, the Secretary of Transportation, EPA administrator, or judge is to consider the seriousness of the violation, the possible economic benefit to the violator, the degree of culpability, prior violations, efforts of the violator to mitigate or minimize the effects of the discharge, and the economic impact of the penalty on the violator.

Failure to comply with the financial responsibility requirements carries a penalty of up to $25,000 per day of violation.[140] Assessment is by written notice. Criteria to be

---

[138]Final Regulations were issued March 30, 1994; (59 Fed. Reg. 15,022 (codified at 33 C.F.R. Part 20 (1996))

[139]59 Fed. Reg. 66,477; Dec. 27, 1995 (codified at 33 C.F.R. Part 1 (1996)).

[140]Section 4303; 33 U.S.C. § 2716a.

used to determine the penalty amount are the nature, circumstances, extent, and gravity of the violation, degree of culpability, prior violation, and ability to pay. In addition to, or in lieu of assessing a civil penalty, the President may request that the attorney general obtain a judicial order to ensure compliance, including such relief as terminating operations of the company or individual.

## 23.0 CONCLUSION

The OPA, as enacted, sets out the general requirements for the progressive oil pollution prevention, liability and compensation regime that Congress adopted. Virtually all of the requirements are subject to further definition and implementation through regulations issued primarily by the U.S. Coast Guard. Many of the OPA requirements for regulations contained dates by which the regulations were to be issued, usually within one or two years of enactment. The OPA schedule was unrealistic. Two years after enactment, most of the regulations have not been issued, although the regulatory process is underway for nearly all of them. A thorough treatment of the OPA requirements will depend on the contents of those regulations.

# CHAPTER 6

# SAFE DRINKING WATER ACT

Stephen E. Williams
Bayh & Connaughton, P.C. and RegNet Environmental Services
Washington, D.C.

## 1.0 OVERVIEW AND BACKGROUND

The Safe Drinking Water Act (SDWA), enacted in 1974,[1] authorized EPA to regulate contaminants in public drinking water systems. Prior to the enactment of the Safe Drinking Water Act, federal control over drinking water was limited to protecting populations from communicable diseases in bottled water and water served to passengers by interstate water carriers such as railroads. The Act significantly expanded federal authority over drinking water by assigning EPA with the responsibility of setting national standards for levels of contaminants in public drinking water systems and regulating underground injection wells and sole source aquifers.

Since its implementation, the Act has taken on considerable importance outside the regulation of public drinking water systems. For example, under section 121 of the Comprehensive Environmental Response Compensation and Liability Act (CERCLA), the health-based goals issued pursuant to the SDWA program are considered relevant and appropriate remedial standards for contaminated drinking water at Superfund sites.[2] Many EPA Regions and states also use the drinking water standards for corrective action at sites under the Resource Conservation and Recovery Act (RCRA) and solid waste regulatory authorities.[3]

More recently, the Act was one of the first pieces of environmental legislation to pass the Republican-led control. The Act was amended to require, among other things, the use of cost-benefit analysis in the regulation of contaminants in drinking water. In the 105th Congress, the SDWA could set the precedent for the reauthorization of other environmental statutes, such as the Resource Conservation and Recovery Act.

### 1.1 Safe Drinking Water Act of 1974

Like other federal environmental statutes, the SDWA of 1974 required EPA to establish national standards to be implemented and enforced by authorized states. However, the regulated entities were not predominantly industrial; rather the SDWA program focused on the regulation of hundreds of large and small municipal drinking water systems. Like the difficulty EPA has encountered in its regulation of municipal

---

[1]Pub.L.No. 93-523, Dec. 16, 1974; 88 Stat. 1660, 42 U.S.C. 300f et seq.; Amended by Pub.L.No. 94-317, June 23, 1976; Pub.L.No. 94-484, Oct. 12, 1976; Pub.L.No. 95-190, Nov. 16, 1977; Pub.L.No. 96-63, Sept. 6, 1979; Pub.L.No. 96-502, Dec. 5, 1980; Pub.L.No. 98-620, Nov. 11, 1984; Pub.L.No. 99-339, June 19, 1986; Pub.L.No. 100-572, Oct. 31, 1988; Pub.L.No. 104-182, Aug. 6. 1996.

[2]42 U.S.C. § 9621(d)(2)(A).

[3]42 U.S.C. §§ 6925(u)-(v) & 6928(h).

wastewater treatment systems under the Clean Water Act, the regulation of public water systems has engendered political controversy and delayed implementation of the program.

The original Act established two avenues for regulating contaminants in drinking water: 1) setting a national primary drinking water standard; and/or 2) setting a secondary drinking water standard. The Act broadly defined "contaminant" to mean "any physical, chemical, biological, or radiological substance or matter in water."[4] Primary standards are designed to regulate contaminants that may cause adverse health effects, while secondary standards are advisory (federally unenforceable[5]) and limited to protecting public welfare from contaminants that may affect, for example, the odor or appearance of drinking water. A contaminant may be subject to both a primary and secondary standard.

Establishment of a primary drinking water standard under the 1974 version of the Act was a protracted process. First, the Act required EPA to propose and then promulgate a "recommended maximum contaminant level" (RMCL). Next, the Act required EPA to propose and promulgate a final primary drinking water standard, either embodied by a maximum contaminant level (MCL) or a water treatment technique.[6]

EPA regulated few contaminants under this scheme. Most of the standards were issued on an interim basis on December 24, 1975.[7] The Interim Primary Drinking Water Regulations established MCLs and monitoring requirements for bacteriological contaminants, turbidity, fluorides, certain pesticides, and heavy metals. The interim standards were largely borrowed from the requirements imposed by the Public Health Service. The Environmental Defense Fund (EDF) challenged the standards as insufficient, because EPA failed to require monitoring for sodium and sulfates and did not control organic chemical contaminants in drinking water. The U.S. Court of Appeals for the District of Columbia upheld the interim standards,[8] and deferred any decision on the failure of EPA to act to regulate organic contaminants, in part, because EPA had issued an Advance Notice of Proposed Rulemaking addressing the issue.[9] Nevertheless, the Court was clearly concerned with delay in regulating drinking water contaminants.

EPA continued to implement the program by promulgating additional MCLs and proposing, but never finalizing, treatment standards, such as Granular Activated Carbon (GAC) filters to remove synthetic organic chemicals. EPA also issued a number of recommended secondary drinking water standards. However, states with primary enforcement authority granted variances and exemptions to drinking water systems in

---

[4]SDWA § 1401(6), 42 U.S.C. § 300f(6).

[5]Although federally unenforceable, states are free to adopt secondary standards as mandatory requirements.

[6]SDWA § 1412(b)(1), 42 U.S.C. § 300g-1(b)(1).

[7]40 Fed. Reg. 59,556 (Dec. 24, 1975). The SDWA actually contemplated the issuance of interim primary drinking water standards, which would be reviewed by the Agency using notice-and-comment rulemaking procedures. The Agency would then issue "revised" primary drinking water standards. No primary drinking water standards were issued by EPA pursuant to the 1974 Act.

[8]*EDF v. Costle*, 578 F.2d 337 (D.C. Cir. 1978).

[9]41 Fed. Reg. 28,991 (July 14, 1976).

their respective states. As a result, many systems remained out-of-compliance with the national protection standards.

## 1.2 The Safe Drinking Water Act Amendments of 1986

The 1986 Amendments to the Safe Drinking Water Act reflected the broad concern regarding several aspects of the Act's implementation, including the slow progress in the development of drinking water standards; a lack of adequate resources for water systems to comply with the requirements of the Act; and, a lack of flexibility given to states to tailor treatment, monitoring, and other requirements to regional needs.[10] Specifically, the 1986 Safe Drinking Water Act Amendments directed EPA to set MCLs for eighty-three priority contaminants in three years and for twenty-five additional contaminants every three years thereafter. The Amendments also: (1) established requirements for certain other types of treatment, such as disinfection and filtration; (2) strengthened the statute's enforcement authorities; (3) expanded ground water protection provisions; and, (4) required public water systems to monitor for unregulated contaminants. Other provisions in the Amendments required EPA to modify the public notification requirements to make them more timely and informative and authorized $10 million per year to provide technical assistance to small systems which had chronic noncompliance problems.

To protect underground sources of drinking water, the 1986 Amendments required EPA to promulgate ground water monitoring regulations for hazardous waste injection operations. In addition, a sole source aquifer demonstration program was established for the purpose of providing protection of particularly critical ground water supplies and assessing the effectiveness of specific protection measures.

The 1986 Amendments also made two changes to the drinking water standard-setting process. The bill eliminated the distinction between "interim" and "revised" standards, removing both terms from the Act, and designated "interim" regulations under existing law as national primary drinking water regulations.[11] The Amendments also changed the term used to refer to the health effects level set before the promulgation of a drinking water standard from "recommended maximum contaminant level" to "maximum contaminant level goal"(MCLG).[12] Finally, the 1986 Amendments provided EPA with new enforcement authority for public water system and ground water protection programs to ensure timely and effective enforcement of existing and new regulatory requirements.

## 1.3 Bull Run Litigation

EPA moved to implement the new legislation, but was quickly overwhelmed with the requirement to address 83 contaminants in only three years. As with so many environmental programs that set deadlines for EPA action, the drinking water program was again in court.

---

[10] The Safe Drinking Water Act Amendments of 1986 are contained in Pub.L.No. 99-339, 100 Stat. 66 (1986).
[11] SDWA § 1412(a)(1); 42 U.S.C. § 300g-1(a)(1).
[12] Id.

In 1989, Citizens Concerned about Bull Run Inc., an activist group based in Oregon, filed a citizen's suit, asking a federal court in Oregon to require EPA to establish a compliance schedule for issuing the remaining drinking water standards. [13] The suit moved control of EPA's regulatory agenda from the Agency to a courtroom in Oregon. Specifically, the Coalition sought an order to compel the Administrator to publish MCLGs and NPDWRs for six inorganic contaminants,[14] radionuclide contaminants,[15] arsenic, lead, and copper. Various consent decrees arising from the suit required EPA to adhere to a strict schedule to achieve the mandates of the Act. EPA's inability to meet these requirements, as well as significant dissatisfaction among municipal drinking water providers, led to the amendment of the Act in 1996.

### 1.4 Amendments of 1996

On August 6, 1996, President Clinton signed into law the Safe Drinking Water Act Amendments (SDWAA) of 1996.[16] The statute enacted by Congress, S. 1316, was a bipartisan compromise that was forged between Senate and House Conferees in an effort to meet an August 1, 1996 deadline, which would have made an additional $725 million available for the drinking water revolving loan fund.[17]

The Amendments make substantial changes to the Safe Drinking Water Act of 1974, especially regarding the regulation of specific drinking water contaminants and the procedures to be followed during the course of rulemaking. Other important provisions include a user "right-to-know" notification requirement, source water protections, revised requirements for special contaminants, such as radon and arsenic, more health-effects drinking water research, and funding to states for drinking water infrastructure improvements. The Amendments will be discussed in the next sections in relation to the changes in the drinking water program.

### 2.0 REGULATION OF PUBLIC WATER SYSTEMS

### 2.1 The Primary Standard-Setting Process Under the 1986 Amendments

The SDWA applies only to "public drinking water systems," although many privately owned drinking water systems fall under the jurisdiction of the Act. A "public water system" means:

> a system for the provision to the public of piped water for human consumption, if such system has at least fifteen service connections or regularly serves at least twenty-five individuals. Such term includes (A) any collection, treatment, storage, and distribution

---

[13]*Miller v. EPA*, No. 89-CV-6328 (D. Ore., filed August 31, 1989).

[14]The six inorganic contaminants, antimony, beryllium, cyanide, nickel, sulfate, and thallium, are listed in section 1412(b) of the SDWA, 42 U.S.C. § 300g-1(b).

[15]The radionuclides, radium 226 and 228, gross alpha particle activity, beta particle and photon radioactivity, uranium, and radon, are listed in section 1412(b) of the SDWA, 42 U.S.C. § 300g-1(b).

[16]Public Law No. 104-182, 110 Stat. 1613 (Aug. 6, 1996).

[17]The deadline, though, was missed and the money reverted to the Clean Water Act revolving fund, until the funding was restored in a subsequent appropriations act.

facilities under control of the operator of such system and used primarily in connection with such system, and (B) any collection or pretreatment storage facilities not under such control which are used primarily in connection with such system.[18]

The goal of the standard-setting process was to identify either an MCL or a treatment standard to prevent adverse health effects. Once EPA determined that a contaminant may be present in public drinking water,[19] the next step was to develop and propose an MCLG. An MCLG was to be "set at the level at which no known or anticipated adverse effects on the health of persons occur and which allows an adequate margin of safety."[20]

In implementing this authority in the past, EPA often relied upon policy as much as science. The list of contaminants in the 1986 Amendments contained substances that presented both acute and chronic health risks. For most acutely toxic or hazardous compounds, animal laboratory studies had identified concentration thresholds below which the compound was found to not cause adverse health effects. For these compounds, EPA took the experimentally determined "no observable adverse effects levels" (NOAELs) and applied various scaling[21] and uncertainty [22] factors and assumptions regarding exposure[23] to the NOAEL for the compound to determine a reference dose (RfD). Scientists expected that even long-term exposure to these compounds at these levels would be safe.

For carcinogens, EPA was not able to reliably determine whether there is an exposure threshold below which a carcinogen will not cause adverse health effects. Although more is known today about the etiology of cancer, EPA maintained there was still considerable doubt about whether a single exposure to a particular carcinogen could cause cancer at some point in the person's lifetime or whether a long-term exposure is needed. Accordingly, EPA adopted the policy that there was no safe exposure level to a carcinogenic substance. The Agency has usually set MCLGs for carcinogenic contaminants at zero, since this is the level at which EPA believes that the statutory criteria of "no known or anticipated adverse effects" is met.[24]

---

[18]SDWA § 1401(4), 42 U.S.C. § 300f(4).

[19]In the 1986 Amendments to the SDWA, Congress itself made the determination that the 83 substances may be present in drinking water.

[20]SDWA § 1401(3), 42 U.S.C. § 300f(3).

[21]Scaling factors are used to account for the differences, for example, in the body weight of test animals to human beings.

[22]Uncertainty factors are usually factors of 10-1000 that are used to adjust NOAELs determined from animal studies for application to humans.

[23]The classic exposure scenario used in developing the SDWA standards is a 70 kilogram person drinking two liters of drinking water each day at his or her residence for a period of 70 years. Although this exposure scenario has been challenged as unrealistic, it remains EPA's basic approach.

[24]This policy decision was upheld in *NRDC v. EPA*, 824 F.2d 1211 (D.C. Cir. 1987).

Once EPA established the MCLG, EPA was required to issue an MCL that was as close to the MCLG as is "feasible." Feasibility means:

> feasible with the use of the best technology, treatment techniques and other means which the Administrator finds, after examination for efficacy under field conditions and not solely under laboratory conditions, are available (taking cost into consideration).... granular activated carbon is feasible for the control of synthetic organic chemicals, and any technology, treatment technique, or other means found to be the best available for the control of synthetic organic chemicals must be at least as effective in controlling synthetic organic chemicals as granular activated carbon.[25]

If it were not "feasible" to issue an MCL, then the Administrator:

> is authorized to promulgate a national primary drinking water regulation that requires the use of a treatment technique in lieu of establishing a maximum contaminant level, if the Administrator makes a finding that it is not economically or technologically feasible to ascertain in the level of the contaminant. In such case, the Administrator shall identify those treatment techniques which, in the Administrator's judgment, would prevent known or anticipated adverse effects on the health of persons to the extent feasible. Such regulations shall specify each treatment technique known to the Administrator which meets the requirements of this paragraph, but the Administrator may grant a variance from any specified treatment technique in accordance with section 1415(a)(3).[26]

EPA considered a technology as "field-tested" if the technology had been used in the field, or if laboratory or pilot studies indicated that the technology would work for the contaminants of concern. Generally, EPA relied upon removal efficiencies in selecting among technologies.

Although EPA determined the cost of available treatment technologies, the Agency considered affordability relative to large municipal drinking water systems. EPA justified this position on the basis that, like other environmental statutes, the SDWA was a "technology-forcing" statute. EPA also looked at the feasibility and costs of monitoring for the presence of the contaminants, although the monitoring requirements proved to be very controversial. Many system operators complained that considerable funds were spent looking for contaminants which were not and would not be expected to be in their drinking water systems.

Indeed, the ability to detect the presence and level of a contaminant became a determining factor in setting MCLs, especially for carcinogens. EPA typically found that it was technically and economically feasible for large water systems to treat drinking water contaminants to the parts-per-billion levels. However, EPA also had to ensure that there were sufficiently accurate tests to measure the concentration of the

---

[25]SDWA § 1412(b)(5)., 42 U.S.C. § 300g-1(b)(5).
[26]SDWA § 1412(b)(7), 42 U.S.C. § 300g-1(b)(7).

contaminant in drinking water, because an MCL is a legally enforceable standard. Many laboratories had analytical equipment and procedures that could detect the presence of a contaminant at minute concentrations. However, this analytical "detection level" was not the same at all laboratories, due to differences in equipment, quality control procedures, and scientific judgment. Therefore, to ensure a fair and enforceable MCL, EPA developed the concept of Practical Quantification Levels (PQLs), which represented the lowest concentration of a contaminant that most laboratories would be able to accurately quantify in a sample of drinking water.[27] Since the determination of the PQL is "feasible" for most laboratories, EPA based MCLs, for many contaminants, using the PQL.[28]

The Act also required the Administrator to request comments from the Science Advisory Board, established under the Environmental Research, Development, and Demonstration Act of 1978, prior to proposal of a maximum contaminant level goal and national primary drinking water regulation.[29] However, the SAB review could not, under any circumstances, delay final promulgation of any national primary drinking water standard.

## 2.2 Changes to the Contaminant Regulatory Process in the 1996 Amendments

EPA efforts to develop drinking water standards for radionuclides and radon highlighted the weaknesses of the standard-setting process. In the 1994 and 1995 appropriations bills, Congress required EPA to reconsider stringent proposed standards and to conduct studies, under the auspices of the EPA Science Advisory Board, to consider whether the regulation of radon in drinking water, a naturally occurring material, represented a significant human health threat and was cost-effective, in light of the fact that there were routes of exposure to radon that appeared to be more significant than in drinking water.

In 1994, Congress considered comprehensive legislation to revise the Safe Drinking Water Act. Although legislation did not pass, the bills formed the basis for the legislation that would become the Safe Drinking Water Act Amendments of 1996. In changing the Act, Congress tackled three of the major complaints regarding the program: (1) appropriate contaminants should be chosen to be regulated; (2) regulation should result in benefits in relation to its cost; and (3) monitoring requirements should not be unduly burdensome.

### 2.2.1 Changes in the Selection of Contaminants for Regulation

The 1996 Amendments repeal the requirement of the 1986 Amendments that EPA promulgate standards for 25 additional contaminants every three years. Instead, EPA

---

[27]This is typically determined by giving a random sample of laboratories drinking water samples with a range of pre-determined concentrations of a contaminant. For example, although some of the laboratories may be able to detect accurately the presence of the contaminant at 2 parts-per-billion (ppb), all or most of the laboratories correctly determined the presence of the contaminant at 8 ppb. The PQL for the compound would be determined to be 8 ppb.

[28]PQLs are commonly used for carcinogens, because the MCLG is zero and the PQL represents the lowest feasible level.

[29] SDWA § 1412(e);42 U.S.C. § 300g-1(e).

must, within 18 months of August 6, 1996 and every five years thereafter, publish a list of contaminants which are not regulated under the Act and are known or anticipated to occur in public drinking water systems. In determining which contaminants should be listed, the Administrator is required to consult with the scientific community and to consider a contaminant occurrence data base which must be established under Section 1445(g). The list is also subject to notice and public comment before it is finalized, but is not subject to judicial review as to the choice of particular contaminants. The unregulated contaminants considered include, but are not limited to, the "hazardous substances" of Section 101(14) of the Comprehensive Environmental Response, Compensation, and Liability Act (CERCLA) and the substances registered as pesticides under the Federal Insecticide, Fungicide, and Rodenticide Act (FIFRA).

The occurrence data base is to be assembled within three years after August 6, 1996 using information on the occurrence of regulated and unregulated contaminants in public drinking water systems. EPA is instructed to consult with the Science Advisory Board, National Academy of Science, the states and interested persons, with respect to the contaminants in the data base. With regard to unregulated contaminants, the data base is to include monitoring information collected by public water systems that serve more than 10,000 persons, monitoring information collected from a representative sample of systems serving less than 10,000 persons, and other reliable information available.

Within five years of August 6, 1996, and every five years thereafter, the Administrator shall select no less than five contaminants from the list and, after notice and public comment, shall decide whether to regulate specific contaminants. In making the decision, the Administrator must rely upon the best available public health information, including the occurrence data base. The Administrator may also decide to regulate a substance that is not on the list of five or more contaminants if the material is either a CERCLA hazardous substance or FIFRA pesticide.

### 2.2.2 Changes in the Standard-Setting Process

The 1996 Amendments retain the basic structure of the MCLG/MCL procedure, but add new requirements that have to be followed in reaching final standards. Not later than 24 months after deciding a particular contaminant should be regulated, the Administrator is required to propose a maximum contaminant goal (MCLG) and a national primary drinking water regulation. Within 18 months thereafter, the Administrator is required to publish the MCLG and promulgate a final drinking water regulation, although this schedule may be extended for up to nine months if the extension is published in the *Federal Register.*

In making regulatory decisions, the Administrator is required to use the best available, peer-reviewed science and supporting studies conducted in accordance with sound and objective scientific practices and data collected by accepted methods or best available methods. For each regulation, in a publicly available document, the Administrator must specify the populations addressed by any estimate of public health effects, the expected risk or central estimate of public health risk, the uncertainties identified in the process of the assessment, and peer-reviewed studies known to the Administrator that are relevant to any estimate of public health effects.

When proposing any national primary drinking water regulation that includes a maximum contaminant level, the Administrator is required, with respect to the proposed level and any alternative levels under consideration, to prepare and use analyses of:

1.  Quantifiable and nonquantifiable health risk reduction benefits likely to occur as the result of treatment to comply with each level;
2.  Quantifiable and nonquantifiable health risk reduction benefits likely to occur from reductions in co-occurring contaminants attributed solely to compliance with the maximum contaminant level;
3.  Quantifiable and nonquantifiable costs likely to occur solely as a result of compliance with the maximum contaminant level, including monitoring, treatment, and other costs;
4.  The incremental costs and benefits associated with each alternative maximum contaminant level considered;
5.  The effects of the contaminant on the general population and on groups within the general population such as infants, children, pregnant women, the elderly, individuals with a history of serious illness, or other subpopulations that are identified as likely to be at greater risk of adverse health effects due to exposure to contaminants in drinking water than the general population;
6.  Any increased health risk that may occur as the result of compliance, including risks associated with co-occurring contaminants;
7.  Other relevant factors, including the quality and extent of the information, the uncertainties in the analyses of the prior six factors, and factors with respect to the degree and nature of the risk.[30]

Moreover, the Amendments require the Administrator to take these analyses and publish a determination at the time that the standard is proposed as to whether the benefits of the maximum contaminant level justify the costs of the levels. If EPA determines in the analysis that the benefits of the standard that would be selected using the traditional rulemaking approach do not justify the costs, EPA may promulgate a standard that maximizes health and risk reduction benefits at a cost that is justified by the benefits.[31] No other environmental statute allows costs and benefits to play such a prominent role in regulatory standard setting.

The Amendments specifically preclude EPA from using this new regulatory procedure for contaminants that are disinfection or disinfectant by-products and for the regulation of cryptosporidium. The Amendments also indicate that EPA may not use its authority to select an alternative standard-setting process, if the benefits of compliance experienced by persons served by large public water systems and systems not likely to receive a variance are justified when using the traditional rulemaking approach. However, the prohibition on the use of the alternative standard- setting process does not apply if the contaminant is found almost exclusively in small systems.

---

[30]SDWA § 1412(b)(3), 42 U.S.C. § 300g-1(b)(3).
[31]SDWA § 1412(b)(6); 42 U.S.C. § 300g-1(b)(6).

### 2.2.3 Changes in the Monitoring Requirements

The Amendments require water systems to provide information to EPA to assist in determining the appropriate monitoring requirements. Within two years, the EPA Administrator must review the monitoring requirements for not fewer than 12 contaminants and promulgate any necessary modifications. For systems serving less than 10,000 persons, a state with primary enforcement authority may modify monitoring requirements on an interim basis.

The Amendments also require the EPA Administrator to promulgate regulations establishing criteria for a monitoring program for unregulated contaminants. Within three years of enactment and every five years thereafter, the Administrator must issue a list of not more than 30 contaminants to be monitored by public water systems and included in the occurrence data base.

### 2.3 Criteria for Granting Variances

The Amendments made limited changes to the variance process. Section 1415 already allowed the EPA Administrator, or a State with primary enforcement responsibility for public water systems, to grant variances from an applicable national primary drinking water regulation to public water systems that could not meet an MCL, because of the characteristics of the raw water sources available to the system.[32] Before granting a variance now, a determination must be made that the MCL cannot be met even if the system uses the best technology, treatment techniques, or other means that EPA has identified in the primary drinking water regulation, taking costs into consideration. In addition, there must be a finding that granting the variance will not result in an unreasonable health risk.

EPA, but not a State, may grant a variance from any treatment technique requirement of a national primary drinking water regulation by showing that an alternative treatment technique not included in such requirement is at least as efficient in lowering the level of the contaminant with respect to which such requirement was prescribed. The variance must require the use of the alternative treatment technique.

The 1996 Amendments allow large public water systems to receive variances before Best Available Technology (BAT) treatment is installed, if the system agrees to install the best technology, treatment techniques or other means that EPA finds is available, taking costs into account. The Amendments also allow EPA to grant variances to systems serving 10,000 or fewer persons if the system agrees to install EPA approved technologies.

### 2.4. Criteria for Granting Exemptions

Under Section 1416, if a public water system could not meet an applicable MCL, for reasons other than its raw water supply or a regulation imposing the use of a treatment technology, the system may be granted an exemption.[33] Under the 1996 Amendments an exemption is only granted for a period of three years beyond the date of compliance with the regulation. Like a variance, an exemption may not be granted if it could result in an unreasonable risk to public health. New public drinking water

---

[32]SDWA § 1415(a); 42 U.S.C. § 300g-4(a).
[33]SDWA § 1416(a); 42 U.S.C. § 300g-5.

systems may not be granted exemptions, unless there are no alternative sources of drinking water.

## 2.5 Enforcement of Drinking Water Regulations

The 1986 Amendments strengthened the original enforcement provisions to: 1) provide additional authority to the Administrator to take enforcement action against public water systems in violation of any regulation; 2) require the Administrator either to issue an order or institute a judicial action against a public water system in violation when the delegated state authority does not take appropriate enforcement action; 3) increase the maximum civil penalty from $5,000 to $25,000 per day of violation; and, 4) eliminate the requirement that a violation of the Act must be willful in order for civil penalties to be assessed.[34] However, the SDWA remains one of the only environmental statutes that has no criminal penalties, other than for tampering with a drinking water system.[35]

Each owner or operator of a public water system is required to give notice to the persons served by it:

1. of any failure to comply with an applicable maximum contaminant level or treatment technique requirement;
2. of any failure to perform required monitoring or testing procedures; and,
3. of any failure to comply with the requirements of any schedule prescribed pursuant to any variance or exemption.

Notification of violations must include notice by general circulation in the newspaper serving the area and, whenever appropriate, include a press release to electronic media and individual mailings. The notice must provide a clear and readily understandable explanation of the violation, any potential adverse health effects, the steps that the system is taking to correct such violation, and the necessity for seeking alternative water supplies, if any, until the violation is corrected. The Administrator may also require the owner or operator of a public water system to give notice to the persons served by it of contaminant levels of any unregulated contaminant required to be monitored under section 1445(a).

The 1996 Amendments further expanded the enforcement authority from violations of Section 1412 (drinking water standards) to include any applicable requirements in Section 1412, 1414, 1415, 1416, 1417, 1441, or 1445. The 1996 Amendments also

---

[34]SDWA § 1414; 42 U.S.C. § 300g-3.

[35]Any person who tampers with a public water system will be imprisoned for not more than 5 years, or fined, or both. Any person who attempts to tamper, or makes a threat to tamper, with a public drinking water system be imprisoned for not more than 3 years, or fined, or both. The Administrator may bring a civil action in the appropriate United States district court against any person who tampers, attempts to tamper, or makes a threat to tamper with a public water system. The court may impose on such person a civil penalty of $50,000. The term "tamper" means to introduce a contaminant into a public water system with the intention of harming persons; or to otherwise interfere with the operation of a public water system with the intention of harming persons.

require fines under $5000 to be assessed after notice and opportunity for public comment and fines from $5000 to $25,000 to be assessed only after a hearing on the record.

## 3.0 NEW FUNDING PROGRAMS AND REQUIREMENTS IN THE 1996 AMENDMENTS

In addition to the standard-setting revisions, Congress also addressed other critical issues associated with drinking water systems, specifically creating new funding mechanisms for compliance and infrastructure improvements, requiring new programs to insure the quality of source water and the competence of drinking water operations, and calling for significant expenditures on research regarding the potential health effects of contaminants in drinking water.

### 3.1 State Revolving Funds

The Amendments authorize $599 million for fiscal year 1994 and $1 billion for each of fiscal years 1995 to 2003 to establish a state Revolving Fund (SRF) from which states may receive capitalization grants, including letters of credit, to improve drinking water infrastructure. To be eligible to receive a grant, a State must establish a drinking water treatment revolving loan fund and enter into an agreement with EPA to meet the applicable requirements. The state must also have the technical, managerial, and financial capability to meet the requirements of the program and cannot be in significant noncompliance with any requirement of a primary drinking water regulation or variance.

The funds will be allotted among the states for fiscal years 1995 to 1997 in accordance with the same formula used to distribute public water system supervision grant funds in 1995, with minor modifications. For fiscal year 1998 and thereon, the allocation formula will be based upon the results of a "needs survey," which is an assessment of water system capital improvement needs of all eligible public water systems in the United States. EPA is also required to prepare and submit to the Congress the "needs survey" within 180 days after the date of enactment of the Safe Drinking Water Act Amendments of 1996 and every 4 years thereafter.

### 3.2 Uses of the Fund

Amounts deposited in a state loan fund, including loan repayments and interest earned on such amounts, are to be used only for loans, loan guarantees, or as a source of reserve and security for leveraged loans. Public water systems can use the assistance only for expenditures, which EPA has determined, through guidance, will facilitate compliance with national primary drinking water regulations applicable to the system or otherwise further health protection. Funds cannot be used for general monitoring, operation, and maintenance expenditures, but can be used to provide loans to systems for installing water treatment. The funds generally may not be used for the acquisition of real property or interests. Fifteen percent of the funds provided the SRF on an annual basis are available solely for providing loan assistance to public water systems, which regularly serve fewer than 10,000 persons.

The loan fund may be used to buy or refinance the debt obligation of a municipality or interstate agency within the state. It can be used to guarantee or purchase insurance for a local obligation, if the guarantee or purchase would improve credit market access or reduce the interest rate applicable to the obligation. Finally, it can be used as a source of revenue or security for the payment of revenue or general obligation bonds issued by the state if the sale proceeds will be deposited into the state loan fund.

A state may combine the financial administration of the state loan fund with any other revolving fund established by the state for the sake of convenience and to avoid administrative costs. Each state may use up to 4 percent of the funds allotted to the state to cover the reasonable costs of administration of the fund. For fiscal year 1995 and thereafter, an additional 10 percent of the funds can be used for public water system supervision programs to administer or provide technical assistance through source water programs, to develop and implement a capacity development strategy, and for operator certification programs, if the state matches the expenditures with at least an equal amount of state funds.

States administering a loan fund and assistance program must submit a report on its activities to EPA every two years, including the findings of the most recent audit of the fund and the state allotment. The EPA Administrator is required periodically to audit all state loan funds.

### 3.3 Intended Use Plans

One of the requirements imposed on water systems receiving grants is the annual preparation of a plan that identifies the intended use of the amounts available to the state loan fund. This plan must be available for public comment before it is finalized.

An intended use plan is to include a list of the projects to be assisted in the first fiscal year, including a description of the project, the expected terms of financial assistance, and the size of the community served. It must also describe the criteria and methods established for the distribution of funds, the financial status of the state loan fund, and the short-term and long-term goals of the fund.

Each state is required to publish and periodically update a list of projects in the state that are eligible for assistance, including the priority assigned to each project and the expected funding schedule for each project. The state loan funds must be established, maintained, and credited with repayments and interest. If amounts in the fund are not committed, the money can be invested in interest-bearing obligations.

### 3.4 Disadvantaged Community Relief

The Amendments provide for special assistance for disadvantaged communities. A "disadvantaged community" is defined as "the service area of a public water system that meets the affordability criteria established after public review and comment by the state in which the public water system is located." EPA is expected to provide guidance to states in establishing affordability criteria. In any case in which a state makes a loan to a disadvantaged community (or a community that is expected to become disadvantaged as a result of a proposed project), the state may provide additional subsidization, including forgiveness of the loan principal. For each fiscal year, a state is limited to providing such loans to disadvantaged communities to an amount that does not exceed 30 percent of the capitalization grant received by the state for the year.

### 3.5 Matching State Funding

Each EPA/state agreement must require the state to deposit in the state loan fund, 20 percent of the total amount of the grant on or before the date the grant payment is made to the state. States are not required to make these prepayments for fiscal years

1994, 1995, 1996, and 1997 if the state deposits the state contribution amounts into the state loan fund prior to September 30, 1999.

### 3.6 State Ground Water Protection Grants

The Amendments authorize $15 million, for each of fiscal years 1997 through 2003, for EPA grants to states for the development and implementation of a state program to ensure the coordinated and comprehensive protection of ground water resources within the state. EPA is required to publish guidance that establishes application procedures and identifies key elements of a state ground water protection program.

After a state applies, EPA determines the grant amount on the basis of an assessment of the extent of ground water resources in the state and the likelihood that the grant will result in protection of ground water quality. EPA may also award a grant for innovative programs for the prevention of ground water contamination, but not for any project to remediate ground water contamination.

As with the SRF, states are required to share in the funding of the program. The federal grant awarded is not to exceed 50 percent of the costs of carrying out the protection program, with the state paying the balance of the program costs. Not later than three years after August 6, 1996, and every three years thereafter, EPA is required to evaluate all protection programs that are the subject of grants and report to the Congress on the status of ground water quality in the United States and the effectiveness of state programs for ground water protection.

### 3.7 Source Water Assessment Program

Within 12 months after August 6, 1996 and after notice and public comment, EPA is required to publish guidance for states to conduct a source water assessment program. These programs are particularly important to states that want to modify their contaminant monitoring program permanently. To be eligible for a permanent modification, a state must have an approved source water assessment program.

A source water assessment program must delineate the boundaries of the areas from which public water systems in the state receive supplies of drinking water. It must also identify, for all contaminants for which monitoring is required, the origins within each delineated area of such contaminants to determine the susceptibility of the public water systems to contamination.

A state source water assessment program must be submitted within 18 months after EPA issues guidance and is deemed approved 9 months after the date of submittal unless the Administrator disapproves the program. States are required to begin implementation of the program immediately after its approval and in accordance with a timetable, established by EPA in consultation with the state, allowing not more than 2 years for completion. The timetable is required to take into consideration the availability to the state of funds from the State loan fund and EPA can extend any timetable by an additional 18 months.

### 3.8 Source Water Petition Program

A state may establish a program under which a community water system or local government may submit a source water quality protection partnership petition to the state requesting assistance in the development of a voluntary, incentive-based partnership, among the waste system, government and other interested persons. A petition is limited to only those contaminants that are pathogenic organisms for which a national primary drinking water regulation has been established and are detected in the source water at levels above the maximum contaminant levels. A petition includes a delineation of the source water area, the origins of the drinking water contaminants addressed by the petition, any deficiencies in information that will impair the development of recommendations by the voluntary local partnership, efforts made to establish the voluntary local partnership, and each person in the source water area who is likely to be affected by recommendations of the partnership. The petition will also address how the partnership will coordinate with voluntary or other activities already being undertaken under federal or state law to reduce the likelihood that contaminants will occur in drinking water and specify the technical, financial, or other assistance that the voluntary local partnership requests of the state to develop the partnership or to implement recommendations of the partnership.

After public comment on the petition, the state must approve or disapprove the petition, in whole or in part, not later than 120 days after the date of submission of the petition. Notice of approval is to include an identification of technical, financial, or other assistance that the state will provide to assist in addressing the drinking water contaminants, any necessary coordination that the state will provide, and the funds available. If a petition is disapproved, it may be resubmitted at any time that new information becomes available, conditions affecting the source water change, or modifications are made in the type of assistance being requested.

### 3.9 Capacity Development

The 1996 Amendments require states to prepare capacity development strategies. The strategies are to identify the methods or criteria that the state will use to identify and prioritize the public water systems most in need of improving technical, managerial, and financial capacity, the governmental factors that encourage or impair capacity development, and the legal authorities and resources to assist public water systems in complying with national primary drinking water regulations. The strategy must also address state assistance for training and certification of operators.

Within two years after a state first adopts a capacity development strategy, and every three years thereafter, the head of the state agency that has primary responsibility for drinking water regulation must submit to the Governor a publicly available report on the efficacy of the strategy and progress made toward improving the technical, managerial, and financial capacity of public water systems in the state. EPA is also required, by August 6, 1998, to publish guidance describing legal authorities and other means to ensure that all new community water systems and new nontransient, noncommunity water systems demonstrate technical, managerial, and financial capacity with respect to national primary drinking water regulations. The Administrator is also required to provide initial funding for one or more university-based environmental finance centers for activities that provide technical assistance to state and local officials in developing the capacity of public water systems.

Beginning in fiscal year 1999, a state will receive only 80 percent of the allotment due from the SRF, unless the state has obtained the legal authority or other means to ensure that all new community water systems and new nontransient, noncommunity water systems, commencing operation after October 1, 1999, demonstrate technical, managerial, and financial capacity with respect to each national primary drinking water regulation in effect, or likely to be in effect, on the date of commencement of operations. States are also required annually to compile a list of community water systems and nontransient, noncommunity water systems that have a history of significant noncompliance with the requirements of the Safe Drinking Water Act and the reasons for noncompliance.

### 3.10 Operator Certification

Not later than 30 months after the date of enactment of the Amendments, and in cooperation with the States, the Administrator is required to publish guidelines specifying minimum standards for certification (and recertification) of operators of community and nontransient noncommunity public water systems. The guidelines are to take into account existing state programs, the complexity of the systems, and other factors aimed at providing an effective program at reasonable cost. Beginning 2 years after the date on which the EPA publishes these guidelines, the Administrator must withhold 20 percent of the funds a state is otherwise due from the SRF unless the state has adopted and is implementing a certification program that meets the requirements of the guidelines or has been properly submitted to EPA and not disapproved. A state exercising primary enforcement responsibility for public water systems or which has an operator certification program, will be allowed to enforce that program in lieu of the guidelines, if the state submits the program to EPA within 18 months after the publication of the guidelines and the program is substantially equivalent to the guidelines. If disapproved, the program may be resubmitted within 6 months after receipt of notice of disapproval.

### 3.11 Consumer Confidence Reports

The new law requires public water systems to mail annually to its users a report as to the source of the water being provided, whether regulated contaminants have been detected in the drinking water, the levels of contaminants in its drinking water, information on compliance with the drinking water regulations, and information on unregulated contaminants for which EPA requires monitoring. EPA is charged to develop regulations specifying how this information is to be communicated, within 24 months of August 6, 1996. The Governor of a state may determine not to require the report to be mailed for systems serving fewer than 10,000 persons, but the system would be required to inform consumers by newspaper or other means that the report will be available.

### 3.12 Research

The 1996 Amendments call for a continuing program of studies to identify groups within the general population that may be at greater risk to adverse health effects from exposure to contaminants in drinking water. For example, the study must examine whether and to what degree infants, children, pregnant women, the elderly, individuals with a history of serious illness, or other subpopulations are likely to experience elevated health risks from contaminants in drinking water. Not later than four years after the date of enactment of the Amendments, and periodically thereafter as new and significant information becomes available, the Administrator is required to report to the Congress on the results of the studies.

The Administrator is also required to conduct biomedical studies to understand the mechanisms by which chemical contaminants are absorbed, distributed, metabolized, and eliminated from the human body, so as to develop more accurate health-effects models. Studies should develop new approaches to the study of complex mixtures found in drinking water to determine the prospects for synergistic or antagonistic interactions.

Not later than 180 days after the date of enactment of the Amendments, EPA must conduct toxicological studies and, if warranted, epidemiological studies to determine the levels of exposure from disinfectants and disinfection byproducts, if any, that may be associated with developmental and birth defects and to quantify the carcinogenic potential from exposure to disinfection byproducts resulting from different disinfectants. Finally, EPA must develop dose-response curves for pathogens, including cryptosporidium and the Norwalk virus. These toxicological and epidemiological studies are to be used to support the development and implementation of Enhanced Surface Water Treatment Rule, Disinfectant and Disinfection Byproducts Rule, and Ground Water Disinfection Rule. Congress specifically authorized $12,500,000 for each of fiscal years 1997 through 2003 for these studies.

The Director of the Centers for Disease Control and Prevention and the Administrator are directed to jointly develop a waterborne disease occurrence study. Within two years after the date of enactment of the Amendments, the two agencies are required to conduct pilot waterborne disease occurrence studies for at least five major United States communities or public water systems and, within five years, prepare a report on the findings of the pilot studies, and a national estimate of waterborne disease occurrence. The Director and Administrator are also jointly to establish a national health care provider training and public education campaign to inform both the professional health care provider community and the general public about waterborne disease and the symptoms that may be caused by infectious agents, including microbial contaminants. Congress authorized $3,000,000, to be appropriated for each of the fiscal years 1997 through 2001 to carry out this waterborne disease program.

The Amendments require that at least $10 million of the SRF annually be reserved for health-effects studies on drinking water contaminants. In allocating these funds, EPA is required to give priority to studies concerning the health effects of cryptosporidium, disinfection byproducts, and arsenic, and the implementation of a plan for studies of subpopulations at greater risk of adverse effects. In a separate section of the Amendments, Congress also indicates that, besides the amounts earmarked for specific studies, an additional $26,593,00 is authorized for drinking water research for fiscal years 1997 through 2003.

## 4.0 CURRENT CONTAMINANTS UNDER EPA CONSIDERATION FOR REGULATION

### 4.1 Radon

Radon is a human carcinogen and is a naturally-occurring substance. Studies have found that radon is present in groundwater in many parts of the country, especially in the Western portion of the United States. Persons can be exposed to waterborne radon by drinking tap water or by inhaling radon released into indoor air from tap water, notably during showering.

While radionuclides in drinking water have been regulated since 1976,[36] these regulations have explicitly excluded control over radon in drinking water. Establishing controls over radon in drinking water has been a difficult and complicated process due to uncertainties associated with evaluating the risks associated with radon in drinking water and the technologies and associated costs capable of removing radon from drinking water.

On July 18, 1991, EPA proposed MCLGs and Primary Drinking Water Regulations for the radionuclides: radon-222, radium-226, radium-228, uranium, alpha emitters, and beta and photon emitters.[37] The proposed MCL for radon was 300 pCi/L, which is below the naturally-occurring levels typically found in the groundwater of many states.

Environmentalists criticized EPA for setting the radon standard too high, and the water industry criticized EPA for setting the standard too low. EPA was also criticized for trying to regulate radon in drinking water when far more significant exposures to radon occur in homes, typically in basement areas. EPA responded to this criticism by claiming that the Agency had no legal authority to regulate such residential radon exposures.

The issue resulted in a debate about the degree to which drinking water contaminants pose a risk to human health and the cost-effective means of regulating these risks. As previously discussed, the passage of appropriations legislation forced EPA to re-evaluate how it would regulate radon in light of the issue of "relative risk."

Under the 1996 SDWA Amendments, the National Academy of Science is directed to prepare a risk assessment for radon in drinking water and an assessment of the health risk reduction benefits associated with possible mitigation measures to reduce radon levels in indoor air. By February 1999, EPA is to publish the NAS health risk reduction and cost analysis. Based on this information, EPA must propose a maximum contaminant level goal (MCLG) and a national primary drinking water regulation for radon by August 1999. After allowing for public comment on the proposal, EPA is mandated by the 1996 Amendments to publish an MCLG and promulgate a final national primary drinking water regulation for radon by August 2000.

States, along with water purveyors, will have an opportunity to be involved with tailoring the final drinking water regulation to meet their specific circumstances. The Amendments also provide for an "alternative maximum contaminant level" (AMCL) for radon if the final MCL for radon in drinking water is more stringent than necessary to reduce the contribution to radon in indoor air from drinking water to a concentration that is equivalent to the national average concentration of radon in outdoor air. EPA is also required to publish guidelines for a state to develop its own multimedia radon mitigation program. If accepted, a program would allow the public water systems within its state to comply with the AMCL. In the event that a state does not have an approved multimedia mitigation program, a local public water system may submit its own program to EPA for approval. EPA is required to approve such a program if the health risk reduction benefits expected to be achieved by the program are equal to or greater than

---

[36]NPDWRs were published for radium-226, radium-228, gross alpha particle radioactivity, and beta particle and photon radioactivity at 41 Fed. Reg. 28404 (July 9, 1976).

[37]56 Fed. Reg. 33,050 (July 18, 1994).

the benefits that would result from compliance with the MCL. An approved state or local program would extend the effective date of the final regulation by 18 months or until February 2005. State or local programs must be approved or disapproved by EPA within 180 days of submission and are required to be reviewed at least once every five years.

## 4.2 Arsenic

Arsenic is also a naturally-occurring contaminant found in some public water systems that rely on groundwater. The current standard for inorganic arsenic in drinking water (50 $\mu g/l$) was established by EPA in 1975,[38] based on studies of Taiwanese that demonstrated an increased risk of skin cancer in areas where drinking water arsenic levels were high. Subsequent studies have suggested that an increased incidence of internal organ cancers may also be related to high levels of arsenic in drinking water. However, many in the scientific community questioned the accuracy of these studies in understanding the health effects of exposure to low doses of arsenic.

Under the Bull Run court order, EPA was required to propose a standard for arsenic in drinking water by November 30, 1995, and to issue a final standard by November 30, 1997.[39] Prior to the 1996 Amendments, EPA was considering lowering the current arsenic standard of 50 $\mu g/l$ to 2 $\mu g/l$ or less. Such a level would have resulted in significant costs for the nation's water systems.[40]

In the 1996 SDWA Amendments, Congress concluded that new research is essential to reduce the existing uncertainty in the scientific database used in the risk assessment and risk management options associated with low-level arsenic exposure. The new law requires that, within 180 days, EPA will develop a comprehensive plan for study in support of drinking water rulemaking to reduce the uncertainty in assessing health risks associated with exposure to low levels of arsenic. The final research program, as it is currently defined, will be jointly funded by the federal government and the private sector.[41] Funds from the federal government have already been appropriated through the Departments of Veterans Affairs and Housing and Urban Development, and the Independent Agencies appropriations process and have further authorized the

---

[38] The NPDWR for arsenic is published at 40 Fed. Reg. 59,566 (December 24, 1975).

[39] *Miller, supra,* Feb. 22, 1994 Order at p. 2.

[40] According to 1993 EPA estimates, if the standard were lowered to 20 $\mu g/l$, as many as 600 systems would been required to install treatment to remain in compliance. This number grew to 12,675 systems, if the standard were lowered to 2 $\mu g/l$. At this level, $6 billion in capital expenditures would be necessary to reach compliance.

[41] On December 24, 1996, EPA announced that there would be a hearing on its draft "Research Plan for Arsenic in Drinking Water," before the Ad Hoc Committee on Arsenic Research of the Board of Scientific Counselors. 61 *Fed. Reg.* 67800. The Board was asked to evaluate the draft Plan and advise EPA as to whether an appropriate research plan had been developed. At the hearings on January 22-23, 1997, members of the public and the Board were critical of the Plan's generality in describing the research to be conducted, the fact that too many projects were assigned a high priority, and the lack of epidemiological research. Although the Board provided general approval of the Plan, considerable doubt was expressed whether implementation of the Plan would provide much useful new information before January 1, 2000, deadline for EPA to propose a new arsenic rule.

SDWA research provisions. In addition, the water industry has worked diligently over the past few months to raise significant funds for arsenic. California water agencies, under the auspices of the Association of California Water Agencies (ACWA), have collected pledges for approximately $500,000. ACWA also received from the American Water Works Research Foundation (AWWARF) a matching $500,000 for a total of $1 million. Between the federal government and the water industry, these two entities have earmarked approximately $3 million for arsenic research. It is envisioned that the EPA will issue a $3 million grant solicitation in October 1996 requesting research proposals.

## 4.3 Sulfates

Like radon and arsenic, sulfates are naturally occurring in water. The significant adverse effect on human health associated with ingestion of drinking water containing sulfates is laxation. Although this is generally not serious in adults, it can present a health threat to infants, small children, and other sensitive subpopulations.

EPA has established a secondary MCL for sulfates of 250 mg/l, based not on health concerns, but the offensive odor caused by high concentrations of sulfates. Pursuant to the 1986 SDWA Amendments, EPA has been considering the adoption of a primary MCL. The World Health Organization recommends a level of 400 mg/l.[42]

The 1996 Amendments require EPA and the Centers for Disease Control to jointly conduct an additional study to establish a reliable dose-response relationship for the adverse human health effects that may result from exposure to sulfate in drinking water, including infants and travelers that may be at a greater risk of adverse health effects within 30 months of August 6, 1996. EPA has to make a determination on whether to regulate sulfates within 5 years (August 6, 2001), and any final drinking water standard must include requirements for public notification and options for the provision of alternative water supplies to populations at risk as a means of compliance in lieu of BAT treatment technologies.

## 4.4 Disinfectants and Disinfection Byproducts

The chlorination process that is used to eliminate the threat of pathogenic organisms in drinking water has been considered a source of health risks for the United States drinking water supply. Chlorine, when used as a disinfectant, can combine with other organic compounds (including decomposing leaves and other natural materials) that are in the raw water supply to form chlorinated, organic compounds like chloroform. As a class of chemicals these compounds are referred to as disinfection byproducts. Health studies have suggested the ingestion of such compounds could pose a risk of bladder and rectal cancers. Although there is, currently, an applicable drinking water standard for trihalomethanes, one class of disinfection byproducts, removing the organic materials before chlorination or using alternative disinfection methods may be potential avenues to reduce the cancer risk.

EPA was required under the 1986 Amendments, every 3 years, to identify a group of 25 additional contaminants for which regulations would be set. Approximately one-half of the contaminants in the first group of 25 were disinfectants or disinfection

---

[42]*Health Effects of Drinking Water Treatment Technologies*, Drinking Water Health Effects Task Force, Lewis Publishers, 1989, at p. 88.

byproducts, many of which are already regulated as trihalomethanes under the standard promulgated in 1979. In partial fulfillment of the obligation to promulgate standards every 3 years, the Agency has been preparing regulations for approximately 12 contaminants that result from the disinfection of drinking water (treatment, generally with chlorine, to remove microbial contaminants).

To facilitate the rulemaking process, the Agency conducted a regulatory negotiation to arrive at a consensus proposal. The negotiation included representatives from state and local government organizations, the drinking water supply community, and public interest groups. The agreement reached included a schedule for the development and promulgation of several regulations including an information collection rule, an enhanced surface water treatment rule, and a two-stage rulemaking for the national primary drinking water regulation for disinfectants and disinfection byproducts. The schedule for completing the two-stage rulemaking was published in the *Federal Register* on February 10, 1994.[43] A proposed rule for Stage I disinfectants and disinfection byproducts was issued on July 29, 1994.[44]

EPA fell behind the schedule set out in the agreement principally because of difficulties in developing analytical methods for Cryptosporidium. The 1996 Amendments require EPA to complete each one of the rulemakings called for in the agreement, including the two-stage rulemaking for disinfectants and disinfection byproducts. The requirement is nondiscretionary and can be enforced by a court pursuant to the citizen suit authorities of section 1449 of the Act. However, since each step in the rulemaking is tied to information gathered in the previous step, the Amendments provide that the schedule for actions can be modified whenever a particular step lags behind the otherwise agreed upon date. In response to a citizen suit, a court may compel EPA to complete a particular action by a date that is determined by reference to the time interval that is provided in the agreement. EPA may accelerate the date for some actions, completing them more quickly than the interval established by the agreement would otherwise provide, but only if EPA has consent from all parties to the agreement.

The Amendments direct the EPA Administrator to promulgate Stage I and II Disinfectants and Disinfection Byproducts Rules in accordance with the schedule published in the February 10, 1994 proposed Information Collection Rule. That schedule requires the promulgation of a Stage I rule in December, 1996 and promulgation of a Stage II rule in June, 2000. However, Congress provided some latitude in meeting those dates, because the February, 1994 schedule contains a number of different deadlines for information collection and public comment. If one of the earlier dates are missed, then the dates of subsequent action will also have to be adjusted. Accordingly, the Amendments provide that "[i]f a delay occurs with respect to the promulgation of any rule in the schedule . . . all subsequent rules shall be completed as expeditiously as practicable but no later than a revised date that reflects the interval or intervals for the rules in the schedule."

Congress also provides EPA with explicit direction on the substance of the rulemakings. For example, in the Amendments, Congress specifically excludes the

---

[43] 59 Fed. Reg. 6332.
[44] 59 Fed. Reg. 38668.

regulation of disinfectants and disinfection byproducts from the new cost-benefit requirements. In addition, Congress includes in the Amendments a statement that "[t]he considerations used in the development of the July 29, 1994, proposed national primary drinking water regulation on disinfectants and disinfection byproducts shall be treated as consistent with such section 1412(b)(5) for purposes of such Stage I and Stage II rules." SDWA Section 1412(b)(5) defines the term "feasible" in the Act, and any maximum contaminant level or treatment technique that EPA adopts must be feasible, both technically and economically. In doing this, Congress may be trying to prevent lawsuits that the final rule is not feasible for smaller systems, should the July 29th proposed rule be adopted.

It should also be noted that on May 14, 1996,[45] EPA promulgated a final Information Collection Rule, which contains requirements for at least 520 public water systems serving more than 100,000 persons to monitor the water system to determine the presence and levels of disinfection byproducts and report the results to EPA. The monitoring is expected to commence in February, 1997 and continue for 18 months.

## 5.0 UNDERGROUND INJECTION CONTROL

The Underground Injection Control (UIC) program, adopted pursuant to the SDWA, regulates the subsurface emplacement of fluids through an injection well.[46] Wells injecting fluids that are either listed or characteristic hazardous waste are also subject to certain requirements adopted pursuant to Subtitle C of the Resource Conservation and Recovery Act (RCRA), most notably, the land disposal restriction program, which limits the injection of hazardous wastes that have not been treated using the best available treatment (BAT) technology.

Unlike many other environmental programs, the UIC program has received relatively less attention than the other provisions of the Safe Drinking Water Act or the regulatory programs adopted pursuant to the Clean Air Act, Clean Water Act, and RCRA. The SDWA Amendments of 1996 did not address the UIC program. However, it is worth noting that, in 1989, of the 197 million metric tons of hazardous waste generated, 95 percent of the wastes disposed of in RCRA units were wastewaters. Much of the wastewater was injected underground. Of the 13.2 billion metric tons of solid waste generated, 1.5 billion tons were generated as "special wastes" in the oil and gas segment of the petroleum industry alone. Many of these oil and gas special wastes were oil field brines and produced waters that were also disposed using injection wells.

According to certain EPA estimates, there are almost 400,000 injection wells subject to UIC requirements. This is almost six times more UIC wells than there are permitted wastewater discharges under the NPDES program of the Clean Water Act.[47] Accordingly, the disposal of fluids under the UIC program is far more extensive than many recognize.

Broadly speaking, underground injection is the subsurface emplacement of fluids by well injection. A "well injection" is fluid emplacement through any bored, drilled

---

[45]61 Fed. Reg. 24354.
[46]SDWA §1421, 42 U.S.C. § 300h.
[47]*See* Jensen, L.J., "Safe Drinking Water Act," *Environmental Law Handbook*, Government Institutes, 12th edition (1993) at p. 259.

or driven shaft or dug hole that is deeper than it is wide.[48] For purposes of the UIC program, even a hose that is pushed into the ground to dispose of water or fluids could be considered to be a well.

The operative concern of the UIC program is well injections that can endanger underground sources of drinking water (USDWs). A USDW is an aquifer or portion of aquifer: (1) which supplies any public drinking water system[49]; or, (2) which contains a sufficient quantity of groundwater to supply a public drinking water system, and either currently supplies drinking water for human consumption, or contains fewer than 10,000 mg/l total dissolved solids (TDS). "Endangerment" is any injection activity that allows the movement of fluid containing any contaminant into underground sources of drinking water, if the presence of the contaminant may cause a violation of any primary drinking water regulation under 40 C.F.R. part 142 or may otherwise adversely affect the health of persons.[50] However, EPA has interpreted this endangerment provision to apply to situations which may allow the "potential" of fluid movement into a drinking water source.

EPA has been criticized for protecting groundwater with TDS levels as high as 10,000 mg/l as "drinking water."[51] Dissolved solids can only be tasted by individuals in drinking water at levels beginning around 1,000 mg/l. Moreover, the secondary drinking water standard for TDS is 500 mg/l, and much of the water consumed in the nation has even lower levels. In adopting such a broad definition of "potential" drinking water, EPA extended the drinking water program to affect industrial operations that engage in deep drilling programs.

EPA has classified wells, in part, in response to the different types of fluids which are injected and to address the groups of wells that inject fluids. In doing so, EPA has identified five classes of wells that are covered under the UIC program:

> *Class I* — wells that inject hazardous waste and industrial or municipal disposal waste wells that inject fluids below the lowermost drinking water formation;
> *Class II* — wells associated with the oil and gas industry, including salt water injection wells, enhanced recovery wells, wells injecting liquid hydrocarbons for storage and certain wells at natural gas plants
> *Class III* — wells injected fluids for the extraction of minerals, e.g. Frasch sulfur mining, insitu production of uranium or other minerals, solution mining of potash and salts
> *Class IV* — wells injecting hazardous waste or radioactive waste into a formation within 1/4 mile from a USDW.

---

[48]40 C.F.R. §146.3.

[49]Individuals that have their own drinking water wells, would not fall under the scope of the program. However, private wells that have been contaminated may be protected under CERCLA (i.e., Superfund) or RCRA depending upon the nature of the contamination.

[50]40 C.F.R. § 144.12(a).

[51]The 10,000 mg/l number appeared in a congressional report prepared during the enactment of the SDWA in 1974 and may have represented the outer boundary of TDS treatment capabilities at the time.

*Class V* — all other injection wells, including: air conditioning return flow wells used to return to the aquifer water used for heating or cooling in a heat pump; cesspools including multiple dwellings, community or regional; cooling water return flow wells; drainage wells used to drain fluids and dry wells used for injection of wastes into subsurface formations; aquifer recharge wells; salt water intrusion barrier wells; septic system wells used to inject waste from multiple dwellings; injection wells associated with geothermal wells.

Class V wells currently have few regulatory requirements, other than a reporting requirement under 40 C.F.R. §144.26, although if such wells endanger drinking water sources, then EPA has authority on a case-by-case basis to impose additional requirements. Class I wells, under the UIC program (especially hazardous waste injection wells), have the most stringent operational requirements. However, with regard to the Class I-III wells, EPA has imposed similar basic construction and operational requirements, particularly for new wells:

- Monitoring Injection Pressure, Volumes and Rate of Fluids Injected, Recordkeeping and Reporting of Fluid Injection — to determine on the basis of these measurements whether wells are leaking fluids from the well or the injection formation;
- Construction Requirements — Cementing and Logging — to ensure that the well is built to prevent fluids from travelling behind the well casing;
- Area of Review — to prevent abandoned wells or open holes from becoming conduits for fluid migration from the injection zone to freshwater strata;
- Mechanical Integrity — to insure that the well is not leaking fluids;
- Corrective Action — to correct any leaks of fluid from the well or through abandoned wells or boreholes;
- Plugging and Abandonment — to prevent existing wells from becoming conduits for contamination in the future.
- Financial Responsibility — to ensure the well can be properly plugged or repaired in the event of a well failure.

All of these provisions are intended to ensure that a well will not itself leak fluids, or provide a conduit for leakage.

These requirements are imposed through a permit system and the States generally operate and enforce the UIC regulations. Class I well permits are issued for a period of ten years, while Class II and III permits are issued for life, but can be reviewed every five years. In most instances, states have been authorized to operate the permitting program; however, the permitting authority is often different for Class I wells and Class II or III wells. For example, Class I wells are generally issued by the state's environmental protection agency. Class II or III permits may be issued by the state's oil or mineral authorities, whose principal concern may be the conservation and use of the state's natural resources rather than preventing environmental contamination. This has led to friction with federal EPA in some instances.

### 5.1 Class I Hazardous Waste Disposal Wells

Class I hazardous waste injection wells are regulated under both the Safe Drinking Water Act and the Resource Conservation and Recovery Act. All Class I wells are subject the most strict construction and operational requirements when compared to the other well classes. Class I hazardous waste wells have also been impacted by the land disposal restriction program imposed under RCRA Section 3004.

Underground injection is considered to be a category of land disposal under RCRA. In amending RCRA in 1984, Congress determined that untreated hazardous waste should not be disposed of on the land. EPA has been implementing the land disposal restrictions over the past 5 years and has finally completed issuing best available treatment (BAT) standards for listed and characteristically hazardous waste. It is interesting to note, though, that for many wastes, application of BAT will make the wastes unamenable to injection, because the materials will no longer be in an aqueous form.

An exception to the land disposal restriction is where an operator can show that no hazardous constituents will migrate from an untreated hazardous waste so long as the waste remains hazardous. This "no migration" exception has been the basis for EPA granting relief from the land disposal ban in the form of a no migration demonstration petition.

Few operators conducting surface land disposal have been able to satisfy the no migration standard, because hazardous constituents can be released to the air. However, injection well operators have been successful in certain instances in showing that hazardous waste placed into particular underground formations will not allow the migration of hazardous constituents.

To obtain a no migration exception, an operator must show, through the use of a computer model, that no waste constituent will migrate vertically or laterally out of the injection zone for 10,000 years.[52] A party can argue for a shorter time period if he can show the wastes will cease to be hazardous at a certain point in time through attenuation, transformation or immobilization of hazardous constituents.

EPA has granted numerous no migration petitions for injection wells, notwithstanding the strict factual showing. Accordingly, Class I wells are likely to continue to be used to disposed of liquid, untreated hazardous wastes.

### 5.2 Class II Oil and Gas Injection Wells

There are two major types of injection wells used in the oil and gas industry: saltwater disposal wells and enhanced recovery injection wells. When oil is produced from a well, water is also produced. Given the depth of the formation, the water will often be briny and contain high levels of TDS. In addition, as an oil field is depleted of petroleum, wells will tend to produce a higher percentage of water relative to oil. Accordingly, a salt water disposal well is needed to place the produced water back into a deep formation.

Enhanced recovery wells are used to flood an oil bearing formation with water or other fluids and to push the oil to a producing well. These enhanced recovery wells are

---

[52] 40 C.F.R. Part 268.

generally carefully located and controlled by the operator to ensure the maximum efficiency in recovering oil.

Although there are UIC regulations regarding the minimum requirements for salt water disposal and enhanced recovery wells, these generally apply only in states in which EPA operates the Class II well program. Every other state which operates its own program received federal approval for its Class II program under Section 1425 of the Safe Drinking Water Act, a provision added to the Act in 1980. Basically, it provides that if the state program meets the statutory criteria in Section 1421 of the Act (the criteria that governs EPA's development of regulations), then EPA should approve the state program. EPA issued guidance regarding the Section 1425 demonstration in 1981.

Recently, though, EPA has been reconsidering whether it should strengthen the requirements for Class II wells, specifically in the areas of construction requirements, monitoring and testing, and area of review for existing wells. No area of review requirements currently apply to existing wells, unless they are imposed by the state's regulations.

### 5.3 Class III and IV Wells

EPA has prohibited injection using Class IV wells, which involves injecting above or into a USDW. The likelihood of endangerment from these wells is well documented and the prohibition has not been controversial.

Class III wells are associated with mining operations and are generally more stringent than those imposed under Class II, but not as stringent as Class I requirements. Most states in which these wells are economically used have assumed responsibility for the permitting and control of the wells.

### 5.4 Class V Wells

Class V wells encompass a significant number of very diverse injection wells. Unless a Class V well is found to be endangering a USDW, no permit is currently required. However, EPA can require a Class I well permit for a particular Class V well if it is determined that the well is being improperly operated or endangers drinking water.

Such was the case with regard to Class V wells located at many gasoline service stations. Service stations that were not connected to a sewer system often had drains and drain pipes in the bay area where they serviced automobiles. These bays were washed down to remove oil and other materials and the drain pipes carried the wash water directly into the ground. EPA found that these drain pipes were Class V wells and brought enforcement actions against a number of major oil companies.

On August 28, 1995, EPA proposed new requirements for Class V wells. 60 Fed. Reg. 44652. In the notice, EPA identified 10 general categories of Class V wells which were:

- "Beneficial Use Wells" which include a variety of well types used either to improve the quality or flow of aquifers or to provide some other benefit, such as preventing salt water intrusion or controlling subsidence.
- "Fluid Return Wells" which are used to inject spent fluids associated with the production of geothermal energy for space heating or electric power, the operation of a heat pump, the extraction of minerals, or aquaculture.

- "Sewage Treatment Effluent Wells" which are used to inject effluent from publicly or privately owned treatment facilities.
- "Cesspools" which are wells that receive untreated sanitary waste. They may have open bottoms, and are typically located in areas not served by sanitary sewers. Under the proposed rule, only those cesspools having the capacity to serve 20 persons or more a day would be considered Class V injection wells subject to the UIC regulations.[53]
- "Septic Systems" which are wells comprised of septic tanks and fluid distribution systems (e.g., leachfields) used to dispose of sanitary waste only. Only those septic systems having the capacity to serve 20 or more persons per day would be considered Class V injection wells subject to the UIC regulations.
- "Experimental Technology Wells" which include any injection well used as part of an unproven subsurface injection technology.
- "Drainage Wells" which consist of a variety of wells used to drain surface and subsurface fluids including storm water and agricultural runoff.
- "Mine Backfill Wells" which are used to place slurries of sand, gravel, cement, mill tailings/refuse, or fly ash into underground mines. Mine backfill wells serve a variety of purposes ranging from subsidence prevention to control of underground fires.
- "In-situ and Solution Mining Wells" which are used to liberate fossil fuels from the geologic formation which contains them or to bring minerals from underground deposits to the surface. They do not include wells specifically listed as Class III wells under Section 146.5.
- "Industrial Waste Discharge Wells" which are used to inject wastewaters generated by industrial, commercial, and service establishments.[54]

In the preamble, EPA analyzed each category of Class V wells and described the associated risks to underground drinking water sources. The principal issue was whether the Agency would adopt a permitting approach for a specific group of Class V wells or rely upon federal and state enforcement efforts to deal with wells that endangered drinking water sources.

EPA concluded that additional federal UIC regulations to protect USDWs would be inappropriate and that the risks posed by these wells were best addressed, using existing authorities. EPA indicated that it would work with the States to implement a comprehensive Class V management strategy. The goal of the strategy would be to speed up the closure of potentially endangering Class V wells using current authorities

---

[53]The current EPA regulations exclude individual single family and non-residential cesspools and septic systems having the capacity to serve fewer than 20 persons per day.

[54]In accordance with the 1986 Amendments to the SDWA, 42 U.S.C. §300h-5(b), EPA had summarized information on 32 categories of Class V wells in a Report to Congress entitled *Class V Injection Wells—Current Inventory; Effects on Ground Water; and Technical Recommendations*, September 1987 (EPA Document Number 570/9-87-006). This report presented a national overview of Class V injection practices and State recommendations for Class V design, construction, installation, and siting requirements.

and to promote the use of best management practices to ensure that other Class V wells of concern do not endanger USDWs.

To achieve these goals, EPA proposed to rely on the existing performance-based standard in 40 C.F.R. §144.12, its other regulatory authorities in subpart C of the UIC rules, and a carefully tailored combination of guidance, education, and outreach. EPA concluded that this approach will be more effective than  promulgating additional design-based Class V requirements.

The Class V management guidance proposes to specifically target the following types of Class V industrial wells for inspection and follow-up enforcement action:

(a)     Disposal wells used by automotive related facilities such as gasoline stations, automobile repair shops, automobile parts supply companies, and motor vehicle dealers;

(b)     Disposal wells used by "light" industrial facilities such as dry cleaners, photographic processors, electro-platers, metal fabricators, and printers.

To support the Implementation Guidance, EPA also proposed to issue technical guidance, some directed at the regulated community and some directed at the States on industrial waste discharge well closure, septic systems, agricultural drainage wells, and storm water drainage well guidance. A final regulation has not been issued.

## 6.0 CRITICAL AQUIFER PROTECTION AREA DEMONSTRATION PROGRAM

The provision for sole source aquifer protection establishes procedures for the development, implementation, and assessment of demonstration programs designed to protect critical aquifer protection areas. A critical aquifer protection area is defined as:

(1) all or part of an area located within an area from which an application or designation as a sole or principal source aquifer (pursuant to section 1424(e)) has been submitted and approved by the Administrator not later than 24 months after the date of enactment and which satisfies the criteria established by the Administrator; and (2) all or part of an area which is within an aquifer designated as a sole source aquifer, as of the date of enactment of these amendments, and for which an area wide ground water quality protection plan has been approved under section 208 of the Clean Water Act prior to such enactment.[55]

An application for a protection plan will be approved or disapproved by the Administrator based on the plan's ability to maintain the quality of the ground water in the critical protection area in a manner reasonable expected to protect human health, the environment, and ground water resources.

Upon approval of an application, the Administrator may enter into a cooperative agreement with the applicant to establish a demonstration program and provide to the applicant, on a matching basis, a grant of 50% of the costs of implementing the plan. The Administrator may also reimburse the applicant of an approved plan up to 50% of

---

[55]SDWA § 1427(b), 42 U.S.C.§ 300h-6(b).

the costs of developing the plan. The total among of grants under section 203 may not exceed $4,000,000 in any one fiscal year.

## 7.0 STATE WELLHEAD PROTECTION PROGRAMS

Within three years of the enactment of the Amendments of 1986, each State is required to adopt and submit to the Administrator a State program to protect wellhead areas within their jurisdiction from contaminants which may cause adverse human health effects. The term "wellhead protection area" is defined as:

> The surface and subsurface area surrounding a water well or wellfield, supplying a public water system, through which contaminants are reasonably likely to move toward and reach such water well or well field.[56]

Within one year after the enactment of the Safe Drinking Water Act Amendments of 1986, the Administrator is required to issue technical guidance which States may use in making wellhead determinations.[57] The guidance should reflect such factors as the radius of influence around a well or wellfield, the depth of drawdown of the water table by such well or wellfield at any given point, the time or rate of travel of various contaminants in various hydrologic conditions, distance from the well or wellfield, or other factors affecting the likelihood of contaminants reaching the well or wellfield, taking into account available engineering pump tests or comparable data, field reconnaissance, topographic information, and the geology of the formation in which the well or wellfield is located.

The program submitted by the State for approval by the Administrator must:

1.  Specify the duties of State agencies, local govern-mental entities, and public water supply systems with respect to the development and implementation of programs required by this section;
2.  For each wellhead, determine the wellhead protection area;
3.  Identify within each wellhead protection area all potential anthro-pogenic sources of contaminants which may have any adverse effect on the health of persons;
4.  Describe a program that contains, as appropriate, technical assistance, financial assistance, implementation of control measures, education, training, and demonstration projects to protect the water supply within wellhead protection areas from such contaminants;
5.  Include contingency plans for the location and provision of alternate drinking water supplies for each public water system in the event of well or wellfield contamination by such contaminants; and,
6.  Include a requirement that consideration be given to all potential sources of such contaminants within the expected wellhead area of a new water well which serves a public water supply system.[58]

---

[56]SDWA § 1428(e); 42 U.S.C. § 300h-7.
[57]SDWA § 1427(d); 42 U.S.C. § 300h-6(d).
[58]SDWA § 1427(e); 42 U.S.C. § 300h-6(e).

In addition to these provisions, States in which there are more than 2,500 active wells at which annular injection is used as of January 1, 1986, must include in their State program a certification that a State program exists and is being adequately enforced that provides protection from contaminants which may have any adverse human health effect and which are associated with the annual injection or surface disposal of brines associated with oil and gas production. The term "annular injection" is defined as "the reinjection of brines associated with the production of oil or gas between the production and surface casings of a conventional oil or gas producing well."

Each State is required to make every reasonable effort to implement the State wellhead area protection program under this section within two years of submitting the program to the Administrator. Each State must submit to the Administrator a biennial status report describing the State's progress in implementing the program.[59]

Unless the State program is disapproved, the Administrator is required to make grants to the State for not less than 50 or more than 90 percent of the costs incurred by the State (as determined by the Administrator) in developing and implementing each State wellhead protection program.

## 8.0 CONCLUSION

The significance of the SDWA has extended far beyond the regulation of public drinking water systems. The implementation of the new primary drinking water standard setting authorities, especially the cost-benefit provisions, will be carefully followed to see if such mechanisms of regulatory reform can function accurately and protect public health. Local water systems also have major new requirements and although considerable funding is available, many water systems need major and costly infrastructure improvements.

Indeed, the amount of resources needed to achieve the goals of the legislation could be staggering. In "Drinking Water Infrastructure Needs Survey: First Report to Congress" (January, 1997), EPA announced that $12.1 billion was needed immediately for water systems to meet health-based standards, $10.2 billion, or 84%, needed to protect water supplies from microbiological contaminants. The 1996 Amendments authorize $9.6 billion through the year 2003. More daunting, though, is EPA's estimate that $138.4 billion will be needed over the next 20 years to replace or upgrade the drinking water infrastructure, including treatment, storage, and delivery, of the Nation's 55,000 community drinking water systems. Whether the system were large, medium, or small, EPA estimated necessary improvements would cost many billions of dollars.

Incidents throughout the country such as the cryptosporidium outbreak in Milwaukee and the new EPA report indicate that the quality of the Nation's drinking water cannot be taken for granted, but requires resources and careful attention by the government and private interests. Let us see that the "Bridge to the 21st Century" spans safe waters.

---

[59]SDWA § 1427(k); 42 U.S.C. § 300h-6(k).

# CHAPTER 7

# TOXIC SUBSTANCES CONTROL ACT

Stanley W. Landfair
McKenna & Cuneo, L.L.P.
Los Angeles, California[1]

## 1.0 INTRODUCTION

The Toxic Substances Control Act (TSCA or the Act), 15 U.S.C. §§ 2601-2629, was enacted on October 11, 1976. The Act has been amended three times, each amendment resulting in an additional title, such that TSCA now contains four titles: Title I—the Control of Toxic Substances; Title II—the Asbestos Hazard Emergency Response Act; Title III—the Indoor Radon Abatement Act; and Title IV—the Lead-Based Paint Exposure Reduction Act. The scope of this chapter, however, is limited to Title I of the Act, the Control of Toxic Substances.

TSCA places on manufacturers the responsibility to provide data on the health and environmental effects of chemical substances and mixtures, and gives EPA comprehensive authority to regulate the manufacture, use, distribution in commerce, and disposal of chemical substances. To implement this authority, TSCA affords EPA the following regulatory tools:

- **Authority to require testing** of chemicals which may present a significant risk or which are produced in substantial quantities and result in substantial human or environmental exposure. (TSCA § 4)
- **Premanufacture review** of new chemical substances prior to their commercial production and introduction into the marketplace. (TSCA § 5)
- **Authority to limit or prohibit** the manufacture, use, distribution, and disposal of existing chemical substances. (TSCA §6)
- **Recordkeeping and reporting** requirements to ensure that the EPA Administrator would continually have access to new information on chemical substances. (TSCA § 8)
- **Export notice** requirements that allow EPA to inform foreign governments of shipments of chemical substances into their countries. (TSCA § 12)
- **Import certification** requirement to ensure that all chemical substances imported into the United States comply with the Act. (TSCA §13)

Unlike other federal statutes that regulate chemical risks after a substance has been introduced into commerce, the major objective of TSCA is to characterize and

---

[1]This chapter is condensed from the *TSCA Handbook* (Govt. Inst. 1997, 3rd. Ed.) co-authored by the many McKenna & Cuneo, L.L.P., partners and associates who practice in this area. Mr. Landfair and Elizabeth Coppage Brown, a partner and associate in the firm's Los Angeles office, have edited and updated this material for the *Environmental Law Handbook*. They gratefully acknowledge the contribution of scientific consultants from Technology Sciences Group Inc., the firm's technical consulting subsidiary.

understand the risks that a chemical poses to humans and the environment before it is introduced into commerce. Before undertaking regulatory action, however, TSCA requires that EPA balance the economic and social benefits derived from the use of a chemical against that chemical's identified risks. Thus, the goal of TSCA is not to regulate all chemicals which present a risk, but only those which present an "unreasonable" risk of harm to human health or the environment.

## 2.0 ACTIVITIES SUBJECT TO TSCA

The varied requirements of TSCA apply to persons and companies that manufacture, process, distribute, use, or dispose of TSCA-regulated chemicals. Thus, it is necessary to determine, case-by-case, whether a particular activity constitutes regulated conduct. Unfortunately, TSCA defines neither "use" nor "dispose," and the definitions of "manufacture," "process," and "distribute" are worded too broadly to provide meaningful guidance. Moreover, EPA's implementing regulations generally define these terms more narrowly than the statute. Consequently, the scope of TSCA jurisdiction often remains unclear. The definition of these important jurisdictional terms and the duties of those who fall within them are discussed below.

### 2.1 Manufacture

TSCA § 3(7) defines "manufacture" to include not only the traditional notions of manufacture and production, but also the importation of TSCA-regulated chemical substances or mixtures. Under TSCA, manufacturers of chemical substances generally must: (1) sponsor tests and submit data to EPA regarding chemicals they manufacture; (2) submit a premanufacture notice (PMN) before manufacturing a chemical substance not on the TSCA Inventory or before manufacturing a chemical for a significant new use; (3) avoid manufacture of PCBs; (4) maintain records and submit reports as required by § 8; (5) submit to EPA inspections and subpoenas as authorized by § 11; and (7) certify compliance with TSCA upon importation as required by § 13.

EPA regulations implementing TSCA § 5 (Premanufacture Notification) and § 8 (Reporting and Recordkeeping) limit jurisdiction to persons who "manufacture for commercial purposes" and define "commercial purposes" as:

. . .the purpose of obtaining an immediate or eventual commercial advantage for the manufacturer, and includes, among other things, . . .

(i)    for distribution in commerce, including for test marketing,

(ii)   for use by the manufacturer, including use for product research and development, or as an intermediate.

[Further, this definition] applies to substances that are produced coincidentally during the manufacture, processing, use, or disposal of another substance or mixture, including both by-products that are separated from that other substance or mixture and impurities that remain in that substance or mixture.[2]

---

[2] 40 C.F.R. §§ 717.3(e), 712.3(h), 704.3, 716.3, and 720.3(r).

EPA has expanded the statutory definition of "manufacture" by including the act of "extracting" a chemical from another chemical substance or mixture of substances.[3] Importantly, a toll manufacturer also is considered a manufacturer under the premanufacture and significant new use notification regulations. The purchasing or contracting company also may be considered a manufacturer, however, if: (1) the toll manufacturer produces the substance exclusively for that purchasing company; and (2) the purchasing company specifies the identity of the substance and controls the amount produced and the basic technology for the plant processes.[4]

## 2.2 Process

TSCA § 3(10) defines "process" to mean:

> . . .the preparation of a chemical substance or mixture, after its manufacture, for distribution in commerce—
>
> (A) in the same form or physical state as, or in a different form or physical state from, that in which it was received by the persons so preparing such substance or mixture, or
> (B) as part of an article containing the chemical substance or mixture.

TSCA § 3(11) further defines the term "processor" as "any person who processes a chemical substance or mixture."

Processors of chemical substances must: (1) provide EPA with data under test rules, in some circumstances; (2) notify EPA prior to processing a chemical for a significant new use; (3) comply with EPA orders issued under §§ 5(e), 5(f) or 6(b) or rules promulgated under § 6(a); (4) avoid processing PCBs except as permitted by EPA; (5) comply with the recordkeeping and reporting requirements of §§ 8(c), 8(d) and 8(e); and (6) submit to EPA inspections and subpoenas, as authorized by § 11.

If EPA's regulations implementing the various subsections of TSCA applied to everyone who fell within the literal language of these broad definitions, TSCA requirements would be imposed on thousands of businesses that Congress never intended the law to touch. To avoid such problems for some reporting requirements under TSCA § 8, EPA has passed implementing rules that apply only to some processors.

Recognizing the need to address this issue in a comprehensive and organized manner, several years ago EPA made available a package of all EPA guidance documents that address the definitions of "process" or "processor."[5] EPA also solicited written comments and held a one-day public meeting to allow interested persons an opportunity to present their views on EPA's interpretation of "process" under TSCA. Several commentors urged EPA to begin formal rulemaking to modify the definition of "processor" and to limit or eliminate application of the term to basic manufacturers and other companies that traditionally have not considered themselves chemical

---

[3]40 C.F.R. §§ 704.3, 716.3 and 720.3(t).
[4]40 C.F.R. § 720.3(t).
[5]57 *Fed. Reg* 38,832 (1992).

processors. At the time, the Agency planned to review all written and oral comments received and address, as appropriate, the issues identified, starting with those that seem to be of the greatest concern to the regulated community and others. Since 1992, however, there has been no significant dialogue or further EPA action on this issue.

## 2.3 Use

TSCA does not provide a definition of "use," nor has EPA issued comprehensive guidance on the distinction between "use" and "process." Nonetheless, users of chemical substances (who are not also manufacturers, processors, or distributors) must: (1) comply with regulations issued under § 6(a); (2) refrain from using PCBs, except as permitted by EPA; (3) refrain from using any chemical substance they know or have reason to know has been manufactured, produced, or distributed in violation of TSCA, as required under TSCA § 15(2); and (4) submit to EPA inspections and subpoenas, as authorized by § 11.

## 2.4 Distribute

Under TSCA § 3(4), the terms "distribute in commerce" and "distribution in commerce" mean to sell, to introduce, or to deliver a chemical substance into commerce or to hold the mixture or article after its introduction into commerce. The term "commerce" is defined in TSCA § 3(3) to mean interstate trade, traffic, transportation, or other activity which affects interstate trade, traffic, transportation, or commerce.

The TSCA definition of "distribution" thus encompasses more than the usual concept of sales or transportation, but its scope is not clear. For example, if applied literally, the portion that defines "holding" a chemical after its introduction in commerce as "distribution" would make any purchaser of a chemical a distributor since the person would necessarily hold the substance briefly before using it. In practice, EPA interprets the term to apply to persons who purchase a chemical and hold it for purposes of later distribution.

Distributors of chemical substances (who are not also manufacturers or processors) must: (1) comply with rules issued under § 6(a); (2) refrain from distributing PCBs except as permitted by EPA; (3) report "substantial risk information" to EPA under § 8(e); and (4) submit to EPA inspections and subpoenas, as authorized by § 11.

## 2.5 Dispose

Disposal is another activity not defined in TSCA. As a result, TSCA imposes no direct obligation on disposers of chemicals, but they may be subject to several types of rules or orders issued pursuant to the Act. Disposers of chemical substances (who are not also manufacturers, processors, distributors, or users) must: (1) comply with regulations issued under § 6(a); (2) dispose of PCBs according to requirements of the PCB disposal regulations; and (3) submit to EPA inspections and subpoenas, as authorized by § 11.

## 3.0 THE TSCA INVENTORY

TSCA § 8(b) requires EPA to compile, keep current, and publish a list of chemical substances manufactured or processed for commercial purposes in the United

States. This "list," known as the TSCA Inventory, forms the basis for distinguishing between "existing" chemicals (those included on the TSCA Inventory) and "new" chemicals (substances that require premanufacture notification under TSCA § 5). Thus, it is critically important to understand the TSCA Inventory and how it is compiled, kept current, and used.

## 3.1 Initial Compilation of the Inventory

The Inventory was developed pursuant to EPA's Inventory Reporting Regulations in December 1977. To be eligible for inclusion in the Inventory, a substance had to be a "reportable chemical substance," defined under the Regulations as: (1) a chemical substance; (2) manufactured, imported, or processed for a commercial purpose in the United States between January 1, 1975 and the date of publication of the Initial Inventory (June 1, 1979); and (3) not specifically excluded from the Inventory.[6] These three criteria are discussed below.

### 3.1.1 Chemical Substance

The statutory definition of the term "chemical substance" was incorporated directly into the Inventory Reporting Regulation, and includes:

. . .any organic or inorganic substance of a particular molecular identity, including (i) any combination of such substances occurring in whole or in part as a result of a chemical reaction or occurring in nature and (ii) any element or uncombined radical.[7]

The Regulations also incorporate the statutory exclusions from the definition of "chemical substance" for: (1) any mixture; (2) any commercial pesticide; (3) tobacco and certain tobacco products; (4) any nuclear source material or by-product; (5) any pistol, firearm, revolver, shells, and cartridges; and (6) any commercial food, food additive, drug, cosmetic, or device.[8]

### 3.1.2 Manufactured or Imported for a "Commercial Purpose"

A chemical substance manufactured or imported "for a commercial purpose" is one manufactured or imported for distribution in commerce (including test marketing) or for use by the manufacturer or importer, including use as an intermediate.[9]

### 3.1.3 Specifically Excluded Substances

"Mixtures" and "chemicals manufactured for a non-commercial purpose" are explicitly excluded from the Inventory by virtue of the definition of "chemical substance" under TSCA § 3(2)(B). The following also are excluded pursuant to § 8(b) and implementing regulations.

---

[6]40 C.F.R. § 710.4.
[7]TSCA §3(2)(A). *See also*, 40 C.F.R. § 710.2(h).
[8]*See* TSCA § 3(2)(A); 40 C.F.R. § 710.2(h).
[9]40 C.F.R. § 710.2(p).

**Research and Development.** Any chemical substance manufactured or processed only in small quantities for research and development (R&D) is excluded from the Inventory under TSCA § 8(b)(1). The R&D exemption is discussed in further detail *infra* at Section 4.3.2.

**Pesticides.** Because pesticides, as defined in the Federal Insecticide, Fungicide, and Rodenticide Act (FIFRA) are specifically excluded from the definition of chemical substances under TSCA § 3(2)(B)(ii) such substances are excluded from the Inventory. If a substance has multiple uses, those uses which are not subject to FIFRA are subject to TSCA, and thus must be included on the Inventory.

**Articles.** EPA defines an "article," for TSCA purposes, as a manufactured item formed into a specific shape or design during manufacture which has an end-use function dependent upon its shape or design during end-use and which has no change of chemical composition during its end-use separate from the purpose of the article.[10] Articles were excluded from Inventory reporting.

**Impurities.** An impurity is defined as "a chemical substance which is unintentionally present in another chemical substance."[11] Impurities are specifically excluded from the Inventory by regulation.[12]

**By-products.** A by-product is a chemical substance produced without a specific commercial intent during the manufacture or processing of another chemical substance(s) or mixture(s).[13] EPA excluded from the Inventory by-products which have no commercial purpose.[14]

**Chemicals Produced from Incidental Reactions.** Chemical substances produced as a result of incidental reactions were excluded from the Inventory because they were not intentionally produced for commercial purposes.[15]

**Non-isolated Intermediates.** Intermediates, defined as chemicals that are both manufactured and partially or totally consumed in the chemical reaction process, or are intentionally present in order to affect the rate of chemical reactions by which other chemical substances or mixtures are being manufactured, are subject to Inventory reporting. Non-isolated intermediates, however, defined as those intermediates that are not intentionally removed from the equipment in which they are manufactured, are excluded from reporting.[16]

### 3.2 Inventory Corrections

In 1980, EPA, recognizing that companies sometimes made errors in reporting substances and that often these errors are not discovered for many years, began to accept corrections to Inventory submissions under the following limited circumstances. Corrections must be submitted by the company that currently owns the rights to the chemical, be accompanied by adequate documentation, and fall into one of the following three

---

[10]40 C.F.R. § 710.2(f).
[11]40 C.F.R. § 710.2(m).
[12]40 C.F.R. § 710.4(d)(1).
[13]40 C.F.R. § 710.2(g).
[14]40 C.F.R. § 710.4(d)(2).
[15]40 C.F.R. § 710.4(d)(3)-(7).
[16]40 C.F.R. § 710.4(d)(8).

categories: (1) corrections of the chemical identity of previously reported materials; (2) corrections to identify previously unrecognized isolated intermediates; and (3) corrections made in response to communications from EPA which identify reporting errors.[17]

### 3.3 Maintaining and Updating the Inventory Data Base

EPA continuously adds to the Inventory new chemicals that have cleared TSCA § 5 PMN review and for which Notices of Commencement of Manufacture have been filed. The Agency also periodically removes, or "de-lists," from the Inventory "orphan chemicals" that are not currently being manufactured or imported for commercial purposes.

Prior to delisting, the Agency publishes a notice of its intent to delist in the *Federal Register* and in its quarterly *Chemicals in Progress Bulletin.* As a result of this process, the Inventory is maintained as a list of chemicals currently in commerce, not just those which were in commercial use during the 1975-1979 reporting period for the initial Inventory.

In June, 1986, EPA issued an Inventory Update Rule requiring manufacturers and importers of certain chemicals listed on the Inventory to report current data on production volume, plant site, and site-limited status.[18] Such reporting is required every four years for all chemical substances listed on the Inventory, except for the following: (1) polymers; (2) micro-organisms; (3) naturally occurring substances; and (4) inorganics.[19]

Under the Rule, any company that manufactures or imports any "reportable substance" for commercial purposes in amounts of 10,000 pounds or more at any time during the most recent complete corporate fiscal year immediately preceding the reporting year is obligated to file the report.[20] Exemptions from reporting under the Rule are available to small manufacturers and for certain chemicals exempt from premanufacture notification requirements.

The Update Rule requires each manufacturer or importer subject to the Rule to maintain specific records documenting the information submitted to EPA.[21] Importantly, production records for substances manufactured at less than 10,000 pounds must be maintained to justify a decision not to report.

### 3.4 How to Use the Inventory

The 1985 edition of the Inventory, with its 1990 Supplement, is the most current hard copy version. In addition, diskette and tape versions are now available that include chemicals added to the Inventory since 1990. These public versions consist of nonconfidential identities and generic names for confidential substances. EPA maintains the Master File that contains both the confidential and the nonconfidential identities.

---

[17] 45 *Fed. Reg* 50,544 (1980).
[18] 51 *Fed. Reg* 21,438 (1986).
[19] 40 C.F.R. § 710.26.
[20] 40 C.F.R. § 710.28.
[21] 40 C.F.R. § 710.37.

There are five volumes in the 1985 TSCA Inventory, each indexed to categorize the TSCA list of chemical substances in different ways. Volume One lists chemical substances in ascending order by CAS Registry Number, the CAS Index, or by Preferred Names. Volumes Two and Three are an alphabetically ordered listing of all CAS Index or Preferred Names, EPA submitter names, and CAS synonyms for the substances in the Chemical Substance Identity section. Volume Four lists all substances appearing in the Chemical Substance Identity section which have determinable molecular formulas. Volume Five lists substances of Unknown or Variable composition, Complex reaction products, and Biological materials (UVCB) substances.

### 3.4.1 Searching the Inventory

Volume One of the 1985 Inventory contains instructions on how to use the Inventory. The appropriate procedure for searching the Inventory depends upon the amount of information known about the substance in question. The easiest way to determine if a substance is listed in the printed Inventory is to search for its CAS registry number in Volume One. If the CAS Registry Number for the substance is already known, then it is necessary only to determine if the substance was included in the Chemical Substance Identities section. If the CAS Registry Number is not known, indices such as the Molecular Formula Index can assist in determining whether the chemical appears on the Inventory.

### 3.4.2 Searches for Confidential Identities: Bona Fide Request

Because confidential chemicals are not listed by specific chemical identity and new confidential chemicals are continually being added, the only way to determine if a substance is or is not on the Inventory is to search the Master File version of the Inventory. This version includes both confidential and nonconfidential chemical identities and is kept current by EPA. EPA will search the confidential Inventory only if the person requesting the search can demonstrate a *bona fide* intent to manufacture or import the substance for a commercial purpose.[22]

A notice of *bona fide* intent to manufacture or import must be submitted in writing and include the following information: (1) the specific chemical identity; (2) a signed statement of intent to manufacture or import for a commercial purpose; (3) a description of the research and development activities conducted; (4) the purpose of the manufacture or import; (5) an elemental analysis; and (6) either an x-ray diffraction pattern (for inorganic substances), a mass spectrum, or an infrared spectrum.[23]

### 4.0 NEW CHEMICAL REVIEW

Under TSCA § 5, any person intending to manufacture or import a chemical substance first must determine whether it is listed on the TSCA Inventory. If it is listed, then manufacture or importation may commence immediately. If the chemical substance is not listed on the Inventory, then the manufacturer or importer must determine whether the chemical substance is excluded altogether from regulation under TSCA or whether it is exempt from the requirements. If the chemical substance is neither excluded nor

---

[22]40 C.F.R. § 720.25(b)(1).
[23]40 C.F.R. § 720.25(b)(2).

exempted, the prospective manufacturer or importer must comply with the premanufacture notice (PMN) requirements before commencing those activities.

### 4.1. PMN Requirements

The PMN must contain: (1) information such as the identity of the chemical, categories of use, amounts manufactured, by-products, employees exposed and the manner or method of disposal to the extent known or "reasonably ascertainable;" (2) any test data related to the chemical's effects on health or the environment in the submitter's possession or control; and (3) a description of any other data concerning the health and environmental effects of the chemical, insofar as they are known to or "reasonably ascertainable" by the submitter.[24]

The policy underlying TSCA is that manufacturers and processors of chemical substances should bear the responsibility for developing adequate data regarding their effects on health and the environment. It is noteworthy that § 5 does not expressly authorize the Administrator to require or obligate the PMN submitter to produce specific tests with a PMN, except where a chemical substance is subject to a rule promulgated under § 4. Thus, unlike comparable laws outside the United States, TSCA does not require a bare set of premarket data on a new chemical.

Under § 5(a), EPA must review the PMN within ninety days of its submission. During its PMN review, EPA must assess the potential risks associated with the manufacture, processing, distribution, use, and disposal of the new substance based upon information supplied by the PMN submitter and available from various Agency data bases and the scientific literature, and, ultimately, based upon the Agency's own professional judgment. If EPA takes no regulatory action on the PMN within the ninety-day review period, the submitter may commence commercial manufacture or importation forthwith and without the need for prior Agency approval. Within thirty days of commencing manufacture or importation, the manufacturer or importer must file a Notice of Commencement (NOC) of Manufacture or Import.[25] The NOC certifies that commercial manufacture or importation actually has occurred. After receiving an NOC, EPA will add the PMN substance to the Inventory, and the new chemical will then become an "existing" chemical under TSCA.

The statute provides EPA with three means to prevent, delay or limit manufacture after the ninety-day review period expires. First, under § 5(c), the Agency may delay manufacture up to an additional ninety days for "good cause." Second, under § 5(e)(1)(A)(i), EPA may issue a proposed order to limit or prohibit manufacture if the Agency determines that available information is "insufficient to permit a reasoned evaluation" of the health and environmental effects of the new chemical substance. Third, under § 5(f)(2), EPA may propose a § 6(a) rule limiting or conditioning manufacture or under § 5(f)(3)(B) may issue a proposed order totally banning manufacture, if there is a "reasonable basis to conclude that the manufacture . . . presents or will present an unreasonable risk of injury to health or the environment." Each of these Agency actions is subject to judicial review, although the scope of review varies under each provision.

---

[24]TSCA § 5(d).
[25]40 C.F.R. § 720.102.

## 4.2 Exclusions from PMN Requirements

The PMN requirements apply to a "new chemical substance" and, once an applicable rule is promulgated, to a "significant new use" of an existing chemical substance. The statutory definition of "chemical substance" excludes any mixture, any pesticide as defined by the Federal Insecticide, Fungicide and Rodenticide Act, and any food, food additive, drug, cosmetic, or device as defined by the Federal Food, Drug and Cosmetic Act, various nuclear materials regulated under the Atomic Energy Act, and any tobacco or tobacco product.[26] Thus, by definition, these substances are excluded from TSCA jurisdiction and, as such, are not subject to the PMN requirements. The PMN requirements nevertheless may apply to such "excluded" substances, if they also are intended for a "TSCA use."

## 4.3 Exemptions from PMN Requirements

TSCA explicitly establishes two exemptions from the PMN requirements–for test marketing and R & D—and grants EPA authority to establish additional exemptions by regulation where the Agency determines that the manufacture, processing, distribution, or use of a chemical substance will not present an unreasonable risk to health or the environment. Pursuant to this authority, EPA has prescribed fifteen exemptions to the PMN requirements. Several of the more important exemptions are discussed below.

### 4.3.1 Test Market Exemption

TSCA § 5(h)(1) authorizes the Administrator to exempt a new chemical substance from the PMN requirements when it is manufactured for test marketing purposes if the Administrator determines that the proposed test marketing activity will not present an unreasonable risk to human health or the environment. The Test Market Exemption (TME) permits a company to assess the commercial viability of a new chemical and to receive customer feedback on product performance before filing a PMN. Under TSCA § 5(h)(1), the test marketer must apply for this exemption and must demonstrate that the proposed activity is legitimate test marketing which will not present an unreasonable risk.

EPA reviews a TME application in essentially the same manner as it does a PMN. Yet, under TSCA § 5(h)(6), EPA must review a TME application within forty-five days of its receipt. According to EPA, however, the Agency's failure to complete its review of a TME application within forty-five days does not constitute an automatic approval. Rather, unlike a PMN submitter, a TME applicant must await EPA approval prior to initiating activity.

### 4.3.2 Research and Development Exemption

TSCA § 5(h)(3) exempts from the PMN and "significant new use rule" (SNUR) requirements small quantities of new chemicals used solely for R&D under the supervision of a technically qualified individual, if the manufacturer or importer notifies persons engaged in R&D of any health risks associated with the substance. Unlike the other exemptions under § 5(h), the manufacturer or importer need not apply for the R&D exemption. EPA regulations establishing requirements for the R&D exemption appear

---

[26]*See* TSCA § 3(2)(B).

at 40 C.F.R. § 720.36. EPA requires that a technically qualified individual supervise the R&D activities and that the manufacturer or importer evaluate any potential risks associated with the R&D substance, notify persons involved in the R&D of those risks, and maintain certain records of their R&D activity. In evaluating risks, the manufacturer or importer must consider all health and environmental effects data in its "possession or control." This includes information in the files of agents and employees engaged in the R&D and marketing of the new chemical. When R&D activity is conducted in laboratories using prudent laboratory conditions, however, this risk assessment need not be performed.

### 4.3.3 Low-Volume Exemptions

Under TSCA § 5(h)(4), EPA has exempted certain low-volume and low-release, low-exposure chemicals from the full PMN requirements by providing an expedited thirty-day review.[27] Although a low-volume exemption (LVE), in one form or another, has existed for some time, EPA significantly modified the low volume exemption in 1995.[28] At the same time, EPA added a new exemption for low-release, low-exposure chemicals (LoREX). In order to grant an LVE or LoREX exemption, EPA must determine that the chemical substance will "not present an unreasonable risk of injury to health or the environment."[29]

Under the now-existing LVE, any manufacturer or importer who intends to produce or import a new chemical substance in quantities of 10,000 kilograms or less per year may be eligible for the LVE. As long as EPA can determine that "the potential human exposure to, and environmental release of, the new chemical substance at the higher aggregate production volume will not present an unreasonable risk of injury to human health and the environment," it should grant multiple LVEs.[30] The application for exemption must be submitted on the standard PMN form.[31] As before, representations in the LVE application regarding human exposure or environmental release controls employed during the manufacture, processing, distribution in commerce, use and disposal of the chemical, the location of manufacture, and the use to which the chemical will be put still are binding, and LVE chemicals still will not be included in the TSCA Inventory.

If new information causes the LVE chemical to become ineligible for the exemption, EPA will revoke it. Before revoking the LVE, however, EPA will notify the manufacturer or importer in writing of the Agency's intent to revoke. After receiving notice of EPA's intent to revoke, the manufacturer or importer within fifteen days may file objections or an explanation of its "diligence and good faith" in attempting to comply with the terms of the exemption.[32] Within fifteen days of receiving the objections or explanation, EPA will make a final determination whether the chemical

---

[27]40 C.F.R. § 723.50.
[28]60 *Fed. Reg* 16,336 (1995).
[29]TSCA § 5(h)(4).
[30]40 C.F.R. § 723.50(f).
[31]40 C.F.R. § 723.50(e)(1).
[32]40 C.F.R. § 723.50(h)(2)(ii).

remains eligible for the LVE.[33] If so, EPA will leave the LVE in effect. If not and EPA also determines that the manufacturer or importer did not act in good faith to meet the terms of the exemption, then within seven days of notification by EPA, all activities involving the LVE chemical must cease.[34] Alternatively, if EPA determines that the manufacturer or importer of the LVE chemical did act in good faith, activities involving the LVE chemical may continue while a PMN for the chemical is prepared and reviewed.[35]

Under the former LVE, annual production or import volume was limited to 1,000 kgs and to a single manufacturer or importer. All exemptions previously granted under the former LVE will remain binding and effective under the superseded provisions, even though such provisions will no longer be contained in the Code of Federal Regulations.[36] If manufacturers or importers wish to upgrade their 1,000 kg-LVE to the new 10,000 kg-LVE, they must submit another exemption application.

The LoREX exemption is available for chemicals that meet stringent and binding release and exposure criteria, regardless of production volume.[37] Briefly, those criteria for consumers and the general population are: (1) no dermal exposure; (2) no inhalation exposure (except that allowed as ambient air releases from incineration); and (3) no exposure in drinking water greater than 1 mg/year.[38] Criteria for workers during the manufacturing, processing, distribution in commerce, use and disposal of the substance are: (1) no dermal exposure; and (2) no inhalation exposure. The ambient surface water criterion is 1 ppb, and the criterion for ambient air releases from incineration is 1 $g/m^3$ maximum annual average concentration.

LoREX chemicals are subject to the same administrative requirements as LVE chemicals, such as a thirty-day review period and mandatory use of the PMN form for submission of the exemption application. In addition, representations in the LoREX application regarding human exposure or environmental release controls used during the manufacture, processing, distribution in commerce, use and disposal of the chemical, the location of manufacture, and the use to which the chemical will be put are binding. Finally, LoREX chemicals will not be included in the TSCA Inventory.

### 4.3.4 Polymer Exemption

Under TSCA § 5(h)(4), EPA also provides a complete exemption from the PMN requirement for certain polymers. As with all exemptions under § 5(h)(4), EPA must find that the exempted polymers will not present an unreasonable risk of injury to human health or the environment. In order to be eligible for the polymer exemption, the new chemical substance must meet three criteria: (1) it must be a "polymer" as defined in 40 C.F.R. § 723.250(b); (2) it must not be specifically excluded by 40 C.F.R. § 723.250(d); and (3) it must meet certain exemption criteria (i.e., have a certain number-average

---

[33] 40 C.F.R. § 723.50(h)(2)(iii).
[34] 40 C.F.R. § 723.50(h)(2)(v).
[35] 40 C.F.R. § 723.50(h)(2)(vi).
[36] 40 C.F.R. § 723.50(m).
[37] 60 *Fed. Reg* at 16,337.
[38] 40 C.F.R. § 723.50(c)(2).

molecular weight or be a polyester of a certain type) as set forth in 40 C.F.R. § 723.250(e).

Effective May 30, 1995, the polymer exemption no longer requires an application. Persons may manufacture or import polymers pursuant to the exemption without prior notification to EPA. All that EPA requires is an annual report, submitted by January 31, indicating the number of new polymers manufactured or imported pursuant to the exemption for the first time during the previous year and by whom they were manufactured or imported.[39] In addition to this annual report, parties that manufacture or import polymers pursuant to the exemption must maintain detailed records documenting that the new chemical substance meets the criteria for an exempt polymer and otherwise demonstrating compliance with the exemption.[40]

Under the new polymer exemption, polymers will no longer be placed on the TSCA Inventory, unless manufacturers or importers elect to proceed under the PMN/NOC process.[41] EPA does not intend to remove polymers from the TSCA Inventory that already are listed.[42] Presumably, manufacturers or importers can submit a PMN for a new polymer at any time, and need not cease manufacture of an otherwise exempt polymer during the pendency of the PMN review period. Manufacturers and importers will have the option, however, of continuing to manufacture or import the polymer pursuant to the former polymer exemption (which includes restrictions on residual monomer and low molecular weight species content) or manufacturing or importing the polymer under the new exemption.[43]

### 4.3.5 "Polaroid" Exemption

In response to a petition from the Polaroid Corporation, EPA exempted new chemical substances used in or for instant photographic and "peel-apart" film articles.[44] Under the terms of the so-called "Polaroid" exemption, manufacturers of instant photographic materials may commence manufacture of new chemical substances for these products immediately upon submitting an exemption notice pursuant to 40 C.F.R. § 723.175. These new chemical substances, however, cannot be distributed in commerce until a PMN is filed and the review period has ended.

### 4.3.6 New Chemicals Imported in Articles

Under 40 C.F.R. § 720.22(b)(1), a manufacturer must file a PMN on any new chemical substances imported into the United States for commercial purposes "unless the substance is imported as part of an article." The term "article" is defined at 40 C.F.R. § 720.3(c). Although EPA's definition of article specifically excludes "fluids and particles . . . regardless of shape or design," importers of articles that contain fluids or particles that are not intended to be removed and that have no separate commercial purpose are excluded from the PMN requirements. Conversely, EPA considers that a substance cannot be "a part" of an article if it is released and, upon release, has a

---

[39]40 C.F.R. § 723.250(f).
[40]40 C.F.R. § 723.250(g) and (j).
[41]60 *Fed. Reg* 16,326 (1995).
[42]*Id.*
[43]40 C.F.R. § 723.250(i).
[44]40 C.F.R. § 723.175.

commercial purpose. Thus, according to EPA, articles that contain fluids designed to be used or released in order for the article to function, like ink in pens, are not encompassed by this exemption.

### 4.3.7 Impurities, By-Products, Non-Isolated Intermediates

EPA has excluded from the PMN requirements impurities, by-products, non-isolated intermediates, and chemicals formed incidentally when exposed to the environment or to other chemicals.[45] These exemptions are essentially identical to exemptions from the initial Inventory, which are found at 40 C.F.R. § 710.4. In fact, EPA often uses its discussion of these exemptions in the Preamble and Response to Comments in its initial Inventory reporting rule to clarify the scope and applicability of these same exemptions from the PMN requirements.

### 4.3.8 Chemicals Formed During the Manufacture of an Article

EPA also exempts from the PMN requirements "any other chemical substance formed during the manufacture of an article destined for the marketplace without further chemical change of the chemical substance except for those chemical changes that occur as described elsewhere in this paragraph."[46] Thus, for example, EPA exempts new chemicals formed upon use of rubber molding or curable plastic compounds, inks, drying oils, adhesives or paints, and metal finishing compounds.[47]

### 4.3.9 Chemicals Formed Incidental to the Use of Certain Additives

Under 40 C.F.R. § 720.30(h)(7), EPA exempts from the PMN requirements new chemicals formed incidental to the use of certain additives intended solely to impart specific physiochemical characteristics when these additives function as intended. Thus, the Agency exempts new chemical substances formed incidental to use of a specific additive–such as a pH neutralizer, stabilizer, or binder–if the additive is used only for the purposes of achieving a specific physiochemical characteristic, and it functions solely to achieve that characteristic. For example, EPA excludes a new chemical substance formed incidental to the addition of bleach to cotton if the manufacturer adds the bleach only to change a specific physiochemical characteristic of the cotton and not to make a major compositional change.[48]

In response to its belief that the regulated community largely has misconstrued the so-called "additives" exemption, EPA disseminated to the regulated community, by letter dated June 29, 1994, guidance for applying this exemption to various manufacturing scenarios. In this letter, EPA states that a substance is excluded from the Inventory or PMN reporting requirements if:

1.   the substance is formed from a chemical reaction that involves the use of a chemical substance of the type described under 40 C.F.R. § 710.4(d)(7) or § 720.30(h)(7);

---

[45]40 C.F.R. § 720.30(h).
[46]40 C.F.R. § 720.36(h)(6).
[47]*Id.*
[48]43 *Fed. Reg* 9256 (1978).

2.  the substance does not function to provide one or more primary properties that would determine the use of the product or product mixture distributed in commerce, even though it may impart certain physicochemical characteristics to the product, product mixture, or formulation of which it is a part; and

3.  the substance is not itself the one intended for distribution in commerce as a chemical substance *per se*. Although it may be a component of the product, product mixture, or formulation actually distributed in commerce, it has no commercial purpose separate from the product, product mixture, or formulation of which it is a component.

EPA's letter also applies the new guidance to a real life manufacturing scenario in the following example:

> Where an acid polymer is converted to its soluble amine salt during an ink formulation process in which other ingredients are added, the polymer salt formed as a result of a chemical reaction that brings the insoluble acid polymer into solution is exempt because (1) it does not itself contribute a primary property that is essential to the functioning of the ink as a viable commercial product, (2) is not itself the product intended for distribution in commerce as a chemical substance *per se*, and (3) has no commercial purpose separate from the ink formulation.

Nevertheless, even with this new guidance, determining whether a particular chemical substance is exempt can be challenging.

## 5.0 PREPARING THE PMN AND SEEING IT THROUGH EPA

Although more than 20,000 new chemical substances have been reviewed through the PMN process and the process has become routine from EPA's perspective, the PMN remains a substantial hurdle to overcome for the manufacturer who wants to market a new chemical quickly and efficiently. The unwary manufacturer may encounter such problems as delays in the review process, or unexpected and costly restrictions on manufacture (which EPA may impose under TSCA § 5(e) or § 5(f)). As discussed below, a manufacturer can minimize many of these potential problems by recognizing them in advance and planning a PMN strategy that is specific to the chemical substance.

### 5.1 Manufacturer's PMN Selection Strategy

For purposes of this discussion, there are four types of PMN: (1) the "standard" PMN for a single chemical substance; (2) the "consolidated" PMN for two or more substances sharing similar molecular structures and use patterns; (3) the "joint" PMN, for use when two companies must jointly submit data; and (4) the "exemption" PMN for substances that are manufactured in low volumes, have low release, low exposure or are manufactured for test marketing purposes. Each of the four types of PMN offers specific advantages and poses special problems to the PMN submitter.

The standard PMN has been used historically in over seventy-five percent of all submissions. With the changes in May 1995 to the low-volume and polymer exemptions and the addition of the low-release, low-exposure exemption, EPA expects this number to drop substantially. The standard PMN is appropriate where the PMN substance has a distinct molecular structure, and the necessary data can be provided by a single company.

A consolidated PMN is appropriate where a company wishes to manufacture several chemicals that are similar in molecular structure and similar in use. A consolidated PMN reduces the need for repetitive filing and requires only a single $2,500 filing fee. Prior to its submission, however, EPA must confirm that the Agency will treat the new chemicals as similar in structure for PMN purposes. The manufacturer must be aware that each chemical so noticed will receive a separate PMN number and that the manufacturer must file a separate Notice of Commencement for each chemical substance subsequently manufactured. Historically, consolidated PMNs are filed most often for certain sodium, lithium, and potassium salts of the same acid.

A joint PMN may be filed by two or more companies where one manufacturer does not possess all the information necessary to complete the PMN form. Such a situation commonly arises in cases where one company develops a new chemical substance that incorporates a second company's proprietary product. Manufacturers also may find joint PMNs useful as a means of sharing or reducing administrative costs and filing fees.

An exemption PMN is appropriate where a chemical substance meets either the low-volume or low-release, low-exposure criteria set forth at 40 C.F.R. § 723.50 or the test marketing exemption criteria set forth at 40 C.F.R. § 720.38. The principal advantage of an exemption PMN is a shortened review period. A manufacturer who relies upon an exemption PMN, however, is bound to its restrictions. Because these limitations are targets of EPA inspection and enforcement activities, exemption PMNs generally are recommended only where time considerations make them especially attractive.

## 5.2 Minimizing Delays

The best means to avoid a delay in manufacturing operations arising from the PMN process is to submit the PMN far in advance of the production schedule. Although such a strategy can reduce production delays, it requires the manufacturer to initiate the PMN process rather early in the product development process. This presents a risk, of course, that some PMNs may be submitted for products that are not produced for intervening reasons.

Manufacturers frequently encounter delays in the PMN process due to the failure to submit required information. If any required information is missing or incomplete, EPA will return the PMN to the submitter. Delays also may result from the inconsistency of information from one section of the PMN to another. Another frequent source of delays arises when a submitter, in attempting to protect confidential business information, fails to supply a generic name for the new chemical or a generic description of its use. Such delays may be avoided only through coordination, planning, and experience

## 5.3 Avoiding Unnecessary Regulation Under TSCA § 5

New chemicals that are delayed during the PMN process or become subject to TSCA § 5(e) Consent Agreements and corresponding SNURs often lose much market value. It is most often the uncertainty arising from insufficient risk assessment data in the PMN that causes EPA to impose such restrictions.

If such restrictions are to be avoided, the PMN submitter must provide a risk assessment that is as comprehensive as possible. Risk is commonly derived by the simple equation: Risk = (Hazard x Exposure). A manufacturer can demonstrate that the "Risk" is low by furnishing information sufficient to show that either the "Hazard" or "Exposure" component of the equation is low.

Hazard information for a new chemical is best supplied as actual human and environmental toxicity information on the specific chemical. Exposure information, although more difficult to quantify, typically includes the expected production volume and uses of the new substance and, when available: (1) certain of the substance's physical properties that impact exposure potential; (2) the numbers and types of human exposure; and (3) the types of release.

Once hazard and exposure information are known, a risk assessment should be developed and included in the PMN. The manufacturer must follow up the risk assessment with a discussion in the PMN of a risk management program, the most common elements of which include routine hazard communication techniques such as appropriate labels and Material Safety Data Sheets.

### 5.4 EPA's Review of the PMN and Use of Check Lists

EPA's PMN review process includes not only the elements of risk assessment, but also includes many technical and administrative details. A submitter thus is well-advised to develop a series of check lists for filing PMNs. These check lists should: (1) ensure that all requested information is included and is consistent throughout the PMN; (2) mirror the items on EPA's own check list, most of which can be obtained from EPA; and (3) address issues that continue after the PMN is submitted, including the obligation to file an NOC within thirty days after commercial manufacture begins, to adhere to any limitations that may apply in the case of exemption PMNs, and to ensure compliance with any TSCA § 5(e) restrictions.

### 6.0 REGULATION OF NEW CHEMICALS AND USES

Under TSCA § 5, once a manufacturer has submitted a PMN, it may commence commercial operations after waiting ninety days without specific EPA approval, unless the Agency exercises one of three statutory options described below. First, under TSCA § 5(a), EPA may delay manufacture for one additional ninety-day review period for "good cause." Second, under TSCA § 5(e), EPA may issue a proposed order limiting or prohibiting manufacture if the Agency makes statutorily prescribed findings regarding risk. Third, under TSCA § 5(f), EPA may propose a § 6(a) rule which becomes immediately effective to limit or condition manufacture, or issue a proposed order totally banning manufacture, if the Agency concludes that manufacture "presents or will present an unreasonable risk of injury to health or [the] environment."

### 6.1 EPA Regulation Under TSCA § 5(e)

TSCA § 5(e) grants EPA authority to issue an administrative order regulating a new chemical substance if the Agency finds that: (1) there is insufficient information to evaluate the risk reasonably; and (2) either the chemical may present an unreasonable risk to health and the environment, or it will be produced in substantial quantities with the result that either substantial quantities will enter the environment or there will be substantial or significant human exposure to the substance. The purpose of a TSCA

§ 5(e) order is to ban or limit manufacture, distribution, use, or disposal of a chemical pending development of sufficient data for EPA to evaluate the risks the chemical poses to human health or the environment. Where EPA acts unilaterally to issue a § 5(e) order, it must be proposed at least forty-five days before the end of the PMN review period. Such unilateral orders become effective on the day the review period ends.

### 6.1.1 EPA's Standard § 5(e) Consent Order

TSCA § 5(e) does not provide explicit authority for EPA to enter into "consent" orders. EPA developed the consent order concept to permit the introduction of new chemicals into the market while controlling any potential risk during the time needed to develop the required data by agreement with the prospective manufacturer, thus avoiding an adversary procedure. Under a § 5(e) consent order, the manufacturer is usually permitted to proceed with commercial manufacture, and in return agrees to certain restrictions on the production, distribution, or disposal of the new chemical, pending development of information that EPA considers necessary to evaluate the potential hazards.

### 6.1.2 EPA Evaluation of § 5(e) Data

After receiving the required test data, EPA may determine that such data are: (1) invalid; (2) equivocal; (3) valid and positive (the chemical poses an unreasonable risk); or (4) valid and negative (the chemical poses no unreasonable risk). EPA interprets § 5 as enabling the Agency to take further action under its standard consent orders based on the submitted data without resorting to procedures required under TSCA §§ 4 or 6.

If EPA determines that the test results are scientifically invalid, the company must cease production or importation of the PMN substance when the aggregate volume reaches the production limit. The company may contest EPA's finding by submitting a report prepared by a "qualified person" (expert) explaining why the data are scientifically valid. If a specific event beyond the control of the company has prevented the development of scientifically valid data, the company may submit a report documenting this extenuating circumstance within several weeks of its occurrence. Upon EPA's concurrence, the company may continue to manufacture beyond the production limit provided a study is initiated, usually within three months, and that the data are submitted within a specified time.

Data are scientifically equivocal if insufficient for the Agency to conduct a reasoned risk evaluation of the substance, when evaluated together with other available information. Upon a finding by EPA that the data are equivocal, a submitter has similar opportunities to refute the EPA finding or to negotiate for new conditions to allow for continued manufacture of the subject chemical.

A finding of valid, positive data indicates that the chemical poses an unreasonable risk. The company may challenge EPA's determination but may not manufacture the chemical until EPA is convinced that the chemical will not present an unreasonable risk, or a court reverses EPA's position.

EPA may determine that the data demonstrate the chemical will not present an unreasonable risk. Despite such negative data, however, the Agency still may decline to modify or revoke the order if EPA finds that the risk may be unreasonable without continued use of engineering or other controls. Often the company must affirmatively petition for such a revocation of the consent order.

### 6.1.3 Preparation of the § 5(e) Consent Order

Because complex consent orders often take so long to negotiate and issue, EPA has created a "two track" system of consent order preparation. The "fast track" is used where the PMN submitter agrees to certain standard terms. Such "fast track" consent orders take an average of seventy working days, compared to 124 working days for a "standard" § 5(e) consent order.

A "standard" consent order is the product of several stages of draft, review, and comment. Once the consent order is signed by all parties, it becomes effective the day following the lapse of the PMN review period. If the review period has been suspended voluntarily beyond the statutory period, EPA and the submitter will revoke jointly any remaining time.

A party to a TSCA § 5(e) consent order may challenge an EPA decision that is based on the data submitted pursuant to the consent order. Companies that disagree with the Agency's determination may challenge the decision by filing: (1) a petition under TSCA § 21 for the "issuance, amendment, or repeal" of the §5(e) order; (2) a petition under the terms of the consent order for modification or revocation of provisions of the consent order; or (3) an action for judicial review under the Administrative Procedure Act (APA).

### 6.1.4 Unilateral § 5(e) Orders

If EPA determines that the potential risk from a PMN substance cannot be reduced to acceptable levels through engineering controls or production limitations or that a mutually agreeable consent order cannot be negotiated, the Agency will issue a proposed unilateral § 5(e) order. The Agency generally uses these orders to ban a PMN substance outright. Because under § 5(e)(1)(B) a unilateral order must be issued no later than forty-five days before the end of the review period, EPA will give priority to its development and issuance.

If the PMN submitter files "objections specifying with peculiarity" the provisions of the order deemed objectionable and stating the grounds therefor, the proposed order will not take effect.[49] A company must address EPA's findings of fact with respect to the PMN chemical and the Agency's resulting conclusion that the issuance of a § 5(e) order is required. In this instance, the Administrator must apply to a federal district court for an injunction to prohibit or limit the commercial manufacture, processing, distribution, use, or disposal.[50] If, after evaluating the objections, the Administrator determines there is no basis to limit or ban the PMN substance under § 5(e), he will not act to finalize the unilateral order.

## 6.2 EPA Regulation Under TSCA § 5(f)

If EPA determines that a new chemical substance presents or will present an unreasonable risk before the Agency can issue a rule under § 6 to protect against such risks, the Administrator may act under § 5(f) to control that risk. Under § 5(f), the Administrator may issue either a proposed rule to limit or delay manufacture,

---

[49]TSCA § 5(e)(1)(C).
[50]TSCA § 5(e)(2)(A)(i).

production, use, or disposal, or a proposed order to ban all use of the substance and apply for a federal injunction to prohibit the chemical from entering commerce.

### 6.2.1 Proposed § 5(f) Rules

Section 5(f)(2) authorizes the Administrator to issue an immediately effective proposed rule under § 6(a) that limits or delays manufacture of a chemical substance undergoing a PMN review. Under § 6(a), EPA has authority to: (1) limit the amount; (2) prohibit particular uses; (3) limit the amount or concentration for a particular use; (4) require specific labels; (5) require recordkeeping; (6) prohibit or regulate commercial use; (7) prohibit or regulate disposal; and (8) give notice of the risk. Such a rule is effective immediately upon publication in the *Federal Register.*

To date, EPA has proposed only three § 5(f) rules covering four chemicals. EPA has not yet "finalized" these proposed rules because the Agency never contemplated rulemaking under TSCA § 6. Nevertheless, the rules were effective as of the date they were published. They were recorded in the *Code of Federal Regulations* and, for all intents and purposes, function as final rules.

Judicial relief from a § 5(f) rule is probably unavailable because TSCA § 6(d)(2)(A) provides that: "[s]uch a proposed rule which is made so effective shall not, for purposes of judicial review be considered final agency action." Presumably, an affected party could challenge EPA's failure to complete the rulemaking in an expeditious manner as directed by TSCA § 6(d)(2)(B). Any challenge to the merits of the rule, however, would have to wait until the final rule was issued

### 6.2.2 Proposed § 5(f) Orders

If EPA determines it necessary to ban a chemical from commercial manufacture, distribution, processing, use, and disposal, the Agency must issue a proposed § 5(f) order and apply for an injunction. The proposed order takes effect upon the expiration of the review period unless the submitter files objections in accordance with TSCA § 5(e)(1)(C). If EPA issues a proposed order, the Agency must apply to federal court for an injunction before the expiration of the review period, unless it determines on the basis of the objections filed that the substance does not or will not present an unreasonable risk.[51] To date, EPA has not proposed any orders under TSCA § 5(f).

## 6.3 Significant New Use Rules

Persons who submitted initial Inventory notices were required to describe the uses to which their chemicals were being put. Similarly, a PMN submitter must describe the intended uses of his new chemical. If EPA determines that a particular use of a chemical already on the Inventory constitutes a "significant new use," the Agency can issue a Significant New Use Rule (SNUR). A SNUR requires anyone who wants to manufacture or process a chemical substance for a use that EPA has determined is a "significant new use" to give EPA ninety calendar days prior notice.[52] This notice is referred to as a "Significant New Use Notice" or SNUN.

---

[51]TSCA § 5(f)(3)(D).
[52]TSCA §§ 5(a)(1)(B) and 5(a)(2); 40 C.F.R. § 721.

If, after reviewing a SNUN, EPA fails to initiate any action under § 5, 6 or 7, then TSCA § 5(g) requires the Administrator to publish a notice in the *Federal Register* giving EPA's reasons for not initiating any action. As is the case with a PMN, a SNUN submitter may manufacture, import, or process the chemical for the "significant new use" without EPA approval or further notice to EPA upon expiration of the ninety-day review period.

### 6.3.1 SNUR Standard

TSCA does not set criteria for determining when EPA may deem a new use "significant," but EPA must consider "all relevant factors."[53] EPA generally defines a "significant new use" broadly as a use that will result in increased production volume, a different or greater extent of exposure, a different disposal method, or even a different manufacturing site.

### 6.3.2 Who Must Report

All persons who intend to manufacture, import, or process for commercial purposes a chemical substance identified at 40 C.F.R. § 721, subpt. E are required to report. In addition, any person who intends to distribute the substance to others must submit a SNUN unless he can document that: (1) he has notified in writing each person who purchases or otherwise receives the chemical from him of the applicable SNUR; (2) each such recipient has knowledge of that specific section of subpt. E; or (3) each recipient cannot undertake any significant new use described in the specific section of subpt. E.[54] Finally, a person who processes a chemical substance listed in subpt. E for a "significant new use" must submit a SNUN unless he can document that: (1) the person does not know the specific chemical identity of the chemical substance being processed; and (2) the person is processing the chemical substance without knowledge of the applicable SNUR.[55]

EPA recognizes certain exemptions from the requirement to make a SNUN report which are identical to those applied to PMNs.[56] EPA never has required manufacturers of non-isolated intermediates to apply for exemptions. Presumably, manufacturers of SNUR-listed chemicals who produce them only as non-isolated intermediates are exempt from the SNUN requirements as well.

### 6.3.3 Alternative Measures to Control Exposure

EPA also has established a procedure whereby a manufacturer or processor may petition the Agency to allow use of alternative measures to control exposure to or environmental release of a chemical substance without submitting a SNUN, if EPA determines that the alternative measure provides substantially the same degree of protection as the methods specified in the SNUR. Persons intending to employ alternative control measures must submit a request to EPA for a determination of equivalency before commencing manufacture, importation, or processing activities with

---

[53]TSCA § 5(a)(2).
[54]40 C.F.R. § 721.5.
[55]*Id.*
[56]40 C.F.R. § 721.45.

the alternative controls. EPA has forty-five days to determine the equivalency of the proposal and will mail a notice of the results to the submitter, who may commence manufacture upon receipt.[57]

### 6.3.4 Obligations of Distributors

If a manufacturer, importer, or processor of a chemical acknowledges that someone who purchases or otherwise obtains the chemical from him is engaged in a significant new use without submitting a SNUN, the distributor must stop supplying the chemical substance and must submit the SNUN, unless the distributor can document: (1) he has notified the recipient and the EPA Office of Enforcement and Compliance Assurance (OECA) in writing within fifteen days of the first time he has knowledge; (2) within fifteen working days after notifying the recipient, the recipient has provided him with written assurance that the recipient is aware of the terms of subpt. E and will not engage in the significant new use; and (3) he has promptly provided OECA with a copy of the recipient's written assurances.[58]

### 6.3.5 Determining Inventory Status

The chemicals listed in 40 C.F.R. § 721, subpt. E are often listed by generic names because the manufacturers have claimed the specific chemical identities as confidential. In order to determine whether a specific chemical is subject to a SNUN, a *bona fide* request may be filed with the Agency.[59]

### 6.3.6 Use of SNURS to Support § 5(e) Consent Orders

When EPA has concerns about a new chemical substance but does not want to prohibit its manufacture completely, the Agency will enter into a consent order with the PMN submitter, allowing limited production under carefully controlled conditions. Once the chemical is placed on the Inventory, however, other manufacturers can begin producing this substance without complying with the restrictions in the consent order, giving them a competitive advantage over the original manufacturer.

As a result, manufacturers subject to § 5(e) consent orders have urged EPA to designate as a "significant new use" any manufacture of such a substance that is not in compliance with the same restrictions placed upon the original manufacturers in the consent orders. Once EPA issues such a SNUR, any manufacturer who intends to depart from the conditions imposed under the SNUR must file a SNUN ninety days before doing so. Because development of even a relatively simple SNUR and its issuance concurrently with a § 5(e) consent order requires commitment of substantial Agency resources, EPA rarely issues such SNURs.

### 6.3.7 Generic SNUR Rule

The Agency's difficulties in developing SNURs to support the § 5(e) consent order program, prompted the Agency to develop the "Generic SNUR Rule." This rule establishes standardized significant new uses, recordkeeping requirements, and two

---

[57] 40 C.F.R. § 721.30.
[58] 40 C.F.R. § 721.5.
[59] 40 C.F.R. § 721.11. *See supra* at Section 3.4.2.

procedures EPA can use to issue SNURs without the usual notice-and-comment rulemaking.[60] The Generic SNUR Rule has five subparts. Subpart A defines terms. Subpart B lists standardized significant new uses that EPA may, by rule, apply to any existing chemical. Subpart C establishes recordkeeping requirements which EPA may impose upon manufacturers, importers, or processors of any chemical subject to a SNUR. Subpart D establishes "expedited" rulemaking procedures that EPA may use to develop SNURs for chemical substances and creates a procedure by which persons affected by the SNUR may petition the Agency to modify or revoke it. Subpart E is a list of chemicals subject to SNURs and their designated significant new uses. EPA may establish significant new uses other than those in subpt. B and can impose recordkeeping requirements other than those in subpt. C but only by notice-and-comment rulemaking.

The Generic SNUR Rule (subpt. B) establishes five categories of standardized significant new uses. These are: (1) commercial activities where a program of appropriate protective equipment has not been established[61]; (2) commercial activities where a worker hazard communication program has not been established[62]; (3) disposal of a listed substance[63]; (4) release to water of a listed substance[64]; and (5) a broad "catch-all" section, designating over two dozen activities that, taken collectively, are so inclusive as to provide EPA the tools to regulate virtually any activity[65].

Section 721.160 (subpt. D) establishes expedited procedures EPA can use to impose SNURs on chemicals that have been the subject of a final order issued under § 5(e). These procedures include: (1) direct final rulemaking; (2) interim final rulemaking; and (3) notice-and-comment rulemaking.

When EPA uses direct final rulemaking procedures to issue a SNUR, it issues a final rule in the *Federal Register*. Unless EPA receives written notice within thirty days of publication that someone wishes to submit adverse or critical comments, the rule will be effective sixty days from the date of publication. If EPA receives such timely notice, however, the Agency must provide for more formal rulemaking procedures.

EPA will use interim final rulemaking procedures when the Agency believes that a significant new use is likely to take place before a direct final rule would become effective. In this case, the Agency will issue an interim final rule in the final rule section of the *Federal Register*. The SNUR will take effect on the date of publication and persons will have thirty days to submit comments. However, such interim rules will cease to be effective 180 days after publication unless, within the 180-day period, EPA issues a final rule in the *Federal Register* that responds to any written comments received.

Although not an "expedited" procedure, EPA also may use traditional notice-and-comment procedures to issue a SNUR. In this case, EPA issues a proposal in the *Federal Register* and allows a thirty day comment period. EPA generally uses notice-and-comment rulemaking where the Agency anticipates adverse comments.

---

[60]*See* 40 C.F.R. § 721 *et. seq.*
[61]40 C.F.R. § 721.63.
[62]40 C.F.R. § 721.72.
[63]40 C.F.R. § 721.85.
[64]40 C.F.R. § 721.90.
[65]40 C.F.R. § 721.80.

### 6.3.8 Expedited SNURs for New Chemical Substances Not Subject to § 5(e) Orders

Section 721.170 of 40 C.F.R. establishes the procedures and criteria under which EPA may use expedited procedures to impose SNURs on a chemical that satisfied the PMN process but was not made subject to a § 5(e) consent order. EPA will promulgate a SNUR for such a chemical only if the substance meets one or more of the concern criteria listed in § 721.170(b). The concern criteria are basically the same criteria EPA uses when determining whether a new chemical substance should be subject to a § 5(e) consent order. Thus, the criteria call for a SNUR if exposure is likely to result from new uses not in the PMN or would have called for a § 5(e) order if they had been in the PMN.

Any person affected by a SNUR may request modification or revocation of any SNUR requirement that has been added to subpt. E by using the expedited procedures. The request must be accompanied by information sufficient to support the request.[66]

## 7.0 BIOTECHNOLOGY

EPA's biotechnology policy under TSCA is developing amidst substantial controversy. The Agency has asserted that it has broad authority under TSCA to regulate genetically engineered microorganisms. Because of the conflicting interests involved and the uncertainty surrounding biotechnology products, the Agency only recently proposed comprehensive biotechnology regulations. Until these regulations become final, EPA is requiring certain researchers, manufacturers, processors, distributors, and importers to comply with selected TSCA reporting requirements.

### 7.1 1986 Framework for Regulation of Biotechnology Products

EPA first asserted TSCA authority over genetically engineered microorganisms in a 1984 proposed policy statement.[67] In 1986, EPA published the final version of the policy statement which established the reporting requirements that are currently in effect for genetically engineered microorganisms.[68] Pursuant to the policy statement, EPA requires compliance with PMN requirements for "new" microorganisms and § 8(e) reporting for all microorganisms. In addition, EPA requests voluntary compliance with other § 8 reporting requirements. The Agency has not provided clear guidance on reporting requirements, however, leaving submitters to rely largely on informal guidance.

### 7.2 Guidance Documents on PMN Submissions for Biotechnology Products

Several sources of information can provide guidance for PMN submitters. The basic reporting requirements for microorganisms are contained in EPA's 1986 policy statement. Also, to assist persons preparing PMNs for biotechnology products under the 1986 policy statement, EPA has prepared an information packet containing several draft guidelines. These guidelines are continuously evolving to reflect changes in policy and additional experience gained through reviewing PMNs on biotechnology products.

---

[66]40 C.F.R. § 721.185.
[67]49 *Fed. Reg* 50,886 (1984).
[68]51 *Fed. Reg* 23,324 (1986).

Some of the guidelines are general and address the administrative details and informational requirements for completing a PMN. One deals with substantiation of confidentiality claims, another with *bona fide* submissions for a search of the Master Inventory File to determine if a microorganism is listed on the confidential portion of the Inventory, and a third with preparing PMNs for closed system, large-scale fermentations. In addition, several 1986 and 1987 guidance documents address the full PMN submission, the sanitized version, and confidentiality claims.

### 7.3 The EPA Biotechnology PMN Review Process

While its policies are still in gestation, EPA is addressing PMN submissions on biotechnology products on a case-by-case basis. The submitter should contact EPA as early as possible in the project development process for a prenotice consultation. Nonetheless, EPA does have a process for reviewing these PMN submissions. In fact, to date, EPA has reviewed thirty PMNs for intergeneric microorganisms used in the manufacture of enzymes or pesticide intermediates, and twenty-five voluntary PMNs for R&D activities involving microorganisms.

Following receipt of the PMN, EPA publishes an announcement in the *Federal Register* describing the submission.[69] EPA then develops hazard and exposure assessments based on information submitted in the PMN, other available scientific information, and consultation with non-Agency experts. These assessments are then combined to form a risk assessment. At this point, EPA may ask for assistance from a Biotechnology Science Advisory Committee (BSAC) Subcommittee containing scientists with expertise relevant to the PMN in question. At the conclusion of a PMN review the Agency may reach one of three decisions: (a) there is sufficient information to determine that the risks are unreasonable; (b) there is sufficient information to determine that the risks are reasonable; or (c) there is insufficient information to make a reasoned evaluation of risk. Finally, the Agency may issue a consent order under § 5(e) wherein it imposes certain restrictions on testing pending development by the PMN submitter of additional information.

### 7.4 The Future of EPA's Biotechnology Policy: The Draft Proposed Rule

In 1988, EPA drafted a proposed biotechnology rule, but the White House Office of Management and Budget (OMB) returned it to EPA for reconsideration of several issues. In response to comments by OMB as well as other government agencies, industry, academia, and public interest groups, EPA continued to revise the draft, and finally, on September 1, 1994, EPA published proposed regulations for the manufacture and processing of microorganisms under TSCA § 5 (premanufacture notification).[70]

**Definition of New Microorganism.** The proposed rule defines microorganism to mean an organism classified in the kingdoms Monera (or Procaryotae), Protista, Fungi, and the Chlorophyta and the Rhodophyta of the Plantae, and a virus or virus-like particle. New microorganisms are those not listed on the TSCA Inventory and that result from deliberate, intergenetic combinations of genetic material from organisms in

---

[69]TSCA § 5(d)(2).
[70]59 *Fed. Reg* 45,526 (1994).

different genera. Consistent with its current policy, EPA proposes to exclude from the definition of "new microorganisms" those resulting from the addition of intergeneric material that is well-characterized and contains only non-coding regulatory regions such as operators, promoters, origins of replication, terminators, and ribosome-binding regions. In addition, naturally occurring microorganisms are implicitly listed on the TSCA Inventory (as are all naturally occurring substances).

**Premanufacture Notification.** EPA proposes to require premanufacture notification for new microorganisms using a microbial commercial activity notice (MCAN). The MCAN must be submitted 90 days prior to commercial manufacture or import of a new microorganism or prior to the manufacture, import or processing of an existing microorganism for a significant new use. At this time, EPA is not requiring the MCAN to be submitted on a specific form. The information required to be submitted with the MCAN is listed in the proposed rule at 40 C.F.R. § 725.155. EPA will add new microorganisms to the inventory upon receipt of a notice of commencement of manufacture or import (NOC). The timing of the NOC for microorganisms is the same as for traditional chemicals. EPA is proposing to identify and list microorganisms on the TSCA Inventory by a taxonomic designation and certain phenotypic and genotypic information.

**Exemptions from MCAN.** EPA proposes to exempt certain microorganisms from all or part of the MCAN requirement based on a finding that the microorganism does not present an unreasonable risk to human health or the environment. These exemptions differ from those available for traditional chemicals. For example, microorganisms will not be eligible for the low volume exemption, but will be eligible for an identical test marketing exemption (TME).

EPA also proposes to establish tiered exemptions for certain microorganisms. The Tier I exemption is a complete exemption from the MCAN requirement. In order to qualify for the Tier I exemption, the recipient microorganism must be listed in 40 C.F.R. § 725.420, the introduced genetic material must be limited in size, of known function and associated nucleotide sequences, poorly mobilizable, and free of certain nucleotide sequences that encode toxins.[71] The site where the microorganism will be used must meet certain containment and control standards.[72] Although manufacturers and importers need not apply for Tier I exemptions, they are required to submit a certification to EPA at least 30 days prior to commercial manufacture or import, stating that the microorganism meets the Tier I exemption criteria.[73]

The Tier II exemption provides for expedited review of microorganisms that meet the recipient organism requirements of § 725.420 and genetic material requirements of § 725.421, but will not meet the containment and control requirements of § 725.422. The exemption application must be submitted 45 days prior to commencing manufacture or import.

**Regulation of R&D Activities.** EPA proposes to regulate microorganisms during commercial research and development (R&D) more closely than traditional chemicals due to the ability of microorganisms to multiply on their own once released into the

---

[71] 40 C.F.R. § 725.421.
[72] 40 C.F.R. § 725.422.
[73] 40 C.F.R. § 725.424.

environment. Provided the R&D takes place in a "contained structure," EPA proposes to exempt such activity from all but recordkeeping, containment, and employee notification requirements.[74] In addition, the R&D must be supervised by a technically qualified individual. This exemption is very similar to the standard R&D exemption for traditional chemicals. If the R&D activity is conducted under the supervision of another federal agency that requires compliance with NIH Guidelines for Research Involving Recombinant DNA Molecules, EPA proposes to exempt such R&D from all regulation under TSCA, even the recordkeeping, containment, and employee notification requirements.[75]

EPA proposes to exempt R&D activities involving intentional testing in the environment of specifically listed microorganisms deemed to be safe. At this time, EPA proposes to list two microorganisms eligible for this exemption.[76] Pursuant to this exemption, EPA proposes to place restrictions on the recipient microorganisms, the introduced genetic material, and the conditions of use. In addition, persons who intend to conduct R&D activities pursuant to this exemption must submit a certification stating compliance with the provisions of the exemption prior to initiation of the activity.[77]

Persons engaged in R&D activities that do not qualify for the contained structure exemption or are not specifically exempted under § 725.239 must submit a TSCA experimental release application (TERA) 60 days prior to commencing such activities. Thus, the TERA process provides a shortened review period compared to the MCAN process, and the data requirements are somewhat less burdensome than the MCAN data requirements. EPA may extend the TERA review period by 60 days for "good cause." Unlike the MCAN or PMN, however, if EPA determines prior to expiration of the TERA review period that the activity does not pose an unreasonable risk to human health or the environment, EPA would allow the R&D activity to proceed prior to expiration of the review period.

## 8.0 TESTING UNDER TSCA

One of Congress' objectives in enacting TSCA was to require chemical manufacturers and processors to develop data on the health and environmental effects of their products.[78] Under the Act, EPA may require manufacturers and processors to develop safety and environmental data when: (1) the chemical may present an unreasonable risk of injury; or (2) substantial quantities of the chemical are produced with the potential for substantial environmental or human exposure.[79]

### 8.1 Selection of Chemicals for Testing

Congress created the Interagency Testing Committee (ITC) "to make recommendations to the Administrator respecting the chemical substances and mixtures

---

[74]*See* 40 C.F.R. §§ 725.234 and 235.
[75]40 C.F.R. § 725.232.
[76]40 C.F.R. § 725.239.
[77]40 C.F.R. § 725.238.
[78]TSCA § 2(b)(1).
[79]TSCA § 4(a)(1).

to which the Administrator should give priority consideration."[80] The ITC consists of designees from eight agencies of the federal government. TSCA requires the ITC to give priority consideration to substances that are suspected of causing or contributing to cancer, gene mutations, or birth defects. Within twelve months after the ITC designates a chemical, the Agency must initiate § 4 rulemaking or publish its reasons for not doing so.

In making its testing recommendations, the ITC must consider eight factors, including: the quantities in which the substance is manufactured or enters the environment; the extent and duration of human exposure; whether the substance is closely related to a chemical substance known to present an unreasonable risk of injury; the existence of data concerning the effects of the substance; and the extent to which testing may aid the Agency to predict the effects of a substance on health or the environment.[81]

The addition of a chemical substance to the TSCA § 4(e) Priority List triggers reporting requirements under TSCA §§ 8(a) and 8(d). Under the § 8(a) Preliminary Assessment Information Rule (PAIR), manufacturers must submit production and exposure data on ITC-listed chemicals within ninety days of publication in the *Federal Register* of the amendment adding the chemical. Under the § 8(d) Health and Safety Data Reporting Rule, manufacturers and processors must submit to EPA unpublished health and safety studies within ninety days of the Agency's listing.[82]

## 8.2 Testing Triggers

Whether a test rule is risk-based or exposure-based will influence the type of testing required. The testing "triggers" are discussed below.

### 8.2.1 TSCA § 4(a)(1)(A): Risk Trigger

EPA may require testing if the Agency finds that: (1) the chemical or mixture may present an unreasonable risk of injury to human health or the environment; (2) existing data on and experience with the chemical or mixture are insufficient to reasonably predict or determine the effects of the chemical substance; and (3) testing is necessary to obtain such data.[83] EPA's first step, therefore, is to make a risk determination. EPA must find that the chemical may present an unreasonable risk.

As EPA uses the term, "risk" is a function of both hazard (toxicity) and exposure. The Agency considers several factors in assessing the possible unreasonable risk of a substance, including knowledge of a chemical's physical and chemical properties, structural relationships to other chemicals with demonstrated adverse effects, data from inconclusive tests, and case history data.[84] Moreover, EPA has advised manufacturers that risk may be significant, even when exposure is extremely low.

Even though a § 4(a)(1)(A) test rule is not exposure-based, the Agency still must demonstrate some possibility of exposure before it may issue a test rule under the

---

[80]TSCA § 4(e).
[81]TSCA § 4(e)(1)(A).
[82]*See* 40 C.F.R. §§ 712, 716.
[83]TSCA § 4(a)(1)(A).
[84]*Id.*

"unreasonable risk" rationale because exposure is a necessary component of risk analysis. In *CMA v. EPA*, however, the D.C. Circuit held that EPA could rely on inferences to establish exposure, "so long as all the evidence—including the industry evidence—indicates a more-than-theoretical probability of exposure."[85]

Not only must EPA determine that the chemical or mixture may present a risk, the Agency also must find that the existing data and experience are insufficient to determine or predict the effects of concern.[86] Data may be insufficient if EPA determines that existing studies are too flawed to be relied upon or otherwise inadequate to determine risk. Additionally, the Agency must affirm that testing is necessary to develop data under TSCA § 4(a)(1)(A)(iii). If the Agency decides that ongoing studies will enable EPA to determine whether a substance presents an unreasonable risk, no further testing will be required. In addition, the Agency will not require chemical testing if no testing methodology exists which would lead to the production of the necessary data.

### 8.2.2 TSCA § 4(a)(1)(B): Exposure Trigger

TSCA § 4(a)(1)(B) provides EPA with an alternative basis for requiring testing founded on an exposure trigger. Using an exposure trigger, EPA can require testing if: (1) a chemical substance is produced in substantial quantities; (2) a substance is reasonably expected to be released into the environment in substantial quantities, or there is or may be significant or substantial human exposure; (3) there are insufficient data or experience upon which to reasonably predict the effects on human health or the environment; and (4) testing is necessary to develop the data.

By its express terms, § 4(a)(1)(B) requires both substantial production and substantial or significant exposure. This trigger requires an exposure finding much higher than that required to satisfy the exposure trigger under § 4(a)(1)(A).[87] This difference is based on the fact that less exposure is necessary when EPA has a scientific basis for suspecting potential toxicity under § 4(a)(1)(A).

Until very recently, EPA had declined to quantify "substantial," contending that it is "neither feasible nor desirable to make strict numerical definitions of substantial exposure or release," and that production and exposure determinations should be made individually for each chemical.[88] On May 14, 1993, EPA published the final policy statement on TSCA § 4(a)(1)(B) findings in which it has quantified "substantial" production, release and exposure.[89] The policy establishes quantitative thresholds to serve as guidance for determining "substantial" production, release, and human exposure. (See Table 7.1)

---

[85]859 F.2d 977, 989 (D.C. Cir. 1988).
[86]TSCA § 4(a)(1)(A)(ii).
[87]45 *Fed. Reg* 48,528 (1980).
[88]50 *Fed. Reg* 20,664 (1985).
[89]58 *Fed. Reg* 28,735 (1993).

**Table 7.1  Quantitive Thresholds for Determining "Substantial" Production, Release, and Human Exposure**

| Category | | Threshold |
|---|---|---|
| Substantial Production | | 1 million pounds total/year |
| Substantial Release | | 1 million pounds total/year |
| Substantial | General Population | 100,000 people |
| Human | Consumers | 10,000 people |
| Exposure | Workers | 1,000 workers |

In addition to making a finding of substantial production volume or exposure under TSCA § 4(a)(1)(B), EPA also must determine that there are insufficient data and that testing is necessary to develop the needed information. These required findings are identical to those in TSCA § 4(a)(1)(A), discussed above.

### 8.3  Tests and Studies Under TSCA § 4

After EPA determines that at least one of the regulatory triggers under TSCA § 4(a) has been met and after a public comment period, EPA publishes the test rule. A TSCA § 4 test rule must identify specifically the chemical substance or mixture to be tested, the standards for the development of test data and, for existing chemicals, the time period during which the test data must be submitted.[90]

TSCA § 4 grants EPA wide latitude in deciding the types and amount of testing it may require: "The health and environmental effects for which standards . . . may be prescribed include carcinogenesis, mutagenesis, teratogenesis, behavioral disorders, cumulative or synergistic effects, and any other effect which may present an unreasonable risk of injury to health or the environment."[91] Generally, EPA requires studies on acute, subchronic, and chronic toxicity; oncogenicity; reproduction; teratogenicity; mutagenicity; neurotoxicity; environmental effects; and chemical fate.

#### 8.3.1  Good Laboratory Practice Standards

Any study whose purpose is to satisfy a TSCA test rule must meet EPA Good Laboratory Practice (GLP) standards. TSCA GLP standards are codified at 40 C.F.R. § 792. TSCA GLP standards prescribe minimum requirements that the laboratory and sponsor must fulfill in areas such as organization and personnel, equipment, test facility operations, and study protocol. Any person who submits to EPA a test required by a § 4 test rule must submit a statement, signed by the submitter and the study director, to the effect that:  (1) the study complies with GLP requirements; or (2) describes the differences between the practices used in the study and TSCA GLP requirements; or

---

[90]TSCA § 4(b)(1).
[91]TSCA § 4(b)(2)(A).

(3) the person was not the sponsor of the study, did not conduct the study and does not know whether the study complies with TSCA GLP requirements.

### 8.3.2 Development and Implementation of Test Rules

EPA in 1985 issued guidelines and procedures for utilization of single-phase rulemaking and now uses this procedure almost exclusively.[92] In the single-phase test rule, EPA proposes the pertinent Office of Toxic Substances (now the Office of Pollution Prevention and Toxics (OPPT)) test guideline as the required test standard in the initial notice of proposed rulemaking. Other methodologies may be proposed during the public comment period. The final rule promulgates as the test standard either the OPPT test guideline or other suitable guidelines. The Agency utilizes single-phase rulemaking for most TSCA § 4 rules, reserving two-phase rulemaking only for testing where there are no well-accepted test methodologies.

### 8.3.3 Letters of Intent

Within thirty days after the effective date of a test rule, each person subject to the rule must either notify EPA by letter of his intent to conduct testing or submit an application for exemption.[93] Manufacturers or processors who continue their activities and who do not submit a letter of intent to test or a request for an exemption will be considered in violation of the rule.[94] Typically, where both manufacturers and processors are subject to the test rule, processors will only participate if specifically directed to do so or if no manufacturer has made known its intent to test. If no manufacturer notifies EPA within thirty days of receipt of EPA's notification, all manufacturers and processors will be in violation of the rule from the thirty-first day after receipt of notification.[95]

### 8.3.4 Test Standards

Each test rule must include standards that prescribe the manner in which data are to be developed and any test methodology or other requirements that are necessary to assure that the manufacturer produces reliable and adequate data.[96] EPA has codified guidelines that may be used to establish test standards in § 4 test rules.[97] These guidelines do not become mandatory test standards until they are promulgated as such in individual § 4 rulemakings.

## 8.4 Exemptions from Testing

Although TSCA § 4 requires any person who manufactures, imports, or processes a chemical subject to a test rule to conduct testing, such a person may seek an exemption. TSCA § 4(c)(2) authorizes EPA to exempt a manufacturer or processor from a test rule if it is determined that the applicant's substance "is equivalent to a

---

[92]50 *Fed. Reg* 20,652 (1985).
[93]40 C.F.R. § 790.45.
[94]40 C.F.R. § 790.45(e), (f).
[95]40 C.F.R. § 790.48(a)(3).
[96]TSCA § 4(b)(1)(B).
[97]40 C.F.R. §§ 796 (Chemical Fate), 797 (Environmental Effects), and 798 (Health Effects).

chemical substance or mixture for which data has been submitted" or for which data are being developed in response to a test rule. Under the exemption, persons subject to a test rule have thirty days within which to either supply a letter of intent to comply or seek an exemption.[98]

EPA will conditionally grant an exemption if the Agency has received and adopted a complete proposed study plan, has determined that the substance that is the subject of the exemption application is equivalent to the test substance for which the required data have been or will be submitted, and has concluded that submission of the required test data would be duplicative of data which have been or will be submitted under the test rule.[99]

EPA may deny an exemption application if: (1) the applicant fails to demonstrate data equivalency; (2) the applicant fails to submit the information required under 40 C.F.R. §§ 790.82 or 790.85; (3) the Agency has not received an adequate study plan for the test rule for which the exemption is sought; or (4) the study sponsor fails to submit the required data.[100]   Although an applicant whose exemption has been denied can appeal the denial, the appeal does not stay the applicant's obligations under TSCA § 4.[101] Moreover, an exemption is only conditional and may be terminated if the Agency determines that equivalent testing has not been initiated timely or the equivalent testing did not comply with the test rules or Good Laboratory Practices.[102]

Persons who manufacture less than 500 kilograms (1,100 pounds) of a chemical annually are exempt from the procedural requirements of a test rule unless the test rule directs them to comply with a rule's testing requirement.[103]  As in the case of processors, such manufacturers still would be legally subject to test rules and would not be exempt from reimbursement claims.

## 8.5  Reimbursement Procedures

Any person receiving an exemption from a testing requirement must reimburse persons who perform required testing for a portion of costs expended in generating the data.[104]   (Because processors are deemed to have fulfilled their testing and reimbursement obligation indirectly "through higher prices passed on by those directly responsible, the manufacturers," processors normally make no direct reimbursement payments.)[105]  Although EPA strongly encourages the parties to reach a voluntary agreement on the amount of reimbursement, the Administrator may issue a reimbursement order directing those who received an exemption "to provide fair and equitable reimbursement" to those who incurred the costs. Reimbursement Orders are developed in consultation with the Department of Justice and the Federal Trade Commission. The Administrator must take into account all relevant factors, including

---

[98]40 C.F.R. § 790.80(b)(1).
[99]40 C.F.R. § 790.87.
[100]40 C.F.R. § 790.88.
[101]40 C.F.R. § 790.90.
[102]40 C.F.R. § 790.93(a).
[103]54 *Fed. Reg* 21,237 (1989).
[104]TSCA § 4.
[105]40 C.F.R. § 791.45(a).

competitive position and market share of the persons providing and receiving reimbursement.[106]

If the parties are unable to agree, they may submit their dispute to arbitration and may request a hearing with the American Arbitration Association (AAA).[107] A hearing notice will be published in the *Federal Register* after which any party may file a written answer in response or to set forth additional claims. However, once a hearing officer is appointed, no additional or different claims can be asserted without the consent of the hearing officer.

After hearing, a proposed reimbursement order will be put forth which, based on a formula, provides that in general, each person's share of the test costs shall be in proportion to its share of the total production volume of the test chemical. EPA has recognized, however, that the allocation of test costs based on market share may not always be equitable. Therefore, any party may propose factors besides market share if their application produces a fair and equitable result.

Cooperative testing reduces costs and avoids duplicative testing. The most frequent form of organization used to conduct cooperative testing is the joint venture, and these are being used with increasing frequency as a means to reduce the costs and risks of developing environmental and toxicological data required by a § 4 test rule. The joint venture is an unincorporated entity that operates much like a partnership but is limited to accomplishing the TSCA testing objectives of the group. Most joint ventures have a business group and a technical group. The latter develops protocols, monitors the studies, and reviews the results. The former typically decides when assessments will be made for expenses and decides if and when the scope of the testing program should be expanded beyond the original tests.

The most important provision in the agreement will be the terms of sharing the costs and testing. Generally the costs can be apportioned on the basis of the market share of each participant, on an equal basis, or on some variant of these two. The joint venture can test only one substance "representative" of all of the members' products and that substance must meet all the requirements of the test rule.

## 8.6 Judicial Review

TSCA § 19 provides for appellate review of EPA test rules that are contested. A court may review, however, only the record of the rulemaking proceeding before the Agency, and the Agency's findings are conclusive, if supported by "substantial evidence."[108]

### 8.6.1 Jurisdiction, Standing and Venue

A petition for judicial review must be filed within sixty days of the final rule. The standing provision of § 19 indicates that "any person" may file a petition seeking review of a final rule. "Any person" would include any producer of a substance, any interested organization, such as a trade association or environmental group; no injury need be shown. A petition may be filed in: (1) the District of Columbia; (2) the circuit in which

---

[106]TSCA § 4(c)(4)(A).
[107]40 C.F.R. § 791.20(a).
[108]TSCA § 19(c)(1)(B)(i).

the petitioner resides; or (3) the circuit in which the petitioner has its principal place of business.[109]

### 8.6.2 The Rulemaking Record

TSCA test rules are promulgated on the basis of the rulemaking record, which the court of appeals will review to determine whether it is supported by substantial evidence. The court will not hold a new (*de novo*) hearing on whether and how a chemical substance or mixture should be tested. The reviewing court will consider only the evidence contained in the rulemaking record consisting of: (1) the final test rule; (2) the necessary findings; (3) transcripts of oral presentations; and (4) written submissions of interested parties. The rulemaking record also includes any other information which EPA considers relevant to the test rule and "which the Administrator identified, on or before the date of the promulgation of such rule, in a notice published in the Federal Register."[110]

### 8.6.3 Standard of Review: "Substantial Evidence"

TSCA § 19(c)(1)(B) also prescribes the standard of judicial review: "[T]he court shall hold unlawful and set aside such rule if the court finds that the rule is not supported by substantial evidence in the rulemaking record . . . taken as a whole." In imposing the substantial evidence test, Congress cautioned that EPA need only demonstrate that the rule is "reasonably" supported.

In reviewing Agency actions, however, courts give close scrutiny to the rulemaking record to assure that factual findings are supported by substantial evidence and that the rulemaking record adequately explains the Agency's decisions. While a reviewing court may defer to EPA on scientific and policy issues, the court will examine the rulemaking record for a full explanation of the Agency's rationale in its adopted approach. The courts agree that judicial review of § 4 test rules should be "demanding" and "fairly rigorous."[111]

### 8.7 TSCA § 4(f) Findings of Significant Risk

The Agency's actions after receipt of test data that indicate a "significant risk" are governed by TSCA § 4(f). If the test data indicate to the Administrator that there may be a "reasonable basis to conclude that a chemical substance or mixture presents or will present a significant risk of serious or widespread harm to human beings from cancer, gene mutations, or birth defects," the Administrator must initiate appropriate rulemaking. If EPA chooses not to initiate rulemaking, the Agency must publish in the *Federal Register* the reasons for not taking action.[112]

---

[109]*See* 28 U.S.C.A. § 1391(c).

[110]TSCA § 19(a)(3)(E).

[111]*CMA v. EPA*, 859 F.2d 977, 992 (D.C. Cir. 1988); *Ausimont U.S.A. Inc. v. EPA*, 838 F.2d 93, 96 (3d Cir. 1988); *Shell Chemical Co. v. EPA*, 826 F.2d 295, 297 (5th Cir. 1987).

[112]TSCA § 4(f)(2).

### 8.7.1 Criteria for Risk

Under TSCA § 4(f), EPA must take regulatory action when the chemical poses "a significant risk of serious or widespread harm to human beings." EPA considers this § 4(f) "significant risk" trigger to present a higher risk threshold than for those actions under TSCA § 6 which require a finding of "unreasonable risk."

EPA will determine that a significant risk of serious harm exists when there is a population whose members are at high individual risk from the substance. If the Agency estimates that humans will be exposed to doses that produced an effect observed in animals or humans, the Agency will make a § 4(f) finding. In addition, EPA will find a "significant risk of serious harm" where an exposed population does not enjoy an adequate margin of safety.

Significant risk of widespread harm is determined to exist when a large number of persons are exposed to the substance at a level on which a significant aggregate population risk is predicated. Although the individual risk may not be as high as that needed under the previous criterion, the harm associated with the risk must be widespread.

### 8.7.2 Review Period

Once EPA determines that the § 4(f) criteria have been met, the Agency has 180 days to decide whether to initiate regulatory action. This 180-day period can be extended for an additional ninety days for "good cause" under TSCA § 4(f)(2). The Agency will begin the 180-day review period when it receives sufficient information to make a § 4(f) finding. In general, EPA will not solicit public comments prior to making a § 4(f) finding and the Final § 4(f) Finding will be made by the Administrator.

## 9.0 REPORTING AND RETENTION OF INFORMATION

TSCA § 8 establishes reporting and recordkeeping requirements to provide EPA with information on which to base regulatory and enforcement actions and to track patterns of adverse reactions to chemicals. EPA uses the information obtained under §8 in other EPA programs to provide chemical information to industry and citizens, to evaluate existing data to determine their adequacy for risk assessment purposes, to identify data gaps, and to monitor ongoing activities with respect to specific chemicals.

### 9.1 TSCA § 8(a): Reports

Under TSCA § 8(a), EPA may require companies to maintain records and submit reports on their chemical manufacturing, importing, and processing activities. The Agency has used its § 8(a) authority to impose recordkeeping and reporting requirements on specific listed chemicals. In implementing its § 8(a) authority, EPA has issued "model" rules that require submission of detailed production and exposure data on certain listed chemicals.

The first of these model rules, the Preliminary Assessment Information Rule (PAIR), issued in June 1982, automatically adds chemicals to the PAIR list thirty days after they are placed on the ITC Priority Testing List.[113] The rule requires manufacturers and importers to submit a two-page PAIR report for each plant site involved in

---

[113] 40 C.F.R. § 712.

manufacturing or importing a listed chemical substance within 60 days of the effective date of the listing of the chemical. Small manufacturers, manufacturers of less than 500 kgs per site, and manufacturers of the substance solely for R&D or as an impurity, non-isolated intermediate, or byproduct are exempt from PAIR reporting.[114]

The second model rule, the Comprehensive Assessment Information Rule (CAIR), issued on December 22, 1988, was intended to elicit far more detailed information about a more narrow group of chemical substances. CAIR was extremely controversial when promulgated, due to the lack of a low volume exemption or a *de minimis* concentration exemption, the amount of information required to be reported, the fact that processors were required to comply, and the requirement that manufacturers of mixtures incorporating CAIR-listed chemicals disclose this information so that processors of these mixtures would be aware of their reporting obligation or, alternatively, report for their customers. Initially, CAIR listed only nineteen chemicals. Persons who manufactured or processed any of these nineteen listed chemicals during the CAIR reporting period (February 1987 to February 1989) were required to prepare and file CAIR reports. Due to the controversy surrounding the rule, EPA has added no other chemicals to the original nineteen on the CAIR list.

In 1993, EPA did publish proposed amendments to CAIR addressing those aspects of the rule that made it so controversial when promulgated.[115] EPA never finalized these amendments, however, and has indicated that it does not anticipate taking any final action on this rule for some time as it "reassesses its TSCA information needs."[116] EPA made these statements in a *Federal Register* notice in which EPA withdrew the CAIR regulations from the C.F.R. Given the current "inactive" status of CAIR (i.e., no one has had to file any CAIR reports since the late 1980s), EPA reasoned that its presence in the C.F.R. is confusing to the public and regulated community and so removed the rule until such time as the CAIR amendments become final.

Also, under its TSCA § 8(a) authority, EPA issued an Inventory Update Rule in June 1986 requiring manufacturers and importers of certain chemicals listed on the Inventory to report current data on the production volume, plant site, and site-limited status of the substances.[117] The requirements under this rule are discussed *supra* at Section 3.3, in conjunction with the TSCA Inventory.

### 9.2 TSCA § 8(c): Records Of Significant Adverse Reactions

TSCA § 8(c) requires manufacturers, processors, and distributors to keep records of significant adverse reactions to health and the environment alleged to have been caused by a chemical substance or mixture they manufacture, process, or distribute. Allegations by employees must be kept on file for thirty years; allegations by others for five years. These allegations do not have to be reported to EPA unless the Agency specifically requests them. EPA may require submission of copies of the § 8(c) records to the Agency, however, and employees can petition the Agency to collect and release § 8(c) information.

---

[114]40 C.F.R. § 712.25.
[115]58 *Fed. Reg* 63,134 (1993).
[116]60 *Fed. Reg* 31,918 (1995).
[117]*See* 40 C.F.R. § 710.

EPA has defined "significant adverse reaction" to mean a reaction that may indicate a substantial impairment of normal activities, or long-lasting or irreversible damage to health or the environment.[118] In order to place some limitation on an otherwise open-ended recording obligation, EPA has provided a narrow exemption for known human health effects.[119] Those environmental reactions which must be recorded include gradual or sudden changes in the composition of animal life or plant life, abnormal numbers of deaths of organisms, reduction of the reproductive success of a species, reduction in agricultural productivity, and alterations in the behavior or distribution of a species.[120]

In order to constitute a recordable allegation under § 8(c), the statement must state clearly the alleged cause of the adverse reaction.[121] An "allegation" is defined as a statement, made without formal proof or regard for evidence, that a chemical substance or mixture has caused a significant adverse reaction to health or the environment. It is important to remember that a series of identical or very similar allegations about a particular substance may indicate a significant risk, which can trigger reporting requirements under § 8(e).

### 9.3 TSCA §8(d): Health and Safety Studies

Section 8(d) requires that, upon request, a person who manufactures, processes, or distributes in commerce any chemical substance or mixture, must submit to the Administrator lists and copies of health and safety studies conducted by, known to, or ascertainable by that person.

Under the § 8(d) Model Reporting Rule, submission of unpublished health and safety studies is required on certain specifically listed chemicals or mixtures. Although TSCA gives EPA the authority to impose this reporting requirement on persons who distribute listed chemical substances in commerce, EPA thus far has chosen not to exercise this authority. Thus, only persons who currently manufacture, import, or process a chemical substance or a mixture listed at 40 C.F.R. § 716.120 (or propose to do so) or who manufactured, imported, or processed (or proposed to do so) within the ten years preceding the effective date of the listing of the chemical are subject to the provisions of the Model Reporting Rule. There are two phases to § 8(d) reporting. First, persons are required to submit copies of all nonexempt studies in their possession at the time they become subject to the rule. Second, EPA must be informed within thirty days of any study on a subject chemical initiated by or for such manufacturer or processor.[122]

In May 1996, EPA announced plans for the first major overhaul of the TSCA § 8(d) Model Reporting Rule, which was adopted in 1982 and then amended in 1986. EPA's goals in undertaking this review of the Model Reporting Rule are to resolve ambiguities in the reporting requirements, balance the reporting burden with the government's need for the data, and provide for electronic filing of reports. Several changes are being contemplated, such as: 1) setting a retrospective search cut-off date

---

[118]40 C.F.R. § 717.3(i).
[119]40 C.F.R. § 717.12(b).
[120]40 C.F.R. § 717.12(c).
[121]40 C.F.R. § 717.10(b)(2).
[122]40 C.F.R. §§ 716.60, 716.65.

for the initial file search; 2) allowing companies to remove certain confidential information before the studies are submitted so that EPA will not have to treat the studies as confidential; 3) shortening the ten-year sunset period; 4) limiting initial reporting to an abstract or uniform cover sheet; and 5) promoting electronic filings. EPA held a public meeting on September 12, 1996 to discuss possible amendments to the rule. The Agency intends to publish a proposed rule in 1997.

## 9.4 TSCA § 8(e): Substantial Risk Information

Section 8(e) requires the manufacturer, processor, or distributor of a chemical substance to report to EPA any information concerning the substance that "reasonably supports the conclusion that the chemical substance or mixture presents a substantial risk of injury to health or the environment." EPA has not issued regulations implementing § 8(e). The Agency has issued other types of formal guidance, however.[123] EPA also provides some limited policy guidance through § 8(e) Status Reports, and from time to time through its monthly publication, *TSCA Chemicals in Progress*. The Status Reports are a summary of EPA's initial review of submitted § 8(e) and "For Your Information" reports and are available for public viewing in the OPPT Public Reading Room at EPA Headquarters in Washington, D.C. Moreover, in the course of the recent TSCA § 8(e) Compliance Audit Program (CAP), EPA has issued publicly a number of responses to inquiries from CAP participants and trade associations.

Although the 1978 Policy Statement remains the fundamental source of specific guidance, EPA has been developing, over the past several years, revised guidance for reporting information regarding nonemergency releases of chemical substances into or chemical contamination of the environment. To date, EPA has issued only proposed revisions to the 1978 Policy Statement on July 13, 1993 and March 20, 1995.[124]

## 10.0 EXISTING CHEMICAL REGULATION

TSCA § 6 grants EPA full authority to regulate existing chemicals that present unreasonable risks to health or the environment. Under TSCA § 6, EPA must place controls and restrictions, including outright bans if necessary, upon the manufacture, use, processing, disposal, or distribution of such chemicals. This is EPA's most extreme regulatory power.

## 10.1 Procedures and Standards for TSCA § 6 Regulation

EPA must initiate § 6 rulemaking to regulate a chemical substance when the Agency finds "a reasonable basis to conclude that the manufacture . . . use, or disposal of a chemical . . . will present an unreasonable risk of injury to health or the environment" and that the risks cannot be addressed by EPA or any other agency under another statute.[125] In determining whether a perceived risk is "unreasonable," the Agency must conduct a risk assessment of the chemical substance. The risk/benefit comparison required by § 6 must consider: (1) the effects on health and the environment; (2) the

---

[123]Statement of Interpretation and Enforcement Policy, 43 *Fed. Reg* 11,110 (1978) ("1978 Policy Statement").

[124]58 *Fed. Reg* 37,735 (1993) and 60 *Fed. Reg* 14,756 (1995), respectively.

[125]TSCA § 6(a).

magnitude of exposure to humans and the environment; (3) the benefits of the substance and the availability of substitutes; and (4) the reasonably ascertainable economic consequences of the rule.[126] Once having found an unreasonable risk, EPA must choose the least burdensome restrictions adequate to protect against the identified risk.[127] In addition to controls on the chemical itself, EPA can order a manufacturer or processor to use approved quality control procedures if EPA determines the chemical substance is manufactured or processed in a manner "which unintentionally causes" it to present an unreasonable risk.

## 10.2 Chemical Specific Regulations

EPA has regulated only six chemical substances under this section since TSCA's inception: asbestos; chloroflourocarbon; dioxins; hexavalent chromium; certain metalworking fluids; and polychlorinated biphenyls. In the case of asbestos, the regulations were ultimately overturned. In the case of polychlorinated biphenyls (PCB), the regulations may be the most widely applicable and best known of any TSCA regulations.

### 10.2.1 Asbestos

EPA's asbestos regulations serve to illustrate some of the difficulties the Agency has experienced implementing TSCA § 6 controls. In 1989, after more than ten years of effort, EPA issued a final rule to ban the manufacture, import, processing, and distribution of virtually all asbestos products. EPA issued the regulations because exposure to asbestos fibers is associated with pulmonary fibrosis (asbestosis), lung cancer, and other cancers and diseases both inside and outside the lungs and because millions of people are exposed to airborne asbestos fibers.[128]

After a bitterly fought challenge to the asbestos regulations brought by industry, the U.S. Court of Appeals for the Fifth Circuit overturned EPA's ban.[129] The court held that EPA failed to justify use of the ban. EPA did not demonstrate that some intermediate alternative action would not be adequate. Nor did the Agency give notice that it intended to predict exposure by use of data on "analogous" substances. Moreover, said the court, EPA failed to consider evidence that available substitutes were toxic also. This failure demonstrates the regulatory hurdles facing EPA under § 6 and suggests why so few TSCA § 6 actions have been initiated.

### 10.2.2 Chlorofluorocarbons (CFCs)

Chlorofluorocarbons (CFCs) had been earmarked for regulation prior to the effective date of TSCA. In 1978, EPA promulgated final regulations prohibiting almost all propellant uses of chlorofluorocarbons (e.g., in aerosol sprays). Under the regulations, the manufacturing, processing, or distribution of fully halogenated chlorofluoroalkanes for aerosol propellant use is prohibited, except for enumerated "essential" uses.

---

[126]TSCA §§ 6(c)(1)(A)-(D).

[127]TSCA § 6(a).

[128]40 C.F.R. § 763.

[129]*Corrosion Proof Fittings v. EPA*, 987 F.2d 1201 (5th Cir. 1991).

EPA also has issued a rule to implement The Montreal Protocol on Substances That Deplete the Ozone Layer. This international agreement calls for a fifty percent reduction in production and consumption of CFCs. EPA did not issue this rule under TSCA, but rather under its Clean Air Act Authority.[130] Although the rule regulates production and consumption of CFCs through an allotment system, it did not modify or rescind the TSCA regulations regarding CFC use as a propellant. In 1995, however, in recognition of the fact that the Clean Air Act provisions have made the TSCA requirements obsolete, EPA withdrew the CFC regulations from the C.F.R.[131]

### 10.2.3 Hexavalent Chromium

EPA prohibits use of hexavalent chromium as a corrosion inhibitor in comfort cooling towers (CCTs) as part of air conditioning and refrigeration systems.[132] EPA determined that hexavalent chromium compounds are human carcinogens and that continued use in CCTs would pose an unreasonable risk to human health. Because the risk of human exposure posed by the use of hexavalent chromium chemicals in industrial cooling towers is low, the rule does not ban such use. To eliminate misuse, distributors of hexavalent chromium-based water treatment chemicals are required to place warning labels on containers and retain records of all shipments of hexavalent chromium-based chemicals intended for use in industrial cooling towers.

### 10.2.4 Metalworking Fluids

On three occasions, EPA has used its § 6(a) authority to address potential hazards that could arise from mixing nitrosating agents with certain amides and salts. The three rules involved PMN substances that were intended for use in metalworking fluids. In each case, EPA determined that, under common metalworking industry practices, use of the new substance would expose employees to incidentally created N-nitrosodiethanolamine. The rules EPA promulgated prohibit mixing nitrosating agents with metalworking fluids that contain the specific PMN substances and require distributors of the PMN substances to affix warning labels to containers of the substances and to send advance warning letters and copies of the regulations to customers.

### 10.2.5 Polychlorinated Biphenyls

TSCA § 6 specifically required EPA to regulate PCBs by establishing a legal presumption under § 6(e) that PCBs pose an unreasonable risk. In general, EPA's PCB regulations, set forth at 40 C.F.R. § 761, cover the following areas: (1) prohibited and authorized commercial activities; (2) marking requirements; (3) storage and disposal requirements; (4) exemptions from the general prohibitions; (5) spill cleanup policy; and (6) recordkeeping requirements. These widely applicable regulations are discussed briefly below.

The manufacture, processing, or distribution of PCBs in commerce for use in the United States is prohibited unless conducted in a manner that EPA has determined is

---

[130]53 *Fed. Reg* 30,566 (1988).
[131]60 *Fed. Reg* 31,919 (1995).
[132]40 C.F.R. § 749.68.

"totally enclosed" or has otherwise specifically authorized. A "totally enclosed" manner is defined as any manner which will ensure that exposure of human beings or the environment to PCBs as a result of the activity will be insignificant.[133]

Standardized PCB warning labels must be affixed to specific types of items such as electrical, hydraulic, and heat transfer equipment, containers, and vehicles. [134] There are formats for large and small PCB labels, and these labels must be used whenever PCB warning marks are required. Marking requirements extend to storage areas, as well as particular PCB articles.

Existing PCBs and PCB articles are to be disposed of gradually through methods by which exposure is virtually eliminated. The regulations define "disposal" so that virtually any release of PCBs to the environment in concentrations of fifty ppm or greater is considered a prohibited act of disposal. Disposal standards exist that encompass the diversity of PCB contaminated waste, including: liquids; electrical equipment; hydraulic machinery; other contaminated articles; dredge and sludge; as well as containers that once held PCBs.

On December 6, 1994,[135] EPA published a proposed rule modifying the PCB disposal rules. If adopted, the proposal is expected to save industry $ 2.0 billion to $ 6.0 billion annually in disposal costs. The proposal would deregulate the disposal requirements for high volume, low PCB-concentration wastes such as contamination at superfund sites, metal shredding facilities, and RCRA corrective action sites. These so-called "mega-amendments" may impact other PCB requirements as well. Therefore, before undertaking any PCB-related activities, make sure you have the most current regulations.

When PCBs and PCB-containing items are removed from use, they may be stored for up to one year while awaiting disposal. All items stored must be marked to indicate the date the item was removed from service, and the storage facility must be constructed to contain spills. In addition, operators must inspect the stored PCBs every thirty days and follow specific recordkeeping requirements.

EPA has issued a policy governing the reporting and cleanup of all spills resulting from the release of materials containing PCBs in concentrations greater than fifty ppm.[136] The Policy classifies PCB spills as either low-concentration spills or high-concentration spills. Low-concentration spills have a PCB concentration less than 500 ppm and involve less than one pound of PCBs. High-concentration spills have a PCB concentration greater than 500 ppm or are low-concentration spills that either involve one pound or more of PCBs or 270 gallons or more of untested mineral oil.[137] Any spill that involves a release of more than ten pounds of PCBs must be reported immediately to the appropriate EPA Regional Office. (CERCLA also requires reporting to the National Response Center.)

The level of cleanup required under the PCB cleanup policy is determined by the following facts: (1) the spill location; (2) the potential for exposure to residual PCBs

---

[133]TSCA § 6(e)(2).
[134]40 C.F.R. § 761.
[135]59 *Fed. Reg* 62,788 (1994).
[136]40 C.F.R. §§ 761.120-135.
[137]52 *Fed. Reg* 10,692 (1987).

remaining after the cleanup; (3) the concentration of PCBs initially spilled; and (4) the nature and size of the population potentially at risk from exposure.[138] In general, the greater the potential human exposure, the more stringent the cleanup standard.

Compliance with the PCB cleanup policy will "create a presumption against both enforcement action for penalties and the need for further cleanup under TSCA."[139] However, when cleanups are required under RCRA, CERCLA, or other statutes, they may have to meet standards different from those imposed by TSCA.

Operators of a facility must prepare and keep at hand an annual report for the previous calendar year if their facility contains forty-five kilograms or more of PCBs in PCB containers, one or more PCB transformers, fifty or more large PCB capacitors, or is used for PCB storage or disposal.[140] Other records described specifically in part 761 must be maintained by persons engaged in activities involving PCBs.

EPA has promulgated a rule that creates a nationwide PCB manifesting system under TSCA.[141] The rule requires all PCB disposal companies, transporters, commercial storers, and generators of PCB wastes who store their own wastes to notify EPA of their activities and identify their facilities. All companies that notify EPA receive an EPA registration number. EPA has attempted to use the least burdensome restrictions by integrating its federal PCB regulations with state regulations under RCRA and by allowing PCB operators to utilize the RCRA Uniform Manifest, which has space designated for additional information required under various state RCRA programs.

## 11.0 RELATIONSHIP BETWEEN TSCA AND OTHER LAWS

Pesticides regulated under the Federal Insecticide, Fungicide, and Rodenticide Act and substances regulated under the Federal Food, Drug, and Cosmetic Act are excluded from jurisdiction under TSCA. Moreover, other statutes administered by EPA, statutes administered by other federal agencies such as the Occupational Safety and Health Act and Consumer Product Safety Act, and toxic substances laws adopted by states or their political subdivisions also regulate chemical risks. The relationship between TSCA and these statutes is discussed below.

### 11.1 Federal Insecticide, Fungicide, and Rodenticide Act (FIFRA)

A chemical must satisfy a two-pronged test to meet the TSCA pesticide exclusion. First, the chemical must fall within the FIFRA definition of a "pesticide." Second, the chemical must be "manufactured, processed, or distributed in commerce for use as a pesticide."[142] Accordingly, EPA considers raw materials and inert ingredients to be subject to TSCA until they become components of a pesticide product, at which time the Agency considers them to be subject to FIFRA.[143] EPA also contends that TSCA's provisions, including the TSCA § 8(e) notification of substantial risk requirements,

---

[138]*Id.* at 10,688-90.

[139]*Id.* at 10,694.

[140]40 C.F.R. § 761.180.

[141]Polychlorinated Biphenyls: Notification and Manifesting for PCB Waste Activities, 53 *Fed. Reg* 37,436 (1988).

[142]TSCA § 3(2)(B)(ii).

[143]42 *Fed. Reg* 64,586 (1977).

apply to R&D candidate pesticides prior to the submission of an application for an Experimental Use Permit or a FIFRA § 3 registration because under FIFRA these chemicals are not yet considered pesticides.[144] EPA also takes the position that a pesticide does not fall within the TSCA § 3(2)(B)(ii) pesticide exclusion during disposal because the chemical is not being "manufactured, processed, or distributed in commerce for use as a pesticide" during the disposal process.

### 11.2 Federal Food, Drug, and Cosmetic Act (FDCA)

TSCA § 3 also excludes foods, food additives, drugs, devices, and cosmetics subject to the FDCA from the TSCA definition of "chemical substance."[145] EPA's position is that a substance should be exempt from TSCA regulation at the point that the Food and Drug Administration (FDA) regulates the substance.[146]

### 11.3 TSCA's Relationship to Other Federal Laws

TSCA § 9 addresses EPA's authority to regulate those chemicals which fall within the purview of both TSCA and other federal statutes. Commonly called TSCA's "referral" provision, § 9 establishes procedures by which EPA can refer regulation of chemical risks to other agencies that have adequate statutory authority to regulate the risks. Referral is accomplished by means of a detailed report which describes EPA's findings. If the referral agency either issues an order declaring that the activities described in EPA's report "do not present the risk" that the Administrator alleged, or initiates within ninety days of its response to EPA "action to protect against such risk," EPA is barred from using TSCA §§ 6 or 7 to regulate the risk.[147] If the referral agency determines, however, that it lacks adequate authority to regulate the risk "to a sufficient extent," explicitly defers the regulatory prerogative back to EPA, or fails to respond within the deadline set by EPA, then EPA remains free to act under TSCA to regulate the risk.

TSCA § 9(b), the intra-agency counterpart of § 9(a), requires the Administrator to "coordinate" actions taken under TSCA with actions taken under other statutes administered "in whole or part" by EPA. If the Administrator determines that a chemical risk "could be eliminated or reduced to a sufficient extent by actions taken under the authorities contained in such other Federal laws, the Administrator shall use such authorities to protect against such risk."[148] If, however, the Administrator in her discretion determines that "it is in the public interest to protect against such risk" by actions taken under TSCA, she is not required to regulate the risk under the other statute.[149]

---

[144]51 *Fed. Reg* 15,098 (1986).
[145]TSCA § 3(2)(B)(vi).
[146]42 *Fed. Reg* 64,586 (1977).
[147]TSCA § 9(a)(2).
[148]TSCA § 9(b).
[149]*Id.*

## 11.4 TSCA Preemption of State and Local Laws

TSCA § 18 governs the relationship between TSCA and state and local laws which regulate chemical risks. Section 18 states that TSCA does not "affect [i.e., preempt] the authority" of states or their political subdivisions to regulate the same chemicals covered by TSCA, subject to two exceptions. First, if EPA adopts a testing rule under TSCA § 4, state and local requirements for testing the same chemical are prohibited.[150] Second, if EPA adopts a rule or order under TSCA §§ 5 or 6, state and local regulations on the same chemical (other than disposal regulations) are prohibited, unless such regulations are identical to EPA's, carry out a federal law (such as the Clean Air Act), or ban the use of the chemical (other than its use in manufacturing or processing of other chemicals).[151]

Despite the foregoing, § 18(b) gives the Administrator authority to allow (by rule) otherwise preempted state or local laws to be adopted or to continue in effect if they are consistent with EPA's actions under TSCA, afford a higher degree of protection than actions taken by EPA under TSCA, and do not unduly burden interstate commerce.

## 12.0 TSCA INSPECTIONS AND ENFORCEMENT

TSCA §§ 11 and 16 authorize EPA to conduct inspections and subpoena documents to monitor for compliance with the Act and provide for the imposition of both civil and criminal penalties for TSCA violations. In addition, EPA may seize products under the authority of §§ 7 or 17(b). The Agency usually limits seizure actions to those instances where a civil penalty action is insufficient to protect human health or the environment. Under § 7, EPA may conduct an "imminent hazard" seizure even absent a violation of TSCA.

## 12.1 Inspections

Under TSCA § 11 an EPA agent may inspect: (1) any establishment in which chemical substances or mixtures are manufactured, processed, stored, or held before or after distribution in commerce; and (2) any conveyance being used to transport such materials in connection with distribution in commerce. An inspection may extend to all things within the premises or conveyances under inspection, including records, files, papers, processes, controls, and facilities, so long as they bear on compliance with the Act.[152] Although TSCA § 11 does not require EPA to obtain a search warrant prior to entry and inspection, independent constitutional considerations may make it necessary for EPA to obtain an administrative search warrant in order to enter the premises when permission is denied.[153] EPA policy presently calls for an inspector to obtain a warrant when lawful entry has been denied.

### 12.1.1 Types of Inspections

A company may undergo any of several "types" of inspections. For example, an inspection may be conducted for § 5 new chemical activity, for § 6(e) PCB violations, for § 8 reporting and recordkeeping compliance, or for any combination of the above.

---

[150]TSCA § 18(a)(2)(A).
[151]TSCA § 18(a)(2)(B).
[152]TSCA § 11(b).
[153]*See Marshall v. Barlow's, Inc.,* 436 U.S. 307, 325 (1978).

In addition, an inspection may be either "specific" (i.e., targeting specific chemicals or regulations) or "general" (i.e., assessing overall compliance).

Often the most extensive inspections are § 8 "verification" inspections. EPA will check to see if the targeted company has set up a centralized system for tracking allegations of adverse effects concerning chemicals under § 8(c) and a well-publicized procedure for its employees to report significant risk information under § 8(e). The absence of such systems and procedures would raise suspicions about a company's TSCA compliance.

### 12.1.2 EPA Inspection Procedures

Inspection procedures fall into the following categories: (1) pre-inspection preparation; (2) notification and entry; (3) opening conference; (4) sampling and documentation; (5) closing conference; and (6) report preparation and follow-up.[154]

**Pre-inspection Preparation.** EPA's appropriate regional office will usually provide written notification to a facility several weeks prior to an actual inspection. The notice will specify the authority for the inspection and discuss what will be covered by the inspection. The inspector also will provide a declaration of confidential business information (CBI) form that the company must use to declare that certain information requested is CBI.

**Notification and Entry.** At the inspection, the investigator will identify himself and present official agency credentials. If the inspector does not have a search warrant he must obtain the consent of the facility officials. Although the company may at any time revoke its permission to enter, all information collected before permission is revoked remains in the possession of the inspector.

**Opening Conference.** The inspector will conduct an opening conference with facility officials where the purpose of the inspection, the parameters of the inspection, and the procedures to be followed are outlined. He will discuss how questions will be handled during the inspection and at the closing conference, and should inform facility officials of their legal rights. If the facility officials have any objections as to how the inspection will be carried out, they should raise them during the opening conference.

**Sampling and Documentation.** In most cases, the inspector will know from pre-inspection preparation which records will be reviewed during the inspection. The investigator will always examine facility records and, when deemed necessary, will take physical samples in order to obtain documentation in support of any contemplated enforcement action.

**Closing Conference.** At the conclusion of the inspection, the EPA inspector will present the facility with a receipt itemizing all samples and documents taken during the inspection. Inspectors will not make statements as to the ultimate status of the facility or discuss the legal consequence of potential noncompliance. However, an inspector may discuss observed deviations from recommended procedures and inform facility personnel of problems that might require immediate attention. Inspectors may offer suggestions based on their preliminary findings. Inspectors also may request additional data and ask follow-up questions regarding their observations and measurements.

---

[154]EPA, *TSCA Inspection Manual* 3-1 to 3-62 (1980).

**Report Preparation and Follow-up.** The inspection report is the compilation of factual information gathered at the compliance inspection. A copy of the final audit report may be obtained through the EPA office that initiated the audit. The regional office will use this report to determine whether follow-up action is appropriate and whether it should pursue criminal charges or civil enforcement.

### 12.1.3 EPA Authority to Issue Subpoenas

TSCA § 11(c) authorizes EPA to issue administrative subpoenas to require the attendance and testimony of witnesses, the production of reports, papers, documents, answers to questions and such other information "that the Administrator deems necessary."[155] EPA interprets its § 11(c) power as an omnibus subpoena authority to support EPA's regulatory activities under other statutes which do not provide subpoena authority so long as a "chemical substance" is involved. Recently, EPA attempted to extend its TSCA § 11 subpoena power to activities conducted entirely outside the United States.

On September 21, 1994, EPA issued subpoenas to ninety-five U.S. companies demanding information about the activities of their subsidiaries operating in Mexicali, Mexico. Several subpoena recipients voluntarily provided the requested data in exchange for EPA withdrawing the subpoena, thereby negating the need to challenge this use of EPA's subpoena power. Subpoena recipients and observers alike, however, remain concerned that this incident not serve as precedent for EPA to hereafter use TSCA § 11 in a similar manner.

## 12.2 Civil Penalties

In determining an appropriate civil penalty for a TSCA violation, the Administrator must take into account nine specific factors that pertain to the nature, circumstances, extent, and gravity of the violation and also pertain to the violator's culpability, compliance history, financial position, and "other matters" as justice requires.[156] The Agency's treatment of these factors is set forth in EPA's Guidelines for the Assessment of Civil Penalties Under Section 16 of the Control Act[157], and other more specific policies, as discussed below.

### 12.2.1 TSCA Civil Penalty Policy

The TSCA Civil Penalty Policy requires a two-stage determination of a proposed civil penalty. First, a penalty matrix is used to calculate a Gravity Based Penalty (GBP). The GBP is based on the nature, extent, and circumstances of the violation. Second, the GBP may be adjusted upward or downward, taking into account several additional factors, including ability to pay, effect on ability to conduct business, any history of prior violations, culpability, and such other factors "as justice may require."

EPA considers two principal criteria for assessing a violator's culpability: (1) the person's knowledge of the TSCA requirement; and (2) the person's degree of control

---

[155]*See EPA v. Alyeska Pipeline Service Co.*, 836 F.2d 443 (9th Cir. 1988) (holding that EPA is required only to show that the documents or testimony sought by the subpoena are relevant to determining whether there is a problem that may be remedied under TSCA).

[156]TSCA § 16(a)(2)(B).

[157]45 *Fed. Reg* 59,770 (1980).

over the violation.[158] Where the violation is "willful" (i.e., the violator intentionally committed an act which he knew was a violation), the TSCA Civil Penalty Policy calls for a twenty-five percent increase in the civil penalty.[159] Criminal penalties may apply as well.[160] EPA considers the culpability of a violator to include the violator's "attitude" after the violation is discovered. Accordingly, the Agency will adjust a proposed penalty upwards or downwards by up to fifteen percent, depending on whether the violator is making "good faith" efforts to comply with the appropriate regulations, the promptness of the violator's corrective actions and any assistance the violator gives EPA to minimize any harm to the environment that was caused by the violation.

The TSCA Civil Penalty Policy lists nine additional matters EPA will consider under its statutory mandate to consider "such other matters as justice may require." EPA takes the position that, regardless of other factors, proposed penalties should be increased when necessary to pay for government investigative and clean-up costs and, in appropriate cases, to ensure that the violator does not profit from noncompliance.[161] On the other hand, EPA will consider reducing proposed penalties where: (1) the violator's cost of cleanup plus penalty seem excessive; (2) there is conflict or ambiguity vis-a-vis other federal regulations; (3) the violator makes voluntary environmentally beneficial expenditures above and beyond those required by law; (4) national defense or foreign policy issues intervene; (5) new owners are burdened with a prior owner's history of violations; and (6) the "extent" of the violation falls very close to the borderline between a significant or a minor violation, and, as a result, the penalty calculated seems disproportionately high.

The issue of whether and what statute of limitations may apply to TSCA enforcement actions can have a dramatic impact on the extent to which EPA may impose civil penalties on a noncompliant company. Until recently, EPA had asserted successfully that TSCA had no statute of limitations. Thus, EPA could bring an enforcement action and assess civil penalties for any violation of TSCA, no matter how stale. On March 4, 1994, however, the D.C. Circuit Court of Appeals issued an opinion holding that the general federal statute of limitations, 28 U.S.C. § 2462, for civil violations applies to TSCA enforcement actions.[162]

The *3M* Court found that 28 U.S.C. § 2462 applies to all administrative civil penalty actions brought before federal agencies, and cited four cases and two Congressional reports supporting this finding.[163] The Court also found that a TSCA enforcement action constitutes a proceeding for the "enforcement of a civil penalty" consistent with the language of § 2462. EPA's contention that "enforcement" connotes only an action to collect a penalty already assessed was rejected.[164] The Court also rejected EPA's contention that the period of limitations did not begin to run until EPA first discovered the violation, not when the violation first occurred. An action, suit or

---

[158] 45 *Fed. Reg* 59,773 (1980).
[159] *Id.*
[160] *See* Criminal Liability section below.
[161] 45 *Fed. Reg* 59,774 (1980).
[162] *3M v. Environmental Protection Agency*, 17 F.3d 1453 (D.C. Cir. 1994).
[163] *Id.* at 1456.
[164] *Id.* at 1458.

proceeding must be commenced within five years of the date of the violation giving rise to the penalty.[165] The decision is now final, as the Department of Justice has decided not to seek certiorari on any part of the ruling.

While the *3M* decision is significant in that it imposes a five year statute of limitations where previously EPA asserted that none existed, many questions remain. For example, the statute of limitations may not apply to cut off entirely the liability from "continuing" violations, such as the failure to report substantial risk information under TSCA § 8(e). The question remains whether other TSCA violations would be considered by EPA to be "continuing" violations and similarly protected from repose by action of the statute of limitations.

### 12.2.2  Regulation-Specific Penalty Policies

The TSCA § 5 Penalty Policy prescribes administrative penalties for non-compliance with TSCA § 5(e) or 5(f) orders, rules, or injunctions, and significant new use rules; for failure to submit PMNs; for submission of false or misleading information; and for commercial use of a substance that was produced without a PMN or valid exemption. The § 5 Policy also addresses violations of the regulations governing NOCs, although those regulations were promulgated under § 8.

The TSCA § 5 Penalty Policy assigns each type of potential violation to one of the three categories, as follows: (1) Chemical Control Violations; (2) Control-Associated Data-Gathering Violations; and (3) Hazard Assessment Violations. TSCA § 5 Penalty Policy at 7. These categories are then used in conjunction with facts pertaining to the specific case to calculate the GBP. After the GBP is calculated, the penalty may be increased or decreased due to the various factors listed in the TSCA Civil Penalty Policy. In a like manner, the TSCA §§ 8, 12 and 13 Penalty Policy addresses § 8 reporting and recordkeeping violations; § 12(b) export notification violations; and § 13 import certification violations.

Both the TSCA § 5 Penalty Policy and the TSCA §§ 8, 12 and 13 Penalty Policy allow violators to reduce penalties by up to eighty percent as a result of confessing and cooperating. The Agency has shown great reluctance, however, to reduce the base penalty by more than eighty percent, even if the self-confessor can show the best of attitudes and substantial steps taken to rectify the violation and to bring itself into full compliance with TSCA. A strict application by EPA of the Civil Penalty Policy is not appropriate in every instance, however. Recently, in an appeal before EPA's chief judicial officer, a company prevailed against the Agency's position that the civil penalty to be assessed must be determined by strict adherence to the Penalty Policy.[166] On appeal by EPA, the hearing officer's downward adjustment of the penalty for "good attitude" and appropriate mitigating steps taken by 3M was upheld. More importantly, however, the appeals officer departed entirely from the Civil Penalty Policy and reduced the penalty by an additional fifteen percent pursuant to TSCA § 16(a)(2)(B), which allows for an increase in the downward adjustment to account for "such other matters as justice may require." The total penalty was thereby reduced ninety-five percent from

---

[165]*Id.* at 1462.

[166]*In the Matter of 3M Company (Minnesota Mining and Mfg.)*, Docket No. TSCA-88-H-06, TSCA Appeal No. 90-3, (Feb. 28, 1992).

that originally proposed. This aspect of the *3M* case has since been utilized successfully by other companies seeking reduced penalties.

Before initiating civil penalty procedures under TSCA, the Agency sometimes will issue a notice of noncompliance (NON), advising a company that a violation of TSCA has been detected or that the Agency is keeping track of the company's actions with respect to correcting a violation. The issuance of a NON is discretionary and may occur when the violation is a minor one, not posing a significant threat to human health, and other positive factors are present.[167]

### 12.2.3 EPA Self-Policing Policy

On December 22, 1995, EPA issued its final environmental "Self-Policing Policy," which took effect on January 22, 1996.[168]  Through the Policy, EPA promises to eliminate all gravity-based penalties for violations of federal environmental laws voluntarily discovered and promptly reported to EPA. In order to qualify for full penalty reduction, a company must satisfy each of the nine conditions outlined in the Policy. In addition, the Policy states that EPA will eliminate 75 percent of the gravity-based penalties for violations that were not "systematically discovered," provided the company meets the Policy's other eight conditions. The Agency, however, reserves the right to impose fines to eliminate any economic benefit a company may have obtained through noncompliance.

EPA also states that the Agency will not recommend criminal prosecution for a company that discovers violations and discloses them under the policy, though the responsible individuals could still be charged. Consistent with its long-held view, the final policy expresses EPA's strong opposition to a statutory evidentiary privilege for environmental audits, but indicates that EPA will not routinely request or use an environmental audit report to initiate a civil or criminal investigation.

To date, more than 70 companies have disclosed violations under the interim and final versions of the Policy. According to EPA sources, TSCA violations constituted more than half of the total number of violations disclosed. Although the Policy applies to violations of all federal environmental statutes, it has quickly become a favorite mechanism for disclosing violations of TSCA. In order to effectively use the Policy, however, a company must be prepared to quickly demonstrate compliance with all nine conditions. For some conditions, this is more easily accomplished with advanced planning.

The Policy's nine conditions are:

| | |
|---|---|
| **Systematic Discovery** | To receive mitigation of *all* gravity-based penalties, a company must discover violations through an environmental audit or through due diligence. |

---

[167]EPA, TSCA Compliance/Enforcement Guidance Manual at 6-3 (July 21, 1984).

[168]60 *Fed. Reg* 66,706 (1995)("Incentives for Self-Policing:  Discovery, Disclosure, Correction and Prevention of Violations").

| | |
|---|---|
| **Voluntary Discovery** | The discovery of violations must be voluntary and not required by order or permit. EPA examples of involuntary discoveries include emissions detected in accordance with a permit's monitoring requirements or emissions detected in accordance with the terms of a judicial or administrative consent order. |
| **Prompt Disclosure** | Violations (or potential violations) must be reported to EPA within *10* calendar days of their discovery. |
| **Independent Discovery** | Violations must be discovered *and* disclosed before the commencement of a government inspection, investigation or request for information; notice of a citizen suit; filing of a third party complaint; filing of a report by a "whistleblower" employee or the imminent discovery of the violation by a regulatory agency. |
| **Correction and Remediation** | Violations must be certified as being corrected within *60* days and the company must takes steps identified by EPA to remedy the violation. |
| **Prevent Recurrence** | A company must agree to take steps to prevent recurrence of the violation. This may include improving audits and due diligence. |
| **No Repeat Violations** | No identical or closely related violations can have occurred at the same facility within the past *3* years, and the violation cannot be part of a parent's pattern of violation within the past *5* years. |
| **Other Violations Excluded** | The violations did not result in serious actual harm or present an imminent and substantial endangerment; or the violations are not ones for which the company previously received penalty mitigation. |
| **Cooperation** | The company cooperates with EPA in its investigation of the violation and any related noncompliance issues. |

Systematic Discovery is the critical condition for full penalty reduction, and is the condition that requires the most forethought and preparation to satisfy. The Self-Policing Policy affords the regulated entity a choice in how it will satisfy this condition —discovery through an "environmental audit" or through "an objective, documented, systematic practice or procedure reflecting the regulated entity's due diligence in preventing, detecting and correcting violations."

The policy defines an environmental audit as "a systematic, documented, periodic and objective review by regulated entities of facility operations and practices related to meeting environmental requirements." In order to show "due diligence," the regulated entity must develop "compliance policies, standards and procedures that identify how employees and agents are to meet the requirements of laws, regulations, permits and other sources of authority for environmental requirements." The policy sets out several additional criteria for due diligence, all of which flow from this fundamental starting point. Beyond compliance policies and procedures, a qualifying compliance program also must include:

- Assignment of overall responsibility for overseeing compliance for the entire company and assignment of specific responsibility for assuring compliance at each facility.
- Mechanisms for assuring that compliance policies are carried out, including monitoring and auditing systems reasonably designed to detect and correct violations.
- Efforts to communicate the regulated entity's compliance program to its employees.
- Incentives to managers and employees to perform consistent with the compliance program.
- Procedures for the prompt and appropriate correction of any violations and modification of the compliance program to prevent future violations.

Whether companies will use the "due diligence" provisions of the policy to any great extent to confess violations remains an open question. To date, most or all of the TSCA violations reported to EPA under the policy have been violations discovered through audits. In part, this may reflect that periodic auditing has become a popular management technique. It also may reflect companies' concerns about whether their compliance programs will meet EPA's criteria for exercise of due diligence and concerns about adverse publicity or revelation of confidential information. EPA has stated that the Agency "may require as a condition of penalty mitigation that a description of the regulated entity's due diligence efforts be made publicly available."[169]

In spite of this trend towards the use of audits to satisfy the first condition, a company probably should not rely solely on audits to uncover TSCA violations. While a company may choose to conduct periodic TSCA audits to cleanse itself of liability for past violations, most entities discover at least some TSCA violations in a less structured way, usually in the course of ordinary business. A comprehensive compliance program that meets the Policy's criteria for due diligence can establish and maintain a high level of compliance and simultaneously set the stage for penalty-free disclosure of the occasional violation that may "slip through the cracks."

Although the Self-Policing Policy provides incentives to audit for environmental compliance, it leaves many problematic issues unresolved. For example, closely related

---

[169]60 *Fed. Reg* 66,708 (1995).

violations that occurred at the subject facility within the past 3 years may preclude application of the Policy, but what constitutes a "closely related" violation is open to question. Similarly, any violations disclosed under the Policy must not be viewed by EPA as part of a pattern of conduct within the past 5 years by any parent organization, but there is no definition of a pattern of conduct. Finally, the Policy gives EPA considerable discretion to dictate the terms of a final consent agreement. For example, under the fifth condition, a company must "take appropriate measures as determined by EPA to remedy any environmental or human harm due to the violation."

In spite of these unresolved issues, however, the climate has never been better to disclose TSCA violations uncovered through "systematic discovery," whether the discovery mechanism is an environmental audit or due diligence. TSCA offenses by their very nature will easily meet several of the nine conditions that might prove problematic when reporting violations under other statutes. For example, TSCA violations are largely paperwork problems which are easily corrected (Condition No. 4) and create no actual harm or endangerment (Condition No. 7). In addition, companies receive little, if any, quantifiable economic benefit from most TSCA violations and therefore probably would not face fines calculated on that basis.

### 12.3 Settlement Procedures

EPA encourages negotiated settlements of civil penalty proceedings.[170] Thus, a settlement conference may be requested at any time during civil enforcement proceedings. A negotiated settlement agreement often will provide for two types of activities. First, it might include a mandatory audit provision, requiring the violator to conduct a self-audit to uncover and report additional TSCA violations and to initiate remedial measures. Second, a negotiated settlement may provide for additional compliance measures designed to further the Agency's policies, for example, a commitment by the defendant to conduct a series of TSCA educational seminars or to prepare a TSCA guidance manual for employees. Generally, a provision is included which places a cap on the total amount of fines.

In certain circumstances, a settlement in an administrative action may be reached that assesses a civil penalty but also provides for the respondent to undertake remedial action as a means of remitting all the assessed penalty. Such a settlement is referred to as a Settlement with Conditions (SWC). The purpose of an SWC is to enhance the level of compliance where violations require complex remedies.

### 12.4 Administrative Hearings

If the Agency considers a violation serious enough or if settlement negotiations are unsuccessful, EPA will institute civil penalty actions leading to an administrative hearing. During the action, EPA will follow the procedures set forth in the Consolidated Rules of Practice (CROP) which govern these administrative actions.[171] Usually a pre-hearing conference intended to facilitate and expedite the proceedings is held where

---

[170]40 C.F.R. § 22.18(a).
[171]40 C.F.R. § 22.

the parties discuss settlement of the case, consolidation of issues, evidence and witnesses to be presented, and any potential method to expedite the hearing.[172]

The administrative hearing is a full evidentiary hearing conducted under the CROP and the Administrative Procedure Act. Witnesses usually are examined orally under oath, but may submit a written statement if the testimony is complicated.[173] The presiding officer may issue a subpoena to compel the attendance of witnesses or the production of documentary evidence.[174]

At the conclusion of the hearing, the parties may detail their position in proposed findings of fact and law, and proposed orders submitted to the presiding officer for consideration in issuing the initial decision. The initial decision becomes a final order within forty-five days unless an adversely affected party makes an appeal to the Administrator, the Administrator determines *sua sponte* that a review of the initial decision is appropriate, or the party files within twenty days a motion to reopen the hearing.[175]

TSCA § 16(a)(3) provides that any person may seek judicial review in the court of appeals of an order assessing a civil penalty. Judicial review under TSCA § 16 is appellate review; that is, the court reviews the record of the civil penalty proceeding before the Agency, and the Agency's findings of fact are conclusive if supported by "substantial evidence."

## 12.5  Criminal Liability

It is a misdemeanor punishable by up to one year's imprisonment and up to $25,000 for each day of violation for any person "knowingly or willfully" to violate any provision of § 15.[176] To obtain a conviction against a company or an individual under § 16(b), the government must prove beyond a reasonable doubt that the defendant violated a requirement of TSCA and that the violation was committed "knowingly or willfully."

Case law indicates that specific knowledge of a TSCA requirement may not be necessary to establish a "knowing and willful" violation when the probability of regulation is so great that anyone handling the substance should be presumed to be aware that it is regulated.[177]

A corporation generally may be found liable for violations of regulations and statutes such as TSCA when such violations are committed by any of its employees, regardless of their position within the company, so long as those employees are acting within the scope of their authority and for the benefit of the corporation. In addition, courts generally will not permit a corporation to assert lack of corporate knowledge as a defense when information was obtained by any one individual who comprehended its full import: a corporation is considered to have acquired the collective knowledge of its

---

[172]40 C.F.R. § 22.19(a).
[173]40 C.F.R. § 22.22(b).
[174]40 C.F.R. § 22.33(b).
[175]40 C.F.R. §§ 22.27, 22.28.
[176]TSCA § 16(b).
[177]*See United States v. International Minerals & Chemical Corp.*, 402 U.S. 558 (1971) (concluding that no actual knowledge of a restrictive shipping regulation was necessary when the shipper was aware that he was shipping sulfuric acid).

employees. Moreover, it makes no difference whether a corporation has instructed its lower level employees to obey the law in performance of their duties. If such an employee disobeys company instructions and violates the law, the corporation is not shielded from criminal liability.[178]

### 12.6 Citizen Actions and Petitions

TSCA contains "private attorney general" provisions, whereby any person may commence a civil action against any other person who is alleged to be in violation of TSCA. In addition, any person may sue to force the Administrator to compel the performance of any non-discretionary act under TSCA.[179] Attorneys fees and other court costs may be awarded if a court determines that such an award is appropriate.

TSCA § 21 likewise permits any person to petition the Administrator to initiate proceedings for the issuance, amendment, or repeal of certain rules.[180] EPA may hold a public proceeding in order to determine the merit of a citizen's petition but must act on the petition within ninety days of its filing.[181] If the petition is granted, the Administrator must promptly commence an appropriate proceeding under §§ 4, 5, 6, or 8.[182] If the petition is denied, the Administrator must publish the reasons for such denial in the *Federal Register*.[183]

An unsuccessful petitioner may seek judicial review by filing an action in a United States district court.[184] The type of Agency action sought in the citizen's petition will determine the legal standard a court will apply to EPA's petition denial. If the subject petition sought the initiation of rulemaking, the petitioner is entitled to *de novo* review.[185] By contrast, if the Administrator denies or fails to act upon a § 21 petition to amend or repeal an existing rule the court will apply the APA's arbitrary and capricious standard.

EPA has issued guidance, including a TSCA check list for preparing citizen petitions under TSCA § 21.[186] With this guidance petitioners should be able to present their requests in a comprehensive and persuasive manner and to facilitate the Agency's review and response.

### 13.0 IMPORTATION AND EXPORTATION

Importers of any chemical substance must comply not only with the same obligations imposed on domestic manufacturers, but also with a certification requirement

---

[178]*See, e.g., Hilton Hotels Corp.*, 467 F.2d 1000 (9th Cir. 1972), *cert. denied*, 409 U.S. 1125 (1973); *but cf. United States v. Beusch*, 596 F.2d 871 (9th Cir. 1979) (existence of company instructions and policies may be considered by the jury in determining whether the employee in fact acted to benefit the corporation).

[179]TSCA § 20.

[180]*See* 40 C.F.R. § 702.

[181]*See* TSCA § 21(b)(2) and (3).

[182]TSCA § 21(b)(3).

[183]*Id.*

[184]TSCA § 21(b)(4)(A).

[185]TSCA § 21(b)(4)(B).

[186]*See* 50 *Fed. Reg* 46,825 (1985).

pursuant to TSCA § 13. Similarly, exporters of chemicals may be subject to export notification obligations pursuant to TSCA § 12.

## 13.1 Import Regulation: TSCA § 13

TSCA § 13 requires the Secretary of the Treasury (the executive branch with authority over the U.S. Customs Service) to refuse entry into U.S. customs territory for a shipment of any chemical substance or mixture, if: (1) it fails to comply with any TSCA rule or regulation; or (2) it is offered for entry in violation of a section 5, 6, or 7 rule order, or action. TSCA § 13(a)(1). The U.S. customs territory includes the fifty States, the District of Columbia and Puerto Rico.[187] Thus, Customs Service regulations require an importer to certify at the port of entry that either: (1) any chemical substance in the shipment is subject to TSCA and complies with all applicable rules and orders thereunder; or (2) is not subject to TSCA.[188] Customs has established approximately ninety ports where entry documents may be filed.[189]

Customs Service regulations establish precise requirements regarding the form of the required certification, including sample statements. According to the regulations, the importer must use one of the statements as worded; no other language may be substituted. The certification may appear either on the appropriate entry document or commercial invoice, or on an attachment to the entry document or invoice. The importer, or its agent, must keep a copy of the import certification along with other Customs entry documentation for five years.[190]

### 13.1.1 Importer Defined

Under Customs Regulations, an "importer" is the "person primarily liable for the payment of any duties on the merchandise, or an authorized agent acting on his behalf." Thus, the importer may be a consignee, the importer of record, or the actual owner of the merchandise.[191] Generally, the consignee will make the certification.

### 13.1.2 Determining TSCA Status of Imported Substance

The importer is responsible for determining whether a chemical substance is on the TSCA Inventory. If the importer does not know whether the chemical substance to be imported is on the Inventory, the importer can file a *bona fide* intent to import request in order to have EPA search the Master Inventory.[192]

If the chemical is not on the Inventory and is being imported for a commercial purpose, the importer must comply with the TSCA § 5 premanufacture notification requirements before importation. If the chemical product is not on the Inventory but is being imported solely for research and development purposes governed by TSCA, the importer still must make a positive certification that the chemical substance is imported in compliance with TSCA.

---

[187] 19 C.F.R. § 101.1(e).
[188] 19 C.F.R. § 12.121(a).
[189] 19 C.F.R. § 101.3(b).
[190] 19 C.F.R. §§ 162.1a(a)(2), .1b, .1c.
[191] *See* 19 C.F.R. § 101.1(1).
[192] 40 C.F.R. § 720.25(b).

### 13.1.3 Exclusions

If a chemical substance is excluded from TSCA jurisdiction under TSCA §3(2)(B), it is subject to a negative certification or to no certification at all, depending on which exclusion applies. EPA takes the position that in order to be excluded from all certification requirements, a chemical substance must be imported solely for an excluded purpose. If, subsequent to importation, a substance is used by the importer for a TSCA purpose, then such use could constitute a TSCA violation. If a shipment is being imported for both a non-TSCA and a TSCA purpose, the importer must identify that portion of the shipment which is subject to TSCA and that which is not. For the former, the importer must certify that it complies with TSCA and for the latter the importer must certify that it is not subject to TSCA.

### 13.1.4 Articles, Samples, and Wastes

A manufacturer of any new chemical substance imported into the United States for commercial purposes must file a PMN "unless the substance is imported as part of an article."[193] EPA interprets this to exempt from the PMN requirement articles containing chemical substances that: (1) are not intended to be removed from the article; and (2) have no separate commercial purpose. Articles containing chemical substances intended to be used or released, such as ink in pens, are not encompassed by this exemption.

Companies occasionally receive unsolicited free samples of chemicals from offshore vendors for R&D purposes. Such samples are subject to TSCA § 13, as well as other TSCA provisions, such as § 5, even though they are unsolicited. To avoid potential liability, many companies refuse to accept such samples and return them to the shipper.

Imported wastes, both hazardous and nonhazardous, are also subject to TSCA because they are "chemical substances" within the meaning of the Act. As such, they require a positive certification, even if accompanied by a hazardous waste manifest pursuant to the Resource Conservation and Recovery Act of 1976 (RCRA).[194]

### 13.1.5 Detention of Shipments by Customs

A shipment may be detained by Customs whenever there exists a reasonable belief that the shipment is not in compliance with TSCA or no certification is filed. When Customs detains a shipment, it must give prompt notice of the detention and specify the reasons therefor to both EPA and the importer.[195] If reasonable grounds exist to believe that the shipment may be brought into compliance with TSCA, the shipment may be released under bond. If released under bond, the shipment must not be used or disposed of until EPA makes a final determination on its entry into the United States.[196]

An importer whose shipment has been detained may submit a written explanation to EPA as to why the shipment should be permitted entry. EPA then, within thirty days

---

[193]40 C.F.R. § 720.22(b)(1).
[194]42 U.S.C. §§ 6901-6992k.
[195]19 C.F.R. § 12.122(c).
[196]19 C.F.R. § 12.123(b).

of the date of notice of detention, will make a decision on whether to allow entry.[197] Only if EPA determines that the shipment is in compliance with TSCA will it be released.[198] If the shipment is not in compliance, however, entry will be refused, or if the shipment has been released on bond, its redelivery will be demanded.[199] Under such circumstances, the importer must bring the shipment into compliance or export the shipment.[200] If the importer decides to export the non-complying shipment the importer must provide written notice of the exportation.[201]

## 13.2  Export Regulation: TSCA § 12

TSCA § 12(a) exempts from most provisions of the Act any chemical substance, mixture, or article manufactured, processed, or distributed solely for export from the United States.[202] In order to qualify for this export exemption, the substance, mixture, or article must bear a stamp or label stating that it is intended solely for export.[203] The recordkeeping and reporting requirements of TSCA § 8, however, continue to apply to such chemical exports.

TSCA § 12(b) requires exporters to notify EPA before exporting any substance for which test data are required under §§ 4 or 5(b), regulatory action has been proposed or taken under §§ 5 or 6, or an action is pending or relief has been granted under §§ 5 or 7. Export notification is required regardless of the intended foreign use of the regulated chemical. EPA does not consider it relevant whether the chemical is being exported for use in a manner that is not regulated domestically under an action, rule, or order.[204] In addition to the export notices required under § 12(b) special notices are required in the case of PCBs.[205]

### 13.2.1  Export Notification Requirement

For chemical substances regulated under TSCA § 4, EPA requires submission of an export notice for the first shipment to each country.[206] For all other chemical substances, EPA requires notification of the first shipment each year to each country.[207] The notice must be postmarked on the date of export or within seven days of forming the "intent to export," whichever is earlier.[208] Intent to export regulated substances "must be based on a definite contractual obligation, or an equivalent intra-company agreement, to export the regulated chemical."[209]

---

[197] 19 C.F.R. § 12.123(a).
[198] 19 C.F.R. § 12.123(c).
[199] *Id.*
[200] 19 C.F.R. § 12.124(a).
[201] 19 C.F.R. § 12.125.
[202] TSCA § 12(a)(1).
[203] TSCA § 12(a)(1)(B).
[204] 45 *Fed. Reg* 82,844 (1980).
[205] *See* 40 C.F.R. § 707.60(c).
[206] 40 C.F.R. § 707.65(a)(2)(ii).
[207] 40 C.F.R. § 707.65(a)(2)(i).
[208] 40 C.F.R. § 707.65(a)(1)-(3).
[209] 40 C.F.R. § 707.65(a)(3).

EPA's Export Notification Rule defines an "exporter" as the "person who, as the principal party in interest in the export transaction, has the power and responsibility for determining and controlling the sending of the chemical substance or mixture to a destination out of the customs territory of the United States."[210]

Within five days of receiving a TSCA § 12(b) export notice, EPA must transmit the following information to the importing country: (1) the name of the regulated chemical; (2) a summary of the regulatory action the Agency has taken; (3) the name of an EPA official to contact for further information; and (4) a copy of the relevant *Federal Register* notice.[211]

### 13.2.2 New Chemicals

A new chemical substance is subject to export notification only if it is subject to a § 4 test rule; is included on the § 5(b)(4) "risk" list; is subject to an order under § 5(e) or 5(f); or is subject to a proposed or final significant new use rule.[212] In the absence of such specific action, the export notification provisions do not apply to new chemical substances intended solely for export. Moreover, export notification need not accompany export of a chemical substance contained in an article, unless the Agency specifically requires export notification for such articles in the context of individual rulemakings.[213]

### 13.2.3 Confidentiality

Exporters may assert confidentiality claims for any information contained in export notices at the time such notices are submitted.[214] No proof of the confidentiality claim is required at the time of submission, but each page must be marked "confidential business information," "proprietary," or "trade secret."[215] Such information is treated by EPA as confidential and may be disclosed to the public only through the procedures set forth at 40 C.F.R. § 2.[216]

---

[210] 40 C.F.R. § 707.63(b).
[211] 40 C.F.R. § 707.70(a), (b).
[212] 45 *Fed. Reg* 82,844 (1980).
[213] 40 C.F.R. § 707.60(b).
[214] 40 C.F.R. § 707.75(a), (b).
[215] 40 C.F.R. § 707.75(b).
[216] 40 C.F.R. § 707.75(c).

# CHAPTER 8

# PESTICIDES

Marshall Lee Miller, Esq.
Baise & Miller
Washington, D.C.

## 1.0 BACKGROUND TO THE FEDERAL REGULATION OF PESTICIDES

The benefits of pesticides, herbicides, rodenticides, and other economic poisons are well known. They have done much to spare us from the ravages of disease, crop infestations, noxious animals and choking weeds. Over the past several decades, however, beginning with Rachel Carson's book *Silent Spring* in 1962,[1] there has been a growing awareness of the hazards as well as the benefits of these chemicals, which may be harmful to man and the balance of nature.

The ability to balance these often conflicting effects is hampered by continuing scientific uncertainties. We still lack full understanding of environmental side effects, the sub-cellular mechanism of human carcinogens, and a host of other factors that are important for a proper evaluation of pesticide suitability. Yet scientific progress, especially in the genetic area, has been so rapid over the past decade or two that we are now realizing that many of our previous assumptions have been wrong, or at least over simplified. The best scientific knowledge is now critical for the agency as it attempts to conduct accelerated reviews of hundreds of chemicals that had been registered earlier under less strict standards.

### 1.1 Overview

Public concern regarding pesticides was a principal cause for the rise of the environmental movement in the United States in the late sixties and early seventies, and therefore was probably the single most important reason for the creation of the EPA. While public attention since then has shifted to various other environmental media, the pesticide issue—with its implications for the safety of food supply and of people in the agricultural area—is still central to the public's notion of environmental protection. Indeed, the fluctuation of interest in this topic is often an accurate barometer of public distrust in the official environmental agencies.

In the last few years this distrust has taken a new and different form. EPA is now being criticized not only by the environmentalists for not doing enough, but also by others for ordering unnecessarily costly or extreme measures. At the heart of both views is the belief that the agency's actions are not always firmly based on good science—a skepticism that is of course by no means limited to EPA's pesticide program.

---

[1]Rachel Carson, *Silent Spring* (New York, 1962).

## 1.2 Early Efforts at Pesticide Regulations

Chemical pesticides have been subject to some degree of federal control since the Insecticide Act of 1910.[2] This act was primarily concerned with protecting consumers, usually farmers, from ineffective products and deceptive labeling, and it contained neither a federal registration requirement nor any significant safety standards. The relatively insignificant usage of pesticides before World War II made regulation a matter of low priority.

The resulting effects on public health and farm production made pesticides a virtual necessity. The agricultural chemical industry became an influential sector of the economy. In 1947, Congress enacted a more comprehensive statute, the Federal Insecticide, Fungicide, and Rodenticide Act (FIFRA).[3] This law required that pesticides distributed in interstate commerce be registered with the United States Department of Agriculture (USDA). It also established rudimentary labeling requirements. This act, like its predecessor, was mostly concerned with product effectiveness; the statute did, however, declare pesticides "misbranded" if they were necessarily harmful to man, animals, or vegetation (except weeds) even when properly used.[4]

Three major defects in the new law soon became evident. First, the registration process was largely an empty formality since the Secretary of Agriculture could not refuse registration even to a chemical he deemed highly dangerous. He could register "under protest," but this had no legal effect on the registrant's ability to manufacture or distribute the product. Second, there was no regulatory control over the use of a pesticide contrary to its label, as long as the label itself complied with the statutory requirements.[5] Third, the Secretary's only remedy against a hazardous product was a legal action for misbranding or adulteration, and—this was crucial—the difficult burden of proof was on the government.

The statute nevertheless remained unchanged for almost two decades. Pesticides were not then a matter of public concern and the Department of Agriculture was under little pressure to tighten regulatory control. Only a handful of registrations under protest were made during that period, and virtually all these actions involved minor companies with ineffective products. The one notable lawsuit involving a fraudulently ineffective product was lost by the USDA at the district court level and mooted by the court of appeals.[6]

In 1964 the USDA persuaded Congress to remedy two of these three perceived defects: the registration system was revised to permit the Secretary to refuse to register a new product or to cancel an existing registration, and the burden of proof for safety

---

[2]36 Stat. 331 (1910).

[3]61 Stat. 190 (1947). The present act is still known by this name, although there have been major changes, especially in 1972, in the law since then. For convenience, we will refer to the pre-1972 version as the "Old FIFRA."

[4]Old FIFRA (pre-1972) § 2(z)(2)(d). See H. Rep. 313 (80th Cong., 1st Sess.). 1947 U.S. Code Cong. Serv. 1200, 1201.

[5]Under FDA practice, doctors may prescribe pharmaceuticals for "off indication" purposes not mentioned on the labels.

[6]*Victrylite Candle Co. v. Brannan*, 201 F.2d 206 (D.C. Cir., 1952).

and effectiveness was placed on the registrant.[7] These changes considerably strengthened the act, in theory, but made little difference in practice. The Pesticide Registration Division, a section of USDA's Agricultural Research Service, was understaffed—in 1966 the only toxicologist on the staff was the division's director—and the division was buried deep in a bureaucracy primarily concerned with promoting agriculture and facilitating the registration of pesticides. The cancellation procedure was seldom if ever used,[8] and there was still no legal sanction against a consumer applying the chemical for a delisted use.

The growth of the environmental movement in the late 1960s, with its concern about the widespread use of agricultural chemicals, overwhelmed the meager resources of the Pesticide Division. Environmental groups filed a barrage of lawsuits demanding the cancellation or suspension of a host of major pesticides such as DDT, Aldrin-Dieldrin, Mirex, and the herbicide 2,4,5-T. This demanding situation required a new approach to pesticide regulations.

### 1.3 Pesticide Regulation Transferred to the Environmental Protection Agency

On December 2, 1970, President Richard Nixon signed Reorganization Order No. 3[9] creating the Environmental Protection Agency (EPA). This order assigned to EPA the functions and many of the personnel previously under Interior, Agriculture, and other government departments. EPA inherited from USDA not only the Pesticides Division but also the environmental lawsuits against the Secretary of Agriculture.

Thus, within the first two or three months of its inception the new agency was compelled to make a number of tough regulatory decisions. The EPA's outlook was considerably influenced by judicial decisions in several of the cases it had inherited from USDA.[10] These court decisions consistently held that the responsible federal agencies had not sufficiently examined the health and environmental problems associated with pesticide use. These helped to shape, indeed force, EPA's pesticide policy during its formative period and ever since.[11]

### 2.0 OVERVIEW OF THE FEDERAL INSECTICIDE, FUNGICIDE AND RODENTICIDE ACT (FIFRA) AND AMENDMENTS

FIFRA is one of the most federal of the environmental laws. Unlike the air, water, and some other statutes which defer or delegate considerable responsibility to the states, at least in theory, under FIFRA states and localities are given little scope. This is deliberate; from the beginning, pesticide regulation has rested on a national system of registration and labeling. Nevertheless, there is a limited state role in registration and

---

[7]Act of May 12, 1964, Pub. L. No. 88-30S, 78 Stat. 190. There were other, less significant, amendments in 1959 (73 Stat. 286) and 1961 (75 Stat. 18, 42).

[8]Instead, a Pesticide Registration Notice would be sent ordering the removal of one or more listed uses from the registration.

[9]Reorganization Order No. 3 of 1970, §2(a)(1), 1970 U.S. Code Cong. Ad. News 2996, 2998, 91st Cong. 2nd Sess.

[10]It also inherited cases concerning pesticide residues from the Food and Drug Administration (FDA) of the Department of Health, Education, and Welfare (HEW), now the Department of Health and Human Services (HHS).

[11]These cases will be discussed in a later section.

an on-going, heated legal controversy over the authority of localities (and tort plaintiffs suing under state law) to impose conditions on pesticides beyond those set forth by EPA.[12]

FIFRA also interacts with the Food and Drug Administration (FDA) in the areas of pesticide residues and disinfectants, and with the Occupational Safety and Health Administration (OSHA) as it applies to workers using or exposed to pesticides.[13]

## 2.1 Background to FIFRA and the 1972 FEPCA

The Federal Insecticide, Fungicide, and Rodenticide Act (FIFRA),[14] as amended by the Federal Environmental Pesticide Control Act (FEPCA) of October 1972 and the FIFRA amendments of 1975, 1978, 1980, 1988, and 1996,[15] is a complex statute. Terms sometimes have a meaning different from, or even directly contrary to, normal English usage. For example, the term "suspension" really means an immediate ban on a pesticide, while the harsher-sounding term "cancellation" indicates only the initiation of administrative proceedings which can drag on for many years. The repeated amending of FIFRA reflects congressional, industry, and environmentalist concern and often discontent about the federal control of pesticide distribution, sale, and use.

The amendments to FIFRA in 1972, known as the Federal Environmental Pesticides Control Act (FEPCA),[16] amounted to a virtual rewriting of the law. FEPCA, not the 1947 FIFRA, is the real pesticide law today.[17] The changes were considered necessary to (1) strengthen the enforcement provisions of FIFRA, (2) shift the legal emphasis from labeling and efficacy to health and environment, (3) provide for greater flexibility in controlling dangerous chemicals, (4) extend the scope of federal law to cover intrastate registrations and the specific uses of a given pesticide, and (5) streamline the administrative appeals process.

EPA was given expanded authority over the field use of pesticides, and several categories of registration were created which give EPA more flexibility in fashioning appropriate control over pesticides.

## 2.2 The Subsequent FIFRA Amendments: An Overview

Amendments to FIFRA since 1972 have been a battleground between environmentalists and various farmer and agricultural chemical interests. The fight has been virtually even; the outcome has oscillated back and forth between one group and the other, while the actual amount of change has been relatively small.

The 1975 amendments are typical. They are significant not for what they actually changed but for the motivations that prompted them—a counterattack by the pesticide

---

[12]See Section 6 of this chapter.

[13]See Section 11 of this chapter.

[14]7 U.S.C. § 135, *et seq.*

[15]Pub. L. No. 96-516, 86 Stat. 973, October 1972; Pub. L. No. 94-140, November 28, 1975; Pub. L. No. 95-396, 92 Stat. 819, September 30, 1978; Pub. L. No. 96-539, 94 Stat. 3194; December 17, 1980.

[16]Pub. L. No. 92-516, 86 Stat. 973, October 21, 1972.

[17]A personal note: We at EPA debated in 1972 whether to continue calling the law FIFRA or to refer to it, more accurately, as FEPCA. We opted for "FIFRA" to preserve the sense of continuity in pesticide regulation.

industry. Not surprisingly, EPA viewed these amendments as, at best, unnecessary and, at worst, a further encumbrance upon an already complicated administrative procedure. EPA was required to consult with the Department of Agriculture and the agricultural committees of Congress before issuing proposed or final standards regarding pesticides. On the other hand, environmentalists were pleased that EPA got the authority to require that farmers take (largely meaningless) exams before being certified as pesticide applicators.

By 1978 Congress had to address the near-collapse of EPA's pesticide registration program. EPA was given the authority to conditionally register a pesticide pending study of the product's safety and was authorized to perform generic reviews without requiring compensation for use of a company's data. The 1980 amendments provided for a two-house veto over EPA rules and regulations, and they required the Administrator to obtain Scientific Advisory Review (SAR) of suspension actions after they were initiated. The 1988 legislation was a victory for the environmentalists, in that it provided for accelerated review of pre-1970 registrations and removed most of the indemnification requirements for canceled pesticides.

And most recently, the 1996 amendments finally repealed the controversial Delaney amendments, as will be discussed in greater detail below.

## 3.0 PESTICIDE REGISTRATION

The heart of FIFRA is the pesticide registration program. Before a pesticide can be manufactured, distributed, or imported, it must be approved by EPA. The data to support registration can take years and millions of dollars of testing, and the submittal to and approval by EPA can require another several years. Registration is thus an expensive and complicated process, more akin to FDA drug registration than the "simple" notification required for non-pesticidal chemicals under the Toxic Substances Control Act (TSCA).

### 3.1 Definition of Pesticides, Pests, and Devices

What is a pesticide? According to the statute, a pesticide is any substance intended for "preventing, destroying, repelling or mitigating any pest," and substances intended for "use as a plant regulator, defoliant, or desiccant."[18] Note that the definition depends upon a use that is intended or claimed.[19] A substance that does not have claims, labels, or advertisements calling it a pesticide, even though it may be very effective as one, is not a pesticide under FIFRA.[20]

---

[18]FIFRA § 2(u), 7 U.S.C. § 136(u).

[19]40 C.F.R. § 152.15. Note that this definition under FIFRA is not consistent with the EPA's interpretation of intent in pesticidal exemptions from the Toxic Substances Control Act, Section 3(2)(B).

[20]EPA has attempted from time to time to challenge this principle, declaring that a substance which makes no pesticidal claims is nevertheless a pesticide if "everybody knows" it affects pests. The most notable attempt, involving citronella candles, was rebuffed by the courts.

Pests are defined as insects, rodents, worms, fungus, weeds, plants, virus, bacteria, micro-organisms, and other animal life.[21]

A pesticide device is an object used for "trapping, destroying, repelling, or mitigating any pest or any other form of plant or animal life."[22] Firearms are excluded by statute, and the Agency has also exempted instruments which depend upon the skill of the person using it. Specifically mentioned in the exemption are fly swatters and traps for vertebrate animals, such as mouse traps; presumably EPA would also exclude spears, baseball bats, and large rocks, although the regulations do not so state.[23]

## 3.2 Pesticide Registration Procedures

All new pesticide products used in the United States, with minor exceptions, must first be registered with EPA. This involves the submittal of the complete formula, a proposed label, and "full description of the tests made and the results thereof upon which the claims are based." The registration is very specific; it is not valid for all formulations or uses of a particular chemical. That is, separate registrations are required for each specific crops and insects on which the pesticide product may be applied, and each use must be supported by research data on safety and efficacy. The term "pesticide product" itself, however, is surprisingly ambiguous. It can mean the active ingredients alone, or the combination of active and inert ingredients.[24]

The Administrator must approve the registration if the following conditions are met:

1. Its composition is such as to warrant the proposed claim for it;
2. Its labeling and other materials required to be submitted comply with the requirements of this act;
3. It will perform its intended function without unreasonable adverse effects on the environment; and
4. When used in accordance with widespread and commonly recognized practice it will not generally cause unreasonable adverse effects on the environment.[25]

The operative phrase in the above criteria is "unreasonable adverse effects on the environment," which was added to the act in 1972. This phrase is defined elsewhere in FIFRA as meaning "any unreasonable risk to man or the environment, taking into account the economic, social, and environmental costs and benefits of the use of the

---

[21]FIFRA § 2(t), 7 U.S.C. § 136(t). Lest that list leaves something out, EPA has declared it has the authority to declare almost anything else a pest subject to FIFRA. 40 C.F.R. § 152.5.

[22]FIFRA § 2(h), 7 U.S.C. § 136(h).

[23]41 Fed. Reg. 51065 (19 November 1976).

[24]49 Fed. Reg. 37916 (September 26, 1984)

[25]FIFRA § 2(bb), 7 U.S.C. § 136(bb). Courts have sometimes simplified the statutory test into two parts, combining the A with B and C with D. *Montana Pole Treating Plant v. I.F. Laucks*, 775 F. Supp. 1399 (D. Mont. 1991), *aff'd* 993 F.2d 676 (9th Cir. 1993).

pesticide."[26] In fact, as "economic poisons," pesticides often cause adverse effects beyond their target species. Balancing this "collateral damage" against the benefits of pesticidal use is a major, continuing EPA policy function.

Registrations are for a limited, five-year period; thereafter they automatically expire unless an interested party petitions for renewal and, if requested by EPA, provides additional data indicating the safety of the product.[27] For the past few years, pre-EPA registrations have been coming up for renewal under much stricter standards than when originally issued. The agricultural chemical companies have justifiably complained that the increased burden of registration is discouraging the development of new pesticides, but there seems no responsible alternative.

Information required for registration includes not only the standard chemical descriptions and specific identification of pests and hosts, but also extensive testing data. Where EPA deems this insufficient, it can and does demand additional testing. This registration procedure, we note, is in marked contrast to TSCA's less rigorous notification process. Petitioners can also rely on public information or, by providing compensation, on data already generated by other companies for the same or similar products.

Even if the pesticide has some negative effects, as many do, these may be balanced against the benefits of usage, such as avoiding the economic damage by insects to crops or the possible threats to public health. (The latter benefit has an enhanced status under the 1996 amendments to FIFRA, discussed below.) A new pesticide may also be beneficial by being less harmful to non-target species than existing pesticides.

### 3.3 Conditional Registration

The near-collapse of EPA's pesticide registration process in the mid-1970s prompted creation of a system of *conditional* registration or reregistration. This could be applied when certain data on a product's safety had either not yet been supplied to EPA or had not yet been analyzed to ensure, according to FIFRA Section 3(a)(5)(D), that "it will perform its intended function without unreasonable adverse effects on the environment." While this was intended as a temporary measure, conditional registrations for new pesticides continue to be almost the rule rather than the exception.

Three kinds of conditional registrations are authorized by Section 6 of the 1978 law which amended FIFRA Section 3(c) with a new section, entitled "Registration Under Special Circumstances": (1) pesticides identical or very similar to currently registered products; (2) new uses to existing pesticide registrations; and (3) pesticides containing active ingredients not contained in any currently registered pesticide for which data need be obtained for registration.

These conditional registrations must be conducted on a case-by-case basis, with the last type of conditional registration further limited both by duration and by the requirement that the "use of the pesticide is in the public interest." Conditional registration is prohibited if a Notice of Rebuttable Presumption Against Registration

---

[26]*Ibid.* The 1975 amendments, as will be discussed, added the specific requirement that decisions also include consideration of their impact on various aspects of the agricultural economy.

[27]FIFRA § 6(a), 7 U.S.C. § 136d(a).

(RPAR) has been issued for the pesticide, and the proposed new use involves use on a minor food or feed crop for which there is an effective registered pesticide not subject to a RPAR proceeding.

Cancellation of conditional registrations must be followed by a public hearing, if requested, within seventy-five days of the request, but must be limited to the issue of whether the registrant has fulfilled its conditions for the registration.[28]

EPA published final regulations implementing conditional registration on May 11, 1979.[29]

### 3.4 Streamlining of Reregistration

EPA's reregistration of pesticides, required every five years, has always been plagued by both a slow regulatory pace and the feeling that much of the safety data underlying the registrations was inadequate by contemporary scientific standards. The 1988 amendments added an entire section, which was renumbered as FIFRA Section 4, covering this topic.[30] This section provided that the data submitted in support of registrations before EPA's creation in 1970 would no longer be considered adequate for reregistration, unless the applicant bears the burden of proof otherwise.[31]

The section set a 48-month timetable for the completion of the studies needed for reregistration. These deadlines were to parallel the time requirements in FIFRA Section 3(c)(2)(B), entitled "Additional Data to Support Existing Registration." These timetables are virtually absolute; they may be extended only in such extraordinary circumstances as a major animal loss, the unintentional loss of laboratory results, or the destruction of laboratory equipment and facilities.

After the Administrator's review is completed, he may ask for additional data to support the reregistration, or declare the pesticide canceled or suspended. Otherwise, he is to approve the reregistration. Under the previous version of FIFRA, no consequences were set for failure of a registrant to provide compensation to the original provider of any data relied upon, or to share in the payments. The 1988 amendments specified that the Administrator, in such a case, must issue a notice of intent to suspend that registrant's registration.

The reregistration continues to lag, despite years of criticism from Congress and environmentalists, and one can safely anticipate these complaints will persist for years to come.

### 3.5 Registration of "Me-Too" Pesticides

For those pesticides which are identical or very similar to other registered products, akin to generic drugs at the Food and Drug Administration, the 1988

---

[28]§ 12 of 1978 amendments, amending FIFRA § 6.

[29]44 Fed. Reg. 27932 (May 11, 1979).

[30]Section 102 of the 1988 amendments, redesignated as Section 4 of FIFRA by Section 801(q) of the 1988 law.

[31]The actual cut-off date is given as January 1, 1970; the EPA was not created until December 2, 1970.

amendments provide that EPA should expedite approvals of these registrations.[32] If proprietary data prepared by competitors is used, financial compensation (indemnification) must be given to the generator, as will be discussed below. To assist the acceleration process, the Administrator is to utilize up to $2 million of the fees collected (see below).[33]

### 3.6 Registration Fees

A one-time registration fee per active ingredient is authorized by the 1988 amendments.[34] The formula is complex, providing for an initial fee of $50,000, a final fee that may be two or three times that amount, and a bulk discount for categories of more than 50 and 200 registrations. In addition, registrants must pay an annual fee through 1997 to supplement EPA's pesticide reregistration budget. The legislation emphasizes, however, that no other fee can be imposed by EPA other than the above. Moreover, the Administrator is empowered to reduce or waive the fees for minor use pesticides where their availability would otherwise be in question. He is to report annually to Congress on the application of this authority.

### 3.7 Generic Pesticide Review

EPA had long complained that registration, and especially reregistration reviews, should be conducted for entire classes of chemicals rather than being limited to examining each particular registration as it comes up for five-year renewal. This authority has always existed under FIFRA, but a district court decision in 1975[35] on compensation for data made this so complicated that the plan was dropped pending a legislative solution.

The amendment that finally emerged under this label in Section 4 of the 1978 act, however, was considerably different in scope: "No applicant for registration of a pesticide who proposes to purchase a registered pesticide from another producer in order to formulate such purchased pesticide into an end-use product shall be required to (i) submit or cite data pertaining to the safety of such purchased product; or (ii) offer to pay reasonable compensation . . . for the use of any such data."[36]

### 3.8 Efficacy

The requirements for submission of test data on a pesticide's efficacy are now discretionary for EPA. Registrants are still expected to conduct all the standard tests. EPA may occasionally ask to review the data, but this is no longer routine except for antimicrobides and rodenticides.[37] The provision is interesting because it marks a complete reversal from the original purpose of federal pesticide legislation earlier in this century, which was to protect farmers from ineffective products and "snake oil" pesticide claims.

---

[32]FIFRA, Section 3(c) (3).
[33]FIFRA, Section 4(k) (3).
[34]FIFRA, Section 4(i).
[35]*Mobay Chemical Corp. v. Train*, 392 F. Supp. 1342, 8 ERC 1227 (W.D. Mo. 1975).
[36]1978 act, amending FIFRA § 3(c)(2).
[37]40 C.F.R. § 158.640.

## 3.9 Modifications and Transfers of Registrations

Minor changes in the pesticide formulation need only be reported to EPA. In this context, however, minor means extremely minor changes, such as different sources for inert ingredients or very small changes in labeling. Anything more significant must be submitted to EPA for approval as an amended registration.[38]

Registrations may not be transferred to another entity with EPA's approval. This also applies whenever a company is acquired by another or broken up.[39] However, a third party may acquire rights to sell or distribute a pesticide product merely by filing a supplemental notice of registration.[40]

## 3.10 Trade Secrets

The issue in FIFRA registration that generated more controversy than any other for many years after the post-1972 amendments involved the treatment of the trade secrets in data submitted to EPA for registration.[41] The judicial protection of commercial trade secrets has gradually eroded during the past few years. Many so-called trade secrets were in fact widely known throughout the industry and did not merit confidential status. Section 10 of FIFRA, added in the 1972 amendments, provides that trade secrets should not be released but, if the Administrator proposes to release them, he should provide notice to the company to enable it to seek a declaratory judgment in the appropriate district court.

Section 10 provides that "when necessary to carry out the provisions of this act, information relating to formulas of products acquired by authorization of this act may be revealed to any federal agency consulted and may be revealed at a public hearing or in findings of fact issued by the Administrator."[42] Consequently, if the public interest requires, a registrant must assume that the formula for his product can be made available, although in practice this may not occur very often.

It is, of course, desirable that scientists and others outside industry and government should be able to conduct tests on the effects of various pesticides. For example, in one case debated by the Agency for several years, a professor needed to know the chemical composition of a particular pesticide to conduct certain medical experiments. The question of whether EPA or a court should furnish this information to a bona fide researcher, with or without appropriate safeguards to preserve confidentiality, was resolved in the experimenter's favor after an investigation revealed that the chemical composition in fact was not a trade secret within the industry.[43]

---

[38]40 C.F.R. § 152.44-46.

[39]40 C.F.R. § 152.135.

[40]FIFRA § 3(e), 7 U.S.C. § 136a(e), and 40 C.F.R. § 152.135.

[41]FIFRA § 10, 7 U.S.C. § 136h. Trade secrets are also a source of contention in the implementation of the Toxic Substances Control Act.

[42]FIFRA § 10(b), 7 U.S.C. § 136h(b). Note that state agencies are not mentioned.

[43]The reverse situation, where a chemical company sought an administrative subpoena of the testing files of two university researchers on pesticides, was raised in *Dow Chemical Co. v. Allen*, 672 F.2d. 1262, 17 ERC 1013 (7th Cir., 1982). The request was rejected as unduly burdensome and not particularly probative, since the EPA had not relied on their data in studies still uncompleted.

Because of the controversy surrounding the disclosure of trade secrets, Congress amended FIFRA in 1975 and 1978. The 1975 amendments[44] cleaned up an ambiguity created by the 1972 amendments by specifying that the new use restrictions applied only to data submitted on or after January 1, 1970. The definition of trade secrets was left to the Administrator.

EPA took the position that the 1972 and 1975 amendments restricted use and disclosure of only a narrow range of data, such as formulas and manufacturing processes, but not hazard and efficacy data. However, the industry challenged this view with some initial success.[45] In 1978, Congress again amended Section 10 to limit trade secrets protection to formulas and manufacturing processes, thus reflecting EPA's position. This was a significant change and has spawned a host of litigation.[46]

In *Ruckelshaus v. Monsanto*,[47] the Supreme Court held almost unanimously (7-1/2 to 1/2) that while a company did have a property right to the data under state law, the key question was whether it had a reasonable expectation that it would not be disclosed or used by other companies, albeit with adequate compensation. This expectation, the Court found, could only be for the period between the 1972 FIFRA amendments and the 1978 amendments, when the interim change in Section 10 of the act first promised strict confidentiality.[48] For this period, compensation is available through the federal Tucker Act, and probably through the statutory arbitration process too. For the periods on either side of those dates, there need be no compensation.

### 3.11 "Featherbedding" or "Me-Too" Registrants

The second most contested provision in FIFRA registration has been the issue of "featherbedding" on registration. The original version in the House stated that "data submitted in support of an application shall not, without permission of the applicant, be considered by the Administrator in the support of any other application for registration."[49] Supporters of the provision, basically the larger manufacturers, claimed that it prevented one company from "free-loading" on the expensive scientific data produced by another company; environmentalists dubbed this the "mice extermination amendment" for requiring subsequent registrants to needlessly duplicate the laboratory experiments of the first registrant.

The groups finally found an acceptable compromise allowing subsequent registrants to reimburse the initial registrant for reliance on its data, adding to the above language the words: "unless such other applicant shall first offer to pay reasonable compensation for producing the test data to be relied upon."

The section originally provides that disputes over the amount of compensation should be decided by the Administrator. The 1975 amendments deleted the unfortunate

---

[44]Pub. L. No. 94-140, 89 Stat. 75 (1975).

[45]*Mobay Chemical Corp. v. Costle*, 447 F.Supp 811, 12 ERC 1228 (W.D. Mo. 1978), appeal dismissed 439 U.S. 320, reh. denied 440 U.S. 940 (1979); *Chevron Chemical Co. v. Costle*, 443 F.Supp 1024 (N.D. Cal. 1978).

[46]Pub. L. No. 95-396, 92 Stat. 812.

[47]104 S. Ct. 2862, 21 ERC 1062 (1984).

[48]28 U.S.C. §1491.

[49]FIFRA, § 3(C)(1)(D), 7 U.S.C. § 136a(C)(1)(D).

clause which ensured that the original registrant should have nothing to lose by appealing to a district court, since "in no event shall the amount of payment determined by the court be less than that determined by the Administrator." The 1978 amendments removed the unwelcome task from the Administrator entirely by providing for mediation by the Federal Mediation & Conciliation Service.[50] The 1975 amendments also pushed back the effective date of the compensation provision from October 1972, the date of the enactment of the FEPCA amendments, to an arbitrary date of January 1, 1970.[51]

The data compensation provision has created many problems in the registration process. Pesticide manufacturers brought several lawsuits to determine the breadth of this provision, the proper use of the data, and the amount of compensation that a manufacturer is entitled for use of its data.[52]

In the case *In re Ciba-Geigy Corp. v. Farmland Industries, Inc.*,[53] EPA set out criteria to be applied in determining what constitutes reasonable compensation under Section 3(c). Plaintiff Ciba-Geigy claimed that it was entitled to $8.11 million in compensation from Farmland Industries for the latter's use of test data to register three pesticides. The defendant argued that it should pay only a proportional share of the actual cost of producing the data based on its share of the market for the products, approximately $49,000. The plaintiff contended that reasonable compensation should be based on the standards used in licensing technical knowledge: an amount equal to the cost of reproducing the data plus a royalty on gross sales for three years.

The administrative law judge hearing the case ruled that a latter, cost-royalty formula was closer to Congress' intent to avoid unnecessary testing costs. He concluded that the reasonable compensation provision was not intended to provide reward for research and development as the plaintiff's formula would do. The fairest compensatory formula, according to the judge, was using the data producer's cost adjusted for inflation and the defendant's market share two or three years after initial registration. Although no reward for research and development was created, this compensation formula does create an incentive to research because the benefits gained from decreased costs of subsequent registrants outweigh the disadvantages of decreasing the original data producer's projects.

In 1984, the United States Supreme Court ruled in *Ruckelshaus v. Monsanto Co.*[54] that pesticide health and safety data was property under Missouri law and thus was protected under the Fifth Amendment of the Constitution. However, as noted above, this was the case where the Court overruled a lower court in finding that data submitted prior to 1972 and after 1978 was not a "taking" since the registrant had no expectation of confidentiality, except for the ambiguous period between the 1972 and 1978 amendments. The Supreme Court decided the remedy was not to find FIFRA

---

[50]Pub. L. No. 95-396 § 2(2), 92 Stat. 819.

[51]Pub. L. No. 94-140, §12, amending FIFRA §3(c)(1)(D). The 1972 amendments had not actually specified an effective date but most authorities assumed it was the date of enactment.

[52]See *Amchem Products Inc. v. GAF Corp.*, 594 F.2d 470 (5th Cir., 1979), reh. den. 602 F.2d 724 (5th Cir. 1979); *Mobay Chemical v. EPA*, 447 F.Supp. 811, 12 ERC 1572 (W.D. Mo., 1975), 439 U.S. 320, 12 ERC 1581 (per curiam) (1979).

[53]Initial Decision, FIFRA Comp. Dockets Nos. 33, 34 and 41 (August 19, 1980).

[54]*Ruckelshaus v. Monsanto Co.*, 104 S.Ct. 2862 (1984).

unconstitutional, as the lower court had done, but to allow a claim against the government for compensation under the Tucker Act.[55]

By statute, EPA is supposed to review and approve or deny a me-too application within 90 days.[56] This compares favorably with the 180-day time period for FDA's me-too generic drug reviews which, in any case, are rarely completed in twice the requisite time.

### 3.12 Essentiality in Registration

Another registration change strongly supported by the pesticide industry was a prohibition against EPA refusing to register a substance because it served no useful or necessary purpose. This is not the same as efficacy, above, nor was this a dispute as to whether a registration application must demonstrate that a product would "perform its intended function." Some chemical companies were apprehensive that EPA might refuse to register a new product because an old one satisfactorily performed its intended function. EPA's best interest, and that of the public, however, lies in having as much duplication of pesticide applications as reasonably possible, since the existence of a similar but safer chemical facilitates the removal of a hazardous pesticide from the market.

The companies were correct, however, in recognizing that the availability of alternative products could have an important bearing on the cancellation-suspension process, as we will see below, but that is another story.

### 4.0 CONTROL OVER PESTICIDE USAGE

### 4.1 Statutory Basis for Control over Pesticide Usage

Until the 1972 FEPCA reforms, the government had no control over the actual use of a pesticide once it had left a manufacturer or distributor properly labeled. Thus, for example, a chemical which would be perfectly safe for use on a dry field might be environmentally hazardous if applied in a marshy area, and a chemical acceptable for use on one crop might leave dangerous residues on another. EPA's only recourse (other than occasional subtle hints to the producer) was to cancel the entire registration—obviously too unwieldy a weapon to constitute a normal means of enforcement. A second problem was that a potential chemical might be too dangerous for general use but could be used safely by trained personnel. There was, however, no legal mechanism for limiting its use only to qualified individuals.

Because of these problems, both environmentalists and the industry agreed that EPA should be given more flexibility than merely the choice between canceling or approving a pesticide. Congress therefore provided for the classification of pesticides into general and restricted categories, with the latter group available only to Certified Applicators. There are several categories of applicators, including private applicators and commercial applicators, who use or supervise the application of pesticides on property other than their own. A pesticide label permitting use only "under the direct supervision of a Certified Applicator" means of course that the chemical is to be applied

---

[55]28 U.S.C. § 1491.
[56]FIFRA § 3(c)(3)(B), 7 U.S.C. § 136a(c)(3)(B).

under the instructions and control of a Certified Applicator who, however, curiously is not required to be physically present when and where the pesticide is applied.

The additional flexibility of the certification program was a principal reason the agro-chemical industry eventually supported the 1972 amendments to FIFRA, but some environmentalists were concerned that the program might become a farce, especially when administered by certain states. Certification standards are prescribed by EPA, but any state desiring to establish its own certification program may do so if the Administrator determines that it satisfies the guidelines and statutory criteria. (See Section 4.3.)

Since 1972, it has been unlawful either "to make available for use, or to use, any registered pesticide classified for restricted use for some or all purposes other than in accordance with" the registration and applicable regulations. Stiff penalties for violations of these restrictions include fines up to $25,000 and imprisonment for up to a year.

The validity of the certification program, however, was considerably undermined by the 1975 amendments to FIFRA. The amendments considerably relaxed the procedures for certification by forbidding EPA to demand any examinations of an applicant's knowledge.[57] Some states may license anyone who applies, but EPA requirements for periodic reporting and inspection provide some degree of control. There would be no objection to every farmer becoming a Certified Applicator if he so desired, provided that he was seriously willing to undergo training.

The Food Quality Protection Act of 1996 (FQPA) established two new categories of pesticide applicators—maintenance applicators, who use or supervise structural or lawn care pesticides, and service technicians, who use or supervise these pesticides on someone else's property for a fee. States are authorized to set minimum training requirements for these new categories.[58]

### 4.2 Experimental Use Permits

FIFRA provides for experimental use permits for registered pesticides.[59] The purpose of this seemingly innocuous section is to permit a registration applicant to conduct tests and "accumulate information necessary to register a pesticide under Section 3."[60] This provision, however, has already been used in at least one successful effort to evade a FIFRA cancellation-suspension order. Under strong political pressure from Western sheep interests and their congressional spokesmen, EPA granted a Section 5 permit for the limited use of certain banned predacides and devices including the "coyote getter."

On July 18, 1979, EPA issued final regulations under which a state may develop its own experimental permits program.[61] A state, by submitting a plan which meets the requirements of EPA's regulations, may receive authorization to issue experimental use

---

[57]Pub. L. No. 94-140 § 5, amending FIFRA § 4(a)(1).

[58]FQPA § 120.

[59]FIFRA § 5, 7 U.S.C. § 136c. The 1975 amendments added a specific provision for agricultural research agencies, public or private.

[60]FIFRA § 5(a), 7 U.S.C. § 136c(a).

[61]44 Fed. Reg. at 41783 (July 18, 1978); 40 C.F.R. § 172.20.

permits to potential registrants under 24(c) of FIFRA (restricted use registration), agricultural or educational research agencies, and certified applicators for use of a restricted use pesticide.

Permits cannot be issued by a state for a pesticide containing ingredients subject to an EPA cancellation or suspension order, or to a notice of intent to cancel or suspend or which are not found in any EPA registered product.[62] The regulations also contain strict limitations on the production and use of a pesticide. Periodic reports must be submitted by the permittee to the state detailing the progress of the research or restricted use. In addition, permits cannot be issued for more than three years.

### 4.3 Self-Certification of Private Applicators

The clearest illustration of Congress' altered view toward FIFRA is their treatment of the certification program which had been a major reason for the enactment of the FIFRA overhaul in 1972. The amendments provided that the pesticides which might be too harmful to the applicators or to the environment if indiscriminately used could continue to be applied by farmers and pesticide operators who had received special training in avoiding these problems.

The program had run into resistance from the beginning from farmers who resented the requirement that they be trained to use chemicals on their own property. The changed law does not remove the examination requirement from commercial applicators, who apply pesticides to property other than their own.[63] It does create an exemption, however, which covers not only the farmer who is applying pesticides to his own land but also his employees. And it must be remembered that the hazards are not necessarily limited to the applicator; organophosphates, which are nerve gases, may be highly toxic to the applicators, but many other substances if improperly used may run off to threaten neighboring farms or the environment in general. The amended law does not seem to recognize this latter problem.

The 1975 amendments also removed the authority of the Administrator to require, under state plans submitted for his approval, that farmers take exams before being certified. In other words, EPA may require a training program but may not require any examination to determine if the information has been learned.[64] In the opinion of the House Agriculture Committee, "The farmer would be more aware of the dangers of restricted use pesticides if each time he makes a purchase he is given a self-certification form to read and sign." One wonders if a similar arrangement for airline pilot certification would be considered acceptable.[65]

---

[62]44 Fed. Reg. at 41788. States may, however, issue permits for products containing ingredients subject to the Rebuttable Presumption Against Review process (RPAR).

[63]See the definition of commercial applicator in FIFRA § 2(e).

[64]States may themselves require an examination of certified applicators but, under the amended FIFRA, EPA could not make this a prerequisite for state plan approval. See Pub. L. 94-140 § 5, amending FIFRA § 4, 7 U.S.C. 136b. See also Senate Report No. 94-452, pp. 7-8.

[65]House Report No. 94-497, p. 9.

### 4.4 Two-House Congressional Veto Over EPA Regulations

The 1980 amendments changed Section 25(a) to provide a two-house congressional veto over EPA rules or regulations.[66] Under the amendments, the Administrator is required to submit to each house of Congress new FIFRA regulations. If Congress adopts a concurrent resolution disapproving the new regulation within ninety days of its promulgation it will not become effective. However, if neither house disapproves the regulation after sixty days and the appropriate committee of neither house has reported out a disapproving regulation, the regulation becomes effective.[67]

### 5.0 REMOVAL OF PESTICIDES FROM THE MARKET

FIFRA is not merely concerned with the registration, or reregistration, of pesticides coming on the market. It also has mechanisms for taking action against products considered to pose a risk to man and the environment.

### 5.1 Cancellation

While the registration process may be the heart of FIFRA, cancellation represents the cutting edge of the law and attracts the most public attention. Cancellation is used to initiate review of a substance suspected of posing a "substantial question of safety" to man or the environment.[68]

Contrary to public assumptions, during the pendency of the proceedings the product may be freely manufactured and shipped in commerce. A cancellation order, although final if not challenged within thirty days, usually leads to a public hearing or scientific review committee, or both, and can be quite protracted; this can last a matter of months or years. A recommended decision from the agency hearing examiner (now called the administrative law judge) goes to the Administrator or to his delegated representative, the chief agency judicial officer, for a final determination on the cancellation. If the decision is upheld, the product would be banned from shipment or use in the United States.[69]

There are several quite different types of action covered under the single term "cancellation."[70] First, there is a cancellation when EPA believes a substance is a highly probable threat to man or the environment but for which there is not yet sufficient evidence to warrant immediate suspension. This is the usual meaning. Second, there can be a cancellation when scientific tests indicate some cause for concern, and a public hearing or scientific advisory committee is desired to explore the issue more thoroughly.

---

[66]Pub. L. No. 96-539, 94 Stat. 3194, 3195 amending 7 U.S.C. § 136w(4).

[67]The constitutionality of congressional vetoes of administrative rules is unsettled. The Supreme Court in 1983 held that one-house vetoes are unconstitutional, and since then legislation has had to be revised to conform to the legislative mode: *both* houses must pass legislation which is then presented to the president for his approval or disapproval. *Immigration & Naturalization Service v. Chadha*, 462 U.S. 919, 103 S.Ct. 2764 (1983), affirming 64 F.d 408 (9th Cir., 1980).

[68]*EDF v. Ruckelshaus*, 439 F.2d 584, 591-92, 2 ERC 1114, 1119 (D.C. Cir., 1971).

[69]The scientific review committee and other features of this process will be discussed later in more detail.

[70]The cancellation-suspension section of the old act was § 4(c); it is § 6 of the post-1972 FIFRA.

And third, there could be a cancellation issued in response to a citizens' suit to enable both critics and defenders of the pesticide to present their arguments.

These distinctions, although not found in the statute, are nevertheless quite important. State authorities, for example, often recommend that farmers cease using a canceled product which they thought had been declared unsafe, although EPA may have considered the action in category two or three above. Conversely, there were occasions when EPA wanted to communicate its great concern over the continued use of a product without resorting to the more immediate and drastic remedy of suspension. This problem is not resolved completely by the amended FIFRA, but two levels of action are distinguished.

The Administrator may issue a notice of his intent either (1) to cancel its registration or to change its classification, together with the reasons (including the factual basis) for his action, or (2) to hold a hearing to determine whether or not its registration should be canceled or its classification changed.[71] This revision of the law may not have solved EPA's communications problem with local officials, but it did provide a basis for a distinction which EPA sometimes needed to make.

## 5.2 Suspension

A suspension order, despite its misleading name, is an immediate ban on the production and distribution of a pesticide. It is mandated when a product constitutes an "imminent hazard" to man or the environment, and may be invoked at any stage of the cancellation proceeding, or even before a cancellation procedure has been initiated. According to the "18th of March Statement," a seminal 1971 EPA pronouncement, "an imminent hazard may be declared at any point in the chain of events which may ultimately result in harm to the public."[72] A suspension order must be accompanied by a cancellation order if one is not then outstanding.

### 5.2.1 Ordinary Suspension

The purpose of an ordinary suspension is to prevent an imminent hazard during the time required for cancellation or change in classification proceedings. An ordinary suspension proceeding is initiated when the Administrator issues notice to the registrant that he is suspending use of the pesticide and includes the requisite findings as to imminent hazard. The registrant may request an expedited hearing within five days of receipt of the Administrator's notice. If no hearing is requested, the suspension order can take effect immediately thereafter and the order is not reviewable by a court.

The original notion was that suspension procedurally "resembles . . . the judicial proceedings on a contested motion for a preliminary injunction,"[73] and that it remains in effect until the cancellation hearing is completed and a final decision is issued by the

---

[71]FIFRA § 6(b), 7 U.S.C. § 136d(b). Note that the administrator himself may request a hearing, a power which he did not have under the old FIFRA, although in fact he assumed this authority in his August 1971 cancellation order on 2,4,5-T.

[72]See EPA's March 18, 1971, Statement, p. 6, prepared by Special Assistant to the Administrator Richard Fairbanks.

[73]*EDF v. EPA* 465 F. 2d 538, 4 ERC 1523, 1530 (D.C. Cir., 1972).

Administrator.[74] This connotation of temporariness does not actually accord with reality but has been the consistent theme of judicial decisions since the agency's inception. According to this view, the function of a suspension order is not to reach a definitive decision on the registration of a pesticide but to grant temporary, interim relief.[75]

The Court of Appeals for the District of Columbia has repeatedly stated this view: "The function of the suspension decision is to make a preliminary assessment of evidence and probabilities, not an ultimate resolution of difficult issues,"[76] and "the suspension order thus operates to afford interim relief during the course of the lengthy administrative proceedings."[77]

The court of appeals has specifically noted that "imminent hazard" does not refer only to the danger of an immediate disaster: "We must caution against any approach to the term 'imminent hazard' used in the statute, that restricts it to a concept of crises."[78] In another case, the court declared that the Secretary of Agriculture has concluded that the most important element of an "imminent hazard to the public" is a serious threat to public health, that a hazard may be "imminent" even if its impact will not be apparent for many years, and that the "public" protected by the suspension provision includes fish and wildlife. These interpretations all seem consistent with the statutory language and purpose.[79]

### 5.2.2 Emergency Suspension

The emergency suspension is the strongest environmental action EPA can take under FIFRA. It immediately halts all uses, sales, and distribution of the pesticide.[80] An emergency suspension differs from an ordinary suspension in that it is *ex parte*. The registrant is not given notice or the opportunity for an expedited hearing prior to the suspension order taking effect. The registrant is, however, entitled to an expedited hearing to determine the propriety of the emergency suspension. The Administrator can only use this procedure when he determines that an emergency exists which does not allow him to hold a hearing before suspending use of a pesticide. This authority has only rarely been invoked.

EPA first used the emergency suspension procedure in 1979 when it suspended the sale and use of 2,4,5-T and Silvex for specified uses. EPA issued the suspension orders based on its judgment that exposure to the pesticides created an immediate and unreasonable risk to human health. EPA's action was reviewed by a Michigan district court in *Dow Chemical Co. v. Blum*,[81] where the plaintiffs petitioned for judicial review of EPA's decision and a stay of the emergency suspension orders. In upholding EPA's

---

[74]*Nor-Am v. Hardin*, 435 F. 2d 1151, 2 ERC 1016 (7th Cir., 1970), *cert. denied* 402 U.S. 935 (1971).

[75]See, *In re Shell Chemical*, Opinion of the Administrator, pp. 8-11, 6 ERC 2047 at 2050 (1974).

[76]*EDF v. EPA, supra*, 465 F. 2d at 537, 4 ERC at 1529.

[77]*EDF v. Ruckelshaus, supra*, 439 F. 2d at 589, 2 ERC at 1115.

[78]*EDF v. EPA, supra*, 465 F. 2d at 540, 4 ERC at 1531.

[79]*EDF v. Ruckelshaus, supra*, 439 F.2d at 597, 2 ERC at 1121-22.

[80]Its counterpart in the Toxic Substances Control Act (TSCA) is Section 7, but that provision has remained virtually unused since inception.

[81]469 F. Supp. 892, 13 ERC 1129 (E.D. Mich., 1979).

order, the court analogized the emergency suspension order to a temporary restraining order and defined the term emergency as a "substantial likelihood that serious harm will be experienced during the three or four months required in any realistic projection of the administrative suspension process."[82]

The court held that this standard required the Administrator to examine five factors: (1) the seriousness of the threatened harm; (2) the immediacy of the threatened harm; (3) the probability that the threatened harm would result; (4) the benefits to the public of the continued use of the pesticides in question during the suspension process; and (5) the nature and extent of the information before the Administrator at the time he makes his decision. The court also held that an emergency suspension order may be overturned only if it was arbitrary, capricious, or an abuse of discretion or if it was not "issued in accordance with the procedures established by law."[83]

The Food Quality Protection Act of 1996 amending FIFRA (see below, Section 11) made one change in the emergency suspension process, allowing a suspension to be issued for no more than 90 days without a simultaneous notice of intent to cancel.[84]

### 5.3 Misbranding and Stop-Sale Orders

EPA has traditionally used the bare charge of "misbranding" for certain unambiguous offenses, notably instances where the pesticide made claims unsupported by the registration. The violation was usually obvious, the appeals uncommon, and the remedy simple—namely, to order the sales halted.

In the early 1990s, however, EPA began for the first time to use the charge of misbranding in cases where the agency questioned the effectiveness of the registered formulation. If the product does not work, it should not be reregistered, or it should be cancelled under Section 6. By using the misbranding approach rather than cancellation, the agency circumvents the procedural safeguards, including the public hearings and scientific advisory committees provided in the statute. For that very reason, this approach should be strongly disfavored.[85]

Ironically, while less procedural protection is afforded by the misbranding approach, the legal consequences can be more severe; unlike with cancellation or even suspension, EPA can prevent a misbranded product from being exported or sold abroad.

### 5.4 The International Effect of EPA Cancellations

EPA cancellation and suspension decisions, as agency administrators have repeatedly noted, are meant to apply only to the United States. The reason is that the risk-benefit calculations applied to challenged pesticides are based on conditions in this

---

[82]*Ibid.* at 902, 13 ERC at 1135.

[83]*Ibid.* The court stated that it arrived at its decision to uphold EPA's order "with great reluctance" and would not have ordered the emergency suspension on the basis of the information before EPA, but was not empowered to substitute its judgment for that of EPA's. 469 F. Supp. at 907, 13 ERC at 1140.

[84]FQPA § 102.

[85]The agency suffered a setback in the first case utilizing this theory, *Metrex v. EPA*, although on the narrower grounds that EPA's test data was invalid.

country and would not necessarily be valid for different risks and different benefits abroad.

This interpretation has not been without its critics. Because of its potential significance, an entire separate part of this chapter (Part 9.0, below) is devoted to this topic.

## 5.5 Disposal and Recall

An important question following a cancellation or suspension action is whether to recall those products already in commerce.[86] "Misbranded" pesticides may be confiscated, and on several occasions EPA has ordered manufacturers to recall a pesticide when the hazard so warranted. But for both practical and administrative reasons cancellation-suspension orders have generally provided that banned pesticides may be used until supplies are exhausted, without being subject to recall.[87] It may seem inconsistent to ban a substance as an imminent hazard and yet allow quantities already on the market to be sold, but repeated challenges by environmentalist groups have been unsuccessful.[88]

This policy was thought necessary, for example, in the mercury pesticides case when EPA scientists concluded that the recall of certain mercuric compounds would result in a concentration more harmful to the environment than permitting the remaining supplies to be thinly spread around the country. In the DDT case, the Administrator decided that his final cancellation order would not go into effect for six months to ensure the availability of adequate supplies of alternative pesticides (namely, organophosphates which can be very hazardous to untrained applicators) and to allow time for training and educational programs to prevent misuse of the new chemicals.

EPA promulgated regulations for the storage and disposal of pesticides in May 1974.[89] These detailed the appropriate conditions for incinerations, soil injection, and other means of disposal, established procedures for shipment back to the manufacturers or to the federal government, directed that transportation costs should be borne by the owner of the pesticide, and provided standards for storage. The regulations devoted considerable attention to the disposal problem of pesticide containers, which have caused a significant proportion of accidental poisonings.

## 5.6 Compensation for Canceled Pesticides

Section 15 of FIFRA provides financial compensation to registrants and applicators owning quantities of pesticides who are unable to use them because of cancellation or suspension. This section was the most controversial in the entire act; the amendment's industry supporters threatened to block passage of the entire 1972

---

[86]FIFRA §§ 19 and 25, 7 U.S.C. §§ 136q and 136w. See also the previous discussion of indemnities.

[87]Compare the recall authority of the Consumer Product Safety Commission under Section 15 of its Hazardous Substance Act, 15 U.S.C. §1274, Pub. L. No. 91-113, which makes recall almost mandatory. The Consumer Product Safety Act, Section 15, on the other hand, provides several options, 15 U.S.C. 2064, Pub. L. No. 92-573.

[88]See, e.g., *EDF v. EPA* 510 F. 2d 1292, 7 ERC 1689 (D.C. Cir., 1975).

[89]39 Fed. Reg. 15236, (May 1, 1974), 40 C.F.R. § 165.

legislation if this section was not attached. Public interest groups complained that it would force taxpayers to indemnify manufacturers for inadequate testing and would encourage the production of unsafe chemicals.[90] To the extent that this provision was intended not so much for indemnification as to deter EPA cancellations,[91] it served to undermine the purposes of this act.

As a partial compromise, a clause was added to bar indemnification to any person who "had knowledge of facts which, in themselves, would have shown that such pesticide did not meet the requirements" for registration and continued thereafter to produce such pesticide without giving notice of such facts to the Administrator. If properly applied, even under the most expedited agency procedures, that saving clause could have disqualified registrants and manufacturers from compensation in virtually all cancellation and suspension actions.

Under this provision, the EPA has paid out $20 million to manufacturers of the two pesticides, 2,4,5-T and ethylene dibromide (EDB). An additional $40 million indemnification is estimated for a third canceled pesticide, dinoseb. These sums come directly from the budget of EPA's Pesticide Office, which last year totaled only $40 million, and thus would require that the agency cut back on other activities.[92]

This indemnities provision was eventually recognized as a mistake. In the 1988 legislation on FIFRA, the House and Senate both voted to remove the section, except for the indemnification of end users (i.e., farmers and applicators), so chemical manufacturers would no longer be covered.[93] Farmers and other users are still eligible for compensation through the federal government's regular Judgment Fund.[94] This reflects the philosophy of an earlier congressional prohibition, contained in the Appropriations Bill for fiscal year 1988, which provided that any sums should be paid from the general U.S. Treasury, not from EPA's budget, so the agency would not be penalized for taking measures it deemed proper.[95]

### 5.7 Balancing Test in FIFRA

The balancing of risks versus benefits is mandated by FIFRA, and its importance warrants a separate discussion. There are some who feel that certain types of pesticides, particularly carcinogens, should be forbidden *per se* as was done under the Delaney Amendment to the Food, Drug, and Cosmetics Act.[96] FIFRA does not require this inflexibility, although the courts have cautioned that the law "places a heavy burden on any administrative officer to explain the basis for his decision to permit the continued use of a chemical known to produce cancer in experimental animals."[97]

---

[90]FIFRA § 15, Pub. L. No. 92-516.

[91]See section 4.1 "Indemnities" in this chapter.

[92]*Washington Post*, September 15, 1988.

[93]See the fuller discussion of the FIFRA Amendments of 1988, *infra*.

[94]Section 501 of the 1988 amendments.

[95]FY 1988 Continuing Appropriation Act, Pub. L. No. 100-202.

[96]FDCA § 409(c)(3)(A), 21 U.S.C. § 348(c)(3)(A). The relationship between the FIFRA and the FDCA will be discussed later in more detail.

[97]*EDF v. Ruckelshaus, supra*, 439 F. 2d at 596, 2 ERC at 1121.

The balancing that is applied during the registration process and, more formally, during the cancellation proceedings is to determine whether there are "unreasonable adverse effects on the environment," taking into consideration the "economic, social, and environmental costs and benefits of the use of any pesticide."

In a suspension proceeding, however, the FIFRA does not require a balancing of environmental risks and benefits. It has nevertheless been EPA's policy since its inception to conduct such an analysis, although in practice the benefits would obviously need to be considerable to balance a finding of "imminent hazard." One Administrator noted that "the Agency traditionally has considered benefits as well as risks . . . and, in his opinion, should continue to do so."[98]

## 5.8 Requirements of Consultation by EPA with USDA

Congress decided in the 1975 amendments to require that EPA engage in formal consultation with USDA and with the Agriculture Committees of the House and Senate before issuing proposals or final standards regarding pesticides. This amended Section 6(b) of the FIFRA to provide that EPA should give 60 days' notice to the Secretary of Agriculture before a notice is made public. The Secretary then must respond within 30 days, and these comments, along with the response of the EPA Administrator, are published in the *Federal Register*.[99] These consultations, however, are not required in the event of an imminent hazard to human health for which a suspension order under Section 6(c) is warranted.

At the same time that the Administrator provides a copy of any proposed regulations to the Secretary of Agriculture, he is also required to provide copies to the respective House and Senate Agricultural Committees. The practical impact of this requirement is that Congress is provided an opportunity to communicate displeasure to the Administrator before a proposal is issued without necessarily having to subject these comments to scrutiny in the public record.[100]

## 5.9 Economic Impact On Agriculture Statement

The 1975 amendments also reflected the increasing trend in government toward requiring impact statements before regulations can be issued. Congress, borrowing from the environmental impact statement process[101] and the economic impact statement requirements,[102] mandated that the Administrator, when deciding to issue a proposal, "shall include among those factors to be taken into account the impact of the action

---

[98]*In re Shell Chemical, supra.*, p. 11, 6 ERC at 2050-51, upheld unanimously by the D.C. Court of Appeals in *EDF v. EPA*, 510 F. 2d 1292, 7 ERC 1689 (April 4, 1975).

[99]These time deadlines may be by agreement between the administrator and the secretary, Pub. L. No. 94-140, § 1.

[100]EPA has often required that congressional communications after the issuance of a proposal be placed on the public record; and where this was not done, as in the DDT proceedings, environmental groups successfully sued to ensure that these contacts and written comments were made public.

[101]National Environmental Policy Act, § 102(2)(c), U.S.C. §§ 4321 *et seq.*, (1969); see also 36 Fed. Reg. 7724 (1971) and 38 Fed. Reg. 20549 (1973).

[102]Presidential Executive Order No. 11821, November 29, 1974.

proposed in such notice on production and prices of agricultural commodities, retail food prices, and otherwise on the agricultural economy."[103]

The necessity for this legal provision is technically questionable since the balancing of risks and benefits is at the heart of FIFRA. No one at EPA or anywhere else has contended that the agricultural benefits of pesticides should not be taken into consideration in this balancing equation. In fact, although the courts have stated that EPA legally need not consider benefits in suspension actions involving an imminent hazard to human health and the environment, EPA from the beginning has always made the agricultural factor an essential element in its determinations.[104] The committees themselves were vague about the actual need for this legislation. Nevertheless, Congress felt that something was lacking. As the Senate report declared, it "concurs in the House position that EPA has not always given adequate consideration to agriculture in its decisions."[105]

### 5.10 Scientific Advisory Committees

Because the Scientific Advisory Committees play such an important role in the cancellation-suspension process, they deserve special attention in this section.

According to the old FIFRA, prior to 1972, a registrant challenging a cancellation order could request either a public hearing or a scientific advisory committee; and in practice, cases involving several registrants usually resulted in both. EPA was also strongly dissatisfied with the vague and often contradictory reports of the advisory committees.

In the 1972 amendments to FIFRA, the advisory committee was transformed into an adjunct of the hearing process, resolving those scientific questions which the administrative law judge or the parties determined were essential to the final decision by the Administrator. The amendments streamlined the process so that Committee deliberations could proceed simultaneously with the administrative hearings, thereby saving time and making them a part of the fact-finding and evaluation system, rather than a separate proceeding with long delays and divisions of responsibility. By meeting outside of the public hearing, the scientists can also avoid being subject to cross examination and other legal burdens they consider unappealing.

The advisory process, however, was again made more formalistic by the 1975 amendments. The use of a scientific advisory committee was mandated both for cancellation actions (where they are usually requested anyway) and for any general pesticide regulations.[106] The amendments required that the Administrator submit proposed and final regulations to a specially constituted scientific advisory panel, separate from the regular Scientific Advisory Committees, at the same time that he provides copies to the Secretary of Agriculture and to the two agricultural committees of Congress. The advisory committee then has 30 days in which to respond. Membership on this committee is prescribed in unusual detail. The Administrator can

---

[103]Pub. L. No. 94-104, § 1, amending FIFRA § 6(b), 7 U.S.C. § 136d.

[104]See the discussion of this in paragraph 2.6 of this chapter.

[105]Senate Report No. 94-452, p. 9.

[106]Pub. L. No. 94-140, § 7, amending FIFRA § 25. A more detailed analysis of the 1975 changes appears in 5.0.

select seven members from a group of twelve nominees—six nominated by the National Science Foundation, and six by the National Institutes of Health.[107]

In 1980, Section 25(d) was amended to allow the chairman of a Scientific Advisory Committee to create temporary subpanels on specific projects.[108] Section 25(d) was also amended to require the Administrator to submit any decision to suspend the registration of a pesticide to a scientific advisory panel (SAP) for its comment.[109] The amendment did not alter the Administrator's authority to issue a suspension notice prior to the SAP review, it only requires him to obtain SAP review after the suspension is initiated. The 1980 amendments also required the Administrator to issue written procedures for independent peer review of the design, protocol and conduct of major studies conducted under FIFRA.[110]

One might question the value of ever more advisory committees when, as EPA Administrator Russell Train pointed out years ago, "EPA is already awash in scientific advisory panels."[111]

## 6.0 ADMINISTRATIVE AND JUDICIAL REVIEW

EPA enforcement actions and other administrative actions usually follow a clearly specified series of internal appeals. The action first goes to an administrative law judge (ALJ), previously called merely a hearing examiner. After discovery and hearings, a process that can take a year or two, the judge renders a decision that can then be appealed within the Agency. The next level used to be the Administrator, or the special assistant acting in his name; then for two decades this role was institutionalized in the Chief Judicial Officer. In the last several years this office has been expanded into a three-member appeals board. After this, the Administrator can personally intervene but now rarely does. Thereafter, the aggrieved party can appeal to the federal courts.

### 6.1 The Scope of the Administrator's Flexibility

The EPA Administrator renders the final agency judgment on administrative actions and appeals.[112] Since issues reach him only after passing through a series of committees, lower level enforcement officials, administrative law judges, and other officials, the question is how much discretion he has to come to a decision at variance with those rendered below.

#### 6.1.1 Concerning the Scientific Advisory Committee

In emphasizing the Administrator's regulatory flexibility, the courts have rejected the contention that he must "rubber stamp" the findings of the Scientific Advisory Committee or the administrative law judge. This is illustrated by *Dow Chemical v.*

---

[107]Pub. L. No. 94-140, § 7, amending FIFRA § 25(d), 7 U.S.C. § 136w.

[108]Pub. L. No. 96-539, 94 Stat. 3195.

[109]*Id.*

[110]No. 96-1020, 96th Cong., 2d Sess. (1980) p. 4.

[111]Statement of EPA Administrator Russell Train to the Senate Agricultural Committee, reprinted in Senate Report No. 94-452, p. 18.

[112]In practice, most appeals to the Administrator are handled and decided by the Chief Judicial Officer, in the office of the Administrator.

*Ruckelshaus*[113] concerning the herbicide 2,4,5-T. In 1970 the USDA suspended some uses of the chemical and canceled others because of the high risk that it, or a dioxin contaminant known as TCDD, had proved a potent teratogen in laboratory tests. Most of these uses were not challenged, but Dow did contest the cancellation of its use on rice. A Scientific Advisory Committee convoked by EPA concluded that the "confused aggregate of observations indicated registrations should be maintained" but that there remained serious questions needing further extensive research. The Administrator reviewed the report in considerable detail and concluded that a "substantial question of safety" existed sufficient to justify an administrative hearing; in the meantime, the cancellation was maintained.[114] Dow appealed, but the Court of Appeals for the Eighth Circuit held that the Administrator was not compelled to follow the recommendations of the advisory committee if—and this is, of course, crucial—he had a justifiable basis for doing otherwise.[115]

### 6.1.2 Concerning the Administrative Law Judge

The Administrator is also not bound by findings of the administrative law judges. This conclusion follows the general principle of administrative law that a hearing examiner's decision should be accorded only the deference it merits. As the Supreme Court said long ago in *Universal Camera*, "we do not require that the examiner's findings be given more weight than in reason and in light of judicial experience they deserve."[116] Only if the decision-maker arbitrarily and capriciously ignored the findings of an examiner, or if the credibility of witnesses was crucial to the case—an infrequent situation in an administrative hearing—would a different conclusion be indicated.

### 6.2 Standing for Registration, Appeals and Subpoenas

FIFRA originally assumed that only registrants would be interested in the continuation of a product's registration or the setting of public hearings and scientific advisory committees. It was increasingly evident, however, that this unintended exclusion of both users and environmentalists needed revision.

Whereas a registrant, when faced with cancellation, might prefer not to contest those minor categories of use which it regarded as financially insignificant, a user might regard them as essential for the protection of his crops.

The law was therefore amended in 1972 by FEPCA to allow not only registrants but any "other interested person with the concurrence of the registrant" to request

---

[113]477 F.2d 1317, 5 ERC 1244 (8th Cir., 1973).

[114]The deficiencies in the advisory report, which was poorly reasoned and internally inconsistent, contributed to the agency's skepticism towards this system of information collection and analysis.

[115]This case is better remembered for its unconscionable delay of the administrative process. Dow appealed first to a district court in Arkansas and obtained an injunction against further EPA action on 2,4,5-T, although the statute explicitly excluded district courts from jurisdiction. The Eighth Circuit reversed, noting that the court below lacked jurisdiction and that in any case Dow was not entitled to an injunction during a period when "the cancellation orders have no effect on Dow's right to ship and market its product until the administration cancellation process has been completed." *Ibid.*, at 1326, 5 ERC at 1250.

[116]*Universal Camera Corp. v. NLRB*, 340 U.S. 474 (1951).

continuation of the registration.[117] While this amendment remedies the problem of legal standing, it does not provide the resources and data which users, particularly small farmers or organizations, would need to support a renewal application.[118]

Another problem of standing relates to the right of environmental and consumer groups to utilize the administrative procedures under cancellation-suspension. The act does not specifically give citizens' groups the right to request a public hearing, but the Administrator himself is now empowered to call a hearing which he might do at the request of such a group. Furthermore, as already discussed, all interested parties may request consent of the administrative law judge to refer scientific questions to a special committee of the National Academy of Sciences for determination, a right which did not exist before.

The issue of standing came up in *Environmental Defense Fund v. Costle* [119] when the D.C. Circuit upheld EPA's denial of standing for an environmental group which requested a Section 6(d) cancellation hearing for the continued use of chlorobenzilate in four states. The Environmental Defense Fund (EDF) requested the hearing after the Administrator issued a Notice of Intent to Cancel the registration of chlorobenzilate for all uses other than citrus spraying in four states. The Administrator denied the hearing, holding that FIFRA was not structured for the purpose of entertaining objections by persons having no real interest in stopping the cancellation from going into effect but who object to the agency's refusal to propose actions.[120]

The D.C. Circuit upheld the Administrator's decision that EDF was not an "adversely affected" party under Section 6(d), stating that a 6(d) hearing may be used only to stop a cancellation proceeding, not initiate one. The proper procedure for EDF in seeking review of EPA's decision to retain the registration for citrus users was to challenge the notice provisions permitting the limited use in district court under Section 16(a) of FIFRA.[121]

## 6.3 Judicial Appeals

Under the old version of FIFRA,[122] appeals from decisions of the Administrator went to the United States court of appeals. According to Section 16 of the amended FIFRA, however, appeals under some circumstances may go to a federal district court.[123] Other appeals go to the court of appeals.

---

[117]FIFRA § 6(a)(1), 7 U.S.C. § 136d(a)(1). See also *McGill v. EPA*, 593 F. 2d 631, 13 ERC 1156 (5th Cir., 1979).

[118]A good example is the Aldrin-Dieldrin suspension proceeding, in which the registrant was almost solely interested in the use for crops, while the USDA had to join the proceeding to insure that other registrations were properly represented. This USDA action under the new FIFRA, however, was necessary not because the users now lacked legal standing, but presumably because they lacked adequate resources. *In re Shell Chemical, supra.*, 6 ERC 2047.

[119]631 F.2d 922, 15 ERC 1217 (D.C. Cir., 1980), *cert. denied* 449 U.S. 1112.

[120]Final Decision, FIFRA Docket No. 411 (August 20, 1979) at 12-22.

[121]631 F. 2d at 935, 15 ERC at 1229. This case is also noteworthy for its treatment of judicial review under Section 16(b): See discussion of Judicial Review in 4.2.

[122]Old FIFRA § 4(d).

[123]FIFRA § 16(a)-(c), 7 U.S.C. § 136n(a)-(c).

This change provoked considerable controversy in EPA during the legislative process. The rationale for change was that courts of appeals are not designed to develop a record if none existed from the proceeding below. It thus seemed logical that in those instances where a record was developed, after public hearing or otherwise, the appeal should be to the court of appeals, whereas in cases where there was no record for the court to review the matter should go to a district court for findings of fact.

Section 16 has been the focus of two courts of appeals decisions which reached contrary holdings on the issue of whether the federal courts or the courts of appeals have jurisdiction to review the denial of a request for a FIFRA Section 6(d) hearing on a notice of cancellation. In *Environmental Defense Fund v. Costle*,[124] the D.C. Circuit Court held that if an administrative record exists in support of a denial of a hearing request, jurisdiction lies exclusively with the courts of appeals. In *AMVAC Chemical Corp. v. EPA*,[125] a divided Ninth Circuit rejected the D.C. Circuit's analysis and held that a denial of a hearing was a procedural action and not an "order" following a "public hearing" within the meaning of Section 16(b). Hence, the Court held that judicial review of hearing request denials lies in the district courts.

In 1996 the Circuit Court of Appeals clarified that a hearing was not always required. Since the distinction between district and appellate jurisdiction turned on whether there was an adequate record for review, the court declared, a pesticide case in which there was a voluminous record was properly before the Court of Appeals even though there might not actually have been a hearing.[126]

On a related point, there has been a growing tendency at EPA to dilute the FIFRA requirements for public hearing to include those situations in the post-1972 law in which only written public comments were submitted. That was not clearly not the intention of Congress in enacting FIFRA; it denies to the parties a fundamental right to be heard. A public hearing is a public session allowing testimony and confrontation with a recorded transcript. It should not be allowed to become anything less.[127]

## 7.0 THE ROLE OF STATES AND LOCALITIES

As the name declares, FIFRA is obviously a federal statute. For all pesticides, nation-wide, it is EPA that controls the registration, labeling, cancellation proceedings, and other regulatory activities. States and local communities, however, are often under strong political pressure from constituents who feel EPA's regulation is inadequate. This feeling may be the result either of skepticism about the agency's motives or competence, or of a belief that specific local conditions exist beyond the scope of federal regulation or interest.

---

[124]631 F. 2d 922, 15 ERC 1217 (D.C. Cir., 1980) *cert. denied* 449 U.S. 1112. This case is also important for its treatment of standing, discussed in the previous subsection.

[125]653 F. 2d 1260, 15 ERC 1467 (9th Cir., 1980) as amended February 5, 1981, *reh. denied*, April 10, 1981.

[126]*National Grain Sorghum Producers Association, Inc. v. EPA*, 84 F.3d 1452 (CADC 1996).

[127]The author of this chapter, while assistant to the Administrator of EPA, helped draft, among others, the hearing and jurisdictional sections of FIFRA in 1971-72 and worked closely with Congress on FEPCA's enactment.

On the other hand, pesticide manufacturers and applicators fear that hundreds of conflicting local pesticide ordinances would create a regulatory nightmare. Resolution of this conflict requires a political determination, by Congress. Unfortunately, Congress has largely avoided the issue. Without adequate guidance, therefore, the courts have had to struggle to guess from existing legislation what Congress intended. For that reason, the various inconsistent judicial decisions have created more confusion than they have solved.

## 7.1 Intrastate Registrations

Under the old FIFRA[128] federal authority did not extend to intrastate use and shipment of pesticides with state registrations. This meant that federal authority could be avoided simply by having manufacturing plants in the principal agricultural states. The 1972 FEPCA amendments broadened the registration requirement to include any person in any state who sells or distributes pesticides.

The states do retain some authority under Section 24 "to regulate the sale or use of any pesticide or device in the state, but only if and to the extent the regulation does not permit any sale or use prohibited by this Act." States, furthermore, cannot have labeling and packaging requirements different from those required by the act—a measure which was popular among some chemical manufacturers who feared that each state might have different labeling requirements. It excludes a feature common to several of the other environmental laws, whereby states may impose stricter requirements than the federal ones on pesticide use within their jurisdiction.

Finally, the section gives a state the authority, subject to certification by EPA, to register pesticides for limited local use in treating sudden and limited pest infestations, without the time and administrative burden required by a full EPA certification.

## 7.2 Greater State Authority

Several sections of the 1978 amendments reflect Congress' intent to give the states greater responsibility in regulating pesticides. This includes not only training and cooperative agreements, but also increasing federal delegation over such matters as intrastate registrations and enforcement. The EPA Administrator, however, retains overall supervisory responsibility and ultimate veto authority.

Because some states, such as California, have promulgated stringent guidelines for pesticide regulations, there has been proposed legislation to limit state authority under Section 24 to gather data about a pesticide for state registration.[129] Pesticide manufacturers have complained for several years that state registration procedures, which may require additional studies and data gathering, are time-consuming and costly. There have been no changes in Section 24 yet, but, Congress may limit the regulatory authority of the states in future legislation.

---

[128]Old (pre-1972) FIFRA § 4(a).

[129]See "Hearings Before the House Agricultural Committee, Federal Insecticide, Fungicide, and Rodenticide Act Amendments," H.R. 5203, Serial No. 97-R, (1982).

## 7.3 Federal Preemption and State Authority

During the past decade no FIFRA subject has inspired more litigation than the question of preemption. The cause, for the most part, has not been attempts by states to infringe upon federal prerogatives; rather, the issue has arisen in private tort suits by injured litigants seeking to sue pesticide manufacturers and applicators. [130]

First, though, the state efforts. There was some justification for the fears of pesticide manufacturers that the states would impose more stringent labeling requirements in spite of the FEPCA amendments. According to Section 24(b), states "shall not impose or continue in effect any requirements for labeling or packaging in addition to or different from those required under this subchapter." [131] California imposed additional data requirements under its restricted-use registration. In *National Agricultural Chemicals Association v. Rominger,*[132] a federal district court declined to issue a preliminary injunction against the state's regulations on the grounds that there was no congressional mandate to occupy the field when Section 24 was enacted, thus there was no federal preemption of restricted-use registrations.[133]

The U.S. Supreme Court attempted to clarify this muddle. In *Wisconsin Public Intervenor v. Mortier,*[134] the court considered a small town ordinance requiring 60 days notice and a permit for applying pesticides on public and some private lands. Warning signs were required 24 hours before spraying. A pesticide sprayer who was denied a permit sued, contended that the ordinance violated both federal and state laws regulating pesticides. The Wisconsin Supreme Court agreed.

However, the U.S. Supreme Court held unanimously that the local ordinance was not preempted by federal law. Since the local restrictions related to usage of a pesticide, not to FIFRA-regulated label claims, states were authorized by FIFRA to regulate certain aspects of pesticide use; these, said the Court, may be delegated to their political subdivisions, towns, and municipalities. Significantly, EPA and the Justice Department, which had traditionally opposed a multiplicity of local regulations on pesticides, in this case felt there was no infringement of FIFRA's federal preemption.

The second, more complicated issue has involved the preemption of private tort suits. In short, the question was whether state or local courts could rule that EPA-approved labels provided the public with inadequate warning of pesticide hazards. This is not a trivial matter. If a judge or jury could decide that a FIFRA label was somehow misleading or inadequate, they could in effect assume EPA's authority over pesticides.

---

[130]Ian M. Hughes, "Does FIFRA Label State Tort Claims for Inadequate Warning 'Preempted?'", 7 *Vill. Envtl. L.J.* 313 (1996); Celeste Marie Steen, "FIFRA's Preemption of Common Law Tort Actions Involving Genetically Engineered Pesticides", 38 *Ariz. L. Rev.* 763 (1996); Kyle W. Lathrop, "Environmental Law—FIFRA After 'Wisconsin Public Intervenor v. Mortier': What Next?", 17 *J.Corp. L.* 887 (1993).

[131]7 U.S.C. §136v(b).

[132]500 F. Supp 465, 15 ERC 1039 (E.D. Cal. 1980).

[133]The court also dismissed challenges to two other provisions of the California laws for lack of ripeness. These challenges were claims that the statute improperly allowed the state to set residue tolerances different from EPA tolerances and that certain labeling requirements for insecticides were improperly imposed.

[134]501 U.S. 597 , 111 S.Ct. 2476 (1991).

After all, states do not have the authority to order labels changes: why should they be allowed to do so indirectly by the threat of tort litigation?

In 1992 the Supreme Court had decided a seemingly-similar preemption case involving health warnings on cigarette packs, the famous *Cipollone v. Liggett Group* decision.[135] When the *Papas* case on FIFRA preemption reached the high court, the justices signaled that they wanted it to follow that model by unanimously remanding the case to the Eleventh Circuit to decide in light of *Cipollone*.[136]

Since then, a deluge of FIFRA cases have raised the same questions and, for the most part, have gotten more or less the same answers: namely that preemption does bar tort suits claiming possible inadequacy of EPA-approved pesticide labels, but it does not claims regarding product defects, faulty tests, or warranties. One wonders why so many judicial resources continue to be devoted to writing original opinions in these cases.[137] One also wonders why Congress did not resolve any uncertainties in its latest 1996 amendments to FIFRA.

## 8.0 LITIGATION ISSUES

Preemption, discussed elsewhere, is clearly the leading litigation issue. Prior to that, during the first decade or so of the new FIFRA, shifted from being concerned with product safety to focusing on data confidentiality and the financial compensation for its use by other companies.[138] That does not necessarily mean that safety is ignored, nor that all sides have reached consensus on what constitutes a health risk, but that the environmental safety issue is now contested more at the staff level within EPA's Pesticide Office than at the Administrator's level or in the courts. The pesticide industry has focused instead on allocating the tremendously expensive costs of developing and registering the few products that survive the testing process and can be marketed. But for that reason, the judicial doctrines set forth in EPA's first half dozen years remain the basis for pesticide regulation.

The extensive litigation about federal preemption has already been summarized in the section above.

---

[135]*Cipollone v. Liggett Group*, 505 U.S.504, 112 S.Ct. 2608 (1992).

[136]*Papas v. Zoecon Corporation*, _ U.S._, 112 S.Ct. 3020 (1992).

[137]Although every appellate court that has addressed the issue of inadequate labeling has held that FIFRA expressly preempts state law, there has nevertheless been a perceptible difference between the circuits in the degree to which they will extend the doctrine. The Tenth and Eleventh Circuits have been most protective of EPA's authority; the Fourth and Fifth have given more latitude to state law; and the others have come out somewhere in the middle. See, e.g., *Arkansas-Platte & Gulf Partnership v. Van Waters & Rogers, Inc.*, 981 F.2d 1177 (10th Cir. 1993); *Papas v. Upjohn Co.*, 985 F.2d 516 (11th Cir. 1993)(*Papas II*); *Lowe v. Sporicidin International*, 47 F.3d 124 (4th Circ. 1995); *Worm v. American Cyanamid Co.*, 5 F.3d 744 (4th Circ. 1993)(Worm II); *MacDonald v. Monsanto*, 27 F.3d 1021 (5th Cir. 1994); *King v. E.I.Dupont De Nemours & Co.*, 996 F.2d 1346 (1st Cir. 1993); *Shaw v. Dow Brands, Inc.*, 994 F.2d 364 (7th Cir. 1993); Bice v. Leslie's Poolmart, Inc., 39 F.3d 887 (8th Cir. 1994).

[138]See, e.g., Rosemary O'Leary, *Environmental Change: Federal Courts and the EPA* (Philadelphia: Temple University Press, 1994), p. 46 et seq.

**8.1 Basic Cases**

The early pesticides cases, originating in the period before EPA's creation, generally resulted in court determinations that the responsible federal agency had not sufficiently examined the health and environmental problems.

A leading case in this respect is the landmark 1970 court of appeals decision by Judge Bazelon in *Environmental Defense Fund v. Hardin*,[139] which not only gave legal standing to environmental groups under the FIFRA but also determined that the Secretary of Agriculture's failure to take prompt action on a request for suspension of the registration of DDT was tantamount to a denial of suspension and therefore was suitable for judicial review.[140]

That same year the Seventh Circuit Court of Appeals held *en banc* in *Nor-Am v. Hardin*[141] that a pesticide registrant could not enjoin a suspension order by the Secretary of Agriculture, since the administrative remedies, namely the full cancellation proceedings, had not been exhausted: "The emergency suspension becomes final only if unopposed or affirmed in whole or in part, by subsequent decisions based upon a full and formal consideration."[142]

An underlying reason for the court's action, which reversed a three-judge court of appeals panel in the same circuit,[143] was the realization that the suspension procedure, which had been designed to deal with imminent hazards to the public, could effectively be short-circuited by injunctions. In the court's view, therefore, a suspension decision is only equivalent to a temporary injunction which shall hold until the full cancellation proceedings are completed.[144]

One of the most important of the earlier cases was decided under the name *EDF v. Ruckelshaus*.[145] The court in another opinion by Judge Bazelon found that the Secretary of Agriculture failed to take prompt action on a request for the interim suspension of DDT registration but that the secretary's findings of fact, such as the risk of cancer and its toxic effect on certain animals, implicitly constituted a finding of "substantial question concerning the safety of DDT" which the court declared warranted a cancellation decision. The suspension issue was remanded once again for further consideration.

The decision is worthy of attention on two additional points. First, Judge Bazelon made the sweeping statement that "the FIFRA requires the secretary to issue notices and thereby initiate the administrative process whenever there is a substantial question about the safety of the registered pesticide, . . . The statutory scheme contemplates that these

---

[139]428 F. 2d 1083, 1 ERC 1347 (D.C. Cir., 1970).

[140]As there was no administrative record underlying the secretary's inaction, however, the court remanded the issue to the department of agriculture "to provide the court with a record necessary for meaningful appellate review."

[141]435 F. 2d 1151, 2 ERC 1016 (7th Cir., en banc, 1970).

[142]*Ibid.*, at 1157, 2 ERC at 1019.

[143]435 F. 2d 1133, 1 ERC 1460 (7th Cir., 1970).

[144]435 F. 2d at 1160-1161.

[145]*EDF v. Ruckelshaus*, 439 F.2d 584, 2 ERC 1114 (D.C. Cir., 1971). This was a sequel to the earlier *EDF v. Hardin* case, supra, but the name of the administrator of EPA was substituted for the secretary of agriculture since the authority of USDA had been transferred to the EPA the month before.

questions will be explored in the full light of a public hearing and not resolved behind the closed doors of the secretary."[146]

Second, the court approved the findings of the secretary that a hazard may be "imminent" even if its effect would not become realized for many years, as is the case with most carcinogens, and that the "public" protected by the suspension provision includes fish and wildlife in the environment as well as narrow threat to human health.

## 8.2 Labels in Theory and Practice

FIFRA is based on labeling. Yet EPA has realized for decades that most people pay little heed to label warnings or directions. As one prominent pesticide official admitted, "Labeling is almost worthless." The head of EPA's pesticide office, Daniel Barolo, voiced an even stronger view on the label issue: "We all agree that the label stinks."[147] Yet, the system is too engrained now to change easily.

One of the most interesting pesticide cases, *In re Stearns*,[148] raised the question of whether a chemical that was too toxic to be safely used around the home could be banned even though it was labeled properly with cautionary statements and symbols such as the skull and crossbones. "Stearn's Electric Paste", a phosphorous rat and roach killer, was so potent that even a small portion of a tube could kill a child and a larger dose would be fatal to an adult. There was no known antidote. An incomplete survey of state health officials indicated several dozen deaths and many serious accidents, most involving young children.

Because of this hazard and the existence of safer substitutes, the USDA canceled the registration of the paste in May 1969, before the creation of EPA, and a USDA Judicial Officer upheld this action in January 1971 by relying on the provision in the old FIFRA that "the term misbranded shall apply. . .to any economic poison. . .if the labeling accompanying it does not contain directions for use which are necessary and, if complied with, adequate for the protection of the public."[149]

A year and a half later, however, the Seventh Circuit Court of Appeals concluded that the statutory test for misbranding was whether a product was safe when used in conformity with the label directions, not whether abuse or misuse was inevitable. The court was impressed with the conspicuous "poison" markings and contended that "disregard of such a simple warning would constitute gross negligence."[150] The hazard of young children left the court unmoved: "such tragedies are a common occurrence in today's complex society and must be appraised as discompassionately as possible." The cancellation order was set aside. Frankly, this decision placed much too much emphasis on the label and not on the environmental safety of the product.

---

[146]*Ibid.*, at 594, 2 ERC at 1119. Because there may be a "substantial question of safety" about most pesticides, administrative necessity has forced EPA to interpret this as requiring cancellation of only the most harmful chemicals.

[147]*Pesticide and Toxic Chemical News*, 20 Nov. 1996, p. 11.

[148]2 ERC 1364 (Opinion of Judicial Officer, USDA, 1971); *Stearns Electric Paste Company v. EPA*, 461 F. 2d 293, 4 ERC 1164 (7th Cir., 1972).

[149]Old FIFRA § 2(z)2(c).

[150]*Stearns Electric Paste, supra.*, 461 F.2d at 310, 4 ERC at 1175.

The issue was confronted more decisively by the Eighth Circuit a year later in another Lindane case, *Southern National v. EPA*.[151] The registrants challenged a proposed EPA label reading in part, "Not for use or sale to drug stores, supermarkets, or hardware stores or other establishments that sell insecticides to consumers. Not for sale to or use in food handling, processing or serving establishments." In EPA's opinion, acceptance of such a label would avoid the necessity of canceling the entire registration. The court questioned whether EPA was within the scope of its powers under the (old) FIFRA in placing the burden on the manufacturer to discourage distribution to homes, but nevertheless sustained the agency action in all respects.

EPA's policy position, both then and now, is that if there are safer alternatives to a product which arguably constitutes a substantial question of safety, the hazardous product should be removed from the market.[152]

## 9.0 EXPORTS AND IMPORTS

Section 17 of FIFRA, in addition to maintaining the provision that imports should be subject to the same requirements of testing and registration as domestic products, also retained the controversial provision excluding U.S. exports from coverage under the act, other than for certain record keeping requirements.[153] The equating of manufacturing and imports is logical, since potential harm to the environment is not dependent on the origin of the pesticides. The exemption of exports is more controversial.

There were two reasons for this treatment of exports. First, the agricultural chemical producers, seeing the market for some of their products such as the chlorinated hydrocarbons drying up in this country, wished to continue exporting the products abroad. They argued that foreign producers would not be stopped from manufacturing these chemicals and they wished to continue to compete, as well as to keep in operation profitable product lines.

A secondary but more compelling reason was that cancellation decisions made in the United States are based upon a risk-benefit analysis that might have little relevance to conditions abroad. For example, DDT is neither needed nor, because of insect resistance, very useful for the control of malaria in the United States. However, the situation in, say, Ceylon, might be quite different and should thus be considered differently there.

One objection to this latter argument is that persistent pesticides may be distributed by oceans and the atmosphere in a world-wide circulation pattern that does not stop at national boundaries. A second problem is that there is no requirement that foreign purchasers relying on EPA registration as proof of a product's safety be notified of cancellation-suspension proceedings. Only after a final agency decision—which may take years—is the State Department legally required to inform foreign governments. The

---

[151]470 F. 2d 194, 4 ERC 1881 (8th Cir., 1972). This case was decided about a month after the enactment of the new FIFRA on October 21, 1972, but that law was not yet applied there. Presumably a different result would have ensued.

[152]See *In re King Paint*, 2 ERC 1819 (Opinion of EPA Judicial Officer, 1971).

[153]FIFRA § 8, 17(c), 7 U.S.C. § 1360(c). The old FIFRA provisions on exports is § 3(a)(5)(b); FIFRA § 8, 7 U.S.C. § 136 f.

1978 amendments did add a requirement that such exports be labeled that they are "not registered for use in the U.S."[154]

In 1980, EPA issued a final policy statement on labeling requirements.[155] Under the 1978 amendments, pesticides which are manufactured for export must have bilingual labeling which identifies the product and protects the persons who come into contact with it. If the pesticide is not registered for use in the United States, the exporter must obtain a statement from the foreign purchaser acknowledging its unregistered status.[156]

The policy statement implements these new requirements by requiring exported products to bear labels containing an EPA establishment number, a use classification statement, the identity of the producer, as well as information about whether the pesticide is registered for use in the United States. In the case of highly toxic pesticides, a skull and crossbones must appear and the word "poison" along with a statement of practical treatment written bilingually.[157]

The policy statement also requires that a foreign purchaser of an unregistered pesticide sign a statement showing that he understands that the pesticide is not registered for use in the United States. The exporter must receive the acknowledgment before the product is released for shipment and submit it to EPA within seven days of receipt. EPA then transmits the acknowledgments to the appropriate foreign officials via the State Department. The acknowledgment procedure applies only to the first annual shipment of an unregistered pesticide to a producer; subsequent shipments of the product to the same producer need not comply with the acknowledgment process.[158]

During the FIFRA amendment and farm bill debates in the early 1990s, there was considerable congressional suport for much stricter controls on the export of American pesticides which have been banned in the United States or have been rejected or never approved for registration. There are only two in the first category, the related pesticides termiticides heptachlor and chloradane; reportedly, there are around eight chemicals currently in the second category.

## 10.0 AMENDMENTS TO FIFRA

The changes in a law over time may not be exciting, but they do show those provisions which have become points of contention. They can also show, in theory, the political trends which can allow predictions as to the future course of the law.

### 10.1 Need for FIFRA Renewal

The authorization for FIFRA under the 1972 act was limited to three years.[159] Congress was therefore provided the opportunity in 1975 and periodically thereafter to review the strengths and shortcomings of the 1972 legislation, even though some portions of that law were not scheduled to go into effect until four years after

---

[154]FIFRA § 17(a)(2), 7 U.S.C. § 136o(e)(f). See also 44 *Fed. Reg.* 4358 (January 19, 1979).

[155]45 Fed. Reg. 50274 (July 28, 1980).

[156]Pub. L. No. 95-396, 92 Stat 833; codified at 7 U.S.C. § 136(o).

[157]45 Fed. Reg. at 50274, 50278 (July 28, 1980).

[158]*Ibid.*, at 50276-77.

[159]FIFRA § 27. Actually the term for the act was less than three years since the act finally went into effect in October 1972 and the authorization expired June 30, 1975.

enactment.[160] This review, however, also provided a chance to redress the balance for those, both within and without Congress, who believed that EPA had been given too much authority.[161]

Two decades of amendments to FIFRA have produced no coherent pattern of improvements to the basic statute. Unlike most other environmental statutes, there has been no clear progress towards greater protection (some amendments, in the 1970s, even went the other way). And those that were more protective, in theory, have not proved very effective.

### 10.2 Hogtie EPA: 1975 Amendments to FIFRA

Congress' 1975 amendments to the FIFRA were significant not for what they actually changed but because of the motivations that prompted them. The amendments themselves were viewed by many as, at best, unnecessary and, at worst, a further encumbrance upon an already complicated administrative procedure. They did, however, indicate a strong desire on the part of Congress—or at least the respective agriculture committees of the House and Senate—to restrict EPA's authority to regulate pesticides. The situation was summarized by an editorial in a Washington, D.C., newspaper captioned, "Trying to Hogtie the EPA."[162]

### 10.3 Data Compensation Changed: 1978 Amendments to FIFRA

The 1978 amendments made changes in a number of areas. Studies showing pesticide efficacy were made optional, relieving EPA of the chore of determining whether a pesticide actually worked for the purposes claimed. The data compensation provisions of the Act were made even more complex, although the EPA Administrator was removed from his role as arbitrator of the financial settlement.

### 10.4 Two-House Veto: 1980 Amendments to FIFRA

FIFRA was amended again in 1980, but the amendments made only minor changes in Section 25 of the act, to provide for a two-house congressional veto of EPA rules and regulations, and some additional tampering with the Scientific Advisory Committee.

### 10.5 FIFRA Lite: 1988 Amendments to FIFRA

FIFRA was amended again in 1988.[163] Dubbed "FIFRA lite", the amendments were notable mostly for what they did not contain; namely, they lacked the hotly-debated provisions sought by environmentalists for protection of the nation's groundwater supplies from contamination by pesticides. The bill also lacked the section sought by the grocery manufacturers to preempt stricter state standards like those under California's Proposition 65 right-to-know law. The legislation did correct a long-

---

[160]One such example is EPA's authority under § 27 to require that a pesticide be registered for use only by a certified applicator.

[161]House Report No. 94-497, "Extension and Amendment of the FIFRA, as Amended," September 19, 1975, for H.R. 8841, p. 5.

[162]*The Washington Star*, October 8, 1975.

[163]The 1988 amendments to FIFRA were signed into law by President Reagan on October 25, 1988.

standing flaw in the act involving compensation for canceled pesticides and streamlined the pesticide reregistration process, but imposed a substantial fee.

### 10.6 Bye-Bye Delaney:1996 Amendments to FIFRA
Prodded by the courts, Congress finally undertook the long-overdue revision of the Delaney Clause. Because of the immediacy and the importance of these amendments, they will be given a special discussion in Section 11, below.

### 11.0 FOOD QUALITY PROTECTION ACT OF 1996
The Delaney Clause was a well-intentioned 1958 amendment to the Food, Drug, and Cosmetic Act (FDCA) that barred any cancer-causing food additive. The problem was two-fold. First, pesticide residues were considered food additives. Second, the increasing sophistication in analytical chemical techniques meant that pesticides could be detected at lower and lower levels. EPA was faced with the prospect of having to ban many common pesticides, under the FDCA's complex residue-tolerance process (described below in Section 12.1), because trace amounts could now be detected in foods.[164]

### 11.1 The Regulatory Dilemma Under the Delaney Clause
EPA has tried to follow a reasonable approach. During the past two decades the agency has tried repeatedly to persuade Congress to correct the situation. Environmentalists opposed this attempt, not so much because they did not recognize the scientific problem but because they feared allowing a regulatory dike to be breached. In any case, EPA's effort failed because, one suspects, congressmen were reluctant to be seen as "soft on cancer."

In October 1988, EPA tried a new approach. It issued a new interpretation of the Delaney Clause with regulations permitting use of four pesticides which were known carcinogens—benomyl, mancozeb, phosmet and trifluralin—under circumstances which the agency concluded would pose only a *de minimis* risk of causing cancer.[165] However, a federal appellate court held in *Les v. Reilly*[166] that EPA had no discretion to permit use of food additives, including pesticides, if those additives are known to be carcinogenic, regardless of the degree of risk. The court declined to expunge the clause by judicial fiat, even if it might be obsolete. That determination was left to Congress. Nor could EPA do what the court could not. As the court explained, "once the finding of carcinogenicity is made, the EPA has no discretion."[167]

---

[164]A good discussion of the residue-tolerance procedure is found in Linda J. Fisher, et al., "A Practitioner's Guide to the FIFRA: Part III",24 *ELR* 10629 (Nov. 1994), Sec. XIII, p. 10646 et seq.

[165]53 Fed. Reg. 41110.

[166]968 F.2d 985 (9th Cir. 1992).

[167]*Ibid*, 988.

## 11.2 The Demise of Delaney

The *Les v. Reilly* case finally prodded Congress into doing what it had long hesitated to do—update the tolerance-residue in the FDCA[168]. According to FQPA rule Section 405, any pesticide residue on a food is considered unsafe unless the agency has set a tolerance for the substance and the residue is below that level. However, EPA is no longer bound to reject insignificant residues of pesticides just because they might be classified as carcinogens. Instead, the agency can grant a tolerance if the product is determined to be safe. As defined in the amendments, "safe" means that "there is a reasonable certainty that no harm will result from the aggregate exposure to the pesticide chemical residue", including both dietary and non-dietary total exposure.[169]

Despite the controversy over whether a distinction should be made, between residues in processed and in raw foods (called raw agricultural commodities, or RAC, in the act), in this section FQPA applied this rule of safety to both types of food.

Even if the Administrator does decide that a particular pesticide is not safe, he is allowed under FQPA to grant a tolerance, if the pesticide (a) provides public health benefits greater than the risk from the dietary residue, or (b) if it was "necessary to avoid a significant disruption in domestic production of an adquate, wholesome, and economical food supply.[170] This could be done if the yearly risk from exposure is no more than ten times the yearly risk which the Administrator had found to be safe.

## 11.3 Other Provisions of FQPA

The FQPA consisted of four other titles which made small changes in FIFRA. Under Title I that included allowing an emergency suspension for 90 days without a simultaneous notice of intent to cancel,[171] the establishment of a standing Science Review Board of 60 scientists that would assist the Science Advisory Panel for FIFRA[172] sets a goal of evaluating the data supporting pesticide registrations every 15 years,[173] and establishes two new categories of pesticide applicators for those handling routine lawn and maintenance work.[174]

Title II deals with special treatment for minor crop uses, which have historically gotten short shrift from both EPA and the leading pesticide companies.[175] This is a welcome addition, though we will have to see how it works in practice. The title also provides special arrangements for antimicrobial pesticide registrations, which are very different from general agricultural pesticides but have hitherto been treated little differently under the law.[176]

Title III establishes a data collection program to assure the safety of infants and children, whose consumption or vulnerability to pesticides might possibly require extra

---

[168]Title IV of the Food Quality Protection Act (FQPA)

[169]FQPA of 1996, § 405, amending FDCA § 408 as § 408(b)(2)(A)(ii).

[170]FQPA, § 405, for FDCA § 408(b)(2)(B).

[171]FQPA § 102.

[172]FQPA § 104.

[173]FQPA § 106.

[174]FQPA § 120.

[175]FQPA § 210.

[176]FQPA § 221 et seq.

measures. Some pesticide manufacturers have claimed that this could present a substantial, costly burden. Title V sets pesticide registration fees.

This legislation, despite its controversial abolishing of Delaney, received unprecedented, bipartisan support. It passed the House of Representatives unanimously. Yet, ironically, the belated complaints from some chemical companies about certain provisions, notably the data collection requirements, have reportedly been so acerbic that some believe the bill might not have passed if the complaints had been registered earlier.

## 12.0 PESTICIDE REGULATION UNDER OTHER FEDERAL STATUTES

Pesticides are not regulated solely under the FIFRA. They may also involve regulatory authority under the Food, Drug and Cosmetic Act (FDCA), under the statutes of several other federal agencies, and under other environmental laws administered by EPA.

### 12.1 Pesticides Under the Food, Drug & Cosmetics Act

One important function of EPA regarding pesticides is not derived from the FIFRA: the setting of tolerances for pesticide residues in food. This authority, originally granted to the Food and Drug Administration (FDA) under the Food, Drug and Cosmetic Act (FDCA),[177] was transferred to EPA by the 1970 Reorganization Plan establishing the agency and, more specifically, by subsequent detailed memos of agreement between EPA and FDA.

The reorganization plan provided that EPA should set tolerances and "monitor compliance", while the Secretary of HEW would continue to enforce compliance. The amendments to FIFRA in 1972 also invested EPA with authority to prevent misuse of registered pesticides. Under Section 408 of the FDCA, the Administrator issues regulations exempting any pesticides for which a tolerance is unnecessary to protect the public health. Otherwise, he "shall promulgate regulations establishing tolerances with respect to . . . pesticide chemicals which are not generally recognized among experts. . . as safe for use . . . to the extent necessary to protect the public health."

Pesticide residues are present in (mostly) negligible levels in most meats, fruits, and vegetables whether or not chemicals are applied to them. Using the most advanced analytical chemical techniques, DDT, for example, is still detectable in most foods, even in mothers' milk. As analytical methods continue to improve, detection of pesticides in anything can become universal.

Before registration of a pesticide, a residue tolerance must be set for the maximum level at which that chemical can be safely ingested. Tolerances are usually set at two orders of magnitude (one-hundredth) below the level at which the pesticide has demonstrated an effect on experimental animals.[178] Some particularly hazardous chemicals are set at "zero residue", but this is causing an increasing problem as the detection capability of analytical equipment is improved.

---

[177]FDCA § 408, 21 U.S.C. § 346a, *et seq.*

[178]This is an oversimplification. The tolerance margin depends on the particular effects of the chemical.

EPA's pesticide jurisdiction is supposed to cover only residues resulting from a chemical's use as a pesticide but not exposure resulting from, say, dust blowing from a factory (this may be covered by EPA's Clean Air Act) or a truck carrying the chemicals. In two major cases involving HCB (hexachlorobenzene) contamination of cattle in Louisiana and sheep in the Rocky Mountains, the HCB was blown from open trucks onto pasture land while being transported from one point to another. EPA assumed responsibility for these cases because the tolerance problems regarding health are really the same whether the chemical entered the food as a result of agricultural use or for some other reason, and FDA was only too glad to oblige.

The question of whether DDT was a food "additive" in fish within the meaning of the FDCA was raised again in *U.S. v. Ewing Bros.*[179] The Seventh Circuit explained that prior to the Delaney Amendment, which banned all additives "found to induce cancer when ingested by man or animal", the term did not cover substances present in the raw product and unchanged by processing. However, after 1958 the definition was expanded so a single tolerance could cover both raw and processed foods. Since DDT was an additive and EPA had not issued a tolerance, DDT was theoretically a food adulterant and contaminated items were liable to seizure.[180]

This could mean, however, that most foods could be seized as adulterated, including the Great Lakes fish at issue in *Ewing*. Realizing this in 1969, the FDA had established an interim action level of 5 ppm DDT in fish, thereby excluding all but the most contaminated samples.[181] This procedure was approved by the Seventh Circuit Court of Appeals in *U.S. v. Goodman*,[182] which held that the Commissioner of FDA had "specific statutory authority in the Act empowering him to refrain from prosecuting minor violations",[183] and that this permitted him to set and enforce action levels in lieu of totally prohibiting the distribution of any food containing DDT at any level.

Recently, the FDA has decided to expand the presumed scope of its authority under the Medical Devices Act of 1976 so as to include disinfectants as "medical devices." These pesticides, which have always been regulated as registered pesticides under FIFRA, have now been subjected to dual jurisdiction. In fact, EPA seems to be uncharacteristically disinterested in retaining authority over this field, even for biocides which have only the faintest connection to medical uses.

---

[179] 502 F.2d 715, 6 ERC 2073 (7th Cir., 1974).

[180] Under FDCA § 402(a)(2)(C), 21 U.S.C. § 342(a)(2)(C), this affects only a substance that "is not generally recognized among experts . . . as having been adequately shown . . . to be safe under the conditions of its intended use . . . ." This category is usually called GRAS, for generally recognized as safe. See FDCA § 201(s), 21 U.S.C. § 321(s). Without a tolerance, "the presence of the DDT causes fish to be adulterated without any proof that it is actually unfit as food." 6 ERC 2073, 2077.

[181] Action levels and enforcement, unlike tolerance setting, remain a prerogative of FDA under Section 306 of the FDCA, 21 U.S.C. § 336.

[182] 486 F.2d 847, 5 ERC 1969 (7th Cir., 1973).

[183] *Ibid.*, at 855, 5 ERC at 1974; FDCA §306, 21 U.S.C. §336, *U.S. v. 1500 Cases*, 245 F.2d 208, 210-11 (7th Cir., 1956); *U.S. v. 484 Bags*, 423 F.2d 839, 841 (5th Cir., 1970).

## 12.2 Clean Air Act of 1970 and Its Progeny

Pesticides in the air may be regulated under Section 112 of the Clean Air Act pertaining to hazardous air pollutants. A hazardous pollutant is defined as one for which "no ambient air quality standard is applicable and which in the judgment of the Administrator may cause, or contribute to, an increase in mortality or an increase in severe irreversible, or incapacitating reversible illness."[184] EPA publishes a list of hazardous air pollutants from time to time and, once a pollutant is listed, proposed regulations establishing stationary source emission standards must be issued unless the substance is conclusively shown to be safe. This section has so far not been applied to pesticides but could acquire more significance in the future.

## 12.3 Federal Water Pollution Control Act of 1972

The Federal Water Pollution Control Act as amended in 1972 has at least three provisions applicable to pesticides. Under Section 301, pesticide manufacturers and formulators, like all other industrial enterprises, must apply for discharge permits if they release effluent into any body of water. These point sources of pollution must apply the "best practicable control technology" by 1977 and by 1983 must use "the best available control technology."[185]

Hazardous and ubiquitous pesticides may be controlled under Section 307 governing "toxic substances."[186] Within one year of the listing of a chemical as a "toxic substance," the special discharge standards set for it must be achieved. There was originally some dispute whether pesticides should properly be regulated under this section because, unless they are part of a discharge from an industrial concern, they generally derive from non-point sources such as runoff from fields and therefore could be controlled under a third provision, Section 208, which is largely under the jurisdiction of the states.[187]

EPA's principal function under Section 208 is to identify and oversee problems of agricultural pollution, regulated at the state and local level. By 1977, according to the statute, state authorities were to have formulated control programs for the protection of water quality, pesticides and other agricultural pollutants such as feed-lots.

The reportedly serious problem of pesticide contamination of groundwater has been hotly debated. Legislation to address this issue was considered in the 1988 amendments to FIFRA but deferred to allow the passage of the other portions of that bill.

In January 1991, EPA issued regulations requiring operators of 80,000 drinking water systems to monitor for the presence of 60 contaminants, including a number of pesticides, and remove those in excess of permitted levels.

---

[184]Clean Air Act, § 112(a)(1), 42 U.S.C. § 1857c-7(a)(1) (1970).

[185]FWPCA § 301, 33 U.S.C. § 1311.

[186]FWPCA § 307, 33 U.S.C. § 1317. The criteria for this list is given in 38 *Fed. Reg.* 18044 (1973).

[187]EPA, however, has not followed this reasoning. The present § 307 list of 299 toxic pollutants contains many of the major pesticides. See *NRDC v. Train* (D.C. Cir., 1976) 8 ERC 2120.

## 12.4 Solid Waste Disposal Acts

The EPA had very limited authority under Section 204 of the Solid Waste Disposal Act (SWDA), as amended by the Resource Recovery Act of 1970,[188] to conduct research, training, demonstrations and other activities regarding pesticide storage and disposal.[189] Enactment of the Resource Conservation and Recovery Act (RCRA) in October 1976 gave EPA an important tool for controlling the disposal of pesticides, particularly the waste from pesticide manufacture.

## 12.5 Occupational Safety and Health Act

The EPA and the Department of Labor share somewhat overlapping authority under FIFRA and the Occupational Safety and Health Act (OSHA) for the protection of agricultural workers from pesticide hazards. This produced a heated inter-agency conflict during the first half of 1973, although the FIFRA and its legislative history clearly indicated that EPA had primary responsibility for promulgating re-entry and other protective standards in this area, and that OSHA specifically yielded to existing standards by other federal agencies.[190] The question was finally settled by the White House in EPA's favor after a court had enjoined Labor's own proposed standards.[191] Since then, the two agencies have cooperated on development of the federal cancer policy in the late 1970s, which grew out of EPA's suspension of the pesticides aldrin and dieldrin. In 1990, they concluded a memorandum of understanding (MOU) to facilitate joint enforcement of their laws.

## 12.6 Federal Hazardous Substances Act

The Federal Hazardous Substances Act of 1970 regulates hazardous substances in interstate commerce. However, pesticides subject to the FIFRA and the FDCA have been specifically exempted by regulation[192] from the definition of the term "hazardous substance." This statute is administered by the mostly-moribund Consumer Product Safety Commission (CPSC), which also administers the Poison Prevention Packaging Control Act of 1970, designed to protect children from pesticides and other harmful substances. It is not yet clear how EPA and the CPSC will divide their overlapping authority in this area.

## 12.7 Federal Pesticide Monitoring Programs

The FDA and USDA assist EPA in monitoring pesticide residues in food. The FDA conducts frequent spot checks and an annual Market Basket Survey in which pesticide residues are analyzed in a representative sampling of grocery items. The FDA's Poison Control Center also compiles current statistics on chemical poisoning. The USDA's Animal and Plant Health Inspection Service conducts spot checks on

---

[188]42 U.S.C. § 3251 *et seq.*, 79 Stat. 997 (1965), 84 Stat. 1227 (1970); RCRA § 204, 42 U.S.C. § 3253.

[189]RCRA § 212, 42 U.S.C. 3241. See also RCRA § 209, 42 U.S.C. § 3254c.

[190]OSHA § 6, 29 U.S.C. § 655.

[191]*Florida Peach Growers Assn. v. Dept. of Labor*, 489 F. 2d 120, (5th Cir., 1974).

[192]16 C.F.R. § 1500 3(b)(4)(ii).

pesticides in meats and poultry based on samples taken at slaughterhouses throughout the country.

The Department of Interior samples pesticide residues in fish and performs experiments to determine the effects of pesticides which may be introduced into the aquatic environment. The Geological Survey Division of Interior also conducts periodic nationwide water sampling for pesticides and other contaminants. The National Oceanic Atmospheric Administration (NOAA) under the Department of Commerce monitors aquatic areas for pesticide levels, and the Department of Transportation's Office of Hazardous Substances records accidents involving pesticides in shipment and distribution.

Several of the FIFRA amendments considered in the early 1990s have been directed toward remedying perceived shortcomings in the pesticide residue system. (See "Legislative Developments" section at end of this chapter.) Unless there is some new evidence of a real need for such legislative protection, this seems to be a solution looking for a problem.

### 12.8 National Environmental Policy Act

The EPA is also not bound by the National Environmental Policy Act (NEPA) to file environmental impact statements on its pesticide decisions. The procedures under the FIFRA are an adequate substitute. Although the strict language of NEPA states that *all* agencies of the federal government should file impact statements, this law was enacted before EPA existed. The courts almost unanimously have found that there is little logic in requiring an agency whose sole function is protection of environment to file a statement obliging it to take into consideration environmental factors.[193] Courts nevertheless hesitated to grant a blanket exemption to EPA, preferring to stress that EPA actions are mandated by a given statute, although this justification has not exempted certain non-environmental agencies; or they have noted that Environmental Protection Agency procedures for articulating its position and providing for public comment were an adequate substitute for the same procedures under NEPA.[194]

### 13.0 BIOTECHNOLOGY

The field of biotechnology promises great advances in human well being, such as the creation of industrial enzymes which would be capable of, among other things, purifying water and degrading toxic chemical wastes. However, because genetic engineering is so new, still being developed, and little understood, it has been surrounded by controversy over both its safeness and who should regulate it.

On June 18, 1986, President Reagan signed the Coordinated Framework for Regulation of Biotechnology, which sets out specific agency roles and statutory authority and ensures the industry's environmental safety and economic viability. Legislation has also been proposed in Congress to set up a regulatory structure for reviewing the safety of genetically engineered products under TSCA.

---

[193]For example, *Essex Chemical Corp. v. Ruckelshaus*, 486 F.2d 427, 5 ERC 1820 (D.C. Cir., 1973), *Portland Cement Assn. v. Ruckelshaus*, 486 F.2d at 375, 5 ERC 1593 (D.C. Cir., 1973).

[194]*EDF v. EPA*, 489 F.2d at 1257, 6 ERC at 1119.

There are some who are dissatisfied that the efforts have not regulated the biotechnology industry enough. Jeremy Rifkin, who heads the environmental group called Foundation for Economic Trends, is one of the most determined opponents. In fact, he believes that biotechnology should be banned altogether. Most of his attention has focused on biotechnology developments and efforts in the pesticides field.

For example, on September 2, 1986, Rifkin filed suit in the U.S. District Court for the District of Columbia against the Department of Defense (DOD) to enjoin the U.S. military from testing, developing and producing toxic biological warfare materials until the military prepares environmental impact statements. The foundation first sued DOD in November 1984 to prohibit the military from building a proposed biological warfare testing facility in Utah. An injunction was granted in May 1985 and is still in effect.

A landmark case decided in 1980, which Rifkin lost and which should be mentioned here, is *Diamond v. Chakrobatry*[195] in which the Supreme Court ruled in June 1980 that genetically altered organisms may be patented. Now when individuals and firms put time and money into biotechnology research they can be assured of earning economic rewards. Rifkin's foundation has filed a "friend of the court" brief supporting the U.S. Attorney General's office in its contention that the federal patent laws should not cover such organisms.

In May 1986, EPA authorized the first permits for the release of a genetically engineered pesticide to a professor from the University of California at Berkeley. The genetically altered bacteria strain, known as "ice-minus" or "Frostban," was developed by the university and licensed by Advanced Genetic Sciences Inc. (AGS).[196]

The court held that this standard required the Administrator to examine five factors: (1) the seriousness of the threatened harm; (2) the immediacy of the threatened harm; (3) the probability that the threatened harm would result; (4) the benefits to the public of the continued use of the pesticides in question during the suspension process; and (5) the nature and extent of the information before the Administrator at the time he makes his decision. The court also held that an emergency suspension order may be overturned only if it was arbitrary, capricious, or an abuse of discretion or if it was not "issued in accordance with the procedures established by law."[197]

In August 1990 a blue-ribbon panel under the direction of then Vice President Dan Quayle concluded that biotech products should be treated no differently from those produced by conventional chemical methods. These risk-based principles, for use by EPA, USDA, FDA, and others, were not much different from those currently in use for FIFRA. In other words, only the end-product is relevant; how it was produced, whether by biochemists or by bacteria, should be irrelevant.

---

[195]100 S.Ct. 2204, 447 U.S. 303.

[196]*Ibid.* at 902, 13 ERC at 1135.

[197]*Ibid.* The court stated that it arrived at its decision to uphold EPA's order "with great reluctance" and would not have ordered the emergency suspension on the basis of the information before EPA, but was not empowered to substitute its judgment for that of EPA's. 469 F. Supp. at 907, 13 ERC at 1140.

The principles are as follows:

1. Federal government regulatory oversight should focus on the characteristics and risks of the biotechnology product not the process by which it is created.

2. For biotechnology products that require review, regulatory review should be designed to minimize regulatory burden while assuring protection of public health and welfare.

3. Regulatory programs should be designed to accommodate the rapid advances in biotechnology. Performance-based standards are, therefore, generally preferred over design standards.

4. In order to create opportunities for the application of innovative new biotechnology products, all regulations in environmental and health areas, whether or not they address biotechnology, should use performance standards rather than specifying rigid controls or specific designs for compliance.[198]

---

[198]*BNA Chemical Reporter*, 17 August 1990, 788

# CHAPTER 9

# RESOURCE CONSERVATION AND RECOVERY ACT

David R. Case
Environmental Technology Council
Washington, D.C.

## 1.0 OVERVIEW

The United States has the most innovative and protective regulatory program for the management of hazardous waste of any country in the world. Since 1980, the adage "out of sight, out of mind" has given way to a comprehensive national program that seeks to encourage source reduction, high-technology treatment, and secure long-term disposal of hazardous wastes. Congress has enacted as national policy the mandate that hazardous wastes will be treated, stored, and disposed of so as to minimize the present and future threat to human health and the environment.[1] EPA and the states have sought to implement this mandate in regulations issued under the Resource Conservation and Recovery Act of 1976 (RCRA), as significantly amended by the Hazardous and Solid Waste Amendments of 1984.[2] Many companies and individuals in the United States who generate over 275 million tons of hazardous waste each year must comply with the RCRA regulatory program.[3]

RCRA is designed to provide "cradle-to-grave" controls by imposing management requirements on generators and transporters of hazardous wastes and upon the owners and operators of treatment, storage and disposal (TSD) facilities. RCRA applies mainly to active facilities that generate and manage hazardous wastes. Congress imposed liabilities and mandated remedies to correct problems at abandoned and inactive sites in the Comprehensive Environmental Response, Compensation, and Liability Act of 1980, commonly known as Superfund,[4] which is discussed in detail in another chapter.

RCRA has been amended several times since its enactment, most importantly by the Hazardous and Solid Waste Amendments of 1984 (HSWA). The 1984 HSWA mandated far-reaching changes to the RCRA program, such as waste minimization and a national land disposal ban program, discussed below. RCRA is currently divided into ten subtitles, A through J. The most significant of these is Subtitle C, which establishes the national hazardous waste management program. Subtitle C, which encompasses

---

[1]Resource Conservation and Recovery Act, 42 U.S.C. §§ 6901 et seq. (1988) (also known as the Solid Waste Disposal Act). Citations throughout this chapter are to sections of the Act, rather than to the U.S. Code. See national policy in § 1003(b).

[2]Pub. L. No. 94-550, 90 Stat. 2796 (1976), as amended, Pub. L. No. 96-482, 94 Stat. 2334 (1980); Hazardous and Solid Waste Amendments of 1984, Pub. L. No. 98-616, 98 Stat. 3221.

[3]U.S. EPA, The Biennial RCRA Hazardous Waste Report (Based on 1994 Data).

[4]42 U.S.C. §§ 9601 et seq.

Sections 3001-3023, establishes the following basic structure for the RCRA program. (See Table 9.1.) Section 3001 requires EPA to promulgate regulations identifying hazardous wastes, either by listing specific hazardous wastes or establishing characteristics of hazardous wastes. Persons managing such wastes are required to notify the U.S. Environmental Protection Agency of their hazardous waste activities.[5]

Persons who generate or produce these wastes (generators) must comply with a set of standards authorized by RCRA Section 3002. These include handling wastes properly and preparing manifests to track the shipment of the waste to treatment, recycling or disposal facilities. Persons who transport hazardous waste (transporters) are required by Section 3003 to comply with another set of regulations dealing with manifests, labeling and the delivery of hazardous waste shipments to designated TSD facilities. Transporters must also comply with the U.S. Department of Transportation (DOT) requirements relating to containers, labeling, placarding of vehicles, and spill response.

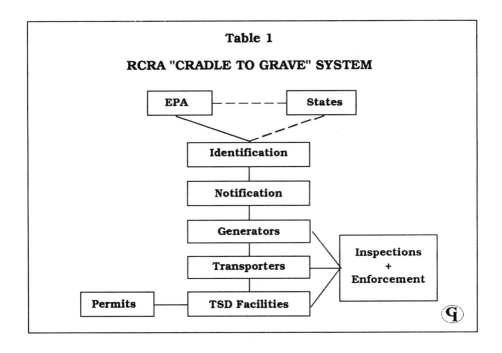

**Table 1**

**RCRA "CRADLE TO GRAVE" SYSTEM**

---

[5]Section 3010(a).

Section 3004 requires TSD facilities to comply with performance standards, including statutory minimum technology requirements, groundwater monitoring, air emission controls, corrective actions, and a prohibition on the land disposal of untreated hazardous wastes. Section 3005 requires owners and operators of TSD facilities to obtain permits which set the conditions under which they may operate. Section 3005(e) establishes the "interim status" provision for existing TSD facilities which allows them to remain in operation until a site-specific permit is issued. Owners and operators of interim status TSD facilities must file a timely application for a RCRA permit under Section 3005(a) in order to qualify, and comply with interim status standards in the regulations.

Section 3006 of RCRA authorizes states to assume responsibility for carrying out the RCRA program, in lieu of the federal program. The state must administer and enforce a program which is consistent with and equivalent to the federal program. States can adopt more stringent requirements, but the state program may be no less stringent than the federal program. Sections 3007 and 3008 authorize site inspections and federal enforcement of RCRA and its implementing regulations.

Other sections of Subtitle C include provisions for compiling a state-by-state hazardous waste site inventory; monitoring and enforcement authority against previous owners of TSD facilities; EPA regulation of recycled oil; controls on the export of hazardous waste; Department of Energy planning for development of treatment technologies and capacity for mixed (hazardous and radioactive) wastes; and provisions for Federally-owned treatment works.[6]

The amendments made by the 1984 HSWA are extensive. They significantly expanded both the scope of coverage and the detailed requirements of RCRA. For example, they required EPA to more fully regulate an estimated 200,000 companies that produce only small quantities of hazardous waste (less than 1,000 kilograms per month). An entirely new regulatory program was created in Subtitle I ("eye") for underground storage tanks containing hazardous substances or petroleum, which affected hundreds of thousands of facilities for the first time.[7] The numerous constraints imposed on those who treat, store or dispose of hazardous wastes in land-based facilities, including restrictions on the disposal of liquid wastes and other common hazardous wastes in landfills, have dramatically changed the way that such wastes are managed in this country.

The 1984 HSWA contain many so-called "hammer provisions" that required EPA to implement new requirements by a deadline or a statutory standard went into effect automatically. For example, if EPA did not promulgate the land disposal restriction for all RCRA hazardous wastes by the statutory deadline of May 1990, the "hammer" would have fallen and the unrestricted wastes would have been prohibited from land disposal by operation of statute. There were 72 major provisions in the 1984 HSWA, by EPA's count, and these new requirements are having a substantial impact on every U.S. business that produces hazardous waste.

---

[6]Sections 3012, 3013, 3014, 3017, 3021, 3022. The latter two provisions were added by the Federal Facility Compliance Act of 1992, Pub. L. No. 102-386, 106 Stat. 1505.

[7]Sections 9001-9010. The underground storage tank program is discussed in a separate chapter.

These major provisions of the Subtitle C program and the impact of the 1984 amendments are discussed in detail below, as are the requirements of other important subtitles of RCRA.

## 2.0 POLICY GOALS AND OBJECTIVES OF RCRA

Subtitle A of RCRA declares that, as a matter of national policy, the generation of hazardous waste is to be reduced or eliminated as expeditiously as possible, and land disposal should be the least favored method for managing hazardous wastes. In addition, all waste that is generated must be handled so as to minimize the present and future threat to human health and the environment.[8]

Subtitle A also includes a series of objectives designed to achieve these goals, including proper management of hazardous waste in the first instance, minimizing the generation and land disposal of hazardous waste, a prohibition on open dumping, state assumption of RCRA programs, promoting research and development activities for waste management, and encouraging recovery, recycling, and treatment as alternatives to land disposal.[9] These national goals and objectives set by RCRA give direction to EPA's regulatory efforts.

## 3.0 DEFINITION OF SOLID AND HAZARDOUS WASTE

The starting point for determining the full scope of RCRA's coverage is the broad definition of "solid waste" in the statute. Section 1004(27) states that:

> The term "solid waste" means *any garbage, refuse, sludge* from a waste treatment plant, water supply treatment plant or air pollution control facility *and other discarded material, including solid, liquid, semisolid, or contained gaseous materials* resulting from industrial, commercial, mining and agriculture activities and from community activities but does not include solid or dissolved material in domestic sewage, or solid or dissolved materials in irrigation return flows or industrial discharges which are point sources subject to permits under section 402 of the Federal Water Pollution Control Act, as amended, or source, special nuclear, or byproduct material as defined by the Atomic Energy Act of 1954, as amended (68 Stat. 923). (Emphasis supplied.)

The statute therefore applies to potentially any waste regardless of its physical form. EPA has further defined "solid waste" by regulation, as discussed below.

The Subtitle C regulatory program of RCRA then covers those solid wastes that are deemed hazardous. As defined in Section 1004(5), the term "hazardous waste" means a solid waste, or combination of solid wastes, which because of its quantity, concentration, or physical, chemical, or infectious characteristics may:

A.  Cause, or significantly contribute to an increase in mortality or an increase in serious irreversible, or incapacitating reversible illness; or

---

[8]RCRA, Sections 1003(b), 1002(b).
[9]RCRA, Section 1003(a).

B.  Pose a substantial present or potential hazard to human health or the environ-ment when improperly treated, stored, transported, or disposed of, or otherwise managed.

These general statutory definitions have been greatly amplified and explained by EPA regulations implementing RCRA, beginning with the framework rule issued on May 19, 1980.[10] These regulations are discussed in the following section which describes the RCRA Subtitle C program in detail.

## 4.0 SUBTITLE C: HAZARDOUS WASTE MANAGEMENT PROGRAM

### 4.1 Identification of Hazardous Wastes[11]

EPA has defined solid waste to include any discarded material, provided a regulatory exclusion or specific variance granted by EPA or an authorized state does not apply.[12] The exclusions from the definition of "solid waste" include:

1.  Any mixture of domestic sewage and other wastes that passes through a sewer system to a publicly-owned treatment works;
2.  Industrial wastewater discharges that are point source discharges under the Clean Water Act;
3.  Irrigation return flows; and
4.  Source, special nuclear or byproduct material under the Atomic Energy Act.

"Discarded material" is in turn defined as any material that is abandoned, recycled, or "inherently waste-like."[13] A material is abandoned if it is disposed of, burned or incinerated, or accumulated, stored or treated prior to or in lieu of abandonment. A material is inherently waste-like if EPA so defines it by regulation.[14]

A material can be a solid waste if it is recycled in a manner constituting disposal, by burning for energy recovery, by reclamation, or by speculative accumulation. Materials that are not solid wastes when recycled are materials that are directly used or reused as ingredients or feedstocks in production processes, or as effective substitutes for commercial products, or that are recycled in a closed-loop production process.[15]

These interlocking definitions result in EPA regulating a universe of materials that may not commonly be understood to be "wastes" for a particular industry or company. In particular, materials that will be reclaimed or recycled, rather than disposed of, may still be considered solid wastes and therefore hazardous wastes subject to RCRA regulation.

---

[10]45 Fed. Reg 33066.

[11]For a more comprehensive description of the regulatory provisions of RCRA, the reader is referred to Hall, et al., *RCRA/Hazardous Wastes Handbook* (Government Institutes).

[12]40 C.F.R. § 261.2(a). See 50 Fed. Reg 664 (January 4, 1985). The list of regulatory exemptions appears at § 261.4(a) and is very limited.

[13]40 C.F.R. § 261.2(a)(2).

[14]40 C.F.R. § 261.2(d). EPA has designated dioxin wastes as inherently waste-like.

[15]The courts have construed the definition of solid waste to exclude certain in-process recycled secondary materials that are part of a continuous production or manufacturing process. See *American Mining Congress* v. EPA, 824 F.2d 1177 (D.C. Cir. 1987).

Once a material is found to be a solid waste, the next question is whether it is a "hazardous waste." EPA's regulations automatically exempt certain solid wastes from being considered hazardous wastes. Generally these regulatory exemptions include:

1.  Household waste;[16]
2.  Agricultural wastes which are returned to the ground as fertilizer;
3.  Mining overburden returned to the mine site;
4.  Utility wastes from coal combustion;
5.  Oil and natural gas exploration drilling waste;
6.  Wastes from the extraction, beneficiation, and processing of ores and minerals, including coal;
7.  Cement kiln dust wastes;
8.  Arsenical-treated wood wastes generated by end users of such wood;
9.  Certain chromium-bearing wastes; and
10. Petroleum-contaminated media and debris that fail the test for the toxicity characteristic and that are subject to corrective action requirements.[17]

EPA has also provided some limited regulatory exemptions under narrowly defined circumstances, such as for hazardous waste that is generated in a product or raw material storage tank, transport vehicle, pipeline or manufacturing process unit prior to removal for disposal. EPA has also adopted a conditional exemption for waste samples collected for testing to determine their characteristics or composition, or to conduct treatability tests.[18]

Finally, EPA has exempted certain "universal wastes" from the Subtitle C program and has promulgated special standards for these wastes, discussed below.[19] Currently, nickel cadmium batteries, certain recalled pesticides, and mercury thermostats are eligible for these special standards.

If a solid waste does not qualify for an exemption, it will be deemed a hazardous waste if it is listed by EPA in 40 C.F.R. Part 261, Subpart D, or if it exhibits any of the four hazardous waste characteristics identified in 40 C.F.R. Part 261, Subpart C.

### 4.1.1 Hazardous Waste Lists

EPA has established three hazardous wastes lists. A hazardous waste number is assigned to each listed waste which can be used to identify the waste on biennial reports and other documents, and for purposes of the land disposal ban program. The first list contains hazardous wastes from nonspecific sources (e.g., spent nonhalogenated solvents, such as toluene or methyl ethyl ketone).[20] The hazardous wastes on this nonspecific source list are assigned an "F" number (e.g. F001 is assigned to various spent solvents).

---

[16]In *City of Chicago v. Environmental Defense Fund*, 114 S. Ct. 1588 (1994), the Supreme Court held that ash from a municipal waste incinerator, which exhibited the toxicity characteristic, was not exempt under Subtitle C.

[17]40 C.F.R. § 261.4(b).

[18]40 C.F.R. § 261.4(c)-(f).

[19]40 C.F.R. Part 273.

[20]40 C.F.R. § 261.31.

The second list identifies hazardous wastes from specific sources (e.g., bottom sediment sludge from the treatment of wastewaters by the wood preserving industry).[21] The hazardous wastes on the specific source list have a "K" number (e.g., K048 - K052 are certain petroleum refining wastes). The first two hazardous waste lists are largely self-explanatory. A company need only compare its solid waste stream to those lists to determine if it manages a hazardous waste.

EPA has continued to expand the F and K lists by promulgating listing determinations for additional hazardous wastes from specific industries; e.g. K156 - K161 wastes from production of carbamates.[22]

The third list sets forth commercial chemical products, including off-specification species, containers, and spill residues, which, when discarded, must be treated as hazardous wastes.[23] This hazardous waste list actually consists of two distinct sublists. One sublist sets forth chemicals deemed acutely hazardous when discarded (40 C.F.R. 261.33(e)). These have a "P" number and are subject to more rigorous management requirements (e.g. P076 is nitric oxide). A second sublist contains "U" listed chemicals which are deemed toxic and, therefore, hazardous when discarded (40 C.F.R. 261.33(f)), and which are regulated like other listed hazardous wastes (e.g., U002 is acetone).

Hazardous waste regulation under the commercial chemical list can be triggered when a company decides to reduce inventory or otherwise discards a listed commercial chemical product in its pure form. Another situation that may trigger regulation is an accidental spill of the chemical.[24] If a listed commercial chemical is spilled, the spilled chemical and any contaminated material, i.e., dirt and other residue, are likely to be discarded and thus become a hazardous waste. Therefore, even companies that generally do not discard or intend to discard any of the commercial chemical products on the list must be prepared to comply with the RCRA hazardous waste regulations in the event of an accidental spill.[25] This may involve, as discussed below, obtaining an EPA identification number and complying, at a minimum, with applicable generator standards. For disposal of small amounts of chemicals or spill materials, the company may qualify as a conditionally exempt "small quantity generator."[26]

Since the RCRA program became effective in 1980, many companies have filed "delisting petitions" with EPA to remove wastes generated at their facilities from the RCRA hazardous waste lists at 40 C.F.R. Part 261. The granting of a delisting petition exempts the waste generated at a particular facility from the RCRA hazardous waste program. A company seeking a delisting must demonstrate that its particular waste does not contain the hazardous constituents for which EPA listed the waste, or any other constituents that could cause the waste to be hazardous.[27]

---

[21] 40 C.F.R. § 261.32.

[22] 60 Fed. Reg. 7824 (1995). A number of the carbamate waste listings were vacated by the court, however, in *Dithiocarbamate Task Force v. EPA*, 98 F.3d 1394 (D.C. Cir. 1996).

[23] 40 C.F.R. § 261.33.

[24] 40 C.F.R. § 261.33(d).

[25] See 45 Fed. Reg. 76629 (November 19, 1980).

[26] 40 C.F.R. § 261.5. Alternatively, a small spill may qualify as a *de minimis* loss exempt from the definition of hazardous waste in § 261.3(a)(2)(iv)(D).

[27] 40 C.F.R. § 260.22.

For example, a company seeking to delist a waste which would otherwise be included under F006 (wastewater treatment sludge from electroplating operations) must show that the concentrations of chromium, nickel, and cyanide for which the waste was listed are below levels of regulatory concern, and also that no other heavy metals or other constituents are present that may cause the waste to be hazardous. EPA or an authorized state must act on a delisting petition within two years of receiving a complete petition.

### 4.1.2 Hazardous Waste Characteristics

If a waste is not listed as hazardous, the waste is still covered by RCRA if it exhibits one of four characteristics: ignitability, corrosivity, reactivity, or toxicity.[28]

The hazardous waste characteristic of ignitability was established to identify solid wastes capable during routine handling of causing a fire or exacerbating a fire once started.[29] A solid waste is deemed to exhibit the characteristic of ignitability if it satisfies one of the following four descriptions. First, if it is a liquid, other than an aqueous solution containing less than 24 percent alcohol by volume, that has a flash point of less than 140 degrees Fahrenheit (60°C). Second, if it is a nonliquid that under normal conditions can cause a fire through friction, absorption of moisture, or spontaneous chemical changes, and burns so vigorously when ignited that it creates a hazard. Third, if it is an ignitable compressed gas as defined by the DOT regulations at 49 C.F.R. 173.300. Finally, a waste exhibits ignitability if it is an oxidizer as defined by the DOT regulations at 49 C.F.R. 173.151. An ignitable hazardous waste has the EPA number of D001.

The hazardous waste characteristic of corrosivity was established because EPA believed that wastes capable of corroding metal could escape their containers and liberate other wastes.[30] In addition, wastes with a pH at either the high or low end of the scale can harm human tissue and aquatic life and may react dangerously with other wastes. Therefore, EPA determined that any solid waste is deemed to exhibit the characteristic of corrosivity if it is (1) aqueous and has a pH of less than or equal to 2.0 or greater than or equal to 12.5, or (2) a liquid and corrodes steel at a rate greater than 6.35 millimeters (.250 inches) per year under specified testing procedures. A waste that exhibits the hazardous characteristic of corrosivity has the EPA number of D002.

EPA established the characteristic of reactivity to regulate wastes that are extremely unstable and have a tendency to react violently or explode during management.[31] The regulation lists a number of situations where this may happen which warrant specific consideration (e.g., when the waste is mixed with water, when heated, etc.). Since test protocols for measuring reactivity are largely unavailable, EPA has promulgated a narrative definition of the reactivity characteristic that must be used. A waste that exhibits reactivity has EPA number D003.

The toxicity characteristic is designed to identify wastes that are likely to leach hazardous concentrations of specific toxic constituents into groundwater under

---

[28]40 C.F.R. § 261.3, § 261.20.
[29]40 C.F.R. § 261.21.
[30]41 C.F.R. § 261.22.
[31]41 C.F.R. § 261.23.

mismanagement conditions.[32] This characteristic is determined based on a mandatory testing procedure which extracts the toxic constituents from a waste in a manner that EPA believes simulates the leaching action which occurs in landfills.[33] A solid waste exhibits the characteristic of toxicity if, using the test methods prescribed by EPA, the extract from a representative sample of the waste contains contaminants at levels of regulatory concern. The test method is called the Toxicity Characteristic Leaching Procedure, or TCLP. It replaces the Extraction Procedure (EP) Toxicity Characteristic that was initially promulgated by EPA in 1980. The TCLP tests for 25 organic chemicals, 8 inorganics, and 6 insecticides/herbicides. The levels that trigger the toxicity characteristic reflect health-based concentration thresholds and a factor for dilution and attenuation that was developed using modeling of the subsurface fate and transport of contaminants in groundwater. These hazardous wastes are given EPA numbers D004-D043, depending on the toxic constituent that causes the waste to be hazardous.

### 4.1.3 Mixtures of Hazardous Wastes and Solid Wastes

Anyone concerned with hazardous waste management must be aware of the "mixture rule."[34] Under this EPA rule, a mixture of a listed hazardous waste and a solid waste must also be considered a hazardous waste, unless the mixture qualifies for an exemption.[35] The exemptions apply if, for example, (1) the listed hazardous waste in the mixture was listed solely because it exhibits a hazardous characteristic and the mixture does not exhibit that characteristic; or (2) the mixture consists of wastewater and certain specified hazardous wastes in dilute concentrations, the discharge of which is subject to regulation under the Clean Water Act; or (3) the mixture consists of a discarded commercial chemical product resulting from *de minimis* losses during manufacturing operations. On the other hand, a mixture of a characteristic hazardous waste and a solid waste will be deemed hazardous only if the entire mixture continues to exhibit a hazardous characteristic. Note that these exemptions apply only when the hazardous waste becomes mixed with other wastes as part of the normal production or waste management process, not when wastes are intentionally mixed to achieve dilution. Such mixing may constitute treatment and could require a RCRA permit.

---

[32]40 C.F.R. § 261.24, as amended, 55 Fed. Reg. 11862 (March 29, 1990).

[33]40 C.F.R. Part 261, Appendix II.

[34]EPA's 1980 mixture rule and derived-from rule (discussed below) were vacated by the U.S. Court of Appeals in *Shell Oil Co. v. EPA*, 950 F.2d 741 (D.C. Cir. 1991). The court held that EPA did not provide adequate notice and opportunity for comment when promulgating these rules in 1980. At the court's suggestion, however, EPA then re-promulgated the mixture and derived-from rules on an interim basis. 57 Fed. Reg. 7628 (March 3, 1992). Congress then directed EPA to promulgate revisions to these rules, if necessary, by October 1, 1994. Pub. L. No. 102-389. Having missed this deadline, EPA's efforts to revise the rules are ongoing pursuant to a court-approved consent decree. *Environmental Technology Council v. Browner*, No. 94-2119 (D.D.C. filed 1994).

[35]40 C.F.R. § 261.3(a)(2).

### 4.1.4 Derived-From Hazardous Wastes

Of equal importance is EPA's so-called "derived-from rule." Under this rule, a waste that is generated from the treatment, storage, or disposal of a hazardous waste (e.g. ash, leachate, or emission control dust) is also a hazardous waste, unless exempted.[36] If the waste is derived from a listed hazardous waste, it is considered a hazardous waste until delisting procedures are followed. If the waste is derived from a characteristic hazardous waste, it is not hazardous if it does not exhibit that characteristic. Materials that are reclaimed from solid wastes for beneficial use are no longer wastes, unless the reclaimed material is burned as a fuel or used in a manner constituting disposal (i.e., applied to the ground).

### 4.1.5 Hazardous Wastes Contained-In Environmental Media and Debris

Another relevant principle is embodied in the "contained-in principle." EPA has long taken the view that soil, groundwater, surface water, and debris that is contaminated with listed hazardous waste must be regulated under RCRA Subtitle C.[37] The contaminated media and debris are said to contain the listed hazardous waste, and thus to require proper management. EPA has now codified this rule, along with the corollary that debris which is treated so that it no longer contains a listed hazardous waste will no longer be subject to Subtitle C regulation.[38]

### 4.1.6 Used, Reused, Recycled or Reclaimed Hazardous Wastes

EPA has defined the term "solid waste" to extend coverage to many recycling and reclamation activities.[39] This aspect of the solid waste definition is complex. Conceptually, it requires consideration of two things—the manner of recycling, and the secondary material being recycled.

The recycling activities that are regulated are (1) use in a manner constituting disposal (e.g. land application), (2) burning for energy recovery, (3) reclamation, and (4) speculative accumulation. Secondary materials that are solid wastes when recycled include spent materials, listed and characteristic sludges, listed and characteristic by-products, commercial chemical products, and scrap metal. These materials are all solid wastes when recycled, with two exceptions. Sludges and by-products that are hazardous only by characteristic are not solid wastes when they are reclaimed. Commercial chemical products are not solid wastes when they are either reclaimed or speculatively accumulated.[40]

---

[36] 40 C.F.R. § 261.3(b).

[37] EPA's position that the contained-in policy was an interpretive gloss on the mixture and derived-from rules was upheld by the court. *Chemical Manufacturers Ass'n v. EPA*, 869 F.2d 1526 (D.C. Cir. 1989).

[38] 40 C.F.R. § 261.3(f), 57 Fed. Reg. 37194 (August 18, 1992).

[39] 40 C.F.R. § 261.2(c).

[40] *Id.* The definition of "sludge" is in § 260.10 and the definitions of "by-product," "scrap metal," "recycled," "reclaimed," and "accumulated speculatively" are found in § 261.1(c). These definitions are critically important to understanding the scope of RCRA's coverage of recycling activities.

Materials are not solid wastes when they are directly used or reused as ingredients in an industrial process to make a product, provided the material is not being reclaimed. A material is also not a solid waste when used as an effective substitute for a commercial product, unless the material is burned as a fuel or applied to the land. Finally, a material is not a waste if it is returned to the original process from which it is generated as a substitute for a raw material feedstock, again provided it is not first reclaimed. These provisions reflect EPA's concern to avoid extending RCRA regulation to production activities, as distinct from waste management.

Generally speaking, hazardous wastes destined for recycling are subject to the Part 262 and 263 regulations for generators and transporters, and to the storage facility requirements in Parts 264 and 265.[41]

## 4.2 Notification of Hazardous Waste Management Activities

RCRA Section 3010(a) requires that any person who manages a hazardous waste (i.e., generators, transporters, and owners and operators of TSD facilities) must file a notification with EPA within 90 days after regulations are promulgated identifying the waste as hazardous. EPA has published Form 8700-12 as the Section 3010(a) notification form. The reporting company must identify itself, its location, and the EPA identification numbers for the listed and characteristic hazardous wastes it manages. Notifications must be filed for each site (e.g., plant) at which hazardous waste is managed.

Persons managing hazardous wastes under EPA's initial RCRA regulatory program should have filed the Section 3010(a) notification form not later than August 18, 1980.[42] Failure to file makes the transport, treatment, storage or disposal of the hazardous wastes unlawful. Companies that failed to file due to excusable oversight may request that EPA exercise its enforcement discretion and permit continued operation if in the public interest.[43]

Persons who produce, market or burn hazardous waste-derived fuels were required to file a notification by February 8, 1985. These notifications also identified the location and description of the facility, the hazardous wastes involved, and a description of the fuel production or burning activity carried out at the facility.

## 4.3 Generators of Hazardous Waste

Generators play a crucial role in the overall RCRA hazardous waste regulatory scheme. The failure of a generator to properly identify and initiate the management of a hazardous waste may mean that the waste never enters the "cradle to grave" hazardous waste program. Thus the requirements imposed on generators under RCRA Section 3002 and EPA's implementing regulations at 40 C.F.R. Part 262 are of key concern.

EPA's regulations define the term "generator" as "any person, by site, whose act or process produces hazardous waste identified or listed in Part 261 of this chapter or whose act first causes hazardous waste to become subject to regulation."[44] This

---

[41]40 C.F.R. § 261.6 Certain exemptions are also set forth in the regulation.
[42]45 Fed. Reg. 33066 (May 19, 1980).
[43]45 Fed. Reg. 76632 (November 19, 1980).
[44]40 C.F.R. § 260.10(a)(26).

definition refers explicitly to the particular site of generation. A corporation with several plants must evaluate and comply with the generator requirements at each facility site.

A generator is initially required to determine whether any of its solid waste is a "hazardous waste" under the criteria described above.[45] The records of any test results, waste analyses, or determinations that a waste is hazardous must be kept for at least three years from the date the waste was last sent to a TSD facility. Most generators retain such records indefinitely. The generator must then obtain an EPA Identification Number before any hazardous waste can be transported, treated, stored or disposed of, and only transporters and TSD facilities that have obtained their EPA Identification Numbers can be used.[46]

The generator has the responsibility for preparing the Uniform Hazardous Waste Manifest, a control and transport document that accompanies the hazardous waste at all times.[47] The generator must specify the name and EPA Identification Numbers of each authorized transporter and the TSD facility or other designated facility that will receive the waste, describe the waste as required by DOT regulations, certify that it is properly packaged and labeled, and sign the manifest certifications by hand.

In the new era of RCRA, companies must develop new management strategies and technologies to reduce the volume and toxicity of their hazardous wastes. As an action-forcing mechanism, Congress now requires that all generators certify on manifests that:

> I have a program in place to reduce the volume and toxicity of waste generated to the degree I have determined to be economically practicable and I have selected the method of treatment, storage or disposal currently available to me which minimizes the present and future threat to human health and the environment.

A sufficient number of copies of the manifest must be prepared so that all parties listed on the manifest as handling the hazardous waste will be provided with a copy, and a final copy can also be returned to the generator by the TSD facility. A copy of the final signed manifest must be kept for at least three years, although most generators retain copies for a much longer period.[48]

If the manifest is not received back by the generator in a timely or properly executed manner, he must file an "exception report" with EPA or the state. The regulations specifically provide that a generator must contact the transporter and/or the TSD facility to determine what happened to the manifest and the hazardous waste. If, after 45 days from shipping the waste, the generator has not received a manifest with the proper signatures back from the TSD facility, the generator must submit an exception report which consists of (1) a copy of the manifest for which the generator does not have

---

[45]40 C.F.R. § 262.11.
[46]40 C.F.R. § 262.12(c).
[47]40 C.F.R. §§ 262.20 - 262.23. See the Uniform Manifest and instructions, 40 C.F.R. Part 262, Appendix.
[48]40 C.F.R. § 262.40.

confirmation of delivery; and (2) a cover letter which describes the efforts taken to locate the waste or manifest and the result of those efforts.[49]

A generator, in addition, must properly prepare the waste for transportation off-site. EPA has adopted the DOT regulations issued under the Hazardous Materials Transportation Act, 49 U.S.C. §§ 1802 et seq., with respect to the packaging, labeling, marking, and placarding of hazardous waste shipments.[50] In addition to the DOT regulations, EPA requires that any container of 110 gallons or less must be specifically marked with the generator's name, address, manifest document number, and the words:

> Hazardous Waste: Federal law prohibits improper disposal. If found contact the nearest police or public safety authority or the United States Environmental Protection Agency.

A generator is allowed to accumulate his own hazardous wastes on site without a RCRA storage permit in two related circumstances. First, the generator can accumulate up to 55 gallons of hazardous wastes at or near the point of generation in "satellite accumulation areas."[51] The containers must be properly marked and maintained in good condition, and the waste must be moved into storage once the 55-gallon limit is reached. Second, a generator is also allowed to store hazardous waste on-site prior to shipment for a period of up to 90 days in tanks or containers, provided certain standards are met.[52] The generator must comply with the Part 265 interim status standards for containers and tanks (e.g., secondary containment structures) and the requirements for personnel training, contingency planning, and emergency preparedness and response.

A generator must file biennial reports with EPA or an authorized state (some states require annual reports). The biennial report is filed on March 1 of even-numbered years for the preceding calendar year, and must include (1) the name, address and EPA identification number of the generator, (2) the EPA identification number for each transporter used, (3) name, address and identification number of each TSD facility to which wastes were sent, and (4) waste identification information including the DOT hazard class, EPA hazardous waste identification number, and the quantity of the wastes.[53] EPA has devised Form 8700-13A for this purpose. The 1984 HSWA requires that the reports now also include information on the "waste minimization" efforts undertaken to reduce the volume and toxicity of the hazardous wastes, and the results actually achieved in comparison with previous years. As a recordkeeping requirement, the generator must maintain copies of the biennial reports (and any exception reports filed) for at least three years.

As a practical matter, in view of the liability imposed by Superfund, discussed in the Superfund Chapter, generators should seriously consider maintaining RCRA waste determinations, test results, manifests, and reports for a lengthy period of time.

---

[49] 40 C.F.R. § 262.42.

[50] 40 C.F.R. § 262.31.

[51] 40 C.F.R. § 262.34.

[52] 40 C.F.R. § 262.34(a). A small quantity generator can store wastes for a longer time period, as discussed below. See 40 C.F.R. § 262.34(d)-(f).

[53] 40 C.F.R. § 262.41.

Special rules have been issued for persons who export or import hazardous wastes.[54] A generator who intends to export his hazardous waste to a foreign country must first notify EPA in writing at least four weeks before the initial shipment in each calendar year. He must then require the foreign consignee to confirm delivery of the waste, such as by returning a signed manifest. If the generator does not receive a manifest signed by the transporter stating the date and place of departure from the U.S. within 45 days, or written confirmation of receipt from the foreign consignee within 90 days, an exception report must be filed. Annual reports of all exports must be submitted to EPA. A person who imports hazardous waste into the U.S. must initiate the manifest procedures as the generator.

### 4.3.1 Small Generators

As directed by the 1984 HSWA, EPA has promulgated special regulations for small quantity generators that produce hazardous wastes in a total monthly quantity of less than 1,000 kilograms (2,200 pounds).[55] The regulations vary somewhat from the standards that currently apply to hazardous wastes of larger quantity generators. For example, small quantity generators of between 100 kg and 1000 kg may accumulate up to 6,000 kilograms (13,200 pounds) of hazardous waste on site for up to 180 days without a permit. If the waste must be shipped over 200 miles, the waste may be stored for up to 270 days.

Besides using the Uniform Manifest, small quantity generators must have their waste treated, stored (except short-term accumulation on site) and disposed of at an interim status or permitted TSD facility, and no longer at a state or municipally licensed landfill. The manifest contains a modified certification of waste minimization for such generators. In almost all other respects, however, small quantity generators of between 100 kg and 1000 kg per month are regulated the same as large generators.

Very small generators of less than 100 kilograms per month are still conditionally exempt from RCRA, but they are subject to certain minimum standards.[56]

### 4.4 Transporters of Hazardous Wastes

A transporter is any person engaged in the off-site movement of hazardous waste by air, rail, highway or water.[57] Off-site transportation includes both interstate and intrastate commerce.[58] Thus, the reach of RCRA includes not only shippers and common carriers of hazardous wastes, but also the company that occasionally transports hazardous wastes on its own trucks solely within its home state.

Anyone who moves a hazardous waste that is required to be manifested off the site where it is generated, or the site where it is being treated, stored and disposed of, will be subject to the transporter standards. The only persons not covered are generators or operators of TSD facilities who engage in on-site transportation of their hazardous waste. Once a generator or a TSD facility operator moves its hazardous waste off-

---

[54]40 C.F.R. § 262.50.
[55]40 C.F.R. § 261.5, § 262.34(d)-(f).
[56]40 C.F.R. § 261.5.
[57]40 C.F.R. § 260.10(a).
[58]Section 3003.

site—which can be any distance along a public road—he is then considered a transporter and must comply with the regulations.[59]

EPA has promulgated standards for all transporters of hazardous wastes at 40 C.F.R. Part 263. These standards are closely coordinated with the standards issued by the U.S. Department of Transportation under the Hazardous Materials Transportation Act for the shipment of hazardous materials.[60] For the most part, EPA's regulations incorporate and require compliance with the DOT provisions on labeling, marking, placarding, using proper containers, and responding to spills. Of course, all transporters must obtain an EPA Identification Number prior to transporting any hazardous waste, and they may only accept hazardous waste which is accompanied by a manifest signed by the generator.[61] The transporter himself must sign and date the manifest acknowledging acceptance of the waste and return one copy to the generator before leaving the generator's property.

The transporter must keep the manifest with the hazardous waste at all times. When the transporter delivers the waste to another transporter or to the designated TSD facility, he must (1) date the manifest and obtain the signature of the next transporter or the TSD facility operator, (2) retain one copy of the manifest for his own records, and (3) give the remaining copies to the person receiving the waste.[62] If the transporter is unable to deliver the waste in accordance with the manifest, he must contact the generator for further instructions and revise the manifest accordingly.[63] The transporter must keep the executed copy of the manifest for a period of three years.[64]

The transporter may hold a hazardous waste for up to ten days at a transfer facility without being required to obtain a RCRA storage permit.[65] A transfer facility generally includes a loading dock, storage area, and similar areas where shipments of hazardous wastes are held during the normal course of transportation.

Transporters of hazardous wastes may become subject to the Part 262 requirements for generators if, for example, the transporter mixes hazardous wastes of different DOT descriptions by placing them into a single container, or if he imports hazardous waste from a foreign country.[66] Also, a hazardous waste that accumulates in a transport vehicle or vessel will trigger the generator standards when the waste is removed.

If an accidental spill or other discharge of a hazardous waste occurs during transportation, the transporter is responsible for its clean up.[67] The transporter must take immediate response action to protect human health and the environment. Such action includes treatment or containment of the spill and notification of local police and fire

---

[59]See the definition of "on-site" in § 260.10(a), which by implication defines transportation off-site as any distance along, as opposed to simply going across, a public or private right-of-way.
[60]49 U.S.C. §§ 1801, et seq., 49 C.F.R. Parts 171-179.
[61]40 C.F.R. § 263.11, § 263.20.
[62]40 C.F.R. § 263.20. Special requirements apply to rail or water transport of hazardous waste, and to persons who transport hazardous waste outside of the United States. 40 C.F.R. § 263.20(e), (f) and (g), § 263.22(b), (c) and (d).
[63]40 C.F.R. § 263.21(b).
[64]40 C.F.R. § 263.22.
[65]40 C.F.R. § 263.12.
[66]40 C.F.R. § 263.10(c).
[67]40 C.F.R. § 263.30.

departments. DOT's discharge reporting requirements are incorporated into the RCRA regulations.[68] They identify the situations in which telephone reporting of the discharge to the National Response Center and the filing of a written report are required. Transporters are subject to both DOT and EPA enforcement.[69]

The 1984 HSWA affected transporters in minor respects. For example, EPA has established requirements for the transportation of hazardous waste-derived fuels.[70] In addition, railroads are shielded from the RCRA "citizen suit" and "imminent hazard" enforcement provisions (discussed below) if the railroad merely transports the hazardous waste under a sole contractual agreement and exercises due care.

### 4.5 Treatment, Storage, and Disposal (TSD) Facilities

The term "TSD" is commonly used to refer to the three management activities that are regulated under RCRA Section 3004, and which thus require a permit under RCRA Section 3005. These activities are treatment, storage and disposal of hazardous wastes. Section 3004 directed EPA to establish a comprehensive set of regulations governing all aspects of TSD facilities, including location, design, operation, and closure. The regulations adopted include standards of general applicability and specific requirements for particular types of TSD facilities.[71]

In 1984, Congress added a number of important provisions to Section 3004. These establish, among other things, a ban on the disposal of liquids in landfills, minimum technological requirements (i.e., double liners) for surface impoundments and landfills, corrective action for continuing releases at permitted TSD facilities, and controls on the marketing and burning of hazardous wastes used as fuels. Congress also directed EPA to make a number of regulatory decisions under Section 3004 in short order. The most significant provisions set a strict timetable under which EPA must implement a land disposal ban of all untreated hazardous wastes, and establish treatment standards for the wastes. The requirements of the current standards and the impact of the new amendments are discussed below.

First of all, certain basic definitions must be understood. A facility will be regulated as a "treatment facility" if the operator utilizes any method, technique, or process designed to change the physical, chemical, or biological character or composition of any hazardous waste so as to neutralize such waste, to recover energy or material resources from the waste, to render the waste nonhazardous or less hazardous, safer to transport, store or dispose of, or amenable for recovery, amenable for storage, or reduced in volume.[72] There is very little that can be done to a hazardous waste that would not qualify as treatment.

A "storage facility" is defined as one which engages in the holding of hazardous waste for a temporary period, at the end of which the hazardous waste is treated,

---

[68]See 49 C.F.R. § 171.15 and § 171.16.

[69]45 Fed. Reg. 51645 (August 4, 1980).

[70]40 C.F.R. § 266.33, discussed below.

[71]See 40 C.F.R. Parts 264 and 265, discussed infra.

[72]40 C.F.R. § 260.10(a). This definition was upheld by the court in *Shell Oil Co. v. EPA*, 950 F.2d 741 (D.C. Cir. 1991).

disposed of, or stored elsewhere.[73] A "disposal facility" is one at which hazardous waste is intentionally placed into or on any land or water, and at which waste will remain after closure.[74] The term "facility" is separately defined to include "all contiguous land, and structures, other appurtenances, and improvements on the land."[75] Clarification of the foregoing definitions can be sought during the permitting process.

A number of different types of TSD facilities and hazardous waste activities are currently exempted from EPA regulation altogether. The list includes the following exclusions:[76]

1. Facilities that dispose of hazardous waste by means of ocean disposal pursuant to a permit issued under the Marine Protection, Research, and Sanctuaries Act (except as provided in a RCRA permit-by-rule).

2. The disposal of hazardous waste by underground injection pursuant to a permit issued under the Safe Drinking Water Act (except as provided in a RCRA permit-by-rule).

3. A Publicly Owned Treatment Works (POTW) that treats or stores hazardous wastes which are delivered to the POTW by a transport vehicle or vessel or through a pipe.

4. TSD facilities that operate under a state hazardous waste program authorized pursuant to RCRA Section 3006, and which are therefore subject to regulation under the state program.

5. Facilities authorized by a state to manage industrial or municipal solid waste, if the only hazardous waste handled by such a facility is otherwise excluded from regulation pursuant to the special requirements for conditionally exempt small quantity generators of less than 100 kilograms.

6. A facility that is subject to the special exemptions for certain recyclable materials, except as provided in Part 266.

7. Temporary on-site accumulation of hazardous waste by generators in compliance with 40 C.F.R. § 262.34.

8. Farmers who dispose of waste pesticides from their own use in compliance with 40 C.F.R. § 262.51.

9. Owners or operators of a "totally enclosed treatment facility."

10. Owners and operators of "elementary neutralization units" and "wastewater treatment units," as defined in the regulations.

11. Persons taking immediate action to treat and contain spills.

12. Transporters storing manifested wastes in approved containers at a transfer facility for 10 days or less.

13. The act of adding absorbent material to hazardous waste in a container to reduce the amount of free liquids in the container, if the materials are added when wastes are first placed in the container.

The regulations should be consulted for the precise scope of these exemptions.

---

[73]*Id.*
[74]*Id.*
[75]*Id.*
[76]See 40 C.F.R. § 264.1 and § 265.1(c).

### 4.5.1 Standards of General Applicability

As discussed more fully in the permits section below, two categories of TSD facilities currently exist—interim status facilities and permitted facilities. Interim status facilities are those that are currently operating without final RCRA permits based upon a legislative decision to allow continued operation of existing facilities until RCRA permits can be issued. These facilities had to meet a three-part statutory test:

1. In existence on November 19, 1980, or the effective date of statutory or regulatory changes that render the facility subject to the need for a RCRA permit,
2. Notify EPA pursuant to RCRA Section 3010(a) of its hazardous waste management activities, and
3. File a preliminary permit application.[77]

A facility's interim status ends when the facility receives a final RCRA permit. This in turn is based upon technical standards issued by EPA, or a state with an approved program, which are incorporated into the permit. As discussed in the next section on permits, the 1984 HSWA specified timetables for issuance of final permits to all interim status TSD facilities. All other TSD facilities must obtain an individual RCRA permit before commencing construction.

Separate standards have been issued for interim status facilities[78] and permitted facilities.[79] Both the Part 264 and Part 265 regulations for TSD facilities include standards of general applicability (e.g., personnel training, security, financial responsibility), as well as specific design and operating standards for each different type of TSD facility (e.g., storage tanks, landfills, incinerators). The standards of general applicability are discussed first. An operator of a TSD facility is required to obtain an EPA identification number.[80] The operator must also obtain or conduct a detailed chemical and physical analysis of a representative sample of a hazardous waste before the waste is treated, stored, or disposed of at the facility.[81] This is to ensure that the operator has sufficient knowledge of the particular waste being handled to be able to properly manage it. The facility's waste analysis plan (WAP) deals with such matters as representative samples, frequency of testing and compliance with land disposal verifications.

Operators must install a security system to prevent unknowing entry, and to minimize the potential for unauthorized entry, of people or livestock to the active portion of the TSD facility.[82] This may be either a 24-hour surveillance system or a barrier around the facility and a means to control entry, and posted "Danger" signs. Operators are required to prepare and implement an inspection plan specifically tailored to the circumstances at their facility.[83] Permitted facilities located in floodplains or areas

---

[77]Section 3005(e).
[78]40 C.F.R. Part 265.
[79]40 C.F.R. Part 264.
[80]40 C.F.R. § 265.11, § 264.11.
[81]40 C.F.R. § 265.13, § 264.13.
[82]40 C.F.R. § 265.14, § 264.14.
[83]40 C.F.R. § 265.15, § 264.15.

prone to seismic activity are subject to location standards designed to reduce the additional risks.[84]

TSD facility personnel are required to be properly trained in the areas to which they are assigned, thus reducing the chances that a mistake due to lack of knowledge of the regulatory requirements might lead to an environmental accident. The training may be by formal classroom instruction or on-the-job training. Facility personnel must be given the training within six months of their employment, and must take part in an annual review thereafter. The program must be directed by a person trained in hazardous waste management procedures.[85] Personnel training should focus on emergency preparations and response procedures.

Special precautions must be taken to prevent accidental ignition or reaction of ignitable, reactive or incompatible wastes. While many of the handling requirements are largely common sense practices, specific steps to protect against mixing of such wastes are included in the regulations. Compliance with the regulations concerning safe management of ignitable, reactive or incompatible wastes must be documented.[86]

Regulations for preparedness and prevention are intended to minimize the possibility or consequences of an explosion, spill, or fire at a TSD facility.[87] Facilities must have, unless unnecessary due to the nature of the wastes handled, the following equipment:

1. An internal alarm or communications system;
2. A device capable of summoning emergency assistance from local agencies;
3. Fire and spill control equipment; and
4. Decontamination equipment.

Operators are required to have a contingency plan for the facility designed to minimize hazards to human health and the environment in the event of an actual explosion, fire, or unplanned release of hazardous wastes.[88] All required equipment must be regularly tested and maintained. Adequate aisle space to allow unobstructed movement of emergency personnel and equipment must also be maintained. Arrangements must be made with local police, fire departments, and hospitals to familiarize them with the facility's layout and hazardous wastes. The TSD facility must also be covered by liability insurance or other financial instruments for claims arising out of injuries to persons or property that result from hazardous waste management operations.[89]

Important recordkeeping requirements apply to TSD facilities.[90] Upon receipt of a manifested shipment of hazardous waste, the operator of a TSD facility must immediately sign, date, and give to the transporter a copy of the manifest prepared by the generator. Within 30 days, the operator must return a completed copy of the manifest

---

[84] 40 C.F.R. § 265.18(b), § 264.17(c), § 264.18(a).

[85] 40 C.F.R. § 265.16, § 264.16.

[86] 40 C.F.R. § 265.17, § 264.17.

[87] *See generally* 40 C.F.R. § 265.30-.49, § 264.30-.49.

[88] *See generally* 40 C.F.R. § 265.50-.56, § 264.50-.56.

[89] 40 C.F.R. § 265.143(e), § 264.143(f).

[90] *See generally* 40 C.F.R. § 265.71-.72, § 264.71-.72.

to the generator, and retain a copy of all manifests at the facility for at least three years from the date of delivery. All TSD facilities must maintain a complete operating record until closure.[91] The operating record must include, among other things, a description and the quantity of each hazardous waste received and the method and date of its treatment, storage and disposal, the location of each waste within the facility, results of waste analyses, trial tests and inspections.

There are also basic reports which the TSD facility operator is obligated to file with the EPA regional administrator or an authorized state. These include a biennial report of waste management activities for the previous calendar year,[92] an "unmanifested waste" report which the operator must file within 15 days of accepting any hazardous waste that is not accompanied by a manifest,[93] and certain specialized reports, e.g. an incident report in the event of a hazardous waste release, fire, or explosion.

There are general closure requirements applicable to all TSD facilities, and additional requirements for each specific type of facility.[94] "Closure" is the period after which hazardous wastes are no longer accepted by a TSD facility and during which time the operator must complete treatment, storage or disposal operations. "Post-closure" is the 30-year period after closure when operators of land disposal facilities, such as landfills, must perform certain monitoring and maintenance activities. Generally, the TSD facility must have a detailed written closure plan and schedule, and a cost estimate for closure. The plan must be approved by EPA or the state. It must be amended when any changes in waste management operations affect its terms, and the cost estimate must be adjusted annually for inflation. The closure plan must be followed when the TSD facility ceases operations at the covered unit(s). Post-closure care must continue for 30 years after the date of completing closure, and includes groundwater monitoring and the maintenance of monitoring and waste containment systems.

Financial responsibility requirements have been established to ensure that funds for closure and post-closure care are adequate and available.[95] TSD facilities must use one of the specified financial instruments, such as a corporate guarantee, to provide the closure and post-closure funds.

### 4.5.2 Standards for Specific Types of TSD Facilities

The standards discussed above are generally applicable to all TSD facilities, from the small drum storage area to the most complex commercial landfill or incinerator. EPA has also promulgated specific design, construction, and operating standards for each different type of TSD facility regulated under RCRA. These include: (1) containers, (2) tanks, (3) surface impoundments, (4) waste piles, (5) drip pads, (6) land treatment units, (7) landfills, (8) incinerators, (9) thermal treatment units, (10) chemical, physical, and biological treatment units, (11) underground injection wells, (12)

---

[91]40 C.F.R. § 265.73, §264.73.
[92]40 C.F.R. § 265.75, § 264.75.
[93]40 C.F.R. § 265.76, § 264.76.
[94]*See generally* 40 C.F.R. § 265.110-.120, § 264.110-.120.
[95]*See generally* 40 C.F.R. § 265.140-.151, § 264.140-.151.

containment buildings, and (13) "miscellaneous units."[96] In the years ahead, additional classes of facilities may also be addressed by distinct sets of standards such as these.

Discussion of the detailed regulatory requirements for all of these types of facilities is beyond the scope of this chapter.[97] The following is an overview of the more significant standards that apply to containers and tanks; surface impoundments, waste piles and landfills; and incinerators and industrial furnaces used for hazardous waste burning.

A container is any portable device for storing or handling hazardous waste, including drums, pails and boxes. Tank systems are stationary devices constructed primarily of non-earthen materials which provide structural support, and any ancillary piping.[98] The RCRA standards for containers and tanks are basically good housekeeping practices.[99] For example, drums must be maintained in good condition and be handled to avoid ruptures or leaks. Containers must always be kept closed, except when adding waste. Tank systems must be constructed of suitable materials and operated so as to contain the hazardous waste during the tank's intended useful life. Tanks must be operated using controls and practices to prevent overflows and spills. Container storage areas must be inspected at least weekly, and tank systems at least daily, for leaks, corrosion, and other problems. More importantly, almost all container and tank storage areas must be constructed or retrofitted with a secondary containment system to collect spills and accumulated rainfall. Generally, a containment system consists of a diked or bermed concrete (impervious) base with sufficient capacity to collect spillage, and a sump or other method for removing collected liquids. For tanks, the operator can use a lined or diked concrete containment facility, a vault system, or double-walled tanks. Tanks without secondary containment must undergo a structural integrity assessment by a professional engineer.

EPA has also issued standards for air emission controls at TSD facilities, particularly for tanks and containers. The Subpart AA standards require controls on process vents associated with distillation, fractionation, air or stream stripping, and similar operations to control volatile organic (VO) emissions.[100] The Subpart BB rules require controls related to leaks from equipment, such as pumps and compressors.[101] The Subpart CC standards require control systems on tanks, containers, and surface impoundments that manage hazardous wastes with VO concentrations greater than 500 ppmw.[102] In general, these rules require an organic reduction efficiency of at least 95%. In addition, the Subpart AA-CC standards apply to 90-day containers and tanks at generator facilities.

---

[96]40 C.F.R. Part 265, Subparts J-R, and Part 264, Subparts J-X, as amended, 57 Fed. Reg. 37265 (August 18, 1992).

[97]These requirements are discussed in detail in Hall, *RCRA Hazardous Wastes Handbook* (Government Institutes), and in Bauer & Kellar, *Managing Your Hazardous Wastes* (Government Institutes).

[98]40 C.F.R. § 260.10.

[99]*See generally* 40 C.F.R. § 265.170-265.199, § 264.170-264.200.

[100]*See generally* 40 C.F.R .§ 264.1030-264.1036, § 265.1030-265.1035.

[101]*See generally* 40 C.F.R. § 264.1050-264.1065, § 265.1050-265.1064.

[102]*See generally* 40 C.F.R. § 264.1080-264.1091, § 265.1080-265.1091, *as amended,* 61 Fed. Reg. 59932 (November 25, 1996).

A surface impoundment is any natural or man-made excavation or diked area designed to hold hazardous wastes containing free liquids, such as pits, ponds, or lagoons. A waste pile is any non-containerized accumulation of solid, non-flowing hazardous waste. A landfill is a disposal facility where hazardous waste is placed in or on the land.[103] The most important performance standards for these land-based facilities are the "minimum technology requirements" (MTRs) enacted in the 1984 HSWA. All new, replacement, and expansion units at surface impoundments and landfills must have double liners, leachate collection systems, leak detection, and groundwater monitoring systems.[104] Waste piles must be constructed with a liner on a supporting base, a leachate collection and removal system above the liner, and surface water run-on controls. The MTR regulations are highly technical and complex, and should be carefully consulted. The groundwater monitoring requirements, for example, call for an extensive scheme for detecting leachate plumes and instituting corrective action when necessary.[105]

Incinerators use controlled flame combustion to destroy hazardous wastes. Recently, industrial furnaces and boilers are increasingly being used to burn hazardous wastes as fuels and for destruction. The RCRA standards for these TSD facilities have become more stringent, in large part as a result of the 1984 HSWA.[106] Basically, an incinerator must conduct a detailed waste analysis and trial burn for waste feeds it intends to handle to establish steady state conditions and demonstrate sufficient destruction of hazardous constituents in the waste. The incinerator must achieve a destruction and removal efficiency (DRE) rate of at least 99.99% for the principal organic hazardous constituents designated by EPA for each waste feed. Emission standards are also applied. The incinerator must have continuous monitoring and automatic controls to shut off the waste feed when operating requirements are exceeded.

EPA has also promulgated standards for industrial furnaces and boilers that burn hazardous wastes.[107] Based on Congress' direction in the 1984 HSWA, EPA now requires all persons who produce, distribute, market or burn hazardous wastes as fuel to notify EPA. The invoice or bill of sale for the fuel must bear the legend: Warning — This Fuel Contains Hazardous Waste (followed by a list of the hazardous wastes). Such fuels cannot be burned except in qualified utility boilers and industrial furnaces, such as cement kilns. Generators, transporters, marketers and burners of hazardous waste fuels are subject to storage standards for containers and tanks, and to other specific RCRA standards. The owners and operators of boilers and industrial furnaces must comply with detailed technical standards similar to incineration standards, including emission controls, and obtain RCRA permits.

---

[103]40 C.F.R. § 260.10.

[104]*See generally* 40 C.F.R. § 265.220-265.230, § 265.300-265.316, § 264.220-264.231, § 264.300-264.317.

[105]*See generally* 40 C.F.R. § 265.90-265.94, § 264.90-264.101.

[106]*See generally* 40 C.F.R. § 265.340-265.352, § 264.340-264.351; 40 C.F.R. § 266.30-266.35.

[107]Section 3004(q)-(s); 40 C.F.R. 266, Subpart D.

### 4.5.3 The Land Disposal Ban Program

Perhaps the most significant provision of the 1984 HSWA are the prohibitions on the land disposal of hazardous wastes. These prohibitions are intended to minimize the country's reliance on land disposal of untreated hazardous wastes, and to require advanced treatment and recycling of wastes. Congress began by banning the disposal of bulk or non-containerized liquid hazardous wastes, and hazardous wastes containing free liquids, in landfills.[108]

Next, Congress required EPA to determine whether to prohibit, in whole or in part, the disposal of all RCRA hazardous wastes in land disposal facilities. These include landfills, surface impoundments, waste piles, injection wells, salt domes, and the like. At the same time, EPA was told to promulgate regulations that establish levels or methods of treatment that minimize threats posed by the hazardous waste. If the waste is first treated in accordance with these treatment standards, the treated waste or residue can then be land disposed. In effect, the so-called "land ban" program is really a waste pretreatment program.

Congress set forth a phased program for EPA to implement these land disposal prohibitions. First, EPA has banned the land disposal of dioxin and solvent containing hazardous wastes effective November 1986, unless the wastes are pretreated.[109] EPA set treatment levels based on incineration of non-wastewater solvents, and based on chemical/physical treatment for dilute solvent wastewaters.

Second, EPA has banned the land disposal of certain hazardous wastes (which California had already banned) effective July 1987, unless the wastes are pretreated. The "California list" includes liquid hazardous wastes, including free liquids associated with any sludge, that (1) contain free cyanides greater than 100 mg/l; (2) contain specified concentrations of heavy metals (arsenic, cadmium, chromium, lead, mercury, nickel, selenium and thallium); (3) are acids below a pH of 2; (4) contain more than 50 ppm PCBs; and (5) are solid or liquid hazardous wastes containing halogenated organic compounds at concentrations greater than 1000 ppm.[110]

Third, EPA published a ranking of all other hazardous wastes based on their intrinsic hazard and volume, with a schedule for determining whether to ban the land disposal of such wastes one third at a time.[111] EPA restricted the land disposal of the first-third of the highest priority hazardous wastes on the ranking list in August 1988. EPA set treatment levels for many of the F and K listed wastes in the first-third. EPA extended the ban to the second-third of the ranked hazardous wastes in June 1989.

---

[108]Congress also directed EPA to minimize the disposal of containerized liquid hazardous wastes in landfills. In order to discourage the use of absorbent materials (e.g., "kitty litter") to reduce free liquids in containerized wastes, EPA's regulations prohibit the landfilling of liquids that have been absorbed in materials that biodegrade or that release liquids when depressed during routine landfill operations. 40 C.F.R. § 264.314-.316.

[109]40 C.F.R. Part 268. The dioxin containing wastes are those chlorinated dioxins, -dibenzofurans, and -phenols listed as F020, F021, F022, F023, F026, F027 and F028. The solvent wastes are those listed as F001-F005 at 40 C.F.R. 261.31. *See generally* Section 3004(d)-(m).

[110]Disposal by deep well injection is subject to special provisions and a different schedule for implementing the ban.

[111]The ranking and schedule are published at 40 C.F.R. 268.

Finally, EPA imposed the land ban restrictions on the third-third wastes, including all characteristic hazardous wastes, in May 1990.

Congress wanted to promote treatment and recycling of hazardous wastes in lieu of or prior to land disposal. Therefore at the same time EPA promulgated these land disposal restrictions, it also promulgated regulations specifying the methods or levels of treatment that substantially diminish the toxicity or reduce the likelihood of migration of the waste from land disposal facilities. Generally, the treatment standards are based on the levels that can be achieved by the Best Demonstrated Available Technologies (BDAT).[112] In most instances, the treatment standards are expressed as concentrations of constituents in the treated waste. Any treatment technology that meets the concentration-based standard can then be used. If EPA prescribes a specific technology, however, then that method must be used. A company that treats its hazardous waste in accordance with these pretreatment standards will not have the treated waste or residue subject to the land disposal ban.

After several years experience with the land ban program, EPA revamped the format of the treatment standards in 1994. To supplement the waste-by-waste standards, EPA has now set "universal treatment standards" for hazardous constituents in certain hazardous wastes.[113] Newly listed or identified wastes are brought under the land ban program in subsequent rulemakings.

In the third-third rule, EPA determined that it had legal authority to establish treatment standards below the characteristic level for the ignitable, corrosive, reactive and toxic wastes. However, EPA used this authority sparingly, and generally required only that characteristic wastes be treated by any method, including dilution, that removed the characteristic. Upon judicial review, the court held that EPA must now revise the treatment standards to address the threats posed by any hazardous constituents in these characteristic wastes.[114] EPA's development of treatment standards for these "underlying hazardous constituents" in hazardous wastes is ongoing.

EPA has limited authority to grant up to a two-year extension of the land ban deadlines for specific hazardous wastes if adequate alternative treatment, recovery, or disposal capacity is not currently available. EPA has granted national capacity variances for certain wastes, such as contaminated soil and debris. EPA can also grant a one-year extension, renewable only once, to a company that demonstrates on a case-by-case basis that a binding contractual commitment has been made to construct or otherwise provide alternative treatment, recovery, or disposal capacity, but due to circumstances beyond its control the alternative capacity cannot reasonably be made available by the ban deadline.

---

[112]EPA's decision to use technology-based standards, rather than risk-based standards, was upheld by the court. *Hazardous Waste Treatment Council v. EPA*, 886 F.2d 355 (1989).

[113]40 C.F.R. § 268.48. 59 *Fed. Reg.* 47982 (September 19, 1994).

[114]*Chemical Waste Management, Inc. v. EPA*, 976 F.2d 2 (D.C. Cir. 1992). The court also ruled that EPA must ensure that hazardous wastes managed in Clean Water Act lagoon systems receive equivalent treatment to that mandated under RCRA. However, Congress then enacted the Land Disposal Program Flexibility Act of 1996 which exempts hazardous wastes managed in Clean Water Act impoundments from the LDR program. Pub. L. No. 104-119, 110 Stat. 830.

Finally, land disposal facilities may submit petitions to EPA which demonstrate, to a reasonable degree of certainty, that there will be no migration of hazardous constituents from a particular disposal unit or injection well for as long as the waste remains hazardous. EPA has granted a number of these so-called "no migration" petitions for deep injection wells.

### 4.5.4 1984 Amendments Relevant to Used Oil

In the 1984 HSWA, Congress also directed EPA to decide whether to identify used automobile and truck crankcase oil or other used oil as hazardous waste.[115] After substantial delay, EPA finally decided not to list used oil that is destined for recycling as a hazardous waste, but instead to promulgate management standards for used oil collection and recycling.[116] These include general facility standards for used oil processors and re-refiners. In addition, EPA decided not to list used oil that is destined for disposal as a hazardous waste, but the hazardous waste characteristics do apply to such used oil.[117]

### 4.5.5 Universal Wastes

EPA has established a separate regulatory program that governs the collection and management of certain widely-generated wastes.[118] At the present time, these "universal wastes" include nickel cadmium batteries, returned pesticides, and mercury thermostats. EPA may add to this list in the future. Small quantity handlers of these universal wastes (less than 5000 kilograms) must comply with streamlined management standards related to preventing releases, employee training, proper packaging and labeling, limiting accumulation time, and tracking off-site shipments. Large quantity handlers must also notify EPA and obtain an identification number. Handlers and transporters must take universal wastes to a qualified destination facility that treats, disposes of or recycles the waste in accordance with regulatory standards, including tracking and record-keeping.

### 4.6 Permits

RCRA requires every owner and operator of a TSD facility to obtain a permit.[119] A TSD facility that was in existence on November 19, 1980, or on the date of any statutory or regulatory change that makes the facility subject to RCRA, need only notify EPA of its hazardous waste management activity and file a Part A application to obtain interim status and continue operations.[120] An interim status TSD facility will be issued a site-specific permit in due course. A new TSD facility, or an existing facility that fails

---

[115]*See* Section 3014(b). EPA proposed the listing of used oil from motor vehicles and industrial manufacturing processes based on a determination that this used oil typically and frequently contains hazardous contaminants at levels of regulatory concern. 50 Fed. Reg. 49258 (November 29, 1985). The final decision was published at 51 Fed. Reg. 41900, (November 19, 1986).

[116]new 40 C.F.R. Part 279.

[117]57 Fed. Reg. 21524 (May 20, 1992).

[118]40 C.F.R. Part 273.

[119]Section 3005.

[120]Section 3005(e). See the interim status standards for TSD facilities in 40 C.F.R. Part 265, discussed above.

to qualify for interim status, must obtain a full RCRA permit before commencing construction, however.

### 4.6.1 The Permitting Procedures and Timetables

A Part A application is a short form containing certain basic information about the facility, such as name, location, nature of business, regulated activities, and a topographic map of the facility site.[121] A Part B application requires substantially more comprehensive and detailed information that demonstrates compliance with the applicable technical standards for TSD facilities.[122] The Part B application may consist of multiple volumes of documentation, including all the written plans and procedures required by the TSD facility regulations.

The final RCRA permit will govern the application of these standards to the particular facility. New facilities must submit Part A and B applications simultaneously; existing facilities that already filed their Part A applications to gain interim status must submit their Part B applications in accordance with statutory deadlines established by Congress, or earlier if requested by EPA or a state.[123]

States authorized under RCRA to administer their own programs are mainly responsible for reviewing applications and issuing permits. EPA regions perform this task in non-authorized states. In the 1984 HSWA, Congress took steps to accelerate the permitting of TSD facilities. Congress provided that interim status for any existing land disposal facility automatically terminated on November 8, 1985, unless the operator submitted a Part B application for a final permit and a certification that the facility was in compliance with groundwater monitoring and financial responsibility requirements. EPA and authorized states were directed to issue final permits for land disposal facilities by November 1988. Similarly, final permits for interim status incinerators were mandated by November 1989, and for all other interim status TSD facilities by November 1992. If EPA or the state fails to meet these deadlines, the TSD facility can continue operations provided a timely Part B application was filed.

After a complete RCRA permit application is filed, the rules in 40 C.F.R. Part 124 establish the procedures for processing the application and issuing the permit. These include preparation of draft permits, public comment and hearing, and the issuance of final decisions. Permit issuance must be based on a determination that the TSD facility will comply with all requirements of RCRA. In HSWA, Congress enacted the RCRA permit "omnibus" provision directing that all permits contain "such terms and conditions as the Administrator determines necessary to protect human health and the environment."[124] EPA has relied on this omnibus authority to develop facility-specific permit conditions that supplement the regulatory standards.

HSWA provides that permits for land disposal facilities, storage facilities, incinerators and other treatment facilities can be issued only for a fixed term not to exceed ten years.[125] While permits may be reviewed and modified at any time during

---

[121] 40 C.F.R. § 270.13.
[122] *See generally* 40 C.F.R. § 270.13-270.21.
[123] Section 3005(c).
[124] Section 3005(c)(3).
[125] Section 3005(c)(3).

their terms, permits for land disposal facilities must be reviewed every five years. At such time, the terms of a permit may be modified to ensure that the permit continues to incorporate the standards then applicable to land disposal facilities.

### 4.6.2 Corrective Action

Congress also imposed new and stringent corrective action requirements on TSD facilities. All RCRA permits must now require the owner or operator of a TSD facility to take corrective action for all releases of hazardous waste and hazardous constituents from solid waste management units at the facility, regardless of when the waste was placed in the unit or whether the unit is currently active.[126] Note that a solid waste management unit can be any tank, lagoon, waste pile, or other unit where any solid waste was placed, and from which hazardous constituents are being released. RCRA permits must contain schedules of compliance for any required corrective action and assurances of financial responsibility for completing such action. If necessary, the operator of the TSD facility may have to take corrective action beyond the facility boundary. This type of authority for cleanup is analogous to Superfund, and will have a very substantial impact on many TSD facilities that need RCRA permits to continue operations.

In fact, EPA estimates there are over 5,000 facilities nation-wide that will require cleanup. Following the 1984 HSWA, EPA codified the basic framework of the corrective action program in regulations, including provisions for corrective action management units (CAMUs).[127] A CAMU is an area within a facility that is designated by the Regional Administrator for the management of remediation wastes.[128] Placement of remediation waste into or within a CAMU does not trigger the land disposal prohibitions or minimum technology requirements. Much of the corrective action program, however, remains the subject of EPA guidance documents.[129] Under this guidance, EPA has tried to take near-term actions to control or abate threats at a greater number of facilities, rather than undertaking comprehensive cleanups at a more limited number of sites. As a result, much corrective action work remains to be completed. EPA has also sought to use environmental indicators and facility-specific performance goals for site cleanups; innovative technical approaches, including voluntary accelerated cleanups; expanded public participation, such as the use of citizen advisory boards; and coordination with state cleanup programs.

### 4.7 State Hazardous Waste Programs

States are authorized by RCRA to develop and carry out their own hazardous waste programs in lieu of the federal program administered by EPA.[130] To obtain EPA

---

[126]Section 3004(u)-(v).

[127]40 C.F.R. §§ 264.90(a)(2), 264.101, 270.60(b) and 270.60(c).

[128]40 C.F.R. § 260.10.

[129]A list of corrective action guidance documents is available in the "RCRA Corrective Action Plan," EPA/520-R-94-004, OSWER Directive 9902.3-2A, May 1994. This Corrective Action Plan, or CAP, provides an overall program implementation framework and model scopes of work for site characterization, interim actions, evaluation of remedial alternatives, and remedy selection, design, and action.

[130]Section 3006; *see generally* 40 C.F.R. Part 271.

approval, the state program must be "equivalent" to the federal program; must be "consistent" with the federal program and other authorized state programs; and must provide adequate enforcement of compliance with the requirements of RCRA Subtitle C.

Ordinarily, states have at least one year to make regulatory changes consistent with the federal program, and two years if statutory changes are necessary. Under the applicable regulations, EPA allows states to consolidate program revisions for EPA review and approval on a periodic basis, and EPA has sought to streamline its approval process. Congress believed the 1984 HSWA provisions were important to implement quickly, however. Therefore, EPA regulations that implement the 1984 HSWA take effect in authorized states on the same day that they take effect under the federal program. EPA is responsible for implementing HSWA provisions until the state takes over authority. The states can then apply for final authorization for the new requirement after promulgating an equivalent regulation.

This dual administration of the RCRA program means that joint permitting is often necessary, with EPA imposing the HSWA provisions and the state taking responsibility for the rest of the permitting.

## 4.8 Inspection

RCRA provides that any officer, employee or representative of EPA or a state with an authorized hazardous waste program may inspect the premises and records of any person who generates, stores, treats, transports, disposes of, or otherwise handles hazardous waste.[131] EPA's inspection authority extends to persons or sites that have handled hazardous wastes in the past but no longer do so. The owner/operator must provide government officials access to records and property relating to the wastes for inspection purposes. Copying and sampling are authorized.

In the 1984 HSWA, Congress has directed EPA and authorized states to improve and regularize RCRA inspections. EPA and the states must now conduct inspections of all privately-operated TSD facilities at least once every two years. Federally-operated TSD facilities must be inspected on an annual basis. Similarly, EPA must conduct annual inspections of TSD facilities which are operated by a state or local government to ensure compliance with the requirements of RCRA.[132]

All organizations should have an established policy and procedure for handling RCRA inspections, including consideration of whether or not a search warrant should be required.

---

[131]Section 3007. EPA's inspection activities under RCRA Section 3007 are subject to the Fourth Amendment's protection against unreasonable searches or seizures, which the Supreme Court has applied in holding that a warrant is generally required for an inspection by an administrative agency. See *Marshall v. Barlow's, Inc.*, 436 U.S. 307 (1978), which involved the inspection provisions of the Occupational Safety and Health Act.

[132]Section 3007(c)-(e).

## 4.9 Civil and Criminal Enforcement Actions

EPA can bring several types of enforcement actions under RCRA. These include administrative orders and civil and criminal penalties.[133] Whenever EPA determines that any person is violating Subtitle C of RCRA (including any regulation or permit issued thereunder), it may either issue an order requiring compliance immediately or within a specified time period, or seek injunctive relief against the alleged violator through a civil action filed in a U.S. District Court. Any person who violates any requirement of Subtitle C is liable for a civil penalty of up to $25,000 for each day of violation, regardless of whether the person had been served with a compliance order. A person subject to RCRA cannot rely on EPA to tell him when he is in violation, then take the required corrective action, and thus avoid a penalty. Failure to comply with an administrative order may also result in suspension or revocation of a permit.

RCRA also imposes criminal penalties of up to $50,000, two years imprisonment, or both for persons who "knowingly" commit certain violations. The 1984 HSWA significantly expanded the list of these criminal violations. Fines and imprisonment can be imposed on generators for knowingly allowing hazardous waste to be transported to an unpermitted facility, for knowing violations of federal interim status standards or counterpart state requirements, for knowing material omissions or the knowing failure to file reports required under RCRA by generators, transporters, and TSD facility operators, and knowing transport of hazardous waste without a manifest.

The "knowing" element of an environmental crime usually requires only that the defendant was aware of his or her own activities, not that the defendant had actual knowledge of EPA regulations or permit requirements. For example, in *United States v. Hayes International Corp.*, 786 F.2d 1499 (11th Cir. 1986), the court upheld a conviction for illegally transporting hazardous wastes in violation of RCRA, rejecting the proposed affirmative defense that the defendants did not know the wastes were classified as hazardous under EPA's regulations. Likewise, in *United States v. Laughlin*, 10 F.3d 961 (2d Cir. 1993), the court held that the defendants were guilty of illegal disposal under RCRA without proof that they had actual knowledge of the lack of a permit or RCRA's permit requirement. Under the Responsible Corporate Officer doctrine, individuals can be criminally liable if they are directly responsible within management for the conduct of subordinate employees, and they knew that the type of improper activity allegedly committed by the subordinate was occurring. *See United States v. MacDonald & Watson Waste Oil Co.*, 933 F.2d 35(1st Cir. 1991).

The statute also creates a crime of "knowing endangerment." The purpose of this sanction is to provide more substantial felony penalties for any person who commits the acts described above and "who knows at that time that he thereby places another person in imminent danger of death or serious bodily injury." Upon conviction, an individual faces a fine of up to $250,000 and/or up to fifteen years' imprisonment. An organizational defendant is subject to a maximum fine of $1 million.[134] All of this is part

---

[133] Section 3008.

[134] The first major conviction for knowing endangerment under RCRA was *United States v. Protex Industries, Inc.*, 874 F. 2d 740 (10th Cir. 1989) (drum recycling plant endangered employees exposed to toxic chemicals)

of the message from Congress to EPA and the Justice Department that more rigorous enforcement of the nation's hazardous wastes laws is the federal policy.

## 4.10 Citizen Suits

Citizen suits are envisioned by Congress and many others as a key enforcement tool for environmental protection. The RCRA citizen suit provision allows any person to bring a civil action against any alleged violator of RCRA requirements, or against the EPA Administrator for a failure to perform a nondiscretionary duty. Any person may also petition the EPA Administrator for promulgation, amendment, or repeal of any regulation. Courts are authorized to award costs including attorneys' fees to a substantially prevailing party.[135]

The 1984 HSWA substantially enhanced the role accorded to these suits. The citizen suit provision has been expanded to authorize suits in cases where past or present management or disposal of hazardous wastes has contributed to a situation that may present an imminent or substantial endangerment. However, citizen suits are prohibited (1) with respect to the siting and permitting of hazardous waste facilities (except by a state or local government); (2) where EPA is prosecuting an action under RCRA or Superfund; (3) while EPA or the state is engaged in a removal action under Superfund or has incurred costs to engage in a remedial action; or (4) where the responsible party is conducting a removal or remedial action pursuant to an order obtained from EPA. Affected parties may be allowed to intervene in ongoing suits. Plaintiffs must notify EPA, the state, and affected parties ninety days prior to commencement of a citizen suit.

## 4.11 Imminent Hazard Actions

In addition, EPA is authorized to bring suits to restrain an imminent and substantial endangerment to health or the environment.[136] EPA construes imminent and substantial endangerment to mean posing a "risk of harm" or "potential harm," but not requiring proof of actual harm.[137]

In response to conflicting federal court decisions, Congress reworded the "imminent hazard" provision in 1984 to clarify that actions which took place prior to the enactment of RCRA are covered by this provision. Thus a non-negligent generator whose wastes are no longer being deposited at a particular site may still be ordered to abate the hazard resulting from the leaking of previously deposited wastes.

The 1984 HSWA also required EPA to provide for public notice and comment, and the opportunity for a public meeting in the affected area, prior to entering into a settlement or covenant not to sue in an imminent hazard action.

## 5.0 STATE SOLID WASTE PROGRAMS UNDER SUBTITLE D

Regulation of non-hazardous waste is the responsibility of the states pursuant to Subtitle D of RCRA. The federal involvement is limited to establishing minimum criteria that prescribe the best practicable controls and monitoring requirements for solid waste disposal facilities.

---

[135]Section 7002.
[136]Section 7003.
[137]*United States v. Vertac Chemical Corp.*, 489 F. Supp. 870 (E.D. Ark. 1980).

In the 1984 HSWA, Congress directed EPA to revise the criteria for facilities receiving hazardous waste from households or from small generators to enable detection of groundwater contamination, provide for corrective action as necessary, and facility siting.[138] Compliance with the minimum requirements determines whether a facility is classified as an "open dump" or not. Disposal of solid waste in "open dumps" (i.e., those facilities not meeting the criteria) is prohibited. Existing dumps were allowed to make modifications that will permit them to meet the requirements, and it is the state's responsibility to ensure that such upgrading occurs or the open dumps are closed.

EPA was not given any enforcement authority, however, for the ban on open dumps. EPA's enforcement authority under RCRA only covers hazardous wastes. EPA cannot take action against a person disposing of non-hazardous wastes in an open dump or against the state for failing to close open dumps, other than terminating certain grant funds available to the state under RCRA. Recognizing this problem, Congress has asked EPA to make recommendations on the need for additional enforcement authorities.[139]

RCRA also envisions that the state, with the help of federal grant funds, will develop regional solid waste management plans. The program is patterned on Section 208 of the Clean Water Act and relies upon a comprehensive regional planning approach to solving solid waste problems. The state is responsible for identifying appropriate management areas, developing regional plans through the use of local and regional authorities, compiling inventories and closing or upgrading existing open dumps, and generally assessing the need for additional solid waste disposal capacity in the area.

Of particular significance is a requirement that states not have any bans on the importation of waste for storage, treatment or disposal, or have requirements that are substantially dissimilar from other disposal practices that would discourage the free movement of wastes across state lines. Although enforcement of this requirement may be difficult, in light of the limited enforcement authority available to EPA, it does evidence a congressional policy for a national approach to solid waste disposal.[140]

## 6.0 OTHER FEDERAL RESPONSIBILITIES

Subtitle E of RCRA gives the Department of Commerce (DOC) responsibility for developing standards for substituting secondary materials for virgin materials, developing markets for recovered materials, and for the promotion of resource recovery technology generally.

The authorities given to DOC are similar to those assigned to EPA in other sections of the act, specifically Subtitle H on Research, Development, Demonstrations and Information. Nevertheless, DOC has not received sufficient funding to support a major role.

Subtitle F of RCRA requires that all federal agencies and instrumentalities comply with all federal, state, interstate, and local requirements stemming from RCRA, unless

---

[138]Section 4010.

[139]*Id.*

[140]In *C & A Carbone, Inc. v. Town of Clarkstown, New York*, 114 S. Ct. 1677 (1994), the Supreme Court held that a New York town's flow control ordinance violated the Commerce Clause because it favored a local operator to the detriment of out-of-state businesses.

exempted by the president. It also requires the federal government to institute a procurement policy that encourages the purchase of recoverable materials which, because of their performance, can be substituted for virgin material at a reasonable price.

## 7.0 RESEARCH, DEVELOPMENT, DEMONSTRATION, AND INFORMATION

In cooperation with federal, state, and interstate authorities, private agencies and institutions and individuals, EPA is directed to conduct, encourage and promote the coordination of research, investigations, experiments, training, demonstrations, surveys, public education programs and studies. These R & D efforts can relate to the protection of health; planning, financing and operation of waste management systems including resource recovery; improvements in methodology of waste disposal and resource recovery; reduction of the amount of waste generated, and methods for remedying damages by earlier or existing landfills; and methods for rendering landfills safe for purposes of construction and other uses.

EPA was also directed to carry out a number of special studies including the following subjects: small-scale and low technology approaches to resource recovery; front-end separation for materials recovery; mining waste; sludge; and airport landfills.

## 8.0 MEDICAL WASTE

Congress added Subtitle J to RCRA with the enactment of the Medical Waste Tracking Act of 1988. In response to the problem of hypodermic needles and other medical wastes washing up on Atlantic Coast beaches, Congress directed EPA to set up a demonstration program for tracking the shipment and disposal of medical wastes in a selected number of states. The states directed to participate were New York, New Jersey, Connecticut, the states contiguous to the Great Lakes.

The demonstration program was concluded in 1992. EPA submitted a report to Congress summarizing the results and making recommendations for adequate control of medical waste shipments and disposal.

## 9.0 CONCLUSION

As the foregoing discussion amply demonstrates, the RCRA program is complex. The 1984 HSWA has added many new requirements which represent a challenge to the will and imagination of the regulated community. Industry has been challenged to find new ways to minimize, treat, recycle and dispose of hazardous waste. These include the use of innovative and emerging treatment technologies, as well as modifications to production processes and raw materials. Never has the incentive been greater to reuse or reclaim wastes, or to search out new products, processes, and raw materials that do not result in the generation of hazardous waste in the first place.

# CHAPTER 10

# UNDERGROUND STORAGE TANKS

Karen J. Nardi[1]
McCutchen, Doyle, Brown & Enersen
San Francisco, California

## 1.0 OVERVIEW

Underground storage tanks (USTs) are widely recognized as a major environmental problem. They have been the cause of soil and groundwater contamination at thousands of sites throughout the United States. Studies have shown that there are many reasons why USTs cause contamination. Some tanks and associated piping simply corroded or structurally failed during years of use. In other cases, poor past practices resulted in spills when tanks were emptied or when they overflowed during filling.[2]

In 1988, the United States Environmental Protection Agency (EPA) estimated that there were over two million UST systems (which include both the underground storage tank and piping connected to it) located at over 700,000 facilities nationwide. EPA judged that roughly 75 percent of such systems posed the greatest potential for leakage and environmental harm because the UST systems were made of steel without any form of corrosion protection.[3]

Since 1984,[4] tremendous resources have been devoted to cleaning up soil and groundwater contaminated from USTs. One study found that, as of March 1995, more than $5 billion had been spent by government and industry remediating leaking underground storage tanks in the previous two years, and that remaining cleanups would

---

[1]The author gratefully acknowledges the contributions of John J. Gregory and Steve Rosen.

[2]53 Fed. Reg 37088-90 (Sept. 23, 1988).

[3]*Id.* at 37095.

[4]In an attempt to address the widespread problems with USTs, Congress enacted the Hazardous and Solid Waste Amendments of 1984, which established in Subtitle I to the Resource Conservation and Recovery Act (RCRA) of 1976 a regulatory program for both new and existing USTs. *See* 42 U.S.C. §§ 6991-6991i. EPA adopted regulations pursuant to the new RCRA Subtitle I in 1988. *See* 53 Fed. Reg. 37082 *et seq.* (Sept. 23, 1988) (adopting final EPA regulations at 40 C.F.R. Part 280). Since 1988, EPA has issued several amendments to its UST regulations. *See, e.g.,* 54 Fed. Reg. 5451 (Feb. 3, 1989); 54 Fed. Reg. 47077 (Nov. 9, 1989); 55 Fed. Reg. 17753 (Apr. 27, 1990); 55 Fed. Reg. 17767 (Apr. 27, 1990); 55 Fed. Reg. 18566 (May 2, 1990); 55 Fed. Reg. 23737 (June 12, 1990); 55 Fed. Reg. 24692 (June 18, 1990); 55 Fed. Reg. 27837 (July 6, 1990); 55 Fed. Reg. 32647 (Aug. 10, 1990); 55 Fed. Reg. 33430 (Aug. 15, 1990); 55 Fed. Reg. 36840 (Sept. 7, 1990); 55 Fed. Reg. 46022 (Oct. 31, 1990); 56 Fed. Reg. 24 (Jan. 2, 1991); 56 Fed. Reg. 38342 (Aug. 13, 1991); 56 Fed. Reg. 40292 (Aug. 14, 1991); 56 Fed. Reg. 49376 (Sept. 27, 1991); 56 Fed. Reg. 66369 (Dec. 23, 1991); 58 Fed. Reg. 9026 (Feb. 18, 1993); 59 Fed Reg 9604 (Feb. 28, 1994); 59 Fed. Reg. 29958 (June 10, 1994); 60 Fed. Reg. 46692 (Sept. 7, 1995); 60 Fed. Reg. 57,747 (Nov. 20, 1995).

cost more than $35 billion.[5] However, some experts now believe we may be spending too much to clean up USTs relative to the magnitude of the environmental problem they create, at least in the case of petroleum releases.[6] Consequently, there is a move to develop a risk-based approach to cleanup.[7] This can include "passive bioremediation," the natural degradation of contaminants without active remediation.[8]

## 1.1 Objectives of the UST Program

In enacting the UST provisions of RCRA in 1984, Congress had several basic public policy objectives. The statute addresses both the problem of existing tanks which may have caused environmental problems and new tanks that should be designed and operated to eliminate the problems of the past.

One objective of the UST program is to identify existing tanks and require that they either be brought up to certain design and operating standards or be closed. Another purpose is to determine whether existing tanks have leaked, causing an environmental problem. If so, the law requires tank owners and/or operators to take corrective action to address the environmental problem.

For new tanks, the law requires that tanks meet strict design and operating standards and that the government be notified when they are installed. Any tanks that continue to be used must be operated in a way that will minimize the possibility of leaks or spills due to filling or emptying.

The RCRA program also requires the reporting, investigation, and cleanup of releases from USTs. Finally, federal law sets standards for closure of USTs and financial responsibility requirements for persons who own and operate petroleum USTs. The regulations, while detailed, were designed to accomplish these basic objectives.

The RCRA UST program, like many federal laws, is a delegated program. States are given an opportunity to adopt laws and regulations that meet the minimum federal standards. EPA has delegated authority to certain states that have adequate UST programs. In such cases, states (not EPA) are the primary permitting and enforcement authorities for USTs. While states may enforce federal law regarding USTs, state and local laws may be stricter than federal law. Thus, it is very important to check to see whether more stringent state and local laws apply.

This chapter describes the various federal requirements that apply to owners and operators of new and existing UST systems. Many state and local authorities have adopted requirements that apply to UST systems. The reader is strongly encouraged to check and verify compliance with such requirements to the extent applicable. The following aspects are discussed in this chapter:

---

[5]Environmental Information, Ltd., *Underground Storage Tank Cleanup: Status and Outlook* (1995) (cited in 25 Environment Reporter (Current Developments) 2290 (Mar. 17, 1995)).

[6]*See Recommendations to Improve the Cleanup Process for California's Leaking Underground Fuel Tanks (LUFTS),* Lawrence Livermore National Laboratory, Oct. 16, 1995 (hereinafter the "Lawrence Livermore Report"), at 16.

[7]*Id.* at 17-18.

[8]*Id.* at 10-11, 19.

**Basic Terminology**: This section describes what UST systems and which owners and operators are subject to the RCRA Subtitle I requirements.

**Implementation and Enforcement**: This section describes which regulatory agencies are responsible for implementation of the RCRA Subtitle I regulations and the mechanisms available for enforcement.

**Summary of Reporting and Recordkeeping Requirements**: This section provides a brief summary of the many reporting and recordkeeping obligations that owners and operators of UST systems must comply with.

**New UST Systems**: This section further describes the notification requirements for owners and operators of new UST systems. A summary of performance standards for new UST systems is also provided.

**Existing UST Systems**: This section further describes the notification requirements for owners and operators of existing UST systems. A summary of upgrading requirements for existing UST systems is also provided.

**General Operating Requirements**: This section describes the various operating requirements covering spill and overfill control, operation and maintenance of corrosion protection systems, substance compatibility, and UST system repairs.

**Release Detection**: This section summarizes the various release detection requirements, methods, and compliance schedules for USTs.

**Release Reporting, Investigation and Response**: This section describes the various procedures for reporting, investigating, confirming, and cleaning up releases from UST systems.

**Closure of UST Systems**: This section summarizes the requirements for temporary and permanent closure and change-in-service of UST systems.

**Financial Responsibility Requirements**: This section briefly summarizes the various financial responsibility obligations facing owners and operators of petroleum USTs.

## 2.0 BASIC TERMINOLOGY

### 2.1 Underground Storage Tank Systems

By legal definition, an underground storage tank (UST) is more than just a tank that is buried underground. Tanks and piping systems that are partially below the ground surface may be subject to the UST regulations. To be specific, an UST is defined as:

> [A]ny one or combination of tanks (including underground pipes connected thereto) that is used to contain an accumulation of regulated substances, and the volume of which (including the volume of underground pipes connected thereto) is 10 percent or more beneath the surface of the ground.[9]

Several systems are specifically excluded from the definition of UST under RCRA Subtitle I, including:

---

[9]40 C.F.R. § 280.12; 42 U.S.C. § 6991(1). Regulated substances are described in section 2.2 below.

a.  Farm or residential tanks of 1100 gallons or less capacity that are used noncommercially for storage of motor fuel;

b.  Heating oil storage tanks that are used on the premises where the tank is stored;

c.  Septic tanks;

d.  Pipeline facilities (including gathering lines) that are regulated under:
    i.   The Natural Gas Pipeline Safety Act of 1968,[10] or
    ii.  The Hazardous Liquid Pipeline Safety Act of 1979,[11] or
    iii. State laws comparable to the provisions of law referred to in subparagraphs (i) or (ii) above;

e.  Surface impoundments, pits, ponds, or lagoons;

f.  Stormwater or wastewater collection systems;

g.  Flow-through process tanks;

h.  Liquid traps or associated gathering lines directly related to oil or gas production and gathering operations;

i.  Storage tanks that are situated in an underground area (for example, basement) if the tank is situated upon or above the surface of the floor in that area; or

j.  Pipes connected to any of the tanks which are described in subparagraphs (a) through (i) above.[12]

In addition to the above, several systems are specifically excluded from regulation under RCRA Subtitle I, including:

a.  UST systems holding hazardous wastes listed or identified under Subtitle C of RCRA, or a mixture of such hazardous wastes and other regulated substances. Such UST systems would be subject to the hazardous waste requirements of RCRA Subtitle C;

b.  Wastewater treatment tank systems that are part of a wastewater treatment facility regulated under Section 402 or 307(b) of the Clean Water Act;[13]

c.  Equipment or machinery that contains regulated substances for operational purposes (for example, hydraulic lift tanks and electrical equipment tanks);

d.  UST systems with capacities of 110 gallons or less;

e.  UST systems that contain a *de minimis* concentration of regulated substances;[14]

f.  Emergency spill or overflow containment UST systems that are expeditiously emptied after use.[15]

---

[10]49 U.S.C. §§ 1671-1684.

[11]49 U.S.C. app. §§ 2001-2015.

[12]42 U.S.C. § 6991(1); 40 C.F.R. § 280.12.

[13]33 U.S.C. §§ 1342, 1317(b), respectively.

[14]In its preamble to the final UST regulations, EPA does not define what a *de minimis* concentration is, but states that the implementing agency shall determine on a case-by-case basis if tanks that hold very low or *de minimis* concentrations of regulated substances are to be excluded from the UST regulations. 53 Fed. Reg. at 37108 (Sept. 23, 1988).

[15]40 C.F.R. § 280.10(b).

In addition to those systems described above that are otherwise exempt or excluded from the UST regulations, EPA has "deferred" several other UST systems from some of its regulations. These deferred UST systems include:

a.    Wastewater treatment tank systems;

b.    UST systems containing radioactive material that are regulated under the Atomic Energy Act of 1954;[16]

c.    UST systems that are part of an emergency generator system at nuclear power generation facilities regulated by the Nuclear Regulatory Commission under 10 C.F.R. Part 50, Appendix A;

d.    Airport hydrant fuel distribution systems; and

e.    UST systems with field-constructed tanks.[17]

No person may install a "deferred" UST system that stores regulated substances unless the system is:

a.    Capable of preventing releases due to corrosion or structural failure throughout the system's operational life;

b.    Cathodically protected against corrosion, or otherwise designed or constructed in a manner to prevent the release or threatened release of any stored substance; and

c.    Constructed or lined with a material that is compatible with the stored substance. Deferred UST systems may be installed at a site without corrosion protection provided a corrosion expert determines that the site is not corrosive enough to cause a release due to corrosion during the operating life of the UST system. For the operating life of the tanks, owners and operators of those systems must maintain records that reflect such a determination.[18]

## 2.2 Regulated Substances

The RCRA UST program applies to tanks that contain "regulated substances." Any "hazardous substance" as defined in Section 101(14) of the Comprehensive Environmental Response, Compensation, and Liability Act (CERCLA) of 1980[19] is regulated under RCRA Subtitle I. Petroleum and petroleum-based substances that are derived from crude oil, such as motor fuels, jet fuels, distillate fuel oils, residual fuel oils, lubricants, petroleum solvents and used oils are also subject to regulation under RCRA Subtitle I.[20] RCRA Subtitle I regulations do not apply to hazardous wastes because they are regulated under RCRA Subtitle C.

---

[16]42 U.S.C. §§ 2011-2286i.

[17]Subparts B, C, D, E, and G of the UST regulations do not apply to any of these deferred systems. 40 C.F.R. § 280.10(c). Also note that Subpart D of the UST regulations does not apply to UST systems that store fuel solely for use by emergency power generators. (40 C.F.R. § 280.10(d)).

[18]40 C.F.R. § 280.11.

[19]42 U.S.C. § 9601(14).

[20]40 C.F.R. § 280.12 (definition of "regulated substance").

## 2.3 Owners And Operators

Owners and operators of USTs have certain responsibilities under RCRA Subtitle I. An "owner" is any person who owns an UST that is used for the storage, use, or dispensing of regulated substances on or after November 8, 1984. In addition, any person who owned an UST immediately before the discontinuation of its use prior to November 8, 1984 is considered an owner.[21] Thus, a person who acquires property containing USTs that were abandoned before acquisition of the property and before November 8, 1984 would not be an owner for purposes of the UST program. Also excluded from the definition of "owner" is "any person who, without participating in the management of an underground storage tank and otherwise not engaged in petroleum production, refining, and marketing, holds indicia of ownership primarily to protect the owner's security interest in the tank."[22] This provision is intended to protect lenders or other persons holding security interests in petroleum UST systems that otherwise do not actively participate in the operation of such UST systems.[23]

RCRA Subtitle I defines "operator" as "any person in control of, or having responsibility for, the daily operation of the underground storage tank."[24] Unlike regulations for owners, which focus on both current and former owners, these regulations, although not entirely clear, appear to focus only on current operators of UST systems.

## 3.0 IMPLEMENTATION AND ENFORCEMENT

### 3.1 Implementation

EPA has primary responsibility for implementation and enforcement of RCRA Subtitle I. However, the UST program allows for delegation of this authority to states. States may implement, subject to EPA approval, their own UST programs in place of the federal requirements if the state's requirements are "no less stringent" than the federal requirements and provide for adequate enforcement.[25] In addition to the federal program, many states and local authorities have adopted their own UST laws and regulations. Such requirements can, in fact, be more stringent than those provided under

---

[21]42 U.S.C. § 6991(3); 40 C.F.R. § 280.12.

[22]42 U.S.C. § 6991b(h)(9). This definition appears to apply only to owners of USTs that contain petroleum as opposed to any regulated substance.

[23]Holders of security interests are permitted to satisfy regulatory obligations as "operators" prior to foreclosure by undertaking specified "minimally burdensome" and "environmentally protective" actions to secure and protect the UST or UST system, while remaining exempt from RCRA's corrective action requirements. 60 Fed. Reg. 46692, 46695 (Sept. 7, 1995). *See also* 40 C.F.R. § 280.230.

[24]42 U.S.C. § 6991(4); 40 C.F.R. § 280.12.

[25]42 U.S.C. § 6991c(a), (b)(1). As of October 1996, 25 states had UST programs that have been approved by EPA. Those states are Alabama, Arkansas, Connecticut, Delaware, Georgia, Iowa, Kansas, Louisiana, Maine, Maryland, Massachusetts, Mississippi, Missouri, Montana, Nevada, New Hampshire, New Mexico, North Dakota, Oklahoma, Rhode Island, South Dakota, Utah, Vermont and Washington. This chapter shall refer to the agency responsible for implementing the federal UST requirements (i.e., either EPA or the state agency with an EPA-approved UST program) as the "implementing agency."

the federal regime. Thus, it is important for owners and operators of UST systems to verify compliance not only with federal requirements, but also with state and local requirements.

## 3.2 Enforcement

EPA has authority under RCRA Section 9006 to issue a compliance order to any person in violation of RCRA Subtitle I.[26] Alternatively, EPA may also commence a civil action in the United States district court for appropriate relief, including the issuance of a temporary or permanent injunction.[27] Failure to comply with an order issued by EPA may result in civil penalties of not more than $25,000 for each day of continued noncompliance.[28] Persons named on an order may request a public hearing to challenge the order within 30 days after the order is served.[29]

EPA may also assess civil penalties against owners and operators who do not comply with UST requirements. An owner who knowingly fails to notify or who submits false information pursuant to the RCRA Subtitle I initial notification requirements shall be subject to a civil penalty not to exceed $10,000 for each tank for which notification is not given or false information is submitted.[30] Owners or operators of USTs may also be subject to civil penalties, not to exceed $10,000 per tank per day of violation for failing to comply with UST requirements relating to leak detection, recordkeeping, reporting, corrective action, closure, and financial responsibility.[31] Similar penalties may be assessed for violations of such requirements in any EPA-approved state UST program.

EPA has authority to order owners and operators of USTs to take corrective action for any releases of petroleum when the EPA (or the state) determines that such corrective action will be done properly and promptly by the owner or operator.[32] Under RCRA Section 9003(h), EPA or the state (for EPA-approved state UST programs) may undertake corrective action itself only if such action is necessary to protect human health and the environment and one or more of the following situations exists:

a. No owner or operator can be found to carry out such corrective action within 90 days or such shorter period as may be necessary to protect human health and the environment;

b. The situation is such that it requires prompt action by EPA or the state to protect human health and the environment;

c. Corrective action costs exceed the amount of coverage required by the RCRA Subtitle I financial responsibility requirements; or

---

[26] 42 U.S.C. § 6991e(a)(1).

[27] For those states with UST programs that have been approved by the EPA, EPA is required to give notice to the state prior to issuing any order or commencing any civil action. 42 U.S.C. § 6991e(a)(2).

[28] 42 U.S.C. § 6991e(a)(3).

[29] 42 U.S.C. § 6991e(b).

[30] 42 U.S.C. § 6991e(d).

[31] 42 U.S.C. §§ 6991b(c), 6991e(d).

[32] *See* 42 U.S.C. § 6991b(h)(1)(A).

d.   The owner or operator of the UST has failed or refused to comply with a compliance order of the EPA under RCRA Section 9006, or with an order of the state to comply with corrective action regulations.[33]

In 1991, EPA issued a final rule establishing procedures relating to the issuance of RCRA Section 9003(h) corrective action orders.[34] The final rule amends regulations provided in 40 C.F.R. Part 24 regarding the issuance of, and administrative hearings on, corrective action orders. Generally speaking, the rule provides that the same administrative procedures employed for issuance of RCRA Section 3008(h) corrective action orders are to be used for the issuance of RCRA Section 9003(h) orders. Such procedures are less formal and resource-intensive than proceedings that would be required for RCRA Section 9006 compliance orders.[35]

## 4.0 SUMMARY OF REPORTING AND RECORDKEEPING REQUIREMENTS

Owners and operators of USTs are subject to myriad reporting and recordkeeping requirements under RCRA Subtitle I. The following is a brief overview of the numerous reporting and recordkeeping obligations. Later sections of this chapter discuss how these requirements apply to new tanks as opposed to existing tanks.

### 4.1 Reporting Requirements

Initial Notification: Owners and operators of existing and new UST systems are required to notify the appropriate designated agency of the use of such systems. Typically, the state or local regulatory agency is designated to receive such initial notification.[36] These owners and operators also must certify compliance with requirements governing UST system installation, cathodic protection, financial responsibility, and release detection.[37]

**Suspected Releases**: Owners and operators of USTs must report any suspected releases to the implementing agency.[38]

**Spills and Overfills**: Owners and operators of USTs must report any spills and overfills from UST systems to the implementing agency.[39]

**Confirmed Releases**: Upon confirmation of any release, owners and operators of USTs must report such release to the implementing agency within 24 hours or within another reasonable period of time determined by the agency.[40] Also note that a release of a hazardous substance equal to or in excess of its reportable quantity must also be reported immediately to the National Response Center and appropriate state and local

---

[33]42 U.S.C. § 6991b(h)(2).

[34]*See* 56 Fed. Reg. 49376 (Sept. 27, 1991).

[35]*Id.* at 49378.

[36]Owners and operators should contact the nearest EPA regional office to determine which agency has been designated for submittal of such notification.

[37]40 C.F.R. § 280.22.

[38]40 C.F.R. § 280.50.

[39]40 C.F.R. §§ 280.30(b) and 280.53.

[40]40 C.F.R. § 280.61.

authorities pursuant to CERCLA and the Superfund Amendments and Reauthorization Act (SARA) of 1986.[41]

**Corrective Action**: Owners and operators of USTs have several reporting obligations when undertaking corrective action involving USTs, including the reporting of initial abatement measures,[42] initial site characterization,[43] removal of free product,[44] results of investigations for soil and groundwater clean-ups,[45] and, if required by the implementing agency, submittal of corrective action plans.[46]

**Permanent Closure/Change-in-Service**: Owners and operators of USTs are required to provide advanced notice of the permanent closure or change-in-service of any UST, unless such action is in response to corrective action.[47]

**Financial Responsibility**: Owners and operators of USTs are required to submit various forms demonstrating financial responsibility for taking corrective action and for compensating third parties for bodily injury and property damage caused by accidental releases arising from the operation of petroleum USTs.[48]

### 4.2 Recordkeeping Requirements

RCRA Section 9005(b), 42 U.S.C. § 6991d(b), provides that any records, reports or information that are provided to implementing agencies shall be made available to the public, except information that has been designated as confidential by the agency.[49] Confidential records, reports or information must be designated as confidential and submitted separately from other records that are otherwise submitted to the regulatory agencies.[50]

**Site Corrosion Potential Analysis**: Owners and operators of metal USTs and piping that are installed at a site without corrosion protection must maintain records that analyze the corrosion potential of the site and UST systems.[51]

**Operation of Corrosion Protection Equipment**: Owners and operators of USTs must maintain records of inspections and testing of cathodic protection systems where used.[52]

**UST Repairs**: Owners and operators of USTs must document and maintain records of UST system repairs.[53]

**Release Detection**: All owners and operators of USTs must maintain records that document performance claims made by manufacturers of release detection equipment, as well as the results of any sampling, testing and monitoring for releases, and records

---

[41] 40 C.F.R. § 280.53, Note.
[42] 40 C.F.R. § 280.62.
[43] 40 C.F.R. § 280.63.
[44] 40 C.F.R. § 280.64(d).
[45] 40 C.F.R. § 280.65.
[46] 40 C.F.R. § 280.66.
[47] 40 C.F.R. § 280.71(a).
[48] 40 C.F.R. § 280.93.
[49] *See* 18 U.S.C. § 1905.
[50] 42 U.S.C. § 6991d(b)(3).
[51] 40 C.F.R. § 280.20(a)(4), (b)(3).
[52] 40 C.F.R. § 280.31(d).
[53] 40 C.F.R. § 280.33(f).

relating to the calibration, maintenance and repair of release detection equipment.[54] To the extent that owners or operators of USTs use other release detection methods than those prescribed by the RCRA Subtitle I regulations, owners or operators must submit documentation that justifies the use of such other methods.[55]

**Permanent Closure**: Owners and operators of USTs are required to maintain records of permanent closure or change-in-service of UST systems for at least three years after completion of the closure or change-in-service.[56]

**Financial Responsibility**: Owners or operators of USTs must maintain evidence of all financial assurance mechanisms used to demonstrate financial responsibility under the RCRA Subtitle I regulations.[57] Owners and operators of USTs must maintain their records either at the UST site or at a readily available alternative site. If an UST is permanently closed, owners and operators may mail closure records to the implementing agency if they cannot be kept at the site or at an alternative site.[58]

## 5.0 NEW UST SYSTEMS

### 5.1 Notification Requirements
Any owner who brings an UST system into use after May 8, 1986 must notify the designated regulatory agency of the existence of such tank system within 30 days of bringing the UST into use. A standard notification form is usually used. Owners and operators of new UST systems must certify in the notification form that they have complied with various UST requirements, including, for example, requirements for installation of tanks and piping, cathodic protection, financial responsibility, and release detection.[59]

The installer of the UST systems must also certify in the notification form that the methods used to install the tank system comply with industry codes of practice developed by a nationally recognized association or independent testing laboratory in accordance with the manufacturer's instructions. The UST regulations refer to several industry codes of practice that may be used by installers to comply with these requirements.[60]

Finally, any person who sells a tank intended to be used as an UST must notify the purchaser of the various notification obligations for owners of USTs under the UST regulations.[61] Companies that sell property with underground storage tanks should be sure that they advise the buyer of the UST notice requirements. Typically this is done in the purchase and sale documentation.

---

[54] 40 C.F.R. § 280.45.
[55] 40 C.F.R. § 280.42(b)(5).
[56] 40 C.F.R. § 280.74.
[57] 40 C.F.R. § 280.111.
[58] 40 C.F.R. § 280.34(c).
[59] 40 C.F.R. § 280.22.
[60] 40 C.F.R. § 280.20(d). *See* 40 C.F.R. 280.22(f).
[61] 40 C.F.R. § 280.22(g).

## 5.2 Performance Standards

Owners and operators of new UST systems are required to meet several performance standards in order to prevent releases of regulated substances from the systems resulting from either structural failure, corrosion, or spills and overfills. The following sections describe these performance standards.

### 5.2.1 Tanks

USTs must be properly designed, constructed and protected from corrosion in accordance with appropriate industry codes of practice.[62] An owner may install an UST and corrosion protection system not specified by the regulations as long as the implementing agency determines that the system is capable of preventing the release or threatened release of any stored regulated substance in a manner that is no less protective of human health and the environment than other prescribed UST systems.[63]

Owners and operators wishing to install tanks constructed of metal *without* corrosion protection must have a corrosion expert determine that the site is not sufficiently corrosive to cause a release due to corrosion from the UST during its operating life. In addition, for the remaining life of the tank, owners and operators of such USTs must maintain records demonstrating such compliance.[64]

### 5.2.2 Piping

As with tanks, UST regulations provide similar guidelines and industry codes of practice to follow in the design, construction and corrosion protection of new piping systems. The regulations provide standards for new piping constructed of fiberglass-reinforced plastic and steel with cathodic protection.[65] Similar regulations are provided for piping constructed of metal without cathodic protection. They require the owner and operator to have a corrosion expert determine that the site is not corrosive and to maintain records that demonstrate that the site will remain noncorrosive for the remaining life of the UST piping.[66]

Piping other than that specifically described by the regulations may be constructed if the regulatory agency determines that it is as capable of preventing the release or threatened release of regulated substances as EPA-approved systems.[67]

### 5.2.3 Spill and Overfill Prevention Equipment

Owners and operators of new USTs must employ spill and overflow prevention equipment to prevent releases that may occur during the filling or emptying of such USTs. Overfill prevention equipment must be capable of either:

---

[62]40 C.F.R. § 280.20(a)(1)-(3) specifically addresses tanks constructed of fiberglass-reinforced plastic, steel with cathodic protection, and steel-fiberglass-reinforced-plastic composite.

[63]40 C.F.R. § 280.20(a)(5).

[64]40 C.F.R. § 280.20(a)(4).

[65]40 C.F.R. § 280.20(b)(1)-(2).

[66]40 C.F.R. § 280.20(b)(3).

[67]40 C.F.R. § 280.20(b)(4).

a. automatically shutting off flow into the tank when the tank is no more than 95-percent full;
b. alerting the transfer operator when the tank is more than 90-percent full by restricting the flow into the tank or triggering a high-level alarm;
c. restricting flow 30 minutes prior to overfilling and alerting the operator with a high-level alarm one minute before overfilling; or
d. automatically shutting off the flow into the tank so that none of the fittings located on top of the tank are exposed to the product due to overfilling.[68]

Spill prevention equipment must be capable of preventing the release of regulated substances into the environment when the transfer hose is detached from the tank's fill pipe.[69] Alternative spill and overflow prevention equipment can be used if owners and operators can satisfactorily demonstrate to the implementing agency that the equipment is no less protective of human health and the environment. No spill and overfill prevention equipment is required if transfers of regulated substances to and from the UST system involve no more than 25 gallons at one time.[70]

### 5.2.4 Installation
All new tanks and pipes must be properly installed in accordance with appropriate industry codes of practice. Owners and operators must certify, test or inspect such installation to demonstrate compliance with such industry codes of practice.[71]

## 6.0 EXISTING UST SYSTEMS

### 6.1 Notification Requirements
Owners of UST systems that were in the ground on or after May 8, 1986 were required to notify the designated regulatory agency of the existence of such tank systems, unless the owner knew that the tank system was subsequently removed from the ground.[72] No notification, however, was required if the UST systems were taken out of operation on or before January 1, 1974. The notice should specify, to the extent known by the owner, the date the tank was taken out of operation, the age of the tank on the date taken out of operation, the size, type and location of the tank, and the type and quantity of substances left stored in the tank on the date the tank was taken out of operation.[73]

Although existing tanks should have been registered by May 1986, states continue to find previously unknown tanks at former gas stations and other businesses. One study

---

[68] 40 C.F.R. § 280.20(c)(1)(ii).
[69] 40 C.F.R. § 280.20(c)(1)(i).
[70] 40 C.F.R. § 280.20(c)(2).
[71] 40 C.F.R. § 280.20(d), (e).
[72] 42 U.S.C. § 6991a(a); 40 C.F.R. § 280.22(a).
[73] 42 U.S.C. § 6991(a)(2)(B).

estimated that as recently as 1995 there were as many as 220,000 existing USTs that were subject to regulation but were still unregistered.[74]

Companies that are considering the purchase of real property typically conduct a "due diligence" review to see whether the property has environmental liabilities that the owner will acquire. One item in an environmental due diligence checklist is underground tanks. A prospective buyer can check agency records to see if the property has any registered tanks. Sometimes unregistered tanks are discovered by a prospective purchaser or his consultant during a site inspection.

## 6.2 Upgrading of Existing UST Systems

All existing UST systems are required, by no later than December 22, 1998, to meet one of the following requirements:

    a.    new UST system performance standards;[75]
    b.    tank upgrading requirements;[76] or
    c.    closure and corrective action requirements.[77]

Existing metal piping systems must also be upgraded to meet the performance standards for new piping systems.[78] Existing UST systems must also comply with new UST system requirements for spill and overfill prevention.[79]

## 7.0 GENERAL OPERATING REQUIREMENTS

### 7.1 Spill and Overfill Control

Owners and operators of USTs must ensure that the volume of the tank is greater than the volume of regulated substance to be transferred into the tank *before* the transfer is made, and that the transfer operation is monitored constantly to prevent overfilling and spilling.[80] The owner and operator must report, investigate and clean up any spills and overflows that occur during transfer operations.[81]

---

[74]Environmental Information, Ltd., *Underground Storage Tank Cleanup: Status and Outlook* (1995) (cited in 25 Environment Reporter (Current Developments) 2290 (Mar. 17, 1995)).

[75]40 C.F.R. § 280.21(a)(1). 40 C.F.R. § 280.20 details the standards.

[76]40 C.F.R. § 280.21(a)(2). 40 C.F.R. § 280.21(b) provides upgrading requirements for steel tanks, including requirements relating to the upgrading of the interior lining of the tanks and cathodic protection. Specific industry codes of practice are referenced.

[77]40 C.F.R. § 280.21(a)(3). 40 C.F.R. § 280 subparts F and G describe the requirements.

[78]40 C.F.R. § 280.21(c) notes that the industry codes of practice and standards listed in 40 C.F.R. § 280.20(b)(2) may be used to comply with the upgrading requirements.

[79]40 C.F.R. § 280.21(d) specifies that the requirements in 40 C.F.R. § 280.20(c) are to be followed.

[80]40 C.F.R. § 280.30.

[81]*See* Section 9.9 of this chapter and 40 C.F.R. § 280.53 for requirements regarding the reporting and clean-up of spills and overfills.

## 7.2 Operation and Maintenance of Corrosion Protection Systems

All owners and operators of steel UST systems that employ corrosion protection must ensure that the corrosion protection systems are operated and maintained to continuously protect those metal components of the UST system that are in contact with the ground.[82] In addition, all UST systems equipped with cathodic protection systems must be inspected for proper operation by a qualified cathodic protection tester in accordance with specific regulatory requirements.[83] Owners and operators of UST systems using cathodic protection must keep and maintain records of the operation of the cathodic protection systems.[84]

## 7.3 Substance Compatibility

Regulations require owners and operators to use UST systems that are made of or lined with materials that are compatible with the regulated substances that are stored in the UST systems.[85]

## 7.4 UST System Repairs

Any repairs made to UST systems must be performed in a manner that will prevent releases due to structural failure or corrosion as long as the UST system is used to store regulated substances. Regulations specify that repairs to UST systems must be properly conducted in accordance with appropriate industry codes of practice.[86] Metal pipe sections and fittings that have released regulated substances as a result of corrosion or other damage must be replaced.[87] Repaired tanks and piping must be tightness tested within 30 days following the date of completion of the repair, except if alternative methods are used to verify the sufficiency of the repair.[88] Cathodic protection systems must be tested within six months following the repair of any cathodically protected UST system.[89] UST regulations require owners and operators to maintain records of each repair for the remaining operating life of the UST system.[90]

## 8.0 RELEASE DETECTION

## 8.1 General Requirements and Schedule

Owners and operators of new and existing UST systems must provide a method or combination of methods of release detection that can detect a release from any portion of the tank and connected underground piping that routinely contains regulated substances. There are several requirements that govern the installation, operation and performance of release detection equipment and methods for tanks.[91] Owners and

---

[82]40 C.F.R. § 280.31(a).
[83]40 C.F.R. § 280.31(b) and (c) provide frequency and inspection criteria.
[84]40 C.F.R. § 280.31(d).
[85]40 C.F.R. § 280.32.
[86]40 C.F.R. § 280.33(a)-(b).
[87]40 C.F.R. § 280.33(c).
[88]40 C.F.R. § 280.33(d).
[89]40 C.F.R. § 280.33(e).
[90]40 C.F.R. § 280.33(f).
[91]*See* 40 C.F.R. § 280.43.

operators of suction and pressurized piping systems must also comply with applicable release detection requirements for those piping systems.[92] The date by which owners and operators of UST systems must comply with release detection requirements depends on when the tank and piping systems were installed.[93] Those requirements are being phased in. One study estimated that some 350,000 active USTs underwent monthly leak detection procedures for the first time in 1993.[94]Any existing UST system that cannot apply a method of release detection that complies with applicable release detection requirements must be closed by the date such compliance was required.[95]

## 8.2 Methods of Release Detection for Tanks and Piping

UST regulations set forth several methods of release detection that may be used for tanks and piping. Such methods for tanks include product inventory control, manual tank gauging, automatic tank gauging, vapor monitoring, groundwater monitoring, interstitial monitoring between the tank and a surrounding secondary barrier, or any other approved method of release detection.[96] Release detection methods for piping include automatic line leak detectors, line tightness testing, vapor monitoring, groundwater monitoring, interstitial monitoring, or any other approved method designed to detect a release from any portion of the underground piping that routinely contains regulated substances.[97] Release detection methods must be capable of detecting a leak rate specified in the regulations for each method with a probability of detection of 95 percent and a probability of false alarm of 5 percent, unless the release detection method was permanently installed prior to December 22, 1990.[98]

## 8.3 Specific Requirements for Petroleum USTs

USTs containing petroleum products must be monitored at least every 30 days for releases.[99] The 30-day monitoring requirement does not apply to those UST systems that (1) meet the performance standards for new and upgraded tank systems,[100] and (2) employ monthly inventory control or monthly manual tank gauging in conjunction with tank tightness testing.[101] UST systems that do not meet the performance standards for new or upgraded USTs may use monthly inventory controls or manual tank gauging in conjunction with annual tank tightness testing until December 22, 1998 when the tank

---

[92]*See* 40 C.F.R. §§ 280.41(b) and 280.44.

[93]*See* 40 C.F.R. § 280.40(c).

[94]Environmental Information, Ltd., *The Underground Storage Tank Market: Its Current Status and Future Challenges*, 3 (1992).

[95]40 C.F.R. § 280.40(d).

[96]*See* 40 C.F.R. § 280.43 for specifications on tank size and appropriate gauging methods.

[97]40 C.F.R. § 280.44.

[98]40 C.F.R. § 280.40(a)(3). Note, however, that the permanent installation date for automatic line leak detectors is September 22, 1991.

[99]40 C.F.R. § 280.41(a).

[100]40 C.F.R. §§ 280.20-280.21.

[101]Tank tightness testing must be performed at least every five years until either December 22, 1998, or ten years after the tank is installed or upgraded, whichever is later. 40 C.F.R. § 280.41(a)(1).

must be upgraded or permanently closed.[102] Owners and operators of tanks with capacities of 550 gallons or less may use weekly tank gauging in lieu of other release detection methods.[103]

Underground piping systems must also be monitored for releases. Underground piping that conveys regulated substances under pressure must be equipped with an automatic line leak detector and have annual line tightness testing or monthly monitoring.[104] Underground piping that conveys regulated substances under suction must either have line tightness testing conducted at least every three years or use monthly monitoring. Suction piping may be exempt from release detection requirements if it meets specific design and construction standards.[105]

### 8.4 Specific Requirements for Hazardous Substance UST Systems

Until December 22, 1998, owners and operators of existing hazardous substance UST systems must employ release detection that at least meets the requirements for petroleum UST systems. After December 22, 1998, all existing hazardous substance UST systems must comply with the release detection requirements for new hazardous substance UST systems.[106] Regulations require new hazardous substance UST systems to have secondary containment systems and be checked for evidence of a release at least every 30 days.[107] Similarly, underground piping that conveys hazardous substances must also be equipped with secondary containment and, if under pressure, must also be equipped with an automatic line leak detector system.[108]

Other methods of release detection for hazardous substance USTs may be used if approved by the implementing agency. Owners and operators, however, must demonstrate to the implementing agency that the alternative method can effectively detect a release of the stored hazardous substance. Owners and operators must provide information to the implementing agency on effective corrective action technologies, health risks, chemical and physical properties of the stored substances, and the characteristics of the UST site, and must obtain agency approval to use the alternative release detection method before installation and operation of the new hazardous substance UST system.[109]

---

[102]40 C.F.R. § 280.41(a)(2).
[103]40 C.F.R. § 280.41(a)(3).
[104]40 C.F.R. § 280.41(b)(1).
[105]40 C.F.R. § 280.41(b)(2).
[106]40 C.F.R. § 280.42(a).
[107]40 C.F.R. § 280.42(b). The regulation notes that the provisions of 40 C.F.R. § 265.193 regarding containment and detection of releases for hazardous waste storage tanks may be used to comply with the release detection requirements for hazardous substance USTs.
[108]40 C.F.R. § 280.42(b)(4).
[109]40 C.F.R. § 280.42(b)(5).

## 9.0 RELEASE REPORTING, INVESTIGATION AND RESPONSE

### 9.1 Overview

EPA has estimated that the nation might spend $32 billion to investigate and clean up chemical releases and spills from underground storage tanks. One study suggests that figure might exceed $41 billion and take over 30 years.[110] Cleanups typically involve excavation of contaminated soil and testing to see whether underlying groundwater has been affected. If groundwater has been contaminated, the cost of a cleanup can escalate rapidly.[111] In many cases, on-site methods of soil treatment such as soil vapor extraction are needed to remove contaminants from areas such as those beneath buildings where excavation is impractical. New studies suggest that the costs of cleaning up petroleum releases from USTs are excessive because fuel hydrocarbons have limited impacts on human health or the environment as they readily biodegrade.[112] As a result, many states have moved towards a risk-based approach to corrective action. This section discusses the legal requirements for reporting, investigating, and cleaning up releases from USTs.

### 9.2 Reporting of Suspected Releases

Owners and operators of UST systems must report any suspected release to the implementing agency within 24 hours or another reasonable time period specified by the implementing agency.[113] UST regulations identify several conditions which would require reporting:

a. The discovery of regulated substances released at the UST site or in the surrounding area.[114]

b. Unusual operating conditions observed by owners and operators, including for example, the erratic behavior of product dispensing equipment, the sudden loss of product from the UST system, or any unexplained presence of water in the UST. Regulations note that the reporting of such unusual conditions is not required if the UST system equipment is found to be defective but not leaking and is immediately repaired or replaced.[115]

c. Monitoring results from any required release detection method which indicate that a release may have occurred. Reporting is not required if the release detection monitoring device is found to be defective and is immediately repaired, recalibrated or replaced, and if additional monitoring does not confirm the initial result or, in the case of inventory control release

---

[110]Environmental Information, Ltd., *The Underground Storage Tank Market: Its Current Status and Future Challenges*, 2-3 (1992).

[111]EPA, concerned that managing petroleum-contaminated media and debris under RCRA would delay cleanups and escalate costs, proposed in February 1993 to exempt from certain portions of EPA's hazardous waste regulations contaminated soils and groundwater generated from UST corrective actions. *See* 58 Fed. Reg. 8504 (Feb. 12, 1993). EPA anticipates taking final action on this rule by December 1996. 61 Fed. Reg. 23670 (May 13, 1996).

[112]*See* Lawrence Livermore Report at 15-16.

[113]40 C.F.R. § 280.50.

[114]40 C.F.R. § 280.50(a).

[115]40 C.F.R. § 280.50(b).

detection monitoring, a second month of data does not confirm the initial result.[116]

## 9.3 Release Investigation and Confirmation

UST regulations require all owners and operators to immediately investigate and confirm *suspected* releases of regulated substances within seven days or another reasonable time period as specified by the implementing agency.[117] Unless another procedure is approved by the implementing agency, owners and operators are required to take additional steps as described in the sections below.

### 9.3.1 System Test

Owners and operators must conduct tightness testing of the UST and associated piping to determine whether a leak exists. Should such testing indicate the presence of a leak, owners and operators must repair, replace or upgrade the UST system and begin corrective action to remedy any release. No further investigation is required if testing results do not indicate the presence of a leak and environmental contamination was not the basis for suspecting a release. Owners and operators must conduct a site check, as described below, if environmental contamination has been observed at the site, even though testing results do not indicate the presence of a leak.[118]

### 9.3.2 Site Check

If environmental contamination is observed at the UST site, owners and operators must evaluate whether a release has occurred from the UST system. If test results indicate that a release has occurred, owners and operators must begin corrective action in accordance with UST regulations. If test results do not indicate that a release has occurred, further investigation is not required.[119]

## 9.4 Initial Release Response

Once a release from an UST system is confirmed, owners and operators must comply with various corrective action requirements. Owners and operators must perform certain initial response actions within 24 hours of a release, or within another reasonable period of time determined by the implementing agency. Those actions include reporting the release to the implementing agency, taking immediate action to prevent any further release of the regulated substance into the environment, and identifying and mitigating any fire, explosion, and vapor hazards that may be associated with the release.[120]

## 9.5 Initial Abatement Measures

Following release confirmation, owners and operators of UST systems must also perform certain abatement measures. Those measures include:

---

[116]40 C.F.R. § 280.50(c).
[117]40 C.F.R. § 280.52.
[118]40 C.F.R. § 280.52(a)(3).
[119]40 C.F.R. § 280.52(b).
[120]40 C.F.R. § 280.61.

a.    removal of as much of the regulated substance from the UST system as is necessary to prevent further release to the environment;

b.    visual inspection of any aboveground or exposed belowground releases and prevention of any further migration of such releases into surrounding soils and groundwater;

c.    continued monitoring and mitigation of any additional fire and safety hazards posed by vapors or free product in subsurface structures;

d.    remediation of any hazards posed by contaminated soils that are excavated or exposed as a result of release confirmation, site investigation, abatement or corrective action activities;

e.    if not already determined, investigation for the presence of a release where contamination is most likely to be present at the UST site; and

f.    investigation to determine the possible presence of free product and removal of free product as soon as practicable.[121]

UST regulations require owners and operators to submit to the implementing agency a report summarizing the initial abatement steps taken and any resulting information or data within 20 days of release confirmation or within another reasonable time period specified by the implementing agency.[122]

### 9.6 Initial Site Characterization

Owners and operators must also assemble information about the site and the nature of the release, including information gained while confirming the release or completing the initial abatement measures. Such information must include at least:

a.    data on the nature and estimated quantity of release;

b.    data from available sources and/or site investigations concerning surrounding populations, water quality, use and approximate locations of wells potentially affected by the release, subsurface soil conditions, locations of subsurface sewers, climatological conditions, and land use;

c.    results of the site check; and

d.    results of the free product investigations.

Owners and operators must submit this initial site characterization to the implementing agency within 45 days of release confirmation or according to a schedule required by the implementing agency.[123]

### 9.7 Free Product Removal

Where investigation has indicated the presence of free product, owners and operators must remove free product to the maximum extent practicable as determined by the implementing agency.[124] Owners and operators must prepare and submit to the

---

[121] 40 C.F.R. § 280.62(a).
[122] 40 C.F.R. § 280.62(b).
[123] 40 C.F.R. § 280.63.
[124] 40 C.F.R. § 280.64.

implementing agency a free product removal report that describes conditions and the measures taken to abate the presence of free product.[125]

## 9.8 Investigations for Soil and Groundwater Cleanup

Owners and operators must also conduct investigations of soil and groundwater at the area of release, the release site, and the surrounding area possibly affected by the release if any of the following conditions exist:

a. Groundwater wells have been affected by the release;
b. Free product is found to need recovery;
c. Contaminated soils may be in contact with groundwater; and
d. The implementing agency requests an investigation, based on the potential effects of contaminated soil or groundwater on nearby surface water and groundwater resources.[126]

Owners and operators are required to submit information collected from such investigations as soon as practicable or in accordance with a schedule established by the implementing agency.

## 9.9 Reporting and Cleanup of Spills and Overfills

Spills and overfills must be contained and immediately cleaned up. Owners and operators must report any spill and overfill incident to the implementing agency within 24 hours, or other reasonable time period specified by the implementing agency, and begin corrective action if there are:

a. spills or overfills of petroleum exceeding 25 gallons or another reasonable amount specified by the implementing agency, or that causes a sheen on nearby surface water; and
b. spills or overfills of hazardous substances that equal or exceed its reportable quantity under CERCLA.[127]

Owners and operators are required to contain and immediately clean up spills and overfills in amounts less than those described above, but are not required to report such incidents. However, the regulations provide that if such cleanup cannot be accomplished within 24 hours or another reasonable time period as specified by the implementing agency, owners and operators must immediately report such incidents.[128]

---

[125]40 C.F.R. § 280.64(d).

[126]40 C.F.R. § 280.65.

[127]40 C.F.R. § 280.53(a). For designation and reportable quantities of hazardous substances under CERCLA, *see* 40 C.F.R. Part 302.

[128]40 C.F.R. § 280.53(b). UST regulations also note that pursuant to 40 C.F.R. §§ 302.6 and 355.40, a release of a hazardous substance equal to or in excess of its reportable quantity must also be reported immediately (rather than within 24 hours) to the National Response Center under Sections 102 and 103 of CERCLA, and to appropriate state and local authorities under Title III of SARA.

## 9.10 Corrective Action Plan

The implementing agency may require owners and operators to submit a corrective action plan for contaminated soils and groundwater.[129] In such instances, owners and operators typically will prepare the plan according to a schedule and format established by the implementing agency. In some instances, owners and operators may choose to voluntarily submit a corrective action plan for contaminated soil and groundwater. The corrective action plan must provide for adequate protection of human health and the environment as determined by the implementing agency. Upon approval of the corrective action plan by the implementing agency, owners and operators must implement the plan and monitor, evaluate and report the results of such implementation in accordance with a schedule and format typically established by the implementing agency.[130]

Owners and operators may begin cleanup of soil and groundwater before a corrective action plan is approved by the implementing agency. However, owners and operators must first notify the implementing agency of their intention to begin clean-up, and they must comply with any conditions imposed by the implementing agency. Owners and operators must then incorporate those self-initiated clean-up measures into the corrective action plan that is submitted to the implementing agency for approval.[131]

## 9.11 The Evolving Approach to Petroleum UST Cleanups

Over the past two years, the American Society for Testing and Materials (ASTM) has worked to develop a standard using risk-based corrective action (RBCA) techniques at petroleum-release sites.[132] EPA supports the use of risk-based approaches that seeks to protect human health and the environment while allowing for consideration of site-specific circumstances.[133] As a result, many states have implemented risk-based corrective action programs for the management of petroleum releases.

The Lawrence Livermore National Laboratory (LLNL), commissioned by the California State Water Resources Control Board to study California's program for remediating leaking underground storage tanks, endorsed the use of risk-based approaches in a recently-published report.[134] After studying the fate and transport characteristics of petroleum leaks in California, LLNL announced several findings and conclusions:

- The public water supply is not threatened with high levels of benzene. Of the 12,150 public water supply wells tested statewide, the LLNL determined that only 48 were reported to have measurable benzene concentrations. The report concludes

---

[129]40 C.F.R. § 280.66(a).

[130]40 C.F.R. § 280.66(c). *See also* 40 C.F.R. § 280.67.

[131]40 C.F.R. § 280.66(d).

[132]*See* American Society for Testing Materials (ASTM) Emergency Standard Guide for Risk-Based Corrective Action Applied at Petroleum Release Sites, ES 38-94.

[133]"FACT SHEET, U.S. EPA Position on LLNL's Report and Recommendations on California's Leaking Underground Storage Tank Program" (undated).

[134]*See generally* Lawrence Livermore Report.

that money spent to remediate low-risk sites over the past decade has not been cost-effective.[135]

- Passive bioremediation acts to naturally complete the cleanup process once the source of petroleum contamination is removed. Passive bioremediation should be used as a remediation alternative "whenever possible."[136]

- A modified ASTM risk-based approach that incorporates tiered decision-making should be implemented at the majority of leaking petroleum UST sites in California.[137]

These conclusions have been accepted by California regulatory agencies.[138] EPA, on the other hand, has taken a more cautious approach and has criticized several aspects of the Lawrence Livermore study, including its emphasis on passive bioremediation as a remedial alternative.[139]

RBCA techniques have dramatically changed the approach to cleanup at a number of UST sites where the selected remedy is now passive bioremediation. Some sites with groundwater contamination that previously would have required the installation of pump-and-treat technology have received approval for regulatory closure without any form of active remediation.

## 10.0 CLOSURE OF UST SYSTEMS

### 10.1 Temporary Closure

Occasionally, owners and operators will discontinue use of USTs for an extended period. However, owners and operators must continue to comply with requirements governing the operation and maintenance of corrosion protection and release detection systems, as well as requirements for release reporting, investigation, confirmation, and corrective action if a release is suspected or confirmed during the period of temporary closure. Compliance with release detection requirements is not necessary as long as the UST is empty.[140]

If an UST system is temporarily closed for 3 months or more, owners and operators, in addition to the above requirements, must leave vent lines open and functioning and cap and secure all other lines, pumps, manways, and ancillary equipment.[141] If an UST system is temporarily closed for more than 12 months and does not meet either performance standards for new UST systems or the upgrading requirements for existing systems (excluding spill and overfill requirements), then

---

[135]*Id.* at 4, 16.

[136]*Id.* at 19.

[137]*Id.* at 18.

[138]*See, e.g.,* Letter dated December 8, 1995, from Walt Pettit, Executive Director of the State Water Resources Control Board to All Regional Water Board Chairpersons concerning the Lawrence Livermore Report.

[139]Comments on LLNL Recommendations to Improve the Cleanup Process for California's Leaking Underground Fuel Tanks, U.S. EPA Region IX (June 6, 1996).

[140]*See* 40 C.F.R. § 280.70(a).

[141]40 C.F.R. § 280.70(b).

owners and operators must permanently close the UST system, unless the implementing agency provides an extension of the 12-month temporary closure period.[142] Owners and operators must complete a site assessment in accordance with 40 C.F.R. § 280.72 before applying for such an extension.

## 10.2 Permanent Closure/Change-in-Service

Before beginning either permanent closure or a change-in-service[143] of an UST system, owners and operators must notify the implementing agency, at least 30 days before beginning such activities, of their intent to undertake such activities unless such action is in response to corrective action associated with any release from the UST system.[144] For permanent closure, tanks must be emptied, cleaned, and either removed from the ground or filled with inert solid material.[145] Before permanent closure or a change-in-service is completed, owners and operators must conduct a site assessment to evaluate whether releases have occurred at the UST site. Corrective action must be undertaken if contamination is encountered during the site assessment.[146]

For UST systems that were permanently closed before December 22, 1988, the implementing agency may direct owners and operators to assess the area involved in the UST closure and may close the UST system in accordance with UST regulations if releases from the UST are determined to pose a current or potential threat to human health and the environment.[147]

Owners and operators must maintain records of closure or change-in-service that are capable of demonstrating compliance with the regulatory requirements. The results of any site assessment must be maintained for at least three years after completion of permanent closure or change-in-service by the owners and operators who took the UST system out of service, the current owners and operators of the UST system site, or by the implementing agency if the records cannot be maintained at the closed facility.[148]

## 11.0 FINANCIAL RESPONSIBILITY REQUIREMENTS

### 11.1 Applicability and Compliance Dates

Owners and operators of all petroleum UST systems that are subject to the UST regulations must demonstrate an ability to pay for cleanups and to compensate third parties for bodily injury and property damage caused by accidental releases arising from the operation of petroleum USTs.[149] Called the "financial responsibility" requirements,

---

[142]40 C.F.R. § 280.70(c).

[143]A change-in-service is described as the continued use of an UST system to store a nonregulated substance. 40 C.F.R. § 280.71(c).

[144]40 C.F.R. § 280.71(a).

[145]40 C.F.R. § 280.71(b).

[146]40 C.F.R. § 280.72.

[147]40 C.F.R. § 280.73.

[148]40 C.F.R. § 280.74.

[149]Financial responsibility regulations state that if the owner and operator of a petroleum UST are separate persons, only one person is required to demonstrate financial responsibility. However, both parties are liable in the event of noncompliance with the financial responsibility regulations. 40 C.F.R. § 280.90(e).

Congress intended that these requirements be phased in over time. EPA has set a time schedule by which owners and operators of petroleum USTs are required to comply with the financial responsibility requirements. Compliance dates depend on the number of USTs that are owned, as well as the net worth of the owner.[150]

UST regulations are silent as to whether financial responsibility requirements are to apply to owners and operators of hazardous substance USTs. EPA has not yet formulated a proposed rule, but it continues to keep the issue on its long-term action agenda.[151]

An owner or operator is no longer required to maintain financial responsibility after the UST has been properly closed or, if corrective action is required, after corrective action has been completed and the tank has been properly closed.[152]

### 11.2 Amount and Scope of Financial Responsibility Required

Owners or operators of petroleum USTs must demonstrate financial responsibility in at least the following *per-occurrence* amounts:

a.  $1,000,000 for owners or operators of petroleum USTs that are located at petroleum marketing facilities, or that handle an average of more than 10,000 gallons of petroleum per month based on annual throughput for the previous calendar year;

b.  $500,000 for all other owners or operators who operate petroleum USTs.[153]

Owners or operators of petroleum USTs must also demonstrate financial responsibility in at least the following *annual aggregate* amounts:

a.  $1,000,000 for owners or operators of 1 to 100 petroleum USTs; and

b.  $2,000,000 for owners or operators of 101 or more petroleum USTs.[154]

### 11.3 Allowable Financial Responsibility Mechanisms

There are several ways owners and operators of UST systems can demonstrate compliance with the financial responsibility requirements. Large companies may self-insure if they meet certain self-insurance requirements.[155] Subsidiaries of large companies may obtain guaranties[156] or letters of credit[157] from a parent company. Other methods of compliance include surety bonds,[158] trust agreements,[159] and EPA-approved state-assurance funds.[160] Local governments may also use a bond rating test, a local

---

[150]*See* 56 Fed. Reg. 66369 (Dec. 23, 1991) (amending 40 C.F.R. § 280.91(d)). *See also* 40 C.F.R. § 280.91.

[151]*See* 61 Fed. Reg. 23674 (May 13, 1996).

[152]40 C.F.R. § 280.113.

[153]40 C.F.R. § 280.93(a).

[154]40 C.F.R. § 280.93(b).

[155]40 C.F.R. § 280.95.

[156]40 C.F.R. § 280.96.

[157]40 C.F.R. § 280.99 *as amended by* 59 Fed. Reg. 29958 (June 10, 1994).

[158]40 C.F.R. § 280.98.

[159]40 C.F.R. §§ 280.102 and 280.103.

[160]40 C.F.R. § 280.101.

government financial test, a government guarantee and maintenance of a fund balance to comply with the requirements.[161]

Nearly all states have set up "tank cleanup funds" to help private parties pay for UST cleanup work.[162] It is estimated that these state funds are collecting nearly $1 billion a year through gasoline taxes and other sources.[163] Many UST owners and operators look to these state funds to comply with the RCRA financial assurance requirements because of the difficulty in obtaining private insurance. These state funds have been an important factor in speeding the investigation and cleanup of the thousands of UST sites throughout the country.

### 11.4 Reporting and Recordkeeping Requirements

Owners or operators must maintain evidence of all financial assurance mechanisms used to demonstrate compliance with financial responsibility requirements until released from the requirements. The type of evidence to be maintained by the owner or operator depends on the financial assurance mechanism used.[164] An owner or operator must maintain an updated copy of a certification of financial responsibility that follows the wording provided in the regulations. The owners or operators must also submit evidence of financial responsibility to the implementing agency, under certain conditions.[165]

### 12.0 CONCLUSION

Finding and cleaning up existing chemical spills from leaking underground storage tanks and enforcing strict standards for new tanks present a serious challenge to the government and to private companies responsible for USTs. The regulations facing owners and operators of UST systems are numerous and can be confusing.

The basic purpose of the federal UST program is five-fold: (1) To identify existing tanks and require that they be removed or upgraded; (2) to clean up past problems caused by USTs; (3) to require new tanks to meet strict new standards; (4) to require that all tanks be operated to minimize the possibility of leaks and be properly closed; and (5) to require the reporting, investigation, and cleanup of UST spills and releases. This chapter has described only the federal requirements for underground storage tanks. More information may be obtained from the nearest regional office of EPA or EPA's RCRA/Superfund UST Hotline.[166] States and local governments may have additional, stricter requirements for USTs. States may also have "tank cleanup funds" to reimburse companies for the cost of cleaning up UST sites.

---

[161]40 C.F.R. §§ 280.104-107.

[162]Hawaii is the only state without a cleanup fund program of any type. In Oregon, funds may be used only by the state for cleanup sites. *See Underground Storage Tank Guide* (Thompson Publishing Group), Tab 900 (Supp. 1996).

[163]Environmental Information, Ltd., *The Underground Storage Tank Market: Its Current Status and Future Challenges*, 2 (1992).

[164]*See* 40 C.F.R. § 280.111(b).

[165]*See* 40 C.F.R. § 280.110-111.

[166]EPA's RCRA/Superfund UST Hotline: 1-800-424-9346.

# CHAPTER 11

# FEDERAL FACILITY COMPLIANCE ACT

Craig Anderson, Esq.
Duvall, Harrigan, Hale & Hassan, P.L.C.
Fairfax, VA

## 1.0 OVERVIEW

The Federal Facility Compliance Act of 1992[1] amended the Resource Conservation and Recovery Act[2] (RCRA), the law governing the handling, transport, treatment, storage and disposal of solid and hazardous waste. (See also Chapter 2, this volume). Passed by Congress and signed by President Bush on October 6, 1992, the primary purpose of the amendment was to ensure that there was a complete and unambiguous waiver of sovereign immunity with regard to the imposition of administrative and civil fines and penalties against federal facilities. This allowed the state environmental agencies and the federal Environmental Protection Agency (EPA) to impose civil penalties and administrative fines on federal facilities under RCRA section 6001[3] for violations of federal, state and local solid and hazardous waste laws.

The amendment also enlarged somewhat the regulatory reach of enforcement by adding in section 6001 of RCRA the words *"and management"* to the definition of solid and hazardous waste activities for which federal facilities would henceforth be held accountable. Paraphrased, it requires compliance with all federal, state, interstate and local requirements ". . . respecting control and abatement of solid waste or hazardous waste disposal *and management* in the same manner, and to the same extent, as any person . . .."

The Federal Facility Compliance Act (FFCA) contains ten sections, most of which either added to or amended various provisions in RCRA. Among the ten sections are provisions clarifying the extent of the waiver of sovereign immunity for civil fines and penalties, provisions describing the manner in which RCRA applies to radioactive mixed wastes, and provisions detailing its application to public vessels, "waste munitions" (to be defined in a new rule), and to federally owned wastewater treatment works. It also provides additional explanation regarding allowable environmental fees and charges, and on issues of personal liability of federal employees for environmental violations.

Federal facilities have long been required to comply with the substantive provisions of most federal, state and local solid and hazardous waste laws. With the passage of the FFCA amendments to RCRA, federal facilities were placed in the same relative position as private or commercial entities for purposes of environmental enforcement using civil fines and administrative penalty actions.

---

[1] Public Law 102-386, 106 Statutes 1505.

[2] Originally, the Solid Waste Disposal Act, now more commonly referred to as "RCRA," 42 U.S.C. Sections 6901 *et seq.*

[3] 42 U.S.C. section 6961.

## 2.0 BACKGROUND

The perceived need for the language in the FFCA was born in the frustration of the enforcement restrictions that seemed, to many in state environmental regulatory agencies, to unfairly "shield" federal facilities from the sting of monetary fines and penalties. Sovereign immunity was a roadblock to the complete use of a state's traditional enforcement tools, and states could not reach the federal treasury unless Congress specifically authorized a waiver of sovereign immunity that would permit civil fines and penalties to be paid.

Congress has, and does, waive federal sovereign immunity in all kinds of cases. The Federal Tort Claims Act, for instance, empowers persons allegedly wronged by a federal agency or employee's negligence to claim for damages. There are administrative and jurisdictional requirements to be sure, but a successful claimant will be paid from the federal treasury. Courts have uniformly upheld the right of Congress to waive sovereign immunity to allow this kind of relief. However, the courts have just as uniformly required that the waiver be expressed in language that is "clear and unequivocal."[4] There can be no ambiguity in the text that proposes to accomplish the waiver, nor can any other reference or outside report be used to assist in conveying or completing the waiver message.

Most federal environmental statutes contain language waiving sovereign immunity. But for the most part, the waivers extended to all of the substantive provisions of the laws, and allowed enforcement for "*requirements and provisions.*" The language of the RCRA waiver section *before* the FFCA amendment was typical of many waiver provisions in environmental laws:

> . . . the Federal Government . . . shall be subject to, and comply with, all Federal, State, interstate, and local requirements, both substantive and procedural (including any requirements for permits or reporting or any provisions or injunctive relief and such sanctions as may be imposed by a court to enforce such relief) . . . in the same manner, and to the same extent, as any person is subject to such requirements . . . .[5]

The language of the RCRA waiver of sovereign immunity prior to the change brought by the FFCA was arguably unclear on whether federal facilities had to pay civil and administrative penalties for violations of hazardous waste provisions.

### 2.1 Judicial History

The judicial history of the FFCA began in 1986 when the state of Ohio sued the Department of Energy (DoE) for violating state and federal hazardous waste laws and water pollution laws at its uranium processing plant in Fernald, Ohio. All of the elements of the lawsuit were eventually settled through a consent decree, except for the issue of civil penalties. The state insisted that DoE pay penalties. DoE insisted that it

---

[4]*Hancock v. Train*, 426 U.S. 167 (1976).
[5]42 U.S.C. 6961.

was not required to pay civil penalties, indeed it could not pay, because there was no waiver of federal sovereign immunity with regard to such payments.[6]

Another relevant judicial decision that contributed to the width and breadth of the FFCA's language was a 1988 decision, *Maine v. Department of the Navy*.[7] The background of this case involved a complicated array of environmental enforcement issues at a U. S. Navy facility that failed and refused to pay what it considered to be impermissible environmental "taxes," as well as the penalties resulting from the nonpayment. These factual issues in the lawsuit were essentially negotiated to the point of a resolution, but neither side would concede the underlying legal issue--whether or not civil fines and penalties could be assessed under RCRA by the state of Maine against the federal installation. The U. S. District Court in Maine ruled that RCRA's sovereign immunity waiver language supported the imposition and payment of civil fines and penalties. Following that decision, the state of Maine and Navy Department agreed that approximately $1.1 million in fees and penalties would be owed should the decision of the District Court of Maine be upheld on appeal. The decision, however, was reversed in part by the First Circuit in 1992, consistent with a Supreme Court decision that year.

In April 1992, the Supreme Court held that the waiver of sovereign immunity in RCRA was not clear enough to allow the states to directly impose civil penalties administratively.[8] In the court's judgment, civil penalties could only be sought after a court had first sanctioned a federal facility (through an injunction or some other type of court order) and the court's order was violated by the federal facility. This ended the position asserted by several states and a few federal district courts that civil penalties were available for any RCRA or Clean Water Act violations at federal facilities within their boundaries and jurisdictions.

## 2.2 Legislative History

Draft language for a Federal Facility Compliance Act was initially introduced in the 100th Congress (1987-1988), but failed to get enough votes in the House of Representatives to pass. Reintroduced in the 101st Congress as H.R. 1056, it passed in the Energy and Commerce Committee by a vote of 38 to 5. It later passed on the floor of the House of Representatives 380 to 39. Companion legislation never reached the

---

[6]DoE conceded that federal agencies might be liable for fines imposed to induce them to comply with judicial orders designed to modify future behavior, that is "coercive fines." But, DoE rejected the argument that either the Clean Water Act or the RCRA statute waived sovereign immunity for fines imposed to punish past violations, e.g., "punitive fines." The district court held in 1988 that both statutes waived federal sovereign immunity for punitive fines. The U.S. Court of Appeals for the Sixth Circuit in 1990 affirmed in part, agreeing that the CWA waiver was adequate to impose fines, but the RCRA waiver was not. The Supreme Court reversed, holding that the state could not recover civil penalties from the federal government for past violations.

[7]*Maine v. Department of the Navy*, 702 F.Supp. 330 (D. Me. 1988), *rev'd and remanded,* 973 F.2d 1007 (1st Cir. 1992).

[8]*United States Department of Energy v. Ohio, et al.*, 112 S.Ct. 1627, 118 L.Ed.2d 255 (1992). The Supreme Court, by a 6-3 vote, rejected the state's contention that the language waiving sovereign immunity in RCRA and the Clean Water Act was sufficiently clear to allow the imposition of punitive administrative and civil fines and penalties.

floor of the Senate, so the measure died (in 1990). The Department of Defense (DoD), the Department of Energy (DoE), and several other executive agencies opposed the legislation, fearing that EPA and the states would use the civil penalty powers to impose large fines on federal facilities, in part to compensate for inadequacies in funding from their own state legislatures. They argued that such a scheme would allow state and regional regulators to dictate the schedule and relative priorities of cleanups at federal facilities across the country, greatly complicating (and subverting) the executive departments' efforts to prioritize cleanup funding on a national, scientifically supported "worst first" basis.[9]

Despite failing to get full support for the RCRA immunity waiver amendment in two prior Congressional sessions, sponsors kept reintroducing the legislation, and it gained support in each successive year. There was a perception of fundamental inequality by those in Congress who continued to hear stories about the slow pace of environmental improvement at federal facilities, and the frustration at state regulatory agencies that couldn't "hammer" federal facilities with civil penalties for environmental program deficiencies. In the 102nd Congress (1991-1992), the legislation (H.R. 2194) was once again introduced, and a number of things suggested that this time some form of the legislation would pass. The Senate Majority Leader, George Mitchell (D-ME), championed the cause and cited specific examples in his state for why this "clarifying"[10] legislation was needed. The National Association of Attorneys General (NAAG) listed passage of the FFCA as their highest national priority. President Bush's promise to make federal facilities "environmental leaders" also prompted DoD and DoE to seek compromise rather than confrontation. An election year was underway and public perceptions were at least as important as finding a way to upgrade federal facility environmental programs to the satisfaction of local and state communities.

Working with the Environmental Protection Agency (EPA), DoD and DoE developed a list of amendments they needed to have in the new legislation. From DoD's perspective, at least three major subject areas needed to be addressed: (1) RCRA's applicability to the demilitarization of ordnance; (2) RCRA's applicability to the sludge

---

[9]In their article, "Federal Facility Compliance Act of 1992: Its Provisions and Consequences," Hourcle and McGowan describe how both DoD and DoE feared that any national priority scheme could be wrecked by a handful of states with aggressive prosecutors who might "bludgeon" federal facilities into quick cleanups at sites that might be relatively unimportant when compared with sites in other states. The threat (or reality) of penalties would subject every national decision to second-guessing by local interests, and reward the most persistent, or outlandish, regulator with funding for a desired project, rather than allocating resources nationally on a scientific "worst first" cleanup basis. *Federal Facilities Environmental Journal*, Winter 1992-93, pp. 359-382, at 362.

[10]Prior to the United States Supreme Court decision in *United States v. Ohio*, several state courts and Federal District Courts expressed the opinion that RCRA and the Clean Water Act waivers of sovereign immunity were sufficiently clear to allow imposition of civil fines and penalties at federal facilities. While not in the majority, these opinions helped define the issue and frame the argument. Senator Mitchell's state, Maine, believed fines could be imposed under existing waiver language. Senator Mitchell did not believe this was a change in the law, but rather a way to make clear to all what was already clear to him, that civil fines and penalties could be imposed against federal facilities.

and wastewater effluent from DoD waste water treatment plants; and (3) RCRA's applicability to hazardous wastes on military seagoing vessels. The Department of Energy needed relief from its most intractable RCRA dilemma, the land ban restrictions on the storage and disposal of mixed radioactive wastes. Since there is currently no viable treatment method for neutralizing or eliminating the hazardous characteristics of mixed radioactive/hazardous wastes prior to disposal, indefinite storage is now the practice.[11] That practice violates RCRA's storage time and land disposal limitations.[12]

The House bill that passed did not incorporate the requested amendments, but the Senate's version did (although not exactly in the same form as the language requested by the federal agencies). For those issues and a variety of other fundamental differences in the language of the two bills, there was a need for a Conference Committee to resolve the differences in the companion bills.[13]

## 3.0 INDIVIDUAL PROVISIONS

### 3.1 Sovereign Immunity Waiver

Drafters of the FFCA wanted to ensure that there was an "unambiguous and complete waiver" of sovereign immunity that would allow states and federal EPA regions to impose civil penalties and administrative fines on federal facilities under RCRA[14] for violations of solid and hazardous waste laws. The text of the sovereign immunity waiver *before* passage of the Federal Facility Compliance Act of 1992 read:

> . . . the Federal Government . . . shall be subject to, and comply with, all Federal, State, interstate, and local requirements, both substantive and procedural (including any requirement for permits or reporting or any provisions or injunctive relief and such sanctions as may be imposed by a court to enforce such relief) . . . in the same manner, and to the same extent, as any person is subject to such requirements. . . . Neither the United States, nor any agent, employee, or officer thereof, shall be immune or exempt from any process or sanction of any State or Federal Court with respect to the enforcement of any such injunctive relief.[15]

---

[11]Scientists at the Oak Ridge National Laboratory are having some success in a project that will use powerful electrodes to melt a pit of nuclear waste and turn it into volcanic glass. The $7 million project would prevent the migration of nuclear pollution by encasing it in a glass mass that would remain intact for millions of years—far beyond the radioactive life of the nuclear waste. *"Scientists Hope to Turn Nuclear Waste to Glass,"* Kingsport-Times News, Monday, Oct. 24, 1994, p. 3A.

[12]RCRA section 3004(j), 42 U.S.C. 6924(j).

[13]For more information, *See*: Conference Report on H.R. 2194, Federal Facility Compliance Act of 1992, H.R. Rep. No. 886, 102d Cong., 2d Sess. (1992), reprinted in 138 Cong. Rec. H8860 (daily ed. Sep. 22, 1992).

[14]RCRA section 6001, 42 U.S.C. 6961.

[15]42 U.S.C. 6961.

The Clean Water Act had similar provisions in its sovereign immunity waiver language.[16] In the conference report accompanying the final language of the FFCA, Congress made it clear that, henceforth, federal facilities would be subject to the full range of enforcement tools available to regulatory agencies at both the state and federal levels. Those tools would include ". . . the mechanisms specifically listed in the language of the amendment, to penalize isolated, intermittent or continuing violations as well as to coerce future compliance."[17] Section 102 of the FFCA added several phrases to the previous RCRA waiver language to clearly indicate that United States departments and agencies would be liable for civil fines and penalties; to wit:

> The Federal, State, interstate, and local substantive and procedural require-ments referred to in this subsection *include*, but are not limited to, *all admin-istrative orders and all civil and administrative penalties and fines*, regardless of whether such penalties or fines are *punitive or coercive* in nature or are imposed for *isolated, intermittent, or continuing* violations. (emphasis added)

> The United States hereby *expressly waives any immunity otherwise applicable to the United States* with respect to any such substantive or procedural requirement (including, but not limited to, any injunctive relief, administrative order or *civil or administrative penalty or fine* referred to in the preceding sentence, or reasonable service charge). (emphasis added)

The practical effect of the phrases added by Section 102 was that states and the Federal EPA were empowered to use the full range of enforcement tools already at their command for any private and corporate entity against a federal facility as well.

Amending language in the FFCA did not affect sovereign immunity provisions in the citizen suit portion of RCRA. Those provisions were intended to fulfill a different purpose. They were designed to give individual citizens a jurisdictional basis for

---

[16]33 U.S.C. 1323, " . . . the Federal Government . . . shall be subject to, and comply with, all Federal, State, interstate, and local requirements, administrative authority, and process and sanctions respecting the control and abatement of water pollution in the same manner . . . as any nongovernmental entity. . . . The preceding sentence shall apply (A) to any requirement whether substantive or procedural (including any record keeping or reporting requirement, any requirement respecting permits and any requirement whatsoever), (B) to the exercise of any Federal, State, interstate, or local administrative authority, and (C) to any process or sanction, whether enforced in Federal, State, or local courts or in any other manner. . . . [T]he United States shall be liable only for those civil penalties arising under Federal law or imposed by a State or local court to enforce an order or the process of such court."

[17]138 Cong. Rec. at H8864 (daily ed., Sept. 22, 1992).

enforcing environmental laws and regulations that, for whatever reason, were not being enforced by governmental regulators.[18]

Another separate and independent provision of RCRA, the underground storage tank regulatory sections in Subtitle I, was not modified by the FFCA. Like the citizen suit provisions, that subtitle contains its own waiver of sovereign immunity.[19]

### 3.1.1 Administrative Fines and Penalties

Congress was mindful of the suspicions of many federal agency leaders regarding the possible abuse of the civil penalty authority. One of the things it did to try to limit an overreaching by regulators was to require that all penalty amounts collected be used for "environmental purposes."

> "Unless a State law in effect on the date of the enactment of the Federal Facility Compliance Act of 1992 or a State constitution requires the funds to be used in a different manner, *all funds collected by a State from the Federal Government from penalties and fines imposed for violation of any substantive or procedural requirement . . . shall be used by the State only for projects designed to improve or protect the environment or to defray the costs of environmental protection or enforcement. . . ."* [20] (emphasis added)

This provision, added to RCRA section 6001, subsection (c), was an apparent attempt to appease the executive branch's concern that states might abuse their penalizing powers to generate income for other purposes. As a practical matter, this appears to have almost no power or influence. Early experience has shown that in many states the funds collected as penalties from federal facilities are deposited into the general revenue account of the state for appropriation by the state's legislature. They are essentially commingled and their "environmental" identity lost.

### 3.1.2 Scope of Federal Employment Protection and Exposure

The FFCA makes an addition to the statutory test of RCRA similar to language already found in the Clean Air Act and Clean Water Act. In something of a "good news-bad news" message, it states:

---

[18]The language of 42 U.S.C. 6928(a) and (g) states: ". . . any person may commence a civil action on his own behalf - (1)(A) against any person (including (a) the United States . . . who is alleged to be in violation of any permit, standard, regulation, condition, requirement, prohibition, or order which has become effective pursuant to this Act and including any past or present generator, past or present transporter, or past or present owner or operator of a treatment, storage, or disposal facility, who has contributed or who is contributing to the past or present handling, storage, treatment, transportation, or disposal of any solid or hazardous waste which may present an imminent and substantial endangerment to health or the environment; . . . The district court shall have jurisdiction . . . to enforce the permit, standard, regulation, condition, requirement, prohibition, or order . . . to restrain any person who has contributed or is contributing to the past or present handling, storage, treatment, transportation, or disposal of any solid or hazardous waste . . . to order such person to take such other action as may be necessary, or both . . . and *to apply any appropriate civil penalties under section 3008(a) and (g).* (emphasis added)

[19]Section 9007, 42 U.S.C. 6991f.

[20]New subsection (c) to RCRA section 6001.

"*No agent, employee or officer* of the United States shall be *personally liable for any civil penalty* under any Federal, State, interstate, or local solid or hazardous waste law *with respect to any act or omission within the scope of the official duties* of the agent, employee, or officer."[21] (emphasis added)

At the other end of the spectrum, another phrase was added by the FFCA to "reaffirm" that federal officials are indeed subject to all criminal laws that apply to the waste management and handling business:

"An agent, employee, or officer of the United States *shall be subject to any criminal sanction* (including but not limited to any fine and imprisonment) under *any* Federal or State solid or hazardous waste law. . ." (emphasis added)

The reason this phrase caused (and still causes) concern among federal officials is that it remains unclear whether anything of substance was changed by the addition of this language. In the Senate report accompanying the bill, it was Congress' belief that this was not a change to, or expansion of, previous law. It may, in part, have been a reaction to the appeal of three federal defendants in the case of *United States v. Dee*,[22] where in their appeal they argued that they should have been entitled to "sovereign immunity" from indictment and prosecution for alleged hazardous waste law violations. The court explained in its opinion that they misunderstood the concept of sovereign immunity, and had confused it with the various kinds of qualified immunity available to government employees who act within the scope of their employment. The court suggested it unlikely that a federal employee could violate a federal statute and still be acting within his or her scope of employment. Nevertheless, there are instances where federal officials are immune from state criminal prosecution for acts within the scope of their official federal duties, a position established in 1890 with a novel Supreme Court decision.[23]

The Senate version of the FFCA contained language that would have allowed federal agencies to defend employees in state criminal proceedings if their conduct fell within the scope of their federal duties (even if they had committed serious errors or mistakes). The conference committee deleted that reference and instead reaffirmed the

---

[21]FFCA, Section 102(a)(4).

[22]*United States v. Dee, Lentz and Gepp, affirmed*, 912 F.2d 741 (4th Cir. 1990). On May 11, 1989, three senior civilian managers of the U.S. Army's Chemical Research and Development Command at Aberdeen Proving Ground, Maryland, were sentenced in the first prosecution of Defense Department employees exclusively based on environmental crimes. They were convicted by a jury of various RCRA violations including illegal treatment, storage, and disposal of hazardous wastes, and several Clean Water Act violations. On appeal from their convictions, they argued that federal sovereign immunity should have protected them from prosecution. That argument was rejected by the appellate court.

[23]*In Re Nagle*, 135 U.S. 1, 34 L.Ed. 55 (1890); where a federal marshall shot and killed a state-employed justice who was attempting to stab a federal justice (apparently over an argument about a woman). The state's attorney charged the federal marshall with murder, but it was determined that he had, in fact, acted properly within the scope of his federal duty to protect the Federal Justice against the attack, and he was never tried.

role of the Department of Justice (DoJ) in protecting federal employees from inappropriate state actions.

DoJ has published guidance[24] detailing the circumstances under which it will come to the legal aid of a federal employee. Basically, it requires that: 1) there is no federal criminal indictment; 2) the facts show that the employee's actions were reasonably within the scope of federal duties and employment; and 3) that providing representation for (or reimbursing a private attorney retained by) the employee, is "in the (best) interests of the United States."

### 3.1.3 EPA Administrative Orders

The FFCA indicates that EPA has explicit authority to issue administrative compliance orders to other federal agencies that are in violation of RCRA. Previously, the discovery of environmental deficiencies at federal facilities was resolved by the negotiation of a "consent agreement," wherein the facility would commit to correcting the problem within a certain period of time and according to a specified schedule. Language in the FFCA's legislative history also makes clear that Congress intended for EPA to issue RCRA 3008(a) administrative complaints to federal facilities for violations similar to those found during private enforcement situations.[25]

In practice, the new administrative order authority begins when EPA issues a complaint and compliance order to the federal agency. The federal agency has 30 days from the filing of the complaint to file an answer.[26] States will likewise use their own rules of practice, and there will be differences from one state to another. If various informal settlement conferences and exchanges prove inadequate for resolving the matter, the case typically proceeds to a hearing before an Administrative Law Judge.

### 3.2 EPA Annual Inspections of Federal Facilities

Section 104(1) of the FFCA[27] requires that EPA conduct an annual inspection of every federal facility that has a RCRA Treatment Storage Disposal (TSD) permit (also referred to as a "Part B permit"). It also provides that federal agencies must reimburse EPA for the costs of the inspection. Authorized states are also given the right, but not the obligation, to inspect federal facilities, either in conjunction with EPA or independently. During the initial visit of these annual inspections, regulators have a mandate to review and comment on the facility's groundwater protection program.

During fiscal year 1993 (October 1992 through September 1993), EPA and authorized states conducted "Compliance Evaluation Inspections" (CEIs) at more than 500 federal facilities. That number includes 371 with permitted TSD facilities. Regulators also conducted "Comprehensive Groundwater Monitoring Evaluations" (CMEs) at 28 federal facilities. Two criteria were used to identify federal facilities that required high priority CMEs: (1) those that required CMEs and had never previously

---

[24]28 C.F.R. 50.15.

[25]H.R. No. 102-886, 102nd Cong. 2nd sess. at 19 (1992).

[26]40 C.F.R. section 22.18 contains guidance for resolving the violation(s). The procedures outlined in this section allow for both administrative hearings and appeals.

[27]Section 104 amended section 3007(c) of the Solid Waste Disposal Act, more commonly referred to as RCRA, that requires annual inspections of federal facilities by EPA.

received an evaluation, and (2) those that had not received a CME in the year prior to enactment of the FFCA.[28] In large part, these annual inspections have proceeded as before enactment of the FFCA, but a high-level Memorandum of Understanding (MoU) between EPA and DoD deals with the cost reimbursement notion included in Section 104.

### 3.3 Three-Year Delay for Radioactive Mixed Wastes

Officials at the Department of Energy, as noted earlier in the legislative history section, were concerned that exposure to civil fines and penalties under RCRA would spell disaster. There is currently no viable process for "treating" radioactive/mixed waste such that it could meet RCRA storage or land disposal restrictions. The result is that storage of low, medium, and high-level radioactive and mixed radioactive/hazardous waste takes place at multiple locations around the country. This activity nominally violates RCRA section 3004(j).[29]

The FFCA provided a three-year moratorium on civil penalty enforcement actions applicable to mixed hazardous and radioactive wastes.[30] The stay began on the date the law was signed, October 6, 1992, and expired on October 6, 1995. This applied to all federal agencies, not just the Department of Energy, although DoE has dominion over the majority of storage sites and situations. Following the end of the three-year delay period, a "conditional delay" continued for just the Department of Energy. To qualify for the continued moratorium, DoE had to develop, and be in compliance with, an approved mixed waste storage plan submitted pursuant to RCRA section 3021(b) and enforceable through an order issued pursuant to RCRA section 3008(a). Section 3021(b) is a new provision in RCRA and the result of FFCA section 105, "Mixed Waste

---

[28]These criteria and other detailed guidance for annual federal facility inspections were provided by March 17, 1993 Office of Federal Facilities Enforcement (OFFE) and Office of Waste Programs Enforcement (OWPE) Guidance for Implementing the Federal Facility Compliance Act. On September 21, 1993, OWPE issued inspections guidance for FY1994 and beyond.

[29]RCRA 3004(j). Storage of Hazardous Waste Prohibited from Land Disposal. In the case of any hazardous waste which is prohibited from one or more methods of land disposal under this section (or under regulations promulgated by the Administrator under any provision of this section), the storage of such hazardous waste is prohibited unless such storage is solely for the purpose of the accumulation of such quantities of hazardous waste as are necessary to facilitate proper recovery, treatment or disposal.

[30]FFCA Section 102(c)(2). Delayed effective date for certain mixed waste. Until the date that is 3 years after the date of the enactment of this Act, the waiver of sovereign immunity contained in section 6001(a) of the Solid Waste Disposal Act with respect to civil, criminal, and administrative penalties and fines . . . shall not apply to departments, agencies, and instrumentalities of the executive branch of the Federal Government for violations of section 3004(j) . . . involving storage of mixed waste that is not subject to an existing agreement, permit, or administrative or judicial order, so long as such waste is managed in compliance with all other applicable requirements.

Inventory Reports and Plan." The FFCA also added a definition for mixed waste to RCRA.[31]

Section 3021(b) required DoE to accomplish an extensive series of reports and procedures, aimed at developing a national inventory of all the mixed waste storage sites and a review of the kinds of treatment technologies that might offer promise. Once an initial draft of the plan for dealing with mixed waste storage issues was reviewed by EPA and the states, a final report was published and DoE created (and must administer) a comprehensive plan to handle and store all mixed wastes at all DoE facilities. Under new section 3021(c), DoE is required to submit annual reports detailing its progress toward compliance with these mandates.

DoE submitted its initial Draft Mixed Waste Inventory Report to EPA and the states in April 1993. The National Governors' Association (NGA) is acting as a facilitator for the states, and coordinating the exchange of comments between all the parties. The statutory deadline established in the FFCA for submission of the final version of the report was December 31, 1993, but that timetable could not be met. DoE timely submitted a revised schedule and proposed process for the development of site-specific treatment plans on April 6, 1993. These plans needed to be final and incorporated into permits and orders by October 1995. DoE committed to completing work on Proposed Treatment Plans by February 1995. Once reviewed and approved by EPA and/or appropriate states, these plans will be incorporated into enforceable RCRA 3008(a) orders.

### 3.4 Public Vessel[32] Exemption from Selected RCRA Requirements

Section 106 is of primary interest to the U.S. Navy. The Navy was concerned by the efforts of some states and EPA regions to individually permit its warships and vessels under RCRA. This would have created an operational and logistical disaster as ships sailed from port to port, or returned from extended deployments in international and foreign waters. Theoretically, it could mean that ships generating hazardous wastes and remaining at sea for more than 90 days would have violated RCRA's unpermitted hazardous waste accumulation restrictions. This amendment gave some relief to the notion that a ship approaching harbor is a legitimate target for routine RCRA compliance inspections as a "generator."

The FFCA amendment adds a new section to RCRA, Section 3022. It provides that public vessels are not subject to RCRA's standard storage, manifest, inspection, or record keeping requirements. Hazardous wastes become regulated only when they are transferred or off-loaded to the shore facility. In practice, the Navy has taken a very conservative approach to its responsibilities under this new provision and considers ship-to-ship transfers of hazardous waste an action sufficient to trigger application of RCRA's coverage.

---

[31]RCRA section 1004(41); 42 USC 6903; The term "mixed waste" means waste that contains both hazardous waste and source, special nuclear, or by-product material subject to the Atomic Energy Act of 1954 (42 U.S.C. 2011 *et seq.*).

[32]A "public vessel" is generally defined as a seagoing vessel owned and operated by the United States government, but also including vessels owned and operated by foreign governments.

## 3.5 RCRA Regulation of Unserviceable Munitions

For many years, opinions have differed, both among regulators and the various military services, over how—and when—military munitions destined for destruction (a process sometimes referred to as "demilitarization") were covered under the "Treatment, Storage, and Disposal" provisions of RCRA. There are also unanswered questions, and confusion, regarding RCRA's applicability to activities that occur at military ordnance firing ranges, and the process of chemical weapons destruction. RCRA rules, since they were developed primarily to deal with various kinds of toxic and chemical wastes, were not a good "fit" on the munitions procedures that had been developed by DoD over the years.

The paramount concern addressed by DoD directives for munitions handling was safety, and the grafting of federal RCRA regulations with this preexisting, comprehensive system of management procedures sometimes results in mutually inconsistent mandates. The "hazardous" part of ordnance destruction from a RCRA perspective often has less to do with the explosive (or reactive) nature of the item than with the residual material remaining after the burning or thermal demolition "treatment." The toxicity of heavy metals and the possibility of carcinogens in the residue following "thermal treatment" are the characteristics that most concern RCRA regulators. One significant potential environmental danger is the possibility that these metals could leach into the soil and contaminate groundwater aquifers.

Congress put EPA under a six-month deadline to propose draft regulations that were to become final within two years of passage of the act.[33] EPA was tasked to propose these regulations in concert with DoD experts and representatives from state regulatory offices. The purpose of the draft regulations was to arrive at some uniform way to specify *when* waste munitions became a regulated hazardous waste under RCRA. Once they were "RCRA wastes," new language was needed to allow a smooth meshing with the existing DoD directives regarding the segregation and storage of "waste munitions," (those awaiting final disposition instructions). If final instructions called for thermal (destructive) treatment, either by burning or detonating, then the new regulations needed to allow or provide for safe transportation to the treatment site (either via a standard RCRA manifest or with some new, uniform federal ordnance manifest). The FFCA provision was designed to address chemical and conventional weapons, but not nuclear weapons.

The six-month and two-year deadlines have both been exceeded,[34] but EPA and the military services are meeting regularly to resolve some fundamental issues. The scope of the discussions has expanded considerably, and now includes activities at military firing ranges unrelated to the routine disposal of "waste ordnance." A close look is being given to activities involving live-fire practice ranges, and the range clearing and "safing" procedures used by military ordnance experts following such

---

[33]Section 107 of the FFCA adds a new subparagraph (y) to section 3004 of RCRA.

[34]After EPA missed the six-month deadline (April 6, 1993) for issuing a proposed rule, it was notified by a citizen's group that a lawsuit would be filed unless progress was forthcoming. EPA is working with that citizen's group, and with a committee of military representatives, to make progress on these issues. The proposed rule was issued November 8, 1995, and the final version of the proposed rule is now scheduled for publication in February 1997.

firings. State regulators and citizens' groups have indicated a high interest in former (closed or closing) military ranges, including those identified as part of the series of installation realignments and closures in the Base Realignment and Closure Commission's work.

The proposed Munitions Rule was published in the *Federal Register* on Wednesday, November 8, 1995 [60 FR 56468]. A summary of the proposed rule (and various alternatives) appears on pages 56469 and 56470. The subject matter of the proposal dealt primarily with five interrelated areas: munitions storage, range operations, the elimination of excess propellant, the transportation of munitions, and emergency operations. On the subject of storage, there was general agreement, in principle, that the procedures and guidance established by the DoD Explosives Safety Board was sufficient to provide the desired degree of security and safety. Considerable historical information was recited confirming the excellent safety record compiled by DoD's management of more than 5.6 million tons of conventional munitions. There were minor disagreements between DoD and EPA and various state delegations participating in the review (Illinois, Michigan, Mississippi, New York, and Utah) when it came to the disposition of excess propellant, transportation issues, and emergency contingencies. The states are significant players in these working groups, and have expressed particular concern over how these new rules will impact the planned destruction of chemical weapons, stockpiled primarily in eight different communities nationwide.

A much wider divergence of opinions existed over range operations. In the proposal, DoD promoted its long-held position that range clearing activities are, and must be, "training" for explosives experts, who perform a similar function during actual combat situations. EPA focused its effort on presenting the position that for ranges where active operations have ceased and clearing activities are required, they should come under the normal considerations and requirements common to a hazardous waste cleanup. Several state and institutional environmental groups went a step further, favoring the position that RCRA regulations would apply to range operations the moment a live explosive charge impacted on (or near) the ground.

The original comment period for the proposed rule proved to be too short to receive and evaluate all of the comments, and was extended several times. Recently, the planned date for publishing the final rule (October 31, 1996) was extended to December 2, 1996. That date too has now been extended at the request of the Department of Justice, to allow for a review of the final rule in light of the litigation status of various challenges to the proposed rule. The final Military Munitions Rule is now expected to be formally published in early February 1997, provided there are no material changes or new judicial challenges.

### 3.6 Regulation of Federally Owned Treatment Works

The goal of this provision was to eliminate the disparity of treatment under RCRA between Federally Owned Wastewater Treatment Works (FOTWs) and similar municipal Publicly Owned Treatment Works (POTWs).[35] Both systems deal with flows that receive most of their volume from domestic sewage, but also include some waste streams from industrial processes and manufacturing. This section borrows its

---

[35]Section 108 of the FFCA creates a new RCRA section, 3023.

underlying premise from the domestic sewage exemption provisions in RCRA.[36] EPA's apparent rationale for the domestic sewage exemption was that the POTW supervisor/manager would insist on adequate pretreatment requirements under the Clean Water Act for any industrial wastes that might enter the system. POTWs are typically regulated under the Clean Water Act, but FOTWs that have, or are receiving, industrial waste could potentially be regulated both under RCRA and the Clean Water Act.

Basically, the new RCRA section provides that if certain conditions are met, an FOTW is essentially exempted from RCRA regulation by virtue of the domestic sewage exclusion to the definition of solid waste.[37] The apparent relief offered by this section, however, is complicated by a provision that prohibits the introduction into an FOTW of any pollutant that is a hazardous waste. Consequently, the distinction is dependent upon careful adherence to new definitions and, in some cases, compliance with Section 307 Clean Water Act permitting requirements. The conditions focus on one of two possible scenarios. The first is the premise that no single sewage source generates more than 100 kilograms of hazardous waste per month, and no acutely hazardous waste at all. In the second alternative, the FOTW could have in place a comprehensive pretreatment system to assure adequate safeguards for treatment of all sewage prior to discharge. For most federal facilities that are currently operating an FOTW, this will mean placing controls on all potentially hazardous wastes to assure that none enter the sanitary sewer system.

Whether this provision is self-implementing has not yet been determined. The intent of the provision was to assure similar treatment for both POTWs and FOTWs. Currently, POTWs have established requirements to regularly self report their compliance status. federal agencies, because of the differences in the manner of past regulation, do not have a similar system.

### 3.7 New Policy on the Payment of Environmental Fees

Section 102 added a sentence to assure federal facility payment of all nondiscriminatory fees that are associated with solid and hazardous waste regulatory programs. Like any other regulated entity, federal facilities will be paying any environmental fees that are not clearly "discriminatory" against them. Discrimination in the past occurred where various state departments and agencies were exempted from having to pay fees while engaged in the same storage and disposal activities as their federal counterparts. The language states that:

> . . . reasonable service charges . . . include . . . fees or charges assessed in connection with the processing and issuance of permits, renewal of permits, amendments to permits, review of plans, studies, and other documents, and inspection and monitoring of facilities, *as well as any other nondiscrimina-*

---

[36] 40 C.F.R. 261.4(a)(1)(ii). EPA specifically excluded industrial wastes that are mixed with sanitary wastes in a sewer system leading to a publicly owned treatment works (POTW) from the definition of "solid waste." Domestic sewage is instead defined as "untreated sanitary wastes that pass through a sewer system."

[37] Section 3023. The lengthy FFCA provision extends the domestic sewage exclusion to FOTW under certain circumstances. The conditions point to compliance with established pretreatment standards and a general allowance for material that would not be prohibited under RCRA land disposal restrictions, among others.

tory charges that are assessed in connection with a Federal, State, interstate, or local solid waste or hazardous waste regulatory program.[38] (emphasis added)

### 3.8 Definition of "Person" Includes Federal Facility

FFCA section 103 amended the definition of "person" under RCRA to specifically include the federal government or, more specifically, "each department, agency and instrumentality of the United States."

## 4.0 EVOLUTION AND EXECUTION OF THE PROVISIONS

### 4.1 Penalty Amounts

While there was initially great concern that states would attempt to "balance their budgets" with federal facility penalties, nothing approaching assessments on that scale has occurred. For the most part, money penalty situations have only resulted where significant environmental violations were discovered. In the majority of cases, violations are administrative and not the result of actual releases and/or damage to the natural environment. Most involve inadequacies with personnel training, records and record keeping procedures, and plan completeness and adherence. As a general practice, the original penalty amount assessments are reduced during the subsequent exchange of information and negotiation process. In many cases, supplemental environmental projects have been substituted for outright penalty payments as a way to achieve "win-win" results.

During the four years since passage of the FFCA, evidence indicates that states assess more penalties, but the amounts are relatively smaller than those assessed by federal regional EPA offices. EPA regional inspectors assess fewer, but relatively larger, penalties. This is consistent with the approximate volume of inspections and extent of resources available to each agency.

### 4.2 EPA Enforcement

The FFCA broadens EPA's enforcement powers against federal facilities. Section 6001(b)[39] of RCRA allows the Administrator to bring enforcement actions under the RCRA authority against federal facilities provided that such an action is brought in the same manner and under the same circumstances as an action would be initiated against any other "person."[40] In July 1993, EPA issued its "Final Enforcement Guidance on Implementation of the Federal Facility Compliance Act." This guidance was official notice that EPA would be applying its RCRA Civil Penalty Policy to federal facility cases in the same manner and to the same extent as it is applied in private party cases. Nevertheless, several differences are identified in subsequent FFCA provisions that point to having a consent order to memorialize the resolution of the enforcement action, and the federal agency is offered a "last resort" to the EPA Administrator prior to any enforcement action being finalized.

---

[38]FFCA, Section 102(3), amending language in RCRA section 6001, 42 U.S.C. 6961.
[39]Added by FFCA section 102(b).
[40]*See* 42 U.S.C. section 6961(b)(1).

### 4.3 EPA's RCRA Civil Penalty Policy of 1990

EPA modified its enforcement policy under RCRA in 1990 in response to an Inspector General report that criticized EPA for inconsistencies in enforcement patterns from one region to another, and generally for assessing too few penalties, and in amounts too low to sufficiently punish the violator. The 1990 policy focuses on determining the proper civil penalty amount that should be sought once the decision has been made that a civil penalty is the proper enforcement remedy to pursue. It does *not* address whether assessment of a civil penalty is the correct enforcement response to a particular violation. Guidance on *when* to assess administrative civil penalties is contained in EPA's "RCRA Enforcement Response Policy," December 21, 1987. The 1990 RCRA policy specifically does *not* apply to penalties assessed under Subtitle I (Underground Storage Tank provisions) of RCRA.

The 1990 RCRA Civil Penalty Policy replaces a 1984 version. The earlier policy was intended to insure that RCRA civil penalties were fair, consistent, and appropriate to the gravity ("seriousness") of the violation. EPA modified its existing policy primarily by revising the procedures for calculating penalties. The overall purpose of the new policy was four-fold. It was designed to ensure that civil penalties in both civil judicial and administrative cases:

1. reflected the gravity of RCRA violations;
2. deterred noncompliance with RCRA and other solid and hazardous waste laws;
3. eliminated economic incentives to violate the law; and
4. were well-documented actions.

The policy was designed to eliminate any economic gain from noncompliance with RCRA by imposing significant punitive penalties. For some violations, the policy required penalties to be assessed not just for the day the violation was discovered, but also for every day of established noncompliance up to 180 days.

Calculating a penalty requires four steps. First, a basic determination is made to establish an appropriate gravity-based penalty considering the "potential of harm" posed by the violation(s), and their "extent of deviation" from regulatory requirements. Next, a calculation is done to find a multi-day component to account for the violations' duration. Third, an "adjustment" is determined, based on a variety of individual factors presented by the overall situation. Some of these are subjective, and some cannot be determined at the point when the penalty is initially assessed. Among the factors that could either increase or decrease a penalty are good faith efforts to comply, the absence of willfulness in creating the violation or discrepancy, a history of generally good compliance, and the presence or existence of environmental engineering projects to be undertaken by the violator to address regulatory problems. Also included in this category is an evaluation by the regulator of the ability of the violator to pay a penalty (e.g., the facility's resources) and the likelihood that risks and costs would be incurred by the regulators if this issue had to be fully litigated. The fourth and final step involves calculating and recapturing the "economic benefit from noncompliance" obtained by the violator.

## Table 11.1: Gravity-Based Penalty Matrix

| Potential For Harm | Extent of Deviation From Regulatory Requirement | | |
|---|---|---|---|
| | MAJOR | MODERATE | MINOR |
| MAJOR | $25,000-$20,000 | $19,999-$15000 | $14,999-$11,000 |
| MODERATE | $10,999 - $8,000 | $7,999 - $5,000 | $4,999 - $3,000 |
| MINOR | $2,999 - $1,500 | $1,499 - $500 | $499 - $100 |

EPA has developed a nine-box matrix (see Table 11.1) to establish the basic penalty amount. Along one axis the question centers on the "potential for harm" created by the violation. Within this category, regulators are looking at the risk of exposure to hazardous waste or constituents presented by a given violation and the relative harm or adverse affect noncompliance may have on the RCRA regulatory program. The risk element includes both the likelihood of exposure and the degree of such potential (or actual) exposure. Along the other axis, the focus is on the "extent of deviation from the regulatory requirement." Within this category, regulators are looking at the relative degree of compliance with the applicable regulatory provision. Comparing the extremes, a violator may be substantially in compliance with the provisions of the requirement but for one small detail, or it may have totally disregarded the requirement.

For both inquiries, the potential for harm and the degree of deviation from established requirements, the measure is broken up into three categories: Major, Moderate, and Minor. Although those terms might at first glance appear to be self-defining, a closer look at the policy indicates curiously similar definitions for the top two categories. A "Major" potential for harm is described as one where the violation poses a substantial risk of exposure of humans or other environmental receptors to hazardous waste or constituents. A "Moderate" potential for harm is one where the violation poses a significant risk of exposure of humans or other environmental receptors to hazardous waste or constituents. Given the possible confusion over where to draw (or argue) the line between substantial and significant, it may be reassuring to know that a "Minor" potential for harm is described as one where the violation poses a "relatively low risk of exposure" of human or other environmental receptors to hazardous waste or constituents.

## Table 11.2 Multi-Day Penalty Matrices

| Potential For Harm | Extent of Deviation from Requirement | | |
|---|---|---|---|
| | MAJOR | MODERATE | MINOR |
| MAJOR | Mandatory | Mandatory | Presumed |
| MODERATE | Mandatory | Presumed | Discretionary |
| MINOR | Presumed | Discretionary | Discretionary |

| Potential For Harm | Extent of Deviation from Requirement | | |
|---|---|---|---|
| | MAJOR | MODERATE | MINOR |
| MAJOR | $5,000 - $1,000 | $4,000 - $750 | $3,000 - $550 |
| MODERATE | $2,200 - $400 | $1,600 - $250 | $1,000 - $150 |
| MINOR | $600 - $100 | $300 - $100 | $100 |

Once a penalty range or amount has been determined by the gravity-based inquiry, the next step is considering and/or calculating a multi-day penalty. Using Table 11.2, regulators are guided by a scheme of "discretionary, presumed, or mandatory" classifications. Depending upon where in the gravity-based matrix (Table 11.1) the basic penalty was classified, that same block will establish both an amount range for the multi-day component and determine whether the regulator has any discretion on whether to add it to the base penalty. The three classifications apply to violations that have a duration of continuous noncompliance of between 2 and 180 days. When multi-day penalties are "presumed" to be appropriate, they must be imposed unless case-specific factors supporting the decision not to assess are well documented.

Some of this decisional information will not be apparent to the facility immediately after receipt of a penalty notification. However, regulations governing the administrative assessment of civil penalties[41] require that the complaint contain a statement which sets forth the regulator's basis for requesting the actual amount of the penalty being sought. Penalties must be broken down to reflect the alleged violation or count each penalty amount represents. Enforcement personnel are allowed to use general language in the complaint, but must be prepared to present at the prehearing conference or

---

[41]40 C.F.R. 22.14(a)(5) and (c).

evidentiary hearing more detailed information reflecting the specific factors weighed in arriving at the selected penalty amount.[42]

Just as with enforcement actions taken against private parties, settlement of the issues identified during an inspection and the amount of any resulting penalty is encouraged. Voluntary resolution or settlement of such actions must be memorialized in a consent agreement or order, setting forth the details of the resolution. Informal settlement discussions or negotiations may begin at any time following the issuance of the complaint, but the fact that negotiations may be ongoing does *not* affect the formal thirty-day deadline for filing an answer to the complaint. That requirement is the same for both private parties and federal facilities.[43]

## 5.0 CONCLUSION

Just over four years have passed since the FFCA amended RCRA, and the early history suggests that while there are disagreements over certain aspects of assessing penalties against federal facilities, most of these are being worked out at relatively low levels of contact. The Republic has not fallen, million dollar penalty assessments have been rare, and the new enforcement options provided by the FFCA have not crippled federal facilities.

Discussion of the "FFCA" as an entity will probably fade in a few years when the changes and amendments it added to RCRA are fully integrated into the routine pattern of dealing with RCRA. Most legislative observers expect subsequent reauthorizations of other major environmental statutes to include language similar to the FFCA's sovereign immunity waiver language for RCRA, and thereby expand the exposure of federal facilities to civil penalties under the Clean Water Act and Clean Air Act, as well as others. It hasn't happened yet, however, as other national legislative priorities consumed the attention of Congress during the last several sessions.

It may still be too early to measure what effect enforcement through the imposition of monetary penalties will have on federal facility environmental programs. There can be no doubt, however, that the mere possibility of even minor penalties has gotten the attention of senior leaders throughout the military departments and other federal government agencies. The argument will continue over whether it makes any sense to impose a civil penalty on an organization that draws from the public treasury, when the penalty amount will be returned to the public treasury for reauthorization and appropriation. But both sides probably would agree that the act of waiving sovereign immunity for civil fines and administrative penalties under RCRA has prompted additional attention, and in many cases resources, on and for environmental programs at federal facilities.

---

[42]The RCRA Civil Penalty Policy specifically states: "Usually the record supporting the penalty amount specified in the complaint should include a penalty computation worksheet which explains the potential for harm, the extent of deviation from statutory requirements, economic benefit of non-compliance, and any adjustment factors applied (e.g., good faith efforts to comply, etc.). Also, the record should include any inspection reports and other documents relating to the penalty calculation."

[43]40 C.F.R. 22.18(a).

# CHAPTER 12

# NATIONAL ENVIRONMENTAL POLICY ACT

James W. Spensley, Esq.
JSC/Spensley
Denver, Colorado

## 1.0 OVERVIEW

The National Environmental Policy Act of 1969 (NEPA)[1] has been heralded as the Magna Carta of the country's environmental movement. It was signed into law on January 1, 1970 to address the need for a national environmental policy to guide the growing environmental consciousness and to shape a national response.

NEPA contains three important elements: (1) the declaration of national environmental policies and goals; (2) the establishment of "action-forcing" provisions for federal agencies to implement those policies and goals; and (3) the establishment of a Council on Environmental Quality (CEQ) in the Executive Office of the President. The essential purpose of NEPA is to insure that environmental factors are given the same consideration as other factors in decision making by the federal agencies. The effectiveness of NEPA has stemmed from its environmental impact statement (EIS) requirement that federal agencies must consider the environmental effects of, and any alternatives to, all proposals for major federal actions that significantly affect the quality of the human environment.

Although CEQ published early guidelines for federal agencies to implement NEPA, it was the federal courts in the early 1970s that had the most influence on shaping NEPA's "action-forcing" provision, section 102(2)(C).[2] Because this provision was virtually ignored during its legislative formulation, judicial interpretations established the basic definitions for section 102(2)(C) concerning who must comply with NEPA, what level of federal involvement triggers an EIS, what constitutes a "major" action that "significantly affects" the environment, and other fundamental issues. This EIS requirement has become the heart of NEPA and has had a profound impact on federal agency decision making.

During this early period, the threat of litigation over the EIS requirement caused many federal agencies to overreact by including in their statements every possible environmental reference that could be found. This resulted in lengthy EISs that neither decision makers nor the public would read. Today, CEQ regulations emphasize the need to reduce excessive paperwork and focus on the essential information that is needed by decision makers and the public. NEPA's emphasis and importance has evolved from a procedural lever used by project opponents to stop or delay proposed federal projects to a more comprehensive framework for documenting and integrating essential environmental information into the federal decision making process.

---

[1] 42 U.S.C. §§ 4321-4370c.
[2] 42 U.S.C. § 4332(2)(C); *see also* Frederick R. Anderson, *NEPA in the Courts: A Legal Analysis of the National Environmental Policy Act* (1973).

The current trend in NEPA compliance has focused on the use of an environmental assessment (EA) to conduct a threshold analysis of whether a full EIS is required. CEQ is placing new emphasis on the use of the EA in order to avoid extensive and duplicative documentation while more effectively integrating key environmental factors in the federal decision making process and opening up the process to outside parties.[3]

## 2.0 NEPA'S DEVELOPMENT

NEPA was enacted at a time when the Congress heard testimony from many quarters of society warning of impending environmental degradation and even disaster.[4] Members of the Congress competed for the popular leadership of this new environmental movement. More than 2,000 legislative proposals having a bearing on environmental matters were introduced into the 91st Congress that passed NEPA.[5] Few congressional members understood or expected that this brief, idealistic NEPA statute would be so successful in reforming federal agency decision making and bringing the public into the process.

### 2.1 Legislative History

The legislative formulation of NEPA principles began years before the statute was enacted.[6] In 1959, Senator James E. Murray (D-Montana) attempted to legislate a national environmental policy when he introduced the Resources and Conservation Act of 1960, which included the creation of a high level council of environmental advisors.[7] However, it was not until the late 1960s that Senator Henry Jackson (D-Wash) and Congressman John Dingell (D-Mich) collaborated to enact the present statute. Early versions of the legislation contained neither policy and goals nor an "action-forcing" provision. It was not until the legislation had passed both houses of Congress and been amended by a House-Senate Conference Committee that the present policy and reporting provisions were included. Although the legislative history is unclear in many respects, Senator Jackson clearly felt that it was the federal government's failures and unresponsiveness that had lead to much of the country's environmental degradation. "The most important feature of the act," according to Senator Jackson, "is that it establishes new decision-making procedures for all agencies of the federal government."[8]

### 2.2 Policy and Goals

NEPA's policies are broad and general and its goals lofty. Indeed, section 101 of the act was written as if to inspire rather than to regulate. It emphasizes the need to

---

[3]Diana Bear, *NEPA at 19: A Primer on an "Old" Law with Solutions to New Problems*, 19 Envtl. L. Rep. (Envtl. L. Inst.) 10060 (1989).

[4]Environmental Quality: Hearings on H.R. 12143 Before the Subcommittee on Fisheries and Wildlife Conservation, Committee on Merchant Marine and Fisheries, 91st Cong., 1st Sess. (1969).

[5]Library of Congress, C.R.S., Env. Policy Div., Congress and the Nation's Environment and Environmental Affairs of the 91st Congress (1971).

[6]Anderson, *supra* note 2, at 4-14.

[7]S.2549, 86th Cong., 2d Sess. (1960).

[8]Henry Jackson, *Environmental Quality, the Courts and Congress*, 68 Mich. L. Rev. 1079 (1970).

recognize "the profound impact of man's activity on the interrelations of all components of the natural environment"[9] and to recognize that "each person should enjoy a healthful environment . . . and to contribute to the preservation and enhancement of the environment."[10] It recognizes the balancing of trade-offs that must occur in the decision-making process by promoting the "use [of] all practicable means and measures . . . [to] fulfill the social, economic, and other requirements of present and future generations of Americans."[11] It goes on to recognize six more specific goals as a guide to the federal government to implement this new policy.[12]

### 2.3 Council on Environmental Quality

The Council on Environmental Quality (CEQ) was created by Title II of NEPA[13] and modeled after the Council of Economic Advisors created by the Employment Act of 1946.[14] The CEQ was placed in the executive office of the president and composed of three members appointed by the president and confirmed by the Senate. Under the statute, CEQ is to assist and advise the president in the preparation of an annual environmental quality report, on the progress of federal agencies in implementing the act, on national policies to foster and promote the improvement of environmental quality, and on the state of the environment. Shortly after signing NEPA into law, President Nixon expanded CEQ's mandate by Executive Order No. 11514 directing it to issue guidelines to federal agencies for the preparation of EISs and to coordinate federal programs related to environmental quality.[15]

This Executive Order further directed federal agencies to develop procedures to ensure timely dissemination of public information concerning federal plans and programs with environmental impacts in order to obtain the views of all interested parties. This public participation mandate, combined with the disclosure requirements of NEPA, has in large part been responsible for the significant and lasting effectiveness of NEPA.

CEQ has played a central role in the development of the EIS process. Its first guidelines were issued in April 1971, and required each department and agency of the federal government to adopt its own guidelines consistent with those from CEQ.[16] Although the guidelines did not have the status of formal agency regulations, the courts often recognized them with considerable deference.[17] Subsequently, President Carter, by Executive Order 11991, authorized CEQ to adopt regulations rather than guidelines on EIS preparation.[18] In 1978, CEQ adopted regulations that reflected its earlier

---

[9]42 U.S.C. § 4331(a).
[10]*Id.* § 4331(c).
[11]*Id.* § 4331(a).
[12]*Id.* § 4331(b).
[13]*Id.* §§ 4341-4347.
[14]15 U.S.C. §§ 1021-1025.
[15]Exec. Order No. 11514, 3 C.F.R. 356 (1972).
[16]36 *Fed. Reg.* 7723 (Apr. 23, 1971).
[17]*See, e.g., Environmental Defense Fund, Inc. v. Hoffman,* 566 F.2d 1060 (8th Cir. 1977).
[18]Exec. Order No. 11991, 3 C.F.R., 1966-1970 Comp., p. 902 (1977).

guidelines and the numerous court decisions that had created NEPA's early "common law."[19]

CEQ has no authority to enforce its regulations. However, it has played a major role in advising agencies on compliance matters. Federal agencies have not availed themselves of CEQ's advice as often as they should, to avoid problems and litigation.

## 3.0 REQUIREMENTS FOR FEDERAL AGENCIES

The requirements of NEPA are mandatory for federal agencies and over the years have been a major force in reforming agency decision-making processes. NEPA contains largely "procedural" requirements that are supplemental to existing statutory responsibilities of the federal agencies.[20] In *Calvert Cliffs' Coordinating Comm. Inc. v. United States Atomic Energy Comm'n*,[21] Judge Skelly Wright writing for the court, notes:

> NEPA, first of all, makes environmental protection a part of the mandate of every federal agency and department. . . . It [the agency] is not only permitted, but compelled, to take environmental values into account. Perhaps the greatest importance of NEPA is to require . . . agencies to *consider* environmental issues just as they consider other matters within their mandates.[22]

Although NEPA's provisions apply only to federal agencies, the pervasiveness of federal decisions affecting state and local matters as well as private actions makes NEPA an issue for many. An applicant should have a direct interest in the successful completion of an agency's EIS so as to avoid potential time-consuming and expensive litigation. Moreover, agencies increasingly are finding ways to shift the costs of NEPA compliance to those requesting some federal action or decision.[23] Therefore, an applicant will want to ensure that the environmental studies and documents are prepared in a cost-effective manner and in accordance with the procedural requirements of NEPA.

The only agency that the courts have recognized as having a limited exemption from NEPA is the Environmental Protection Agency (EPA). Although there is no reference to an exemption for EPA in the statute, EPA has argued that it should be exempt for the reason that it has statutory responsibility for protection of the environment. Some legislation has specifically exempted EPA from NEPA compliance. Under the Energy Supply and Environmental Coordination Act of 1974, an exemption is provided to EPA for its actions under the Clean Air Act.[24] Similarly, under the Clean Water Act, EPA is exempted from the obligation to prepare an EIS on some actions such

---

[19]43 Fed. Reg. 55,978 (1978).

[20]*See Vermont Yankee Nuclear Power Corp. v. Natural Resources Defense Coun.*, 435 U.S. 519 (1978), *cert. granted*, 459 U.S. 1034 (1982), *rev'd on other grounds*, 462 U.S. 87 (1983).

[21]449 F.2d 1109 (D.C. Cir. 1971).

[22]*Id.* at 1112 (emphasis in original).

[23]*See Alumet v. Andrus*, 607 F.2d 911 (10th Cir. 1979); *see also* David Sive and Frank Friedman, *A Practical Guide to Environmental Law* §§ 7.01(a), 7.02(k) (1987).

[24]15 U.S.C. § 793(c)(1).

as discharge permits for existing sources of water pollution.[25] Other EPA non/regulatory actions require NEPA compliance, such as the issuance of construction grants for water treatment facilities.

## 3.1  CEQ Regulations

The CEQ regulations begin by calling for agencies to integrate NEPA requirements with other planning requirements at the earliest possible time to ensure that plans and decisions reflect environmental values, avoid delays later in the process, and head off potential conflicts.[26] Agencies are to utilize a "systematic, interdisciplinary approach" as required by section 102(2)(A) and to study and develop appropriate alternatives to recommended courses of action for unresolved conflicts in the use of available resources as provided in section 102(2)(E).[27]

NEPA's action-forcing provision, section 102(2)(C), requires that an EIS shall be "include[d] in every recommendation or report on proposals for legislation and other major Federal actions significantly affecting the quality of the human environment. . . ."[28] The key terms in this statement are defined in the CEQ regulations and have been the most judicially interpreted words of NEPA.

CEQ states its intention that judicial review of agency compliance with these regulations should not occur before an agency has filed a final EIS or has made an appropriate finding of no significant impact, or takes action that will result in irreparable injury.[29] Furthermore, CEQ suggests that a trivial violation of these regulations should not give rise to an independent cause of action.

The regulations require each agency to adopt procedures consistent with these regulations for implementing NEPA's provisions. Specifically, the agencies are to identify typical classes of action:

(i)   which normally require an EIS;

(ii)  which normally do not require either an EIS or an environmental assessment (categorical exclusions (§ 1508.4)); and

(iii) which normally require environmental assessments but not necessarily an EIS.[30]

Agency procedures may provide specific criteria for limited exceptions to classified proposals.[31]

The first question is whether a federal agency must prepare an EIS. As noted earlier, each of the key words in section 102(2)(C) has been the subject of judicial interpretation in answering that question. Is there an agency "proposal" for an "action"?

---

[25]33 U.S.C. § 1371(c)(1).
[26]*Id.* § 1501.2.
[27]*Id.*
[28]42 U.S.C. § 4332(2)(C).
[29]40 C.F.R. § 1500.3 (1991).
[30]*Id.* § 1507.3(b)(2).
[31]*Id.* § 1507.3(c).

Is the action "federal"? Is it "major"? Is it "significant"? Does the action "affect the human environment"? The CEQ regulations define each of these statutory terms.[32]

The EIS requirement is not triggered unless there is a "proposal" for action by a federal agency.[33] Because agencies are constantly involved in planning and program formulation, it is not always easy to determine when a proposal has been made. If a proposal is made too early in the planning process, it will contain insufficient information to provide the necessary environmental disclosure.[34] On the other hand, if the agency prepares an EIS too late in the planning process, it becomes simply a post hoc justification for a decision already made. The regulations have addressed this timing question by defining the term "proposal" as that which:

> . . .exists at the stage in the development of an action when an agency subject to the Act has a goal and is actively preparing to make a decision on one or more alternative means of accomplishing that goal and the effects can be meaningfully evaluated. Preparation of an environmental impact statement on a proposal should be timed (§ 1502.5) so that the final statement may be completed in time . . . to be included in any recommendation or report on the proposal.[35]

If there is a proposal, it must be a "federal" proposal in order for an EIS to be required. Clearly, policies, plans, programs and projects proposed by federal agencies meet this definition.[36] CEQ regulations also address actions with "effects" that may be major and which are potentially subject to federal control and responsibility.[37] Further, private, state and local actions which have sufficient federal involvement may also require an EIS. Such non/federal actions that are regulated, licensed, permitted or approved by federal agencies generally are considered "federal" for NEPA purposes.[38] The need for federal permits, licenses and other approvals from a federal agency program are examples where seemingly non/federal actions have triggered NEPA compliance.

Federal assistance to a non/federal project or action may also trigger NEPA. The primary determinant in these cases is the extent to which the federal control is or may be exercised. Generally, there have been three forms of federal assistance: categorical grants, block grants and some form of revenue sharing. Federal categorical grants to non/federal projects usually require NEPA compliance. Block grants and revenue

---

[32]*Id.* § 1508.

[33]*Id.* § 1502.5; *see also Kleppe v. Sierra Club*, 427 U.S. 390 (1976).

[34]*See Scientists' Inst. for Public Information, Inc. v. Atomic Energy Commission*, 481 F.2d 1079 (D.C. Cir. 1973) (for discussion of timing); *see also Aberdeen and Rockfish R.R. Co. v. Students Challenging Regulatory Agency Procedures (SCRAP)*, 422 U.S. 289 (1975).

[35]40 C.F.R. § 1508.23 (1991).

[36]*Id.* § 1508.18.

[37]*Id.*

[38]*Id.*; *see generally* D. Mandelker, *NEPA Law and Litigation* § 8.16 (1984).

sharing arrangements are typically exempt from NEPA when there is limited federal involvement in these programs.[39]

There are two other key words that require definition in the threshold determination of NEPA application—one must determine whether the federal action is "major" and "significantly" affects the quality of the human environment. These two terms have been the subject of considerable judicial discussion without establishing a universally accepted definition. CEQ regulations provide that the term "major" reinforces but does not have a meaning independent of the term "significantly".[40] Agencies have defined "major actions" in their program-specific regulations. CEQ regulations have attempted to define "significantly" by suggesting consideration of both the "context" and the "intensity" of the specific circumstances.[41] The context refers to the surrounding circumstances where the action is proposed and its impact upon society as a whole, the affected region, the affected interests and the locality. The term "intensity" refers to the severity of the impact. The regulations refer to a list of considerations which an agency should take into account when weighing the significance of the impacts.[42]

The last key term is "quality of the human environment." At the time Congress enacted NEPA, primary attention was focused on improving and preserving the natural environment as reflected in the policies and goals section of NEPA. However, this phrase has been given broad definition.[43] In *Hanly v. Mitchell*,[44] where the plaintiffs were concerned about a detention center planned for downtown Manhattan, the court recognized that NEPA applied to protection of the urban quality of life as well. Although other cases have supported this broad definition of impacts upon the human environment, at least one case has concluded that "pure economic impacts" without other accompanying physical impacts do not trigger NEPA's application.[45] In one case, aesthetic impacts on the urban environment were sufficient to trigger a NEPA review.[46] The CEQ regulations advise that economic and social effects are not intended by themselves to require preparation of an EIS, but when they are interrelated with natural or physical environmental effects, then they must be discussed.[47]

## 3.2 Relationship to Other Federal Laws

NEPA is a policy and procedural statute that has been interpreted by the courts to make environmental protection a part of the mandate of every federal agency and department.[48] The court in *Calvert Cliffs* cites Senator Jackson, NEPA's principal sponsor, as stating that "no agency will be able to maintain that it has no mandate or no

---

[39]*Carolina Action v. Simon*, 389 F. Supp. 1244 (M.D.N.C. 1975), *aff'd*, 522 F.2d 295 (4th Cir. 1975).

[40]40 C.F.R. § 1508.18 (1991).

[41]*Id.* § 1508.27.

[42]*Id.*

[43]42 U.S.C. § 4331(a).

[44]460 F.2d 640 (2d Cir. 1972), *cert. denied*, 409 U.S. 990 (1972).

[45]*Breckinridge v. Rumsfeld*, 537 F.2d 864 (6th Cir. 1976), *cert. denied*, 429 U.S. 1061 (1977).

[46]*Save the Courthouse Comm. v. Lynn*, 408 F. Supp. 1323 (S.D.N.Y. 1975).

[47]40 C.F.R. § 1508.14 (1991).

[48]*Calvert Cliffs Coordinating Committee Inc.*, 449 F.2d at 1112.

requirement to consider the environmental consequences of its actions."[49] Further, the court interpreted the congressional intent of NEPA to indicate that environmental factors must be considered throughout agency review processes. It went on to underscore the act's requirement that environmental consideration be given "to the fullest extent possible," finding that this language set a high standard for agencies to meet.

Courts have also recognized that, in some limited circumstances, federal actions may be wholly or partially exempt from compliance with NEPA due to statutory conflicts. These conflicts may arise from explicit statutory exemptions as well as implied conflicts. As noted previously, EPA has been expressly exempted from NEPA compliance for all of its actions under the Clean Air Act and specific actions under the Clean Water Act.[50] Congress has also expressly exempted specific agency projects or programs from NEPA compliance, such as the Alaskan Pipeline.[51]

A more controversial situation arises where NEPA is determined to be inapplicable because of agency statutory duties that preclude compliance with NEPA's procedural requirements. In *Flint Ridge Dev. Co. v. Scenic Rivers Ass'n of Oklahoma*,[52] the Supreme Court held that an agency's specific statutory directive to review a matter within 30 days was mandatory and that compliance with NEPA would frustrate this legislative directive. However, the Court did not relieve the agency of all NEPA duties under this conflicting legislation. It specifically noted that the agency had the authority and obligation to require additional environmental information and to consider environmental factors in its decision-making process.

Some federal agencies have claimed an implied exemption from NEPA for actions taken under the cloak of national security or national defense. Although such an implied exemption has not been recognized, the Supreme Court has upheld a Freedom of Information Act exception to disclosure in the EIS process.[53] The Court specifically noted that public disclosure under NEPA is governed by the Freedom of Information Act while agencies must prepare NEPA documentation even for classified proposals. Agencies may include specific criteria for providing limited exceptions to the disclosure provisions of the CEQ regulations for classified proposals.[54]

Perhaps the most important relationship of NEPA to other environmental laws is the role the EIS plays as the public repository of the combined environmental assessment of all applicable environmental laws. Most agency regulations require the EIS to identify and discuss possible violations of the standards established by other more substantive environmental statutes.

---

[49]*Id.* at 1113.

[50]*See supra*, Section 3.0.

[51]15 U.S.C. § 719H(c)(3).

[52]426 U.S. 776 (1976); *see also cf. Jones v. Gordon*, 792 F.2d 821 (9th Cir. 1986).

[53]*Weinberger v. Catholic Action of Hawaii/Peace Education Project*, 454 U.S. 139 (1981); *see also*, F.L. McChesney, *Nuclear Weapons and "Secret" Impact Statements: High Court Applies FOIA Exemptions to EIS Disclosure Rules*, 12 Envtl. L. Rep. (Envtl. L. Inst.) 10007 (1982).

[54]40 C.F.R. § 1507.3(c) (1991).

## 3.3 Functional Equivalency

The courts have been asked, in several cases, to determine whether compliance with other environmental laws which require environmental analyses similar to NEPA constitutes the "functional equivalent" of the NEPA process. In a few cases, the courts have recognized such an exception to NEPA compliance for the EPA only.

For a court to apply the functional equivalency exception, it must find that the statute creating the agency, as well as the specific statute being applied, together provide sufficient substantive and procedural standards to ensure a full and adequate consideration of all pertinent environmental issues by the agency.[55] The key is the consideration of the issues by the *agency*; thus courts have rejected arguments for applying the exception where the environmental consequences of the actions were, or were not, considered by agency outsiders.

The functional equivalency exception is "not . . . a broad exemption from NEPA for all environmental agencies or even for all environmentally protective regulatory actions of such agencies. Instead, [it is] a narrow exemption from the literal requirements for those actions which are undertaken pursuant to sufficient safeguards so that the purpose and policies behind NEPA will necessarily be fulfilled."[56]

Courts have held that the functional equivalency exception to NEPA has been met with respect to EPA actions under the Clean Air Act,[57] the Federal Insecticide, Fungicide and Rodenticide Act,[58] the Resource Conservation and Recovery Act,[59] the Toxic Substances Control Act,[60] the Safe Drinking Water Act,[61] and the Ocean Dumping Act.[62] Courts have not yet addressed whether EPA Superfund cleanup actions under the Comprehensive Environmental Response, Compensation and Liability Act (CERCLA) fall within the functional equivalency exception.

One of the primary arguments against applying the exception to CERCLA is that often the agency which caused the contamination is the one which is cleaning it up, albeit under EPA supervision. In such a case, the agency with primary responsibility does not have the mandate in its organic statute to protect the environment. Indeed, courts have not yet applied the exception to agencies other than EPA, even where the

---

[55]*See, e.g., Alabama v. United States Environmental Protection Agency*, 911 F.2d 499 (11th Cir. 1990); *Environmental Defense Fund v. Environmental Protection Agency*, 489 F.2d 1247 (D.C. Cir. 1973).

[56]*EDF v. EPA*, 489 F.2d at 1257.

[57]*Portland Cement Ass'n v. Ruckelshaus*, 486 F.2d 375 (D.C. Cir. 1973), *cert. denied*, 417 U.S. 921 (1974).

[58]*EDF v. EPA*, 489 F.2d at 1256-57.

[59]*Alabama v. EPA*, 911 F.2d at 504.

[60]*Warren County v. State of North Carolina*, 528 F. Supp. 276, 286-87 (E.D.N.C. 1981).

[61]*Western Nebraska Resources Coun. v. United States Environmental Protection Agency*, 943 F.2d 867, 871-72 (8th Cir. 1991).

[62]*Maryland v. Train*, 415 F. Supp. 116, 121-22 (D. Md. 1976).

agency arguably has substantial environmental responsibilities,[63] and have rejected arguments to extend the exception to actions by the Forest Service,[64] the National Marine Fisheries Service,[65] the National Institutes of Health,[66] and the Bureau of Land Management,[67] among others.

However, it has been suggested that NEPA procedures could be easily melded with the early "remedial investigation and feasibility study" (RI/FS) required by CERCLA,[68] perhaps, in view of the importance CERCLA places on prompt remedial actions, by using the expedited process allowed by NEPA in cases of emergency.[69] Indeed, this is the approach taken by the Department of Energy, which has decided to prepare a programmatic EIS to address the agency/wide implications of its CERCLA cleanup efforts, which can be tiered to "sitewide" EIS's which analyze the environmental impacts of treatment, storage and disposal facilities and the cumulative impacts of DOE clean-up actions.[70] NEPA compliance for individual DOE/CERCLA projects will be accomplished through the use of categorical exclusions or EA/FONSIs[71] (FONSI: finding of no significant impact) drafted during the RI/FS process.[72]

## 4.0 STRATEGIC APPROACHES TO NEPA COMPLIANCE

The strategy for successful compliance with NEPA's provisions is achieved by integrating environmental awareness and environmental factors early in the planning and decision-making process. Recognizing that NEPA is largely a procedural statute, compliance with its provisions calls for planning and analysis which fully considers and documents on a timely basis the environmental considerations and alternatives to the proposed action. Sound environmental planning provides opportunities for the federal agency to design proposals early in the process that meet both the agency's programmatic and environmental objectives and help insure successful NEPA compliance.

### 4.1 Non-Major Actions

The first step in planning for an agency proposal or private action is to determine whether that proposal or action will be subject to NEPA. Agency regulations developed in accordance with CEQ directives should assist in defining those proposals or actions

---

[63]*Compare Wyoming v. Hathaway*, 525 F.2d 66, 71-72 (10th Cir. 1975) *cert. denied, sub nom. Wyoming v. Kleppe*, 426 U.S. 906 (1976), *with Texas Comm. on Natural Resources v. Bergland*, 573 F.2d 201, 208 (5th Cir.) ), *cert. denied*, 439 U.S. 966 (1978) *and Jones v. Gordon*, 621 F. Supp. 7, 13 (D. Alaska 1985) ), *aff'd in part, rev'd in part*, 792 F.2d 821 (9th Cir. 1986).

[64]*Texas Committee on Natural Resources*, 573 F.2d at 208.

[65]*Jones*, 621 F. Supp. at 7.

[66]*Foundation on Economic Trends v. Heckler*, 587 F. Supp. 753, 765-66 (D.D.C. 1984), *aff'd in part, vacated in part on other grounds*, 756 F.2d 143 (D.C. Cir. 1985).

[67]*Sierra Club v. Hodel*, 848 F.2d 1068, 1094-95 (10th Cir. 1988).

[68]42 U.S.C. § 9620(e)(1).

[69]40 C.F.R. § 1506.11 (1991).

[70]Dept. of Energy, Guidance on Implementation of the DOE NEPA/CERCLA Integration Policy (Nov. 15, 1991).

[71]*See infra*, Section 4.4.

[72]*Id.* DOE expects only a relatively few projects will require the preparation of an EIS during the RI/FS for individual projects.

which may be excluded from NEPA documentation. The "categorical exclusion" is the method by which an agency identifies a category of actions which "do not individually or cumulatively have a significant effect on the human environment" and which have been found to have had no such effect in past instances.[73] Proposals or actions which fit these exclusion categories do not require an EA, an EIS or other documentation unless unique circumstances create the possibility that significant impacts could occur. However, categorical exclusion is not an exemption from compliance with NEPA, but merely an administrative tool to avoid paperwork for those actions without significant environmental effects.[74]

If a non-federal action has some "minor" federal involvement, a court may determine that the federal action is a minor action not subject to NEPA. To be subject to NEPA, the action must be one over which the federal agency has sufficient discretion and control to make NEPA application meaningful.[75]

## 4.2 Formulating the Proposal

It is important in the early planning stages to clearly define the "need" to be addressed by the proposed action. The definition of need is often closely aligned with the definition of the required "no-action" alternative which must be discussed in the EIS. If the need is ill-defined or vague, the proposed action and any alternatives may also suffer and will likely be difficult to assess. This result may weaken the proposal and increase its vulnerability to a potential challenge in the EIS process.

If early scoping and consultation with affected parties is accomplished, a notion of the environmental concerns will be known. To the extent that the proposed action can be designed or formulated to incorporate mitigation measures which address these concerns, it is more likely that the proposed action will have a sound footing for acceptance and will avoid significant impacts. This fulfills NEPA's intent.

In formulating the proposed action, the agency must be careful to include all of the actions related to the proposed action which constitute the proposal.[76] The problem of "segmentation" or "piece-mealing" has arisen in projects which involve various stages of development or where agencies have attempted in the past to avoid "major actions" by splitting up a proposed action. The proposed action must include all of these connected actions as part of the proposal. CEQ provides guidance in the definition of the "scope" of the EIS on such "connected actions" which are "closely related" and should be considered together in a single EIS.[77] The regulations state:

Actions are connected if they:
(i)     automatically trigger other actions which may require EISs.
(ii)    cannot or will not proceed unless other actions are taken previously or
        simultaneously.

---

[73]40 C.F.R. § 1508.4 (1991).
[74]*See* Bear, *supra* note 3, at 10063.
[75]*See Macht v. Skinner*, 916 F.2d 13 (D.C. Cir. 1990); see also Daniel R. Mandelker, *NEPA Law and Litigation* § 8:16 (1984); *Winnebago Tribe of Nebraska v. Ray*, 621 F.2d 269, 272 (8th Cir.), *cert. denied*, 449 U.S. 836 (1980).
[76]40 C.F.R. § 1502.4(a) (1991).
[77]*Id.* § 1508.25(a).

(iii)   are interdependent parts of a larger action and depend on the larger action for their justification.[78]

For example, in highway cases where this issue originally arose,[79] a project planned between two points may involve the construction of several highway segments over time. Under the Federal Highway Administration NEPA regulations, in order to avoid segmentation, a project must (1) connect logical termini; (2) have independent utility or independent significance; and (3) not restrict future transportation improvement alternatives.[80]

## 4.3  Tiering

There are various levels in the planning and decision-making process where an EIS may be required. Federal decisions made at the national level among competing programmatic alternatives and policies which affect the entire federal effort may require the preparation of a "programmatic" EIS (PEIS). Proposals for federal actions may also be made at a regional level requiring an EIS which is focused on regional considerations and which must be more specific than the national PEIS. Finally, a proposed project at a specific site may require an EIS more detailed than the regional EIS or national PEIS.

"Tiering" is an approach whereby the very site-specific project EIS can incorporate by reference and without repetition the broader considerations of a regionwide EIS, or even a national PEIS, if they are relevant. CEQ regulations note that tiering is appropriate when the sequence of EIS's is from a program, plan or policy EIS to a site-specific statement or from an EIS on a specific action at an early stage (such as a need and site selection) to a subsequent statement at a later stage. Tiering in such cases is appropriate when it helps the responsible federal agency focus on the issues which are ripe for discussion, and exclude from consideration issues already decided or not yet ripe.[81]

An example is the Federal Aviation Administration (FAA) which might prepare a programmatic EIS on its nationwide systems airport plan to evaluate choices and alternatives to providing national aviation services. On a regional or statewide basis, the FAA may focus on providing air service improvements within that region, utilizing a regionwide or statewide EIS. Finally, for a specific airport proposal, a project EIS would be developed which could incorporate by reference any relevant information from the regionwide or statewide EIS, or information from the nationwide PEIS.

Tiering is a useful tool when new federal programs are initiated which must later be delegated to regional programs and finally become site-specific activities. Tiering can be used in the NEPA compliance process to avoid duplication and provide the appropriate detail required for the level of action under consideration. Using the tiered system, a project specific EA or EIS need only focus on potential environmental impacts of the project that are not covered by earlier, broader statements.

---

[78]*Id.* § 1508.25(a)(1).

[79]*See Named Individual Members of the San Antonio Conservation  Soc'y v. Texas Highway Dept.*, 446 F.2d 1013 (5th Cir. 1971), *cert. denied*, 406 U.S. 933 (1972).

[80]23 C.F.R. § 771.111(f)

[81]*Id.* § 1508.28.

## 4.4 Environmental Assessments

An environmental assessment (EA) is used as a screening document to determine whether an agency must prepare an EIS or make a finding of no significant impact (FONSI). CEQ regulations describe an EA as a concise public document that also serves to aid an agency's compliance with NEPA when no EIS is necessary and to facilitate preparation of an EIS when one is necessary.[82] An EA should include a brief discussion of the need for the proposal, of alternatives as required by section 102(2)(E), of the environmental impacts of the proposed action and alternatives, and a listing of agencies and persons consulted.

Although most agency procedures do not require public involvement prior to finalizing an EA document, it is advisable for agencies to consider facilitating public comment at the draft EA stage. Early public input will help the agency prepare a final EA which addresses adequately and completely the environmental issues likely to be raised by opponents of an agency action. Moreover, it will assist the agency in preparing the FONSI, which becomes the record for review by a court if challenged.

A FONSI briefly presents the reasons why an action, not otherwise categorically excluded, will not have a significant effect on the human environment. It must include the EA or a summary of the EA in supporting the FONSI determination.[83] Although EAs and FONSIs are public documents, they are not filed in a central location like EISs.

CEQ regulations require that, in certain limited circumstances, the agency must make the FONSI determination available for public review by some means, including state and areawide clearinghouses, for thirty days before the agency makes its final determination of whether to prepare an EIS, and before any action may begin.[84] Those circumstances are:

(i)    The proposed action is, or is closely similar to, one which normally requires the preparation of an EIS under the procedures adopted by the agency; or

(ii)   The nature of the proposed action is one without precedent.

EAs need to be of sufficient length to insure that the underlying decision about whether to prepare an EIS is sound, but should not attempt to be a substitute for an EIS.[85] A thorough EA provides a good information base early in the process for both agency and public consideration.

## 5.0 EIS PREPARATION

If it is determined that a proposed federal action, or non federal action having sufficient federal involvement, does not fall within a designated categorical exclusion or does not qualify for a FONSI, then the responsible federal agency or agencies must prepare an EIS.

---

[82]*Id.* § 1508.9.

[83]*Id.* § 1508.13.

[84]*Id.* § 1501.4(e)(2).

[85]*See* Bear, *supra* note 3, at 10063.

## 5.1 Lead Agency

The proposed action may be one where several agencies have some responsibility and all must comply with NEPA. CEQ regulations provide for a "lead agency" to take primary responsibility for the preparation of the EIS and to supervise the process.[86] Other agencies which have a responsibility by law for the joint action then become "cooperating agencies."[87] If a disagreement should arise among the agencies as to who should be the lead, CEQ regulations provide guidance based upon the magnitude of the agency's involvement, their project approval authority, expertise, duration of involvement and sequence of agency's involvement.[88] If a determination cannot be made on these factors, the CEQ can be asked to make the necessary determination.

The lead agency concept avoids duplication and enhances cooperation among the agencies. In addition, where there are state or local environmental reporting requirements, the lead agency can team with state or local agencies in the preparation of one EIS or environmental document to satisfy all requirements, thereby reducing duplication.[89]

At this stage in the process, sufficient environmental planning should have been completed to clearly identify the proposed action and reasonable alternatives thereto. Further, if an EA has been prepared for this proposed action, some early coordination with affected agencies and interest groups will have already occurred. Thus, the agency should be prepared to publish a notice of intent to prepare an EIS and initiate the first step—the scoping process.[90]

## 5.2 Scoping and Early Coordination

The scoping process is the first opportunity for the agency to involve the public by describing the agency's planning efforts to address the needs identified and to solicit comments on the scope of actions, alternatives and impacts which need to be considered. The CEQ regulations require that this be an early and open process conducted as soon as practicable after its decision to prepare an EIS.[91] The lead agency must invite the participation of affected federal, state and local agencies, any affected Indian tribes, the proponents of the action, and other interested persons (including those who might not be in accord with the action on environmental grounds).[92]

This scoping process is used to identify the significant issues requiring in-depth analysis in the EIS and to eliminate from detailed study those issues which are not significant or have been covered by prior environmental reviews. The scoping process is also used by the agency to make preliminary assignments between the lead agency and cooperating agencies concerning the EIS preparation, to identify other public EAs or

---

[86]40 C.F.R. § 1501.5 (1991).

[87]*Id.* § 1501.6.

[88]*Id.* § 1501.5(c).

[89]*Id.* § 1506.2.

[90]*Id.* § 1501.7. The "notice of intent" must (I) describe the proposed action and possible alternatives; (ii) describe the proposed scoping process; and (iii) provide the name and address of a person within the agency to contact concerning the EIS. *Id.* § 1508.22.

[91]*Id.* § 1501.7

[92]*Id.* § 1501.7(a).

EISs which are being or will be prepared that are related to the EIS under consideration, to identify other environmental review and consultation requirements that need to be integrated into this process, and finally, to establish a schedule for the timing of the EIS and the ultimate decision on the proposed action.

The CEQ regulations allow the agencies flexibility in several other areas, such as setting page limits on environmental documents, setting time limits, adopting procedures to combine the EA process with the scoping process, and holding early scoping meetings or meetings which may be integrated with other early planning meetings.[93]

The scoping process is important because it sends a signal to the public about both the agency's attitude toward public involvement and its planning for the proposal at hand. It also provides an opportunity for the agency to set reasonable boundaries on the timing, content and process that will be used for the EIS. It may also be used to restrict new subjects from being introduced later to challenge the agency's decision.[94]

The scoping process also offers an opportunity for the agency to investigate the criteria which commenting agencies will use in determining the environmental factors that are important and what impacts are likely to be considered significant.

### 5.3 Use of the EA and Applicant's Information

After the scoping process is completed, the lead agency must begin to prepare for collecting and assimilating the environmental information needed for the EIS. A starting point for this process is to review the material prepared for the EA or supplied by the applicant.

CEQ regulations provide that an agency may require an applicant to submit environmental information for possible use by the agency in preparing an EIS. The agency must assist the applicant in outlining the types of information required and must independently evaluate the information submitted in order to take responsibility for its accuracy.[95] Similarly, if an agency permits an applicant to prepare an EA, the agency must undertake a similar evaluation of its own and assume responsibility for the scope and content of the EA.[96]

### 5.4 Delegation

The responsibility for preparing the EIS belongs to the lead federal agency pursuant to section 102(2)(C). Under many federal programs, delegation to the states has been a common practice, particularly where the state acts as an applicant for federal funding. The Federal Highway Administration is one agency that delegated to the states many of the responsibilities under the Federal Aid Highway program. In 1975, this practice was challenged by an environmental group in *Conservation Soc'y of S. Vermont v. Secretary of Transportation*.[97]

---

[93]*Id.* § 1501.7(b).

[94]*See Vermont Yankee Nuclear Power Corp.*, 435 U.S. at 551-54.

[95]40 C.F.R. § 1506.5 (1991).

[96]*Id.* § 1506.5(b).

[97]508 F.2d 927 (2d Cir. 1974), *vacated*, 423 U.S. 809 (1975) (vacated as a result of subsequent legislation).

In holding that the Federal Highway Administration could not delegate its NEPA responsibility to the state, the court noted that:

A state agency is established to pursue defined state goals. In attempting to serve federal approval of a project, "self-serving assumptions" may ineluctably color a state agency's presentation of the environmental data or influence its final recommendation. Transposing the federal duty to prepare the EIS to a state agency is thus unlikely to result in as dispassionate an appraisal of environmental considerations as the federal agency itself could produce.[98]

The surrounding states interpreted this decision to prohibit any delegation to state highway agencies and thus stopped all highway construction in the Northeast. Congress responded in 1975 with the only substantive amendment to NEPA since its enactment by adding a new section to address the delegation issue, section 102(2)(D).[99]

This section provides that an EIS may be prepared by a state agency having statewide jurisdiction so long as the responsible federal official furnishes guidance, participates in the preparation, and independently evaluates the EIS prior to its approval and adoption. Further, the amendment provides that if the proposed action has any impacts on an adjoining state or federal land management entity, the responsible federal official must solicit that state's or entity's views on potential impacts.[100]

An earlier court case had disapproved the preparation of an EIS by a private applicant on account of the potential self-serving interest of the applicant in receiving an approval from the agency.[101] However, this decision did not prevent an applicant from assisting the agency by submitting environmental information or by participating in environmental studies that form the basis for an EIS.[102]

Similarly, the use of consultants in the preparation of an EIS is a common practice and is acceptable so long as the federal agency retains sufficient control of their work product.[103] The CEQ regulations state that the agency should avoid conflicts of interest and require a disclosure statement from the contractor indicating that it has no financial or other interest in the project. Further, the federal agency is to provide guidance and participate in the preparation of the EIS, evaluate it independently, and take responsibility for its scope and content.[104]

## 5.5 Content of EIS

The purpose of an EIS is to help public officials make informed decisions that are based on an understanding of environmental consequences and the reasonable

---

[98]*Id.* at 931.

[99]42 U.S.C. § 4332(2)(D).

[100]*Id.* § 4332(2)(D)(iv).

[101]*Green County Planning Bd. v. Federal Power Comm'n.*, 455 F.2d 412 (2d Cir.), *cert. denied*, 409 U.S. 849 (1972).

[102]*Sierra Club v. Lynn*, 502 F.2d 43 (5th Cir. 1974), *cert. denied*, 421 U.S. 994, 422 U.S. 1049 (1975).

[103]*Natural Resources Defense Coun. v. Callaway*, 524 F.2d 79 (2d Cir. 1975).

[104]40 C.F.R. § 1506.5(c) (1991).

alternatives available to them. "[EISs] shall be concise, clear, and to the point, and shall be supported by evidence that agencies have made the necessary environmental analyses."[105]

Section 102(2)(C) requires an EIS to describe: (I) the environmental impacts of the proposed action; (ii) any adverse environmental impacts which cannot be avoided should the proposal be implemented; (iii) the reasonable alternatives to the proposed action; (iv) the relationship between local short-term uses of man's environment and the maintenance and enhancement of long-term productivity; and (v) any irreversible and irretrievable commitments of resources which would be involved in the proposed action should it be implemented.

EISs have evolved so that they place more emphasis on a description of the affected environment, the alternatives to the proposed action, and possible mitigation measures than on what is outlined in the statute. The CEQ regulations outline a recommended format for EIS preparation.[106]

The alternatives section of the EIS is the "heart" of the EIS.[107] Once the affected environment and environmental consequences are described, the discussion of the proposed action and alternatives should be presented in a comparative form in order to sharply define the issues and provide a clear basis for the choice among options by the decision maker and the public. CEQ regulations require that all "reasonable" alternatives, within or outside the jurisdiction of the lead agency, including the no-action alternative, be discussed.[108] CEQ has provided guidance on the range of alternatives agencies must consider.[109] This discussion should also include appropriate mitigation measures not already included in the proposed action and alternatives.

The environmental consequences section of the EIS provides the scientific and analytic basis for the comparison of alternatives. It must include a discussion of direct effects of the proposed action and alternatives, indirect effects, possible conflicts with objectives of federal, regional, state, and local (including Indian tribes) land use plans, policies and controls of the area concerned, and other key areas outlined in the CEQ regulations.[110]

When evaluating reasonably foreseeable significant adverse effects in the EIS, if there is incomplete or unavailable information on account of the costs of obtaining such information, the agency is directed to include within the EIS a statement that such information is incomplete or unavailable, the relevance of such information, a summary of existing credible scientific evidence which is relevant to evaluating the reasonably foreseeable adverse impacts, and the agency's evaluation of such impacts based upon theoretical approaches or research methods generally accepted in the scientific commu-

---

[105]*Id.* § 1500.2(b).

[106]*Id.* § 1502.10.

[107]*Id.* § 1502.14.

[108]*Id.* § 1502.14.

[109]46 *Fed. Reg.* 18026, 18027 (1981) (Council on Environmental Quality, Forty Most Asked Questions Concerning CEQ's National Environmental Policy Act Regulations, Question 1).

[110]40 C.F.R. § 1502.16 (1991).

nity.[111] Earlier CEQ regulation had required a "worst case analysis" in such situations, but revoked this analysis requirement with a 1986 amendment to the regulations after considerable debate.[112] The Supreme Court later approved this revocation of the CEQ regulation noting that it was not a prior codification of any judicial determination and thus the Court should give substantial deference to CEQ's revocation amendment.[113]

The discussion of indirect effects or impacts has been the most vulnerable to challenge. Indirect effects include economic growth-inducing effects of the proposed action, changes in land use patterns induced by the action, anticipated changes in population density or growth areas, and related impacts on air, water and other natural systems, including ecosystems. Effects also include those resulting from actions which may have both beneficial and detrimental effects, even if, on balance, the agency believes that the effect will be beneficial.

Finally, "cumulative" impacts must also be covered in an EA or EIS which requires analysis of the "incremental impact of the action when added to other past, present, and reasonably foreseeable future actions, regardless of what agency (federal or nonfederal) or person undertakes such other actions. Cumulative impacts can result from individually minor but collectively significant actions taking place over a period of time."[114] This language from the CEQ regulations substantially expands the discussion of impacts in the EIS, but allows considerable discretion by the agency in defining some of the key terms in its definition. Further, the regulation defining "significantly" requires the federal agency to consider "actions related to other actions with individually insignificant, but cumulatively significant, impacts."[115] The courts have scrutinized closely cumulative impact analyses in EAs and EISs and appear willing to find them inadequate on this basis.[116]

## 5.6 Commenting and Public Involvement

The NEPA statute makes public involvement in the process an essential element in ensuring informed decision making at the federal level. Section 102(2)(C) requires that "[c]opies of [the EIS] and the comments and views of the appropriate Federal, state and local agencies, which are authorized to develop and enforce environmental standards, shall be made available to the President, the Council on Environmental Quality and *to the public* as provided by [the Freedom of Information Act]."[117] Further, section 102(2)(G) requires that the federal agencies must make available to the states, counties, municipalities, institutions, and *individuals*, advice and information useful in restoring, maintaining, and enhancing the quality of the environment.[118]

---

[111]*Id.* § 1502.22.

[112]51 Fed. Reg. 15625 (1986).

[113]*Robertson v. Methow Valley Citizens*, 490 U.S. 332, 356 (1989).

[114]40 C.F.R. § 1508.7 (1991).

[115]*Id.* § 1508.27(b)(7).

[116]*See Fritiofson v. Alexander*, 772 F.2d 1225 (5th Cir. 1985); *Thomas v. Peterson*, 753 F.2d 754 (9th Cir. 1985).

[117]42 U.S.C. § 4332(2)(C) (Emphasis added).

[118]*Id.* § 4332(2)(G) (Emphasis added).

Public involvement was expanded by both Executive Order 11514[119] and the CEQ Guidelines[120] (now regulations). The CEQ regulations provide for involvement by requiring "public notice of NEPA-related hearings, public meetings, and the availability of environmental documents" so that interested persons and agencies can be informed.[121]

Public involvement can occur at three stages in the EIS process: initial scoping, commenting on the draft EIS, and commenting on the final EIS prior to a record of decision. At the scoping stage, public involvement is valuable to identify the potential environmental impacts, to judge the breadth of potential controversial issues, and to observe the public's reaction to the need for action and the alternatives that may exist to satisfy the need. Effective public involvement can also assist the agency in prioritizing the issues that need to be addressed in the EIS. At the draft EIS comment stage, the public can provide valuable feedback to the agency in identifying both the impacts which have not been adequately addressed and areas where gaps of information or analysis may exist. Comments regarding potential mitigation measures from the public may also be helpful to the agency at this juncture. Lastly, public comments on the final EIS assist the agency in making its final decision and preparing a formal record of decision. This is the last opportunity the public has to ensure that the agency has all the relevant information and analyses before it, and that significant issues have been properly addressed.

The CEQ regulations direct the agency, after preparing a draft EIS and before preparing a final EIS, to obtain the comments of any federal agency which has jurisdiction by law or special expertise with respect to environmental impacts involved or which is authorized to develop and enforce environmental standards.[122] Further, the agency must request the comments of appropriate state and local agencies which are authorized to develop and enforce environmental standards; Indian tribes, when effects may occur on a reservation; and any agency which has requested that it receive comments on actions of the kind proposed.[123] Finally, the agency must request comments from the applicant, if any, and from the public, affirmatively soliciting comments from those persons or organizations who may be interested or affected.[124]

The lead agency preparing the final EIS must then assess and consider the comments both individually and collectively and respond by making necessary changes in the EIS, making factual corrections or explaining why the comments do not warrant further agency response.[125] All of the substantive comments received on the draft EIS must be attached to the final EIS whether or not the comment is thought to merit individual discussion by the agency.

The CEQ regulations require agencies to make diligent efforts to involve the public in the NEPA process by providing public notice of NEPA-related hearings, public meetings and the availability of environmental documents, and holding or sponsoring

---

[119]*See supra*, note 15.
[120]*See supra*, note 16.
[121]40 C.F.R. § 1506.6(b) (1991).
[122]*Id.* § 1503.1.
[123]*Id.*
[124]*Id.*
[125]*Id.* § 1503.4.

public hearings or public meetings whenever appropriate or in accordance with statutory requirements applicable to the agency.[126]

### 5.7 Mitigation of Impacts

Appropriate mitigation measures must be included in the EIS.[127] Once an agency decision is made, any mitigation measures or other conditions established in the EIS or during its review and committed as part of the decision must be implemented by the lead agency or other appropriate consenting agency.[128] CEQ lists five generic mitigation measures in their regulatory definition of "mitigation."[129]

Whether NEPA requires agencies to commit to mitigation measures in the first instance was addressed by the Supreme Court in *Robertson v. Methow Valley Citizens.*[130] The Court of Appeals had held that NEPA imposes a substantive duty on agencies to take action to mitigate the adverse effects of major federal actions, which entails the further duty to include in every EIS a detailed explanation of specific actions that will be employed to mitigate the adverse effects.[131] The Supreme Court reversed the finding, noting the difference between a requirement that mitigation be discussed and a substantive requirement that a complete mitigation plan be formulated and adopted. "[I]t would be inconsistent with NEPA's reliance on procedural mechanisms—as opposed to substantive, result-based standards—to demand the presence of a fully developed plan that will mitigate environmental harm before an agency can act."[132] The Court found no substantive requirement or duty to include in an EIS a detailed explanation of specific measures which will be employed to mitigate adverse impacts of a proposed action.

### 5.8 Proposals for Legislation

Section 102(2)(C) requires the preparation of an EIS for proposals for legislation as well as for major federal actions.[133] CEQ regulations require that a legislative EIS be transmitted to Congress within thirty days of the formal transmittal of a legislative proposal to Congress.[134] The intent is to provide a document that can serve as the basis for public and congressional debate. A scoping process is not required as part of a legislative EIS, and normally only a draft EIS will be required.[135]

Very little attention has been given to proposals for legislation under NEPA, primarily because most legislative proposals come from the president or the executive

---

[126]*Id.* § 1506.6.
[127]*Id.* § 1502.14(f).
[128]*Id.* § 1505.3.
[129]*Id.* § 1508.20.
[130]490 U.S. 332 (1989).
[131]*Methow Valley Citizens Coun. v. Regional Forester*, 833 F.2d 810 (9th Cir. 1987), *cert. granted*, 47 U.S. 1217 (1988), *rev'd*, 490 U.S. 332 (1989).
[132]*Robertson*, 490 U.S. at 353.
[133]42 U.S.C. § 4332(2)(C).
[134]40 C.F.R. § 1506.8 (1991).
[135]*Id.* § 1506.8(b).

office of the president, which are not included in the definition of "federal agency."[136] Further, in the extensive communication which occurs between the Congress and the executive branch, it is often very difficult to determine when a "proposal" will trigger the need for an EIS.

The Supreme Court has addressed the question of whether an EIS is required for an appropriations request from an agency. In *Andrus v. Sierra Club*,[137] the Court held that an EIS was not required when the Office of Management and Budget proposed a significant reduction in the Fish and Wildlife Service appropriation for the operation of the National Wildlife Refuge System. The Court referenced CEQ regulations, which define "legislation" as "a bill or legislative proposal" and omit any reference to "appropriation requests."[138] Therefore, the Court held that an EIS was not required, and further, that requiring an EIS on appropriation proposals would circumvent and eliminate "the careful distinction Congress had maintained between appropriations and legislation."[139]

## 6.0 NEPA'S EXTRATERRITORIAL APPLICATION

International application of NEPA has been a matter of controversy since the statute does not explicitly indicate whether it applies outside the United States. Some agencies have argued that compliance with NEPA could present obstacles to meeting certain foreign policy objectives. While section 102(2)(F) requires that "all agencies of the federal government shall . . . recognize the worldwide and long-range character of environmental problems and . . . lend appropriate support . . . to maximize international cooperation," it appears to impose a duty on federal agencies only to "recognize" worldwide environmental problems. In a D.C. Court of Appeals decision reversing an early District Court decision, the Court held that the operation of an incinerator in the Antarctica by the National Science Foundation required an EIS, holding explicitly that the presumption against extraterritorial application does not apply where the effect will occur in Antarctica, as Antarctica has no sovereign, and the United States has a measure of legislative control over the continent."[140]

In 1979, President Carter issued Executive Order No. 12114 on the environmental effects abroad of major federal actions, based on his independent executive authority rather than on NEPA. Nevertheless, the objective of the Executive Order was to further the purposes of NEPA by providing procedures for ensuring that pertinent environmental considerations were given to actions having effects outside the geographical boundaries of the United States.[141] Although it does not create a cause of action in the courts, it provides for environmental analysis and documentation for actions affecting

---

[136]*Id.* § 1508.12. The presidential exemption applies only to the president and immediate staff, not to offices in the EOP like CEQ.

[137]442 U.S. 347 (1979).

[138]*Id.* at 357.

[139]*Id.* at 364.

[140]*Environmental Defense Fund v. Massey*, 986 F.2d 528, 529 (D.C. Cir. 1993).

[141]Executive Order No. 12114, 3 C.F.R. 356 (1980).

the global commons or for actions in which foreign nations are not participating with the United States; and for certain actions which could create a serious public health risk.[142]

In February 1991, the United States signed a Convention on Environmental Impact Assessment with European countries obligating the signatories to consult when an activity is likely to cause adverse transboundary environmental impacts. The Department of State, EPA and CEQ are designing the implementation strategy for the convention.[143]

## 7.0 ENVIRONMENTAL JUSTICE

Environmental justice is a new NEPA consideration that was introduced by President Clinton on February 11, 1994 in Executive Order (E.O.) 12898 entitled "Federal Actions to Address Environmental Justice in Minority Populations and Low-Income Populations". This E.O. was designed to focus the attention of federal agencies on the human health and environmental conditions in minority communities and low income communities. The President emphasizes that existing laws, including the National Environmental Policy Act, provide opportunities for federal agencies to address environmental hazards in minority and low-income communities. Thus, the E.O. requires federal agencies to adopt strategies to address environmental justice concerns within the context of agency operations.

In July, 1996, the EPA published, draft guidance[144] to implement its environmental justice goals into EPA's preparation of environmental impact statements and environmental assessments under NEPA. In this draft guidance, EPA's Office of Environmental Justice offers the following definition of environmental justice:

> The fair treatment and meaningful involvement of all people regardless of race, color, national origin, or income with respect to the development, implementation, and enforcement of environmental laws, regulations, and policies. Fair treatment means that no group of people, including racial, ethnic or socioeconomic group should bear a disproportionate share of the negative environmental consequences resulting from industrial, municipal, and commercial operations or the execution of federal, state, local and tribal programs and policies.

The Presidential Memorandum accompanying the E.O. calls for a variety of actions. Four specific actions were directed to NEPA-related activities, including:

1. Each federal agency must analyze environmental effects, including human health, economic, and social effects, of federal actions, including effects on minority communities and low-income communities, when such analysis is required by NEPA.
2. Mitigation measures outlined or analyzed in EAs, EISs or Records of Decision, whenever feasible, should address significant and adverse environmental effects of proposed federal actions on minority communities and low-income communities.

---

[142]*Id.* §§ 2-3.
[143]Council on Environmental Quality 22nd Annual Report, p.136 (1992).
[144]61 FR 36727 (1996)

3.  Each federal agency must provide opportunities for community input in the NEPA process, including identifying potential effects and mitigation measures in consultation with affected communities and improving accessibility of publicmeetings, official documents, and notices to affected communities.

4.  In reviewing other agencies' proposed actions under Section 309 of the Clean Air Act, EPA must ensure that the agencies have fully analyzed environmen tal effects on minority communities and low-income communities, including human health, social and economic effects.

## 8.0  EPA REVIEW AND COMMENT

The Environmental Protection Agency (EPA) has specific authority and responsibility under Section 309 of the Clean Air Act[146] to review and comment in writing on the environmental impact of any matter relating to the duties and responsibilities granted pursuant to the Act or other provisions of the authority of the Administrator. Such review and comment authority relates to (1) legislation proposed by a federal department or agency; (2) newly authorized federal projects for construction and any major federal action subject to Section 102(2)(C) of the National Environmental Policy Act; and (3) proposed regulations published in any department or agency of the federal Government. Such written comments must be made public at the conclusion of any review.

EPA adopted an Environmental Review Process to implement this authority and responsibility in a set of policies and procedures.[147] These policies and procedures define the review process, assign internal responsibilities, and outline mechanisms for resolving problems that arise in the Environmental Review Process.

As part of their Environmental Review Process, EPA has developed a rating system for draft EISs which summarizes EPA's level of concern about the adequacy of the document. The rating system uses an alpha numeric system the alphabetical categories LO (Lack of objections), EC (Environmental Concerns), EO (Environmental Objections), and EU (Environmental Unsatisfactory) signify EPA's evaluation of the environmental impacts of the proposal. The numerical categories 1 (Adequate), 2 (Insufficient Information) and 3 (Inadequate) signify an evaluation of the adequacy of the information and assessment in the EIS. Depending upon the ratings, EPA may initiate follow-up discussions with the lead agency. If the EIS receives an "Unsatisfactory" rating and significant issues are not resolved with the lead agency, EPA may refer the proposed regulation or major action to the Council on Environmental Quality, along with their assessment for resolution. CEQ has only received some 26 referrals in its history from all agencies including EPA. In such cases, if CEQ cannot resolve the issue, it may refer the matter to the President, although that has never been done[148].

---

[146]42 U.S.C. 7609, Public Law 91-604 12(a), 84 Stat. 1709

[147]"Policy and Procedures for the Review of Federal Actions Impacting the Environment",U.S. EPA, Office of External Affairs, Office of Federal Activities, Washington, D.C.

[148]Elizabeth Blaug, General Counsel's Office, CEQ.

EPA should provide comments to the lead agency within 45 days from the start of the official review period. In general, EPA's comments should be focused on the proposal, but may also review the complete range of alternatives, identifying those that are environmentally unacceptable to EPA and identifying EPA's preferred alternative. EPA's comment letter on the draft EIS should reflect all of EPA's responsibilities that may bear on the action including measures to avoid or mitigate damage to the environment, or to protect, restore, and enhance the environment.

Finally, EPA's policy is to conduct detailed reviews of final EISs which have had significant issues raised by EPA at the draft EIS stage. The detailed review and submission of comments will be done for those actions rated EO, EU, or 3 at the draft stage. These EPA reviews and comments are almost always important indicators to the public of what the acceptability of the proposed action should be in the community.

## 9.0 JUDICIAL REVIEW OF NEPA

The courts have played a crucial role in enforcing NEPA's environmental mandates. Judicial review is not expressly provided for in the statute, but federal agencies have held that judicial review of agency decisions is implied under NEPA.[149] Judicial review usually occurs when the agency either decides not to file an EIS or makes a final decision after completing the EIS process. Generally, the courts review an agency's EIS to determine whether it is "adequate" under NEPA's statutory provisions.

The court case most often cited in setting the standard of review for agency decisions under NEPA is *Citizens to Preserve Overton Park, Inc. v. Volpe.*[150] Although this case was not a NEPA case, the Supreme Court indicated that courts must conduct a "substantial inquiry" into agency decisions to determine whether the agency has taken a "hard look" at the issues. This "hard look" doctrine has become the hallmark of judicial review in environmental law.

However, this "hard look" does not mean that a court can substitute its own judgment for that of the agency. Under NEPA, as in administrative law generally, once a court is satisfied that the agency has given fair and adequate consideration to the relevant evidence, the agency decision will not be set aside absent a finding that the decision was "arbitrary, capricious, an abuse of discretion, or otherwise not in accordance with law."[151] In essence, this means that the agency decision will not be set aside unless the court is convinced there has been "a clear error of judgment" by the agency.[152] The reason for this deferential standard of review is that the agency's decision turns on the resolution of factual disputes—an inquiry which the agency, by virtue of its substantial technical expertise, is more qualified to conduct than the court. Thus, the Supreme Court in 1989 held that an agency's decision not to prepare a supplemental EIS based on new information was not a clear error of judgment, inasmuch as there were conflicting views in the scientific community with respect to the significance of that

---

[149]*Calvert Cliffs Coordinating Committee, Inc.*, 449 F.2d at 1115; *see also Environmental Defense Fund v. Corps of Engineers of the United States Army*, 470 F.2d 289 (8th Cir. 1972), *cert. denied*, 412 U.S. 931 (1973).

[150]401 U.S. 402 (1971).

[151]5 U.S.C. § 706(2); *Marsh v. Oregon Natural Resources Coun.*, 490 U.S. 360 (1989).

[152]*Marsh*, 490 U.S. at 377-78, 385.

information and the agency could only decide which side to believe based on its own scientific expertise.[153]

By contrast, where the outcome of the dispute turns on the agency's *legal* interpretation of applicable statutes or regulations, a court will conduct a less deferential review, and may substitute its own judgment for that of the agency. The reason for this is clear—in matters of legal interpretation, as opposed to matters of fact, the agency has no special expertise that makes its decision preferable to that of a court. There is one important qualification to this rule, however. A court will give effect to an agency's interpretation of its *own* organic statute or regulations, as long as that interpretation is a "reasonable" one.[154] In addition, the courts have accorded "substantial deference" to CEQ's regulations regarding the implementation of NEPA.

An important issue in obtaining judicial review is "standing." Most environmental challenges under NEPA are brought by environmental organizations or third parties who may not have participated in the agency decision that is the subject of litigation. Their standing or access to the courts has been routinely granted under NEPA, although it may become more difficult in the future.

While the courts apply the basic "significant injury" test for standing under the Constitution and the Administrative Procedures Act (APA),[155] at least one court has suggested that when this test is applied to NEPA litigation, there is perhaps a lower threshold for standing than is typically required.[156] This is because the nature of rights created by NEPA may compel an unusually broad definition of the act's zone of interest, thus making it easier to obtain standing under NEPA than under most statutes.

In general, plaintiffs have successfully maintained standing by alleging their use of areas that may be affected by an agency's failure to prepare an EIS, or areas in close proximity to those areas.

In 1990, however, the Supreme Court held that plaintiffs failed to satisfy the specific injury requirement if they could only allege that they use certain lands "in the vicinity of" the potentially affected areas.[157] The Supreme Court acknowledged that NEPA does not provide a private right of action for violations of its provisions, but rather that an injured party must seek relief under the APA.

To demonstrate standing under the APA, a plaintiff must identify some final agency action that affects him or her and must show that he or she has suffered a legal wrong because of the agency action or has been adversely affected by that action within the meaning of the relevant statute. To be "adversely affected within the meaning of the statute," a plaintiff must be within a "zone of interest" sought to be protected by the statutory provision that forms the basis of the complaint. Using this test of standing, the court found that the plaintiffs' interests were within the zone of interest to be protected by NEPA, but that the plaintiffs' claiming use "in the vicinity" of the agency action was not enough to render them "adversely affected." Given these findings, the court ruled

---

[153]*Id.*

[154]*Robertson v. Methow Valley Citizens Council*, 490 U.S. at 358-59.

[155]5 U.S.C. §§ 551-559.

[156]*Public Citizen v. Nat'l Highway Traffic Safety Admin.*, 848 F.2d 256, 261 (D.C. Cir. 1988).

[157]*Lujan v. National Wildlife Federation*, 487 U.S. 871 (1990).

that the plaintiffs had not set forth "specific facts" in their affidavit sufficient to survive the agency's motion for summary judgment.

While proving significant injury is certainly the most difficult part of establishing standing, a plaintiff must also show that the alleged significant injury will occur as a result of the agency's action. By characterizing the threatened injury as a chance that the agency, by failing to comply with NEPA, would overlook serious environmental harm, courts have found the causation element to be easily met. For example, in *City of Los Angeles v. Nat'l Highway Traffic Safety Admin.*,[158] the federal Court of Appeals for the District of Columbia granted standing to an environmental group that claimed the government, by failing to prepare an EIS, risked overlooking the impact of proposed federal fuel economy standards on global warming. The court held that as long as there is a "real possibility" that the agency would have reached a different decision if it had complied with the requirements of NEPA, standing should be granted. One judge disagreed, focusing instead on the alleged injury in the form of the "environmental nightmare" that would result from global warming. Because the agency's activity would, at most, have only an insignificant impact on global warming, the judge would have denied standing on the grounds that the agency's failure to prepare an EIS "appears to be but an insignificant tributary to the causal stream leading to the overall harm that petitioners have alleged."[159]

## 10.0 CONCLUSION

NEPA continues to serve as the cornerstone environmental law whose mandates have been more fully integrated into the decision-making process of federal agencies. Environmental concerns have shifted from agency implementation issues to use NEPA to address global problems of biodiversity, pollution prevention, global warming, stratospheric ozone depletion and sustainable growth. President Clinton announced at the end of 1994 that the Office of Environmental Policy, created early in his administration, would be merged with the CEQ, which had been targeted in proposed legislation to be abolished and its functions split between EPA and the new White House Office of Environmental Policy. Since 1994, the budget for CEQ has steadily increased to approximately $2.5 million in FY 97 which supports almost 20 FTE. Katie McGinty, who formerly headed the Office of Environmental Policy, was confirmed as the new Chairman of CEQ in December, 1995.

---

[158]912 F.2d 478, 498 (D.C. Cir. 1990).
[159]*Id.* at 483-84.

# CHAPTER 13

# COMPREHENSIVE ENVIRONMENTAL RESPONSE, COMPENSATION, AND LIABILITY ACT

Robert T. Lee
Ogletree, Deakins, Nash, Smoak & Stewart P.C.
Washington, D.C.

## 1.0 INTRODUCTION

### 1.1 CERCLA's History and Objectives

The Comprehensive Environmental Response, Compensation, and Liability Act,[1] commonly referred to as "CERCLA" or "Superfund," was enacted by Congress in 1980. CERCLA's impetus was the emerging realization—as most directly evidenced by the Love Canal tragedy—that inactive hazardous waste sites presented great risk to public health and the environment and that existing law did not address these abandoned disposal sites. CERCLA was designed to respond to situations involving the past disposal of hazardous substances. As such, it complements the Resource Conservation and Recovery Act (RCRA)[2], which regulates on-going hazardous waste handling and disposal.

Throughout its history, CERCLA has been roundly criticized by industry as a draconian system that hinders economic growth and penalizes individual companies by requiring them to perform extensive and costly cleanups without regard to when the original disposal took place or the fact that a company may have exercised due care in handling hazardous materials. At the same time, Congress and the American public have vented frustration over the slow pace of cleanup and the reported waste of taxpayer monies. To many on both sides of these issues, CERCLA has been an expensive failure. During 1994, for the first time since 1986, Congress made a serious effort to modify CERCLA. (See Section 8.0 below). This effort failed to produce change in the 103rd Congress. Serious efforts to reform CERCLA continued in the 104th Congress.

This chapter will discuss CERCLA's most significant features. It is organized into eight major sections. The first section is an introductory overview of CERCLA. Subsequent sections will discuss CERCLA's primary terms and concepts, remedial provisions, liability provisions, settlement procedures, release reporting requirements, federal facility requirements, and CERCLA's future.

### 1.2 Overview of CERCLA's Provisions

When originally enacted, CERCLA was far less complex than it is today. In 1986, CERCLA was extensively amended by the Superfund Amendments and Reauthorization

---

[1]42 U.S.C. §§ 9601 *et seq.*
[2]42 U.S.C. §§ 6901 *et seq.*

Act (SARA).[3] SARA added many provisions to CERCLA and clarified much of what was unclear in the original act. However, even after SARA, CERCLA's major emphasis has remained the cleanup of inactive hazardous waste sites and the distribution of cleanup costs among the parties who generated and handled hazardous substances at these sites.

CERCLA's major provisions are designed to address comprehensively the problems associated with hazardous waste sites. CERCLA provides EPA the authority to clean up these sites under what may be generically called its "response" or "remedial" provisions. In doing so, it details the procedures and standards that must be followed in remediating these sites. CERCLA, like most environmental statutes, also contains enforcement provisions. These provisions identify the classes of parties liable under CERCLA, detail the causes of action that will lie under the statute, and provide guidance on settlements with EPA. In addition, CERCLA contains provisions specifying when releases of hazardous substances must be reported and the procedures to be followed for the cleanup of federal installations.

## 1.3 The Superfund

One of the most important features of CERCLA is the creation of the Hazardous Substance Superfund to be used by EPA in cleaning up hazardous waste sites. It is to this fund that CERCLA owes its "Superfund" nickname. The Superfund is created by taxes imposed upon the petroleum and chemical industries as well as by an environmental tax on corporations. In addition, general tax revenue is contributed to the Superfund.[4]

The Superfund may be used not only to pay EPA's cleanup and enforcement costs and certain natural resource damages, but also to pay for certain claims of private parties. Private parties are entitled to payment from the Superfund for EPA-approved cleanups that they have performed.[5] In addition, private parties may file claims for reimbursement when they have performed a cleanup but have been unable to obtain payment from the facility owner or operator,[6] or when EPA has administratively required them to conduct a cleanup which is deemed to be arbitrary and capricious or for which they are not liable.[7] However, the Superfund may not be used to finance the remediation of federal facilities.[8]

## 1.4 Sources of CERCLA Law

For those unfamiliar with CERCLA law and lore, finding, let alone understanding, CERCLA's provisions can often be difficult. Many of the procedures that apply in the typical CERCLA matter are set forth in layers of statutory, regulatory, and policy making documents. While it is true that the foundation for CERCLA is the statute itself,

---

[3]Pub. L. No. 99-499, Oct. 17, 1986; 126 Cong. Rec. S13112 *et seq.* (daily ed. Sept. 19, 1986).

[4]*See* Title V of the Superfund Amendments and Reauthorization Act of 1986.

[5]42 U.S.C. § 9611(a)(2).

[6]42 U.S.C. § 9612.

[7]42 U.S.C. § 9606(b)(2).

[8]42 U.S.C. § 9611(e)(3).

forecasting the government's actions is possible only when one understands the myriad of regulations, policy letters, and papers issued by EPA. These materials detail everything from EPA procedures for remediating contaminated groundwater to collecting stipulated penalties in settlements. Often, EPA staff level employees are *not* aware of many of these policy statements.

## 2.0 IMPORTANT CERCLA TERMS

An understanding of CERCLA's key terms and phrases is essential in interpreting both the remedial and liability features of CERCLA. Among the most critical terms are those discussed below.

### 2.1 "Hazardous Substance" and "Pollutant or Contaminant"

CERCLA is designed to address problems and redress complaints associated with "hazardous substances." With the single exception relating to "pollutants or contaminants," discussed below, if a matter does not involve a CERCLA "hazardous substance," it does not fall within the scope of CERCLA. Understanding what a CERCLA "hazardous substance" constitutes is therefore critical.

#### 2.1.1 Definition of "Hazardous Substance"

"Hazardous substances" are defined in CERCLA section 101(14). They are defined by reference to substances that are listed or designated under other environmental statutes. They include "hazardous wastes" under RCRA, "hazardous substances" defined in section 311 of the Clean Water Act, "toxic pollutants" designated under section 307 of the Clean Water Act, hazardous air pollutants listed under section 112 of the Clean Air Act, substances designated under section 102 of CERCLA which "may present substantial danger to public health or welfare or the environment," characteristic hazardous wastes under section 3001 of RCRA, and imminently hazardous chemical substances or mixtures that EPA has addressed under section 7 of the Toxic Substances Control Act (TSCA).

In order to facilitate the identification of CERCLA hazardous substances, EPA has prepared a list of these substances, which is located at 40 C.F.R. Part 302.

#### 2.1.2 Quantity of Hazardous Substance

It is important to note that CERCLA, unlike most other environmental statutes, contains no requirement that a specified amount of a hazardous substance be present before a response action can be taken or a party found liable for a release or threat of release of such substance.[9] This is true in spite of the fact that CERCLA's reporting requirements mandate reporting a release of hazardous substances only when a specified

---

[9]*But see United States v. Alcan Aluminum Corp.*, 964 F.2d 252 (3d Cir. 1992)(suggesting concentration might affect apportionment of liability). *See also Acushnet Co. v. Coaters, Inc.*, Civ Action No. 93-11219-REK, 1996 U.S. Dist. Lexis 11370 (D. Mass. July 24, 1996.) (Individual company not liable as its waste could not have leached out of groundwater at higher than background levels).

quantity is released.[10] (*See infra* section 6.0). This so-called "reportable quantity" has no effect on a party's liability.[11] The release of any quantity of a hazardous substance is sufficient to establish liability. The rationale for the distinction is that CERCLA's response and enforcement provisions are designed to deal with a "release," which is defined as "any spilling, leaking. . .,"[12] while CERCLA's reporting requirements specifically require a minimum quantity be discharged before a report need be filed.[13]

### 2.1.3 Petroleum Exclusion

Excluded from the definition of hazardous substance is "petroleum, including crude oil or any fraction thereof."[14] This exception, which has become known as the "petroleum exclusion," plays a significant role in CERCLA since many sites contain petroleum contamination. In many cases, the companies responsible for the petroleum contamination are not liable for CERCLA cleanup costs.[15] This is true even though petroleum contamination *is* addressed under RCRA. The result has been situations in which sites, particularly former gasoline service stations, cannot be the subject of CERCLA actions but can be the subject of actions brought under RCRA.[16]

The meaning of the petroleum exclusion has been the subject of considerable debate as petroleum frequently contains other listed "hazardous substances." The most common of these are the so-called "BTX" compounds—benzene, toluene, and xylene. Whether these substances, when present in petroleum, are "hazardous substances" has been the source of controversy. In 1987, EPA's general counsel issued an opinion addressing when such substances, if present in petroleum, are considered hazardous. The opinion states that such substances are not hazardous as long as they are found in refined petroleum fractions, or they are not present at levels which exceed those normally found in such fractions.[17] In short, indigenous, refinery-added hazardous substances are exempted. The opinion indicates that substances *added* to petroleum as a result of *contamination during use* are not within the petroleum exclusion and that in such cases the substances are considered CERCLA "hazardous substances." This test has met favorable reaction from several courts considering the issue.[18]

### 2.1.4 Pollutant or Contaminant

While the vast majority of actions taken under CERCLA relate to CERCLA hazardous substances, CERCLA also provides authority for EPA to respond to "a

---

[10]42 U.S.C. § 9602.

[11]*Uited States v. Wade*, 577 F. Supp. 1326 (E.D. Pa. 1983).

[12]42 U.S.C. § 9601(22).

[13]42 U.S.C. § 9603.

[14]42 U.S.C. § 9601(14).

[15]*Wilshire Westwood Assocs. v. Atlantic Richfield Corp.*, 881 F.2d 801 (9th Cir. 1989).

[16]*Compare Wilshire Westwood Assocs.*, 881 F.2d at 801 (9th Cir. 1989)(CERCLA) *with Zands v. Nelson*, 779 F. Supp 1254 (S.D. Cal. 1991)(RCRA).

[17]United States Environmental Protection Agency, Memorandum from Francis S. Blake to J. Winston Porter, *Scope of the CERCLA Petroleum Exclusion Under Sections 101(14) and 104(a)(2)* (July 31, 1987).

[18]*E.g.*, *Wilshire Westwood Assocs. v. Atlantic Richfield Corp.*, 881 F.2d 801 (9th Cir. 1989); *Washington v. Time Oil Co.*, 687 F. Supp. 529 (W.D. Wash. 1988).

release or substantial threat of release ... of *any pollutant or contaminant* which may present an imminent and substantial danger to public health or welfare. . .".[19] Under CERCLA "pollutants or contaminants" encompasses just about anything. By definition, such substances include compounds which upon exposure "will or may reasonably be anticipated to cause" certain specified harmful health effects.[20] While EPA can respond to and clean up a site polluted by either a hazardous substance or a pollutant or contaminant, the statute does not authorize EPA to recover its cleanup costs from private parties or to issue an order directing the parties to perform a cleanup when the substance involved is only a pollutant or contaminant. Only sites contaminated with hazardous substances are subject to such actions.[21] Consequently, while the definition of a pollutant or contaminant is broad, this breadth of coverage has no practical impact on private parties.

## 2.2 Release or Threat of Release

In order for EPA to undertake a response action under CERCLA, and for liability to attach, there must be a "release" or "substantial threat" of a release of a hazardous substance into the environment. The discharge of a certain quantity of a hazardous substance need not occur for a "release" or "substantial threat of release" to exist. Any quantity, however small, is adequate to trigger CERCLA.[22]

Under CERCLA, the term "release" is defined broadly to include virtually any situation leading to a hazardous substance being freed from its normal container. A release thus occurs whenever there is "any spilling, leaking, pumping, pouring, emitting, emptying, discharging, injecting, escaping, leaching, dumping, or disposing into the environment. . .".[23]

Excluded from the definition of release are: releases occurring in the workplace covered by employer claims procedures; emissions from the exhausts of motor vehicles, rolling stock, aircraft, vessels, or pipeline pumping station engines; certain nuclear releases; and the normal application of fertilizer.[24] These exceptions are designed to ensure that workplace-related incidents, nuclear incidents, and exhaust emissions remain regulated by laws other than CERCLA and to avoid interference with agricultural activities. While not specifically excluded from the definition of release, federally permitted releases (such as releases pursuant to an NPDES permit under the Clean Water Act) are treated differently than other releases. The only remedy provided under CERCLA for such a release is that under existing law relating to the permit issued.[25]

As with a release, the term "substantial threat of a release" is interpreted broadly. Cases that have determined whether such a threat exists have had little difficulty

---

[19]42 U.S.C. § 9604 (emphasis added).

[20]42 U.S.C. § 9601(33).

[21]*See* 42 U.S.C. §§ 9606, 9607.

[22]*United States v. Conservation Chem. Co.*, 619 F. Supp. 162, 233 (W.D. Mo. 1985). *But see Amoco Oil Co. v. Borden, Inc.*, 889 F.2d 664, 670 (5th Cir. 1989)(release of any quantity not sufficient to create liability unless hazard justified response action).

[23]42 U.S.C. § 9601(22).

[24]*Id.*

[25]42 U.S.C. § 9607(j).

agreeing with the subjective appraisal of EPA. Corroding tanks, the presence of a hazardous substance in a location where it might freely move in the environment, and abandoned tanks have all been deemed examples of threatened releases.[26]

### 2.3 Facility or Vessel

Before a party can be liable under CERCLA's cost recovery and abatement sections, there must first be a release or threatened release from a "facility" or "vessel."[27] Interestingly enough, there is no corresponding requirement for EPA response actions.[28] While this would appear to create situations where EPA might perform a cleanup and be unable to recover its costs, court decisions have so broadly interpreted the definition of "facility" that there is virtually no possibility that such a situation could arise.

CERCLA defines a facility in two parts. First, it lists a variety of things that constitute facilities (e.g., building, structure, installation, equipment, pipe or pipeline, or well) and, second, it provides that a facility is also "any site or area where a hazardous substance has . . . come to be located."[29] Perhaps it is easier to consider what is not a facility. Specifically excluded are consumer products in consumer use and vessels. Under CERCLA, the term "vessel" means any craft used as a means of transportation on water.[30]

### 2.4 Environment

The term "environment" under CERCLA is important because a release requires the freeing of a hazardous substance into the environment. Absent this, CERCLA's response and enforcement provisions are not triggered. Like all other CERCLA terms, "environment" is defined broadly to include any surface water, groundwater, drinking water supply, land surface, subsurface strata, and ambient air.

### 2.5 National Priorities List

The "National Priorities List," otherwise known as the "NPL," is an important facet of CERCLA's response procedures. First established in 1981 under section 105(a)(8)(B) of CERCLA, the NPL is part of the National Contingency Plan (NCP) and must be updated annually. CERCLA requires that EPA develop criteria for determining priorities among the various "releases or threatened releases" throughout the nation. These criteria are to be based on risks to public health, welfare, or the environment, taking into account a variety of factors including the extent of population at risk, the hazard potential of the facility's hazardous substances, the potential for contamination

---

[26]*United States v. Metate Asbestos Corp.*, 584 F. Supp. 1143 (D. Ariz. 1984)(asbestos lying on ground); *New York v. Shore Realty Corp.*, 759 F.2d 1032, 1045 (2d Cir. 1985)(cor-roding tanks, failure to license facility); *United States v. Northernaire Plating Co.*, 670 F. Supp. 742, 747 (W.D. Mich. 1987)(abandoned drums), *aff'd sub nom.*, *United States v. R.W. Meyer, Inc.*, 889 F.2d 1497 (6th Cir. 1989), *cert. denied*, 494 U.S. 1057 (1990).

[27]42 U.S.C. § 9607.

[28]42 U.S.C. § 9604.

[29]42 U.S.C. § 9601(9).

[30]42 U.S.C. § 9601.

of drinking water supplies, and the threat to ambient air.[31] Applying these criteria, EPA scores and ranks the various sites for possible listing on the NPL.

EPA's original scoring system was issued in 1980. In 1990 EPA revised its hazardous ranking scoring system pursuant to the 1986 SARA Amendments.[32]

EPA's decision to list a site on the NPL is considered an action pursuant to the Administrative Procedure Act[33] and subject to notice and public comment. Parties challenging a site listing by EPA must do so within 90 days after EPA's final decision.[34] The failure to challenge a listing during this period operates as a bar to any subsequent challenges.[35]

It is important to recognize that only sites listed on the NPL qualify for long-term remedial actions financed by the Superfund.[36] A site not listed on the NPL may still be the subject of a more short-term removal action.[37]

## 2.6 National Contingency Plan

The primary guidance document for CERCLA response actions is the National Contingency Plan (NCP). The NCP sets forth the procedures that must be followed by EPA and private parties in selecting and conducting CERCLA response actions.

The NCP has been present in various forms since it was first promulgated in 1973. At that time, it was prepared pursuant to the Federal Water Pollution Control Act[38] and designed to address the removal of oil and other hazardous substances. With CERCLA's passage in 1980, EPA was required to expand the NCP to place greater emphasis on the procedures for responding to releases of hazardous substances.[39] The NCP has been revised several times. The current version of the NCP is far more comprehensive than all of its predecessors.[40]

The NCP sets forth the responsibilities of the various organizations (e.g., National Response Teams, Regional Response Teams, On Scene Coordinators, Remedial Project Managers)that take part in responses to releases, describes how coordination among these various organizations is to occur, establishes methods and criteria for determining the appropriate extent of response, outlines the procedures to be followed in performing cleanups (remedial actions or removals), and establishes the method by which EPA is to prepare an administrative record to support its actions. What the NCP fails to do is tell EPA the specific type of remedy to employ in each situation. This is largely a matter left to the discretion of EPA in each instance. The vagueness of the NCP on this issue means that the subject of remedy selection is sometimes hotly contested in CERCLA proceedings.

---

[31]42 U.S.C. § 9605(a)(8)(A).

[32]55 Fed. Reg. 51,532 (1990).

[33]*See* 5 U.S.C. § 553.

[34]*See* 42 U.S.C. § 9613(a).

[35]*See Washington State Dep't of Transp. v. United States Envtl. Protection Agency*, 917 F.2d 1309 (D.C. Cir. 1990), *cert. denied*, 501 U.S. 1230 (1991).

[36]40 C.F.R. § 300.425(b)(1).

[37]*Id.*

[38]33 U.S.C. §§ 1251 *et seq.*

[39]42 U.S.C. § 9605(a).

[40]40 C.F.R. Part 300. The NCP was last amended in 1994. 59 Fed. Reg. 47,384 (1994).

## 3.0 CERCLA'S REMEDIAL PROVISIONS

Whenever confronting a situation involving the need to conduct a cleanup, EPA has two basic options under CERCLA. It may conduct the cleanup itself and later seek to recover its costs from potentially responsible parties (PRPs) in a subsequent cost recovery action, or it can compel the PRPs to perform the cleanup (either voluntarily or involuntarily) through administrative or judicial proceedings.

### 3.1 EPA's Authority To Act

At CERCLA's core are its provisions setting forth EPA's authority and the procedures EPA must follow in responding to releases. Section 104(a)(1) sets forth the authority to act. Under this section, EPA is authorized, consistent with the NCP, to remove and provide for remedial actions relating to hazardous substances or pollutants or contaminants whenever:

1. Any hazardous substance is released or there is a substantial threat of such release into the environment, or
2. There is a release or substantial threat of release into the environment of any pollutant or contaminant that may present an imminent and substantial danger to the public health or welfare.

Thus, this section sets forth the two broad categories of response actions available—"remedial actions" and "removals."

### 3.2 Categories of Response Actions

#### 3.2.1 Removal

Under CERCLA, "removal" actions are undertaken to deal with environmental emergencies.[41] Such actions could include the providing of alternate water supplies to persons whose groundwater has been polluted, the immediate cleanup of hazardous waste spilled from a container, or the erection of a fence around a hazardous waste site. In short, just about any action that tends to diminish the threat of a hazardous waste site and that can be done promptly qualifies as a removal.

Removal actions can occur at a site not listed on the NPL, or they can occur as part of the initial response to a seriously contaminated NPL site that will later be the subject of a more formal and extensive remedial action. For example, investigations of a site that will be the subject of a more extensive remedial action are considered removal actions.[42]

Because the administrative requirements imposed on an EPA removal action are far less than those for a remedial action, removals are frequently done in conjunction with more formal remedial actions.

There are, however, some limitations on removals. Ordinarily a removal action must be capable of being completed within one year and cost no more than $2 million.[43] Exceptions are situations in which:

---

[41] 42 U.S.C. § 9601(23).
[42] *Id.*
[43] 42 U.S.C. § 9604(c)(1).

1. Continued action is necessary to respond to an emergency,
2. There is an immediate risk to public health or the environment,
3. The action is part of a larger approved remedial action, or
4. Continuation of the removal is consistent with the remedial action to be taken.[44]

The breadth of these exceptions generally means that in situations where EPA wants to continue a removal action beyond one year or above $2 million, it can find a basis for doing so.

### 3.2.2 Remedial Actions

Unlike removals, remedial actions are long-term, permanent cleanups. Thus, while a removal may alleviate an immediate threat to human health or the environment, a remedial action is designed to permanently eliminate any threat that a site might pose. While a removal can be accomplished in a matter of weeks, remedial actions take years or, in some cases, decades to complete. Examples of remedial actions include constructing dikes, trenches, or clay covers; excavations; and the permanent destruction or neutralization of hazardous substances.[45]

## 3.3 Steps In The Remedial Process

Because remedial actions are significantly more complex and costly, more detailed requirements are set forth in CERCLA and the NCP for such actions than for removals. Not surprisingly, PRP's are also very concerned with the process by which remedial actions are selected and conducted by EPA and will often seek to participate in the process used to select such remedies.

### 3.3.1 Site Identification and Initial Evaluation

Sites are brought to EPA's attention in numerous ways. Site information may be contained in reports of releases submitted either under section 103(a) of CERCLA (*see infra* section 6.0), or under other federal reporting requirements. Citizens' complaints, investigations by government agencies, and submissions by state agencies are also potential sources of information.[46]

Once brought to EPA's attention, sites with releases or threatened releases are listed in the Comprehensive Environmental Response and Liability Information System (CERCLIS) for subsequent evaluation. CERCLIS contains the official inventory of CERCLA sites and supports EPA's site planning and tracking process.[47]

EPA then assembles information on the site and conducts a preliminary assessment (PA) to determine the scope of the potential environmental problem. The PA, which provides the initial screening of sites, focuses on determining whether the site presents a risk of a release of hazardous substances. A PA may be performed merely by reviewing existing data on the site; if appropriate, a site inspection may also be

---

[44]*Id.*
[45]42 U.S.C. § 9601(24).
[46]40 C.F.R. § 300.405.
[47]40 C.F.R. § 300.5.

conducted. The PA may or may not result in a recommendation that further investigation be done.

If, after the performance of a PA, it appears that the site presents a threat and that it will score high enough to be listed on the NPL, EPA conducts additional site investigations to gather more data about the hazardous substances at the site, possible human and environmental receptors, and migration pathways. This information is then combined with the information developed in the PA to score the site in accordance with the NPL's hazardous ranking system.

### 3.3.2 NPL Listing

Formal site scoring is conducted using EPA criteria and scoring procedures set forth in the hazardous ranking system. Among the criteria applied are toxicity of the substances, the location of potential receptors, exposure pathways, threats to the human food chain, and threats to ambient air and groundwaters. Site listing occurs when a score greater than 28.5 is achieved.[48]

Once listed on the NPL, CERCLA's expensive remedial process is committed. Because NPL listing guarantees prolonged and expensive government response actions, challenges to site listing occasionally occur. They have largely been unsuccessful.[49]

### 3.3.3 Planning Remedial Actions—SCAP

EPA's remedial action timing is tied not only to the nature of each individual site, but also to EPA's concern with meeting congressionally mandated cleanup numbers.[50] This so-called "bean counting" is an integral part of the overall CERCLA process and explains in part why certain sites appear to languish for years and then suddenly generate a great deal of EPA activity.

EPA's nationwide strategic plan for addressing hazardous waste sites is set forth in its "Superfund Comprehensive Accomplishments Plan" (SCAP). This document provides details on each site in a computer printout format and specifies those activities that are expected to occur during each fiscal quarter. Analysis of the SCAP can provide any party concerned with a particular site a preview of EPA's long-term planning for the site. In many cases, information will appear in the SCAP before it is widely known to the public.

### 3.3.4 Remedial Investigation/Feasibility Study

The first major event in the remedial action process after NPL listing is the performance of the Remedial Investigation/Feasibility Study (RI/FS). The RI/FS is the most important facet of any remedial action, because it determines the scope of remedial action to be undertaken. The purpose of the RI/FS is to assess site conditions and

---

[48] 40 C.F.R. Part 300 (Appendix A).

[49] *Compare Stoughton v. United States Envtl. Protection Agency*, 858 F.2d 747 (D.C. Cir. 1988) (unsuccessful challenge) *with Tex Tin Corp. v. United States Envtl. Protection Agency*, 992 F.2d 353 (D.C. Cir. 1993) (successful challenge).

[50] *See* 42 U.S.C. § 9616(d),(e).

evaluate alternatives to the extent necessary to select a remedy.[51] EPA then selects one of the alternatives discussed in the RI/FS as the remedy for the site.

As the name implies, the RI/FS consists of two phases, although in practice they are often very interrelated. The first phase is the remedial investigation (RI).[52] The RI, which in many cases can take years to perform, is designed to assess the nature and extent of releases of hazardous substances and determine those areas of a site where releases have created damage or the threat of damage to public health or the environment.

It is during the RI process that extensive soil and groundwater sampling is performed and voluminous reports detailing the results of these investigations are prepared. The purposes of these investigations include determining the nature of the site's geology and hydrogeology, locating the sources of contamination, identifying the type and mobility of contaminants present, and defining the nature of any threat to human health and the environment. In short, the overall purpose of the RI is to collect data necessary to adequately characterize the site for the purpose of developing and evaluating effective remedial alternatives. At the conclusion of the RI, it is expected that EPA will have a reasonably good idea of the sources of contamination, the nature and extent of contamination, and the actual and potential exposure routes.

When enough technical information about the site is available to analyze potential remedies, EPA will then prepare a Feasibility Study (FS).[53] The objective of the FS is to develop a range of remedial alternatives for consideration. As such, the FS evaluates in detail potential remedies for the site, taking into account the findings of the RI. In evaluating options, EPA considers the extent to which each complies with the cleanup criteria specified in CERCLA section 121.[54] (*See infra* section 3.3.5.2).

The entire RI/FS process can be extremely costly and time-consuming. Costs, which can range as high as several million dollars, may increase if EPA elects to remediate a site in what are known as "operable units." The use of operable units which represents nothing more than a phased approach to site cleanups—began in the mid-1980s. It is now rare that a major site cleanup does not include the use of operable units. When operable units are used, they ordinarily represent the remediation of a segment of the site. For example, a single site may include three operable units: one operable unit may be designed to address the cleanup and isolation of the sources of contamination at the site; a second operable unit may pertain to remediation of groundwater at the site; and a third operable unit may relate to the remediation of areas adjoining the site. EPA prefers this approach in order to begin remediation of certain portions of the site, while other portions are undergoing study and evaluation.[55]

---

[51]40 C.F.R. § 300.430(a)(2).
[52]*See generally* 40 C.F.R. § 300.430(d).
[53]*See generally* 40 C.F.R. § 300.430(e).
[54]42 U.S.C. § 9621.
[55]40 C.F.R. § 300.430(a)(1)(ii)(A).

### 3.3.5 Determining the Appropriate Level of Cleanup

#### 3.3.5.1 General Considerations

One of the most controversial issues at any CERCLA site is the level or degree of cleanup that must be achieved before the site is considered "clean." At each site, the scope and variety of contamination varies. Moreover, each site's relationship to the public and the environment differs. The bottom line questions are whether the site must be cleaned up to pristine predisposal conditions and, if not, what levels of cleanup are adequate.

The issues that arise with regard to cleanup standards include the level of groundwater remediation required, the level of residual soil contamination that will be permitted to remain, and the extent to which site remediation will require excavation of contaminated soils and debris. At the crux of these issues is the question: What levels of risk are acceptable? Since cleanups resulting in the removal of all, or nearly all, risks are more costly and take longer to complete, all parties with a stake in the CERCLA process have concern about how cleanup standards are established.

#### 3.3.5.2 CERCLA Section 121

History shows that CERCLA cleanups have become significantly more expensive with each passing year. Costs have been driven upward by the discarding of many formerly acceptable procedures for remediating sites and the substitution of remedies that are designed to achieve far greater permanence and far less residual risk. This trend continued with the 1986 SARA Amendments, which set forth much stricter requirements, making cleanups more conservative and costly. As these costs have risen, many have questioned the need for such expensive cleanups in situations where the risk factors applied are stricter in some cases than risks people encounter every day.

Section 121 of CERCLA sets forth the statutory requirements for cleanup standards. It provides that CERCLA-based remedial actions be in accordance with its precepts and, to the extent practicable, with the National Contingency Plan.[56] Section 121 also requires remedial actions to be cost-effective. This latter requirement appears to have become a secondary factor applied by EPA in selecting remedies.

In setting forth the factors to be applied, section 121 evidences a clear preference for remedies that are permanent and involve the treatment of hazardous substances to reduce their volume, toxicity or mobility.[57] This has meant that remedies involving the construction of man-made barriers to "contain" contamination within a designated area are disfavored. At the same time, section 121 clearly indicates that the off-site transport and disposal of hazardous substances without treatment should be EPA's least favored remedial approach. Reading section 121 as a whole, it is clear that Congress' preferred approach is the permanent destruction of hazardous substances through treatment. Various procedures are set forth that drive EPA's remedial decisions in that direction. For example, when hazardous substances are left on-site, section 121 requires that EPA

---

[56] 42 U.S.C. § 9621(a). While Section 121 lists general factors to be applied, the NCP attempts, consistent with the factors listed in section 121, to provide more detailed cleanup requirements.· *See* 40 C.F.R. Part 300.
[57] 42 U.S.C. § 9621(b).

review the adequacy of the remedy every five years. If the review indicates that the remedy is inadequate, EPA must select a new remedy.[58]

CERCLA's greatest impetus towards permanent treatment is the requirement that a remedy achieve all Applicable or Relevant and Appropriate Requirements (ARARs) where hazardous substances are left on-site. Section 121 states that the following are ARARs for the hazardous substance, pollutant, or contaminant concerned:

1.  Any standard, requirement, criteria, or limitation under any federal environmental law; and

2.  Any promulgated standard, requirement, criteria, or limitation under a state environmental or facility siting law that is more stringent than any federal standard.[59]

Application of ARARs at CERCLA sites has meant that remedies must achieve the highest cleanup levels established by other federal and state standards. By incorporating requirements from other state and federal environmental statutes and regulations into CERCLA, section 121 ensures that CERCLA remedies will be extremely conservative and costly. CERCLA 121, however, does not specify just what ARARs pertain to a specific site. As a result, the selection of ARARs has become a part of the RI/FS process.

### 3.3.5.3 Remedy Selection Criteria and ARARs under the NCP

The NCP attempts to fill in some of the gaps left by section 121 and provide more detail regarding the criteria to be used in both selecting remedies and applying ARARs.

The NCP provisions regarding remedy selection clearly diminish section 121's mandate that selected remedies be cost-effective. While section 121(a) emphasizes that remedies be cost-effective and does not suggest that cost-effectiveness be less of a factor than other considerations, the NCP relegates cost-effectiveness to merely a measure by which certain other factors are to be evaluated.

The NCP sets forth nine criteria that must be applied in evaluating remedies. These nine criteria are in turn divided into three major categories. The first of these three major categories is labeled threshold criteria.[60] There are two threshold criteria: (1) overall protection of human health and the environment and (2) compliance with ARARs.

Should a proposed remedy fail to meet both threshold criteria, it will not be selected. If the proposed remedy does meet the criteria, it is then evaluated by application of the second major category of criteria, which is known as "primary balancing criteria." Primary balancing criteria consist of the following:

1.  Long-term effectiveness and permanence;
2.  Reduction of toxicity, mobility, or volume through treatment;
3.  Short-term effectiveness;

---

[58]42 U.S.C. § 9621(c).
[59]42 U.S.C. § 9621(d)(2)(A).
[60]*See generally* 40 C.F.R. § 300.430(f).

4.  Implementability; and
5.  Cost.

It is during the application of the primary balancing criteria that the NCP provides for the consideration of cost-effectiveness. Cost-effectiveness is determined by evaluating the first three primary balancing criteria to assess overall effectiveness of the remedy. A remedy is deemed cost-effective if its costs are proportional to its overall effectiveness as established by these three criteria.[61] Obviously, this appraisal is very subjective, and results can vary widely from site to site.

The final major category of criteria is modifying criteria. Two criteria fall within this category. They are "state acceptance" and "community acceptance." Both modifying criteria are clearly of limited importance since they are merely required to be *considered* by EPA in selecting a remedy.[62] Since that consideration occurs at the very end of the evaluation process—presumably after EPA has a reasonably firm idea of what it desires based upon the other criteria—it can be expected that very strong public and state disapproval would have to exist for a remedy to be discarded.

Since compliance with ARARs is a threshold criterion, determining what ARARs are and whether a remedy will comply with them assumes critical importance. The NCP therefore attempts to expand on the discussion of ARARs contained in section 121. As the phrase implies, ARARs consist of both "applicable" and "relevant and appropriate" standards or requirements. The NCP states that an "applicable" requirement is one which "specifically addresses a hazardous substance, pollutant, contaminant, remedial action, location, or other circumstance found at a CERCLA site."[63] Thus, applicable requirements at a site with releases into the air or surface water would include those standards addressing air emissions or surface water discharges.

Determining what constitutes a "relevant and appropriate" standard is more difficult. This is largely because of the greater subjectivity involved. The NCP lists several factors to apply in determining whether a standard is relevant and appropriate:

1.  The purpose of the requirement being considered and the purpose of the CERCLA action;
2.  The medium (groundwater, surface water, soil, etc.) regulated or affected by the requirement and the medium contaminated at the site;
3.  The substances regulated by the requirement and the substances at the site;
4.  The activities regulated by the requirement and the remedial action contemplated;
5.  Any variances, waivers, or exemptions of the requirement and their availability for the circumstances at the site;
6.  The type of place regulated and the type of place affected by the release or CERCLA action;
7.  The type and size of the structure or facility regulated and the type and size of the structure affected by the release or contemplated by the CERCLA action; and

---

[61] 40 C.F.R. § 300.430(f)(1)(ii)(D).
[62] 40 C.F.R. § 300.430(f)(1)(ii)(E).
[63] 40 C.F.R. § 300.400(g)(1).

8.  Any consideration of use or potential use of the affected resources in the requirement and the use or potential use of the affected resource at the site.[64]

Once determined to apply, an ARAR must be met unless it is waived. CERCLA contains a list of the limited circumstances in which EPA may select a remedy not meeting an ARAR but still permitting hazardous substances to remain on-site.[65] These circumstances are as follows:

1.  The selected remedy is only part of a total remedy that will attain the ARAR;
2.  Compliance with the ARAR will lead to greater risk to human health or the environment than alternative actions;
3.  Compliance is technologically impracticable from an engineering perspective;
4.  The remedy will attain an equivalent standard of performance to the ARAR through use of another approach;
5.  With respect to state standards, the state has not consistently applied the standard itself under similar circumstances; and
6.  With respect to situations involving Superfund-financed remedies, the need to retain sufficient monies in the Superfund to respond to other sites overrides application of the ARAR to protect public health, welfare, and the environment.

### 3.3.6 Record of Decision

After completion of the RI/FS, EPA issues a Record of Decision (ROD), which sets forth EPA's selected remedy as well as the factors which led to its selection. The ROD must set forth all facts, analyses of facts, and site-specific policy determinations in sufficient detail for the situation. It must explain how the remedy is protective of human health and the environment, detail applicable ARARs and how they will be attained (or why they are waived), and set forth how the remedy is cost-effective and uses permanent solutions to the maximum extent possible.[66] The ROD must also respond to any public comments on the remedy selected by EPA. Once issued, the ROD must be placed in the administrative record supporting EPA's action at the site.

### 3.3.7 Administrative Record

The entire remedial process is subject to public notice and comment. In addition, EPA must compile an administrative record. The public,[67] as well as the state,[68] may review and comment on EPA's proposed remedial actions; such comments must be included in the administrative record. The administrative record must also contain EPA's responses to all public comments received[69] and all documents considered and relied upon by EPA in selecting its remedy.

---

[64]40 C.F.R. § 300.400(g)(2).
[65]42 U.S.C. § 9621(d)(4).
[66]40 C.F.R. § 300.430(f)(5).
[67]42 U.S.C. §§ 9613(k), 9617.
[68]42 U.S.C. § 9621(f)(1)(E),(H).
[69]42 U.S.C. § 9617(b).

The administrative record is critical, not only to the decision-making process, but also to any subsequent judicial review of EPA's preferred remedy. Judicial review of EPA's remedy selection decision is limited to the administrative record.[70] Unless review of the administrative record shows EPA's decision to be arbitrary and capricious, the decision will be upheld.

### 3.3.8 Implementation of the Cleanup Decision

After issuance of the ROD, EPA completes a remedial design (RD). It is through the RD that the ROD's conceptual remedy is reduced to a detailed design permitting its construction and operation. The remedial action (RA) phase involves the construction and operation of the remedy in accordance with the RD. Costs to implement a remedy at a CERCLA site can vary considerably. Seldom will they be less than $1 million. Not infrequently they can exceed $50 million. More costly remedies are likely in situations of extensive groundwater contamination where long-term aquifer restoration is attempted.

### 3.3.9 Prerequisites to EPA Conducting Remedial Action—State Involvement

As indicated earlier, CERCLA requires that EPA consult with affected states before selecting an appropriate remedial action.[71] CERCLA also provides that EPA cannot proceed with a remedial action using Superfund monies unless EPA first receives certain assurances from the state involved. These required assurances are set forth in CERCLA section 104(c)(3). This section provides that EPA shall not undertake a remedial action unless the state in which the release has occurred first enters into a contract or cooperative agreement with EPA providing that the state will provide future maintenance of the remedial action, ensure the availability of a hazardous waste disposal facility for any necessary off-site disposal, and pay or assure payment of ten percent of the cost of the remedial action, including all future maintenance.[72] A state's inability or unwillingness to meet the ten percent funding requirement can pose a significant barrier to EPA's ability to conduct a Superfund-financed remedial action.

## 4.0 CERCLA'S LIABILITY PROVISIONS

### 4.1 Overview

CERCLA contains two basic liability provisions:

1. A provision permitting EPA and private parties to recover their cleanup costs,[73] and

---

[70]42 U.S.C. § 9613(j)(1).
[71]42 U.S.C. § 9604(c)(2).
[72]42 U.S.C. § 9604(c)(3).
[73]42 U.S.C. § 9607.

2. A provision permitting EPA to seek a judicial order requiring a liable party to abate an endangerment to public health, welfare, or the environment.[74]

In addition to its two major liability provisions, CERCLA also includes provisions: (1) permitting EPA to take certain administrative actions to compel private parties to undertake actions necessary to protect public health, welfare or the environment; (2) permitting private parties to bring "citizen suits" to enforce CERCLA's provisions; and (3) providing authority for natural resource trustees to bring actions for damages to natural resources.

## 4.2 CERCLA's Operative Concepts

It is important to understand that there are certain key operative concepts that permeate CERCLA's liability provisions. These concepts, while most directly applicable to CERCLA's cost recovery provisions (section 107), have also been found applicable to CERCLA's abatement provisions (section 106).

### 4.2.1 Strict, Joint and Several, and Retroactive Liability

Courts have found that CERCLA imposes strict and, in most cases involving multiparty sites, joint and several liability with *no* requirement that a party's hazardous substances have been the cause for the cleanup or response action.

CERCLA's strict liability scheme has been uniformly endorsed by the courts.[75] The basis for CERCLA's strict liability is found in its requirement that "liability" be construed in accordance with the liability standard for section 311 of the Clean Water Act (CWA). Because the courts have interpreted CWA section 311 as imposing strict liability, they have had little problem reaching a similar result under CERCLA.[76] Consequently, claims that a party was not negligent or that its activities were consistent with standard industry practices provide no defense to liability.[77]

While CERCLA contains no statutory mandate that liability be joint and several, courts in practice have freely found such liability. In many cases, this has occurred despite the existence of a strong basis for apportionment and despite Congress having *deleted* provisions imposing joint and several liability from CERCLA before its enactment. The deletion, however, has not been viewed as removing the *possibility* of joint and several liability on a case-by-case basis, but instead as not mandating joint and several liability in all instances.[78] Nevertheless, courts have for the most part readily found joint and several liability whenever there is any evidence of the commingling of

---

[74]42 U.S.C. § 9606.

[75]*E.g., Levin Metals Corp. v. Parr-Richmond Terminal Co.*, 799 F.2d 1312 (9th Cir. 1986); *United States v. Northeastern Pharmaceutical & Chem. Co. ("NEPACCO")*, 810 F.2d 726 (8th Cir. 1986), *cert. denied*, 484 U.S. 848 (1987).

[76]*United States v. Chem-Dyne Corp.*, 572 F. Supp. 802 (S.D. Ohio 1983); *New York v. Shore Realty Corp.*, 759 F.2d 1032 (2d Cir. 1985).

[77]*United States v. Conservation Chem. Co.*, 619 F. Supp. 162, 204 (W.D. Mo. 1985).

[78]*United States v. Chem-Dyne Corp.*, 572 F. Supp. 802 (S.D. Ohio 1983).

hazardous substances by different parties.[79] (*See infra* section 4.8.4). The practical result of this presumptive joint and several liability has been EPA's ability to sue a few PRP's at major Superfund sites and obtain judicial decisions that each is individually responsible for *all* cleanup costs at the site. While this stance has greatly simplified EPA's task, it has burdened defendants not only with total cleanup costs, but also with the prospect of pursuing costly contribution actions against parties EPA has elected not to sue. (*See infra* section 4.11).

CERCLA's standard of causation is minimal. In fact, based on some decisions, there is arguably no causation requirement with regard to individual defendants at multiparty sites where there has been a release.[80] In CERCLA section 107 cost recovery actions, for example, the issue of causation has been reduced to whether a release or threatened release has caused a plaintiff to incur response costs. It has been stated that a "causal link between a defendant's release and the plaintiff's response . . ." must be established for liability to attach.[81] However, at multiparty sites it has typically not mattered whether a party's own waste was released or threatened to have been released as long as some hazardous substance at the site has been discharged.[82]

Finally, the vast majority of courts addressing the issue have found that CERCLA liability is retroactive. Under these decisions, parties may be found liable as a result of actions they took long *before* CERCLA's enactment.[83]

### 4.2.2 Individual and Corporate Liability

One of the unique features of CERCLA's liability scheme is that liability has been found in situations where application of traditional notions of corporate law, such as concepts of limited liability, would exempt individual corporate officers and parent corporations. This breadth of coverage is attributable in part to the flexibility of CERCLA's liability language. In other respects, it is due to the willingness of the courts

---

[79]*E.g.*, *O'Neil v. Picillo*, 682 F. Supp. 706 (D.R.I. 1988), *aff'd*, 883 F.2d 176 (1st Cir. 1989), *cert. denied sub nom.*, *American Cyanamid Co. v. O'Neil*, 493 U.S. 1071 (1990). A recent trend in several federal circuit courts asserts that commingled waste may, nevertheless, be divisible. *See, United States v. Alcan Aluminum Corp.*, 964 F.2d 252 (3d Cir. 1992); *In re Bell Petroleum Servs, Inc.*, 3 F.3d 889 (5th Cir. 1993).

[80]*But see* discussion regarding causation in Natural Resource Damage Claims, *infra* section 4.10.

[81]*See Dedham Water Co. v. Cumberland Farms, Inc.*, 689 F. Supp. 1223, 1224 (D. Mass. 1988), *rev'd on other grounds*, 889 F.2d 1146, 1151-1154 (1st Cir. 1989).

[82]*United States v. South Carolina Recycling & Disposal, Inc. ("SCRDI")*, 653 F. Supp. 984, 992 (D.S.C. 1984), *aff'd in part and vacated in part sub nom.*, *United States v. Monsanto Co.*, 858 F.2d 160 (4th Cir. 1988), *cert. denied*, 490 U.S. 1106 (1989). *See also Acme Printing Ink Co. v. Menard, Inc.*, 870 F. Supp. 1465 (E.D. Wis. 1994) (proper test for causation is whether release or threatened release caused incurrence of response costs, not whether defendant's hazardous waste caused response cost).

[83]*United States v. NEPACCO*, 810 F.2d 726, 732-733 (8th Cir. 1986), *cert. denied*, 484 U.S. 848 (1987); *Kelley v. Thomas Solvent Co.*, 714 F. Supp 1439, 1443-1445 (W.D. Mich. 1989). *But see United States v. Olin Corp.*, 927 F. Supp. 1502 (S.D. Ala. 1996) (finding CERCLA not retroactive.)

to use this language to cast the liability net widely in order to achieve what they view as CERCLA's remedial purpose.[84]

CERCLA section 101(20)(A) provided the initial impetus for the courts to discard traditional concepts of individual and corporate liability. This section defines the term "owner or operator" under CERCLA. In so doing, it indicates that the term "does not include a person, who without participating in the management of a vessel or facility, holds indicia of ownership primarily to protect his security interest in the vessel or facility."[85] Courts have derived from this provision the affirmative implication that a person who *does* participate in management and owns an interest in a business is liable under CERCLA for his company's waste disposal practices.[86]

Based on sections 101(20)(A) and 107(a)(3), which renders liable "[a]ny person who . . . arranged for disposal . . . of hazardous substances owned or possessed by such person . . . ," courts have evolved what is termed the "control" test. The control test has been used in determining to what extent individual corporate officers and parent corporations may be found liable. This control test has come to mean that an individual corporate officer or a parent corporation can be found liable if either has exercised control over a corporation's hazardous waste handling and disposal activities.[87] In some cases, courts have held that direct control over waste handling need not be shown as long as control over the overall business operations, including environmental matters, of the corporation is shown.[88] Most disturbing, from the perspective of the individual corporate officer and parent corporations, has been the suggestion, in at least one case, that simply having the *authority to control* waste disposal activities may be sufficient to create liability—even though such ability to control was *never exercised.*[89] Other decisions have found this *authority to control* test to be too expansive and require an actual nexus with disposal activities.[90]

While some courts have continued to follow traditional notions of corporate law in assessing the liability of parent corporations or individual officers,[91] the clear trend has been to determine liability based on CERCLA's developing control test.

---

[84]*See United States v. Mottolo*, 695 F. Supp. 615, 624 (D.N.H. 1988), *aff'd*, 26 F.3d 261 (1st Cir. 1994).

[85]U.S.C. § 9601(20)(A).

[86]*United States v. NEPACCO*, 810 F.2d 726, 742 (8th Cir. 1986), *cert. denied*, 484 U.S. 848 (1987); *United States v. Bliss*, 20 Envtl. L. Rep. 20,879 (E.D. Mo. 1988).

[87]*United States v. NEPACCO*, 810 F.2d 726 (8th Cir. 1986), *cert. denied*, 484 U.S. 848 (1987); *New York v. Shore Realty Corp.*, 759 F.2d 1032 (2d Cir. 1985).

[88]*Vermont v. Staco Inc.*, 684 F. Supp. 822, 831-832 (D. Vt. 1988); *United States v. Kayser-Roth Corp.*, 910 F.2d 24 (1st Cir. 1990), *cert. denied*, 498 U.S. 1084 (1991).

[89]*See United States v. Fleet Factors Corp.*, 901 F.2d 1550, 1556 (11th Cir. 1990), *cert. denied*, 498 U.S. 1046 (1991). *See also, United States v. Nicolet*, 712 F. Supp. 1193 (E.D. Pa. 1989) (familiarity with and capacity to control subsidiary's waste disposal practices).

[90]*United States v. TIC Inv. Corp.*, 68 F.3d 1082 (8th Cir. 1995), *reh'g denied* (8th Cir 1996) (nexus test applied in "arranger" liability case.)

[91]*E.g., United States v. Cordova Chem, Co.*, 59 F.3d 584 (6th Cir. 1995); *Joslyn Corp. v. T.L. James & Co.*, 696 F. Supp. 222 (W.D. La. 1988), *aff'd*, 893 F.2d 80 (5th Cir. 1990), *cert. denied*, 498 U.S. 1108 (1991).

### 4.2.3 Bar Against Pre-Enforcement Review

As indicated above, the process of selecting a remedial action is lengthy and tremendously expensive. Frequently, PRPs, persons living near a site, and environmental groups disagree with EPA's method of performing its studies or with the cleanup plan EPA has selected. For this reason, before EPA incurs the tremendous costs of implementing the remedial action it has selected, one or more of these groups may wish to challenge the action selected by filing a civil suit to enjoin performance of the remedy. CERCLA's provisions facilitating EPA's ability to obtain liability determinations against PRPs are complimented by provisions that, quite literally, make it impossible for these same PRPs, as well as citizens or environmental groups, to challenge EPA's remedial actions until a time of EPA's own choosing.

Section 113(h) limits the jurisdiction of courts to hear challenges to EPA response actions or administrative orders requiring PRPs to perform cleanups. (*See infra* section 4.7). Courts have jurisdiction to hear such matters *only* in the following situations:

1. Section 107 cost recovery actions or actions for contribution;
2. Actions to enforce a CERCLA section 106 administrative order or to seek penalties for violation of such an order;
3. Actions for reimbursement under section 106(b)(2) (actions for private party reimbursement from the Superfund);
4. Citizen suits under section 310 alleging that a removal action or remedial action violated CERCLA's provisions *after* such actions have been completed, except where a removal action is to be followed by a remedial action, in which case the action may not be heard until the remedial action is concluded; or
5. Actions brought by EPA under section 106 in which EPA is seeking an order compelling a party to perform a cleanup.

The courts have typically held that section 113(h) removes from their jurisdiction any cases seeking to challenge EPA's actions in situations other than those listed above.[92] Indeed, some courts have suggested that any judicial action that might interfere with EPA's ongoing cleanup actions cannot be heard, even if such actions do not directly challenge the remedial action selected.[93]

### 4.3 EPA's Enforcement Policy

EPA has always used its enforcement authority to pursue the recovery of cleanup costs and to seek judicial orders (consensual or involuntary) requiring PRPs to perform

---

[92]*E.g.*, *Alabama v. United States Envtl. Protection Agency*, 871 F.2d 1548 (11th Cir.), *cert. denied sub nom.*, *Alabama ex rel. Siegelman v. United States EPA*, 493 U.S. 991 (1989); *Barmet Aluminum Corp. v. Thomas*, 730 F. Supp. 771 (W.D. Ky. 1990), *aff'd sub nom.*, *Barmet Aluminum Corp. v. Reilly*, 927 F.2d 289 (6th Cir. 1991). *But see United States v. Princeton Gamma-Tech, Inc.*, 31 F.3d 138 (3d Cir. 1994) (review and injunctive relief may be available when a property owner asserts bona fide allegations that an EPA cleanup will cause irreparable harm to public health or environment).

[93]*North Shore Gas Co. v. United States Envtl. Protection Agency*, 753 F. Supp. 1413 (N.D. Ill. 1990), *aff'd*, 930 F.2d 1239 (7th Cir. 1991); *United States v. Cordova Chem. Co. of Michigan*, 750 F. Supp. 832 (W.D. Mich. 1990).

cleanups. However, within the last several years, EPA has adhered to a more aggressive enforcement policy. This policy evolved from a 1989 management review of the CERCLA program conducted by EPA.[94] In essence, EPA's announced policy is one of "enforcement first." Accordingly, when a site requires remediation and PRPs are identified, it is EPA's stated policy to require the PRPs to clean up the site, rather than conduct the cleanup with Superfund monies. EPA's policy is to issue administrative orders under CERCLA section 106 to PRPs prior to the performance of a cleanup by EPA. (*See infra* section 4.7). To support its "enforcement first" policy, EPA has increased its enforcement staff to handle the projected increase in enforcement actions.

EPA's "enforcement first" policy has probably lead to increased PRP-financed cleanups. This has been largely because of the threat of penalties associated with failure to comply with EPA's administrative orders.

## 4.4 Identifying Responsible Parties

### 4.4.1 PRP Search

Before it can initiate an enforcement action, EPA must first identify those parties responsible for a site's cleanup. Because many CERCLA sites are the result of disposal activities by hundreds of companies, EPA has developed a highly structured procedure for identifying these companies. EPA initially conducts what is referred to as a "Potentially Responsible Party (PRP) Search." This search is ordinarily performed by an EPA contractor. The process involves obtaining and organizing all available documents associated with the site's operation (*e.g.*, invoices, manifests, trip tickets) to determine which entity sent a certain substance to the site.[95] A computer data base, reflecting the quantity and nature of wastes contributed by each responsible party, is often created as a result of this process.

### 4.4.2 CERCLA Section 104(e)

EPA is aided in its ability to identify PRPs by section 104(e) of CERCLA. This section authorizes EPA to issue information requests requiring a party to provide information to EPA concerning: the nature and quantity of materials it may have disposed of at a site; the nature and extent of any release of a hazardous substance at the site; and information concerning its ability to pay for the cleanup.[96] Section 104(e) also gives EPA the authority to obtain access to vessels and facilities to inspect and copy documents,[97] to enter and conduct sampling at such locations,[98] and to issue orders

---

[94]United States Environmental Protection Agency, *A Management Review of The Superfund Program* (June 1989).

[95]*See* United States Environmental Protection Agency, OSWER Directive 9834.6, *Potentially Responsible Party Search Manual* (1987).

[96]42 U.S.C. § 9604(e)(2).

[97]*Id.*

[98]42 U.S.C. § 9604(e)(4).

directing compliance with such requests.[99] Penalties for failure to comply with any request made pursuant to CERCLA section 104(e) can amount to $25,000 per day.[100]

EPA's use of CERCLA section 104(e) information requests is a routine step in the investigative process. Section 104(e) responses form a significant basis for EPAs judgment as to the relative liability of parties. Moreover, since responses to these requests are publicly available, the information they contain may be used by PRP's at multiparty sites to institute contribution actions or allocate damages in cost-recovery actions brought by the government.[101]

EPA has been successful in obtaining sizable penalties from parties who have failed to respond to section 104(e) requests for information.[102] The failure of a party to allow access or properly respond to a CERCLA section 104(e) request for information can result in significant penalties regardless of whether the denial was willful.[103]

## 4.5 Response Cost Recovery Actions

### 4.5.1 Overview

The vast majority of litigation under CERCLA is brought pursuant to section 107. This section permits the United States, individual states, or private parties to bring an action to recover costs they have incurred in responding to a release or a threatened release of a hazardous substance. At the same time, section 107 has been recognized as setting forth the basic liability scheme applicable to all causes of action under CERCLA. Traditionally, courts have found that the categories of parties liable under section 107 are also liable under CERCLA's other liability provisions.[104]

### 4.5.2 Categories of Liable Parties Under CERCLA

A liable party under CERCLA section 107(a) can generally be viewed as any party having some involvement with the creation, handling, or disposal of a hazardous substance at a site. The categories of liable parties include:

1. Current owners and operators of the facility or vessel involved;
2. Former owners and operators of a facility who were involved with the facility during the time any hazardous substance was disposed at the facility;
3. Persons who arranged for disposal or treatment of hazardous substances that they owned or possessed at a facility; and
4. Persons who accepted hazardous substances for transport to disposal or treatment facilities or sites that they selected.[105]

---

[99]42 U.S.C. § 9604(e)(5).

[100]*Id.*

[101]42 U.S.C. § 9604(e)(7).

[102]*United States v. Crown Roll Leaf, Inc.*, 29 Env't Rep. Cas. (BNA) 2025 (D.N.J. 1989)($142,000 penalty).

[103]*B.F. Goodrich Co. v. Murtha*, 697 F. Supp. 89 (D. Conn 1988); *United States v. Crown Roll Leaf, Inc.*, 29 Env't Rep. Cas. (BNA) 2025 (D.N.J. 1989).

[104]*United States v. Bliss*, 667 F. Supp. 1298, 1313 (E.D. Mo. 1987).

[105]42 U.S.C. § 9607(a)(1)-(a)(4).

Since CERCLA 107(a) does little more than generally identify the categories of liable parties, it has been left to the courts to address in detail how a party may fit within each category.

### 4.5.2.1 Current Owners and Operators

The first category of liable parties, current facility owners and operators, is the easiest type of liable party to identify. A current owner or operator is the owner or operator at the time a cleanup is performed or at the time litigation is initiated.[106] A current owner or operator is statutorily liable regardless of whether it had any involvement in the handling, disposal, or treatment of hazardous wastes at the facility or whether hazardous substances were disposed of at the facility during its period of ownership or operation.[107] Where statutory liability is broad, EPA has issued enforcement guidance narrowing the scope of liability in certain instances.[108]

There are few statutory exceptions to current owner/operator liability under CERCLA. One exception exists for state or local governments. Unless they have caused a release or threatened release, state and local governments are not liable as owners or operators where they acquire ownership or control of property involuntarily through bankruptcy, tax delinquency, abandonment, or other circumstances associated with their function as sovereign.[109] An additional exception exists to protect the banking industry. Under the exception, those parties "who, without participating in the management of a vessel or facility, [hold] indicia of ownership primarily to protect [their] security interest . . ." are exempted from owner/operator liability.[110]

Because in some cases it is inequitable to find current owners and operators liable where they have merely acquired a facility after all disposal activities have ceased, Congress created in the 1986 SARA amendments what is known as the "innocent purchaser" defense. This defense is available when a current owner or operator can establish that it did not know or have reason to know at the time of purchase that any hazardous substance had been disposed of at the facility. In establishing this lack of knowledge, the current owner or operator must show that, before buying the property, it undertook "all appropriate inquiry into the previous ownership and uses of the property consistent with good commercial or customary practice. . .."[111] The defense becomes unavailable if the property is later transferred to another party without the owner/operator disclosing any knowledge of on-site waste disposal gained during his ownership or possession.[112]

---

[106]*Philadelphia v. Stepan Chem. Co.*, 18 Envtl. L. Rep. 20133 (E.D. Pa. 1987).

[107]*United States v. Tyson*, 25 Env't Rep. Cas. (BNA) 1897, 1908 (E.D. Pa. 1986).

[108]*E.g.*, EPA Lender Liability Policy, 60 *Fed. Reg.* 63517 (Dec. 11, 1995); EPA Guidance on Agreements with Prospective Purchasers of Contaminated Property, 60 Fed. Reg. 34792 (July 3, 1995). EPA's Lender Liability Policy was enacted into law by Congress in the Asset Conservation, Lender Liability and Deposit Insurance Protection Act of 1996, Pub. L. No. 104-208 (1996).

[109]42 U.S.C. § 9601(20)(D).

[110]42 U.S.C. § 9601(20)(A).

[111]*See* 42 U.S.C. § 9601(35).

[112]42 U.S.C. § 9601(35)(C).

As one may imagine, the "innocent purchaser" defense has created a windfall for environmental consulting firms. An entire industry has been built around the defense as corporations have increasingly called upon these firms to conduct the "due diligence" investigations necessary to establish the "appropriate inquiry" required by the defense.

The expansive nature of current owner and operator liability is best reflected in CERCLA's caselaw. Courts have found lessees liable as "owners."[113] Courts also have found corporate officials who actively participated in their companies' management and disposal activities as "operators" under CERCLA.[114] In some cases, this liability has been found merely when the corporate official had the authority to control disposal of hazardous wastes.[115] Parent corporations have been found liable as operators at sites held by subsidiaries where it has been shown that the parents exercised influence over the subsidiaries' management and waste disposal.[116] It has been held that a lender who actively participates in the business of its borrower or whose "involvement with the management of the borrower's facility is sufficiently broad to support the inference that it could affect hazardous waste-disposal decisions . . ." can be an owner or operator of the borrower's facility.[117] While some courts have found that state agencies may be liable as owner/operators when they have actively engaged in activities at sites that have made site conditions worse or led to further releases,[118] recently the U.S. Supreme Court has found that, absent their consent, states may not be sued by private plaintiffs.[119]

### 4.5.2.2 Former Owners and Operators

CERCLA's liability provisions addressing former owners and operators are ostensibly designed to reach former owners and operators who owned the facility when the disposal of hazardous substances occurred.[120] Unless "disposal" occurred while these parties owned or operated the site, the courts have found them not liable.[121]

---

[113]*United States v. South Carolina Recycling & Disposal Inc. ("SCRDI")*, 653 F. Supp. 984, 1003 (D.S.C. 1984), *aff'd in part and vacated in part sub nom.*, *United States v. Monsanto Co.*, 858 F.2d 160 (4th Cir. 1988), *cert. denied*, 490 U.S. 1186, (1989). *But cf., Long Beach Unified Sch. Dist. v. Dorothy B. Godwin Living Trust*, 32 F.3d 1364 (9th Cir. 1994) (owning an easement alone, with no more of an active role, does not render the easement holder an owner or operator under CERCLA).

[114]*New York v. Shore Realty Corp.*, 759 F.2d 1032 (2d Cir. 1985).

[115]*United States v. Carolina Transformer Co.*, 978 F.2d 832 (4th Cir 1992)

[116]*United States v. Kayser-Roth Corporation*, 910 F.2d 24 (1st Cir. 1990). *But see Joslyn Mfg. Co. v. T.L. James & Co.*, 893 F.2d 80, 83 (5th Cir. 1990), *cert. denied*, 490 U.S. 1108 (1991).

[117]*United States v. Fleet Factors Corp.*, 901 F.2d 1550, 1557 (11th Cir. 1990). *But see*, EPA Lender Liability Policy, 60 Fed. Reg. 63517 (Dec. 11, 1995) (requiring actual participation instead of mere influence).

[118]*CPC Int'l Inc. v. Aerojet-General Corp.*, 731 F. Supp. 783, 788 (W.D. Mich. 1989). *But see United States v. Dart Indus.*, 847 F.2d 144 (4th Cir. 1988)(government entity not liable under CERCLA for activities related to regulatory function).

[119]*Seminole Indian Tribe of Florida v. Florida*, 517 U.S. ____, 116 S.Ct. 1114, 134 L.Ed.2d 252 (1996).

[120]42 U.S.C. § 9607(a)(2).

[121]*E.g., New York v. Shore Realty Corp.*, 759 F.2d 1032, 1044 (2d Cir. 1985).

Logically one might conclude that a former owner or operator cannot be liable unless there has actually been waste handling and discharge of hazardous substances into the environment during its period of ownership or operation. However, such has not always been the case, in part because the courts have disagreed on what constitutes "disposal."

Some courts have given the term "disposal" a broad meaning. They have suggested that disposal can occur in situations where previously discharged hazardous substances continue to migrate at a site.[122] This interpretation is based upon the fact that, under CERCLA, disposal is defined by reference to its definition under RCRA and includes "the discharge, deposit, injection, dumping, spilling, leaking or placing of any solid waste or hazardous waste into or on any land or water. . .."[123] Under this definition, courts have found that continued migration of hazardous substances constitutes "disposal."[124] Thus, under this concept, former owners/operators can be liable regardless of whether they had any role in disposal activities or even knew that hazardous substances were migrating while they owned the property.

Other courts have taken a more restrictive view of disposal for purposes of former owner/operator liability. They have found that continued migration of hazardous substances alone is not adequate. Rather, liability attaches, in their view, only if hazardous substances were introduced into the environment during the former owner's or operator's association with the site.[125]

### 4.5.2.3 Generators or Arrangers

At most CERCLA sites, the "deepest pockets" fall within the third category of liable parties: "generators" or "arrangers." This is because, at most major CERCLA sites, many of these parties are Fortune 500 companies.

This category of liable parties encompasses more than those who have merely produced or generated hazardous substances. By definition, it includes "any person who by contract, agreement, or otherwise *arranged for disposal or treatment* . . . of hazardous substances *owned or possessed* by such person. . .."[126] Thus, the major issues associated with this category of liable parties involve what constitutes (1) an arrangement for disposal and (2) ownership or possession of hazardous substances.

Courts have broadly interpreted an "arrangement for disposal or treatment" to reach practically any situation where there has been a relationship between two entities involving the handling and ultimate disposal of a waste containing hazardous substances.

---

[122]*CPC Int'l Inc. v. Aerojet-General Corp.*, 759 F. Supp. 1269 (W.D. Mich. 1991); *Nurad, Inc. v. William E. Hooper & Sons Co.*, 966 F.2d 837 (4th Cir.), *cert. denied sub nom.*, *Mumaw v. Nurad, Inc.*, 113 S.Ct. 377 (1992).

[123]42 U.S.C. § 6903(3).

[124]*United States v. Waste Indus.*, 734 F.2d 159, 164 (4th Cir. 1984).

[125]*Ecodyne Corp. v. Shah*, 718 F. Supp. 1454 (N.D. Cal. 1989).

[126]42 U.S.C. § 9607(a)(3).

Indeed, to be liable as a generator or arranger, a party need not have intended or known that the disposal of hazardous substances would result from the arrangement.[127]

Aside from the traditional situation where the generator of a hazardous substance has arranged for its disposal, "arrangements" deemed sufficient to trigger liability have included: selling a waste material containing hazardous substances to another party for its use in its business;[128] contracting for the disposal of hazardous substances as fill at a construction site;[129] and entering into an agreement for the production of chemicals from furnished raw materials while knowing that the second party's production would lead to the disposal of hazardous substances.[130]

There have been few situations where courts have not found an arrangement to exist where the ultimate disposal of a hazardous substance has occurred. One situation where an arrangement has not been found is the sale by one company to another of a useful product (as opposed to a waste) containing hazardous substances.[131] Thus, it appears that characterizing the material sold as a "waste" is important in determining liability under this aspect of the generator or arranger provision.

Generally, courts have tended to ignore CERCLA's apparent requirement that a generator or arranger must have *owned or possessed* the hazardous substance for which there has been an arrangement for disposal. In order to find liability, courts have relied on concepts such as "constructive possession." "Constructive possession" exists when a party has the authority to control the handling and disposal of hazardous substances. Consequently, a waste broker who arranges for disposal can be liable as a generator or arranger despite the lack of actual ownership or possession.[132]

Responding to the nearly impossible burdens of proof which would arise if they had to do so, courts have universally held that plaintiffs need not "fingerprint" a generator's or arranger's hazardous substances at a site. It is sufficient to show that there are hazardous substances "like" those of the generator or arranger at the site and that there is evidence showing that the generator's or arranger's hazardous substances were sent to the site.[133]

---

[127]*Florida Power & Light v. Allis Chalmers Corp.*, 893 F.2d 1313 (11th Cir. 1990). *But see Amcast Indus. Corp. v. Detrex Corp.*, 2 F.3d 746, 751 (7th Cir. 1993) (the words "arranged for" imply intentional acts), *cert. denied*, 114 S.Ct. 691 (1994); *United States v. Cello-Foil Prods., Inc.*, 848 F. Supp. 1352 (W.D. Mich. 1994) (for a party to be liable as an arranger, it must intend to dispose of a hazardous substance).

[128]*United States v. A & F Materials Co.*, 582 F. Supp. 842 (S.D. Ill. 1984).

[129]*Jersey City Redevelopment Auth. v. PPG Indus.*, 655 F. Supp. 1257 (D.N.J. 1987).

[130]*United States v. Aceto Agricultural Chem. Corp.*, 699 F. Supp. 1384 (S.D. Iowa), *aff'd in part and rev'd in part*, 872 F.2d 1373 (8th Cir. 1988).

[131]*Florida Power & Light Co. v. Allis Chalmers Corp.*, 893 F.2d 1313 (11th Cir. 1990). *But cf., Catellus Dev. Corp. v. United States*, 34 F.3d 748 (9th Cir. 1994) (recyclable used automotive batteries are a waste for purposes of arranger liability).

[132]*United States v. Bliss*, 667 F. Supp. 1298 (E.D. Mo. 1987).

[133]*E.g., United States v. Wade*, 577 F. Supp. 1326 (E.D. Pa. 1983).

### *4.5.2.4 Transporters*

The final category of liable parties under CERCLA encompasses those who have transported a hazardous substance to a site from which there has been a release or threatened release.[134] Parties in this category are typically commercial waste haulers.

Section 107(a)(4), which addresses transporter liability, defines a liable party as one "who accepts or accepted any hazardous substances for transport to disposal or treatment facilities or sites selected by such person from which there is a release or a threatened release." Thus, under this section a transporter is liable *only if it selected the disposal or treatment site.*[135]

Determining whether transporter site selection has occurred is largely a case-by-case analysis. Any involvement in helping a generator select where to dispose its waste may be sufficient. The mere fact that a transporter has taken waste to the only state-licensed disposal facility available does not necessarily mean that a transporter did not participate in site selection, particularly when the transporter helped smaller generators identify the facility.[136] Both private haulers and common carriers can be found liable as transporters if they participated in site selection.[137]

### 4.5.3 Elements of CERCLA Cost Recovery

In addition to establishing that a party fits within one of the categories of liable parties, the elements of liability in CERCLA section 107 cost recovery action include the following:

1. A release or threatened release
2. Of a hazardous substance
3. From a vessel or facility
4. Which has led to the incurrence of response costs.

Elements 1, 2, and 3 have been discussed in depth earlier in this chapter. The fourth element—incurrence of response costs—warrants greater discussion at this point.

### *4.5.3.1 What Constitutes Recoverable Response Costs?*

What constitutes a recoverable response cost is largely determined with reference to CERCLA's definition of "response." CERCLA section 101(25) defines "response" as meaning "remove, removal, remedy, and remedial action, [where] all such terms (including the terms removal and remedial action) include enforcement activities related thereto."[138] Response costs thus incorporate any costs associated with a removal or remedial action.

Specific examples of recoverable response costs include costs associated with sampling and monitoring to assess and evaluate the extent of a release or threatened

---

[134]42 U.S.C. § 9607(a)(4).

[135]*E.g.*, *United States v. Hardage*, 761 F. Supp. 1501 (W.D. Okla. 1990). *See also* United States Environmental Protection Agency, *Policy For Enforcement Actions Against Transporters Under CERCLA* (December 23, 1985).

[136]*See generally United States v. Hardage*, 750 F. Supp. 1444 (W.D. Okla. 1990).

[137]*Id.*

[138]42 U.S.C. § 9601(25).

release;[139] costs associated with detecting, identifying, controlling, and disposing of hazardous substances;[140] and costs associated with investigating the extent of danger to the public or environment.[141] While some courts have found otherwise,[142] the majority have also held that EPA's indirect costs (e.g., administrative and overhead) are also recoverable response costs.[143] Certain costs have been found not to be recoverable response costs. They include medical monitoring costs[144] as well as lost profits and general damages.[145]

Whether attorney fees are recoverable as response costs in a CERCLA 107 action will depend, to some extent, on whether a private party or the government is seeking to recover these costs. Since the definition of "response" includes costs associated with "enforcement," courts have universally held that Department of Justice (DOJ) and EPA attorney fees and litigation costs associated with bringing a CERCLA action are recoverable response costs.[146]

On the other hand, attorney fees are not recoverable by a private party when they are incurred while negotiating with EPA or during litigation.[147] A private party may recover attorney fees for work that is "closely tied to the actual cleanup."[148]

The government may not necessarily recover all costs it incurs regarding the cleanup of a contaminated site. For example, Courts disagree over whether EPA is entitled to recover costs associated with monitoring a PRP's cleanup performed under the authority of a settlement with EPA.[149]

As indicated in section 4.2.1, before any response cost is recoverable under section 107, it must be shown that the release or threatened release caused the incurrence of the costs. For example, a landowner whose land adjoins a site with a threatened release would not be entitled to response costs for the installation of monitoring wells if the

---

[139]*E.g., Cadillac Fairview/California, Inc. v. Dow Chem. Co.*, 840 F.2d 691, 695 (9th Cir. 1988).

[140]*NL Indus. v. Kaplan*, 792 F.2d 896, 898 (9th Cir. 1986).

[141]*Brewer v. Ravan*, 680 F. Supp. 1176 (M.D. Tenn. 1988).

[142]*United States v. Ottati & Goss*, 694 F. Supp. 977, 994-994 (D.N.H. 1988), *aff'd in part and vacated in part, remanded*, 900 F.2d 429 (1st Cir. 1990).

[143]*United States v. Hardage*, 733 F. Supp. 1424, 1438-1439 (W.D. Okla. 1989) *aff'd in part, rev'd in part*, 982 F.2d 1436 (10th Cir. 1992), *cert. denied*, 114 S.Ct. 300 (1993); *United States v. R.W. Meyer, Inc.*, 889 F.2d 1497, 1503 (6th Cir. 1989), *cert. denied*, 110 S.Ct. 1527 (1990).

[144]*Coburn v. Sun Chem. Corp.*, 28 Env't Rep. Cas. (BNA) 1665 (E.D. Pa. 1988).

[145]*Mola Dev. Corp. v. United States*, 22 Env't Rep. Cas. (BNA) 1443 (C.D. Cal. 1985).

[146]*E.g., United States v. South Carolina Recycling & Disposal, Inc. ("SCRDI")*, 653 F. Supp. 984, 1009 (D.S.C. 1984), *aff'd in part and rev'd in part sub nom., United States v. Monsanto*, 858 F.2d 160 (4th Cir. 1988), *cert. denied*, 490 U.S. 1106 (1989).

[147]*Key Tronic Corp. v. United States*, 514 U.S. ____, 114 S.Ct. 1960, 128 L.Ed. 2d 797 (1994).

[148]*Id.*

[149]*Compare United States v. Rohm & Haas Co.*, 2 F.3d 1265 (3d Cir. 1993) (costs not recoverable) *with United States v. Lowe*, No. H-91-830, 1994 WL 518025 (S.D. Tex. Sept. 20, 1994) (costs recoverable).

wells were installed in response to another unrelated event.[150] This causation requirement is particularly applicable to private cost recovery actions since the CERCLA section authorizing such actions limits recovery to "necessary costs of response."[151] Presumably, "unnecessary" costs are not recoverable; in fact, some courts have suggested that if an action after objective evaluation is not reasonable, the costs should not be recoverable.[152]

### 4.5.3.2 Compliance With the NCP

In both private and EPA cost recovery actions, an essential element is that the party seeking such costs must have complied with the provisions of the NCP in incurring such costs. While both EPA and private parties must comply with the NCP, courts have interpreted CERCLA to create a different burden of proof with regard to establishing NCP compliance in each instance. CERCLA provides that EPA is entitled to all costs "not inconsistent" with the NCP,[153] while in private actions such costs must be "consistent" with the NCP.[154] This statutory difference has meant that a defendant must prove response costs were inconsistent with the NCP in EPA's cost recovery actions,[155] while the plaintiff seeking response costs in private actions bears the burden of establishing its costs were consistent with the NCP.[156]

While courts have uniformly found that the failure to comply with the NCP is a barrier to the recovery of response costs,[157] the extent of compliance necessary has been subject to differing interpretations. Since the government is accorded a presumption of consistency, and challenges to its actions are limited to an administrative record—reversible only when arbitrary and capricious—it is not surprising that cases addressing the issue of NCP consistency have largely been in the context of private cost recovery actions. Two approaches for assessing the degree of necessary compliance have evolved. One approach holds that a private party must *strictly* comply with the NCP in order to recover its response costs.[158] Other courts have taken a less restrictive view. They have held that only "substantial compliance" with the NCP is required.[159] This more reasonable approach will likely be the standard of review in the future, particularly because the NCP sets forth a "substantial compliance" requirement for private response actions.[160]

---

[150]*See Dedham Water Co. v. Cumberland Farms, Inc.*, 22 Chem. Waste Litig. Rept. 1130 (D. Mass. 1991).

[151]42 U.S.C. § 9607(a)(4)(B).

[152]*Amoco Oil Co. v. Borden, Inc.*, 889 F.2d 664 (5th Cir. 1989).

[153]42 U.S.C. § 9607(a)(4)(A).

[154]42 U.S.C. § 9607(a)(4)(B).

[155]*See United States v. NEPACCO*, 810 F.2d 726 (8th Cir. 1986), *cert. denied*, 484 U.S. 848 (1987).

[156]*Amland Prop. Corp. v. ALCOA*, 711 F. Supp. 784, 801 (D.N.J. 1989).

[157]*E.g., Carroll v. Litton Sys, Inc.*, No. 92-2219 (4th Cir. Jan. 13, 1995) 1995 U.S. App. LEXIS 2015 *cert. denied* ____ U.S. ____, 116 S.Ct. 70, 133 L.Ed. 2d 31 (1995).

[158]*Amland Prop. Corp. v. ALCOA*, 711 F. Supp. 784 (D.N.J. 1989).

[159]*Wickland Oil Terminals v. ASARCO, Inc.*, 792 F.2d 887 (9th Cir. 1986).

[160]40 C.F.R. § 300.700(c)(3)(i).

It should be noted the NCP creates a presumption that private party costs incurred in complying with a cleanup mandate from EPA are consistent with the NCP.[161] This presumption has been accepted by some courts.[162]

## 4.6 CERCLA Section 106 Abatement Actions

The second major cause of action available under CERCLA arises under CERCLA section 106.[163] This section authorizes EPA to seek judicial relief requiring a PRP to abate an imminent and substantial endangerment to the public health, or welfare, or the environment because of an actual or threatened release of a hazardous substance from a facility. Such an action may be maintained only by EPA and is not available to private parties.[164] The purpose of a CERCLA section 106 action for judicial relief is to require liable parties at a site to pay for a cleanup, thus avoiding commitment of Superfund monies for the cleanup.

Most courts have found the general classes of liable parties and elements of proof under CERCLA section 106 the same as those under section 107.[165] The most significant difference is that under section 106 there must also be a situation which "may" present an "imminent and substantial endangerment." To date, this difference between the two causes of action has had little apparent impact. EPA has routinely filed suits containing both causes of action. While paying lip service to the "imminent and substantial endangerment" requirement of section 106, courts have had little difficulty finding that such an endangerment exists since the standard necessary to establish an imminent and substantial endangerment is minimal. Caselaw has construed "imminent" to mean not that the harm must be immediate, but that it could arise in the future if unabated.[166] Similarly, "endangerment" has been construed to mean not actual harm but only a threat of a potential harm.[167] It is therefore difficult to imagine a situation with a release or threatened release without there also being an imminent and substantial endangerment.

Notwithstanding the above, there are differences between CERCLA sections 106 and 107 that can lead to different results. Section 106 provides for equitable relief and states that district courts "shall have jurisdiction to grant such relief as the public interest and the *equities of the case* may require." As a result, some courts have held that certain equitable defenses not available in a section 107 action are available in section 106

---

[161]40 C.F.R. § 300.700(c)(3)(i).

[162]*United States v. Western Processing Co.*, 1991 U.S. Dist. LEXIS 16021, 34 Env't Rep. Cas. (BNA) 1175 (W.D. Wash. July 31, 1991).

[163]42 U.S.C. § 9606.

[164]*Velsicol Chem. Corp. v. Reilly Tar & Chem. Corp.*, 21 Env't Rep. Cas. (BNA) 2118, 2121 (E.D. Tenn. 1984).

[165]*E.g.*, *United States v. Price*, 577 F. Supp. 1103, 1113 (D.N.J. 1983). *But see United States v. Wade*, 546 F. Supp. 785, 794 (E.D. Pa. 1982), *appeal dismissed*, 713 F.2d 49 (3d Cir. 1983).

[166]*B.F. Goodrich v. Murtha*, 697 F. Supp. 89, 95 (D. Conn. 1988).

[167]*United States v. Conservation Chem. Co.*, 619 F. Supp. 162, 175 (W.D. Mo. 1985).

cases.[168] A minority of courts have also refused to limit their review of a remedy in a CERCLA section 106 action to EPA's administrative record. In doing so, they have stressed the equitable nature of a section 106 action and the fact that CERCLA section 113's language prohibiting pre-enforcement review limits the scope of judicial review to EPA's administrative record only in situations "concerning the adequacy of any response action *taken or ordered"* by EPA.[169]

Finally, the type of cleanup available under section 106 is arguably different from that available under section 107. Section 106 is designed to *abate* an endangerment, while section 107 is designed to obtain costs associated with responding to a release or threatened release. Full site remediation, which is clearly available under section 107, may not be warranted to abate an endangerment in every case. Some courts have noted this limitation.[170] Thus, despite the fact that EPA has indicated it can use section 106 to obtain the same types of cleanups available under section 107, the scope of cleanup under section 106 remains at issue.[171]

### 4.7 CERCLA Section 106 Administrative Orders

#### 4.7.1 Recent Popularity of Administrative Orders
In addition to authorizing the injunctive relief mechanism (*see supra* section 4.6), section 106 of CERCLA authorizes EPA to issue a unilateral administrative order to compel a private party to undertake a response action. This enforcement tool was seldom used before SARA's enactment. By 1989, however, in response to criticism that its enforcement program was not sufficiently aggressive and a clearly expressed congressional desire to encourage settlement of lawsuits and private funding of cleanup work, EPA began to use section 106 orders routinely as part of its "enforcement first" policy.

The section 106 order is EPA's most potent enforcement tool and a powerful settlement incentive. CERCLA authorizes EPA to impose stiff penalties for a party's failure to comply with an order, including potential treble damages. Moreover, judicial review is unavailable until EPA decides to initiate an enforcement or cost recovery action. EPA will normally issue section 106 administrative orders only to those parties that are the largest contributors of waste to a site, are financially viable, and against which there is substantial evidence of liability.

---

[168]*United States v. Hardage*, 116 F.R.D. 460, 26 Env't Rep. Cas. (BNA) 1049 (W.D. Okla. 1987).

[169]*United States v. Hardage*, 663 F. Supp. 1280 (W.D. Okla. 1987).

[170]*E.g.*, *United States v. NEPACCO*, 579 F. Supp. 823, 840 n.17 (W.D. Mo. 1984), *aff'd in part and rev'd in part*, 810 F.2d 726 (8th Cir. 1986), *cert. denied*, 484 U.S. 848 (1987).

[171]*See* United States Environmental Protection Agency, *Memorandum On Use and Issuance of Administrative Orders Under Section 106(a) of CERCLA* (September 8, 1983), *reprinted in* 41 Env't Rep. 2931, 2935.

### 4.7.2 Authority To Issue Administrative Orders

Authority for the issuance of a unilateral administrative order is contained in section 106. This section sets forth the following legal prerequisites for issuance of an order:

a.  The existence of:
    i.   an actual or threatened "release"
    ii.  of a hazardous substance
    iii. from a facility;
b.  An administrative finding that there is or may be an imminent or substantial endangerment; and
c.  Relief that "may be necessary" to abate the imminent hazard.

EPA's finding of imminent and substantial endangerment and its determination of "necessary relief" required to abate the endangerment may well be in dispute. However, PRPs have little opportunity to challenge the existence of these requirements until after the recipient fulfills its obligation under the order or EPA seeks enforcement of the order against a noncomplying party.

### 4.7.3 Judicial Review of Administrative Orders

A party believing it may have good cause for its refusal to comply with a section 106 order cannot immediately obtain judicial relief to set aside the order. Under CERCLA, the timing of judicial review is essentially determined by EPA. As indicated, section 113 provides that no federal court shall have jurisdiction to review any order issued under section 106 until EPA seeks to enforce its order or sues to recover the costs of undertaking the response action directed in the order. (*See supra* section 4.6).

In addition, CERCLA does not provide a party with a formal opportunity to file public comments that criticize findings made in the order. Instead, it is EPA's policy to offer the respondent a limited opportunity to meet with the agency to discuss the order. The scope of this conference is very narrow. According to an EPA policy statement, the conference is "not intended to be a forum for discussing liability issues or whether the order should have been issued. Instead, the conference is designed to ensure that the order is based on complete and accurate information, and to facilitate understanding of implementation."[172]

Once a party is able to obtain judicial review, the district court will use a deferential standard of review in considering any arguments the recipient might have about the merit of or necessity for EPA's selected response action. The court's review will be limited to material in the administrative record, and the selected response action will be upheld unless the court finds it to be arbitrary, capricious, or not in accordance with law.[173] If not already determined, issues of liability would be tried *de novo*. To the extent they are not connected to the merits or "adequacy" of EPA's chosen response action, issues relating to the existence of "sufficient cause" should also be tried *de novo*.

---

[172]United States Environmental Protection Agency, *Guidance on CERCLA Section 106(a) Unilateral Administrative Orders for Remedial Design and Remedial Action*, OSWER Dir. # 9833.01-a (March 13, 1990).
[173]*See* 42 U.S.C. §§ 9613(j), 9621(a).

(*See infra* section 4.7.5). It is unclear under what standard issues relating to the EPA's legal authority to issue the order—the existence of an imminent and substantial endangerment, for instance—would be determined.

### 4.7.4 Reimbursement from the Superfund

In an attempt to encourage expeditious compliance with section 106 orders, CERCLA provides that a party who complies with a cleanup order may file a claim against the Superfund to recover costs of complying with the order. However, a party may recover only if that party can show that it was not a liable party under section 107, or that the response action ordered was arbitrary, capricious, or contrary to law. EPA has established procedures for filing, evaluating, and resolving claims against the Superfund.[174]

### 4.7.5 Penalties for Failure to Comply; Defenses

A party that refuses or fails to comply with a section 106 order may be assessed up to $25,000 per day of the violation.[175] In addition, an unjustified failure or refusal to comply may also result in punitive damages equal to, but not more than, three times the amount of costs incurred as a result of the party's failure to take the action required by the order.[176] Passages in CERCLA's legislative history indicate that the amount of punitive damages will be set by the court exercising its equitable discretion.[177]

A party may avoid the imposition of penalties by establishing that it had "sufficient cause" for its failure to comply with the order.[178] Only a few cases to date have had occasion to construe the term "sufficient cause"; those that have, rely heavily upon statements contained in CERCLA's legislative history.[179] Under these decisions, the party which has failed to comply with the order bears the burden of demonstrating that it has a *reasonable, objectively grounded* belief that:

1. It was not a liable party (as defined in section 107) under CERCLA, or that it had a defense to such liability under section 107(b);
2. It was a *de minimis* contributor to the release or threatened release;
3. The order was legally invalid for some reason (*e.g.*, no evidence of an imminent or substantial endangerment);

---

[174]58 Fed. Reg. 5,460 (1993) (to be codified at 40 C.F.R. pt. 307).

[175]42 U.S.C. § 9606(b)(1).

[176]42 U.S.C. § 9607(c)(3). *See also United States v. Lecarreaux*, 1992 U.S. Lexis 9365 (D.N.J. Feb. 18, 1992); *EPA Policy on Civil Penalties*, 17 Env't L. Rep. 35083 (February 16, 1984).

[177]*See Solid State Circuits v. United States Envtl. Protection Agency*, 812 F.2d 383 (8th Cir. 1987).

[178]42 U.S.C. §§ 9606(b)(1), 9607(c)(3).

[179]*See Solid State Circuits v. United States Envtl. Protection Agency*, 812 F.2d 383 (8th Cir. 1987)(providing extensive discussion of defense).

4.  Financial, technical, or other inability prevented compliance with the order[180]; or
5.  The response action ordered was not cost-effective as required by CERCLA section 121(b) or otherwise inconsistent with the NCP.[181]

Consequently, in order to challenge a section 106 order, "a party must show that the applicable provisions of CERCLA, EPA regulations and policy statements, and any formal or informal hearings or guidance the EPA may provide, give rise to an objectively reasonable belief in the invalidity or inapplicability of the cleanup order."[182]

Given the provisions described above, parties who receive an administrative 106 order have few options under the statute. A party may either comply with the order or face judicial action by EPA. If a party chooses to comply with the order, he may, after fulfilling his obligations under the order, seek reimbursement under section 106(b)(2)(A). The major advantage of this approach is the avoidance of penalties. However, this advantage may be offset by unpredictability about the size of the financial commitment necessary to comply and the lengthy period that funds will be tied up before a reimbursement claim is considered. In the event of noncompliance, the issues would be addressed in a later district court action by EPA to enforce the order or, if EPA funds and implements the response action itself, to recover its response costs plus penalties and punitive damages.

### 4.8 Defenses To Liability

Generally speaking, there are few affirmative defenses available in a CERCLA action. This is particularly true with regard to CERCLA section 107 cost recovery actions. While the defenses available in a section 106 abatement action appear to be broader, and may include certain equitable defenses, the case law in the area is unsettled.

#### 4.8.1 Statutory Defenses

CERCLA section 107 limits affirmative defenses to situations where a release was caused solely by:

1.  An act of God;
2.  An act of war; or
3.  An act or omission of a third party (other than an employee, agent, or party with whom there is a contractual relationship) as long as the defendant exercised due care and took precautions against foreseeable acts of the third party.[183]

---

[180]*See e.g., United States v. Parsons*, 723 F. Supp. 757, 763 (N.D. Ga. 1989), *vacated*, 936 F.2d 526 (11th Cir. 1991).

[181]*Solid State Circuits v. United States Envtl. Protection Agency*, 812 F.2d 383, 391 n.11 (8th Cir. 1987).

[182]*Solid State Circuits v. United States Envtl. Protection Agency*, 812 F.2d 383, 392 (8th Cir. 1978).

[183]42 U.S.C. § 9607(b).

Many courts have found that these are the only affirmative defenses available in a CERCLA section 107 action.[184] For this reason, EPA has often been successful in having any other defenses raised by a defendant struck early during enforcement proceedings.[185] Nevertheless, in most CERCLA actions, a variety of defenses, including many equitable defenses (*e.g.*, due care, compliance with existing standards, estoppel), have been raised. In some cases, the courts have appeared willing to go beyond CERCLA's three statutory defenses and consider these additional defenses on the theory that they raise issues relating to apportionment.[186] Thus, despite CERCLA's limited statutory defenses, it is always to a defendant's advantage to raise additional defenses.

The necessity of asserting other equitable defenses is more apparent when one considers the limited instances in which the statutory defenses are available. Each defense is narrowly written and has been narrowly construed by the courts.

There is little case law interpreting the *act of God defense*. What case law exists suggests that it is to be interpreted narrowly. For example, the defense requires more than mere natural occurrences, but rather exceptional events.[187]

There has also been little discussion of the *act of war defense* by the courts. It remains unclear whether the defense will be limited to releases caused by combat or whether it may extend to releases caused by increased production demands resulting from a war. Consistent with the narrow interpretation given other defenses, it can be expected that the act of war defense will be limited to releases caused by combat.[188]

Most litigation concerning these defenses has focused on the *third party defense*. Since the defense is available only when the third party "solely" caused the release, any involvement, however slight, that the defendant may have had in contributing to the release will make the defense unavailable.[189] In addition, few situations will arise in which the third party will not have had a direct or indirect[190] contractual relationship with the defendant in some way. Leases, employment contracts, waste hauling contracts, and real estate sales contracts can each constitute a connection to the third party that will nullify the defense.[191] The third party defense's most useful application appears to arise in the innocent purchaser situation. (*See supra* section 4.5.2.1).

### 4.8.2 Equitable and Other Defenses

As indicated, defendants frequently will raise many defenses in addition to the three statutory defenses. Some of these defenses have been based upon alleged procedural violations by EPA. Others could be generically categorized as "equitable"

---

[184]*E.g.*, *United States v. Rohm & Haas Co.*, 669 F. Supp. 672, 675 (D.N.J. 1987).

[185]*E.g.*, *United States v. Dickerson*, 640 F. Supp. 448, 450-451 (D. Md. 1986).

[186]*United States v. Hardage*, 116 F.R.D. 460, 463 (W.D. Okla. 1987).

[187]*United States v. Alcan Aluminum, Corp.*, 892 F. Supp. 648 (M.D. Pa. 1995); *United States v. Stringfellow*, 661 F. Supp. 1053, 1061 (C.D. Cal. 1987).

[188]*See FMC Corp. v. United States Dep't of Commerce*, 786 F. Supp. 471 (E.D. Pa. 1992), *aff'd* 10 F.3d 987 (3d Cir. 1993), *vacated, reh'g granted en banc* 10 F.3d 987 (3d Cir. 1994), *aff'd* 29 F.3d 833 (3d Cir. 1994).

[189]42 U.S.C. § 9607(b).

[190]*United States v. Hooker Chems. & Plastics Corp.*, 680 F. Supp. 546 (W.D.N.Y. 1988)(suggesting indirect relationship sufficient to bar third-party defense).

[191]*E.g.*, *United States v. Tyson*, 25 Env't Rep. Cas. (BNA) 1897 (E.D. Pa. 1986).

defenses. Courts have divided over the availability of these additional defenses. Generally, defenses raising procedural omissions (e.g., failure to provide a private party the opportunity to perform a cleanup, failure to notify responsible parties, failure to list a site on the NPL) have been unsuccessful.[192]

Defendants have had more success in raising equitable defenses such as estoppel, unclean hands, and laches. While some courts have ruled that these defenses are unavailable in a CERCLA section 107 action,[193] others have suggested that they may be asserted.[194] Regardless, equitable defenses are more likely to be available in a CERCLA section 106 proceeding since the court is required to render its decision based on the "equities" of the case.[195]

### 4.8.3 Statute of Limitations

CERCLA contained no specific statute of limitations provision prior to the 1986 SARA amendments. This omission was remedied with the addition of section 113(g), which contains limitation periods for cost recovery actions, natural resource damages, and contribution actions.

With regard to cost recovery actions, section 113(g)(2) sets forth two limitation periods—one for removals and another for remedial actions. It also contains a "tacking" provision which extends the limitation period for removals when they are followed by a remedial action. Response cost claims flowing from a removal action must ordinarily be brought within three years after completion of the removal. However, the government may extend this period by finding that a waiver for continued response is needed. Claims flowing from a remedial action must be brought within six years "after initiation of physical on-site construction of the remedial action." The "tacking" provision arises when a remedial action is initiated within three years after completion of the removal action. In such a case, costs associated with the removal can be recovered with the remedial action costs. Thus, it is theoretically possible that the period to recover removal costs may extend up to nine years. Because the limitations periods are tied to whether an event is a "removal" or "remedial action," correctly categorizing an action becomes critical to evaluating the appropriate limitations period.

The limitations period for natural resource damage claims (*see infra* section 4.10), is three years after the latter of either: (1) the "date of the discovery of the loss and its connection with the release," or (2) the date of promulgation of natural resource damage assessment regulations.[196] Since the government's initial effort at promulgating final natural resource damage assessment regulations has been struck by the courts, there has been debate over when the limitations period actually begins to run.[197] In the most important decision on the subject to date, the Circuit Court for the District of Columbia

---

[192]*E.g.*, *New York v. Shore Realty Corp.*, 759 F.2d 1032, 1046 (2d Cir. 1985). *But see Bulk Distribution Ctrs. v. Monsanto Co.*, 589 F. Supp. 1437, 1448 (S.D. Fla. 1984).

[193]*Kelley v. Thomas Solvent Co.*, 714 F. Supp. 1439, 1451 (W.D. Mich. 1989).

[194]*Mardan Corp. v. C.G.C. Music, Ltd.*, 600 F. Supp. 1049 (D. Ariz 1984), *aff'd*, 804 F.2d 1454 (9th Cir. 1986).

[195]*United States v. Hardage*, 116 F.R.D. 460 (W.D. Okla. 1987).

[196]42 U.S.C. § 9613(g)(1).

[197]*Ohio v. United States Dep't of Interior*, 880 F.2d 432 (D.C. Cir. 1989).

has held that, notwithstanding their later nullification, for purposes of the limitations period prescribed in the statute, natural resource damage assessment regulations were promulgated when originally published.[198]

Contribution actions for response costs or damages must be brought no more than three years after: (1) the date of judgment in any action under CERCLA for recovery of such costs or damages, or (2) the date of an administrative order or entry of a judicially approved settlement with respect to such costs or damages.

### 4.8.4 Divisibility

Traditionally, joint and several liability does not exist where the "harm" is divisible or reasonably capable of apportionment.[199] In such cases, each tortfeasor is liable only for the harm or portion of harm that it individually caused.

At most multiparty sites, responsible parties have had little success in avoiding joint and several liability by arguing that the harm caused is divisible or capable of apportionment.[200] Rather than hear a defendant's arguments on divisibility of harm during the liability phase of the case, many courts have tended to accept EPA's argument that the commingling of wastes renders the harm indivisible. Accordingly, in most cases involving multiparty sites, defendants have been unable to raise divisibility of harm as a partial or total defense to liability. Instead, they have been forced to raise the issue during secondary proceedings to allocate costs among those parties deemed jointly and severally liable. Thus, at sites where several parties have contributed high levels of a hazardous substance and others contributed *de minimis* levels of a far less hazardous substance, each is jointly and severally liable irrespective of its actual contribution.

Some courts have demonstrated disapproval of the above approach. One federal circuit court found that commingled waste is not synonymous with "indivisible" harm and suggested that a PRP should be permitted a hearing during the liability phase of a proceeding to establish that the harm was divisible and that its waste could not have contributed to the release because of its relative toxicity, migratory potential, and synergistic capacity.[201] Another federal circuit court held that the imposition of joint and several liability was improper when the defendants had demonstrated that "a reasonable and rational approximation of each defendant's individual contribution to the contamination [could] be made."[202] Should other courts follow these decisions, defendants will be provided a real opportunity in future CERCLA litigation involving multiparty sites to avoid the imposition of joint and several liability. In some cases, they may be able to avoid liability altogether. Needless to say, EPA is quite concerned about these decisions' impact on its enforcement efforts since more liability hearings to assess divisibility are anticipated.

---

[198]*Wennecott Utah Copper Corp. v. United States Dept of Interior*, 88 F.3d 1191 (D.C. Cir 1996). *See also, United States v. Montrose Chem. Corp.*, 883 F. Supp. 1396 (C.D. Cal. 1995) (same holding).

[199]Restatement (Second) of Torts, Sections 433A, 433B.

[200]*E.g., United States v. Chem-Dyne Corp.*, 572 F. Supp. 802 (S.D. Ohio 1983). *But see United States v. A & F Materials Co.*, 578 F. Supp. 1249 (S.D. Ill. 1984).

[201]*United States v. Alcan Aluminum Corp.*, 964 F.2d 252 (3d Cir. 1992).

[202]*In re Bell Petroleum Servs., Inc.*, 3 F.3d 889, 903 (5th Cir. 1993).

## 4.9 Citizen Suit Provisions

CERCLA, as do other environmental statutes,[203] contains a "citizen suit" provision. This provision permits any "person" to initiate a civil action in two instances: (1) against any other person (including the United States) for violations of any standard, regulation, condition, requirement, or order effective under CERCLA; and (2) against any officer of the United States for failure to perform a nondiscretionary act under CERCLA.[204] With respect to the first type of action, a United States District Court may enforce the standard, regulation, condition, requirement, or order and impose civil penalties for such a violation. In the second type of action, the appropriate district court may order the officer to perform the act or duty.[205]

Prior to initiating a citizen suit, one must first provide 60-days notice of the intended action to EPA, the alleged violator and, in certain instances, the state involved.[206] This requirement is jurisdictional.[207]

Both responsible parties and environmental groups have attempted to use the citizen suit provisions to obtain, either directly or indirectly, review of EPA's remedial action process. These attempts have consistently failed. CERCLA and decisions from the courts make clear that the provisions of CERCLA section 113(h), which limit judicial review of EPA's remedial actions, take precedence over the citizen suit provisions, even when the challenge is only to EPA's procedures in selecting a remedy and not to the remedy itself.[208]

### 4.10 Natural Resources Damages

The majority of CERCLA actions to date have involved the assessment of liability and damages for costs related to response actions associated with a release. However, the government is increasingly invoking claims under CERCLA's natural resources damages provision to recover costs associated with the loss of a contaminated area's natural resources.

#### 4.10.1 Statutory Provision

Section 107(a)(4)(C) of CERCLA provides that responsible parties may be held liable for "damages for injury to, destruction of, or loss of natural resources, including the reasonable costs of assessing such injury, destruction, or loss resulting from such a release."[209] While the definition of natural resources is broad in scope and encompasses not only more commonly considered resources such as land, wildlife, fish, and biota, but also air, water, groundwater, drinking water supplies, and any other resources, it is limited to those resources owned, held in trust, or otherwise controlled by a state, the

---

[203]*See* 42 U.S.C. § 7604 (Clean Air Act); 33 U.S.C. § 1365 (Clean Water Act).
[204]42 U.S.C. § 9659.
[205]42 U.S.C. § 9659(c).
[206]42 U.S.C. § 9659(a),(d)(1),(e).
[207]*Roe v. Wert*, 706 F. Supp. 788, 792 (W.D. Okla. 1989).
[208]*Schalk v. Reilly*, 900 F.2d 1091 (7th Cir.), *cert. denied sub nom.*, *Frey v. Reilly*, 498 U.S. 981 (1990).
[209]42 U.S.C. § 9607(a)(4)(C).

federal government, or Indian tribe. Hence, damages to private property where no government interest is involved are not recoverable.[210]

Monies recovered for natural resources damages are to be used for restoration or replacement of the resource or for acquisition of an equivalent resource.[211] Regulations interpreting CERCLA's natural resource provisions clearly indicate that natural resource damages are compensatory, rather than punitive, in nature.[212]

Although the government is not required to provide notice to a private party when it initiates a claim against the Superfund for natural resources,[213] CERCLA does contain further limitations on the recovery of natural resources damages. Section 107(f) prohibits recovery for natural resources losses identified in an environmental assessment and thus authorized by permit or license.[214] Moreover, unlike response actions, actions for the recovery of natural resources damages have limited retroactivity; under the Act, "[t]here shall be no recovery . . . where such damages and the release of a hazardous substance from which such damages resulted have occurred wholly before [December 11, 1980, the date of CERCLA's enactment]."[215]

### 4.10.2 Potential Plaintiffs

CERCLA identifies those parties that may assert natural resource damages claims. Specifically, CERCLA provides for designation of federal or state "trustees" who are authorized to assess natural resource damages and bring actions for recovery of damages.[216] Although certain courts have extended "trusteeship" to include those municipalities specifically designated by a state, a municipality's ability to pursue natural resource damages remains questionable.[217] Double recovery is not permitted either where there are multiple trustees or where both cleanup and resources restoration costs are claimed.[218]

---

[210]42 U.S.C. § 9601(16). *See also Lutz v. Chromatex, Inc.*, 718 F. Supp. 413, 419 (M.D. Pa. 1989); *Ohio v. United States Dep't of Interior*, 880 F.2d 432, 460-461 (D.C. Cir. 1989).

[211]42 U.S.C. § 9607(f)(1).

[212]*See* 51 Fed. Reg. 27,674, at 52,127-52,128 (1986); *see also Ohio v. United States Dep't of Interior*, 880 F.2d 432, 474 (D.C. Cir. 1989).

[213]42 U.S.C. § 9612(a). *See also Idaho v. Howmet Turbine Component Co.*, 814 F.2d 1376, 1377 (9th Cir. 1987).

[214]42 U.S.C. § 9607(f). *See also Idaho v. Hanna Mining Co.*, 882 F.2d 392, 395 (9th Cir. 1989).

[215]42 U.S.C. § 9607(f). *See also United States v. NEPACCO*, 579 F. Supp. 823, 839 (W.D. Mo. 1984), *aff'd in part and rev'd in part*, 810 F.2d 726 (8th Cir. 1986)(pre-CERCLA costs are not recoverable); *United States v. Wade*, 577 F. Supp. 1326 (E.D. Pa. 1983). *But see United States v. Shell Oil Co.*, 605 F. Supp. 1064 (D. Colo. 1985)(retroactivity permitted where damages continued after enactment).

[216]42 U.S.C. § 9607(f)(2).

[217]*Compare New York v. Exxon Corp.*, 633 F. Supp. 609, 619 (S.D.N.Y. 1986)(permitting municipal trusteeship); *Boonton v. Drew Chem. Corp.*, 621 F. Supp. 663, 667 (D.N.J. 1985)(same) *with Bedford v. Raytheon Co.*, 755 F. Supp. 469 (D. Mass. 1991) (disallowing municipal trusteeship).

[218]42 U.S.C. § 9607(f)(1).

### 4.10.3 Historical Inactivity

Throughout the 1980s, the federal and the state governments initiated few actions to recover natural resource damages. This lack of activity resulted in part from section 107's prescription against retroactive application. (*See supra* section 4.8). Moreover, until enactment of SARA, the federal and state governments had relatively easy access to Superfund monies to resolve natural resource damage claims. The monies could be used both to assess the injury to the natural resources as a result of a release and to restore or replace such resources.[219] However, as amended by SARA, CERCLA currently provides that "[n]o natural resource claim may be paid from the Superfund unless the President determines that the claimant has exhausted all administrative and judicial remedies to recover the amount of such claim from the person who may be liable under section 107."[220]

Further contributing to the limited use of CERCLA's natural resource provisions was the difficulty in characterizing the value of natural resources damaged or lost as a result of a release. Although CERCLA included provisions requiring assessment regulations at its enactment, the first of such regulations were not promulgated until 1986.

### 4.10.4 Assessment Regulations

Section 111 of CERCLA indicates that natural resource damages shall be assessed by those individuals indicated in the National Contingency Plan.[221] In keeping with this mandate, regulations governing such assessments were to be promulgated, including: identify[ing] the best available procedures to determine such damages, including both direct and indirect injury, destruction or loss and . . . tak[ing] into account consideration of factors, including, but not limited to, replacement value, use value and the ability of the ecosystem or resource to recover.[222]

In 1986 and 1987, the Department of Interior (DOI)[223] promulgated two types of assessment regulations dependant upon the associated release: (1) Type A regulations ostensibly for assessing damages resulting from minor releases but actually limited to coastal and marine environment damage[224] and (2) Type B regulations for individual cases whose damages have been caused by more serious discharges.[225] Both sets of

---

[219]42 U.S.C. § 9611(c)(1)(2).

[220]42 U.S.C. § 9611(b)(2)(A).

[221]42 U.S.C. § 9611.

[222]42 U.S.C. § 9651(c)(2).

[223]*See* Exec. Order No. 12,316, 46 Fed. Reg. 42,237, 42,240 (1981)(designating Department of Interior as party to promulgate assessment regulations), *superseded by* Exec. Order No. 12,580, 52 Fed. Reg. 2923 (1987). *See also* 42 U.S.C. § 9651(c).

[224]52 Fed. Reg. 9,042 (1987), *amended* at 53 Fed. Reg. 9,769 (1988); 53 Fed. Reg. 20,143 (1988); 54 Fed. Reg. 39,015 (1989). *See also Colorado v. United States Dep't of Interior*, 880 F.2d 481, 490 (D.C. Cir. 1989)(limited application of Type A regulations to marine and coastal environments not arbitrary or capricious).

[225]51 Fed. Reg. 27,674 (1986), *amended* at 53 Fed. Reg 5,166 (1988).

regulations became the subject of intense litigation, resulting in their being struck down and remanded to the Department of Interior for revision.[226]

On March 25, 1994, DOI issued a final rule revising the Type B rule to comply with all but one aspect of the court's order. The rule establishes a procedure for calculating natural resource damages based on costs of restoring, replacing or acquiring the equivalent of injured resources. It also allows for the assessment of all use values of injured resources that are lost to the public pending completion of restoration of equivalent resources.[227] DOI proposed revisions to Type A assessments in coastal/marine areas later in 1994.[228] EPA's 1994 Type B rule was also subjected to judicial challenge. In the resulting court decision the majority of the rule was upheld.[229]

### 4.10.5 Prospect of Increased Use

Coupled with the stricter natural resource provisions enacted by SARA, the promulgation of the assessment regulations has substantially increased the likelihood of natural resource damage litigation. Individuals identified as trustees in the National Contingency Plan are required to assess natural resources damage, and restoration costs cannot be borne by the Superfund until all administrative and judicial remedies are exhausted. (*See supra* section 4.10.3). Moreover, assessments conducted in compliance with the assessments regulations are entitled to a rebuttable presumption in proceedings to recover damages from responsible parties.[230] Given these powerful incentives, the federal government or its state counterpart has little reason not to initiate a natural resource action against responsible parties. Moreover, as technical studies increasingly indicate that once-hailed remedial practices such as pump-and-treat technologies cannot return a resource to its original condition or that such restoration is technically impracticable, litigation for "lost use" of natural resources will probably increase.

### 4.10.6 Proof Issues

The standard for natural resource litigation is significantly different than that for response actions. Under section 107(a) of CERCLA, liability for release of a hazardous substance is based in strict liability and requires no element of causation. The Department of Interior, however, has interpreted natural resources damage actions as requiring a traditional causation analysis typical of tort actions. This interpretation has been affirmed by the courts.[231] Consequently, to prevail on a claim for injury to a natural resource, the trustee must show by a preponderance of the evidence[232] that the defendant's hazardous substance release "was the sole or substantially contributing cause

---

[226]*See Ohio v. United States Dep't of the Interior*, 880 F.2d 432 (D.C. Cir. 1989); *Colorado v. United States Dep't of Interior*, 880 F.2d 481, 490-491 (D.C. Cir. 1989).

[227]59 Fed. Reg. 14,262 (Mar. 25, 1994).

[228]59 Fed.Reg. 63,300 (Dec. 8, 1994).

[229]*Kennecott Utah Copper Corp. v. U.S. Department of Interior*, 88 F.3d 1191 (D.C. Cir. 1996)

[230]42 U.S.C. § 9607(f)(2)(C).

[231]*Ohio v. United States Dep't of Interior*, 880 F.2d 432, 470-472 (D.C. Cir. 1989).

[232]*Idaho v. Southern Refrigerated Transport, Inc.*, No. 88-1279 (D. Idaho Jan. 24, 1991) (natural resource damages must be proved by preponderance of the evidence).

of each alleged injury to natural resources."[233]  In so doing, the trustee must show (1) what resource was injured, (2) at what specific locations of the natural resource the injury occurred, (3) when the injury occurred, (4) which release of what substance caused the injury, and (5) by what pathway the natural resource was exposed to the substance.[234]  Conversely, defendants carry the burden of proof when asserting as a defense that damages being sought are exempt.[235]

### 4.11 Contribution Actions

In view of CERCLA's liability scheme, including strict, joint and several liability (in most cases), and few defenses, it is not surprising that contribution actions assume a major role in CERCLA litigation.

Prior to the 1986 SARA amendments, some question existed whether a right of contribution existed under CERCLA.  The 1986 SARA amendments resolved the matter by adding section 113(f).  This section specifically provides for contribution actions among jointly and severally liable parties and states that in resolving such claims, courts should apply such "equitable factors" as they deem appropriate.  This language gives the courts broad discretion in determining cost allocation among jointly and severally liable parties in a contribution action.  The factors which appear to be relevant include:

1.  The volume of hazardous substances contributed by each party;
2.  The relative degree of toxicity of each party's wastes;
3.  The extent to which each party was involved in the generation, transportation, treatment, storage, or disposal of the substances involved;
4.  The degree of care exercised in handling the hazardous substances; and
5.  The degree of cooperation by the parties with government officials in order to prevent any harm to public health or the environment.[236]

While courts are free to apply any other "equitable" factors they deem appropriate, most allocations derive from applying the above factors.

Contribution actions may be brought either during or following a CERCLA section 107 cost recovery action or CERCLA section 106 abatement action.[237]  However, in most government enforcement actions, contribution actions are set for hearing after the government's liability case against the primary defendants is resolved.[238]

At many multiparty sites, certain PRPs desire to settle with EPA while others, for whatever reasons, feel that a settlement is not in their best interests.  In these cases, EPA may see fit to settle with the first group for less than the full amount of its claim, while

---

[233]*United States v. Montrose Chem. Corp. of California*, 22 Chem. Waste Litig. Rept. 237 (C.D. Cal. 1991).

[234]*Id.*

[235]*In re Acushnet River & New Bedford Harbor:  Proceedings re Alleged PCB Pollution*, 716 F. Supp. 676, 686 (D. Mass. 1989).

[236]*See* H.R. Rep. No. 253, 99th Cong., 1st Sess., pt. 3, 19, *reprinted in* 1986 U.S. Code Cong. & Admin. News 3038, 3042.

[237]42 U.S.C. § 9613(f)(1).

[238]*E.g., United States v. Bell Petroleum Serv.*, 19 Chem. Waste Litig. Rept. 152 (W.D. Tex. 1989).

reserving the remainder of its claim for an action against the non-settlors. In such instances, CERCLA provides what is known as "contribution protection" for the settlors. It does so by stating that a party "[which] has resolved its liability to the United States or a State in an administrative or judicially approved settlement shall not be liable for claims for contribution regarding matters addressed in the settlement." [239] A settling party may, however, be liable for costs outside the scope of "matters addressed in the settlement."[240]

## 5.0 SETTLEMENTS WITH EPA

### 5.1 Overview

Although certain CERCLA cases have proceeded through trial, these cases are the exception rather than the rule. Settlement is the norm in CERCLA cases, and this preference can be explained for several reasons. From EPA's perspective, settlement is preferable because it conserves Superfund monies as well as EPA's limited resources. Settlements also free EPA's personnel to work on other cleanups. From the perspective of PRPs, settlement is often preferred because it permits them to exercise greater control over the selection and implementation of remedial actions, presumably minimizing costs. PRPs also often prefer settlement to avoid the tremendous costs of litigating a CERCLA case.

This is not to say that the settlement process is smooth or produces results uniformly acceptable to PRPs. Indeed, negotiations can be protracted, contentious, and extremely costly. This scenario is particularly likely at multiparty sites where PRPs must not only negotiate with EPA but also with each other and, in some cases, with the State where a site is located. While it is EPA's policy to settle, increasingly it has demonstrated inflexibility both with regard to the remedial action selected and with the terms of the settlement agreement. Consequently, many PRPs have begun to question whether settlement is necessarily the best course. Given EPA's policy of routinely issuing section 106 administrative orders, some PRPs have decided to perform cleanups under these orders rather than under a settlement agreement.

### 5.2 Controlling Authority

Parties attempting to negotiate a CERCLA settlement with EPA often find that the flexibility of the EPA negotiators is constrained both by CERCLA's settlement provisions and by a variety of guidance documents issued by EPA. Moreover, EPA has prepared "model" settlement documents for use by its staff level negotiators. Because of these constraints, truly "negotiated" settlements are not likely to occur.

The SARA amendments added section 122 entitled "settlements." This section sets forth procedures which EPA may follow if it attempts to settle a CERCLA case. EPA's decision whether to invoke the procedures under CERCLA section 122 is discretionary and not subject to judicial review.[241] However, section 122 codifies many of the settlement policies that EPA had followed prior to the SARA amendments. The section

---

[239] 42 U.S.C. § 9613(f)(2).
[240] *See Akzo Coatings v. Aigner Corp.*, 30 F.3d 761 (7th Cir. 1994).
[241] 42 U.S.C. § 9622(a).

should therefore be consulted in detail by any party attempting to settle a CERCLA case, because in many instances it provides specific instructions when and how various settlement provisions may be used. For example, section 122(f) provides detailed requirements addressing the circumstances in which EPA can provide a covenant not to sue in a settlement agreement. Other sections address such issues as partial funding by the Superfund ("mixed funding"), *de minimis* settlements, and public participation in settlements.

Section 122 also contains extensive discussion of "special notice procedures" that EPA may follow when it determines that a period of negotiation would "facilitate an agreement."[242] These procedures provide that if EPA elects to pursue settlement under section 122, it must provide PRPs notice including the names and addresses of all other PRPs, the volume and nature of substances each party contributed to the site (if known), and a ranking of the responsible parties by volume contributed. These special notice procedures also contain provisions authorizing EPA to prepare a "nonbinding preliminary allocation of responsibility" (NBAR) for the PRPs to use in their attempts to allocate costs among themselves. To date, however, EPA has not seen fit to use this provision extensively. This agency reluctance is probably due to the fact that EPA would prefer not to be bound by the notice provision's requirements or lose its flexibility in dealing with potential settlors.

Throughout CERCLA's history, EPA has from time to time issued guidance documents on various issues associated with settlements. In 1985, EPA issued what continues to be its primary settlement policy.[243] This document, which pre-dates the SARA amendments, is generally consistent with CERCLA section 122. It remains the only comprehensive treatment of overall CERCLA settlement policy by EPA. Since 1986, EPA has issued a variety of guidance documents addressing individual settlement topics. Among the topics these guidance documents address are: covenants not to sue,[244] *de minimis* party settlements,[245] stipulated penalties in consent decrees,[246] and "mixed funding."[247] In any negotiation it can be expected that EPA's negotiators will attempt to comply with any applicable guidance document.

### 5.3 Consent Decrees and Consent Orders

Settlements with EPA are ordinarily memorialized in a consent decree or an administrative order on consent ("consent order"). The difference between the two forms of agreement is that a consent decree is filed with and signed by a federal court,

---

[242]42 U.S.C. § 9622(e).

[243]50 Fed. Reg. 5,034 (1985).

[244]52 Fed. Reg. 28,038 (1987).

[245]57 Fed. Reg. 29,313 (June 2, 1992); United States Environmental Protection Agency, *Streamlined Approaches for Settlement with De Minimis Waste Contributors Under CERCLA Section 122(g)(1)(A)*, OSWER Directive No. 9834.7-1D (July 30, 1993).

[246]United States Environmental Protection Agency, *Office of Enforcement and Compliance Monitoring, Guidance on the Use of Stipulated Penalties In Hazardous Waste Consent Decrees*, OSWER Directive No. 9835.2b (1987).

[247]53 Fed. Reg. 8,279 (1988).

while a consent order does not involve any judicial action. Moreover, any settlement and consent order involving total response costs greater than $500,000 requires approval by the United States Department of Justice.[248] Not surprisingly, most parties prefer to have a settlement memorialized through a consent decree as there will be a neutral third party—the judge—available to resolve disputes.

Until recently, the terms and conditions of consent orders and consent decrees were often the source of extensive negotiations between EPA and potential settlors. The recent issuance of model consent orders and consent decrees by EPA has severely hindered the opportunity for meaningful negotiations.[249] Experience to date with these model documents suggests that staff level negotiators will be unwilling to vary from most of their provisions.

### 5.4 Major Settlement Issues

While no two CERCLA settlement negotiations involve precisely the same issues, there are several issues that commonly arise. The frequency with which these issues occur is reflected in the fact that they are the subject of discussion in both section 122 and EPA guidance documents.

#### 5.4.1 Mixed Funding and Carve Outs

As discussed earlier, at every multiparty CERCLA site there are parties that wish to settle with EPA and those that cannot or do not. At the same time, there may be a vast quantity of wastes at the site that came from defunct or bankrupt companies. Wastes from these defunct or bankrupt companies have traditionally been referred to as a site's "orphan share." Thus, at most sites, those parties that settle will ordinarily account for less than 100 percent of the volume of hazardous substances at the site. In fact, it is not uncommon for many settlements to involve settlors whose cumulative volume of waste represents less than 50 percent of that present at the site.

Settlors in the situations described above are quite naturally interested in avoiding 100 percent of the liability for site remediation and EPA's past response costs. Consequently, they have often sought EPA's payment for a portion (usually the orphan share) of these costs through use of Superfund monies—a process referred to as "mixed funding." At the same time, these settlors will seek to have EPA "carve out" part of its remedial action or costs from their liability and proceed against the non-settlors for the portion "carved out."

Section 122(b)(1) gives EPA the authority to enter into mixed funding agreements whereby EPA agrees to use the Superfund to reimburse settlors a portion of the costs they incur in performing an agreed-upon remedial action. EPA's guidance on mixed funding acknowledges that Congress recognized the need to consider settlements for less than 100 percent and to use Superfund monies for shares of parties "unknown, insolvent, similarly unavailable, or [which have] refuse[d] to settle." The guidance, which encourages the use of mixed funding in appropriate situations, lists the following factors

---

[248]42 U.S.C. § 9622(h)(1).

[249]*See* United States Environmental Protection Agency, *Model Administrative Order on Consent for CERCLA Remedial Investigation/Feasibility Study*, OSWER Directive No. 9835.3-1A (January 30, 1990); United States Environmental Protection Agency, Superfund Program, *Model CERCLA RD/RA Consent Decree*, 56 *Fed. Reg.* 30,996-31,012 (July 8, 1991).

as considerations in evaluating mixed funding settlements: (1) the strength of the liability case against both nonsettlors and settlors, (2) those options the government may have if a settlement is not reached, (3) the size of the share to be covered by the Superfund, and (4) the good faith of the settlors.[250] The guidance identifies the best situations for mixed funding as those where the settlors offer a substantial portion of remediation costs and where the government has a strong case against financially viable nonsettlors.

EPA's use of mixed funding has been uneven. Despite explicit authority in both CERCLA and EPA's guidance documents, mixed funding has been unavailable to deal with the problems of "orphan shares" and nonsettlors at many sites. However, EPA has been more receptive to carving out a portion of its costs for the remedial action for nonsettling parties to absorb.

### 5.4.2 *De Minimis* Settlements

At most multiparty sites there are a large number of companies who disposed of relatively small quantities of hazardous substances. Section 122(g) addresses these so-called "*de minimis*" parties. It encourages EPA to "as promptly as possible" reach a final settlement with such parties and identifies the following types of situations in which a *de minimis* settlement is appropriate:

1.  Situations where both the amount and toxicity of hazardous substances contributed by a party are minimal compared with other hazardous substances at the facility; or

2.  Situations where a party is the owner of the property where the facility is located but did not conduct or permit the generation, handling or disposal of hazardous substances at the facility; contribute to the release or threatened release from the facility; or acquire the facility with knowledge that it had been used to store, handle or dispose of hazardous substances.[251]

Aside from the opportunity of an early settlement, *de minimis* parties are ordinarily offered a settlement with *real finality*. In return for what is known as a "premium payment," EPA will ordinarily provide *de minimis* parties a complete covenant not to sue, which is revocable only if subsequent information reveals that the party's waste contribution was not truly *de minimis*. This guarantee means that should future problems develop at a site, these *de minimis* parties will not be required to participate in or fund future remediation efforts.

### 5.4.3 Covenants Not To Sue and Reopeners

For most settlors, a settlement with EPA that entails subsequent remediation actions does not represent finality. Because there is great uncertainty at most sites whether the remedial action selected will prove effective, neither CERCLA nor EPA guidance provides a complete release from future liability.

CERCLA section 122(f) provides that settlements may contain a covenant not to sue. There is no provision for the use of a release. In considering whether to issue a

---

[250]*See* 53 Fed. Reg. 8,279 (1988).
[251]42 U.S.C. § 9622(g)(1).

covenant not to sue, EPA is to consider: whether such a covenant is in the public interest, whether it would expedite a response action, whether the settlor is in compliance with the consent decree, and whether the response action has been approved by EPA.

In most cases, however, EPA's covenant not to sue is illusory. CERCLA provides that, except in certain designated instances, a covenant not to sue must be accompanied by an additional provision—known as a "reopener"—which allows EPA to sue for future liability resulting from *unknown conditions*.[252] EPA guidance on covenants not to sue also requires that the reopener provision permit a subsequent suit in situations where *additional information* reveals that the remedy is "no longer protective of public health or the environment." This reopener is required in all settlements except those involving:

1. *De minimis* parties;
2. "Extraordinary circumstances" where reasonable assurances exist that public health and the environment will be protected from future releases and where certain enumerated factors (e.g., nature of risks, toxicity, strength of evidence, ability to pay, litigation risks, etc.) are considered; and
3. Portions of a remedial action that entail:
    a. The offsite transport of hazardous substances to RCRA-approved disposal facilities where EPA has required offsite disposal after rejecting an alternative permitting on-site or other disposal; or
    b. The treatment of hazardous substances "so as to destroy, eliminate, or permanently immobilize the hazardous constituents of such substances" such that they no longer present a significant threat.[253]

### 5.4.4 Stipulated Penalties

CERCLA settlements, whether consent orders or consent decrees, routinely contain provisions for stipulated penalties in the event that a settlor fails to meet certain designated milestone events. The use and amount of these penalties are the subjects of negotiation, but generally EPA seeks to extract a penalty amount deemed sufficient to motivate the settlor to meet the deadline set by the agreement.

CERCLA section 121(e)(2) provides for the use of stipulated penalties in consent decrees. EPA's guidance on the use of stipulated penalties in consent decrees has interpreted this provision to require that all consent decrees involving a remedial action contain provisions for stipulated penalties.[254] It is EPA's policy to tie stipulated penalties to compliance schedules, performance standards, and reporting requirements. However, stipulated penalties do not arise if delay is occasioned by a *force majeure* event or, in some situations, where an interim deadline is missed but a final deadline is met.

---

[252]42 U.S.C. § 9622(f)(6).
[253]*Id.*
[254]United States Environmental Protection Agency, Office of Enforcement and Compliance Monitoring, *Guidance on the Use of Stipulated Penalties In Hazardous Waste Consent Decrees* (1987).

One of the policy's more disturbing features to settlors is EPA's insistence that stipulated penalties continue to accrue during any delay caused by a dispute under the consent decree. Where the dispute is resolved in EPA's favor, a settlor forfeits the accrued amount. Thus, the policy effectively hinders settling parties from effectively using a consent decree's dispute provisions.

## 6.0 RELEASE REPORTING REQUIREMENTS

CERCLA sections 102 and 103 provide the basis for requiring certain parties to give notice of a release of hazardous substances. Section 103(a) requires that any person in charge of a vessel or facility notify the National Response Center, (*see* 33 U.S.C. § 1251 *et seq.*), as soon as that person has knowledge of any "release" from the vessel or facility of a hazardous substance *equal to or greater than the reportable quantity for that substance.* As indicated in section 2.2, a "release" is defined broadly to include the escape of a hazardous substance into the "environment."[255]

The crux of CERCLA's reporting requirements is the concept of "reportable quantities." Simply stated, a reportable quantity is the amount of a substance which must be reported if released. Reportable quantities for hazardous substances are established by EPA pursuant to section 102. Where EPA has not indicated a listed substance's reportable quantity, section 102 further specifies that the quantity shall be one pound, unless the hazardous substance has a reportable quantity under the Clean Water Act, in which case the latter will be used.

EPA has promulgated regulations listing the various hazardous substances regulated under CERCLA and specifying their reportable quantities.[256] These regulations should be consulted in detail when determining whether a release must be reported because the reportable quantities for hazardous substances vary significantly. The regulations also provide detailed guidance on assorted issues that arise in determining whether a report must be filed, including the calculations for a reportable release. As a general rule, to ascertain whether a substance's release has equalled or exceeded its reportable quantity, the person in charge of the facility or vessel must calculate the total amount released during any twenty-four-hour period. If the total amount equals or exceeds the reportable quantity during that twenty-four-hour period, it must be reported.[257]

Failure to report a release involving a reportable quantity of a hazardous substance can result in both civil and criminal penalties. The maximum criminal penalty is three years in prison for a first conviction and five years for a subsequent conviction.[258] Fines may also be imposed. Civil penalties equal to $25,000 per day for failure to report may be assessed.[259]

Since there are more listed hazardous substances under CERCLA than under other environmental laws, it is important that parties do not assume a report need not be filed merely because it is not required under another statute.

---

[255]*See supra* section 2.4 for definition of "environment."
[256]40 C.F.R. § 302.
[257]40 C.F.R. § 302.5(b).
[258]42 U.S.C. § 9603(b).
[259]42 U.S.C. § 9609(b),(c).

Notwithstanding the above discussion, certain *types* of releases are exempted from CERCLA's notice requirements, irrespective of the quantity released. Pursuant to CERCLA section 103(a), the following types of releases need not be reported:

1. Releases resulting from application, handling, or storage of pesticides registered under the Federal Insecticide, Fungicide, and Rodenticide Act;[260]
2. Federally permitted releases;[261]
3. Releases regulated under subtitle C of RCRA which have been or need not be reported pursuant to RCRA;[262] and
4. Continuous releases from a facility for which notification has been given previously.[263]

## 7.0 FEDERAL FACILITIES

As with the private sector, years of inattention to the environmental harm posed by certain activities have caused many federal facilities serious environmental problems. The greatest problems exist for facilities associated with the massive military-industrial complex—Department of Energy and Department of Defense facilities—which was constructed in response to World War II and the Cold War. Past disposal practices contributing to pollution at these facilities include the use of unlined pits, holding ponds, drying beds, landfills, discharge to the ground, and on-site burning of wastes. The estimated costs of cleanup are staggering. Citizens, states, and environmental groups have expressed outrage at the conditions of many of these facilities and have sought to inject themselves in determining appropriate cleanups.

CERCLA contains broad waivers of sovereign immunity, which permit individuals and states to bring cost recovery actions against federal facilities,[264] and to bring "citizen suits" for the facilities' compliance with the statute.[265] The authority of citizens and states to bring action against these facilities has been a spur toward their cleanup.

The 1986 SARA amendments reflected Congress' great concern for federal facilities by creating an entire section—section 120—devoted to their cleanup. Section 120(a) provides for federal facility compliance, both substantively and procedurally, to the same extent as any private entity.[266] This compliance includes requirements related to listing on the NPL (e.g., site assessments, hazardous ranking, and evaluation procedures).

Section 120 also addresses hazardous waste cleanup at federal facilities and establishes requirements that are unique to federal facilities. These requirements include the creation of a Federal Agency Hazardous Waste Compliance Docket listing facilities, which manage hazardous waste or have potential hazardous waste problems. This list is then used to provide timetables for addressing the problems at each facility. A preliminary assessment and, as needed, site inspection are required within 18 months of

---

[260]42 U.S.C. § 9603(e).
[261]42 U.S.C. § 9603(a).
[262]42 U.S.C. § 9603(f)(1).
[263]42 U.S.C. § 9603(f)(2).
[264]42 U.S.C. § 9620(a).
[265]42 U.S.C. § 9659(a).
[266]42 U.S.C. § 9620(a).

a facility being listed. Subsequently, the facility is scored under the hazardous ranking system to determine whether it should be placed on the NPL. If listed on the NPL, the facility must begin a remedial investigation/feasibility study (RI/FS) within six months of its NPL listing. While performing the RI/FS, consultation with EPA and the state must occur. Within 180 days of EPA's review of the RI/FS, an interagency agreement must be entered into with EPA for the performance of the selected remedy.[267]

In response to the various hazardous waste problems at their facilities, both the Departments of Defense (DOD) and Energy (DOE) have formulated extensive long-term cleanup plans. DOD's plan—the Defense Environmental Restoration Program—is funded by monies set aside by Congress under the Defense Environmental Restoration Account (DERA). The 1984 Defense Appropriations Act created DERA as a set-aside fund to pay for DOD response actions under CERCLA and the NCP. The use of DERA funds is limited to addressing past disposal problems, not correcting currently useable facilities.

## 8.0 SUPERFUND'S FUTURE

Throughout its history many aspects of Superfund have been controversial. Nearly everyone finds fault with at least part of it. Few find all of its features acceptable. For this reason, future modifications to Superfund can be expected. It is also why there is constant pressure on EPA to develop policies that ameliorate some of Superfund's most counterproductive features.

The most serious effort at Superfund reform occurred in 1994 during the 103d Congress when the "Superfund Reform Act of 1994"[268] was debated. This bill addressed several aspects of Superfund that many feel are the most troubling. Included among its provisions were the following:

- Implicit elimination of joint and several liability by provisions making it possible for PRP's to achieve final settlements with EPA based upon their proportionate share of responsibility. EPA would have had responsibility for covering any "orphan shares" from nonviable (e.g., bankrupt) parties and for pursuing nonsettling PRPs for their share of responsibility.
- Creation of a formal allocation structure with a neutral allocator responsible for assigning liability shares to PRPs, based on a number of factors. These factors would have included volume, toxicity, and the degree of care taken in handling the hazardous substances.
- Elimination of any liability for parties contributing extremely small amounts of hazardous substances to a site. These so-called *de micromis* parties would have no liability to EPA or other PRPs. EPA would have been required to offer other small volume contributors not qualifying for *de micromis* treatment ("*de minimis*" PRPs) early settlements based on their volume contribution and a settlement premium.

---

[267]42 U.S.C. § 9620(c),(d),(e).
[268]*See* S. 1834, 103d Cong., 2d Sess. (1994) *and* H.R. 4916, 103d Cong., 2d Sess. (1994).

- Establishment of a 10-percent overall cleanup liability ceiling for generators and transporters of municipal wastes.
- Modification of CERCLA's stringent cleanup standards. EPA would have been required to develop national cleanup standards and generic remedies. Future land use was to be considered in setting these cleanup standards. The current remedy preference for treating waste would have been limited to the most contaminated parts of a site ("hot spots"). Containment without extensive treatment was to be a more accepted remedy.
- Creation of an environmental insurance resolution fund to settle insurance claims.
- Establishment of more formal procedures designed to increase community involvement.

During the 104th Congress (1995-1996) Superfund reform once again was on the agenda. While many of the features of the 1994 legislation were considered, consensus for how to affect comprehensive modification to Superfund failed to emerge as many in industry demanded a provision limiting Superfund's retroactive liability. Actual legislative change was limited to a provision extending liability protection to lenders. It is anticipated that Superfund reform will be reconsidered during the 105th congress. Many of the above provisions may resurface.

While Congress has found it difficult to make legislative change, EPA, through a series of administrative reforms has sought to limit some of the most frustrating effects of Superfund. These reforms have included: modifying enforcement procedures to make it easier for *de minimis* PRPs to settle earlier and for PRPs to obtain information on other PRPs at a site; increasing community involvement by providing more information and funding to local groups; and, establishing guidance for ensuring that cleanups are more cost-effective by addressing actual risks and that sites or portions of sites are more quickly removed from the National Priority List.[269] Moreover, because industry has been reluctant to redevelop contaminated sites due to the potential of owner/operator liability, EPA has developed a so-called "Brownfields Initiative." In addition to a number of pilot projects, this initiative has included entering into liability limiting agreements with prospective purchasers of contaminated properties[270] and guidance limiting the liability of lenders in certain instances.[271]

---

[269] *See* 60 Fed. Reg. 55466 (Nov. 1, 1995) (Partial Delisting Policy).
[270] 60 Fed. Reg. 34792 (July 3, 1995).
[271] 60 Fed. Reg. 63517 (Dec. 11, 1995)

# CHAPTER 14

# EMERGENCY PLANNING AND COMMUNITY RIGHT-TO-KNOW ACT

Wayne T. Halbleib
Counsel
Mays & Valentine, L.L.P.
Richmond, Virginia

## 1.0 OVERVIEW

On October 17, 1986, the Superfund Amendments and Reauthorization Act of 1986 (SARA) was signed into law. One part of the SARA legislation is Title III, otherwise known as the Emergency Planning and Community Right-To-Know Act of 1986 (EPCRA). EPCRA requires states to establish a process for developing local chemical emergency preparedness programs and to receive and disseminate information on hazardous chemicals present at facilities within local communities.

EPCRA has four major components: (1) emergency planning (Sections 301-303); (2) emergency release notification (Section 304); community right-to-know reporting (Sections 311-312); and toxic chemical release inventory reporting (Section 313). Each component has its own facility and chemical substance reporting requirements. The information submitted by facilities under these four reporting requirements allows States and local communities to develop a broad perspective of chemical hazards for the entire community as well as for individual facilities.

## 2.0 EMERGENCY PLANNING

### 2.1 Overview

Section 301 of EPCRA requires the governor of each state to designate a State Emergency Response Commission (SERC). The SERC is required to designate emergency planning districts within each state to facilitate the preparation and implementation of the emergency plans required under Section 303. In addition, Section 301 requires the SERC to appoint a local emergency planning committee (LEPC) in each of those districts.[1]

### 2.2 Covered Facilities and Substances

Section 302 of EPCRA requires any facility that produces, uses or stores any of the substances on the United States Environmental Protection Agency's (EPA's) List of Extremely Hazardous Substances in quantities equal to or greater than the threshold planning quantity established for each substance to notify the SERC.[2] A list of the

---

[1]*See*, 42 U.S.C.A. § 11001(a)-(c).
[2]See 42 U.S.C.A. § 11002(b)-(c); 40 C.F.R. § 355.30.

extremely hazardous substances and their threshold planning quantities is contained in the EPA's *Title III List of Lists*.[3]

If a facility is covered by Section 302, the owner or operator of the facility should have notified the SERC by May 17, 1987, that the facility is subject to the emergency planning requirements. After May 17, 1987, the owner or operator must notify the SERC and the LEPC, within 60 days, if an extremely hazardous substance (EHS) becomes present at the facility in a quantity that equals or exceeds the established threshold planning quantity (TPQ).[4]

A covered facility must designate a facility representative who will participate in the local emergency planning process as a facility emergency response coordinator. In addition, the facility owner or operator must submit additional information to the LEPC upon request and notify the LEPC of any changes occurring at the facility that may be relevant to emergency planning (e.g., change in person designated as facility emergency response coordinator; any material change in the inventory of EHSs maintained by the facility).[5]

EHSs that are solids are subject to two threshold planning quantities as shown on the *Title III List of Lists* (i.e., 500/10,000 pounds). The lower quantity applies only if the solid exists in powdered form and has a particle size less than 100 microns; or is handled in solution or in molten form; or meets the criteria for a National Fire Protection Association (NFPA) rating of 2, 3, or 4 for reactivity. If the solid does not meet any of the above-mentioned criteria, it is subject to the upper (10,000 pound) threshold planning quantity.[6]

### 2.3 Comprehensive Emergency Response Plans

Each LEPC is responsible for reviewing the information submitted by facilities covered by the emergency planning requirements and developing a plan to respond to local hazardous chemical emergency releases.[7] The local emergency response plan must:[8]

1.  Identify all the facilities subject to the emergency planning requirements within the emergency planning district;
2.  Identify all routes within the emergency planning district used to transport extremely hazardous substances;
3.  Identify all risk-related facilities near covered facilities, such as natural gas facilities, power stations/high transmission towers, or schools or hospitals, within the emergency planning district;
4.  Describe the methods and procedures that will be followed by emergency response personnel to respond to a chemical release within the emergency planning district;

---

[3]See EPA's *Title III List of Lists*, Document No. EPA 740-R-95-001 or Appendix A or Appendix B to 40 C.F.R. Part 355 for a list of the extremely hazardous substances.
[4]See 42 U.S.C.A. § 11002(c); 40 C.F.R. § 355.30(b).
[5]See 42 U.S.C.A. § 11003(d); 40 C.F.R. § 355.30(c) and (d).
[6]See 40 C.F.R. § 355.30(e)(2)(i).
[7]See 42 U.S.C.A. § 11003.
[8]See 42 U.S.C.A. § 11003(c).

5.  Designate the community emergency response coordinator and identify all the facility emergency response coordinators within the emergency planning district;

6.  Describe the emergency notification procedures to be used to notify the public of a chemical release and the evacuation plans to be implemented in the event a chemical emergency requires an evacuation;

7.  Specify the methods for determining whether a chemical release has occurred and the probable affected area and population;

8.  List all community and facility emergency equipment or facilities available and their location as well as the persons responsible for them; and

9.  Describe the training program used to train emergency response personnel for chemical emergencies and list a schedule for exercising the emergency response plan within the emergency planning district.

Although the primary responsibility for emergency planning rests with the LEPC, the SERC must review each local chemical emergency response plan. The SERC must review each plan to determine whether all required plan elements have been included. In addition, the SERC's review will include recommendations to the LEPC on revisions to the plan that may be necessary to ensure coordination of the plan with the emergency response plans of other emergency planning districts.[9]

## 3.0 EMERGENCY RELEASE NOTIFICATION

### 3.1 Covered Releases

Under Section 304 of EPCRA, the owner or operator of a facility that either produces, uses or stores a hazardous chemical must immediately notify the SERC and the LEPC if there is a release of a listed hazardous substance that is not federally permitted and ,that exceeds the reportable quantity (RQ) established for that substance and results in exposure to persons off-site.[10] Substances subject to this notification requirement include substances on the EPA's List of EHSs and hazardous substances subject to the emergency notification requirements under Section 103(a) of the Comprehensive Environmental Response, Compensation and Liability Act of 1980 (CERCLA).[11]

### 3.2 Notification Requirements

The initial notification of a release can be made by telephone, radio, or in person. The owner or operator of a covered facility must immediately notify the community emergency coordinator for the LEPC of any area likely to be affected by the release and the SERC of any state likely to be affected by the release.[12] In addition, when there is a reportable release of a CERCLA listed hazardous substance, notification must be given

---

[9]See 42 U.S.C.A. § 11003(e).
[10]See 40 C.F.R. § 355.40(a).
[11]*Ibid.*
[12]See 40 C.F.R. § 355.40(b).

to the National Response Center (NRC) in Washington, D.C. at 1-800-424-8802.[13] The notifications made under EPCRA are in addition to the notifications normally made to local emergency response or fire personnel.

### 3.3 Contents of Notice

The emergency notification must include, to the extent known at the time of the release, the following information:[14]

1. Name of the chemical substance involved;
2. Indication of whether it is an extremely hazardous substance;
3. Estimate of the amount released into the environment;
4. Time and duration of the release;
5. Environmental media into which the release occurred;
6. Known or anticipated acute or chronic health risks associated with the release and advice regarding medical attention necessary for exposed individuals;
7. Proper precautions to be taken as a result of the release, including evacuation; and
8. Name and telephone number of a person at the facility to be contacted for further information.

### 3.4 Written Follow-up Emergency Notice

Section 304 further requires that the owner or operator of a covered facility provide a written follow-up emergency notice as soon as possible after the release.[15] The notice must be sent to the appropriate SERC(s) and the appropriate LEPC(s). The follow-up notice must include the following information:[16]

1. An update of the information included in the initial release notification;
2. Information on actions taken to respond to and contain the release;
3. Any known or anticipated acute or chronic health risks associated with the release; and
4. Where appropriate, advice regarding medical attention for exposed individuals.

The written follow-up notice must be sent to the appropriate SERC(s) and the appropriate LEPC(s).

### 3.5 Transportation-Related Releases

The owner or operator of a facility from which there is a transportation-related release can satisfy the emergency release notification requirements under Section 304 by providing the above-mentioned information required during the initial notification to the 911 operator, or in the absence of a 911 emergency telephone, providing such

---

[13]See 40 C.F.R. § 302.6(a).
[14]See 40 C.F.R. § 355.40(b)(2).
[15]See 42 U.S.C.A. § 11004(c); 40 C.F.R. § 355.40(b)(3).
[16]*Ibid.*

information to the operator.[17] A "transportation-related release" includes a release during transportation, or storage incident to transportation if the stored substance is moving under active shipping papers and has not reached the ultimate consignee.[18]

### 3.6 Continuous Release Reporting

Reporting requirements for "continuous" releases of hazardous substances under CERCLA were issued by the EPA on July 24, 1990. Under the final rule, which became effective on September 24, 1990, releases that qualify as continuous and that are "stable in quantity and rate" are subject to reduced reporting under CERCLA § 103(f)(2).[19]

The final rule defines "continuous" broadly to include a "release that occurs without interruption or abatement or that is routine, anticipated, and intermittent and incidental to normal operations or treatment processes." The definition of "stable in quantity and rate" includes a "release that is predictable and regular in amount and rate of emission."[20]

### 3.7 Continuous Release Notification

The new rule requires a minimum of one telephone call to the NRC under CERCLA § 103(a) and to the appropriate SERC(s) and LEPC(s) under EPCRA § 304. In addition, within 30 days of the initial telephone notification, an initial written notification must be made to the appropriate EPA Regional Office, the appropriate SERC(s), and the appropriate LEPC(s).

### 3.8 Initial Telephone Notification

To satisfy the initial telephone notification requirement, the person in charge of a facility or vessel must identify the release in the telephone call to the NRC, the appropriate SERC(s), and the appropriate LEPC(s) as a report under CERCLA § 103(f)(2) of a continuous release above the RQ.[21] The following information must be provided for each release:[22]

1. The name and location of the facility or vessel; and
2. The name(s) and identity(ies) of the hazardous substance(s) being released.

### 3.9 Initial Written Report

The initial written report must include the following information:[23]

1. The name of the facility or vessel; the location, including the longitude and latitude; the case number assigned by the NRC or the EPA; the Dun & Bradstreet number of the facility, if available; the port of registration of the vessel; the name and telephone number of the person in charge of the facility or vessel.

---

[17]See 42 U.S.C.A. § 11004(b)(1); 40 C.F.R. § 355.40(b)(4)(ii).
[18]See 40 C.F.R. § 355.40(b)(4)(ii).
[19]See 55 Fed.Reg. 30185 (July 24, 1990); 40 C.F.R. § 302.8.
[20]See 40 C.F.R. § 302.8(b).
[21]See 40 C.F.R. § 302.8(d)(3).
[22]See 40 C.F.R. § 302.8(d)(3)(i)-(ii).
[23]See 40 C.F.R. § 302.8(e)(1).

2.  The population density within a one-mile radius of the facility or vessel, described in terms of the following ranges: 0-50 persons; 51-100 persons; 101-500 persons; 501-1,000 persons; more than 1,000 persons.

3.  The identity and location of sensitive populations and ecosystems within a one-mile radius of the facility or vessel (e.g., elementary schools, hospitals, retirement communities, or wetlands).

4.  The name/identity of the hazardous substance; the Chemical Abstracts Service (CAS) Registry Number for the substance, if available. If the substance being released is a mixture, the components of the mixture and their approximate concentrations and quantities by weight.

5.  The upper and lower bounds of the normal range of the release (in pounds or kilograms) over the previous year.

6.  The source(s) of the release (e.g., valves, pump seals, storage tank vents, stacks). If the source is a stack, the stack height (in feet or meters).

7.  The frequency of the release and the fraction of the release from each release source and the specific period over which it occurs.

8.  A brief statement describing the basis for stating that the release is continuous and stable in quantity and rate.

9.  An estimate of the total annual amount of the hazardous substance that was released in the previous year (in pounds or kilograms).

10. The environmental media affected by the release:
    a.  If surface water, the name of the surface water body.
    b.  If a stream, the stream order or average flowrate (in cubic feet/second) and designated use.
    c.  If a lake, the surface area (in acres) and average depth (in feet or meters).
    d.  If on or under ground, the location of public water supply wells within two miles.

11. A signed statement that the hazardous substance release(s) described is(are) continuous and stable in quantity and rate and that all reported information is accurate and current to the best knowledge of the person in charge.

**3.10 Follow-up Notification**

Within 30 days of the first anniversary date of the initial written notification, the person in charge must evaluate the reported releases and submit a one-time follow-up report to the appropriate EPA Regional Office. The purpose of this report is to verify or update the information submitted in the initial written report.[24]

**3.11 Annual Evaluation of Continuous Releases**

After the submission of the follow-up report, the person in charge must reevaluate annually each reported hazardous substance release within 30 days of the anniversary date of the initial written notification to determine whether there have been changes in

---

[24]See 40 C.F.R. § 302.8(f).

the release that require modification of the information previously submitted.[25] Each annual evaluation must be documented, but no annual report or notification of the annual evaluation is required. Notification subsequent to the written follow-up report must be made to the appropriate EPA Regional Office only if there is a change in any of the information submitted previously.[26]

### 3.12 Change in the Composition or Source of the Release

If there is a change in the composition or source(s) of the release, the release is considered a "new" release. To qualify a "new" release for reduced reporting under CERCLA § 103(f)(2), both the initial telephone notification and the initial written notification must be made. The initial telephone notification should be made as soon as there is a sufficient basis for asserting that the "new" release is continuous and stable in quantity and rate.[27]

### 3.13 Notification of a Statistically Significant Increase

A "statistically significant increase" must be reported immediately by telephone to the NRC, the appropriate SERC(s) and the appropriate LEPC(s). A statistically significant increase in a release is defined as "an increase in the quantity of the hazardous substance released above the upper bound of the reported normal range of the release."[28] The normal range is defined to include all releases of a hazardous substance reported or occurring during any 24-hour period under normal operating conditions during the previous year.[29]

Because such a release is considered episodic, it must be reported under CERCLA § 103(a) and EPCRA § 304(b). The release must be identified by the person in charge as a statistically significant increase in a continuous release. The written follow-up emergency notice required under § 304 of EPCRA must also be made to the appropriate SERC(s) and LEPC(s) after the initial telephone notification of a statistically significant increase.[30]

### 3.14 Changes in Other Reported Information

If there is a change in any information submitted in the initial written notification or the follow-up notification other than a change in the source, composition, or quantity of the release, the person in charge of the facility or vessel must provide written notification of the change to the appropriate EPA Regional Office within 30 days of determining that the information submitted previously is no longer valid.[31]

---

[25]See 40 C.F.R. § 302.8(i).
[26]See 40 C.F.R. § 302.8(g).
[27]See 40 C.F.R. § 302.8(g)(1).
[28]See 40 C.F.R. § 302.8(b).
[29]Ibid.
[30]See 40 C.F.R. § 355.40(b).
[31]See 40 C.F.R. § 302.8(g)(3).

### 3.15 Use of the EPCRA Section 313 Form

In lieu of an initial written report or a follow-up report on a continuous release, owners or operators of facilities subject to the EPCRA Section 313 reporting requirements can submit to the appropriate EPA Regional Office, a copy of the relevant Toxic Chemical Release Inventory Reporting Form submitted to EPA the previous July 1st. If this option is selected, however, facility owners or operators must submit the following additional information:[32]

1. The population density within a one-mile radius of the facility or vessel, described in terms of the following ranges: 0-50 persons; 51-100 persons; 101-500 persons; 501-1,000 persons; more than 1,000 persons;

2. The identity and location of sensitive populations and ecosystems within a one-mile radius of the facility or vessel (e.g., elementary schools, hospitals, retirement communities, or wetlands);

3. The upper and lower bounds of the normal range of the release (in pounds or kilograms) over the previous year;

4. The frequency of the release and the fraction of the release from each release source and the specific period over which it occurs;

5. A brief statement describing the basis for stating that the release is continuous and stable in quantity and rate; and

6. A signed statement that the hazardous substance release(s) is(are) continuous and stable in quantity and rate and that all reported information is accurate and current to the best knowledge of the person in charge.

The person in charge can rely on recent release data, engineering estimates, the operating history of the facility or vessel, or other relevant information, including best professional judgment, to support notification. All supporting documents, materials, and other information shall be kept on file at the facility, or in the case of a vessel, at an office within the United States in either a port of call, a place of regular berthing, or the headquarters of the business operating the vessel. Supporting materials must be kept on file for one year. These materials must be made available to the EPA upon request.[33]

### 4.0 COMMUNITY RIGHT-TO-KNOW REPORTING

There are two community right-to-know reporting requirements contained within Sections 311 and 312 of EPCRA. Facilities covered under Section 311 are covered also under Section 312.

### 4.1 MSDS/List of Hazardous Chemicals

#### 4.1.1 Overview

Section 311 requires the owner/operator of a facility that must prepare or have available material safety data sheets (MSDSs) under the Occupational Safety and Health Administration's (OSHA's) Hazard Communication Standard regulations to submit either copies of its MSDSs or a list of hazardous chemicals to the SERC, the LEPC and

---

[32]See 40 C.F.R. § 302.8(j).
[33]See 40 C.F.R. § 302.8(k).

the local fire department (LFD) with jurisdiction over the facility.[34] Most SERCs either require or encourage owners or operators of covered facilities to submit a "list" of hazardous chemicals grouped by health and physical hazard categories as defined by EPA in lieu of submitting the MSDS on each hazardous chemical.

### 4.1.2 Submission of a List of Hazardous Chemicals

If the facility owner or operator elects to submit a list of hazardous chemicals, the list must include the chemical or common name of each substance and it must identify the applicable hazard categories. The hazard categories are as follows:

1. *Immediate (acute) health hazard* (which includes the OSHA health hazard categories: "highly toxic," "toxic," "corrosive," "irritant," and "sensitizer");
2. *Delayed (chronic) health hazard* (which includes the OSHA-defined "carcinogen");
3. *Fire hazard* (which includes the OSHA physical hazard categories: "combustible liquid," "flammable," "oxidizer," and "pyrophoric");
4. *Sudden release of pressure hazard* (which includes the OSHA physical hazard categories: "compressed gas," and "explosive"); and
5. *Reactive hazard* (which includes the OSHA physical hazard categories: "organic peroxide," "unstable reactive," and "water reactive").[35]

If the facility elects to submit a list, it must submit a copy of the MSDS for any chemical on the list upon the request of the SERC or the LEPC within 30 days of the receipt of such request.[36] EPA has established minimum threshold quantities for reporting hazardous chemicals present at a facility. The threshold levels are as follows:

1. "Hazardous chemicals" present in amounts equal to or greater than 10,000 pounds; and
2. "Extremely hazardous substances" present in amounts equal to or greater than 500 pounds or the threshold planning quantity established for the substance, whichever is lower.

### 4.1.3 Reporting Requirements

The owners or operators of facilities subject to the reporting requirements under Section 311 had until October 17, 1990 to submit the required information. The owners or operators of new facilities (i.e., those opening after October 17, 1990), that are covered by the OSHA regulations, must submit MSDSs or a list of MSDS chemicals within three months after they first become subject to the OSHA regulations.[37]

The owner or operator of a covered facility must provide within three months either MSDSs or a revised list of MSDS chemicals when new hazardous chemicals become present at a facility in quantities at or above the established threshold levels

---

[34]See *also*, 40 C.F.R. § 370.21.
[35]See 40 C.F.R. § 370.2.
[36]See 40 C.F.R. § 370.21(d).
[37]See 55 *Fed. Reg.* 30646 (July 26, 1990); 40 C.F.R § 370.20(b)(1).

after the deadline.[38] The owner or operator of a covered facility must provide a revised MSDS within three months after discovery of significant new information concerning the hazardous chemical.[39]

### 4.1.4 Mixture Reporting

The vast majority of chemicals subject to reporting under Section 311 will be mixtures. The owner or operator of a covered facility has two options with respect to reporting hazardous mixtures. The first option is to provide the required information on the mixture itself. The second option is to provide the required information on each hazardous chemical component in the mixture.[40]

The above-mentioned threshold levels apply to the *total quantity* of either the hazardous mixture, or each hazardous component that is present at the facility at any time during the preceding calendar year. A hazardous component of a mixture which is present in an amount greater than 1% of the mixture (or 0.1% if carcinogenic) must be included when calculating the total quantity of the chemical subject to reporting.

The regulations require the owner or operator of a covered facility to *aggregate* (i.e., total) each extremely hazardous substance, whether it is present as a mixture component, or in its pure form, to determine whether the reporting threshold for an extremely hazardous substance has been met.[41] Aggregation of hazardous chemicals that are not extremely hazardous substances present in mixtures and in their pure form is not required, but may be done if a facility is reporting all hazardous chemicals in mixtures by component.

Once the determination is made that an extremely hazardous substance must be reported, the owner or operator of the facility has the option of reporting the extremely hazardous substance separately, as a component of one or several different mixtures, or reporting the mixture(s) as a whole.[42]

## 4.2 Tier One/Tier Two Reporting

### 4.2.1 Overview

Section 312 requires the owner or operator of a covered facility to submit an emergency and hazardous chemical inventory form to the SERC, the LEPC, and the LFD. The hazardous chemicals covered by Section 312 are the same chemicals for which facilities are required to submit MSDSs or a list of MSDS chemicals under Section 311. In addition, the threshold levels established for reporting under Section 312 are the same as those established for reporting under Section 311.[43]

---

[38]See 40 C.F.R. § 370.21(c)(2).
[39]See 40 C.F.R. § 370.21(c)(1).
[40]See 40 C.F.R. § 370.28(a).
[41]See 55 *Fed. Reg.* 30646 (July 26, 1990); 40 C.F.R § 370.28(c)(1).
[42]See 40 C.F.R. § 370.28(c)(2).
[43]See 40 C.F.R. § 370.20(b).

**4.2.2 Reporting Requirements**

The inventory form incorporates a two-tier approach. Under Tier One, the owner or operator of a covered facility must submit for each health and physical hazard category the following aggregate information:

1. An estimate (in ranges) of the maximum amount of hazardous chemicals for each category present at the facility at any time during the preceding calendar year;
2. An estimate (in ranges) of the average daily amount of hazardous chemicals in each category; and
3. The general location of hazardous chemicals in each category.

Tier One information must be submitted on or before March 1st of the first year after a covered facility becomes subject to the reporting. The owner or operator of a covered facility is required to submit the Tier One information every year on or before March 1st.[44]

The public may also request additional information on specific facilities from the SERC or the LEPC. In addition, upon the request of the SERC, the LEPC or the LFD, the facility must provide for each substance covered by the request the following information:

1. The chemical name or the common name of the chemical and the CAS registry number as provided on the MSDS;
2. An indication of whether the hazardous chemical is an extremely hazardous substance;
3. An indication of whether the hazardous chemical is present at the facility in its pure state or in a mixture and whether it is a solid, liquid, or gas;
4. The applicable health and physical hazard categories;
5. An estimate (in ranges) of the maximum amount of the hazardous chemical present at the facility at any time during the preceding calendar year;
6. An estimate (in ranges) of the average daily amount of the hazardous chemical present at the facility during the preceding calendar year;
7. The number of days the hazardous chemical was found on-site at the facility;
8. A brief description of the manner of storage of the hazardous chemical at the facility;
9. A brief description of the precise location of the hazardous chemical at the facility; and
10. An indication of whether the owner or operator of the facility elects to withhold location information on a specific hazardous chemical from disclosure to the public.

This information is usually submitted as a Tier Two report. A covered facility may submit a Tier Two report to the SERC, the LEPC, and the LFD in lieu of the Tier One report. EPA published a uniform format for the inventory forms on July 26, 1990.[45]

---

[44]See 40 C.F.R. § 370.20(b)(2).
[45]See 55 *Fed. Reg.* 30632 (July 26, 1990); 40 C.F.R. §§ 370.40 and 370.41.

The Tier Two report is preferred by most SERCs, LEPCs, and LFDs because of the chemical specific information it contains.

If the owner or operator of a covered facility elects to withhold location information on a specific chemical from disclosure to the public, the facility owner or operator must complete a separate Tier Two Confidential Location Information Sheet. When the Tier Two submissions are made, the Tier Two Confidential Location Information Sheet(s) must be attached to the Tier Two Inventory Form. The information contained on the Tier Two Confidential Location Information Sheet(s) is not subject to public disclosure.

## 5.0 TOXIC CHEMICAL RELEASE INVENTORY REPORTING

### 5.1 Overview

Section 313 of EPCRA requires the owners or operators of certain manufacturing facilities to submit annual reports on the amounts of listed "toxic chemicals" their facilities release into the environment, either routinely or as a result of an accident. The owners or operators of facilities subject to this reporting requirement must report releases to the air, water, and land as well as discharges to publicly owned treatment works (POTWs) and transfers to off-site locations for proper treatment, storage, or disposal. The initial reports were required to be submitted to EPA and a designated state official on or before July 1, 1988, and annually thereafter on July 1st, reflecting releases during each preceding calendar year.

### 5.2 Reporting Requirements

The Section 313 reporting requirement applies to owners and operators of facilities that are in Standard Industrial Classification (SIC) Codes 20 through 39 (see Table 1 on the following page); that have the equivalent of ten or more full-time employees; and that manufacture, import, process or otherwise use a listed toxic chemical in excess of established threshold.[46]

A "full-time employee," for purposes of Section 313 reporting, is defined as 2,000 work hours per year. This definition is dependent *only* upon the number of hours worked by all employees at the facility during the calendar year and *not* the number of persons working. A facility must calculate the number of full-time employees by totaling the hours worked during the calendar year by all employees, including contract employees and sales and support staff working for the facility, and dividing that total by 2,000 hours.[47] If the total number of hours worked by *all* employees is 20,000 hours or more, the facility meets the ten-employee threshold.

Section 313 requires that reports be filed by the owners or operators of "facilities," which are defined as "all buildings, equipment, structures, and other stationary items which are located on a single site or on contiguous or adjacent sites and which are owned or operated by the same person." The SIC code system, however, classifies business "establishments," which are defined as "distinct and separate economic

---

[46]See 40 C.F.R. § 372.65(a) for a list of the chemicals subject to reporting under Section 313.

[47]See 40 C.F.R. § 372.3.

activities [that] are performed at a single physical location." Many facilities may include multiple establishments that have different primary SIC codes. Such facilities should calculate the *value* of the products produced or shipped from each establishment within the facility and determine whether the facility meets the SIC code criteria by using the following rules:

1.  If the total value of the products shipped from or produced at establishments with primary SIC codes between 20 and 39 is greater than 50 percent of the value of the entire facility's products and services, the entire facility meets the SIC code criteria; and

2.  If any one establishment with a primary SIC code between 20 and 39 produces or ships products whose value exceeds the value of products and services produced or shipped by any other establishment within the facility, the facility meets the SIC code criteria.[48]

The term "manufacture" means to produce, prepare, compound, or import a listed toxic chemical. The term also includes coincidental production of a toxic chemical (e.g., as a by-product or impurity) as a result of the manufacture, processing, use, or treatment of other chemical substances.[49] In the case of coincidental production of an "impurity" (i.e., a chemical that remains in the product that is distributed in commerce), the *de minimis* limitation applies. Thus, if a listed toxic chemical is present as an impurity in a concentration of 1 percent (0.1% if the listed toxic chemical meets the OSHA carcinogen standard) or less, the quantity of that chemical need not be considered for purposes of determining whether a reporting threshold has been met.[50]

The *de minimis* limitation does *not* apply to the coincidental production of a by-product (e.g., a chemical that is separated from a process stream and further processed or disposed).

Certain listed toxic chemicals may be manufactured as a result of wastewater treatment or other treatment processes. For example, neutralization of nitric acid wastewater with ammonia can result in the coincidental manufacture of ammonium nitrate solution as a by-product. If the ammonium nitrate solution is produced in a quantity that exceeds the manufacturing threshold, the facility must report the ammonium nitrate under the nitrate compounds category. The aqueous ammonia is considered to be otherwise used and 10 percent of the total aqueous ammonia would be counted toward the "otherwise use" threshold.

The term "import" is defined as causing the listed toxic chemical to be imported into the customs territory of the United States.[51] When a facility orders a listed toxic chemical (or a mixture containing the chemical) from a foreign supplier, then the facility has imported the chemical when that shipment arrives at the facility directly from a source outside of the United States.

---

[48]See 40 C.F.R. § 372.22.
[49]See 40 C.F.R. § 372.3.
[50]See 40 C.F.R. § 372.38.
[51]See 40 C.F.R. § 372.3.

## TABLE 1
## TRI INDUSTRY CATEGORIES

| SIC Code | Industry |
|---|---|
| 20 | Food and Kindred Products |
| 21 | Tobacco Products |
| 22 | Textile Mill Products |
| 23 | Apparel and Other Finished Products Made from Fabrics |
| 24 | Lumber and Wood Products |
| 25 | Furniture and Fixtures |
| 26 | Paper and Allied Products |
| 27 | Printing, Publishing and Allied Industries |
| 28 | Chemicals and Allied Products |
| 29 | Petroleum Refining and Related Industries |
| 30 | Rubber and Miscellaneous Plastic Products |
| 31 | Leather and Leather Products |
| 32 | Stone, Clay, Glass and Concrete Products |
| 33 | Primary Metal Industries |
| 34 | Fabricated Metal Products |
| 35 | Industrial and Commercial Machinery and Computer Equipment |
| 36 | Electronic and Other Electrical Equipment and Components |
| 37 | Transportation Equipment |
| 38 | Measuring, Analyzing, and Controlling Instruments; Photographic, Medical and Optical Goods; Watches and Clocks |
| 39 | Miscellaneous Manufacturing |

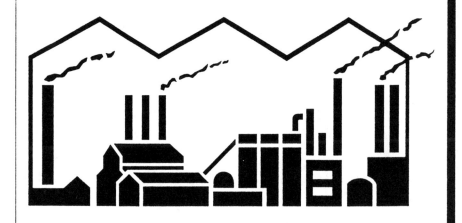

The term "process" means the preparation of a listed toxic chemical, after its manufacture, for distribution in commerce. Processing is usually the intentional incorporation of a toxic chemical into a product. Processing includes preparation of the chemical in the same physical state or chemical form as that received by the facility, or preparation that produces a change in physical state or chemical form. The term also applies to the processing of a mixture or other trade name product that contains a listed toxic chemical as one component.[52]

The term "process" includesuse of the listed toxic chemical as (1) a reactant; (2) a formulation component; or (3) a component of an article distributed for industrial, trade, or consumer use. The term also includes the repackaging of a listed toxic chemical for distribution in commerce in a different form, state, or quantity.

The term "otherwise use" encompasses any use of a listed toxic chemical at a facility that is not covered under the definitions of "manufacture" or "process."[53] A chemical that is otherwise used by a facility is *not* intentionally incorporated into a product distributed in commerce. The term includes use of the listed toxic chemical as (1) a cleaner; (2) a degreaser; (3) a fuel; (4) a lubricant; (5) a chemical used for treating waste; (6) a chemical processing aid (e.g., process solvents, catalysts, inhibitors, initiators, reaction terminators, and solution buffers); or (7) as a manufacturing aid (e.g., process lubricants, metalworking fluids, coolants, refrigerants, and hydraulic fluids).

## 5.3 Exemptions

Certain uses of listed toxic chemicals are specifically exempted: (1) use as a structural component of the facility; (2) use in routine janitorial or facility grounds maintenance, provided the product is similar in type or concentration to consumer products; (3) personal uses by employees or other persons at the facility of foods, drugs, cosmetics, or other personal items containing listed toxic chemicals; (4) use of products containing toxic chemicals for the purpose of maintaining motor vehicles operated by the facility; and (5) use of listed toxic chemicals contained in intake water (used for processing or noncontact cooling) or in intake air (used either as compressed air or for combustion).[54]

The owner or operator of a covered facility does not have to factor into threshold or release determinations the quantities of a listed toxic chemical contained in an "article" when that article is processed or otherwise used at the facility. An "article" is defined as a manufactured item (1) which is formed to a specific shape or design during manufacture; (2) which has end use functions dependent in whole or in part upon its shape or design during end use; and (3) which does not release a toxic chemical under normal conditions of processing or use of that item at the facility.[55]

If the processing or otherwise use of similar articles results in a total release of less than 0.5 pound of a listed toxic chemical in a calendar year to any environmental media, EPA will allow this release quantity to be rounded to zero and the manufactured items remain exempt as articles. EPA requires the owners or operators of covered facilities

---

[52]See 40 C.F.R. § 372.3.
[53]See 40 C.F.R. § 372.3.
[54]See 40 C.F.R. § 372.38.
[55]See 40 C.F.R. § 372.3.

to round off and report all estimates to the nearest whole number. The 0.5 pound limit does not apply to each individual article, but applies to the sum of all releases from processing or the otherwise use of like articles.

The article exemption applies to the normal processing or otherwise use of an article. It does not apply to the manufacture of an article. Listed toxic chemicals that are incorporated into articles produced at a facility must be factored into threshold and release determinations.[56] For example, if a facility services a transformer containing PCBs by replacing the PCBs, the PCBs added during the reporting year must be counted in making the threshold and release calculations.

The article exemption is not applicable when the processing or otherwise use of an item generates fumes, dust, filings, or grindings. The listed toxic chemicals in the item must be counted toward the appropriate threshold determination, and the fumes, dust, filings, and grindings must be reported as releases or wastes. In addition, scrap pieces of a manufactured item that are recognizable as an article do not constitute a release.

## 5.4 Threshold Levels

Section 313 reporting is required if established threshold quantities are exceeded. Separate threshold quantities apply to the amount of the listed toxic chemical that is manufactured, imported, processed or otherwise used.[57]

The owner or operator of a facility that otherwise used any of the listed toxic chemicals in amounts equal to or in excess of 10,000 pounds in a calendar year is required to submit a toxic chemical release form on each listed chemical by July 1 of the following year. Such reporting began with the 1987 calendar year. Similarly, owners or operators of facilities that manufacture, import, or process any of the listed toxic chemicals in amounts equal to or in excess of 25,000 pounds in a calendar year are required to report by July 1 of the following year.[58]

## 5.5 Alternate Threshold Rule

EPA has established a reduced reporting option for facilities meeting Section 313 reporting thresholds for a listed chemical, but whose total annual reportable amount does not exceed 500 pounds for that chemical. A facility that does not exceed the 500 pound criteria is eligible to apply an alternate manufacture, process, or otherwise use threshold of 1 million pounds to the chemical. If the facility does not exceed the 1 million pound threshold, then the facility is eligible to submit a certification statement in lieu of a full Form R for activities beginning January 1, 1995.[59]

## 5.6 Mixture Reporting

Listed toxic chemicals in mixtures and trade name products must be factored into threshold and release determinations. If the owner or operator of a facility processed, or otherwise used mixtures or trade name products during the preceding calendar year,

---

[56]See 40 C.F.R. § 372.3.
[57]See 42 U.S.C.A. § 11023(f).
[58]See 40 C.F.R. § 372.25.
[59]See 40 C.F.R. § 372.27.

the owner or operator is required to use the best information available at the facility to determine whether the components of a mixture are above the *de minimis* concentration. If the owner or operator knows that a mixture or trade name product contains a listed toxic chemical, the owner or operator must combine the amount of the listed chemical in the mixture or trade name product with the other amounts of the same chemical processed or otherwise used at the facility for threshold and release determinations.[60]

If the owner or operator of a facility knows that a mixture contains a listed toxic chemical but no concentration information is provided by the supplier, then the facility does not have to consider the amount of the listed toxic chemical present in that mixture for purposes of threshold and release determinations.[61]

If the owner or operator of a facility only knows the lower bound concentration of a listed toxic chemical present in a mixture, he should first subtract out the percentages of any other known components of the mixture to determine a reasonable upper bound concentraton, and then determine a midpoint. If the owner or operator only knows the lower bound concentration, he should calculate a midpoint assuming an upper bound concentration of 100 percent. If the owner or operator only knows the upper bound concentration, he must use it for threshold determinations. The owner or operator should use an average of the low and high concentration numbers for threshold determinations if only a range of concentrations is available for a listed toxic chemical present in a mixture.

A listed toxic chemical does not have to be considered if it is present in a mixture at a concentration below the *de minimis* level.[62] If a mixture contains more than one member of a listed chemical category, the *de minimis* level applies to the aggregate concentration of all such members and not to each individually. In making threshold determinations, the *de minimis* exemption applies to the following:

1. A listed toxic chemical in a mixture or trade name product received by the facility; and
2. A listed toxic chemical manufactured during a process where the chemical remains in a mixture or trade name product distributed by the facility.

The *de minimis* exemption does *not* apply to a listed toxic chemical manufactured at the facility that does not remain in a product distributed by the facility. A threshold determination must be made on the annual quantity of the listed chemical manufactured regardless of the concentration. For example, quantities of formaldehyde produced as a result of waste treatment must be applied toward the threshold for manufacture of this chemical, notwithstanding the concentration of this chemical in the wastestream.

### 5.7 Supplier Notification Requirement

EPA requires some suppliers of mixtures and trade name products containing one or more of the listed toxic chemicals to notify their customers. This requirement has been in effect since January 1, 1989. The supplier notification requirement applies to facilities in SIC codes 20 through 39 that manufacture, import, or process a listed toxic

---

[60]See 40 C.F.R. § 372.30(b)(3)(i).
[61]See 40 C.F.R. § 372.30(b)(3)(iii).
[62]See 40 C.F.R. § 372.38(a).

chemical which is *sold or otherwise distributed* in a mixture or trade name product containing the listed chemical to either a facility that must report under Section 313, or a facility that, in turn, sells the same mixture or trade name product to a firm in SIC codes 20 through 39.[63]

Supplier notification is required if a waste mixture containing a listed toxic chemical is sold to a recycling or recovery facility. If, however, the waste mixture containing a listed toxic chemical is sent off-site as a waste for treatment or disposal, no supplier notification is required.

The supplier notification must include the following information:

1. A statement that the mixture or trade name product contains a listed toxic chemical subject to the reporting requirements of Section 313 and 40 C.F.R. Part 372;

2. The name of each listed toxic chemical and its Chemical Abstracts Service registry number, if applicable; and

3. The percentage, by weight, of each listed toxic chemical (or all toxic chemicals within a listed category) contained in the mixture or trade name product.

The required notification must be provided at least *annually* in writing. Acceptable forms of notice are a letter, product labeling, and product literature distributed to customers. The owners and operators of facilities that are required to prepare and distribute a MSDS for the mixture under the OSHA Hazard Communication Standard must either attach their supplier notification to the MSDS or modify their MSDS to include the required information. Suppliers subject to the notification requirement must make it clear to their customers that any copies or redistribution of the MSDS must include the Section 313 notice.[64]

Suppliers must notify each customer receiving a mixture or trade name product containing a listed toxic chemical with the *first shipment of each calendar year*. Once customers have been furnished with a MSDS containing the Section 313 information, a supplier may refer to the MSDS by a written letter in subsequent years if the MSDS is current.[65]

Whenever a supplier's products contain newly listed toxic chemicals, the supplier must notify customers with the *first shipment made during the next calendar year* following EPA's final decision to add the chemical to the list.[66] Suppliers must send a *new notice* to their customers *within 30 days* when they discover that their previous notification did not properly identify the listed toxic chemical(s) in the mixture or correctly indicate their percentage by weight. Suppliers must identify in the new notice the prior shipments of the mixture or product in that calendar year to which the new notification applies.[67]

---

[63]See 40 C.F.R. § 372.45.
[64]See 40 C.F.R. § 372.45(c)(5).
[65]See 40 C.F.R. § 372.45(c)(1).
[66]See 40 C.F.R. § 372.45(c)(2).
[67]See 40 C.F.R. § 372.45(c)(4).

Suppliers must send a *revised notice* to their customers when they change a mixture or trade name product by adding, removing, or changing the percentage by weight of a listed chemical. The revised notice must be sent with the *first shipment* of the changed mixture or trade name product to the customer.[68]

Supplier notification is *not* required for a "pure" listed toxic chemical unless a trade name is used. Suppliers are not required to make a "negative declaration" (i.e., to indicate that a product contains no listed toxic chemicals). Supplier notification is also *not* required if the mixture or trade name product does not contain a listed toxic chemical in an amount greater than the applicable *de minimis* level established for that chemical. Likewise, supplier notification is *not* required if the mixture or trade name product is an "article;" food, drug, cosmetic, alcoholic beverage, tobacco, or a tobacco product packaged for distribution to the general public; or a "consumer product" as defined in the Consumer Product Safety Act packaged for distribution to the general public.[69]

If a supplier considers the specific identity of a listed toxic chemical in a mixture or trade name product to be a trade secret, the notice must contain a generic chemical name that is descriptive of the structure of that chemical (i.e., halogenated aromatic).[70] Similarly, if a supplier considers the specific percent by weight composition of a toxic chemical in the mixture or trade name product to be a trade secret under the Restatement of Torts, the notice must contain a statement that the listed chemical is present at a concentration that does not exceed a specified upper bound concentration value. The upper bound value chosen must be no larger than necessary to adequately protect the trade secret.[71]

Suppliers are required to retain for *three years* records of the following:
1. Copies of the notifications sent to customers;
2. All supporting materials and documentation used to determine whether a notice was required;
3. All supporting materials and documentation used to develop the notice;
4. All supporting materials and documentation that explain why a specific chemical identity is considered a trade secret and why the generic chemical name provided in the notification is appropriate; and
5. All supporting materials and documentation that explain why a specific concentration is considered a trade secret and the basis for the upper bound concentration limit.[72]

## 5.8 Reporting Form

Facilities covered by the Section 313 reporting requirements must use the Toxic Chemical Release Inventory Reporting Form (Form R) to report the following information:

1. The name, location, and principal business activities at the facility;

---

[68]See 40 C.F.R. § 372.45(c)(3).
[69]See 40 C.F.R. § 372.45(d).
[70]See 40 C.F.R. § 372.45(e).
[71]See 40 C.F.R. § 372.45(f).
[72]See 40 C.F.R. § 372.10(b).

2.  Off-site locations to which any waste that contains the listed chemical is transferred;
3.  Whether the listed chemical is manufactured, imported, processed, or otherwise used and the general use categories of the chemical;
4.  An estimate (in ranges) of the maximum amounts of the listed chemical present at the facility at any time during the preceding year;
5.  The quantity of the listed chemical entering each environmental medium-- air, water and land--annually;
6.  Waste treatment and disposal methods and the efficiency of such methods for each waste stream;
7.  Information on source reduction and recycling or pollution prevention; and
8.  A certification by a senior management official that the report is complete and accurate.

## 5.9 Mandatory Pollution Prevention Reporting On EPA Form R

The Pollution Prevention Act of 1990, passed in October 1990 as part of the Budget Reconciliation Act of 1990, requires the owners or operators of facilities that must report under Section 313 to provide information on source reduction and recycling activities with each annual toxic chemical release inventory report beginning with the 1991 calendar year.

The pollution prevention report on each chemical reported includes the following information:

1.  Amount entering the wastestreams before recycling, treatment, or disposal and the percentage change from the previous year;
2.  Amount recycled, the percentage change from the previous year, and the recycling process used;
3.  Amount treated on-site or off-site and the percentage change from the previous year;
4.  Estimate of the amount that will be reported as entering any wastestream prior to recycling, treatment, or disposal for the next two years;
5.  Estimate of the amount that will be reported as recycled for the next two years;
6.  Specific source reduction practices used by the facility (e.g., equipment, technology, process, or procedure modifications; reformulation or redesign of products; substitution of raw materials; improvement in management, training, inventory control, or materials handling;
7.  Techniques used to identify source reduction opportunities (e.g., employee recommendations, external and internal audits, participative team management, and material balance audits);
8.  Ratio of production in the reporting year to production in the preceding year; and
9.  Amount released because of accidents or other one-time events (e.g., catastrophic event or remedial action) not associated with production processes.

The pollution prevention data can give some indication of whether changes in the quantity of listed toxic chemicals released are due to shifting of chemicals off-site for energy recovery, treatment, or recycling; decrease in economic activity or production levels; or source reduction.

## 5.10 Recordkeeping Requirements

The owner or operator of a facility covered by the Section 313 reporting requirements (excluding the supplier notification requirements) must retain the following records:

1. A copy of each toxic chemical release inventory report;
2. All supporting materials and documentation used to make the compliance determination that the facility or establishments within the facility is a covered facility;
3. Documentation supporting any determination that a claimed allowable exemption applies;
4. Data supporting the determination of whether a reporting threshold applies for each reported chemical;
5. Documentation supporting the calculations of the quantity of each reported chemical released to the environment or transferred to an off-site location;
6. Documentation supporting the activities and use classifications and quantity on site reported for each reported chemical, including the date of manufacture, processing, or use;
7. Documentation supporting the basis of estimate used in developing any release or off-site transfer estimates for each reported chemical;
8. Receipts or manifests associated with the transfer of each reported chemical in waste to off-site locations; and
9. Documentation supporting reported waste treatment methods, estimates of treatment efficiencies, ranges of influent concentration to such treatment, the sequential nature of treatment steps, if applicable, and the actual operating data, if applicable, to support the waste treatment efficiency estimate for each reported chemical.[73]

The records must be maintained at the facility for three years from the date each report was submitted and they must be readily available for inspection by EPA officials.[74]

In view of the data requirements mandated by the Pollution Prevention Act of 1990, several new records should be maintained under Section 313.[75] Those records include the following:

1. Documentation supporting the estimates of the amounts of the chemical entering any wastestream, recycled on-site, sent off-site for recycling or

---

[73]See 40 C.F.R. § 372.10(a).
[74]See 40 C.F.R. § 372.10(c).
[75]See 56 *Fed. Reg.* 48475 (September 25, 1991).

treatment, and entering any wastestream as a result of remedial actions, catastrophic, or one-time events;

2.  Documentation supporting the estimates for the previous year and the first and second years following the reporting year of the amounts of the chemical entering any wastestream or otherwise released to the environment, recycled on-site, and recycled off-site;

3.  Documentation supporting the estimates for the previous year of the amounts of the chemical entering treatment on-site and sent off-site for treatment;

4.  Documentation supporting the validity of the method used to estimate the amount that would have been generated in waste if source reduction had not been implemented, and the calculation of the estimate of that quantity, including index of production or activity level in the reporting year to the prior year level;

5.  Documentation supporting the determination of whether changes in accounting practices, estimation methods, or point of measurement occurred in the reporting year versus the previous year;

6.  Documentation supporting the type of recycling process used on-site and off-site;

7.  Documentation of the implementation of source reduction and recycling activities, including receipts for new capital equipment; and

8.  Documentation demonstrating how the production ratio or activity index was calculated.

## 6.0 FEDERAL COMPLIANCE WITH RIGHT-TO-KNOW LAWS AND POLLUTION PREVENTION REQUIREMENTS

### 6.1 Overview

On August 3, 1993, President Clinton signed Executive Order 12856 requiring government-owned and government-operated federal facilities (GOGOs) that manufacture, process, or otherwise use listed toxic chemicals to comply with the reporting requirements under EPCRA. The Order sets a goal for all federal agencies to reduce toxic releases and off-site transfers of listed Section 313 toxic chemicals by 50 percent by 1999. The Order also calls for changes in the procurement of hazardous substances and requires federal facilities to work with neighboring communities to develop local emergency response plans.[76]

### 6.2 Planning Requirements

The Order requires each federal agency to develop a written pollution prevention strategy for the entire agency. Each agency's pollution prevention policy statement must designate the principal responsibilities for development, implementation, and evaluation of the strategy. The policy statement also must designate an individual responsible for

---

[76]See Executive Order 12856, "Federal Facility Compliance with Right-to-Know and Pollution Prevention Laws," 58 *Fed. Reg.* 41981 (August 6, 1993).

coordinating the agency's pollution prevention efforts. The written strategy must be submitted to the EPA Adminstrator by August 3, 1994.[77]

The Order required each federal agency to provide the EPA Administrator with a preliminary list of facilities that potentially meet the reporting requirements under EPCRA. The list was required to be submitted by December 31, 1993.[78]

### 6.3 TRI Reduction Goals

The Order directs each federal agency to develop voluntary goals to reduce total releases and off-site transfers of listed Section 313 toxic chemicals by 50% by 1999. The Order further directs each federal agency head to ensure that each of the agency's covered facilities develops a written pollution prevention plan by December 31, 1995.[79]

Under the Order, each federal agency may choose to expand their toxic chemical reduction goals to achieve a 50 percent reduction for all toxic pollutants by 1999. Baseline for measuring reductions will be either 1993 or 1994, depending on when each federal agency first began Section 313 reporting.[80]

### 6.4 Acquisition and Procurement of Goods and Services Goals

The Order requires all federal agencies to establish a plan and goals for eliminating or reducing the unnecessary acquisition of products containing extremely hazardous substances or toxic chemicals. Moreover, the Order directs each federal agency to establish a plan and goals for voluntarily reducing its own manufacturing, processing, and use of products containing extremely hazardous substances or toxic chemicals.[81]

The Order further requires the Department of Defense (DOD) and the General Services Administration (GSA), and other agencies, as appropriate, to review their specifications and standards and identify opportunities to eliminate or reduce acquisition and procurement of extremely hazardous substances or toxic chemicals. Such review and identification was required to be completed by August 3, 1995. By 1999, DOD, GSA and other affected agencies must make all appropriate revisions to their specifications and standards.[82]

Any revisions to the Federal Acquisition Regulation that are necessary to implement the Order were required to be made by August 3, 1995.[83]

The Order encourages federal agencies to develop and test innovative pollution prevention technologies at their facilities to promote the development of strong markets for such technologies. The Order further encourages partnerships between industry, federal agencies, government laboratories, academia, and others to assess and deploy innovative environmental technologies for domestic use and markets abroad.[84]

---

[77] *See Ibid.*, Section 3-301.
[78] *See Ibid.*, Section 5-501.
[79] *See Ibid.*, Section 3-302(d).
[80] *See Ibid.*, Section 3-302(b) and (c).
[81] *See Ibid.*, Section 3-303(a).
[82] *See Ibid.*, Section 3-303(b).
[83] *See Ibid.*, Section 3-303(c).
[84] *See Ibid.*, Section 3-303(d).

## 6.5 EPCRA Reporting Requirements

Under the Order, all federal facilities meeting the EPCRA definition of "facility"[85] and exceeding the thresholds for manufacture, use or processing of toxic chemicals must report under Section 313, as amended by the Pollution Prevention Act of 1990. Such reporting applies even if the facilities do not fall within SIC Codes 20-39.[86] Section 313 requirements became effective at such facilities no later than January 1, 1994. The first reports were due July 1, 1995.[87]

All federal facilities are subject also to the other EPCRA requirements (i.e., Sections 302-312). The compliance dates are as follows:[88]

| | |
|---|---|
| •January 1, 1994 | Effective date for Emergency Notification of Releases of Extremely Hazardous Substances under Section 304 that occur on or after January 1, 1994. |
| •March 3, 1994 | Submit Emergency Planning Notification under Section 302. |
| •August 3, 1994 | Submit information for the preparation of Comprehensive Emergency Response Plans under Section 303. |
| •August 3, 1994 | Submit MSDSs under Section 311. |
| •March 1, 1995 | Submit Tier I/Tier II Inventory Form for 1994 under Section 312 |

The Order does not apply to government-owned/contractor-operated facilities (GOCOs) not within SIC Codes 20-39 since they are not currently covered by Section 313. However, overall agency reports must take into account such activities. Future contract revisions will require GOCOs not within SIC Codes 20-39 to provide their agencies with the information necessary for TRI reporting.[89]

## 7.0 FEDERAL ACQUISITION AND COMMUNITY RIGHT-TO-KNOW EXECUTIVE ORDER

### 7.1 Overview

On August 8, 1995, President Clinton signed Executive Order 12969 mandating that, to the extent practicable, each federal agency shall contract only with those companies that have committed to continue reporting their releases of toxic chemicals under Section 313 and Section 6607 of the Pollution Prevention Act of 1990. To achieve this goal, the Order requires prospective contractors to include in their bids a

---

[85]EPCRA defines the term "facility" as follows: "all buildings, equipment, structures, and other stationary items which are located on a single site or on contiguous or adjacent sites and which are owned or operated by the same person (or by any person which controls, is controlled by, or under common control with, such person). For purposes of Section 304 (i.e., emergency release notification), the term includes motor vehicles, rolling stock, and aircraft. See 42 U.S.C.A. § 11049(4).

[86]The Order does not apply to federal agency facilities outside the customs territory of the United States, such as the United States diplomatic and consular missions abroad. *See supra.,* Executive Order 12856, Section 1-102.

[87]*See supra.,* Executive Order 12856, Section 3-304(a)-(c).

[88]*See Ibid.,* Section 3-305(a)-(d).

[89]*See Ibid.,* Sections 1-103 and 1-104.

certification that, if awarded the contract, they will continue to report as required under Section 313, unless an exemption provided by the Order applies. The Order applies to all competitive contracts expected to exceed $100,000. The certification requirement also applies to first-tier subcontractors.[90]

Executive Order 12969 does not extend the Section 313 reporting requirements to facilities that are not currently subject to the requirements. The Order only mandates that contractors already required to report under Section 313 certify that they will continue to do so for the life of the contract or face termination of their contracts. Federal contractors not required to report can simply indicate in their proposals that they are not subject to the Section 313 requirements.[91]

## 8.0 TRADE SECRETS

### 8.1 Overview

Only the specific chemical identity of a covered chemical can be claimed as a trade secret in submissions to EPA, the SERC, the LEPC, or the LFD required under Sections 303, 311, 312, and 313. EPCRA provides no trade secret protection for Section 304 submissions. When claiming confidentiality, the owner or operator of a covered facility must submit all other required information, including a generic name for the chemical whose identity is claimed as a trade secret, on the MSDS (or list of MSDS chemicals) and the Tier Two report.[92]

### 8.2 Substantiation Required

Substantiation for the claim must be provided to EPA, in both sanitized and unsanitized form, at the same time the Section 303, 311, 312 or 313 submission is made to the SERC, the LEPC or the LFD. The substantiation must include the following information:

1. Specific measures taken to safeguard the confidentiality of the chemical identity claimed as a trade secret and whether these measures will continue in the future;

2. Whether the chemical identity claimed as a trade secret has been disclosed to any other person (other than a member of a LEPC, officer, or employee of the U.S. or a state or local government, or an employee) who is not bound by a confidentiality agreement to refrain from disclosing this trade secret information to others;

3. All local, state and federal government entities to which the specific chemical identity claimed as a trade secret has been disclosed;

4. Indication of whether a confidentiality claim for the chemical identity was asserted at the time of disclosure to the local, state, and federal government entities and whether the government entity denied that claim;

---

[90]See Executive Order 12969, "Federal Acquisition and Community Right-to-Know," 60 *Fed. Reg.* 40989 (August 10, 1995).

[91]See "EPA Guidance for Implementing Executive Order 12969," 60 *Fed. Reg.*. 50738 (September 29, 1995).

[92]See 42 U.S.C.A. § 11042(a); 40 C.F.R. § 350.5.

5. The specific use of the chemical claimed as a trade secret, including the product or process in which it is used;

6. Whether the company's or the facility's identity has been linked to the specific chemical identity claimed as a trade secret in a patent, or in publications or other information sources available to the public or competitors;

7. Explanation of how competitors could deduce the use of the chemical claimed as a trade secret from disclosure of the chemical identity together with other information on the SARA Title III submission;

8. Explanation of why the use of the chemical claimed as a trade secret would be valuable information to competitors;

9. Indication of the nature of the harm to the company's competitive position that would likely result from disclosure of the specific chemical identity and why such harm would be substantial;

10. The extent to which the chemical claimed as a trade secret is available to the public or competitors in products, articles, or environmental releases; and

11. Whether the chemical claimed as a trade secret is in pure form or is mixed with other substances.[93]

**8.3 Trade Secret Disclosure**

All information for which a trade secrecy claim is not ultimately upheld is available to the public on request with one exception. Under Section 324, the SERC, the LEPC, and the LFD are required to withhold information regarding the location within a facility of any specific chemical contained in a Tier Two report if requested to do so by the owner or operator of a facility submitting the report.

Information concerning the specific chemical identity of a substance must be provided to health professionals upon request in the following situations:

1. The information is needed by a health professional for the purpose of diagnosis or treatment;

2. The information is needed by a health professional working for a local government to assess exposure; conduct sampling, periodic medical surveillance, or studies on the health effects of exposure; or provide medical treatment to exposed individuals or population groups; _or_

3. The information is needed by doctors or nurses in order to treat exposed individuals in a medical emergency.

The owner or operator of a covered facility is required to furnish the specific chemical identity in the first two situations described above only if the request for the information is *in writing* and is accompanied by a *written confidentiality agreement.* In a medical emergency, however, no written statement of need or written confidentiality agreement is required as a precondition to disclosure. The owner or operator of a

---

[93]See 40 C.F.R. § 350.7(a).

covered facility may require a written statement of need and written confidentiality agreement as soon as circumstances permit.[94]

## 9.0 PUBLIC AVAILABILITY OF EPCRA INFORMATION

The information submitted by facilities under Sections 304 311, 312 and 313 must generally be made available to the public by the SERC and the LEPCs during normal working hours.[95] Each SERC must have established written guidelines on receiving and processing requests for information under EPCRA.[96]

As a general policy, the SERCs and LEPCs will make the fullest possible disclosure of records to the public consistent with the provisions of EPCRA and their State Freedom of Information Act. All SERC and LEPC records are available to the public unless they are specifically exempt from the disclosure requirements.

## 10.0 ENFORCEMENT AUTHORITIES AND PENALTIES

### 10.1 Overview

EPCRA contains a complex set of administrative, civil, and criminal penalties for violations of its various provisions. Sections 325 and 326 authorize the EPA, the SERCs, the LEPCs, and citizens to take legal action against owners or operators of facilities who fail to comply with the law.

The enforcement authorities vary for each requirement in EPCRA. In some instances, federal authority is primarily administrative, in other instances it is judicial. For some requirements, but not all, there is express authority for state and local suits. Similarly, for some requirements, but not all, there are citizen suits.

Congress intended that the implementation of EPCRA be mainly a state and local function with the notable exception of Section 313 pertaining to toxic chemical release inventory reporting. The EPCRA enforcement authorities are summarized below.

### 10.2 Violations of Sections 302 and 303

Section 325 of EPCRA authorizes the Administrator of the EPA to order the owner or operator of a covered facility to comply with Sections 302 and 303. The local U.S. district court has jurisdiction to enforce the order and impose a penalty.[97]

Under Section 326, the SERC and the LEPC can bring a civil action against the owner or operator of a covered facility for failing to report that the facility is covered by the emergency planning requirements.[98] The SERC and the LEPC can bring a civil action against the owner or operator of a covered facility for failing to notify the LEPC of a facility representative who will participate in the emergency planning process or for failing to provide information promptly upon request by the LEPC.[99] The local U.S.

---

[94]See 40 C.F.R. § 350.40.
[95]See 42 U.S.C.A. § 11044(a).
[96]See 42 U.S.C.A. § 11001(a).
[97]See 42 U.S.C.A. § 11045(a).
[98]See 42 U.S.C.A. § 11046(a)(2)(A).
[99]See 42 U.S.C.A. § 11046(a)(2)(B).

district court has the authority to impose civil penalties provided by EPCRA in such suits.[100]

Violations of Sections 302 and 303 subject the violator to civil penalties of up to $25,000 per day for each day the violation or failure to comply with the order continues.[101]

## 10.3 Violations of Section 304

The CERCLA Section 109 and EPCRA Section 325 enforcement provisions for emergency notification are very similar. Both establish administrative penalties and the authority to bring actions judicially to assess penalties for failing to notify the proper authorities at the time of an emergency release of a listed hazardous substance subject to reporting.[102]

CERCLA and EPCRA both provide criminal fines for knowingly failing to provide notice of a reportable release or providing false or misleading information.[103] Section 326(a) of EPCRA authorizes any citizen to file a civil action in the local U.S. district court for failure to submit a written follow-up report of a release required to be reported to the SERC and the LEPC under Section 304(c).[104] The SERC and the LEPC may bring a civil action under the citizen suit provisions for Section 304 violations.[105]

Under Section 325 of EPCRA and CERCLA Section 109, a Class I administrative penalty of up to $25,000 per violation and a Class II administrative penalty of up to $25,000 per day for each day during which the violation continues may be assessed for each violation of Section 304.[106] This penalty also may be assessed judicially.[107]

In the case of a second or subsequent violation of Section 304, civil penalties of up to $75,000 per day for each day during which the violation continues may be assessed.[108] Both penalties also may be assessed judicially.[109]

Any person who knowingly and willfully fails to provide notice in accordance with EPCRA Section 304 can, upon conviction, be fined up to $25,000 or imprisoned for up to two years, or both.[110] In the case of a second or subsequent conviction, the violator is subject to a fine of up to $50,000 or imprisonment for up to five years, or both.[111]

---

[100]See 42 U.S.C.A. § 11046(b)(1).

[101]See 42 U.S.C.A. § 11045(a).

[102]See 42 U.S.C.A. § 9609 and 42 U.S.C.A. § 11045.

[103]See 42 U.S.C.A. § 9603(b) and 42 U.S.C.A. § 11045(b)(4).

[104]See 42 U.S.C.A. § 11046(a)(1)(A)(i).

[105]See 42 U.S.C.A. § 11049(7) and 42 U.S.C.A. § 11046(a). The term "person" used in Section 326 of EPCRA is defined to include, among others, "any ... State, municipality, commission, political subdivision of a State, or interstate body."

[106]See 42 U.S.C.A. § 11045(b)(1) and (2); and 42 U.S.C.A. § 9609(a) and (b).

[107]See 42 U.S.C.A. § 11045(b)(3) and 42 U.S.C.A. § 9609(c).

[108]See 42 U.S.C.A. § 11045(b)(2) and 42 U.S.C.A. § 9609(b).

[109]See 42 U.S.C.A. § 11045(b)(3) and 42 U.S.C.A. § 9609(c).

[110]See 42 U.S.C.A. § 11045(b)(4).

[111]*Ibid.*

## 10.4 Violations of Sections 311-313

Under Section 325 of EPCRA, the Administrator of the EPA can assess civil penalties for violations of Sections 311, 312, and 313 through the issuance of administrative orders or bring actions to enforce compliance and assess penalties in the local U.S. district court.[112]

Under Section 326 of EPCRA, the SERC and the LEPC can bring civil actions for failing to submit MSDSs or Tier One/Tier Two Inventory Reports under Sections 311 and 312.[113] Under the citizen suit provisions of Section 326, the SERC and the LEPC can bring a civil action for failing to submit toxic chemical release inventory reports under Section 313.[114]

Section 326 gives citizens the authority to bring a civil action against an owner or operator of a covered facility for violations of Sections 311, 312, and 313.[115] The local U.S. district court has the authority to enforce the reporting requirements and to impose any civil penalty provided for violation of the requirements.[116]

A violation of Section 311 subjects the violator to a civil penalty of up to $10,000 per day for each such violation.[117] Each day a violation continues constitutes a separate violation.[118]

A violation of Sections 312 or 313 subjects the violator to a civil penalty of up to $25,000 per day for each such violation.[119] Each day a violation continues constitutes a separate violation.[120]

## 11.0 CONCLUSION

Compliance with EPCRA presents a continuing challenge to those facilities subject to its planning and reporting requirements. EPA recently began the regulatory development process for the reporting of chemical use information under the Toxic Release Inventory.[121] Data elements that may be added as part of a chemical use program could include amounts of the listed toxic chemical produced or brought on-site, amounts consumed in the manufacturing process, amounts contained in products and waste, the amount of waste prevented by source reduction, and the number of workers potentially exposed to each listed toxic chemical.

Facilities subject to the emergency planning provisions should participate actively in the local planning process as a matter of good community relations and to provide the technical expertise needed by the LEPCs. Facilities subject to the reporting requirements need clearly written and rigorously implemented compliance plans and information management programs to avoid enforcement actions for noncompliance.

---

[112]See 42 U.S.C.A. § 11045(c).
[113]See 42 U.S.C.A. § 11046(a)(2).
[114]See 42 U.S.C.A. § 11046(a)(1)(A)(iv).
[115]See 42 U.S.C.A. § 11046(a)(1).
[116]See 42 U.S.C.A. § 11046(c).
[117]See 42 U.S.C.A. § 11045(c)(2).
[118]See 42 U.S.C.A. § 11045(c)(3).
[119]See 42 U.S.C.A. § 11045(c)(1).
[120]See 42 U.S.C.A. § 11045(c)(3).
[121]See "EPA Advance Notice of Proposed Rulemaking on the Addition of Reporting Elements for Toxic Chemical Release Reporting," 61 Fed.Reg. 51321 (October 1, 1996).

# CHAPTER 15

# POLLUTION PREVENTION ACT

John M. Scagnelli[1]
Whitman, Breed, Abbott & Morgan
Newark, New Jersey

## 1.0 OVERVIEW

In July 1994, the United States Environmental Protection Agency (EPA or Agency) introduced its new approach towards protecting human health and the environment, the "Common Sense Initiative" (CSI). The Common Sense Initiative was launched to encourage industry, regulators and environmental interest groups to develop strategies for pollution prevention and other innovations in environmental policy. The Common Sense Initiative, which has been evolving over the past few years, represents a new era for the EPA. In the past, when an environmental crisis arose, laws were passed. Frequently, these laws had the effect of shifting pollution from one place to another—from land to air, from air to water, from water to land. Under the Common Sense Initiative, the Agency focuses on an industry-by-industry approach to regulatory policy.

This chapter highlights the Common Sense Initiative and other EPA programs which involve innovative regulatory compliance and regulatory reinvention. Specifically, this Chapter looks at EPA's Environmental Leadership Program and EXcellence in Leadership (XL) Program. After reviewing the federal pollution prevention strategy, this chapter addresses the pollution prevention programs of several states, and the cooperative efforts between EPA and the states toward a new regulatory structure incorporating pollution prevention.

## 2.0 THE FEDERAL POLLUTION PREVENTION STRATEGY

### 2.1 Background

The Federal Pollution Prevention Act of 1990[2] (PPA or Act) establishes pollution prevention as a national objective. The PPA required the EPA to develop and implement a strategy to promote source reduction.[3] In the Act, Congress declared that pollution prevention is the highest tier in a hierarchy of acceptable practices. The pollution that cannot be prevented should be recycled. If it is not feasible to prevent or recycle, pollution should be treated; disposal or other release into the environment

---

[1]The author gratefully acknowledges the contributions of Kathleen A. Pierce, co-author.

[2]The Pollution Prevention Act of 1990, Omnibus Budget Reconciliation Act of 1990, 42 U.S.C.A. 13101 *et seq.*, Pub. L. 101-508 (November 5, 1990), section 6601 *et seq.*

[3]Source reduction means any practice which (i) reduces the amount of any hazardous substance, pollutant, or contaminant entering any waste stream or otherwise released into the environment (including fugitive emissions) prior to recycling, treatment or disposal; and (ii) reduces the hazards to public health and the environment associated with the release of such substances, pollutants, or contaminants. 42 U.S.C.A. 13101(b).

should be used as a last resort. The PPA defined pollution prevention to mean source reduction and other practices that reduce or eliminate the creation of pollutants through increased efficiency in the use of raw materials, energy, water or other resources or protection of natural resources by conservation.[4]

The Act required EPA to identify measurable goals, consider the effect of Agency programs on source reduction and evaluate existing barriers to source reduction.[5] The Act amended the reporting requirements of the Emergency Planning and Community Right-to-Know Act (EPCRA)[6] through its Toxic Chemical Release Inventory (TRI). Under the Act, facilities required to file an annual toxic chemical release form pursuant to 313 for any toxic chemical are also required to provide information on pollution prevention and recycling for each facility and for each toxic chemical.[7] The PPA required the Administrator of the EPA to submit biennial reports to Congress detailing the steps it has taken to implement the strategy to promote pollution prevention.[8]

### 2.2 Pollution Prevention Strategy

The EPA published its Pollution Prevention Strategy to incorporate pollution prevention objectives into every aspect of its already existing programs in February 1991.[9] The Strategy was designed to respond to the PPA's requirement that measurable source reduction goals be established. Although not an official rule-making, the Strategy sets forth a national pollution prevention model and a voluntary program for companies to reduce aggregate environmental releases of specific chemicals. The EPA will use the data from the Toxic Release Inventory established under the EPCRA to track industrial pollution prevention efforts.

### 2.3 EPA's Environmental Leadership Program

EPA's Environmental Leadership Program (ELP) focuses on encouraging, not directing, companies to develop and implement pollution prevention management practices and to establish environmental goals beyond those set for regulatory compliance. The ELP seeks to reward companies, through public recognition and other incentives, for voluntarily incorporating pollution prevention into high level corporate decisions and facility practices and systems. The ELP includes an element of public accountability to encourage companies' progress toward meeting the ELP's goals.

#### 2.3.1 Scope of Program

EPA will establish national risk reduction goals for participation in the ELP. The TRI will provide the basis for setting national goals and measuring progress at the source. However, TRI varies in the quality of reported data and does not include reporting of all significant pollutants or sources. EPA will therefore seek to gather

---

[4] 42 U.S.C.A. 13102(5)(A).
[5] 42 U.S.C.A. 13103 (b).
[6] 42 U.S.C.A. 11001 *et seq.* Section 11023 requires facilities subject to EPCRA to complete a toxic chemical release form.
[7] 42 U.S.C.A. 13106.
[8] 42 U.S.C.A. 13107(a).
[9] 56 *Fed. Reg.* 7849 (February 26, 1991).

additional pertinent information through the two components of the ELP: (1) the Corporate Statement of Environmental Principles and (2) the Model Facility Program.

*Corporate Statement of Environmental Principles.* EPA, in cooperation with corporations and industry, will develop environmental principles governing the way corporations design, manufacture, market and distribute products. Companies will be required to conduct their operations in accordance with those principles and commit to specific pollution prevention goals by subscribing to a written commitment to abide by the principles. These Corporate Statements of Environmental Principles would be maintained in a public docket to allow other public access to examine the contents.

The facilities subscribing to the Corporate Statement of Environmental Principles will be required to observe disclosure, testing and reporting principles concerning substances required to be listed on the TRI; publish a plan for pollution prevention in accordance with the method prescribed under the PPA; provide information to employees and the public concerning pollution prevention practices; and commit to assessing environmental factors and incorporating pollution prevention strategies at each stage of a product's life cycle. The facilities will also be required to pledge to institute facility-wide environmental compliance management systems to promote and monitor environmental compliance.

*The Model Facility Program.* The second component of the ELP provides for public recognition of facilities that meet strict environmental criteria as "Model Facilities." Participation in the Model Facilities Program differs from the Corporate Statement of Environmental Principles because EPA will certify that the facility meets stringent environmental compliance standards. The facilities that participate in the Model Facilities Program will have to subscribe to a Statement of Environmental Principles, and provide EPA with comprehensive data regarding all facility activities which have a potentially significant impact on the environment, including sources not covered by the TRI or PPA reporting requirements.

The enhanced reporting requirements include supplying data related to the EPA national risk reduction goals regarding the facility's consumption of energy, water and other raw materials. Facilities must also develop a plan for achieving the national risk reduction goals by emphasizing the measures that reduce waste through pollution prevention practices, performing a product life cycle assessment, and enacting an environmental cost accounting approach which can reflect the impact of pollution activities. Worker participation and facility compliance through implementation of a comprehensive environmental compliance management system will be required and the facility's compliance record will be stringently screened for acceptance into the Model Facility Program.

The major incentive for ELP participation is public recognition. The EPA will announce the Model Facilities and provide a flag or seal bearing the Model Facility Program logo. Other incentives include a commitment by EPA to accelerate the permit and product registration process, reduce monitoring and reporting requirements, issue multi-media permits and allow companies to off-set voluntary actions against future regulatory requirements.

### 2.3.2 Status of the Proposed Program

In 1994, the EPA initiated a pilot project to test parts of the ELP and explore ways both the EPA and the States could encourage facilities to develop innovative auditing and compliance programs and reduce the risk of noncompliance through pollution prevention practices.

In 1996, EPA completed a one-year pilot project. The pilot program involved the participation of ten private sector facilities and two federal facilities. The EPA's Office of Compliance, within the reorganized Office of Enforcement and Compliance Assurance, coordinated the pilot projects with regional and state partner involvement. The pilot project will be utilized by the EPA to develop the full-scale Environmental Leadership Program. It is anticipated that EPA will issue a proposed framework for the Program in late 1996, and begin accepting applications for participation in the ELP in early 1997. Under the most recent draft of EPA's proposal, facilities would have to commit to six years of ELP participation. Participation would be renewed every six years.

### 2.3.3 The Criteria Used for Facility Pilot Projects

The proposals for pilot projects addressed seven criteria. This criteria is set forth below. Although it is not clear at the time of this writing whether this criteria will be used to review potential applicants for approval for participation in the Program, the criteria should provide some guidance to facilities interested in participating in the Program in the future.

A.   Facilities must describe their local, state and federal compliance history and provide an explanation about resolution of past compliance issues, unresolved compliance issues and how they would go beyond compliance;

B.   Facilities must describe their existing or proposed environmental management and auditing programs, their systems to resolve issues raised by these programs in a timely manner and their systems to evaluate and adjust these programs on a regular basis;

C.   Facilities must be willing to disclose in some manner the results of their environmental audits;

D.   Facilities must describe their existing or proposed comprehensive, multimedia pollution prevention program that is part of their overall operations. Facilities must describe their pollution prevention planning process, their State pollution prevention plan, their systems for implementing pollution prevention projects, how resources are allocated to pollution prevention and how they measure pollution prevention progress.

E.   Facilities must show that they are using or are willing to use their auditing, pollution prevention or environmental management programs as models for other facilities within their company or industry, or for their customers, suppliers and contractors. In addition, facilities must include how they will help others learn from their experience and the type and extent of information they will be willing to share.

F.   Facilities must propose quantitative and/or qualitative measures that will track the compliance improvements and pollution prevention results that would accrue from their participation in the pilot project. Facilities must include descriptions of additional performance objectives that they are striving to meet and of the systems they use to track and monitor progress toward these goals.

G. Facilities must demonstrate that their employees and their communities are involved in developing and implementing their environmental management programs and mechanisms to verify this involvement.

### 2.3.4 Benefits of the ELP

The EPA believes the ELP will benefit the public because it encourages industry to monitor itself. This can lead to improved compliance, pollution prevention and environmental protection. Industry will benefit because its leaders have an opportunity to be recognized by the EPA for their outstanding environmental management practices. The program gives industry a chance to reform barriers to self-monitoring and compliance efforts. Further, the program benefits government by allowing federal-state partnerships to prosper, while also giving the EPA the ability to gather empirical data on environmental compliance measures and methodology.

### 2.4 EPA'S Common Sense Initiative

A major development that has had a greater impact on pollution prevention is the Common Sense Initiative. On July 20, 1994, the EPA Administration announced this program that changed the way the EPA protects human health and the environment through an industry-by-industry approach to environmental policy. This program is evidence of the EPA's commitment to pollution prevention.

The CSI replaced the previous system of environmental protection, which used the pollutant-by-pollutant approach, with an industry-by-industry approach. The CSI brings together all levels of government officials, environmentalists and industry leaders to create strategies that will work cleaner, cheaper and smarter to protect the health of people of this country and its natural resources. The EPA believes the CSI will have a cleaner effect because participating industries will achieve true environmental protection. It is cheaper because tailoring environmental protection on an industry-by-industry basis is thought by the EPA to save billions of dollars. It is believed to be smarter because the program utilizes people who have a stake in the outcome working together to protect the environment.

The CSI, which is currently evolving, examines environmental protection in industries from top to bottom and comes up with a blueprint for achieving real environmental protection. The six industries that are the focus of the CSI's first phase are auto manufacturing, computers and electronics, iron and steel, metal plating and finishing, oil refining and printing.

The CSI is based on the premise that the environment is best protected when tough environmental goals are set, while using flexibility and innovation to reach those goals. The EPA hopes to implement this premise by assembling teams of industry executives, environmental and community representatives and federal, state and local officials to improve the environmental regulation and performance of the six pilot industries. By using teams working together, the EPA seeks to avoid an adversarial approach to environmental protection. Additionally, the teams consist of those individuals with a stake in the outcome. By utilizing the expertise of industry; environmental leaders and grassroots activists; and local, state, and federal government officials, the EPA believes the CSI will drastically improve the environmental regulation and performance of the six pilot industries.

**2.4.1 Blueprint to Achieve Real Environmental Protection**

Each CSI team is responsible for examining how EPA and its state partners interact with an industry and locate areas for improvement. There are six key areas for improvement, and they make up the EPA's blueprint for achieving real environmental protection:

A.   Each team will conduct a review of every major regulation applicable to their industry and improve new regulations through increased coordination. The CSI marks the first time in EPA history that such a comprehensive review will take place.

B.   The CSI wants to avoid the mistakes of the past that shifted pollution from one area to another. In its place, the CSI intends to make pollution prevention part of normal business practices in every industry. The CSI wants to encourage industry to exceed pollution prevention standards as opposed to simply meeting the minimum standards.

C.   Each team must make environmental information collection easier for industry and allow the public greater access.

D.   With the help of the newly reorganized Office of Enforcement and Compliance Assurance, each team will offer those companies motivated to achieve real environmental protection a more flexible way to obtain this goal. Significantly, those companies not motivated will suffer the consequences because of a strong enforcement program. A strong enforcement program prevents companies that are complying with the law from suffering a competitive disadvantage to companies not complying.

E.   The permit process will be improved so that it is responsive to the needs of the public and industry.

F.   Industry will have the incentives and flexibility to create new technology that meet and exceed environmental standards while cutting costs.

The CSI begins a new and aggressive approach for EPA to protect our environment. It removes an adversarial system and in its place brings together people with the knowledge to find environmental solutions. The CSI moves beyond media-specific regulations to viewing an industry as a whole. The EPA believes the CSI can produce greater environmental protection for the public that is cheaper than we previously received.

**2.5 EPA'S Regulatory Reinvention (XL) Program**

On May 23, 1995, the EPA announced a set of actions directed toward giving regulated sources greater flexibility to develop alternative strategies for environmental compliance. The program, called the EXcellence in Leadership (XL), is part of President Clinton's "Reinventing Environmental Regulation" initiative, announced by the President in March, 1995. In his report, President Clinton announced twenty-five high-priority actions to improve the regulatory system as it exists today. The most notable of these is the Project XL. The XL Program is another example of EPA's commitment to incorporating pollution prevention strategies into its policies.

The XL Program goes beyond command and control regulatory systems by granting industrial participants flexibility in meeting regulatory requirements in exchange for an enforceable commitment by the participants to attain greater environmental results than what would have been achieved through full compliance. The first eight participants in the XL Pilot Project were approved by President Clinton in December 1995. EPA is targeting fifty XL projects for eventual selection.

The XL Pilot Projects test potential avenues for facilities to achieve environmental compliance by implementing technologically innovative and cost-effective alternatives to regulatory requirements. Project XL establishes a process for individual companies to develop unique environmental strategies for their particular facilities through collaboration with governmental officials and the interested public and other "stakeholders."

### 2.5.1 Criteria For Participation in the (XL) Program

To be selected for participation in Project XL, projects must meet specific criteria. The criteria, as published by the EPA in May, 1995, includes the following.[10]

A.  Environmental Results. Projects should be able to achieve "cleaner results" than what would be achieved through compliance with current and reasonable anticipated future regulations. Such results can be achieved directly through the environmental performance of the project or through the reinvestment of the cost savings from the project in activities that produce greater environmental results. Explicit measures for achieving the cleaner results will be included in the project agreement negotiated among stakeholders.

B.  Stakeholder Support. Applicants must gain the support of parties that have a stake in the environmental impacts of the project. Stakeholders include communities near a project, local or state governments, business, environmental and other public interest groups.

C.  Innovative Strategies. The project must test innovative alternatives, including processes, technologies, or management practices, for achieving environmental results and pollution prevention. Projects should systematically test these alternatives against several regulatory requirements and involve more than one environmental medium. Pilot projects should reflect EPA's pollution prevention objectives for protecting the environment by preventing the generation of pollution rather than controlling pollution once it has been created.

D.  Transferability. The pilots should be transferable or amenable to implementation into EPA's programs or in other industries or other facilities in the same industry.

### 2.5.2 Status of the (XL) Program: Growing Pains

In December 1995, eight pilot projects were selected for participation in Project XL. The initial six corporate participants included Anheuser-Busch, the 3M Company, Intel Corporation, HADCO Corporation, and Lucent Technologies (a former AT&T unit). The project proposals selected included emissions trading, facility emission caps, multi-media permitting and elimination of obsolete requirements.

---

[10]See 60 *Fed. Reg.* 27282 (May 15, 1995).

To date, at least one of the proposed projects has gained approval for the XL pilot program. This project, the Berry project, will focus on preparing a comprehensive multi-media operating permit that will encompass all of the facility's emissions. In return for its operating flexibility, Berry will reduce water consumption, increase use of non-hazardous pest controls, reserve acreage for habitat conservation and use process wastewater for irrigation.

The evolving XL Project has, however, experienced some growing pains. Two of the initial corporate participants, Anheuser-Busch and 3M Company, have, at the time of this writing, withdrawn their project proposals. Both companies were unwilling to provide the EPA with an up-front guarantee that their facilities would achieve superior environmental performance standards in exchange for regulatory flexibility. According to 3M Company, whose XL project involved a multi-media permit with emission caps and below regulatory levels, EPA's restriction would have been burdensome and would have allowed the failure of a single superior environmental performance standard to constitute grounds for permit amendment or revocation before the end of the permit's five-year term.

Despite varying expectations as to the purpose of the Project, Project XL has gained widespread support from the business community. EPA intends to learn from the pilot projects and promote cooperation and forge closer ties among the regulators and the regulated community. The goal is to establish at least fifty partnerships with the XL participants.

### 2.6    Multi-Media Permitting

Another important pollution prevention initiative is multi-media permitting. Launched as part of President Clinton's "Reinventing Environmental Regulation" initiative, multi-media permitting will provide an opportunity for selected industries to submit one application for one permit.

EPA has organized a Permits Improvement Team (PIT) to meet with the regulated community, regulators and the public to develop strategies for the innovative regulatory program. The PIT process will involve obtaining detailed input from the public and the regulated community, and developing a permitting program which should (i) incorporate performance-based standards rather than the command and control requirements; (ii) improve methods of data collection; and (iii) streamline permitting techniques, such as group permits and de minimis exemptions.

Permittees at pilot facilities would submit a single application for a single permit, setting forth all the pollution control and cleanup requirements for that facility. This approach will promote "common sense" solutions to multi-media pollution problems and encourage the use of pollution prevention.

### 3.0 THE POLLUTION PREVENTION PROGRAMS OF SEVERAL STATES

### 3.1 Mandatory Waste Reduction Programs

A number of states have passed mandatory waste reduction statutes requiring companies to reduce the generation of hazardous waste. In Iowa, for example, the legislature passed the Waste Minimization Act in 1989 requiring reductions in the generation of hazardous wastes through recycling and source reduction.[11] Massachusetts[12] and Tennessee[13] have passed similar waste reduction programs mandating significant reductions in statewide hazardous waste. In 1991, Iowa's pollution prevention activities were strengthened by the passage of the Toxics Pollution Prevention Program.[14] The statute encourages, not requires, certain toxic users[15] to develop a facility-wide multi-media toxics pollution prevention plan.

In 1991, the Arizona legislature passed its Amendments to Hazardous Waste Management Statutes.[16] The statute requires a person who owns or operates a facility, that meets certain conditions, to prepare and implement a pollution prevention plan that addresses a reduction in the use of toxic substances and the generation of hazardous wastes.[17] On July 25, 1994, the Director of the Arizona Department of Environmental Quality announced a statewide goal of reducing hazardous waste by 25 percent by the year 2000. This announcement fulfilled the mandate of Section 963, requiring the Director to establish a numeric goal for the state for waste minimization by January 1, 1994.[18] The Director has until January 1, 1999 to establish a numeric goal for the state for toxic use reduction.[19]

New York has a statewide goal for hazardous waste reduction of 50 percent by 1999.[20] In 1992, New York State's Department of Environmental Conservation (DEC) published its Multi-Media Pollution Prevention Initiative (M2P2).[21] M2P2 marks a new approach to environmental quality management in New York State. The program seeks to help facilities use multi-media pollution prevention through source reduction.

Other states have passed mandatory waste reduction planning and reporting statutes. The Alabama Hazardous Waste Management Act[22] requires waste generators to report annually on efforts to reduce the volume and toxicity of wastes generated. In 1989, California enacted the Hazardous Waste Reduction and Management Review Act requiring industries which generate 12,000 kilograms or more of hazardous wastes to

---

[11]Iowa Code 455B.481.

[12]Toxics Use Reduction Act, Mass. Gen. Laws, Chapter 21 I. The Act mandates a 50 percent reduction in toxic and hazardous byproducts by 1997.

[13]Tennessee Hazardous Waste Reduction Act of 1990, House Bill No. 2217. The Act mandates a 25 percent reduction in hazardous waste by June 30, 1995.

[14]Iowa Code 455B.518.

[15]Toxic user means a large quantity generator as defined pursuant to the Federal Resource Conservation and Recovery Act, 42 U.S.C. 6901 *et seq.* or a person required to report pursuant to Title III of the Federal Superfund Amendments and Reauthorization Act of 1986. Iowa Code 455 B. 516.

[16]House Bill 2121.

[17]49 Az Rev. Statutes §963.

[18]The July announcement refined the Director's January, 1994 announcement calling for a reduction of waste by 25-50 percent by the year 2000.

[19]49 Az. Rev. Statutes §963.

[20]27 N.Y. ECL Section 27-908.

[21]The Multimedia Pollution Prevention Initiative is the result of two Department of Environmental Conservation Organization and Delegation Memoranda. The first memorandum was the Reduction and Integrated Facility Management, DEC O&D Memo 92-13. The second was the Pollution Prevention Initiative, DEC O&D Memo 92-24.

[22]Alabama Code Section 22-30 *et seq.*

annually review their operations for potential waste reduction measures and to prepare an implementation schedule.[23] A similar statute was passed in Louisiana.[24]

## 3.2 Multi-Media Permit Programs and Other Regulatory Innovations

New Jersey passed its Pollution Prevention Act (NJPPA)[25] to focus the State's approach to waste minimization and pollution prevention. The NJPPA established an Office of Pollution Prevention in the New Jersey Department of Environmental Protection (NJDEP) and authorized regulations which encourage voluntary pollution prevention. New Jersey has established a statewide goal of a 50 percent reduction in the use, discharge or generation of hazardous substances over a five-year period. Covered industrial facilities must prepare Pollution Prevention Plans to be kept at the facility, and Pollution Prevention Plan Summaries and Progress Reports for submittal to the NJDEP.[26] Pollution Prevention Plans and Plan Summaries must address the use and discharge of New Jersey Right-to-Know substances, New Jersey Toxic Catastrophe Prevention Act substances, EPCRA Section 313 and Superfund substances.

In December 1993, under a pilot program pursuant to the NJPPA and associate regulations, the NJDEP selected priority industrial facilities to test multi-media permits. Each selected priority industrial facility received facility-wide permits which incorporate all formerly held facility permits[27] under the Solid Waste Management Act,[28] the Air Pollution Control Act,[29] the Water Pollution Control Act[30] and the NJPPA. The facility-wide permit program is designed to incorporate pollution prevention planning into all NJDEP permit programs integrating use, output, release and compliance data for facilities.

Other states are developing similar innovative regulatory programs to encourage pollution prevention. For instance, since 1995, Minnesota has been authorized by EPA to take the lead in the selection and implementation of the XL Program at the state level. Massachusetts is launching a pilot program to test a self-certification program intended to replace low-risk environmental permits at the state level. Companies involved in this program, called the "Environmental Results Program," will be asked to commit to meeting environmental performance standards and to provide annual certifications of compliance with such standards in exchange for suspended permit requirements. California environmental officials are also preparing to implement a pilot program to test the idea of replacing environmental permits with facility-wide compliance plans.

---

[23]1989 Hazardous Waste Reduction and Management Review Act. (Senate Bill 14); 1992 Amendments to the Hazardous Waste Source Reduction and Management Review Act of 1989. (Senate Bill 1726).

[24]1987 Louisiana Waste Reduction Law, Act No. 657.

[25]N.J.S.A. 13:1D-35 *et seq.* (1991). Pollution Prevention Rules, N.J.A.C. 7:1K-1.1 *et seq.* (1993).

[26]*See* Pollution Prevention Program Rules, N.J.A.C. 7:1K *et seq.* (March 1, 1993).

[27]N.J.S.A. 13:1D-4 *et seq.* and N.J.A.C. 7:1K-7 *et seq.*

[28]N.J.S.A. 13:1E-1 *et seq.*

[29]N.J.S.A. 26:2C-1 *et seq.*

[30]N.J.S.A. 58:10A-1 *et seq.*

### 3.3 Voluntary Technical Assistance Programs

A majority of states that have considered pollution prevention, but have not enacted regulatory programs, utilize some form of technical assistance. These programs include establishing technology centers through a consortium of local colleges and research institutions, source reduction programs and generator seminars or multi-media waste reduction programs and include both public and private participation and funding. The states which have enacted such programs include Florida,[31] Illinois[32] and Ohio.[33]

### 4.0 THE NATIONAL ENVIRONMENTAL PERFORMANCE PARTNERSHIP SYSTEM

In an effort to provide more flexibility to states, the EPA and state officials have launched a program called the National Environmental Performance Partnership System (NEPPS). The NEPPS represents a new era of environmental protection by allowing states to step out of EPA's shadow and establish their own environmental goals and indicators and address local needs and problems.

Under the program, states will negotiate annual agreements with their regional EPA office, instead of submitting traditional workplans, and set consensus based environmental goals and mechanisms for measuring their success in meeting these goals. The program is intended to assist states and the EPA in understanding the nature of environmental problems and think more broadly about how to address them. Further, the program is intended to eventually give the states the necessary flexibility to develop innovative environmental programs that respond to local needs and problems.

Five states are currently participating in the program — New Jersey, Colorado, Delaware, Utah and Illinois. State and EPA officials expect that all states will participate in the NEPPS by 1997. For the regulated community, the NEPPS could provide a mechanism for implementing new environmental approaches that offer flexibility in return for increased performance. For example, states will eventually be authorized to implement innovative regulatory programs including the XL Project and the Common Sense Initiative.

### 5.0 CONCLUSION

The CSI, ELP and XL programs are evidence of the EPA's intention to promote pollution prevention. These programs also are evidence of the EPA's intent to encourage, rather than dictate, to facilities the importance of pollution prevention measures. Moreover, the EPA is keenly aware that strong enforcement of its programs is needed for those facilities that do not comply, so that those facilities that do comply are not placed at an unfair competitive disadvantage. These new programs are a giant

---

[31]The Florida Department of Environmental Regulation has received one of fourteen Federal Resource Conservation and Recovery Act grants to develop a State Training Action Plan for Florida state personnel and hazardous waste generators.

[32]The 1989 Illinois Toxic Pollution Prevention Act, (SB 1044), established a voluntary toxic pollution prevention program within the Illinois Environmental Protection Agency.

[33]The Ohio Technology Transfer Organization and the Fisher/Troy Toxic Use Bill establish the funding for a hazardous waste assistance center.

step forward in uniting the efforts of the EPA and the states towards pollution prevention.

Further, the NEPPS, the new cooperative arrangement between EPA and state officials, should foster a partnership relationship between the EPA and participating states, and represents a giant step toward achieving consensus based standards and goals. The NEPPS will also provide states the necessary flexibility to implement innovative programs which address pollution prevention, including the authority to implement the XL Project and Common Sense Initiative. As such, the NEPPS should work toward resolving conflicting state and federal goals and toward continuous improvement of environmental programs.

# CHAPTER 16

# OCCUPATIONAL SAFETY AND HEALTH ACT

Marshall Lee Miller
Baise & Miller
Washington, D.C.

## 1.0 INTRODUCTION

The U.S. Occupational Safety and Health Administration (OSHA) was once called the most unpopular agency in the federal government. It was criticized for its confusing regulations, chronic mismanagement, and picayune enforcement. With somewhat less accuracy, business groups likened it to an American gestapo, while labor unions denounced it as ineffective, unresponsive, and bureaucratic.

Most damning of all, OSHA was often simply ignored. It no longer is. Although OSHA is still technically weak and many of its standards outmoded, its penalties have sharply increased in severity. This has caught the attention of labor and management alike.

It is not often recognized, however, that OSHA is also perhaps the most important environmental health agency in the government. Even the Environmental Protection Agency (EPA), with far greater resources and public attention, deals with a smaller range of much less hazardous exposures than does OSHA. After all, individuals are more likely to be exposed to high concentrations of dangerous chemicals in their workplaces than in their backyards.

### 1.1 Comparison of OSHA and EPA

There are several distinct differences between OSHA and EPA, besides the obvious occupational jurisdiction. First, OSHA has major responsibility over safety in the workplace as well as health. Second, OSHA is essentially an enforcement organization, with a majority of its employees as inspectors, performing fifty thousand or more inspections a year. This "highway patrol" function, inspecting and penalizing thousands of businesses large and small, has been the major reason for OSHA's traditional unpopularity. At EPA, on the other hand, inspections and enforcement are a relatively smaller part of the operation.

Third, whereas EPA is an independent regulatory agency, albeit headed by presidential appointees, OSHA is a division of the Department of Labor. This organizational arrangement provides not only less prestige and less independence for OSHA, but poses an internal conflict whether OSHA should be primarily a health or a labor-oriented agency. Nevertheless, OSHA and EPA regulate different aspects of so many health issues—asbestos, vinyl chloride, carcinogens, hazard labeling, and others—that it is reasonable to regard them both as overlapping environmental organizations.

## 2.0 LEGISLATIVE FRAMEWORK

OSHA was created in December 1970—the same month as EPA—with the enactment of the Occupational Safety and Health Act (OSH Act),[1] and officially began operation in April 1971. When compared with other environmental acts, the OSH Act is very simple and well drafted. This does not mean that one necessarily agrees with the provisions of every section, but it is clearly and concisely written so that details can be worked out in implementing regulations. And unlike the other environmental laws which have been amended several times, becoming more tangled each time, the OSH Act has scarcely been amended or modified since its original passage.[2]

### 2.1 Purpose of the Act

The act sets an admirable but impossible goal: to assure that "*no* employee will suffer material impairment of health or functional capacity" from a lifetime of occupational exposure.[3] It does not require a balancing test nor a risk-benefit determination. The supplementary phrase in the OSH Act, "to the extent feasible," was not meant to alter this. This absolutist position, comparable only to one provision in the Clean Air Act,[4] reflects Congress' displeasure at previous, overly-permissive state standards which traditionally seemed always to be resolved against workers' health. In fact, the concession to "feasibility" was added almost as an afterthought.

Business groups did obtain two provisions in the law as their price for support. First, industry insisted that states should be encouraged to assume primary responsibility, in order to minimize the role of the federal OSHA. Second, because of their distrust for the allegedly pro-union bias of the Department of Labor, responsibility for first-level adjudication of violations would be vested in an independent, three-member panel of judges in a separate Occupational Health and Safety Review Commission (OSHRC). Both of these assumptions may have been mistaken, and (as discussed below), the first has openly been acknowledged as such by many industry leaders.

Congress did reject an industry effort to separate the standard setting authority from the enforcement powers of the new organization, but it gave a special role to the National Institute for Occupational Safety and Health (NIOSH) in the standard-setting process.

Thus, the three main roles of OSHA are (1) setting of safety and health standards, (2) their enforcement through federal and state inspectors, and (3) public education and consultation.

---

[1]Occupational Safety and Health Act of 1970, PL 91-596, 84 Stat. 1590.

[2]Its annual appropriations legislation, however, has been modified several times to restrict OSHA authority over small businesses, farming, hunting, and other subjects.

[3]OSH Act § 6(b)(5), emphasis added.

[4]Clean Air Act § 112, 42 U.S.C. § 1857, the National Emission Standards for Hazardous Air Pollutants (NESHAP).

## 2.2 Coverage of the Act

In general, coverage of the act extends to all employers and their employees in the fifty states and all territories under federal government jurisdiction.[5] An employer is defined as any "person engaged in a business affecting commerce who has employees but does not include the United States or any State or political subdivision of a State."[6] Coverage of the act was clarified by regulations published in the *Federal Register* on 21 January 1972.[7] These regulations interpret the coverage as follows:

1. The term "employer" excludes the United States and states and political subdivisions.
2. Any employer employing one or more employees is under its jurisdiction, including professionals, such as physicians and lawyers; agricultural employers; and nonprofit and charitable organizations.
3. Self-employed persons are not covered.
4. Family members operating a farm are not regarded as employees.
5. To the extent that religious groups employ workers for secular purposes, they are included in the coverage.
6. Domestic household employment activities for private residences are not subject to the requirements of the Act.
7. Workplaces already protected by other federal agencies under other federal statutes (discussed later) are also excluded.

In total, OSHA directly covers approximately 100 million workers in 6 million workplaces.

## 2.2 Exemptions from the Act

The OSH Act and regulations exempt a number of different categories of employees. The most important exemption is for workplaces employing 10 or fewer workers. What often is not recognized is that this exemption is only partial; these smaller establishments are still subject to accident and worker complaint investigations and the hazard communication requirements (discussed below).

Federal and state employees are also exempted from direct coverage by OSHA. As discussed below, however, the former are subject to OSHA rules under OSH Act Section 19 and several presidential Executive Orders, and most states having their own state OSHA plans also cover their state and local government workers.

Workers are also exempted if they are covered under other federal agencies, such as railroad workers under the Federal Railroad Administration or maritime workers subject to Coast Guard regulations. This exemption has generated much intergovernmental friction where the other agency has general safety and health regulations but not the full coverage of OSHA regulations. In other words, is the exemption absolute or only proportional? Under OSH Act Section 9, OSHA is supposed to defer to the other agency if it can better protect the workers and, similarly, the other agency is expected

---

[5]OSH Act § 4(a)-4(b)(2).

[6]OSH Act § 3(5). Congress' annual appropriations language has excluded several "peripheral" categories of employers in the past few years.

[7]37 FR 929, 21 January 1972, codified at 29 CFR § 1975.

to recede when the situation is reversed. Of course, considerations of turf and politics are often paramount.[8]

## 3.0 THE SCOPE OF OSHA STANDARDS

To give the reader an idea of the areas covered by the standards, the following is a subpart listing from the Code of Federal Regulations, Part 1910, Occupational Safety and Health Standards. The health standards are contained in Subpart Z; the others are safety-related, except for Subparts A, C, G, and K which cover both.

### 3.1 Areas Covered by the OSHA Standards

*Subpart A*: General (purpose and scope, definitions, applicability of standards, etc.)

*Subpart B*: Adoption and Extension of Established Federal Standards (construction work, ship repairing, longshoring, etc.)

*Subpart C*: General Safety and Health Provisions (preservation of records)

*Subpart D*: Walking-Working Surfaces (guarding floor and wall openings, portable ladders, requirements for scaffolding, etc.)

*Subpart E*: Means of Egress (definitions, specific means by occupancy, sources of standards, etc.)

*Subpart F*: Powered Platforms, Manlifts, and Vehicle-Mounted Work Platforms (elevating and rotating work platforms, standards organizations, etc.)

*Subpart G*: Occupational Health and Environmental Control (ventilation, noise exposure, radiation, etc.)

*Subpart H*: Hazardous Materials (compressed gases, flammables, storage of petroleum gases, effective dates, etc.)

*Subpart I*: Personal Protective Equipment (eye and face, respiratory, electrical devices, etc.)

*Subpart J*: General Environmental Controls (sanitation, labor camps, safety color code for hazards, etc.)

*Subpart K*: Medical and First Aid (medical services, sources of standards)

*Subpart L*: Fire Protection (fire suppression equipment, hose and sprinkler systems, fire brigades, etc.)

*Subpart M*: Compressed Gas and Compressed Air Equipment (inspection of gas cylinders, safety relief devices, etc.)

*Subpart N*: Materials Handling and Storage (powered industrial trucks, cranes, helicopters, etc.)

*Subpart O*: Machinery and Machine Guarding (requirements for all machines, woodworking machinery, wheels, mills, etc.)

*Subpart P*: Hand and Portable Powered Tools and Other Hand-Held Equipment (guarding of portable power tools

*Subpart Q*: Welding, Cutting and Brazing (definitions, sources of standards, etc.)

---

[8]EPA learned this lesson in 1984 when Deputy Administrator James Barnes quite properly deferred to OSHA on certain asbestos workplace matters. Congressional critics, who believed OSHA would not treat the matter seriously or competently, raised such furor that EPA retained jurisdiction.

*Subpart R*: Special Industries (pulp, paper and paperboard mills, textiles, laundry machinery, telecommunications, etc.)

*Subpart S*: Electrical (application, National Electrical Code)

*Subpart T*: Commercial Diving Operations (qualification of team, pre- and post-dive procedures, equipment, etc.)

*Subpart U-Y*: [Reserved]

*Subpart Z*: Toxic and Hazardous Substances (air contaminants, asbestos, vinyl chloride, lead benzene, etc.)

### 3.2 Overview of Health Standards

Health issues, notably environmental contaminants in the workplace, have increasingly become OSHA's concern over the past few years. Health hazards are much more complex, more difficult to define, and because of the delay in detection, perhaps more dangerous to a larger number of employees. Unlike safety hazards, the effects of health hazards may be slow, cumulative, irreversible, and complicated by non-occupational factors.

If a machine is unequipped with safety devices and maims a workers, the danger is clearly and easily identified and the solution usually obvious. However, if workers are exposed for several years to a chemical that is later found to be carcinogenic, there may be little help for those exposed.

In the nation's workplaces there are tens of thousands of toxic chemicals, many of which are significant enough to warrant regulation. Yet OSHA only has a list of less than 500 substances with simple threshold limits adopted from the recommended lists of private industrial hygiene organizations, although this list is now finally being revised.

The promulgation of health standards involves many complex concepts. To be complete, each standard needs medical surveillance requirements, recordkeeping, monitoring, and multiple physical reviews, just to mention a few. At the present rate, promulgation of standards on every existing toxic substance could take centuries.

### 3.3 Overview of Safety Standards

This chapter emphasizes the health aspects of OSHA, for most press attention and the agency's own public emphasis since the mid-1970s has been on toxic hazards. Nevertheless, OSHA is also an occupational safety organization. The two parts of the organization are quite distinct: there are separate inspectors and standards offices for each, and the two groups are different in terms of background, education, and age. There are also far more safety than health inspectors.

Safety hazards are those aspects of the work environment which, in general, cause harm of an immediate and sometimes violent nature, such as burns, electrical shock, cuts, broken bones, loss of limbs or eyesight, and even death. The distinction from health hazards is usually obvious, with mechanical and electrical considered as safety problems, while chemicals are considered health problems. Only noise is difficult to categorize; it is classified as a health problem.

The Section 6(a) adoption of national consensus and other federal standards, created chaos in the safety area. It was one thing for companies to follow industry or association guidelines that, in many cases, had not been modified in years; it was another thing for those guidelines actually to be written down as law. In the two years the act provided for OSHA to produce standards derived from these existing rules, the agency should have examined these closely, simplified them, deleted the ridiculous and unnecessary ones, and promulgated final regulations that actually identified and eliminated hazards to workers. But in the commotion of organizing an agency from scratch, it did not happen that way.

Almost all of the so-called "Mickey Mouse" standards were safety regulations, such as the requirements that fire extinguishers had to be attached to the wall exactly so many inches above the floor. Undertrained OSHA inspectors often failed to recognize major hazards while citing industries for minor violations "which were highly visible, but not necessarily related to serious hazards to workers' safety and health."[9]

Section 6(g) of the OSH Act directs OSHA to establish priorities based on the needs of specific "industries, trades, crafts, occupations, businesses, workplaces, or work environments." The Senate report accompanying the OSH Act stated that the agency's emphasis initially should be put on industries where the need was determined to be most compelling.[10] OSHA's early attempts to target inspections, however, were sporadic and, for the most part, unsuccessful. The situation has improved somewhat in recent years, for both health and safety, in part because of the recent requirement that some priority scheme be used that could justify search warrants, but that has brought its own problems.[11]

## 4.0 STANDARD SETTING

We can all recognize the amount of time that could be expended in setting standards. There are thousands of chemical substances, electrical problems, fire hazards, and many other dangerous situations prevalent in the workplace for which standards needed to be developed.

To meet the objectives defined in the act, three different standard setting procedures were established:

1. Consensus Standards, under Section 6(a).
2. Permanent Standards, under Section 6(b).
3. Emergency Temporary Standards, under Section 6(c).

## 4.1 Consensus Standards: Section 6(a)

Congress realized that OSHA would need standards to enforce while it was developing its own. Section 6(a) allowed the agency, for a two-year period which ended on 25 April 1973, to adopt standards developed by other federal agencies or to adopt consensus standards of various industry or private associations.[12] This resulted in a list of around 420 common toxic chemicals with maximum permitted air concentrations specified in parts per million (PPM) or in milligrams per cubic meters ($mg/M^3$).

---

[9]Statement of Basil Whiting, Deputy Assistant Secretary of Labor for OSHA, before the Committee on Labor and Human Resources, U.S. Senate, 21 March 1980, pp. 5-6.
[10]For the legislative history of the act, see especially the Conference Report 91-1765 of 16 December 1970, as well as H.R. 91-1291 and S.R. 91-1282.
[11]See *Marshall v. Barlow's Inc.*, 436 U.S. 307 (1978), which will be discussed later in this chapter.
[12]39 FR 23502, 27 June 1974.

There are several problems inherent in these standards. First, these threshold values are the only elements to the standard. There are no required warning labels, monitoring, or medical recordkeeping, nor do they generally distinguish between 8-hour, 15-minute, peak, annual average, and other periods of exposure. Second, being thresholds, they are based on the implicit assumption that there are universal "no effect" levels, below which a worker is safe. This is controversial and, for carcinogens, quite questionable.

Third, most of the standards were originally established not on the basis of firm scientific evidence but, as the name implies, from existing guidelines and limits of various industry, association, and governmental groups. Before OSHA's creation, they were intended to be general, non-binding guidelines, and had been in circulation for a number of years with no urgency to keep them current. Consequently, neither industry nor labor bothered to comment when OSHA first proposed the consensus standards. Many of these "interim" standards were out of date by the time they were adopted by OSHA, and they are now frozen in time until OSHA goes through the full Section 6(b) administrative rulemaking procedure.

Fourth, OSHA consensus standards often involve "incorporation by reference," especially in the safety area. In some cases, these pre-1972 publications were not standards or even formal association guidelines but mere private association pamphlets that are no longer in print and not easily obtainable anywhere. For example, the general regulation on compressed gases merely states that the cylinders should be in safe condition and maintained "in accordance with Compressed Gas Association pamphlet P-1-1965" and several similar documents.[13]

Whatever disadvantages, Congress was undoubtedly correct in requiring the compilation of such a list. Otherwise, there would have been no OSHA health standards at the beginning; there are virtually no others even now.

### 4.1.1 Standards Completion Process

The agency has attempted to deal with one of the shortcomings of the consensus standards by what is called the Standards Completion Process. Over a number of years, OSHA has taken some threshold standards and added various medical, monitoring, and other requirements.[14] At least a broader range of protection is offered to exposed workers.

### 4.2 Permanent Standards: Section 6(b)

Permanent standards must now be developed pursuant to Section 6(b). This is the regular standard-setting process. Permanent standards may be initiated by a well-publicized tragedy, court action, new scientific studies, or (theoretically) the receipt of a criteria document from the National Institute of Occupation Safety and Health (NIOSH), an organization described later in this chapter. The criteria document is a compilation of all the scientific reports on a particular chemical, including epidemiological and animal studies, along with a recommendation to OSHA for a standard. The

---

[13]29 C.F.R. § 1910.101.
[14]Since the 6(a) process ended in April 1972, the standards promulgated thereunder cannot be modified or revised without going through the notice and comment administrative procedures under Section 6(b).

recommendation, based supposedly only on scientific health considerations, includes suggested exposure limits (8-hour average, peaks, etc.) and appropriate medical monitoring, labeling, and other proscriptions.

Congress apparently assumed that NIOSH would be the standard-setting arm of OSHA, although the two are in different government departments (HHS and Labor, respectively). That is, OSHA would presumably take the scientific recommendations from NIOSH, factor in engineering and technical feasibility, and then promulgate as similar a standard as possible. However, the system has never worked this way. Instead, OSHA's own standards office has regarded NIOSH's contribution as just one step in the process—and not one entitled to a great deal of deference. NIOSH criteria documents vary considerably in quality, depending in part on to whom they were subcontracted, but another problem is that too often they are insufficiently discriminating in evaluating questionable studies. That is, one study is regarded as good as any other study, without regard to the quality of the data or the validity of the protocols. Of course, another factor in OSHA's attitude just might be the "not invented here" syndrome.

Following receipt of the criteria document, or some other initiating action, OSHA will study the evidence and then possibly publish a proposed standard. Most candidate standards never get this far: the hundreds of NIOSH documents, labor union petitions, and other serious recommendations have resulted in (depending on the count) only slightly over a dozen health standards since 1970.[15]

The proposed standard is then subjected to public comment for (typically) a ninety-day period, after which the reactions are analyzed and informal public hearings are scheduled. In a few controversial instances, there may be more than one series of hearings and comments. Then come the post-hearing comments, which are perhaps the most important presentations by the parties. After considerable further study, a final standard is eventually promulgated. The entire process might be accomplished in under a year, but in practice it takes a minimum of several years and, as with asbestos, even decades.

The following is a list of the final health standards which OSHA has promulgated to date:

1. Asbestos
2. "14 carcinogens"
   - 4-Nitrobiphenyl
   - alpha-nephthylamine
   - methyl chloromethyl ether
   - 3,3'-dichlorolenzidine
   - bis-chloromethyl ether
   - beta-naphthylamine
   - benzidine
   - 4-aminodiphenyl

---

[15]This meager number does *not* reflect OSHA's scientific judgment that the other candidates are unworthy or that the agency has sharply different priorities, although these may be partial factors. More important reasons are: poor leadership, technical inexperience, and a bit of politics.

- ethyleneimine
- beta-propiolactone
- 2-acetylaminofluorene
- 4-dimethylaminozaobenzene
- N-nitrosodimethylamine
- (MOCA - stayed by court action)
3. Vinyl chloride
4. Inorganic arsenic
5. Lead
6. Coke oven emissions
7. Cotton dust
8. 1,2-dibromo-3-chloropropane
9. Acrylonitrile
10. Ethylene oxide
11. Benzene
12. Field Sanitation

## 4.3 Emergency Temporary Standards

The statute also provides for a third standard-setting approach, specified for emergency circumstances where the normal, ponderous rulemaking procedure would be too slow. Section 6(c) gives the agency authority to issue an emergency temporary standard (ETS) if necessary to protect workers from exposure to "grave danger" posed by substances "determined to be toxic or physically harmful or from new hazards."[16]

Such standards are effective immediately upon publication in the *Federal Register*. An ETS is only valid, however, for six months. OSHA is thus under considerable pressure to conduct an expedited rulemaking for a permanent standard before the ETS lapses. For this reason, a quest for an emergency standard has been the preferred route for labor unions or other groups seeking a new OSHA standard.

These ETSs have not fared well, however, when challenged in the courts.

## 4.4 The General Duty Clause, 5(a)(1)

There is actually a fourth type of enforceable standard, one that covers situations for which no standards currently exist.

Since OSHA has standards for only a few hundred of the thousands of potentially dangerous chemicals and workplace safety hazards, there are far more situations than the rules cover. Therefore, inspectors have authority under the "General Duty" clause to cite violations for unsafe conditions even where standards do not exist.[17] Agency policy has shifted back and forth between encouraging the use of "Section 5(a)(1)," as the clause is often termed, since this ensures that unsafe conditions will be addressed, and discouraging its use on the theory that employers should be liable only for compliance with specific standards.

However, the agency has acknowledged that many of the standards which do exist are woefully out of date and thus cannot be relied upon for adequate protection of

---

[16]OSHA Act § 6(c)(1).
[17]OSH Act § 5(a)(1), 29 U.S.C. 654(a)(1).

worker safety and health. The traditional notion was that compliance with an existing specific standard, even if demonstrably unsafe, precluded an OSHA citation,[18] has been called in question by the courts. In April 1988, a federal appellate court allowed OSHA to cite for violations of the General Duty clause even where a company was in full compliance with a specific numerical standard on the precise point in question.[19] Bare compliance with the standards on the books, therefore, would not be responsible management.

### 4.5 Feasibility and the Balancing Debate

There has been a continuing debate over feasibility and balancing in OSHA enforcement. The important issues include the following:

1. Can OSHA legally consider economic factors in setting health or safety standards levels?
2. If so, is this consideration limited only to extreme circumstances?
3. Does the Occupational Safety and Health Act provide for a balancing of costs and benefits in setting standards?
4. Can OSHA mandate engineering controls although they alone would still not attain the standard?
5. And, can OSHA require engineering controls even if personal protective equipment (such as ear plugs) could effectively, if often only theoretically, reduce hazards to a safe level and at a much lower cost?

These questions have been extensively litigated before the Occupational Safety and Health Review Commission (OSHRC) and the courts; most of the debate has been over the interpretation of "feasibility" in Section 6(b)(5) of the act.

One must remember that OSHA legislation was originally seen by Congress in rather absolutist terms: any standard promulgated should be one "which most adequately assumes . . .that no employee will suffer material impairment of health." Only late in the congressional debate was the Department of Labor able to insert the phrase "to the extent feasible" into the text. This was intended to prevent companies having to close

---

[18]This is exemplified by *Phelps Dodge Corporation* (OSHRC Final Order, 1980), 9 OSHC 1222, which found no violation of the act to expose workers to "massive amounts of sulphur dioxide for short periods of time" since there was no maximum ceiling value in the standard and the employer was complying with the eight-hour average value required in the specific sulphur dioxide regulation. The citation for violation of § 5(a)(1) was therefore vacated.

[19]*International Union, UAW v. General Dynamics Land System Division*, 815 F.2d 1570, 13 OSHC 12-1 (CADC 1988). The Court held that employer's knowledge was the crucial element; if he knew that the OSHA standard was not adequate to protect workers from a hazard, he could not claim he was maintaining a safe workplace within the meaning of § 5(a)(1), the "General Duty" clause, even if he were adhering to a standard he knew was outmoded. The Court thereby dismissed the argument that the employer would not know what is legally expected of him; he was expected to maintain a safe workplace, specific regulations notwithstanding. There was no specific provision in the statute which prevented a general duty citation when a specific standard existed.

because unattainable standards were imposed on them, but it was not spelled out to what extent economic as well as technical feasibility was included.[20]

Since the term "feasibility" was not clearly defined, there has been much confusion over how to interpret what Congress intended, as the earlier cases show. In *Industrial Union Department, AFL v. Hodgson*, the D.C. Circuit accepted that economic realities affected the meaning of "feasible", but only to the extent that "a standard that is prohibitively expensive is not 'feasible.'"[21] It was Congress' intent, the court added, that this term would prevent a standard unreasonably "requiring protective devices unavailable under existing technology or by making financial viability generally impossible." The court warned, however, that this doctrine should not be used by companies to avoid needed improvements in their workplaces:

Standards may be economically feasible even though, from the standpoint of employers, they are financially burdensome and affect profit margins adversely. Nor does the concept of economic feasibility necessarily guarantee the continued existence of individual employers.[22]

A similar view was adopted in 1975 by the Second Circuit in *The Society of the Plastics Industry v. OSHA*, written by Justice Clark, who cited approvingly the case above.[23] He held that "feasible" meant not only that which is attainable technologically and economically now, but also that which might reasonably be achievable in the future. In this case, which concerned strict emissions controls on vinyl chloride, he declared that OSHA may impose "standards which require improvements in existing technologies or which require the development of new technology, and . . . is not limited to issuing standards based solely on devices already fully developed."[24]

Neither court undertook any risk-benefit analysis, such as attempting to compare the hundreds of millions of dollars needed to control vinyl chloride with the lives lost to angiosarcoma of the liver. Those who have attempted to develop such equations have generally concluded the task is undoable, at least for most such chronic health effects.[25]

A third federal appeals court, however, took a strongly contrary position in a case involving noise. In *Turner Co. v. Secretary of Labor*, the Seventh Circuit Court of Appeals decided that the $30,000 cost of abating a noise hazard should be weighed

---

[20]This account of the behind-the-scenes machinations is based largely on the views of the late Congressman William Steiger (R-Wisc.), a principal author of the act, and of Judge Lawrence Silberman, then Solicitor of Labor. The legislative history is relatively unhelpful on this subject. See, for example, hearings before the Select Subcommittee on Labor, Committee on Education and Labor, "Occupational Safety and Health Act of 1969", two vols., 1969.

[21]499 F.2d 467, 1 OSHC 1631 (D.C. Cir., 1974).

[22]1 OSHC 1631 at 1639.

[23]509 F.2d 1301, 2 OSHC 1496 (2nd Cir., 1975), cert. den. 421 U.S. 922.

[24]509 F.2d at 1309, 2 OSHC at 1502 (2nd Cir., 1975).

[25]See, for example, the conclusions of the National Academy of Sciences report, "Government Regulation of Chemicals in the Environment," 1975.

against the health damage to the workers, taking into consideration the availability of personal protective equipment to mitigate the risk.[26]

This holding is not unreasonable, but is based on a highly tenuous interpretation of the law. The court, without providing any clear rationale for its view, held that "the word 'feasible' as contained in 29 CFR § 1910.95(6)(1) must be given its ordinary and common sense meaning of 'practicable.'" (This may be so, but is of no analytical value.) From this the court concluded:

Accordingly, the Commission erred when it failed to consider the relative cost of implementing engineering controls...versus the effectiveness of an existing personal protective equipment program utilizing fitted earplugs.[27]

This interpretation does not follow from the analysis. In fact, since the Turner Company had both the financial resources and the technical capability to abate the noise problem, compliance with the regulation would appear to be "practicable." The court, however, considered this term to mean that a cost-benefit computation should be made.

In 1982, the U.S. Court of Appeals for the Ninth Circuit, in the case of *Donovan v. Castle & Cooke Foods and OSHRC*,[28] also held that the Noise Act and the regulations permit consideration of relative costs and benefits to determine what noise controls are feasible.

OSHA gave the plant a citation on the grounds that, although Castle & Cooke required its employees to wear personal protective equipment, its failure to install technologically feasible engineering and administrative controls[29] constituted a violation of the noise standard, and that the violation could only be abated by the implementation of such controls. OSHA argued that engineering and administrative controls should be considered economically infeasible only if their implementation would so seriously jeopardize the employer's economic condition as to threaten continued operation.

On appeal, OSHA argued that neither the OSHC nor the courts are free to interpret "economic feasibility," because its definition is controlled by the Supreme Court's

---

[26]561 F.2d 82, 5 OSHC 1970 (7th Cir., 1977). The Occupational Safety and Health Review Commission (OSHRC) decisions on *Turner* and the related *Continental Can* case can be found at 4 OSHC 1554 (1976) and 4 OSHC 1541 (1976), respectively.

[27]5 OSHC 1790 at 1791.

[28]692 F.2d 641, 10 OSHC 2169 (1982).

[29]Engineering controls are those that reduce the sound intensity at the source of that noise. This is achieved by insulation of the machine, by substituting quieter machines and processes, or by isolating the machine or its operator. Administrative controls attempt to reduce workers' exposure to excess noise through use of variable work schedules, variable assignments, or limiting machine use. Personal protective equipment includes such devices as ear plugs and ear muffs provided by the employer and fitted to individual workers.

decision in *American Textile Manufacturers Institute, Inc. v. Donovan*.[30] The appeals court, however, decided that the Supreme Court's interpretation of the term "feasible" made in *American Textile* was not deemed controlling for the noise standards. It also affirmed that economic "feasibility" should be determined through a cost-benefit analysis, and that in the case of Castle & Cooke the costs of economic controls did not justify the benefit that would accrue to employees. Thus, the decision to vacate the citation was upheld.

## 5.0 VARIANCES

Companies who complain that OSHA standards are unrealistic are often not aware that they might be able to create their own version of the standards. The alternative has to be at least as effective as the regular standard, but it can be different.

### 5.1 Temporary Variances

Section 6(b)(6)(A) of the OSH Act establishes a procedure by which any employer may apply for a "temporary order granting a variance from a standard or any provision thereof." According to the act, the variance will be approved when OSHA determines that the requirements have been met and establishes that (1) the employer is unable to meet the standard "because of unavailability of professional or technical personnel or of materials and equipment," or because alterations of facilities cannot be completed in time; (2) that he is "taking all available steps to safeguard" his workers against the hazard covered by the standard for which he is applying for a variance; and (3) he has an "effective program for coming into compliance with the standard as quickly as practicable."[31]

This temporary order may be granted only after employees have been notified and, if requested, there has been sufficient opportunity for a hearing. The variance may not remain in effect for more than one year with the possibility of only two six-month renewals.[32] The overriding factor an employer must demonstrate for a temporary variance is good faith.[33]

### 5.2 Permanent Variances

Permanent variances can be issued under Section 6(d) of the OSH Act. A permanent variance may be granted to an employer who has demonstrated "by a preponderance" of evidence that the "conditions, practices, means, methods, operations

---

[30]101 S.Ct. 2478, 9 OSHC 1913 (17 June 1981). In this case, representatives of the cotton dust industry challenged proposed regulations limiting permissible exposure levels to cotton dust. Section 6(b)(5) of the act requires OSHA to "set the standard which most adequately assures, to the extent feasible...that no employee will suffer material impairment of health..." The industry held that OSHA had not shown that the proposed standards were economically feasible. However, the Supreme Court upheld the cotton dust regulations, holding that the "plain meaning of the word 'feasible' is capable of being done, executed, or effected," and that a cost-benefit analysis by OSHA is not required because a feasibility analysis is.

[31]OSH Act § 7(b)(6)(A).

[32]*Ibid.*

[33]E. Klein, Variances, in *Proceedings of the Occupational Health and Safety Regulations Seminar* (Washington, D.C.: Government Institutes, 1978), p. 74..

or processes used or proposed to be used" will provide a safe and healthful workplace as effectively as would compliance with the standard.

## 6.0 COMPLIANCE AND INSPECTIONS

OSHA is primarily an enforcement organization. In its early years both the competency of its inspections and the size of the assessed fines were pitifully inadequate; they were the primary reason OSHA was not taken seriously by either labor unions or the business community. That picture has now changed significantly.

### 6.1 Field Structure

The Department of Labor (DOL) has divided the territory subject to the OSH Act into ten federal regions, the same boundaries that EPA also uses. Each region contains from four to nine area offices. When an area office is not considered necessary because of a lack of industrial activity, a district office or field station may be established. Each region is headed by a regional administrator; each area by an area director. In the field, compliance officers represent area offices and inspect industrial sites in their vicinity, except in unique situations where a specialist or team might be required.

### 6.2 Role of Inspections

The only way to determine compliance by employers is inspections, but inspecting all the workplaces covered by the OSH Act would require decades. Each year there are over fifty-thousand federal inspections, and as many or more state inspections, but there are several million workplaces. Obviously, a priority system for high-hazard occupations is necessary, along with random inspections just to keep everyone "on his toes."

Inspections are supposed to be surprises; there are penalties for anyone alerting the sites beforehand. The inspections may be targeted at random, triggered by worker complaints, set by a priority system based on hazardous probabilities, or by events such as a fatality or explosion. Inspectors expect admittance without search warrants, but a company has the right to refuse admittance until OSHA obtains a search warrant from a federal district court.[34] Such refusal is frankly not a good idea except in very special circumstances.

### 6.3 Training and Competency of Inspectors

There has been a major problem with OSHA inspectors in the past—the training program did not adequately prepare them for their tasks, and the quality of the hiring was uneven. In the early days there was tremendous pressure from the unions to get an inspection force on the job as soon as possible, so recruitment was often hurried and training was minimal. Inspectors would walk into a plant where, for example, kepone dust was so thick workers could not see across the room, yet, because there was no standard as such, the inspectors would not think there was a problem. Yet had there been a fire extinguisher in the wrong place, and had the inspector been able to see it through the haze, he would have cited the plant for a safety violation.

---

[34]See a later section in this chapter on the Supreme Court's *Barlow's* decision interpreting the Fourth Amendment to the U.S. Constitution.

Competency among staff has markedly improved since the early days of the program. Both in-house training efforts by OSHA and increased numbers of professional training programs conducted by colleges and universities have contributed to these improvements. There is also a greater sensitivity towards workers and their representatives.[35]

## 6.4 Citations and Proposed Fines

If the inspector discovers a hazard in the workplace, a citation and a proposed fine are in order. Citations can be serious, nonserious, willful, or repeated. A serious violation is found if there is "substantial probability that death or serious physical harm could result from a condition which exists, or from one or more practices, means, methods, operations, or processes which have been adopted by or are in use, in such place of employment unless the employer did not, and could not with the exercise of reasonable diligence, know of the presence of the violation."[36]

A penalty is mandatory for a serious violation; penalties for nonserious violations are discretionary. Even several nonserious violations considered together do not make up a serious violation unless the combination somehow would be likely to lead to death or serious physical harm to an employee.

## 6.5 Willful Violations

Any employer who is aware of a hazardous condition in his plant, or should be aware, yet makes no effort to rectify it, may be held to be a willful violator and penalized as such. A "willful" violation is "properly defined as an act or omission which occurs consciously, intentionally, deliberately or voluntarily as distinguished from accidentally."[37]

The critical element of proof necessary is that of knowledge. OSHA would have to establish that the employer was aware that a hazardous condition existed and then took no reasonable steps to eliminate the condition.[38]

Penalties for willful violations considerably exceed those for serious or nonserious violations; a penalty of $10,000, now potentially raised seven-fold, may be assessed for each violation.

## 6.6 Repeat Violations

The same penalty may be applied for repeated violations, with each day being in theory a separate violation. A citation for a repeated violation cannot be issued unless the employer has been cited for a violation, has abated the violation, and has thereafter again violated the same standard or permitted the same hazard to exist in his plant. In the case of a company having multiple sites or plants in different states or OSHA regions, the issue of repetition is more complex. OSHA has changed its definitions several times, and the policy is not yet firm.

---

[35]Statement of Lane Kirkland, President, AFL-CIO, before the Senate Committee on Labor and Human Resources on Oversight of the Occupational Safety and Health Act, 1 April 1980.
[36]OSH Act § 17(k).
[37]*Guidebook to Occupational Safety and Health* (Chicago: CCH, 1974), p. 149.
[38]OSH Act § 17(d).

When enough time has been allowed for the correction of a violation, OSHA may reinspect the plant to verify compliance with the issued citation. If the employer has failed to abate, a penalty will be assessed "for each day during which such failure or violation continues."[39]

## 6.7 Egregious Violations

OSHA believes that some really bad companies deserve fines much higher than under the standard calculations. The idea therefore arose that rather than counting a violation once, in special cases it should be multiplied by the total number of workers who were thereby endangered. This policy has naturally created enormous controversy. It is not set forth in the statute, and on pragmatic grounds is less justifiable since Congress increased OSHA potential penalties by seven fold.

## 6.8 Communicating and Enforcing Company Rules

Many, arguably, even most, accidents are due to human negligence, usually involving an act which is contrary to company policy. Merely claiming a firm policy, however, is not enough. For employers to plead employee misconduct as a defense to an OSHA citation, however, the company must first demonstrate three things. First, of course, is to prove the existence of such rules. [40]

Second, an employer must prove that these rules were effectively communicated to the employees. Proof can include written instructions, evidence of required attendance at education sessions, the curriculum of training programs, and other forms which should be documented. [41]

Third, many companies which can demonstrate the above two principles can fall short on the third, namely that there should be evidence the policies are effectively enforced. [42] For this, evidence of disciplinary action taken against infractions of the rules, though not necessarily the precise rule that would have prevented the accident under investigation, is necessary. The closer to the actual circumstance, of course, the more that proof of active company enforcement is dispositive. [43]

If the above three principles can all be demonstrated, they constitute a reasonable defense to charges of violating the regulations, even in cases of death or serious injury. Note that this defense is not limited to the misconduct of a low-ranking employee. Misconduct of a supervisor, although it may suggest inadequate company policy and direction, can also be shown as an isolated and personal failing. According to an appellate court, the proper focus of a court is on the effectiveness of the employer's implementation of his safety program, and not on whether the unforeseeable conduct was by an employee or by supervisory personnel. [44]

---

[39]*Ibid.*
[40]*The Carborundum Company* (OSHRC Judge, 1982), 10 OSHC 1979.
[41]*Schnabel Associates, Inc.* (OSAHRC Judge, 1982), 10 OSHC 2109.
[42]*Galloway Enterprises, Inc.* (OSAHRC Judge, 1984) 11 OSHC 2071.
[43]*Bethlehem Steel Corporation, Inc.* (OSAHRC Judge, 1985), 12 OSHC 1606. *Dover Electric Company, Inc.* (OSAHRC Judge, 1984) 11 OSHC 2175.
[44]*Brock v. L. E. Myers Company*, 818 F.2d 1270, 13 OSHC 1289 (6th Cir., 1987).

## 7.0 RECORDKEEPING

For an agency that seems grounded in practical workplace realities, OSHA's regulations increasingly emphasize recordkeeping and paperwork requirements. Moreover, recent OSHA enforcement efforts have been directed heavily towards paperwork violations.

### 7.1 Accident Reports

Any workplace accident requiring treatment or resulting in lost work time must be recorded within six working days on an OSHA Form 200. This is officially entitled the Log and Summary of Recordable Occupational Injuries and Illnesses, although no one uses that longer term. This document is supposed to provide insight to accident types and causes for both the company and for OSHA inspectors. It must be retained for five years. Criminal penalties apply to any "knowing false representation" on these and other required records.[45]

A second document is the OSHA Form 101, which describes in detail the nature of each of the recorded accidents. All the supporting information does not have to be on this one form, provided that the material is available in the file. This form is entitled the Supplementary Record of Occupational Injuries and Illnesses.

A third required document is the annual summary of accidents and illnesses, statistics based on the Form 200 data. This summary must be signed by a responsible corporate official and posted in some conspicuous place by the following 1st of February each year.

### 7.2 Monitoring and Medical Records

OSHA's health standards increasingly contain provisions calling for medical records, monitoring of pollution, and other information. Safety as well as health standards may also require periodic inspections of workplaces or equipment which must be recorded. These medical and exposure records must be retained for 30 years; a company going out of business or liquidating must transfer these records to NIOSH.[46]

For example, the OSHA noise standards mandate baseline and periodic hearing tests[47], the lead standard requires measuring of blood lead levels and other data which can be the basis for removal from the workplace until the levels go down, and the ionizing radiation regulation requires careful recording of exposure and absorption information.

A host of safety (and some health) regulations require (1) written safety programs, (2) specified training, (3) documented routine inspections, or combinations of all three. There is no clear pattern to these requirements; they must be checked separately for each regulation. For example, derricks don't require the first but do the second and third,

---

[45] OSH Act § 17(g).

[46] 29 C.F.R. § 1910.20.

[47] OSHA's noise monitoring and recordkeeping requirements for hearing loss and standard threshold shift (STS, previously "significant threshold shift") are particularly complex and have been subject to considerable litigation.

while cranes require only the third.[48] Some safety standards, such as fire protection, lockout/tagout, process safety management, and employee alarms require all three.[49] The health standards tend to require all three as well, including those for bloodborne pathogens and for hazard communications.[50]

### 7.3 Hazard Communication

The OSHA hazard communication program, which is described more fully elsewhere in this chapter, requires companies making or using hazardous chemicals to provide information to their workers on possible exposure risks. The program provides for (1) the labeling of toxic chemicals, (2) warning signs and posters, (3) material safety data sheets (MSDS) on hazardous chemicals, (4) a written policy setting forth the company's handling of issues under the hazcom program, and (5) a list of hazardous chemicals on premises.[51]

### 7.4 Access to Records

Employees and their designated legal or union representatives have the right to obtain access to their records within 15 working days. They may not be charged for duplication or other costs. Former employees are also given this access.

There are certain limited exceptions to disclosure dealing with psychiatric evaluation, terminal illness, and confidential informants. Otherwise the view is that even the most secret chemical formulas and business information must be revealed to the employees or former employees if they are relevant to exposure and toxicity. This could be a godsend for industrial espionage, but so far there have been few claims that this is a practical problem.

OSHA inspectors also have access to these records. From time to time some company challenges this access as a violation of the Fourth Amendment unless the inspector produces an easily-obtained search warrant.

### 8.0 REFUSAL TO WORK AND WHISTLEBLOWING

Employees have a right, where they believe company policy or a supervisor's orders are unsafe, and OSHA regulations protect them from discrimination. And if employees see unsafe or unhealthy workplace conditions, they have a right to report them to OSHA without fear of reprisals or discrimination.

### 8.1 Refusal to Work

OSHA has ruled, and the Supreme Court has unanimously upheld, the OSHA principle that workers have the right to refuse to work in the face of serious injury or death. [52] The case was a simple one. Two workers refused to go on some wire mesh screens through which several workers had fallen part way and, two weeks before,

---

[48]29 C.F.R. § 1910.181, and § 1910.178-179.
[49]29 C.F.R. §§ 1910.156 et seq., 1910.147, 1910.119, and 1910.165.
[50]29 C.F.R. § 1910.1030, and 29 C.F.R. § 1200.
[51]29 CFR 1910.1200
[52]29 C.F.R. § 1977.12 (1979); *Whirlpool Corp. v. Marshall*, 445 U.S. 1, 8 OSHC 1001 (1980).

another worker had fallen to his death. When reprimanded, the workers complained to OSHA. The Supreme Court had no difficulty in finding that the workers had been improperly discriminated against by their employer in this case. How a court would rule in less glaring circumstances is harder to predict. Interestingly, there has not been a swarm of such cases, despite dire predictions of wholesale refusal and consequent litigation.

## 8.2 Protection of Whistleblowing

If a worker is fired or disciplined for complaining to governmental officials about unsafe work conditions, he has a legal remedy under the OSH Act for restoration of his job or loss of pay. [53] Similar provisions, administered also by OSHA's "Eleven-C" staff, have been inserted into other federal statutes, including EPA's Emergency Planning and Community Right-to-Know Act (EPCRA) in the Superfund legislation. [54]

Congress assumed that the employees in a given workplace would be best acquainted with the hazards there. It therefore statutorily encouraged prompt OSHA response to worker complaints of violations.[55] Since this system could be undermined if employers penalized complaining employees, the act in Section 11(c) provides sanctions against such retaliation or discrimination:

No person may discharge or in any manner discriminate against any employee because such employee has filed any complaint or instituted or caused to be instituted any proceeding under or related to this Act or has testified or is about to testify in any such proceeding or because of the exercise by such employee on behalf of himself or others of any right afforded by this Act.[56]

If discrimination occurs, particularly if an employee is fired, a special OSHA team intervenes to obtain reinstatement, back wages, or—if return to the company is undesirable—a cash settlement for the worker. If agreement cannot be reached, the agency resorts to litigation.

This entire system has not worked as expected. First, the worker complaints have surprisingly not been a very fruitful source of health and safety information. Far too many of the complaints came in bunches, coinciding with labor disputes in a particular plant. OSHA has therefore finally abandoned its policy of trying to investigate every complaint.

Second, the Title 11(c) process has worked slowly and uncertainly, so even though an employee may receive vindication, the months (or even years) of delay and anguish are a strong disincentive for workers to report hazards.

Third, it is often difficult to determine whether a malcontented worker was fired for informing OSHA or for a number of other issues which might cloud the employer-employee relationship. Does the complaint have to be the sole cause of dismissal or discrimination, or can some (fairly arbitrary) allocation be made.

---

[53]OSH Act § 11(c), 29 U.S.C.660.

[54]Title III of the Superfund Amendment and Reauthorization Act of 1986 (SARA). These amendments are designed to "prevent future Bhopals" by informing community fire and emergency centers what chemicals a company has on site.

[55]OSH Act § 8(f)(1).

[56]OSH Act § 11(c)(1).

Fourth, there is continuing controversy over whether 11(c) should protect workers complaining of hazards to those other than OSHA, even if the direct or indirect result is an OSHA inspection. In the Kepone tragedy of 1975, an employee complained of hazardous chemicals to his supervisor, was fired, and only then went to OSHA. Not only was he declared unprotected by the act, but his complaint, no longer a worker complaint, was not even investigated at the time. Although agency officials have sworn not to repeat that mistake, the issue of what triggers 11(c) protection, (a) a complaint of unsafe workplace conditions, or (b) reporting that matter to OSHA, is a continuing one.

A related current issue is whether an employee who reports a hazard to the press, whose ensuing publicity triggers an OSHA investigation, was protected by 11(c). In one notable instance, OSHA regional officials decided in favor of the worker and won the subsequent litigation in federal district court. The Solicitor of Labor, however, disagreed, and attempted to withdraw the agency from a winning position.[57]

For all these reasons, therefore, a worker can never really predict how he might fare if he does complain.

## 9.0 FEDERAL AND STATE EMPLOYEES

The exclusion of federal and state employees has been the topic of much discussion and debate.

### 9.1 Federal Agencies

Federal employees are not covered directly by OSHA, at least not to the extent that federal agencies are subject to fines and other penalties. However, the presumption was that the agencies would follow OSHA regulations in implementing their own programs. Section 19 of the OSH Act designates the responsibility for providing safe and healthful working conditions to the head of each agency. A series of Presidential Executive Orders have emphasized that this role should be taken seriously. Nevertheless, many commentators feel the individual agencies' programs are inadequate and inconsistent.

In 1980 the leading Presidential Executive Order[58] was issued, which broadened the responsibility of federal agencies for protecting their workers, expanded employee participation in health and safety programs, and designated circumstances under which OSHA will inspect federal facilities. In the operation of their internal OSHA programs, agency heads have to meet requirements of basic program elements issued by the Department of Labor and comply with OSHA standards for the private sector unless they can justify alternatives.

### 9.2 State Employees

The OSH Act excludes the employees of state governments. Virtually all states with their own OSHA programs, however, cover their state and local employees. Some labor unions believe this exclusion of state workers is one of the most serious gaps in the OSH Act, and recent proposed legislation has attempted to remedy the perceived omission.

---

[57]*Washington Post*, "About Face Considered in OSHA Suit", 20 October 1982.
[58]Executive Order 12196, signed 26 February 1980, 45 FR 12769, superseding E.O. 11807 of 28 September 1974.

## 10.0 STATE OSHA PROGRAMS

The federal OSHA program was intended by many legislators and business only to fill the gaps where state programs were lacking. The latter were to be the primary regulatory control. It has not happened that way, of course, but approximately two dozen state programs, albeit often limping, are still important.

### 10.1 The Concept

The OSH Act requires OSHA to encourage the states to develop and operate their own job safety and health programs, which must be "at least as effective as" the federal program.[59] Until effective state programs were approved, federal enforcement of standards promulgated by OSHA preempted state enforcement,[60] and continue to do so where state laws have major gaps. Conversely, state laws remain in effect when no federal standard exists.

Before approving a submitted state plan, OSHA must make certain that the state can meet criteria established in the act.[61] Once a plan is in effect, the secretary may exercise "authority...until he determines, on the basis of actual operations under the State plan, that the criteria set forth are being applied."[62] But he cannot make such a determination for three years after the plan's approval. OSHA may continue to evaluate the state's performance in carrying out the program even after a state plan has been approved. If a state fails to comply, the approval can be withdrawn, but only after the agency has given due notice and opportunity for a hearing.

### 10.2 Critiques

The program has not developed as anticipated into an essentially state-oriented system, although almost half the states have their own system. Industry has cooled to the local concept, which requires multi-state companies to contend with a variety of state laws and regulations instead of a uniform federal plan. Moreover, state OSHAs are often considerably larger than the local federal force, so there can be more inspections.

Organized labor has never liked the state concept, because of its poor experience with the previous local organizations and a realization that its strength could more easily be exercised in one location—Washington, D.C.—than in all fifty states and the territorial capitals, many of which are traditionally hostile to labor unions. This has meant, ironically, that some of the better state programs, in areas where unions had the most influence, were among the first rejected by state legislators under strong union pressure.

It was therefore never clear what incentive a state had to maintain its own program, since a governor could always terminate his state's plan and save the budgetary expenses, knowing that the federal government would take up the slack. California Governor Dukmejian came to this conclusion in 1987 and terminated the state Cal-OSHA. However, the notion did not stick and, surprisingly, the virus has not spread.

---

[59]OSH Act §§ 2(b)(11) and 18(c)(2).
[60]OSH Act § 18(a).
[61]OSH Act § 18(c)(1)-(c)(8).
[62]OSH Act § 18(c).

Organized labor and industry are not alone in their criticism of the state programs. Health research organizations, OSHA's own national advisory committee (NACOSH), and some of the states themselves have also voiced disapproval of the state program policy. Ineffective operations at the state level, disparity in federal funding, and the lack of the necessary research capability are just a few of the criticisms lodged.[63]

OSHA had not developed articulate, coherent programs for achieving fully effective enforcement. State plans, in other words, are likely to be defective because they have been formed around defective criteria. OSHA must now go back and redo, to a certain extent, those criteria and reevaluate the state plans.[64]

There is some defense of state control, however. "To the extent that local control increases the responsiveness of programs to the specific needs of people in that area, this [a state plan] is a potentially good policy."[65] But reevaluation and revision will be necessary in the next several years if OSHA's policy for state programs is to be accepted by all the factions involved.

## 11.0 CONSULTATION

Employers subject to OSHA regulation, particularly small employers, would benefit from on-site consultation to determine what must be done to bring their workplaces into compliance with the requirements of the OSH Act. This was particularly true during the agency's formative years. Although OSHA's manpower and resources are limited, this assistance, where rendered, should be free from citations or penalties.

As in so many other areas of OSHA regulation, there has been a great deal of controversy surrounding the consultation process. Union leaders have always feared that OSHA could become merely an educational institution rather than one with effective enforcement. But Section 21(c) of the act does mandate consultation with employers and employees "as to effective means of preventing occupational injuries and illnesses."[66]

Along with the consultation provisions, the statute provides for "programs for the education and training of employers and employees in the recognition, avoidance, and prevention of unsafe or unhealthful working conditions in employments covered" by the act.[67] OSHA produces brochures and films to educate employees about possible hazards in their workplaces. But, there are problems at every stage of the information process, from generation to utilization.

In 1979, OSHA experimented with a New Directions Training and Education Program, which made available millions in grants to support the development and strengthening of occupational safety and health competence in business, employee, and educational organizations. This program supported a broad range of activities, such as

---

[63]Robert Hayden, "Federal and State Rules" in *Proceedings of the Occupational Health and Safety Regulation Seminar*, Washington, D.C.: Government Institutes, 1978), pp. 9-10.

[64]*Ibid.*, p. 11.

[65]Nicholas A. Ashford, *Crisis in the Workplace: Occupational Disease and Inquiry* (Boston: MIT Press, 1976), p. 231.

[66]OSH Act § 21(c)(2).

[67]OSH Act § 21(c)(1).

training in hazard identification and control; workplace risk assessment; medical screening and recordkeeping; and liaison work with OSHA, the National Institute for Occupational Safety and Health, and other agencies. "The goal of the program was to allow unions and other groups to become financially self-sufficient in supporting comprehensive health and safety programs."[68] This program, criticized by some as a payoff to constituent groups, especially labor unions, was a natural target of the budget cutters during the Reagan administration, but the concept of increased consultation has been given even greater emphasis.

There is also a provision that state plans may include on-site consultation with employers and employees to encourage voluntary compliance.[69] The personnel engaged in these activities must be separate from the inspection personnel and their existence must not detract from the federal enforcement effort. These consultants not only point out violations, but also give abatement advice.

## 12.0 OVERLAPPING JURISDICTION

There are other agencies involved with statutory responsibilities that affect occupational safety and health. These agencies indirectly regulate safety and health matters in their attempt to protect public safety.

One example of an overlapping agency is the Department of Transportation and its constituent agencies, such as the Federal Railroad Administration and the Federal Aviation Administration. These agencies promulgate rules concerned with the safety of transportation crews and maintenance personnel, as well as the traveling public, and consequently overlap similar responsibilities of OSHA.

Section 4(b)(1) of the OSH Act states that when other federal agencies "exercise statutory authority to prescribe or enforce standards or regulations affecting occupational safety or health," the OSH Act will not apply to the working conditions addressed by those standards. Memorandums of understanding (MOUs) between these agencies and OSHA have eliminated much of the earlier conflict.

The Environmental Protection Agency is the organization that overlaps most frequently with OSHA. When a toxic substance regulation is passed by EPA, OSHA is affected if that substance is one that appears in the workplace. For instance, both agencies are concerned with pesticides, EPA with the general environmental issues surrounding the pesticides and OSHA with some aspects of the agricultural workers who use them. During the early 1970s, there was a heated interagency conflict over field reentry standards for pesticides (see the chapter on Pesticides), a struggle which spilled over into the courts and eventually had to be settled by the White House in EPA's favor.[70]

Thus, although the health regulatory agencies generally function in a well-defined area, overlap does occur. As another example, there are toxic regulations under

---

[68]U.S. Department of Labor, "OSHA News", 12 April 1978.

[69]29 CFR § 1902.4(c)(2)(xiii).

[70]*Florida Peach Growers Assn. v. Dept. of Labor*, 489 F.2d 120 (5th Cir., 1974). To avoid this type of confrontation, in 1976 Congress provided in Section 9 of the Toxic Substances Control Act the detailed coordination procedures to be followed when jurisdictional overlap occurs.

Section 307 of the Federal Water Pollution Control Act, Section 112 of the Clean Air Act, and under statutes of the FDA and CPSC. These regulatory agencies realized the need for coordination, particularly when dealing with something as pervasive as toxic substances, and under the Carter administration combined their efforts into an interagency working group called the Interagency Regulatory Liaison Group (IRLG). Although the IRLG was abolished at the beginning of the Reagan administration, the concept of interagency working groups is a good one. The federal agencies involved in regulation should rid themselves of the antagonism and rivalry of the past and cooperate with one another to meet the needs of the public.

## 13.0 OCCUPATIONAL SAFETY AND HEALTH REVIEW COMMISSION

The OSH Act established the Occupational Safety and Health Review Commission (OSHRC) as "an independent quasi-judicial review board"[71] consisting of three members appointed by the President to six-year terms. Any enforcement actions of OSHA that are challenged must be reviewed and ruled upon by the Commission.[72]

### 13.1 OSHRC Appeal Process

Any failure to challenge a citation within fifteen days of issuance automatically results in an action of the Review Commission to uphold the citation. This decision by default is not subject to review by any court or agency. When an employer challenges a citation, the abatement period, or the penalty proposed, the Commission then designates a hearing examiner, an administrative law judge, who hears the case; makes a determination to affirm, modify or vacate the citation or penalty; and reports his finding to the Commission.[73] This report becomes final within thirty days unless a Commission member requests that the Commission itself reviews it.

The employer or agency may then seek a review of the decision in a federal appeals court.

### 13.2 Limitations of the Commission

One of the major problems with the Review Commission is the question of its jurisdiction. "The question has arisen of the extent to which the Commission should conduct itself as though it were a court rather than a more traditional administrative agency."[74] The Commission cannot look to other independent agencies in the government for a resolution of this problem "because its duties and its legislative history have little in common with the others."[75] It cannot conduct investigations, initiate suits, or prosecute; therefore, it is best understood as an administrative agency with the limited duty of "adjudicating those cases brought before it by employers and employees who seek review of the enforcement actions taken by OSHA and the Secretary of Labor."[76]

---

[71]Ashford, *Crisis*, p. 145.
[72]OSH Act § 12(a)-(b).
[73]OSH Act § 12(j).
[74]Ashford, *Crisis*, p. 145.
[75]*Ibid.*, pp. 281-82.
[76]*Ibid.*

Another problem inherent in the organization of the Commission is the separation from the President's administration. There has been a question of where the authority of the administration ends and the authority of the Commission begins. Because of the autonomous nature of the Review Commission, it cannot always count on the support of the Executive agencies. In fact, OSHA has generally ignored Review Commission decisions, and few inspectors are even aware of the Commission interpretations on various regulations.

## 14.0 NATIONAL INSTITUTE OF OCCUPATIONAL SAFETY AND HEALTH

Under the act, the Bureau of Safety and Health Services in the Health Services and Mental Health Administration was restructured to become the National Institute for Occupational Safety and Health (NIOSH), so as to carry out HEW's responsibilities under the act.[77] (HEW—The Department of Health, Education, and Welfare—has since become the Department of Health and Human Services, HHS.) For the past two decades NIOSH has reported, illogically, to the Center for Disease Control (CDC), and the two organizations have headquarters in Atlanta.

Since mid-1971, NIOSH has claimed the training and research functions of the act, along with its primary function of recommending standards. For this latter task, NIOSH provides recommended standards to OSHA in the form of criteria documents for particular hazards. These are compilations and evaluations of all available relevant information from scientific, medical, and (occasionally) engineering research.

The order of hazards selected for criteria development is determined several years in advance by a NIOSH priority system based on severity of response, population at risk, existence of a current standard, and advice from federal agencies (including OSHA) as well as involved professional groups.[78]

The criteria documents may actually have some value apart from the role in standards-making. Even though they do not have the force of law, they are widely distributed to industry, organized labor, universities, and private research groups as a basis to control hazards. The criteria documents also serve as a "basis for setting international permissible limits for occupational exposures."[79]

To the extent that certain criteria documents may be deficient, as discussed earlier, this expansive role for them among laymen poses a real problem. This problem may unfortunately become worse, if NIOSH declines in both funds and morale. Nevertheless, there is some benefit in having the two organizations separate. NIOSH has on occasion criticized OSHA for regulatory decisions which the former believed was scientifically untenable.[80]

---

[77]OSH Act § 22(a).
[78]John F. Finklea, "The Role of NIOSH in the Standards Process," in *Proceedings of the Occupational Health and Safety Regulation Seminar*, p. 38.
[79]*Ibid.*, p. 39.
[80]See, for example, G. Fishbein, op. cit., 8 June 1982 on formaldehyde.

## 15.0 WARRANTLESS INSPECTIONS: THE *BARLOW* CASE

Litigants have challenged OSHA's constitutionality on virtually every conceivable grounds from the First Amendment to the Fourteenth.[81] The one case that has succeeded has led to the requirement of a search warrant, if demanded, for OSHA inspectors.

The Supreme Court in *Marshall v. Barlow's Inc.*[82] decided that the Fourth Amendment to the Constitution, providing for search warrants, was applicable to OSHA, thereby declaring unconstitutional Section 8(a) of the Act, in which Congress had authorized warrantless searches.[83]

While the court held OSHA inspectors are required to obtain search warrants if denied entry to inspect, it added that OSHA meet only a very minimal "probable cause" requirement under the Fourth Amendment in order to obtain them. As Justice White explained:

Probable cause in the criminal sense is not required. For purposes of an administrative search such as this, probable cause justifying the issuance of a warrant may be based not only on specific evidence of an existing violation but also on a showing that "reasonable legislative or administrative standards for conducting an...inspection are satisfied with respect to a particular [establishment]".[84]

Moreover, if too many companies demanded warrants so that the inspection program was seriously impaired, the Court indicated it might reconsider its ruling. This ironically would make enjoyment of a Constitutional right partly contingent on few attempting to exercise it. It is therefore not surprising that commentators, both liberals and conservatives, were critical of the decision. Conservative columnist James J. Kilpatrick declared flatly:

If the Supreme Court's decision in the *Barlow* case was a "great victory," as Congressman George Hansen proclaims it, let us ask heaven to protect us from another such victory anytime soon.[85]

## 16.0 HAZARD COMMUNICATIONS REGULATION

OSHA's output of health standards has never been an impressive volume. In recent years, it has tried three new approaches to get around this bottleneck. The first was the abortive cancer policy designed to create a template for dealing in an expedited fashion with a number of hazardous chemicals. The second was the wholesale review initiated in 1988 of all the Z-1 list consensus standards—an effort struck down by the courts.

---

[81]A good, if dated summary of these challenges is found in Volume I of Walter B. Connolly & David R. Cromwell, II, *A Practical Guide to the Occupational Safety and Health Act* (New York: New York Law Journal Press, 1977).

[82]436 U.S. 307 (1978).

[83]There are circumstances in which warrants are not required, such as federal inspection of liquor dealers, gun dealers, automobiles near international borders, and in other matters with a long history of federal involvement.

[84]*Marshall v. Barlow's Inc.*, supra, quoting *Camara v. Municipal Court*, 387 U.S. 523 at 538 (1967).

[85]*Washington Star*, 2 June 1978.

The third, characterized by one OSHA official as the agency's most important rulemaking ever, is the hazard communication (hazcom) regulation issued in November 1983.[86]

## 16.1 Reason for the Regulation

This standard, sometimes known as the "worker right-to-know" rule, provides that hazardous chemicals must be labeled, material safety data sheets (MSDS) on hazards be prepared, and workers and customers should be informed of potential chemical risks.

How could a rule with such far-reaching consequences be issued from an Administration that so stressed deregulation and deliberately avoided issuing other protective regulations? The answer lies in an almost unprecedented grassroots movement at the state and municipal level to enact their own "worker right to know" laws which, many businessmen felt, could be a considerable burden on interstate commerce. They therefore lent their support to OSHA in its confrontation with the Office of Management and Budget (OMB) at the White House. A federal regulation on this subject would arguably preempt the multiplicity of local laws.

The rule was originally presumed to apply to only a few hundred, perhaps a thousand, particularly hazardous chemicals. The individual employers would evaluate the risk and then decide for themselves which products merited coverage. Most employers were unable or unwilling to make such scientific determinations. Within a year or two, this limited program expanded into a universal coverage.

## 16.2 Scope and Components

Published on 25 November 1983, OSHA's Hazard Communication or "Right-to-Know" Standard[87] went into effect two years later, in November 1985, for chemical manufacturers, distributors, and importers, and May of 1994 for manufacturers that use chemicals. It required that employees be provided with information concerning hazardous chemicals through labels, material safety data sheets, training and education, and lists of hazardous chemicals in each work area. Originally it covered only manufacturing industries classified in SIC codes 20-39, but by court order in 1987 it was extended to virtually all employers.[88]

Every employer must assess the toxicity of chemicals it makes, distributes, or uses based on guidelines set forth in the rule. Then it must provide this material downstream to those who purchase the chemicals through MSDSs.[89] The employers are then required to assemble a list of the hazardous materials in the workplace, label all chemicals, provide employees with access to the MSDSs, and provide training and education. While *all* chemicals must be evaluated, the "communication" provisions

---

[86]49 FR 52380, 25 November 1983.

[87]48 FR 53280; 29 CFR 1200.

[88]52 FR 31852, 24 August 1987, in response to *United Steelworkers of America, AFL-CIO v. Pendergrass*, 819 F.2d 1263 (3rd Cir., 1987).

[89]There is some legal question whether OSHA, which has jurisdiction over employer-employee health and safety relations, has authority over the relationship between a company and its downstream customers.

apply—in theory—only to those chemicals known to be present in the workplace in such a way as to potentially expose employees to physical or health hazards.

Special provisions apply to the listing of mixtures which constitute health hazards. Each component which is itself hazardous to health and which comprises one percent or more of a mixture must be listed. Carcinogens must be listed if present in quantities of 0.1 percent or greater.

The Hazard Communication Standard is a performance-oriented rule. While it states the objectives to be achieved, the specific methods to achieve those objectives are at the discretion of the employer. Thus, in theory, employers have considerable flexibility to design programs suitable for their own workplaces. However, this may mean the employers will have questions on how to comply with the standard.

The purpose of labeling is to give employees an immediate warning of hazardous chemicals and a reminder that more detailed information is available. Containers must be labeled with identity, appropriate hazard warnings, and the name and address of the manufacturer. The hazard warnings must be specific, even as to the endangered body organs. For example, if inhalation of a chemical causes lung cancer, the label must specify that and cannot simply say "harmful if inhaled" or even "causes cancer." Pipes and piping systems are exempt from labeling, as are those substances required to be labeled by another federal agency.

Material safety data sheets (MSDSs), used in combination with labels, are the primary tools for transmitting detailed information on hazardous chemicals. A MSDS is a technical document which summarizes the known information about a chemical. Chemical manufacturers and importers must develop a MSDS for each hazardous chemical produced or imported and pass it onto the purchaser at the time of the first shipment. The employer must keep these sheets where employees will have access to them at all times.

The purpose of employee information and training programs is to inform employees of the labels and MSDSs and to make them aware of the actions required to avoid or minimize exposure to hazardous chemicals. The format of these programs is left to the discretion of the individual employer. Training programs must be provided at the time of initial assignment and whenever a new hazard is introduced into the workplace.

### 16.3 Hazard Evaluation

Chemical manufacturers are required to evaluate all chemicals they sell for potential health and physical hazards to exposed workers. Purchasers of these chemicals may rely on the supplier's determination or may perform their own evaluations.

There are really no specific procedures to follow in determining a hazard. Testing of chemicals is not required, and the extent of the evaluation is left to the manufacturers and importers of hazardous chemicals. However, all available scientific evidence must be identified and considered. A chemical is considered hazardous if it is found so by even a single valid study.

Chemicals found on the following "master" lists are automatically deemed hazardous under the standard:

• the International Agency for Research on Cancer (IARC) monograph;

- the *Annual Report on Carcinogens* published by the National Toxicology Program (NTP);
- OSHA's "Subpart Z" list, found in Title 29 of the Code of Federal Regulations, Part 1910; or
- *Threshold Limit Values for Chemical Substances and Physical Agents in the Work Environment*, published by the American Conference of Governmental Industrial Hygienists.

If a substance meets any of the health definitions in Appendix A of the standard, it is also to be considered hazardous. The definitions given are for a carcinogen, a corrosive, a chemical which is highly toxic, an irritant, a sensitizer, a chemical which is toxic, and target organ effects.

Appendix B gives the principal criteria to be applied in complying with the hazard determination requirement. First, animal as well as human data must be evaluated. Second, if a scientific study finds a chemical to be hazardous, the effects must be reported whether or not the manufacturers or importers agree with the findings.

Appendix C of the standard gives a lengthy list of sources which may assist in the evaluation process. The list includes company data from testing and reports on hazards, supplier data, MSDSs or product safety bulletins, scholarly text books, and government health publications.

In practice, as noted above, companies have begun requiring MSDSs from manufacturers for *all* chemicals they purchase, so the evaluation aspect of the standard has become unimportant.

## 16.4 Trade Secrets

Although there is agreement that there must be a delicate balance between the employee's right to be free of exposure to unknown chemicals and the employer's right to maintain reasonable trade secrets, the exact method of protection has been considerably disputed.

Under the standard, a trade secret is considered to be defined as in the Restatement of Torts; i.e., something that is not known or used by a competitor. However, OSHA had to revise its definition to conform with a court ruling which said that a trade secret may not include information that is readily discoverable through reverse engineering.

Although the trade secret identity may be omitted from the MSDS, the manufacturer must still disclose the health effects and other properties about the chemical. A chemical's identity must immediately be disclosed to a treating physician or nurse who determines that a medical emergency exists.

In non-emergency situations, any employee can request disclosure of the chemical's identity if he demonstrates through a written statement a "need to know" the precise chemical name and signs a confidentiality agreement. The standard specifies all purposes which OSHA considers demonstrate a need to know a specific chemical identity.

The standard initially limited this access to health professionals, but on 24 May 1985, the U.S. Court of Appeals for the Third Circuit ruled that trade secrets protections must be narrowed greatly, allowing not only health professionals, but also workers and their designated representatives the same access as long as they follow the required procedures.[90] In response, OSHA issued a final rule on trade secrets on 30 September 1986[91] which narrows the definition of "trade secret." It denies protection to chemical identity information that is readily discoverable through reverse engineering. It also permits employees, their collective bargaining representatives, and occupational nurses access to trade secret information.

Upon request, the employer must either disclose the information or provide written denial to the requestor within 30 days. If the request is denied, the matter may be referred to OSHA, whereupon evidence to support the claim of trade secret, and alternative information that will satisfy the claimed need.

### 16.5 Federal Preemption Controversy

Several states and labor groups have filed suits challenging state laws which are more protective. New Jersey, for example, has enacted the toughest labeling law in the nation, requiring industry to label all its chemical substances, whether they are hazardous or not, and supply the information to community groups and health officials, as well as to workers.

They were also concerned that, because the original OSHA standard only covered the manufacturing sector, more than 50 percent of the workers (such as those workers in the agricultural and construction fields) would be unprotected, and OSHA did not cover (and still does not) such groups as state employees and consumers. Moreover, they argued that OSHA would be incapable of enforcing worker protection because of the staff cuts made by the Reagan administration.

The chemical industry, on the other hand, favored a uniform federal regulation because they believed it would be less costly and easier to comply with one federal rule as opposed to several state and local rules that would often conflict or be confusing.

On 10 October 1985, the U.S. Court of Appeals for the Third Circuit ruled that the federal Hazard Communication Standard does not preempt all sections of New Jersey's right-to-know laws designed to protect workers and the public from chemical exposure—only those which apply to groups the agency's rules covered, which was then only the manufacturing sector.[92] Thus, while some parts of a state law may be preempted, other provisions may not be.

On 12 September 1986, the Third Circuit also found that the federal Hazard Communication Standard did not entirely preempt requirements under Pennsylvania's right-to-know act pertaining to worker protection in the manufacturing industry where the state rules relate to public safety generally and for protection of local government officials with police and fire departments. However, on 17 September 1986, the U.S. Court of Appeals for the Sixth Circuit ruled that a right-to-know ordinance enacted by the city of Akron, Ohio, is preempted by the federal standard in manufacturing sector workplaces.

---

[90]*United Steelworkers of America, AFL-CIO-CLC v. Auchter, et al.*, 763 F.2d 728; 12 OSHC 1337 (3rd Cir., 1985).

[91]51 FR 34590.

[92]*New Jersey State Chamber of Commerce v. Hughey*, 774 F.2d 587, 12 OSHC 1589 (3rd Cir., 1985).

In 1992, the Supreme Court came down strongly on the side of preemption. *The Gade v. National Solid Waste Management Association* case, although it involved OSHA's so-called HAZWOPER regulations[93] rather than hazard communication, involved a state law requiring more additional training for heavy equipment operators on hazardous waste sites. The high court found that the OSHA regulations preempted the state despite arguments that the federal rules only set a minimum which the state could exceed—the situation in most environmental laws—and the more transparent claim that the state laws had a dual purpose in protecting the public as well as workers.[94]

## 17.0 LEGISLATION

The OSH Act has remained virtually untouched since its passage in 1970. With the inauguration of a Democratic president, William Clinton, in 1993 and Democratic control of both houses of Congress, the expectation was that the labor unions would secure the passage of the first significant revisions in the law.

Under the circumstances, the proposed legislation was surprisingly innocuous. It included verbose and often unnecessary sections on enforcement, refusal to work, and other issues. Among them was a seemingly innocuous section providing for labor-management safety committees in the workplace. Both employers and employees have found these committees quite useful, but some manufacturers' organizations perceived the language as forcing a much greater role for labor unions.

With the Republican election victories in the House and Senate in late 1994, these Democratic legislative plans not only collapsed but the victors prepared their own onslaught on the OSH Act. To the surprise of many, the draconian Republican plans to curtail or even eliminate OSHA got no further than the previous Democratic plans. However, the Republicans' hostile scrutiny of OSHA paralyzed the agency leadership and led to a sharp decline in both enforcement and standard setting.

---

[93]Hazardous Waste Operations and Emergency Response (HAZWOPER) regulations in 29 C.F.R. § 1910.120.
[94]*Gade v. National Solid Wastes Management Ass'n*, 112 S.Ct. 2374 (1992).

# INDEX

# References from Government Institutes

## Books

For more information on these books and others, please call our Publishing Department at (301) 921-2355. A Note: Prices subject to change without prior notice. We can also be found on the Internet—http://ww.govinst.com our e-mail address is giinfo@govinst.com

### Federal/State Environmental Law

**Environmental Statutes, 1997 Edition**
Softcover, 1200 pages, Mar' 97, ISBN: 0-86587-562-6 $69

**Environmental Regulatory Glossary, 6th Edition**
Edited by Thomas F.P. Sullivan
Hardcover, 544 pages, 1993, ISBN: 0-86587-353-4 $69

We carry the entire Code of Federal Regulations. Call for details.

We also have State Environmental Law Handbooks for more than 40 states.

### Environmental Management

**Environmental Audits, 7th Edition**
By Lawrence B. Cahill, Senior Prgram Director, ERM Inc.
Softcover, 727 pages, 1996, ISBN: 0-86587-525-1 $79

**Industrial Environmental Management: A Practical Approach**
By Jack Daugherty, MSChE, PE, CIH, CHMM, Environmental and Safety Engineer, Vickers, Inc.
Hardcover, Index, 572 pages, 1996, ISBN: 0-86587-515-4 $79

**ISO 14000: Understanding the Environmental Standards**
By Dr. W. M. von Zharen, Coordinator of Texas A & M Coastal & Ocean Management Studies Program
Softcover, 226 pages, 1996, ISBN: 0-86587-510-3 $69

**ISO 14001: An Executive Report**
By Gordon West, Pilko & Associates, and Joseph Manta, Manta & Wedge
Softcover, 124 pages, 1996, ISBN: 0-86587-551-0 $55

**Principles of Environmental, Health and Safety Management**
Edited by Gordon A. West, Arthur Andersen & Company and Ronald W. Michaud, Pilko Associates
Softcover, 1995, 360 pages, ISBN: 0-86587-478-5 $69

**California Spill Reporting Manual**
By Charles F. Timms, Jr. LeBoeuf, Lamb, Greene & MacRae, L.L.P. and Sandra H. Waddell,
McCutchen, Doyle, Brown & Enersen, LLP
Softcover, 500 pages, 1996, ISBN: 0-86587-528-6 $125

**Lead Regulation Handbook**
By Edward E. Shea, Partner, Windels, Marx, Davies, & Ives
Softcover, 254 pages, 1996, ISBN: 0-86587-518-9 $79

**Environmental Guide to the Internet, 2nd Edition**
By Carol Briggs-Erickson and Toni Murphy
Softcover, 236 pages, 1996, ISBN:0-86587-517-0 $55

# Environmental Science & Engineering

**Environmental Engineering and Science: An Introduction**
By Ram S. Gupta, Roger Williams University, PhD, PE
Hardcover, Index, 400 pages, April 1997, ISBN: 0-86587-548-0 $79

**Fate and Transport of Organic Chemicals in the Environment:**
**A Practical Guide, 2nd Edition**
By Ron E. Ney, Jr. Ph.D, Northern Virginia Community College
Softcover, Index, 302 pages, 1995, ISBN: 0-86587-470-0 $55

# RCRA Hazardous Waste

**Waste Generator's Compliance Manual**
By Ethan S. Naftalin, attorney, Hunton & Williams
Softcover, Index, 452, 1995, ISBN: 0-86587-507-3 $89

**RCRA Hazardous Wastes Handbook, 11th Edition**
By Ridgway M. Hall, Jr. et al, Crowell & Moring
Softcover, 616 pages, 1995, ISBN: 0-86587-503-0 $115

**Pollution Prevention Strategies and Technologies**
By Mark S. Dennison, LLM, JD, Dennison Legal Services
Hardcover, Index, 463 pages, ISBN:0-86587-480-8 $79

# Water Pollution Control

**Clean Water Handbook, 2nd Edition**
By Lynn A. Gallagher, and Leonard A. Miller, Swidler & Berlin
Softcover, 452 pages, 1996, ISBN: 0-86587-512-X $89

**Comprehensive Water Planning and Regulation:**
**New Approaches for Workable Solutions**
By William Whipple, Jr.
Softcover, 200 pages, 1996, ISBN: 0-86587-513-8 $69

## Air Pollution Control

**Clean Air Handbook, 2nd Edition**
By F. William Brownell et al, Hunton and Williams
Softcover, 340 pages, 1993, ISBN: 0-86587-343-7 $89

## OSHA

**Making Sense of OSHA Compliance**
By Jeffrey Vincoli, J.W. Vincoli Associates, a safety consulting firm
Hardcover, Index, 250 pages, 1996, ISBN: 0-86587-535-9 $59

**Safety Made Easy: A Checklist Approach to OSHA Compliance**
By W. A. "Tex" Davis, Texas State Technical College, John R. Grubbs, Monarch Tile Inc., and
SeanM. Nelson, Safety Consultant
Softcover, Index, 192 pages, 1995, ISBN: 0-86587-463-8 $49

**TSCA Handbook, 3rd Edition**
By Charles O'Connor III et al, McKenna
Softcover, 500 pages, April 1997, ISBN: 0-86587-566-9 $95

## Natural Resources

**Wetland Mitigation: Mitigation Banking and Other Strategies for Development and
Compliance**
By Mark S. Dennison, LLM , JD, Dennison Legal Services, and James A. Schmid
Hardcover, Index, 272 pages, 1996, ISBN: 0-86587-534-0 $75

**Wetlands: An Introduction to Ecology, the Law & Permitting**
By Theda Braddock, Attorney & L. Reed Huppman, Geomophologist, Plant Ecologist
Softcover, Index, 185 pages, 1995, ISBN: 0-86587-467-0 $69

**Property Rights: Understanding Government Takings and Environmental Regulations**
By Nancie G. Marzulla, president of Defenders of Property Rights, and Roger J. Marzulla,
Akin, Gump, Strauss, Hauer & Feld, Former Assistant District Attorney
Hardcover, 350 pages, 1996, ISBN: 0-86587-554-5 $79

# Electronic Products

Please ask for the Electronic Publishing Department for more information
on a full list of electronic products (301) 921-2355.

**Environmental, Health & Safety CFRs on CD ROM** (Includes Title 29, Title 40, Title 49)
CD ROM for Windows, Macintosh or DOS, 1996
Single Issue-Latest Release- Product Code #4020 $395
LAN License-Latest Release- Product Code #4000 $1,185
Single Issue-One Year Subscription- Product Code #4020 $$980
LAN License-One Year Subscription- Product Code #4000 $2,940

**Environmental Statutes on Disk, 1997**
CD ROM for Windows, February 1997, Product Code #4060
Single User, $135; LAN License $405

# Continuing Education Credit Available
## through the Environmental Law Self-Study Course

The Environmental Law Handbook seerves as the text for a new self-study course, now available from Government Institutes.

**The U.S. Environmental Laws and Regulations Self-Study Course** is based on Government Institutes' traditional classroom course that has trained more than 12,0000 environmental professionals since 1973.

The Self-Study Course uses the Environmental Law Handbook and a 300-page companion guide prepared by distance learning experts. The study guide includes learning objectives, self-assessment tests, and a master exam.

Students may return the master exam to Governmenta Institutes for grading and course credit. Those who successfully complete the exam will earn continuing education credits and receive a personalized Certificate of Achievement.

"This course represents a unique opportunity for anyone at any site in the world to learn about U.S. environmental law at his or her own pace," says Jay Collert, author of the study guide an a 18-year veteran environmental manager and trainer.

Designed for practicing environmental specialists, international business professionals, and students preparing for a career in environmental compliance, the Self-Study Course is one of many distance learning tools available from Government Institutes.

The study guide can be ordered for $195 (U.S.), plus $10 shipping and handling. Additional copies of the Enviromental Law Handbook are available at the current list price.

To order or receive further information, contact:
Government Institutes, 4 Research Place, Rockville, Maryland 20850.
Tel. (301) 921-2345   Fax (301) 921-0373